For Reference

Not to be taken from this room

FILMARAMA

Volume I

The Formidable Years,
1893 - 1919

compiled by

JOHN STEWART

76610

The Scarecrow Press, Inc.

Metuchen, N. J.   1975

Library of Congress Cataloging in Publication Data

Stewart, John, 1920-
  Filmarama.

  CONTENTS: v. 1. The formidable years, 1893-1919.
  1. Moving-picture actors and actresses. 2. Moving-
pictures--Indexes. I. Title.
PN1998.A2S67   791.43'028'0922 [B]   75-2440
ISBN 0-8108-0802-1 (v. 1)

To America's Sweetheart

MARY PICKFORD

INTRODUCTION

For eighty years motion picture patrons have laughed
at and learned from, cried and cringed at, loved and loathed
what and whom they saw from Nickelodeons to Cinerama. The
many players became heroines, heroes, villains, and clowns.
From the tinkling emotions of piano accompaniment through
the dramatic tones of an organ to stereophonics came an aura
of mystery and intrigue. Whatever the private lives of the
screen greats, near-greats, and little-knowns, these players
contributed to the great society of man the world over.

From the sneezing of Fred Ott to the vamping of Theda
Bara to the teasing of Raquel Welch have come fascinating
personalities along the enchanted road to stardom.

This road, which every player travels, is a heartbreak-
ing, two-way path--up or down: for many it is and was more
down than up. Those who reached the top found there a pre-
carious perch, and the trip down, a greased slide.

Whether up or down, thousands of boys and girls, men
and women have traveled the road. Filmarama is intended as
a record of those travelers. Unfortunately in the early days
records were rarely kept and those that were might as well
have been written on the wind, for they have disappeared.

Searching existing records and talking with actors and
actresses, while fascinating, has been a monumental task. A
task that has been both rewarding and disappointing. Rewarding because of the quantity of information compiled; disappointing because of the information not available. This work, however, should prove invaluable to librarians, drama teachers
and students, writers, researchers, movie buffs, and the ever-
curious general public.

Where obtainable, the player's real name is given and
a representative record of stage, radio, and television work.
The index is an alphabetical film list giving the date of

v

release and the releasing company or producer.

In addition to this volume, when completed, Filmarama will consist of the following volumes:

Vol. II	The Flaming Years	1920-1929
Vol. III	The Golden Years	1930-1939
Vol. IV	The Blue Years	1940-1949
Vol. V	The Dark Years	1950-1959
Vol. VI	The Explosive Years	1960-1969

Each volume will contain special material such as Academy Award winners with brief biographies. Famous movie animals of each era are included, as are cartoons, and a complete listing of films by the top director of each decade.

Many players will appear in several volumes because of the span of their active careers. Numbering of name entries is for index reference. Films are listed alphabetically in the index, and the numbers following these entries refer to the players in the film. For example if you know the name of a picture, but none of the players, check the index first and the numbers following the film title refer to the players; in many instances the entire cast may be located in this manner.

Vital statistics in these formidable early years are as vague and shadowy as the players themselves. Films then reflected a variety of public interests, plus classics of the stage, and a few stories designed especially for the new media--but cast lists were not given.

Film history along with that of its players is full of contradictions. Many have been perpetuated by critics, journalists, and biographers. Records of vital statistics have suffered from the irresponsibility of press agents and studio heads, from faulty memories, even from too much "ego" in the players' makeup.

A complete compilation is beyond the realm of possibility, because between 1893 and 1969, the scope of this work, there were more than 150,000 films produced. The main source of recorded material comes from The Film Index, The Film Daily Year Book of Motion Pictures, and The International Motion Picture Almanac.

Another method of research has been to trace people, directly or indirectly, involved with the films listed. This form of detective work involved ferreting out personalities who have long since left the industry, writing letters and interviewing those kind enough to respond. I discovered an interesting fact over the months of work--actors and actresses have rather clouded memories. One prominent personality, although gracious and cooperative, offered information which further research proved to be inaccurate. Some, fortunately, kept rather detailed written records.

My judgment in selecting names for this compilation may have been faulty in the minds of some, but selection in this type of work is necessary. Names that may appear inconsequential were, after all, consequential to the cast of a film. I certainly do not consider myself a motion picture personality expert, and apologize for whatever errors appear. I shall be grateful for corrections and additions sent to me through the publisher. In this way it will be possible for later revised and more comprehensive editions. This first volume covers those uncertain, experimental years.

Formidable years, indeed, for what began as a joke backfired into a multi-million dollar industry and the development of an art form peculiarly American, yet universal.

The lives of motion picture personalities may be summed up in the following lines from an unfinished poem by Richard Henry Wilde around 1815:

> My life is like the Summer Rose
> That opens to the morning sky
> But ere the shades of evening close
> Is scattered on the ground to die.

John Stewart

Covina, California
1973

FILMARAMA

- A -

1
AARONSON, Max see ANDERSON, Gilbert

2
ABBE, Charles*
Niobe†
Stage:††
Battle, The 1908
Come On Charlie 1919
Eyes of Youth 1917
Help Wanted 1914
His Majesty, Bunker Bean 1916
Jimmy, the Carrier 1905
Lost River 1900
No. 13 Washington Square /aka/
    No. 33 Washington Square 1915
Roundup, The 1907
Silent Call, The 1911
Squaw Man, The 1911
What Happened at 22? 1914

3
ABBEY, May*
Othello in Jonesville

4
ABE, Utake*
Cheat, The (Tori's Valet)†††

5
ABELES, Edward*
Brewster's Millions

Stage:
Brewster's Millions 1906-07
Cousin Billy 1905
Dictator, The 1904
Diplomat, The 1902
Glad of It 1903
Goddess of Liberty, The 1909
Lady Margaret 1902
Lasso, The 1917
Last Laugh, The 1915
Man and Superman (Henry Straker)
    1905
Master 1916-17
My Wife's Husbands 1903
Oh, Lady! Lady! 1918
On with the Dance 1917
Pair of Queens, A 1916
Rich Mrs. Repton, The 1904
Sprightly Romance of Morsoc, The
    1900
Under Two Flags 1901
West Point Cadet, The 1904
Whitewashing of Julia, The 1903

6
ABINGDON, W. B.*
Henry VIII (servant)

7
ACKER, Jean*
Checkers
Lombardi, Limited

8
ACKERMAN, Walter*

---

*Indicates vital dates are unknown; if death date is known and birth date is not, it will simply be indicated as, e.g., "(d.1933)."
†Dates of film production or release and producing companies are given in the index listing of films.
††Stage credits represent New York productions, unless otherwise indicated. Stage credits are representative only, not complete.
†††Information appearing in parentheses after a film or stage play title normally will indicate the role the actor played; alternatively, it will sometimes indicate that the film is a serial; less often, other clarifying bits of information.

Midsummer Night's Dream, A
   (Demetrius)

9
ACORD, Art (1890-1931)
Back to the Prairie
Buck Parvin series
Cleopatra (Kephren)
Man Afraid of His Wardrobe, A
Moon Riders, The (serial)
Squaw Man, The

10
ACROBATS OF THE FOLIES
   BERGERE
Trip to the Moon, A (The Selenites)

11
ADAIR, Robyn*
Hazards of Helen (serial)

12
ADAMS, Claire*
Key to Power
Spirit of the Red Cross

13
ADAMS, Kathryn*
Baby Mine

14
ADAMS, Mildred*
Great Pearl Tangle, The

15
ADAMS, Peggy*
Spirit of the Red Cross

16
ADAMS, Stella*
Seminary Scandal, A
Stage:
Miss Prinnt 1900
Mocking Bird, The 1902-03

17
ADENEY, Eric*
Hamlet (Francisco & Reynaldo)

18
ADLER, Jacob*
Michael Strogoff

19
ADOLFI, John G. *
Othello (Roderigo)
Romeo and Juliet (Romeo)
Stage:

Ranger, The 1907
Silver Box, The 1907

20
AHERN, George*
Charity Castle
Stage:
Isle O'Dreams, The 1913

21
AICKEN, Elinor*
Richard III (Duchess of York)

22
AINLEY, Henry (1879-1945)
Bachelor's Love Story, A
Brother Officers
Called Back
Great Adventure, The
Henry VIII (Buckingham)
Iris
Jeffs
Manxman, The
Marriage of William Ashe
Outrage, The
Prisoner of Zenda, The
Quinneys
Rupert of Hentzau
She Stoops to Conquer
Sowing the Wind
Sweet Lavender
Stage:
Pretty Sister of Jose, The 1903

23
AINSLEY, Charles*
Adventures of Dollie, The (Evil Gyp-
   sy; serial)

24
AINSWORTH, Sydney /aka/ Sidney
   (1872-1922)
Crimson Gardenia, The
Girl From Outside, The
Heartease
Man and His Money, A
Romance of an American Duchess,
   The
Strange Case of Mary Page, The
   (serial)
White Sister, The
Stage:
Arizona (Lt. Young) 1900
Classmates 1907
Fortune Hunter 1909
Ransom's Folly 1904
Strongheart 1905

25
AITKEN, Spottiswoode (d. 1933)
Americano, The
Avenging Conscience (the Uncle)
Battle, The
Big James' Heart
Birth of a Nation, The (Dr. Cameron)
Broken Commandments
Captain Kidd, Jr.
Captain Machlin
Evangeline
Fighting Through
Hay Foot, Straw Foot
Her Kingdom of Dreams
Home Sweet Home (Apple Pie Mary's
   Father)
How Could You, Jean?
Intolerance (Brown Eyes' Father)
Jane Goes A-Wooing
Liberty Bells
Macbeth (Duncan)
Man of Courage
Old Maid, The
Stage Struck
Thunderbolt
Wharf Rat, The
White Heather, The
Who Cares?
Wicked Darling, The (Fanem)
Woman of Pleasure, A
Stage:
Billy 1909

26
ALBERTSON, Coit*
Carter Case, The (the Craig Ken-
   nedy serial)
$1,000,000 Reward

27
ALDEN, Mary*
Acquitted
Another Glance
Argyle Case, The
Battle of the Sexes, The (Mrs. Frank
   Andrews)
Big James' Heart
Birth of a Nation, The (Lydia Brown)
Bred in the Bone
Broken Butterfly, The
By Right of Possession
Common Clay
Erstwhile Susan
Ghosts
Hell-to-Pay Austin
Her Mother's Daughter
Home Sweet Home (the mother)
Intolerance (an uplifter)

Land of Promise, The
Less Than the Dust
Little Country Mouse, The
Macbeth (Lady Macduff)
Naulahka, The
Second Mrs. Roebuck, The
Straight Path, The
Unpardonable Sin, The
Stage:
Personal 1907
Rule of Three, The 1914
War Brides 1915

28
ALEXANDER, Ben (Nicholas Benton
   Alexander) (1911-1969)
Battle of Youth
Better Wife
Each Pearl a Tear
Heart of Rachel
Hearts of the World (Doug's little
   brother)
Hushed Hour
Joselyn's Wife
Little American, The
Macbeth
Tangled Threads
Turn in the Road, The
White Heather, The

29
ALEXANDER, Edward*
Uncle Tom's Cabin

30
ALEXANDER, Gus*
Safe for Democracy
Stage:
His Majesty 1906

31
ALEXANDER, Queen*
Great Love, The (herself)

32
ALEXANDRE, Rene*
Les Enfants d'Edouard (Tyrrell)
Notre Dame de Paris

33
ALLARDT, Arthur*
Louisiana

34
ALLEN, Alfred*
Flashlight Girl, The (John Peterson)
Grand Passion, The (Mackay)
Hell Morgan's Girl (Oliver Curwell)

Lion's Claw, The (serial)
Red Glove, The (serial)

35
ALLEN, Jack Major*
Bear Hunt, The

36
ALLEN, Joseph*
Essanay player 1912
Stage:
District Leader, The 1906
My Innocent Boy 1899
Red Widow, The 1911
Royal Chef, The 1904
Seven Keys to Baldpate (Peters)
  1913-14
Three Twins 1908
When Knights Were Bold 1907

37
ALLEN, Phyllis*
Caught in a Cabaret /aka/ The Jazz
  Waiter
Dough and Dynamite
Fatty's Jonah Day
Fickle Fatty's Fall
Gentlemen of Nerve
Getting Acquainted
Giddy, Gay and Ticklish /aka/ A
  Gay Lothario
Gussie's Wayward Path
His Musical Career
His Trysting Place
Judge, The
Movie Star, A
No One to Guide Him
Property Man, The /aka/ The
  Roustabout
Rounders, The
Shot in the Excitement
Submarine Pirate, A
Tillie's Punctured Romance

38
ALLEN, Ricca*
Runaway June (serial)
Stage:
Fires of St. John, The 1904
Hedda Gabler (Berta) 1904
Judith of Bethulia 1904
Magda (Franziska) 1904
Uncle Tom's Cabin (Ophelia) 1907
Up and Down Broadway 1910

39
ALLEN, Tex*
Vengeance and the Woman (serial)

40
ALLEN, Viola (1869-)
Essanay play 1915
Stage:
Cymbeline (Imogen) 1906
Daughter of Heaven, The 1912
Eternal City, The 1902
Hunchback, The 1902
Importance of Being Earnest, The
  (Gwendolen Fairfax) 1895
In the Palace of the King 1900
Irene Wycherley 1908
Lady of Coventry, The 1911
Macbeth (Lady Macbeth) 1916
Toast of the Town, The 1905
Twelfth Night (Viola) 1904-05
White Sister, The 1909
Winter's Tale, The (Hermione and
  Perdita) 1904

41
ALLISON, May (1895-)
Almost Married
Big Tremaine
Castles in the Air
Comeback, The
Fair and Warmer
Fool There Was, A (Fool's wife's
  sister)
Governor's Lady
Her Inspiration
In for Thirty Days
Isle of Intrigue
Last Card, The
Peggy Does Her Darndest
Promise, The
Return of Mary
River of Romance
Secret Wire, The
Shop Girls
Social Hypocrites
Successful Adventure, A
Testing of Mildred Vane
Uplifters, The
Winning of Beatrice
Stage:
Apartment 12-K 1914
Iole 1913

42
ALMROTH, Grete*
Song of the Red Flower

43
AMES, Gerald (1881-1933)
Adam Bede
Arsene Lupin
Black Spot, The

Boundary House
Brother Officers
Cage, The
Christian, The
Comradeship
Derby Winner, The
Difficult Way, The
England's Menace
Forest on the Hill, The
Fortune at Stake, A
Fringe of War, The
Gamble for Love, A
Game of Liberty, The
Greater Need, The
Highwayman's Honour, The
Irresistible Flapper, The
Jeffs
King's Daughter, The
King's Outcast, The
Kitchen Countess, The
Love in a Wood (Orlando)
Masks and Faces
Me and My Moke
Middleman, The
Missing the Tide
Morals of Weybury, The
Nature of the Beast, The
On His Majesty's Service
Paste
Peep behind the Scenes, A
Possession
Princess of Happy Chance, The
Prisoner of Zenda, The
Ragged Messenger, The
Red Pottage
Revenge of Mr. Thomas Atkins, The
Rupert of Hentzau
Sheba
Shulamite, The
Sons of Satan, The
Sunken Rocks
Turf Conspiracy, A
When Knights Were Bold
Whoso Diggeth a Pit
You

44
ANDEAN, Richard*
Hamlet (Bernardo and Second Player)

45
ANDERSON, Andy*
Oriental Love
Saved by Wireless

46
ANDERSON, Claire*
Bath Tub Perils

Cinders of Love
Clever Dummy, A
Late Lamented, The
Object of Affection
She Loved a Sailor

47
ANDERSON, Cora*
Dizzy Heights and Daring Hearts

48
ANDERSON, Dave*
Dizzy Heights and Daring Hearts
His Last Laugh

49
ANDERSON, George*
Little Pal

50
ANDERSON, Gilbert M. "Bronco
    Billy" (Max Aaronson) (1882-1970)
Across the Plains
Alkali Ike in Jayville
Alkali Ike Plays the Devil
Alkali Ike Stung!
Alkali Ike's Auto
Alkali Ike's Boarding House
Alkali Ike's Close Shave
Alkali Ike's Homecoming
Alkali Ike's Misfortune
Alkali Ike's Motorcycle
Alkali Ike's Pants
Away out West
Awful Skate, An
Bad Man's Christmas, The
Bad Man's Downfall, The
Bandit's Wife, The
Bearded Bandit, The
Best Man Wins
Black Sheep, The
Border Ranger, The
Boss of the Katy Mine
Bronco Billy and the Baby
Bronco Billy and the Bad Man
Bronco Billy and the Card Sharp
Bronco Billy and the Claim Jumpers
Bronco Billy and the Escaped Bandit
Bronco Billy and the False Note
Bronco Billy and the Land Grabber
Bronco Billy and the Lumber King
Bronco Billy and the Maid
Bronco Billy and the Mine Shark
Bronco Billy and the Outlaw's Mother
Bronco Billy and the Posse
Bronco Billy and the Rattler
Bronco Billy and the Red Hand
Bronco Billy and the Rustler's Child

Bronco Billy and the Settler's Daughter
Bronco Billy and the Sheriff
Bronco Billy and the Sheriff's Kid
Bronco Billy and the Squatter's Daughter
Bronco Billy and the Step-sisters
Bronco Billy and the Vigilante
Bronco Billy Begins Life Anew
Bronco Billy Evens Matters
Bronco Billy--Guardian
Bronco Billy--Gunman
Bronco Billy Misled
Bronco Billy Outwitted
Bronco Billy--Sheepman
Bronco Billy Steps In
Bronco Billy Well Repaid
Bronco Billy's Adventure
Bronco Billy's Bible
Bronco Billy's Brother
Bronco Billy's Christmas Deed
Bronco Billy's Close Call
Bronco Billy's Cowardly Brother
Bronco Billy's Cunning
Bronco Billy's Duty
Bronco Billy's First Arrest
Bronco Billy's Gratefulness
Bronco Billy's Greaser Deputy
Bronco Billy's Gunplay
Bronco Billy's Heart
Bronco Billy's Jealousy
Bronco Billy's Last Deed
Bronco Billy's Leap
Bronco Billy's Love Affair
Bronco Billy's Marriage
Bronco Billy's Mexican Wife
Bronco Billy's Outlaw
Bronco Billy's Parents
Bronco Billy's Promise
Bronco Billy's Protege
Bronco Billy's Punishment
Bronco Billy's Redemption
Bronco Billy's Secret
Bronco Billy's Sentence
Bronco Billy's Sermon
Bronco Billy's Sister
Bronco Billy's Squareness
Bronco Billy's Teachings
Bronco Billy's True Love
Bronco Billy's Vengeance
Bronco Billy's Ward
Bronco Billy's Way
Bronco Billy's Word of Honor
Bronco's Surrender
Calling of Jim Barton
Carmencita the Faithful
Champion, The (an extra)
Corporation and the Ranch Girl, The

Count and the Cowboy, The
Cowboy and the Squaw, The
Cowboy Coward
Cowboy's Mother-in-law, A
Cowboy's Vindication, A
Cowpuncher's Ward, The
Cutting California Redwoods
Dance at Silver Gulch
Deputy's Love Affair, The
Desperado, The
Dumb Half-breed's Defense, The
Faithful Indian, The
Flower of the Ranch, The
Forest Ranger, The
Gambler of the West, A
Girl of the West, A
Girl on the Triple X, The
Golden Trail, The
Good-for-Nothing, The
Great Train Robbery, The
Heart of a Cowboy
Hidden Mine, The
His Reformation
Indian Friendship, An
Indian Girl's Love
Indian Maiden's Lesson, The
Indian Trailer, The
Infant of Snakeville, The
Influence on Bronco Billy
Interference of Bronco Billy
Judgement
Last Roundup, The
Love on the Luck Ranch
Lucky Card, The
Marked Trail, The
Mexican's Gratitude, A
Millionaire and the Girl, The
Mistaken Bandit, The
Mother of the Ranch, The
On the Desert's Edge
Outlaw and the Child, The
Outlaw's Sacrifice, The
Pals of the Range
Patricia of the Plains
Pony Express Rider, The
Prospector, The
Puncher's New Love, The
Ranch Girl's Legacy, The
Ranch Girl's Trail, The
Ranchman's Feud, The
Ranchman's Rival, The
Red Blood and Yellow
Red Riding Hood of the Hills
Reward of Bronco Billy
Romance of Bar "O"
Sheriff's Brother, The
Sheriff's Child, The
Sheriff's Chum, The

Sheriff's Honeymoon, The
Sheriff's Inheritance, The
Sheriff's Luck, The
Sheriff's Sacrifice, The
Sheriff's Story, The
Shootin' Mad
Shotgun Ranchman, The
Silent Message, The
Smuggler's Daughter, The
Snakeville's New Doctor
Spanish Girl
Take Me out to the Ball Game
Tale of the West, A
Tenderfoot Messenger, The
Three Gamblers, The
Thwarted Vengeance, A
Tomboy on Bar Z, The
Tout's Remembrance, The
Trailed by the West
Treachery of Bronco Billy's Pal
Tribe's Penalty, The
Two Reformations
Under Western Skies
Unknown Claim, The
Western Chivalry
Western Girls
Western Maid, A
Westerner's Way, A
When Love and Honor Called
Why Bronco Billy Left Bear Country
Stage:
Life 1902
Big Show, The 1916

51
ANDERSON, Mary (1859-   )
Change in Baggage, A
False Faces (Cecelia Brooks)
Father's Flirtation
Magnificent Meddler, The
Tangled Tangoists
Train of Incidents, A
Stage:
Miss Innocence 1908

52
ANDERSON, Mignon*
Merchant of Venice, The (Jessica)
Two Little Dromios (dual role)

53
ANDERSON, Nellie*
Scarlet Runner, The (serial)

54
ANDERSON, Robert*
Common Property
Fires of Faith

Heart of Humanity, The
Hearts of the World (Monsieur
   Cukoo)

55
ANDRÉ, Victor*
Trip to the Moon, A (member of
   Scientific Congress)

56
ANIBUS, Pearl*
Hazards of Helen, The (serial)

57
ANKEWICH, Camille (Marcia
   Mannon)*
Stella Maris

58
ANNABELLE see WHITFORD,
   Annabelle

59
ANNARD, J.*
Romeo and Juliet (Tybalt)

60
AOKI, Tsuru (1892-1962)
Alien Souls
Ashes of Desire
Bonds of Honor
Call of the East, The
Courageous Coward, The
Curse of Iku, The
Dragon Painter, The
Gray Horizon
Hearts in Pawn
His Birthright
Typhoon, The

61
APFEL, Oscar C.*
Squaw Man, The
Stage:
Optimist, The 1906

62
APPLING, Bert*
Grand Passion, The (Red Pete
   Jackson)

63
ARBUCKLE, Andrew*
Hoodlum, The

64
ARBUCKLE, Macklyn (1866-1931)
County Chairman, The

It's No Laughing Matter
Stage:
Better 'Ole, The (Old Bill) 1918
County Chairman, The 1903
Home Again 1918
Lord and Lady Algy 1917
Merchant of Venice, The (Antonio)
  1901
Misalliance (John Tarleton) 1917
Round Up, The 1907
Skipper and Co., Wall Street 1903
Sprightly Romance of Morsco, The
  1900
Triumph of Love, The 1904
Under Two Flags 1901
Welcome to Our City 1910
Why Smith Left Home 1899

65
ARBUCKLE, Roscoe "Fatty" (Roscoe
  Conklin Arbuckle) (1887-1933)
Alarm, The
At the San Diego Exposition
Back Stage
Bandit, A
Barnyard Flirtations
Bath House Beauty, A
Bell Boy, The
Brand New Hero, A
Bright Lights, The /aka/ The Lure
  of Broadway
Butcher Boy, The
Camping Out
Caught in a Cabaret
Chicken Chaser, The
Coney Island
Cook, The
Creampuff Romance, A /aka/ His
  Alibi
Desert Hero
Eavesdropper, An
Faithful Taxicab, The
Fatal Flirt, A
Fatty Again /aka/ Fatty the Four
  Flusher
Fatty and Mabel
Fatty and Mabel Adrift
Fatty and Mabel at the San Diego
  Exposition
Fatty and Mabel's Married Life
Fatty and Mabel's Simple Life
Fatty and Minnie-He-Haw
Fatty and the Broadway Stars
Fatty and the Heiress
Fatty at San Diego
Fatty in Coney Island
Fatty Joins the Force
Fatty on the Job

Fatty's Affair of Honor
Fatty's Chance Acquaintance
Fatty's Day Off
Fatty's Debut /aka/ Fatty Butts In
Fatty's Faithful Fido
Fatty's Feature Film
Fatty's Finish
Fatty's Flirtation
Fatty's Gift
Fatty's Hoo-Doo Day
Fatty's Jonah Day
Fatty's Magic Pants /aka/ Fatty's
  Suitless Day
Fatty's New Role
Fatty's Plucky Pup
Fatty's Reckless Fling
Fatty's Sweetheart
Fatty's Tin Type Tangle
Fatty's Wine Party
Fickle Fatty's Fall
Film Johnny, A /aka/ Movie Nut
  and Million Dollar Job
Flirt's Mistake, A
For the Love of Mabel
Gangsters, The
Garage, The
Goodnight Nurse
Gypsy Queen, The
Hayseed, The
He Did and He Didn't /aka/ Love
  and Lobsters
He Would a Hunting Go
Help! Help! Hydrophobia!
His Favorite Pastime
His Sister's Kids
His Wedding Night
His Wife's Mistake
In the Clutches of a Gang
Incompetent Hero, An
Knockout, The
Leading Lizzie Astray
Little Teacher, The /aka/ A Small
  Town Bully
Love
Love and Courage
Love in Armor
Lover's Luck
Lover's Post Office
Mabel and Fatty Viewing the World's
  Fair at San Francisco
Mabel and Fatty's Wash Day
Mabel, Fatty and the Law /aka/
  Fatty's Spooning Day
Mabel's Dramatic Career /aka/
  Her Dramatic Debut
Mabel's New Hero
Masquerader, The
Misplaced Foot, A

Miss Fatty's Seaside Lovers
Moonshine
Mother's Boy
Noise from the Deep, A
Oh, Doctor!
Other Man, The
Out West
Passions, He Had Three
Quiet Little Wedding, A
Rebecca's Wedding Day
Reckless Romeo, A
Riot, The
Robust Romeo, A
Rounders, The
Rural Demon, A
Sea Nymphs /aka/ His Diving Beauty
Sheriff, The
Shotguns That Kick
Sky Pirate, The
Speed Queen, The
Surf Girl, The
Suspended Ordeal, A
Tango Tales
Teddy Telzlaff and Earl Cooper,
    Speed Kings
Telltale Light, The
That Little Band of Gold
That Minstrel Man
Their Ups and Downs
Those Country Kids
Those Happy Days
Undersheriff, The
Village Scandal, The
Waiter's Ball, The
Waiter's Picnic, The
Water Dog, The
When Love Took Wings
Where Hazel Met the Villain
Woman Haters, The
Zip, the Dodger

66
ARCHER, Harry*
Red Ace, The (serial)

67
ARDEN, Edwin*
New Exploits of Elaine, The (serial)
Stage:
Any House 1916
Aztec Romance, An 1912
Caleb West 1900
Caste 1910
Fedora (Loris Ipanoff) 1905
Frederick Wagner 1913
Happy Marriage, The 1909
Hearts Are Trumps 1900
His Wife's Family 1908

House of Silence, The 1906
Irene Wycherley 1908
Israel 1909
L'Aiglon-Metternick 1900
Marriage Game, The 1901
Merely Mary Ann (Lancelot) 1903-04
Ninety and Nine, The 1902
Question, The 1912
Redskin, The 1906
Regeneration, The 1908
Romeo and Juliet 1903
Thief, The 1911
Truth Wagon, The 1911
Via Wireless 1908
Whirlwind, The 1911
You Never Can Tell (Fergus
    Crampton) 1915

68
AREY, Wayne*
King Lear (Albany)
Stage:
Blue Grass 1908
Princess Players, The (repertory)
    1913
Vik 1914

69
ARLEY, Cecil see ARNOLD, Cecil

70
ARLING, Charles*
Court House Crooks
Crooked to the End
Favorite Fool, A
Footlight Parade, A
Oily Scoundrel, An
Rascal of Wolfish Ways, A
Stage:
Erminie 1903

71
ARMSTRONG, Billy*
Bank, The
By the Sea
Hula Hula Land
Lover's Might, A /aka/ The Fire
    Chief
Police
Royal Rogue, A
Shanghaied
Shanghaied Jonah
Tramp, The
Triple Trouble
Woman, A
Work

72
ARMSTRONG, Marguerite see
 [Miss] DuPONT

73
ARNOLD, Cecile*
Dough and Dynamite /aka/ The
 Doughnut Designers
Face on the Barroom Floor, The
 /aka/ The Ham Artist
Game Old Knight, A
Getting Acquainted
Gussle's Day of Rest
His Last Scent
His Prehistoric Past
Masquerader, The
Those Love Pangs

74
ARNOLD, Edward (Guenther Schnei-
 der) (1890-1956)
Primitive Strain, The
Stage:
Mid-Channel (Cole) 1910
She Would and She Did 1919
Storm, The (Burr Winton) 1919

75
ARNOLD, Helen*
Witching Hour, The

76
ARONSON, Gustaf*
Sir Arne's Treasure

77
ARTHUR, Julia (1869-)
Common Cause, The
Woman the Germans Shot, The
Stage:
Eternal Magdalene, The 1915
More Than Queen 1899
Out There 1918
Seremonda 1917

78
ARTHUR, Paul*
Real Thing At Last, The

79
ARVIDSON, Linda (Linda Johnson/
 Mrs. D. W. Griffith) (1884-1949)
Adventures of Dollie, The (Dollie)
Awful Moment, An
Balked at the Altar
Barbarian, Ingomar, The
Charity
Comata, the Sioux

Converts, The
Convict's Sacrifice, A
Cord of Life
Corner in Wheat, A
Cricket on the Hearth, The
Curtain Pole, The
Day After, The
Death Disc, The
Deception, The
Drunkard's Reformation, A
Edgar Allan Poe
Enoch Arden, Part I, Part II
Fair Rebel, A
Fisher Folks
Greaser's Gauntlet, The
Heart Beats of Long Ago
Helping Hand, The
Her First Biscuits
House that Jack Built
In a Hamper Bag
Lines of White on a Sullen Sea
Lucky Toothache, A
Man and the Woman, The
Mills of the Gods
Mission Bells
Peach Basket Hat, The
Pippa Passes
Planter's Wife, The
Politician's Love Story, The
Rocky Road, The
Salvation Army Lass, The
Scarlet Letter, The
1776, or The Hessian Renegades
Test of Friendship
Tragic Love
Unchanging Sea, The
When Knights Were Bold
Wife, The

80
ASH, Jerry*
Purple Mask, The (serial)

81
ASHER, Max (1880-1957)
Almost an Actor (the director)
Cheese Special, The
Lady Baffles and Detective Duck
Mike and Jake at the Beach
Traffic in Soles

82
ASHLEY, Arthur*
Summer Girl, The

83
ASHTON, Sylvia*
Dash through the Clouds, A

Don't Change Your Husband (Mrs.
  Huckney)
For Better, For Worse (Sylvia's Aunt)
For the Defense
Her Fame and Shame
Lottery Man, The
Men, Women and Money
Nick of Time Baby
Old Wives for New (Sophy Murdock)
Pair of Silk Stockings, A
Secrets of a Beauty Parlor
We Can't Have Everything (Kedizie's
  Mother)
Would-Be Shriner, The

84
ASQUITH, Miss Elizabeth*
Great Love, The (herself)

85
ASTAIRE, Adele (Adele Austerlitz)*
Fanchon the Cricket
Stage:
Apple Blossoms (Molly) 1919
Over the Top 1917
Passing Show of 1918, The 1918

86
ASTAIRE, Fred (Frederick Austerlitz)
  (1899-)
Fanchon the Cricket
Stage:
Apple Blossoms (Johnny) 1919
Over the Top 1917
Passing Show of 1918, The 1918

87
ASTOR, Camille*
Chimmie Fadden (Hortense)
Chimmie Fadden Out West (The
  Duchess)

88
ASTOR, Gertrude (1906-)
Bondage (Eugenia Dawn)
Cheyenne's Pal
Gray Ghost, The (serial)
Lion Man, The (serial)
Lion's Claw, The (serial)
Rescue, The
Wicked Darling, The (Adele Hoyt)

89
ATKINS, Robert*
Hamlet (Marcellus and First Player)

90
ATKINSON, Josephine (Mrs. Paul

Panzer)*
Romeo and Juliet (bit part)

91
ATWILL, Lionel (1885-1946)
Marriage Price, The
Stage:
Another Man's Shoes 1918
Doll's House, A (Torvald Helmer)
  1918
Eve's Daughter 1917
Hedda Gabler (George Tesman) 1918
Indestructible Wife, The 1918
L'Elevation 1917
Lodger, The 1917
Mrs. Thompson 1915
Tiger! Tiger! 1918
Walls of Jericho, The (stage debut)
  1904

92
AUBREY, Jimmy*
Footlights and Fakers
Heinie and Louie comedies:
  Merry Chase, A
  Monkey Shines
Mules and Mortgages

93
AUEN, Signe see OWEN, Seena

94
AUER, Florence (1880-1962)
King Lear (wicked sister)
Richard III
Snow Man, The
Stage:
Ranger, The 1907
Robert B. Mantell Repertory 1915

95
AUGUST, Edwin (Philip Von der
  Buts) (1883-1964)
Blot on the 'Scutcheon
Bondwoman
Broadway Scandal, A (David Kendall)
Child's Impulse, A
City of Tears
Eternal Mother, The
From out the Shadows
Fugitive, The
Getting Even
Girl and Her Trust, A
Hand that Rocked the Cradle, The
His Daughter
Lesser Evil, The
Lion's Claw, The (serial)
Madame Rex

Mortgaged Wife
Old Actor, The
One Is Business, the Other Is
    Crime
Poison Pen
Primitive Man
Renunciation, The
Romance of an Actor, The
Sands of Dee, The
School Teacher and the Waif, The
Simple Charity
Tale of the Wilderness, A
Tale of Two Cities, A
Tale of Two Nations, A
White Roses
Winning Back His Love
Yellow Passport
Stage:
Mr. and Mrs. Daventry 1910

96
AUGUST, Hal*
Romance of an Actor, The

97
AUSTIN, Albert*
Adventurer, The
Behind the Screen
Bond, The
Count, The
Cure, The
Day's Pleasure, A
Dog's Life, A
Easy Street
Fireman, The
Floorwalker, The
Immigrant, The
One A. M. (taxi driver)
Pawnshop, The
Rink, The (dual role)
Shoulder Arms (dual role)
Sunnyside
Triple Trouble
Vagabond, The

98
AUSTIN, Jere*
School for Scandal, The

99
AVERY, Charles*
Cohen's Outing
Sleuth's Last Stand, The
Telltale Light, The
Stage:
David Harum (Peleg Hopkins) 1900
Miss Elizabeth's Prisoner 1903

100
AYERS, Cleo*
Third Judgement, The

101
AYERS, Sydney*
Trapped in a Forest Fire

102
AYRES, Agnes (Agnes Hinkle)
    (1896-1940)
Bottom of the Well
Defeat of the City, The
Enchanted Profile, The
Forbidden Fruit
Girl and the Graft, The
His New Job (an extra)
O. Henry series (25)
$1,000
Purple Dress, The
Richard the Brazen
Sacred Silence

- B -

103
BACKNER, Arthur*
Taming of the Shrew, The
    (Petruchio)

104
BACKNER, Constance*
Taming of the Shrew, The
    (Katherina)

105
BACON, Frank (1864-1922)
Corner in Cotton, A
Rosemary
Silent Voice, The
Stage:
Barbara 1917
Cinderella Man, The 1916
Lightnin' (Lightnin' Bill Jones) 1918
Miracle Man, The (Hiram Higgins)
    1914
Stop Thief 1912

106
BACON, Lloyd (1890-1955)
Bank, The
Behind the Screen
Champion, The
Corner in Cotton, A
Fireman, The
Floorwalker, The
In the Park

Jitney Elopement, The
Rink, The
Tramp, The
Vagabond, The

107
BADGELY, Helen*
Dog's Love, A

108
BAGGOTT, King (1880-1948)
Absinthe
Across the Atlantic
City of Terrible Night
Corsican Brothers, The (dual role)
Crime's Triangle
Dr. Jekyll and Mr. Hyde (dual role)
Eagle's Eye, The
Hawk's Trail, The
Human Hearts
Ivanhoe
Jane and the Stranger
Kildare of the Storm
Lady Audley's Secret
Man Who Stayed at Home, The
Scarlet Letter, The
Wishing Ring, The
Stage:
Mrs. Wiggs of the Cabbage Patch
   (Mr. Bob) 1906

109
BAILEY, Gordon*
Romeo and Juliet (Mercutio)

110
BAILEY, William*
Eagle's Eye, The
Snare, The
Stage:
Forbidden (Count Robert von Eckdorf)
   1919

111
BAIRD, Leah (1887-)
Absinthe
As a Man Thinks
Bunny and the Bunny Hug
Chumps
Cure for Pokeritus
Echo of Youth
Hearts of the First Empire
Ivanhoe
Life of Honor
Locket, The
Moral Suicide
Neptune's Daughter
One Law for Both

People vs. John Doe, The
Souls in Bondage
Stenographer Wanted (the brunette)
Sunset, A
There's Music in the Hair
Tried for His Own Murder
Volcano, The
When a Woman Wars
Window Opposite, The
Wolves of Kultur (serial)
Working for Hubby

112
BAKER, Gene*
Carter Case, The (the Craig Kennedy
   serial)

113
BALFOUR, Sue*
Great Secret, The (serial)

114
BALLIN, Mabel (1885-1958)
Illustrious Prince, The
Lord and Lady Algy
Quickening Flame, The
White Heather, The

115
BANKHEAD, Tallulah (1902-1968)
Thirty a Week
Virtuous Vamp, The
When Men Betray
Wishful Girl, The
Stage:
Footloose 1919
Squab Farm, The 1918
39 East 1919

116
BARA, Theda (Theodosia Goodman)
   (1890-1955)
Camille (Camille)
Caravan
Carmen (Carmen)
Clemenceau Case, The (Iza)
Cleopatra (Cleopatra)
Darling of Paris, The (Esmeralda)
Destruction (Ferdinande)
Devil's Daughter, The (La Gioconda)
East Lynne (Isabel)
Eternal Sapho (Sapho)
Fool There Was, A (the vampire)
Forbidden Path, The (Mary Lynde)
Galley Slave, The (Francesca Bra-
   bout)
Gold and the Woman (Juliet DeCor-
   dova)

Heart and Soul (Jess)
Her Double Life (Mary Doone)
Her Greatest Love (Vera Herbert)
Kathleen Mavourneen (Kathleen)
Kreutzer Sonata (Celia Friedlander)
La Belle Russe (La Belle)
Lady Audley's Secret (Helen Devenaut)
Light, The (Blanchette Dumonde)
Lure of Ambition, The (Olga Dolan)
Madame DuBarry (Countess DuBarry)
Message of the Lillies
Price of Silence, The
Romeo and Juliet (Juliet)
Rose of the Blood (Liza Tapenko)
Salome (Salome)
Serpent, The (Vania Lazar)
She-Devil, The (Lolette)
Sin (Rosa)
Siren's Song, The (Marie Bernais)
Soul of Buddah, The (Bavahari)
Stain, The (an extra)
Tiger Woman, The (Princess Petro-
    vitch)
Two Orphans, The (Henriette)
Under the Yoke (Maria Valverde)
Under Two Flags (Cigarette)
Vixen, The (Elsie Drummond)
When a Woman Sins (Lillian Marchard)
When Men Desire (Marce Lohr)
Wolves of Kultur (serial)
Woman There Was, A (Zara)
Stage:
Devil, The (under name Theodosia
    deCappet) 1908
Quaker Girl, The 1911

117
BARCLAY, Adela*
Romeo and Juliet (nurse)

118
BARCLAY, Don*
Ambrose's Little Hatchet
Ambrose's Lofty Perch
Home Breaking Hound, A
Stage:
Ziegfeld Follies of 1916

119
BARCLAY, Lola*
Seven Sisters

120
BARKER, Bradley*
Erstwhile Susan

121
BARKER, Eric*

Toilers, The

122
BARKER, Florence*
Call, The
Chosing a Husband
Dancing Girl of Butte, The
Diamond Star, The
Faithful
Fool's Revenge, A
Her Terrible Ordeal
His Daughter
His Sister-in-Law
Last Deal, The
Two Paths, The
Usurer, The
Wreath of Orange Blossoms, A

123
BARLEON, Amelia*
Winter's Tale, A (Princess of Sicilia)
Stage:
Anthony and Cleopatra (Canidius) 1909
Arrow Maker, The 1911
Bluebird, The (Daddy Tyl) 1910-11
Children of Earth 1915
Cock O' the Walk 1915
Flower of the Palace of Man, The
    1912
Nigger, The 1909
Noah's Flood 1911
Old Lady 1916
Pigeon, The (a humble man) 1912
Prunella (Scarmel) 1913
Sins of Society, The 1909
Sister Beatrice 1910
Strife 1909
Tempest, The 1916
Terrible Meek, The 1912
Twelfth Night 1910
Votes for Woman 1909
What Happened at 22? 1914
Winter's Tale, The 1910
Yellow Jacket, The (Tai Fah Min
    and Uin Suey Gong) 1912

125
BARNES, George*
Great Train Robbery, The

126
BARNES, J. H.*
Hamlet (Polonius)
Stage:
Betty at Bay 1918
Henry Irving-Ellen Terry Co (reper-
    tory) 1901
Hypocrites, The 1906

Mrs. Leffingwell's Boots 1905
Wife without a Smile, A 1904

127
BARNES, Justice D. *
Country Girl, The

128
BARNETT, Battling*
Griffo-Barnett Fight

129
BARNETT, Charles*
Old Dutch

130
BARNETT, Chester*
Heart of the Blueridge
La Boheme
Law of Compensation, The
Trilby

131
BARRIE, Eddie*
Seminary Scandal, A

132
BARRIE, Nigel /aka/ Nigel Barre
  (1889-)
Beatrice Fairfax (serial)
Better Wife
Charge It
Marionettes, The
Widow by Proxie

133
BARRINGTON, Herbert*
Three Musketeers, The (Duke of
  Buckingham)

134
BARRISCALE, Bessie (1884-1965)
All of a Sudden Norman
Beckoning Roads
Blindfolded
Brewster's Millions
Cast-Off
Corner in Coleen's Home, A
Cup of Life, A
Eileen of Erin
Heart of Rachel
Her Purchase Price
Home
Joselyn's Wife
Maid O' the Storm
Not My Sister
Painted Soul, The
Patriotism

Payment, The
Plain Jane
Ready Money
Rose of Paradise
Rose of the Rancho, The (Juanita)
Tangled Threads
Those Who Pay
Trick of Fate
Two Gun Betty
White Lie
Within the Cup
Woman Michael Married, The
Wooden Shoes
Stage:
Cape Cod Folks 1906
We Are Seven 1913
What Would You Do? 1914

135
BARROWS, Henry*
Kaiser, The Beast of Berlin, The
  (General Pershing)
Lion Man, The (serial)

136
BARRY, Pauline*
Gold and the Woman (Ethel)

137
BARRY, Viola see PEARCE,
  Peggy

138
BARRY, Wesley (1907-)
Amarilly of Clothesline Alley
Daddy Long Legs
Her Kingdom of Dreams
Male and Female (Boots)
Rebecca of Sunnybrook Farm
Unpardonable Sin, The
Woman of Pleasure, A

139
BARRYMORE, Ethel (Ethel Blythe)
  (1879-1959)
American Widow, An
Awakening of Helena Ritchie
Call of Her People
Divorcee, The
Eternal Mother, The
Final Judgment, The
Kiss of Hate
Lady Frederick
Life's Whirlpool
Lifted Veil, The
Nightingale, The
Our Mrs. McChesney
Super Woman

Test of Honor
White Raven, The
Stage:
Alice Sit-by-the-Fire (Mrs. Grey)
   1905; 1911
Belinda 1918
Carrots 1902
Country Mouse, A 1902
Cousin Kate (Kate Curtis) 1903; 1907;
   1912
Captain Jinks of the Horse Marines
   (Madame Tretoni) 1901; 1907
Declassée (Lady Helen Haden) 1918
Doll's House, A (Nora) 1905
Her Sister 1907
His Excellency, the Governor 1907
Lady Frederick (Lady Frederick) 1908
Lady of the Camelias, The (Mar-
   guerite Gautier) 1917
Mid-Channel (Zoe Blundell) 1910
Off Chance, The 1918
Our Mrs. McChesney 1915
Scrap of Paper (Susanne DeRuseville)
   1914
Shadow, The 1915
Silver Box, The 1907
Slice of Life, A (Mrs. Hyphen-Brown)
   1912
Sunday 1904
Tante-Madame Okraska 1913
Trelawny of the Wells (Rose Trelawny)
   1911
Twelve Pound Look, The (Kate) 1905;
   1911
Witness for the Defense 1911

140
BARRYMORE, John (John Blythe)
   (1882-1942)
American Citizen, An
Are You a Mason?
Dictator, The
Here Comes the Bride
Incorrigible Dukane
Lost Bridegroom, The
Man from Mexico, The
Nearly a King
On the Quiet
Raffles, the Amateur Cracksman
Red Widow, The
Test of Honor, The
Stage:
Affairs of Anatol, The (Anatol) 1912
Alice-Sit-by-the-Fire (Stephen Rollo)
   (1905)
Believe Me, Xantippe (George Mac-
   Farland) 1913
Boys of Company B, The 1907

Dictator, The 1904
Fortune Hunter, The 1909
Glad of It 1903
His Excellency, the Governor 1907
Jest, The (Giannetto Malespini) 1919
Justice (William Falder) 1916
Kick In (Chick Hewes) 1914
Pantaloon (Clown) 1905
Peter Ibbetson (Peter) 1917
Redemption (Fedor Vasilyevich
   Protosova) 1918
Slice of Life, A (Mr. Hyphen-Brown)
   1912
Stubborn Cinderella, A 1909
Toddles 1908
Uncle Sam 1911
Yellow Ticket, The (Julian Rolfe)
   1914
Yvette 1904

141
BARRYMORE, Lionel (Lionel Blythe)
   (1878-1954)
Adventure in the Autumn Woods, An
Battle, The
Brand of Cowardice, A
Brutality
Burglar's Dilemma, The
Chief's Blanket, The
Classmates
Cry for Help, A
Death's Marathon
Exploits of Elaine, The (serial)
Face in the Fog
Fate
Fighting Blood
Friends
God Within, The
Gold and Glitter
Great Green Eye
His Father's Son
House of Darkness, The
House of Discord
Informer, The
Judith of Bethulia
Just Gold
Lady and the Mouse, The
Life's Whirlpool
Love in an Apartment Hotel
Men and Women
Millionaire's Double, The
Misunderstood Boy, A
Musketeers of Pig Alley, The
My Baby
My Hero
Near to Earth
New York Hat, The
Oil and Water

One She Loved, The
Perfidy of Mary, The
Peter Ibbetson
Power of the Press
Ranchero's Revenge, The
Romance of Elaine, The (serial)
Sheriff's Baby, The
So Near, Yet So Far
Strongheart
Tenderhearted, The
Timely Interception, A
Three Friends
Vengeance of Galora, The
Wanderer, The
Yaqui Cur, The
Yellow Streak
Stage:
Arizona (Sgt. Kellar) 1900
Bachelor's Baby (St. Jones) 1895
Best of Friends, The (Kid Garvey)
    1903
Bob Acres (scenes from "The
    Rivals") 1911
Brixton Burglary, The 1901
Cooperhead, The (Milt Shanks) 1918
Cumberland 61 (Adolfus Drayton
    Lenox) 1897
East Lynne (Richard Hare)
    (Minneapolis) 1898
Fires of Fate, The (Abdulla) 1909
Honorable John Rigsby (Harold
    Marson) 1898
Jail Bird, The 1910
Jest, The (Neri Ciaramantesi) 1919
Magda (Max) (Minneapolis) 1898
Mary Pennington, Spinster (Watson)
    1896
Mummy and the Hummingbird, The
    1902-03
Other Girl, The (Mr. Sheldon)
    1903-04
Pantaloon (Pantaloon) 1905
Peter Ibbetson (Col. Ibbetson) 1917
Rivals, The 1893
Road to Ruin, The (footman) 1894
Sag Harbor 1900
Second in Command, The 1901
Squire Kate (Lord Silversnake) 1896
Still Voice, The 1912
Uncle Dick (Lawrence Sherman) 1898
White Slaver, The (Italian laborer)
    1910-11

142
BARTET, Julia*
Le Retour d'Ulysse

143
BARTHLEMESS, Richard (1895-1963)

Bab's Burglar
Bab's Diary
Boots
Broken Blossoms (the Chinaman)
Eternal Sin, The
Girl Who Stayed at Home, The
    (Ralph Grey)
Gloria's Romance (serial)
Hit the Trail Holiday
Hope Chest, The
I'll Get Him Yet
Nearly Married
Peppy Polly
Rich Man, Poor Man
Scarlet Days (Alvarez)
Seven Swans
Three Men and a Girl
War Brides

144
BARY, Leon*
Mystery of the Double Cross, The
    (serial)
Seven Pearls, The (serial)
Shielding Shadow, The (serial)

145
BASQUETTE, Lina (Lina Belcher)
    (1907-)
Juvenile Dancer
Prince for a Day
Shoes
Supreme

146
BASSETT, Russell*
Behind the Scenes
Best Man Wins, The
Hit the Trail Holiday
Hulda from Holland
Jim, the Penman
Less than the Dust
Little Pal
Such a Little Queen
Stage:
Other Fellow, The 1910
Rip Van Winkle (Nick Vedder) 1905
Top o' th' World, The 1907-08

147
BATEMAN, Victory*
Romeo and Juliet (Lady Montague)
Stage:
Yellow Jacket, The 1916-17

148
BATES, Blanche (1873-)
Border Legion, The
Stage:

Children of the Ghetto 1899
Darling of the Gods, The (Princess
Yo-San) 1902
Diplomacy 1914
Famous Mrs. Fair, The (Nancy
Fair) 1919
Fighting Hope, The (Anna) 1908-09
Getting Together 1918
Girl of the Golden West, The (the
girl) 1905; 1908
Moliere (Francoise Marquise de
Montespan) 1919
Naughty Anthony 1900
Nobody's Widow (Roxana Clayton)
1910
Under Two Flags 1901

149
BATLEY, Dorothy (1902-   )
Child Mother, The
Child's Strategy, A
Christmas without Daddy
Girl Boy Scout, The
Little Child Shall Lead Them, A
Master Crook Outwitted by a Child,
The
Those Children
Three Little Orphans

150
BATLEY, Ernest G. (Ethyle Batley)
(1879-1917)
Across the Wires
Answering the Call
Boys of the Old Brigade
Charles Peace, King of Criminals
Child Mother, The
Child's Strategy, A
Christmas without Daddy
Deliver the Goods
Enemy Amongst Us, The
Englishman's Home, An
Future Safeguard
Girl Boy Scout, The
Great Red War, The
Guy Fawkes and the Gunpowder Plot
Into the Light
Keep the Home Fires Burning
Kleptomania Tablets
Little Child Shall Lead Them, A
Master Crook Outwitted by a Child,
The
Master Crook Turns Detective, The
Midnight Wedding, The
One Shall Be Taken
Out of Evil Cometh Good
Peggy Gets Rid of the Baby
Pressure of the Poster, The

Red Cross Pluck
Revolution
Tattooed Will, The
There's Good in the Worst of Us
Those Children
Three Little Orphans
Through the Flames
Two Father Christmases
War Is Hell
When London Sleeps
When the Germans Entered Loos
Woman Pays, The

151
BATTISTA, Miriam (1914-   )
Blazing Love
Eye for Eye
Stage:
Daddy Long Legs 1918
Freedom 1918
Papa 1919
Red Dawn, The 1919
Whirlwind, The (Mariquita) 1919

152
BAUER, Harry (1881-1941)
Shylock (Shylock)

153
BAXTER, Warner (1893-1951)
All Woman
Traitor, The
Stage:
Lombardi, Ltd. (Riccardo Tosello)
1917

154
BAYLEY, Eva*
Life of William Shakespeare, The
(Shakespeare's mother)

155
BAYLISS, Blanche*
Miss Jerry

156
BAYNE, Beverly (1896-   )
Adopted Son, The
Billy the Bear Tamer
Blood Will Tell
Brass Check, The
Cyclone Higgins, D. F.
Daring Hearts
God's Outlaw
Good Catch, A
Graustark
Great Secret, The (serial)
Loan Shark, The

Magic Wand, The
Of Conscience
One Wonderful Night
Pair of Cupids, A
Poor Rich Man
Red White and Blue Blood
Romeo and Juliet (Juliet)
Snare, The
Social Quicksands
Their Compact
Under Royal Patronage
Under Suspicion
With Neatness and Dispatch

157
BEAUDET, Louise (1861-1948)
Battle Cry of Peace
Bunny's Mistake
Father's Flirtation
Love's Way
Mr. Bunny in Disguise
Model Wife, A
Price for Folly, The
Setting the Style
Tangled Tangoists
Stage:
Flo-Flo 1917
One Night in Rome (Mrs. Redlynch)
    1919

158
BEAUMAR, Constance*
Getting Mary Married (Matilda
    Bussard)

159
BEAUMONT, Harry*
Active Life of Dolly of the Dailies,
    The

160
BEBAN, George (1873-1928)
Alien, The
Hearts of Men
Italian, The
Jules of the Strong Heart
Lost in Transit
One More American
Pasquale
Stage:
About Town 1906
All Star Variety Jubilee 1913
American Idea, The 1908
Bunty, Bulls and Strings 1912
Fantana 1905
Girl Behind the Counter, The 1907
Hokey-Pokey 1912
Moonshine 1905

Nancy Brown 1903
Sign of the Rose, The 1911

161
BECHTEL, William*
Lurking Peril, The (serial)
Three Musketeers, The (King
    Louis XIII)
Stage:
DeLancey 1905
Toymaker of Nuremberg, The 1907

162
BECK, Cornish*
Broadway Bill
Stage:
Moloch 1915

163
BECKLEY, Beatrice*
Prisoner of Zenda, The
Stage:
Caliban of the Yellow Sands 1916
Declassée (Charlotte Ashley) 1919
Freedom of Suzzane, The 1905
Ideal Husband, An (Lady Chiltern)
    1918
John Gladye's Honour 1907
Knife, The 1917
Walls of Jericho, The 1906
Why Marry? (Lucy) 1917

164
BEECH, Frances*
Mirandy Smiles

165
BEERY, Noah (1884-1946)
Believe Me, Xantippe
Hostage, The
In Mizzoura
Less Than Kin
Louisana
Red Lantern
Source, The
Squaw Man, The (Tabywana)
Valley of the Giants
Whispering Chorus, The (Long-
    shoreman)
Woman Next Door, The
Stage:
As Ye Sow 1905
Siberia 1905

166
BEERY, Wallace (1886-1949)
Broken Pledge, The
Cactus Nell

Clever Dummy, A (vaudeville
  manager)
Dash of Courage, A
Johanna Enlists
Life Line, The
Little American, The
Love Burglar, The
Maggie's First False Step
Romany Rye
Sweedie Comedies
Sweedie Goes to College
Teddy at the Throttle (rascally
  guardian)
Unpardonable Sin, The
Victory (Schomberg)
Stage:
Yankee Tourist, A 1907

167
BEERY, William*
Soldiers of Fortune

168
BEHRENS, William*
Railroad Raiders, The (serial)

169
BELASCO, David (1854-1931)
Star over Night, A

170
BELASCO, Jay*
Bobbie of the Ballet
Gilded Spider, The
Grasp of Greed
Grip of Jealousy, The
Price of Silence, The (Billy Cupps)
Some Nurse
Tangled Hearts

171
BELCHER, Frank*
Gloria's Romance (serial)
Stage:
Dream City 1906
My Best Girl 1912
Skylark, A 1910
Sweethearts 1913
When Sweet Sixteen 1911

172
BELFORD, Hazel*
Deserter, The (Mary)

173
BELL, Digby (Digby Valentine Bell)
  (1851-1917)
Father and the Boys

Stage:
Debtors, The 1909
Education of Mr. Pipp, The (J.
  Wesley Pipp) 1905
Gilbert and Sullivan Opera Company
  1915
International Marriage, An 1909
Mr. Pickwick (Sam Weller) 1903

174
BELL, Gaston*
Destruction (Jack Froment)

175
BELL, Montana*
Adventurer, The

176
BELL, Tula*
Bluebird, The
Deliverance

177
BELLEW, Dorothy (Dorothy Falck)
  (1891-   )
At the Hour of Three
Avenging Hand, The
Behind the Scenes
Convent Gate, The
Disraeli
Face to Face
Family Solicitor, The
Father and Son
Foiled by a Girl
For Her Mother's Sake
Gardner's Daughter, The
Hard Times
Her Guardian
House of Mystery, The
In Peace and War
In the Blood
Jealous Cavalier, The
King Charles
Lead Kindly Light
Lt. Rose and the Stolen Submarine
Locket, The
Lost Cord, The
Love of an Actress, The
Master of Men
Master of the Merripit, The
Maud
Miraculous Recovery, A
Night and Morning
Profligate, The
Saved by Fire
Secret Life
Seventh Word, The
Southern Blood

Strong Man's Love, A
Treasure of Heaven, The
Under the German Yoke
When East Meets West
Wreck and Ruin

178
BELLEW, Kryle (1855-1911)
Gentleman of France, A
Stage:
Brigadier Gerard 1906
Builders of Bridges, The 1909
Gentleman of France, A 1901
Lady of Lyons, The (Claude Melnotle)
  1902
Marriage of Reason, A 1907
Raffles, The Amateur Cracksman
  (A. J. Raffles) 1903; 1910
Romeo and Juliet (Romeo) 1903
Sacrament of Judas, The (Jacques
  Bernez) 1903
Scandal, The 1910
School for Scandal (Charles Surface)
  1902
She Stoops to Conquer (Young
  Marlowe) 1905
Thief, The (Richard Voysin) 1907
Two Orphans, The (Chevalier
  DeVaudrey) 1904

179
BELMONT, Joseph*
A La Cabaret
Bath House Blunder
Better Late Than Never /aka/
  Getting Married
Dollars and Sense /aka/ The Twins
Her Circus Knight /aka/ The Circus
  Girl
Love Comet
Oriental Love
Skidding Hearts
Wife and Auto Trouble
Wings and Wheels

180
BELMORE, Lionel*
Romeo and Juliet

181
BENEDICT, Kingsley*
Burgler of Algiers, The
Mystery Ship, The (serial)
Stage:
Under Southern Skies 1901

182
BENHAM, Dorothy*
Thanhouser player as a child 1913

183
BENHAM, Ethyle*
Thanhouser player 1913

184
BENHAM, Harry
Cecilia of the Pink Roses (Harry
  Twombly)
Dr. Jekyll and Mr. Hyde
Merchant of Venice, The
Zudora (The Twenty Million Dollar
  Mystery) (serial)
Stage:
Peggy from Paris 1903
Rainbow Girl, The 1918

185
BENHAM, Leland*
Thanhouser player as a child 1913

186
BENNETT, Belle (1891-1932)
Ashes of Hope
Atom, The
Because of a Woman
Bond of Fear
Charmer, The
Devil Dodger, The
Fires of Rebellion
Fuel of Life
Hellcat of Alaska, The
Judgment of the Guilty
Last Rebel, The
Lonely Woman, The
Mayor of Filbert, The
Reckoning Day
Soul in Trust, A
Sweet Kitty Bellairs

187
BENNETT, Billie*
Best of Enemies, The
Cinders of Love
Hearts and Sparks
His Last Laugh
Tillie's Punctured Romance

188
BENNETT, Charles*
Adventures of Ruth, The (serial)
Tillie's Punctured Romance (Uncle
  and 2 minor roles)

189
BENNETT, Enid (1894-1969)
Aryan, The
Biggest Show on Earth
Carmen of the Klondike
Desert Wooing, A

Extravagance
Fuss and Feathers
Happy Though Married
Haunted Bedroom, The
Italian, The
Keys of the Right House
Law of Men
Marriage Ring
Naughty Naughty
Partners Three
Princess in the Dark
Stepping Out
Vamp, The
Vive La France!
What Every Woman Learns
When Do We Eat?
Wrath of the Gods, The
Stage:
Cock o' the Walk 1915

190
BENNETT, Frank*
Intolerance (Charles IX)
Reggie Mixes In (Cafe owner's
    assistant)
Stage:
Winter's Tale, The 1904

191
BENNETT, Hugh*
Secret of the Submarine, The (serial)

192
BENNETT, Joseph*
Crown Jewels
Golden Fleece
Indiscreet Corrine
Limousine Life
Man's Desire
Marked Cards
Rose of Hell
Terror, The
Stage:
Love Mill, The 1918

193
BENNETT, Richard (1873-1944)
And the Law Says
Damaged Goods
Gilded Youth
Stage:
Best of Friends, The 1903
Bosom Friends 1917
Brass Bottle, The 1910
Damaged Goods (George Dupont) 1913
Deep Purple, The (William Lake)
    1911
Diana of Dobson's 1908

For the Defense (Christopher
    Armstrong) 1919
His Excellency, the Governor
    1899; 1902
Hypocrites, The 1906
Imprudence 1902
Lion and the Mouse, The (Jefferson
    Ryder) 1905; 1907
Man and Superman (Hector Malone,
    Jr.) 1905
Maternity 1915
Morris Dance, The 1917
Other Girl, The (Mr. Taylor)
    1903-04
Passers-by 1911
Rio Grande 1916
Royal Family, A 1900
Stop Thief 1912
Sweet and Twenty 1901
Twelve Months Later 1900
Twenty Days in the Shade 1908
Unknown Purple, The 1918
Very Idea, The (Alan Camp) 1917
What Every Woman Knows (John
    Shand) 1908

194
BENNETT, Wilda (1899-   )
Good Little Devil, A
Stage:
Apple Blossoms (Nancy) 1919
Everywoman 1911
Girl behind the Gun, The 1918
Good Little Devil, A (Queen Mab)
    1913
Only Girl, The 1917
Riviera Girl, The 1917

195
BENOIT, Victor*
Devil's Daughter, The (Cosimo
    Dalos
Fool There Was, A (Young Parmalee)

196
BENSON, Frank R.*
Julius Caesar (Mark Anthony)
Macbeth (Macbeth)

197
BENSON, Frank R., Mrs.*
Julius Caesar (Portia)
Macbeth (Lady Macbeth)

198
BENTLEY, D. B.*
Beloved Adventurer, The (serial)

199
BENTLEY, Grendon*
Hamlet (Fortinbras)
Stage:
Forbes-Robertson Repertory 1913
Light that Failed, The (Gilbert
    Belling Torpenhow) 1913

200
BERANGER, Andre (1895-)
Birth of a Nation, The (Wade Cam-
    eron)
Flirting with Fate
Good Bad Man
Half Breed, The
Home Sweet Home
Manhattan Madness
Mixed Blood
Pillars of Society
Sandy
Those without Sin

201
BERANGER, George*
Broken Blossoms (the spying one)
Manhattan Madness (the butler)

202
BERGER, Bror*
Sir Arne's Treasure

203
BERGER, Grete /aka/ Greta Berger*
Midsummer Night's Dream, A (Puck)
Student Von Prag

204
BERGMAN, Henry*
Adventurer, The
Behind the Screen
Cure, The
Day's Pleasure, A
Dog's Life, A
Easy Street
Floorwalker, The
Immigrant, The (dual role)
Kreutzer Sonata (Raphael Friedlander)
Pawnshop, The
Rink, The (dual role)
Shoulder Arms (dual role)
Sunnyside
Stage:
Daughter of Heaven, The 1912
Easterner, The 1908
Firm of Cunningham, The 1905
Frou-Frou 1902
Gentleman from Number 19, The
    1913

Last Appeal, The 1902
Mam'selle Napoleon 1913
Milady's Boudoir 1914
Military Maid, The 1900
My Lady's Maid 1906
Papa's Wife 1899
Passing Show of 1917, The 1917
Pearl and the Pumpkin, The 1905
Pearl Maiden, The 1912
Prince of Peace, The 1902
Prodigal Son, The 1905
Red Rose, The 1911
Soul Kiss, The 1908
Sprightly Romance of Morosac, The
    1900
Step this Way 1916
Sword of the King, The 1902
Temperamental Journey, The (Prof.
    Babcock Roland) 1913
Typhoon, The 1912
Vanderbilt Cup, The 1906
Yankee Girl, The 1910

205
BERKELEY, Gertrude*
Two Orphans, The (Mother Frochard)
War Brides
Stage:
Embarrassment of Riches, The 1906
Game of Love, The 1909
Little Eyolf 1910
Little Women (Mrs. March) 1912
Master Builder, The (Mrs. Solness)
    1907
Old Friends 1917

206
BERLE, Milton (1908-)
Easy Street
Little Brother
Perils of Pauline, The (serial)
Tillie's Punctured Romance

207
BERNA, Elsa*
Madame DuBarry

208
BERNARD, Barney (1877-)
Prince in a Pawnshop, A
Stage:
Abe and Mawruss 1915
Boy and the Girl, The 1909
Business before Pleasure 1917
His Honor, Abe Potash (Abe) 1919
La Belle Paree 1911
Potash and Perlmutter (Abe Potash)
    1913

Silver Star, The 1909
Soul Kiss, The 1908
Vera Violetta 1911
Whirl of Society 1912

209
BERNARD, Dorothy (1890-1955)
Awful Moment, An
Blot on the 'Scutcheon, A
Cord of Life
Cricket on the Hearth, The
District Attorney, The
Failure, The
Fate's Turning
Female of the Species, The
Fine Feathers
Girl and Her Trust, A
Girls and Daddy, The
Goddess of Sagebrush Gulch, The
Heaven Avenges
His Lesson
Jones and His Neighbor
Jones and the Lady Book Agent
Jones' Burglar
Jonesy
Les Miserables
Little Gypsy
Little Women
Man of Sorrow, A
Mr. Jones at the Ball
Mrs. Jones' Lover
One Is Business, the Other Is Crime
Root of Evil, The
Sins of the Man, The
Siren of Impulse, A
Sister's Love, A
Smoked Husband, A
Sporting Blood
Summer Idyll, A
Sunshine through the Dark
Tale of the Wilderness, A

210
BERNARD, Harry*
Battle of Ambrose and Walrus
Crossed Love and Swords
Dirty Work in a Laundry
Our Daredevil Chief

211
BERNARD, Sam (1863-1927)
Because He Loved Her
Fatty and the Broadway Stars
Great Pearl Tangle, The
Stage:
Belle of Bohemia, The 1900
Belle of Bond Street, The 1903; 1914
Casino Girl, The 1900

Century Girl, The 1916
Friendly Enemies (Henry Block)
   1918
Girl and the Wizard, The 1909
Girl from Kay's, The 1903
He Came from Milwaukee 1910
Hoity Toity 1901
Modiste Shop, The 1913
Nearly a Hero 1908
Rich Mr. Hoggenheimer, The 1906
Rollicking Girl, The 1905
Silver Slippers, The 1902

212
BERNHARDT, Sarah (Rosalie
   Bernard) (1845-1923)
Adirenne Lecouvreur
Hamlet
Jeanne Dore
La Dame Aux Camelias (Camille)
La Tosca
Mothers of France
Queen Elizabeth
Tosca
Stage:
Adrienne Lecouvreur 1880
Bernhardt-Coquelin Repertory
   1900-01
Madame Sarah Bernhardt Repertory
   1910; 1916; 1917

213
BERRY, James*
Richard III (King Henry VI)

214
BERTHOLDI, Mme.*
Contortionist, A

215
BERTINI, Francesca*
Merchant of Venice, The (Portia)
Romeo and Juliet (Juliet)

216
BERWIN, Isabel*
Prunelia

217
BERYL, Edwin /aka/ Eddie Beryl*
Open Your Eyes
Stage:
Awakening, The 1918

218
BESSERER, Eugenie (-1934)
Auction of Souls
Carpet from Bagdad

Count of Monte Cristo, The
Crisis
Greatest Question, The (Mrs. Hilton)
Little Orphan Annie
Scarlet Days (Rosie Nell)
Turning the Tables

219
BETCHEL, William*
Lurking Peril, The (serial)

220
BEVAN, Billy (1887-1957)
L-KO comedies (supporting roles)
    1917-19

221
BEYERS, Clara*
Mignon

222
BIANCHI, Mario*
Purple Mask, The (serial)

223
BILLINGS, Billie*
Arsene Lupin
Enemy, The
Scarlet Runner, The (serial)

224
BILLINGS, Florence*
Probation Wife, The

225
BILLINGTON, Francelia*
Children of the Sea
Blind Husbands (wife)

226
BINNEY, Constance (1900-)
Erstwhile Susan
Sporting Life, The
Test of Honor
Stage:
Oh, Lady! Lady! 1918
Saturday to Monday 1917
39 East 1919

227
BINNEY, Faire*
Here Comes the Bride
Open Your Eyes
Sporting Life, The
Woman, The

228
BINNS, George*
Late Lamented, The

229
BITNER, W. W.*
Runaway Romany (Zelaya, Chief of
    the Gypsies)

230
BLACK, Bill*
Fatal Fortune, The (serial)

231
BLACKWELL, Carlyle (1888-1955)
Battle for Freedom
Bell of Penance, A
Beloved Blackmailer, The
Burglar, The
By Hook or Crook
Cabaret, The
Captain Barnacle's Messmate
Case of Becky, The
Courage for Two
Dixie Mother, A
Doctor Cupid
First Violin, The
Golden Wall, The
His Royal Highness
Hit or Miss
Indian Uprising at Santa Fe
Invaders, The
Kentucky Girl
Key to Yesterday, The
Leap to Fame
Love in a Hurry
Man Who Could Not Lose, The
Marriage Market, The
Mrs. Reynolds
Parasite, The
Perils of the Sea
Road to France, The
Secret Orchard, The
Spitfire, The
Stolen Orders
Struggle, The
Such a Little Queen
Three Green Eyes
Uncle Tom's Cabin
Way Out, The
Woman's Way, A

232
BLAKE, A. D.*
Where Are My Children?

233
BLAKE, Loretta*
His Picture in the Papers (Christine
    Cadwaller)

234
BLAKE, Tom*

Great Secret, The (serial)

235
BLANCHARD, Eleanor*
Essanay player 1912

236
BLAND, R. Henderson*
From the Manger to the Cross
  (Christ)

237
BLANKE, Kate*
Tiger Woman, The (Marion's Mother)

238
BLINN, Genevieve*
Cleopatra (Ventiduis)
Madame DuBarry (Duchess de
  Gaumont)
Rose of Blood, The (governess)
Salome (Queen Marian)
When a Woman Sins (Mrs. West)

239
BLINN, Holbrook (1872-1928)
Ballet Girl, The
Boss, The
Butterfly on the Wheel
Empress, The
Family Cupboard, The
Hidden Scar, The
Husband and Wife
Ivory Snuff Box, The
McTeague
Madam of the Slums
Pride
Prima Donna's Husband, The
Unpardonable Sin, The
Weakness of Man, The
Stage:
Arnold Daly Repertory 1907
Boss, The 1911
Candida (Rev. Morell) 1907
Cat and the Cherub, The 1897
Clansman, The 1906
Challenge, The (Harry Winthrop) 1919
Duchess of Dantzic, The 1905
Getting Together 1918
Green Cockatoo 1910
Hannele 1910
Ib and Little Christina 1900
Lady of the Camellias, The (George
  Duval) 1917
L'Elevation 1917
Lights o' London, The 1911
Man and His Angel 1906
Merely Mary Ann (Mr. Peter) 1907

Moliere (Louis XIV) 1919
Moloch 1915
Pillars of Society (Karsten Bernick)
  1910
Princess Players Repertory, The
  1913; 1914
Salomy Jane 1907
Salvation Nell (Jim Platt) 1908
To Have and to Hold 1901
Trap, The 1915
Woman of No Importance, A 1916

240
BLOCK, Sheridan*
Two Orphans, The (Count de Linere)

241
BLOOMER, Raymond J. *
Belle of New York, The (Jack
  Bronson)
Stage:
Baron Trenck 1912
Good Little Devil, A (Hon. Percy
  Cusack Smith) 1913
Naughty Marietta (Sir Harry Blake)
  1910
Revue of Revues, The 1911
Squab Farm, The 1918

242
BLUE, Monte (1890-1963)
Betrayed
Betsy's Burglar
Birth of a Nation, The (extra)
Come Back To Me
Everywoman
Ghosts
Goddess of Lost Lake
Hands Up!
His Pal
In Mizzoura
Intolerance (strike leader)
Johanna Enlists
Man Behind, The
Man from Painted Post, The
Microscope Mystery, The
M'Liss
100% American
Only Road, The
Pettigrew's Girl
Prince of Power
Romance and Arabella
Romance of Tarzan, The
Rustling a Bride
Squaw Man, The (Hoppy)
Till I Come Back To You (an
  American soldier)
Told in the Hills

Wild and Wooly

243
BLYTHE, Betty (Elizabeth Blythe
    Slaughter) (1893-)
All Man
Charge It
Dust of Desire
Game with Fate, A
Green God
His Own People
Miss Ambition
Over the Top
Tangled Lives
Undercurrent

244
BOARDMAN, True*
Social Pirates
Stringaree
Tarzan of the Apes

245
BOLAND, Eddie (1885-)
Lucille Love (serial)
Mysterious Rose, The
Peg O' the Ring (serial)

246
BOLAND, Mary (1880-1965)
Big John Garrity
Edge of the Abyss
His Temporary Wife /aka/ The
    Contrary Wife
Prince of Happiness, The
Prodigal Wife, The
Stepping Stone, The
Woman's Experience, A
Stage:
Backfire 1916
Case of Lady Camber, The 1917
Clarence (Mrs. Wheeler) 1919
Inconstant George 1909
Jack Straw 1908
Matinee Hero, The 1918
Much Ado about Nothing (Hero) 1913
My Lady's Dress 1914
Perplexed Husband, The 1912
Ranger, The 1907
Scrap of Paper, A (Louise De La
    Glaciere) 1914
Sick-a-Bed 1918
Single Man, A 1911
Smith-Smith 1910
Tyranny of Tears, The 1913
Will, The 1913

247
BOLDER, Robert*

Strictly Confidential
Stage:
Olga Nethersole Repertory 1908

248
BONAFE, Mlle. Pepa*
Shylock (Portia)

249
BOND, Frederick*
She-Devil, The (Apollo)

250
BOOKER, Harry*
Bombs
Feathered Nest, The /aka/ Girl
    Guardian /aka/ Only a Farmer's
    Daughter
Game Old Knight, A
Great Vacuum Robbery, The
Her Fame and Shame
Her Marble Heart
Her Painted Hero
Her Torpedoed Love
His Hereafter /aka/ Murray's
    Mixup
His Uncle Dudley
Judge, The
Love Riot, The
Maggie's First False Step
Maid Mad /aka/ The Fortune Teller
Pills of Peril
She Needed a Doctor

251
BOOTH, Elmer*
Mrs. Black Is Back
Musketeers of Pig Alley, The (the
    gangster)
Narrow Road, The
So Near, Yet So Far
Two Daughters of Eve
Unseen Enemy, An
Unwelcome Guest, The
Stage:
Cub, The (Charley Hall) 1910
45 Minutes from Broadway 1912
Gentleman of Leisure, A 1911
Sylvia Runs Away 1914

252
BOOTH, Marie*
Romeo and Juliet

253
BORDEAUX, Joe*
Fatty and Mabel Adrift
Goodnight Nurse

His Musical Career
Moonshiners, The
Other Man, The
Tillie's Punctured Romance
Waiter's Ball, The

254
BORGSTROM, Hilda*
Phantom Carriage, The

255
BORING, Edwin*
Romeo and Juliet

256
BORZAGE, Frank*
American Beauty comedies 1915
That Gal of Burke's

257
BOSS, Yale*
Active Life of Dolly of the Dailies,
    The (serial)

258
BOSWORTH, Hobart (Hobart Van
    Zandt Bosworth) (1867-1943)
Behind the Door
Border Legion, The
Code of Honor, The
Count of Monte Cristo, The
Country Mouse, The
Fatherhood
Freckles
Jackanapes
Joan, the Woman (General LaHire)
John Barleycorn
Little American, The (German
    Commander)
Oath, The
Odyssey of the North, An (Naass)
Oliver Twist
Profligate, The
Roman, The
Sea Wolf, The
Sultan's Power, The
Wise Old Elephant
Woman God Forgot, The (Cortez)
Stage:
Hedda Gabler (Eilert Lovberg) 1903
Marta of the Lowlands (Manelich)
    1903

259
BOTELER, Wade*
Crooked Straight, The
Twenty-Three and a Half Hours'
    Leave

Stage:
Silent Voice, The 1914

260
BOTTOMLEY, Roland*
Grip of Evil, The (serial)
Neglected Wife, The (serial)
Stage:
All Star Variety Jubilee 1913

261
BOULDEN, Edward*
Edison player 1915

262
BOURCHIER, Arthur*
Henry VIII (Henry)
Macbeth (Macbeth)

263
BOURNE, Adeline*
Hamlet (Gertrude)
Stage:
Caesar and Cleopatra 1906
Forbes-Robertson Repertory 1913
Light that Failed, The (the red
    haired girl) 1913
Mrs. Patrick Campbell Repertory
    1902
Olga Nethersole Repertory 1908

264
BOWER, Robert*
Beauty Market
Edison Player 1911
Hawthorne of the U. S. A.
Lottery Man, The

265
BOWERS, John (1891-1936)
Betsy Ross
Darkest Russia
Daughter of Mine
Day Dreams
Divorce Game, The
Eternal Grind, The
Hulda from Holland
Joan of the Woods
Madame X
Maternity
Oldest Law, The
Pest, The
Self-Made Widow, A
Sis
Sis Hopkins
Spurs of Sybill
Strictly Confidential
Through the Wrong Door

Stage:
Life 1914
Little Miss Brown 1912
Rich Man, Poor Man 1916

266
BOWES, Cliff*
Cactus Nell
Thirst

267
BOWES, Lawrence A.*
Charlie Chaplin's Burlesque on
    Carmen
Shanghaied

268
BOWMAN, William J.*
False Faces (Submarine Captain)
Merchant of Venice, The (Shylock)

269
BOYD, William "Bill" (1898-1972)
Exit the Vamp
Michael O'Halloran
Money Mad
New Loves for Old
Old Wives for New

270
BOYLE, John*
Kick In
Stage:
Cohan Revue of 1916, The 1916
Miss Daisy 1914
Passing Show of 1915, The 1915

271
BRACY, Clara T.*
Awakening, The
Decree of Destiny, A
Eloping with Auntie
Ressurection
Three Sisters
Stage:
Agnes 1908
Aphrodite (Chimeris) 1919
Colonel Newcome 1917
Humpty Dumpty 1918
Off Chance, The 1918
Old Lady Shows Her Medals, The
    1917 (1st N. Y. Production)
Seven Sisters 1911
Single Man, A 1911

272
BRACY, Sidney*
Crime and Punishment

Deemster, The
Elusive Isabel
Invisible Ray, The (serial)
Long Trail, The
Merely Mary Ann
Million Dollar Mystery, The (serial)
Miser's Reversion, The
Social Buccaneers
Sporting Blood
Temptation and the Man
Zudora (The Twenty Million Dollar
    Mystery) (serial)
Stage:
Robin Hood 1912

273
BRADY, Alice (1893-1939)
As Ye Sow
At the Mercy of Men
Ballet Girl
Betsy Ross
Better Half
Boss, The
Bought and Paid For
Cup of Chance, A
Danger's Peril, The
Dark Lantern, A
Darkest Russia
Death Dance
Divorce Game, The
Guilded Cage, The
Her Great Chance
Her Silent Sacrifice
His Bridal Night
Hungry Heart, The
In the Hollow of Her Hand
Indestructible Wife
Knife, The
La Boheme
Lure of a Woman, The
Marie, Ltd.
Maternity
Miss Petticoats
Ordeal of Rosetta
Rack, The
Redhead, The
Self-Made Widow, A
Spurs of Sybill
Tangled Fates
Then I'll Come Back to You
Trap, The
Whirlpool
Woman Alone
Woman and Wife
Woman in 47, The
World to Live In, The
Stage:
Balkan Princess, The 1911 (N. Y.

debut under name Marie Rose)
Family Cupboard, The 1913
Forever After 1918
Gilbert and Sullivan Opera Company
  1915
H. M. S. Pinafore 1911; 1912
Little Women (Meg) 1912
Mikado, The 1912
Patience 1912
Pirates of Penzance, The 1912
School 1913
Sinners 1915
Sylvia Runs Away 1914
Things that Count, The 1913
What Is Love? 1914

274
BRADY, Edwin J. (1889-)
Almost a Husband
Edge of Heart's Desire
Fires of Rebellion, The
Fount of Courage
Great Radium Mystery (serial)
Neal of the Navy (serial)
Out of the Shadow
When Bearcat Went Dry (Rattler
  Webb)
Who Pays?
Stage:
Spy, The 1913

275
BRAHAM, Lionel*
Diana the Huntress
Stage:
Androcles and the Lion (Ferrovius)
  1915
Caliban of the Yellow Sands 1916
Doctor's Dilemma, The (Sir Patrick
  Cullen) 1915
Garden of Paradise, The 1914
King Henry VIII 1916
Man Who Married a Dumb Wife, The
  1915
Midsummer Night's Dream, A (Snout)
  1915
Wanderer, The 1917

276
BRAMBRICK, Gertrude*
Virtue Its Own Reward (Alice)

277
BRANDT, Charles*
Fortune Hunter, The
Road of Strife, The (serial)
Sporting Duchess, The
Stage:

Madame X (President of the Court)
  1910

278
BRANSCOME, Lilly*
Snare, The

279
BRAWN, John P.*
Dream of a Rarebit Fiend, The

280
BRAY, Helen*
Danger Girl, The /aka/ Love on
  Skates
Haystacks and Steeples
Nick of Time Baby, The
Safety First Ambrose /aka/ Sheriff
  Ambrose

281
BREAMER, Sylvia (1896-)
Cold Deck
Common Cause, The
Family Skeleton, The
House Divided, A
Millionaire Vagrant, The
Missing
My Husband's Other Wife
Narrow Trail, The
Pinch Hitter
Sudden Jim
We Can't Have Everything (Zada
  L'Etoile)

282
BREEN, Harry*
Dog Catcher's Love, A
Stage:
Girlies 1910

283
BREESE, Edmund (1871-1935)
Chains of Evidence
Common Level
Early Bird
Lure of Heart's Desire, The
Master Mind, The
Someone Must Pay
Song of the Wage Slave, The
Spell of the Yukon, The
Temporary Wife
Walls of Jericho, The
Weakness of Strength, The
Stage:
Just a Wife 1910
Lion and the Mouse, The (John B.
  Ryder) 1905; 1907

Man of Honor, A 1911
Master Mind, The 1913
Moloch 1915
Monte Cristo (Danglars) 1900
Right to Be Happy, The 1912
Romeo and Juliet (Romeo) 1903
Scarecrow, The 1911
Shepherd King, The 1904
Spendthrift, The 1910
Strongheart 1905
Third Degree, The (Richard
    Brewster) 1909
Why Marry? (John) 1917

284
BRENNAN, Johnny*
Kalem player 1912

285
BRENON, Herbert (1880-1958)
Ivanhoe
Two Orphans, The (Pierre)

286
BRENT, Evelyn (Mary Elizabeth
    Riggs) (1899-)
Fool's Gold
Glorious Lady, The
Harbor Bar
Help! Help! Police
Iron Woman, The
Lure of Heart's Desire, The
Millionaire's Double, The
Other Man's Wife, The
Soul Market, The
Spell of the Yukon
Who's Your Neighbor?

287
BRIAN, Donald (1875-1948)
Smugglers, The
Voice in the Fog, The
Stage:
Belle of Broadway, The 1902
Buddies (Sonny) 1919
Dollar Princess, The 1909
Floradora (Donegal) 1902
45 Minutes from Broadway 1906
Girl behind the Gun, The 1918
Girl from Utah, The 1914
Her Regiment 1917
Little Johnny Jones 1904; 1907
Marriage Market, The 1939
Merry Widow, The (Prince Danilo)
    1907
Siren, The 1911
Supper Club, The 1901
Sybil 1916

288
BRICE, Rosetta*
Fortune Hunter, The
Road of Strife, The (serial)

289
BRIGNONE, Mercedes*
Hamlet (Gertrude)

290
BRINDLEY, Charles*
Red Ace, The (serial)

291
BRISCOE, Lottie (1883-1950)
Beloved Adventurer, The (serial)

292
BRITTON, Edna*
Master Mystery, The (serial)

293
BRITTON, Hutin*
Merchant of Venice, The (Portia)

294
BROCKWELL, Billie*
Love Will Conquer
Village Vampire, The /aka/ The
    Great Leap

295
BROCKWELL, Gladys (1893-1930)
Bird of Prey
Branded Soul, A
Broken Commandments
Call of the Soul
Chasing Rainbows
Conscience
Devil's Riddle, The
Devil's Wheel, The
Divorce Trap, The
Double Trouble
Flames of the Flesh
For Liberty
Forbidden Room, The
Her One Mistake
Moral Law, The (dual role)
One of the Discard
One Touch of Sin
Pitfalls of a Big City
Scarlet Road, The
She-Devil, The
Sins of the Parents
Sneak, The
Strange Woman, The
Wolves of Kultur, The
    (serial)

296
BRODY, Anna (1894-   )
Girl at Bay
Jeweled Hand, The (serial)
Mrs. Wiggs of the Cabbage Patch
Perfect Lover, The
Princess of Park Row
Suspect, The
Who's Your Brother?
Yellow Ticket, The

297
BROOKE, Van Dyke*
Barrier of Faith
Billy's Burglar
Captain Barnacle's Baby
Captain Barnacle's Courtship
Criminal, The
Crown Prince's Double, The
Cupid vs. Money
Daughter of Israel, A
Daughter's Strange Inheritance, A
Doctor's Secret, The
Elopement at Home, An
Elsa's Brother
Fanny's Conspiracy
Father's Hat Band
Goodbye Summer
Helpful Sisterhood, The
Hidden Letters, The
His Little Page
His Silver Bachelorhood
Honorable Algernon, The
Ida's Christmas
Janet of the Chorus
John Rance, Gentleman
Leading Lady
Loan Shark King, The
Memories in Men's Souls
Mr. Murray's Wedding Present
Moonshine Trail
My Old Dutch
Officer John Donovan
O'Hara Helps Cupid
Old Reliable
Peacemaker
Pillar of Flame
Politics and the Press
Question of Clothes, A
Right of Way, The
Sawdust and Salome
Soul in Bondage, A
Stormy Petrel, The
Sunshine and Shadow
Under the Daisies
Vavawert Ball, The
Wanted a Strong Hand

298
BROOKES, Charles*
King Lear (Cornwall)

299
BROOKS, Marion*
Martin Chuzzlewit
Stage:
Cousin Billy

300
BROTHERHOOD, William*
Dark Star, The (Steward)

301
BROWN, Charles D. (1887-1948)
Fates and Flora Fourflush (The Ten
    Billion Dollar Vitagraph Mystery)
    (serial)
John Tobin's Sweetheart
Private Bunny
Stage:
American Maid, The 1913
Captain Kidd, Jr. 1916
C. O. D. 1912
Fancy Free 1918
Gentleman from Number 19, The
    1913
La Belle Marseillaise 1905
Little Simplicity 1918
Luck in Pawn 1919
Marriage a la Carte 1911
Peggy 1911
See-Saw (Lord Harrowby) 1919
That Sort 1914

302
BROWN, Edward*
Graft (serial)

303
BROWN, Fred*
She Needed a Doctor 1917
Stage:
Uncle Tom's Cabin 1907

304
BROWN, Hal*
Open Your Eyes

305
BROWN, Lucille*
Intolerance (Uplifter)

306
BROWN, Milton*
Arab, The (Abdullah)

Call of the North (Me-en-gan)
Trail of the Lonesome Pine (a
    Tolliver man)

307
BROWN, W. H. *
Whispering Chorus, The (Stauberry)
Stage:
Henry V 1900

308
BROWN, William*
Intolerance (Father of the bride)

309
BROWNE, Kathryn*
Pride of the Clan, The

310
BROWNE, W. Graham*
Mrs. Plumb's Pudding

311
BROWNING, Tod (1882-1962)
Intolerance (a crook)

312
BROWNLEE, Frank*
Brass Buttons
Paid in Advance (Gold Dust Barker)
Stage:
Brother Officers (Jarvis) 1900
Brother Officers (Waiter) 1901
Daughters of Men, The 1906
Diplomacy (Antonio) 1901
Girl with the Green Eyes, The (a
    guide) 1902
Granny 1904
Great Divide, The (an architect) 1907
Importance of Being Earnest, The
    1902
Lady Rose's Daughter 1903
Lord and Lady Algy 1899
Man and His Wife, A 1900
Mrs. Dane's Defense (Adams) 1900
Twin Sister, The 1902
Wilderness, The 1901
Yvette 1904

313
BRUCE, Belle*
Great Secret, The (serial)

314
BRUCE, Clifford*
Fool There Was, A (the friend)
Lady Audley's Secret (George
    Talboys)

Perils of Pauline, The (serial)
Seven Deadly Sins
Stage:
Chains 1912
Mere Man 1912
William Gillette Repertory 1910

315
BRUCE, Kate*
As It Is in Life
At the Altar
Awful Moment, An
Battle at Elderbush Gulch, The
Better Way, The
Betsy's Burglar
Betty of Greystone
Choosing a Husband
Civilization
Corner in Wheat, A
Dash through the Clouds, A
Death's Marathon
Exam Day at School
Feud in the Kentucky Hills, A
Fighting Blood
Fugitive, The
Girl Who Stayed at Home, The
    (Mrs. Edward Gray)
Girls and Daddy, The
Golden Louis
Greatest Thing in Life, The
    (Jeanette's Aunt)
Gretchan, the Greenhorn
Hearts of the World (Mrs. Hamilton)
Her Father's Pride
His Trust Fulfilled
Home Folks
Hun Within, The
In a Hamper Bag
In Old Kentucky
Indian Summer, An
Informer, The
Intolerance (Old Babylonian woman)
Judith of Bethulia
Just Gold
Light That Came, The
Little Tease, The
Look Up
Microscope Mystery, The
Midnight Adventure, A
My Hero
Old Actor, The
One Is Business, the Other Is Crime
One Touch of Nature
Punishment, The
Rocky Road, The
Romance of Happy Valley, A (Mrs.
    Logan)
Romance of the Western Hills, A

Scarlet Days
1776 or the Hessian Renegades
Sheriff's Baby, The
Susan Rocks the Boat
Tender-Hearted Boy, The
True Heart Tessie (Bettina's Aunt)
Two Brothers, The
Usurer, The
Wilful Peggy
Would-Be Shriner, The
Yaqui Cur, The
Stage:
Starbucks, The 1903
Votes for Woman 1909

316
BRULE, André*
Werther

317
BRUNDAGE, Mathilde*
New Moon, The

318
BRUNETTE, Fritzi (1894-1943)
Beware of Strangers
City of Purple Dreams, The
Jacques of the Silver North
Jaguar's Claw, The
Playthings
Sealed Envelope
Selig player 1913
Sporting Chance, A
Still Small Voice, The
Velvet Hand, The
Whitewashed Walls
Who Shall Take My Life?
Woman under Cover

319
BRUNTON, William*
Lost Express, The (serial)
Railroad Raiders, The (serial)
Squaw Man, The (Shorty)

320
BRYAN, Ruth*
Beloved Adventurer, The (serial)

321
BRYANT, Charles E. (1887-1948)
Brat, The
Eye for Eye
Out of the Fog
Red Lantern, The
Revelation
Stronger Than Death
Toys of Fate

Train of Incidents, A
Stage:
Aunt Jeannie 1902
Bella Donna 1912
Captain Jinks of the Horse Marines
   (Charles LaMartine) 1907
'Ception Shoals 1917
Driven 1914
Hedda Gabler (Judge Brack) 1918
Joy of Living, The 1902
Mrs. Patrick Campbell Repertory
   1902
Second Mrs. Tanqueray, The 1902
That Sort 1914

322
BRYANT, James*
Bright Lights, The /aka/ The Lure
   of Broadway
Fatty and Mabel Adrift

323
BRYDONE, Alfred*
Richard III (King Edward IV)

324
BUCHANAN, Jack (1891-1957)
Auld Lang Syne
Her Heritage

325
BUCKHAM, Hazel*
Liberty, a Daughter of the U. S. A.
   (serial)

326
BUCKINGHAM, Lillian*
Diamond from the Sky, The (serial)

327
BUCKLEY, Floyd*
Exploits of Elaine, The (serial)
Fatal Fortune, The (serial)
Fatal Ring, The (serial)
House of Hate, The (serial)
Master Mystery, The (serial)
Patria (serial)
Pearl of the Army (serial)
Seven Pearls, The (serial)

328
BUCKSTONE, Roland /aka/ Rowland
   (1862-1922)
Enemy to the King, An
Stage:
Anthony and Cleopatra (M. Aemilius
   Lepidus) 1909
Beau Brummell 1916

E. H. Sothern Repertory 1909
Greatest Nation, The 1916
Hamlet 1900; 1902; 1903
Hamlet (first grave digger) 1919
If I Were King (Guy Tabarie) 1901
Pretty Soft 1919
Proud Prince, The 1903
Richard Lovelace 1901
Romeo and Juliet 1915
Song of the Sword, The 1899
Sothern and Marlowe Repertory
    1904-05; 1907-08; 1910; 1911
Strife 1909
Sunken Bell, The 1900
Taming of the Shrew, The (Grumio)
    1919
Twelfth Night (Sir Toby Belch) 1919

329
BUHLER, Richard*
Lubin Player 1913
Stage:
Ben Hur (Title role) 1911
Evangeline 1913
Ghetto, The 1899
Quo Vadis (Plautius) 1900
Return of Eve, The 1909

330
BUHLER, William*
Railroad Radiers, The (serial)

331
BUNDEL, Raymond*
Tess of the D'Urbevilles

332
BUNNY, John (1863-1915)
And His Wife Came Back
At Scrogginses' Corner
Autocrat of Flapjack Junction, The
Awakening of Jones, The
Bachelor Buttons
Blarney Stone, The
Bunco Bill's Visit
Bunny All at Sea
Bunny and the Bunny Hug
Bunny and the Dogs
Bunny and the Twins
Bunny As a Reporter
Bunny at the Derby
Bunny Attempts Suicide
Bunny Backslides
Bunny Buys a Harem
Bunny Dips into Society
Bunny for the Cause
Bunny in Disguise
Bunny vs. Cutey

Bunny's Birthday
Bunny's Birthday Surprise
Bunny's Dilemma
Bunny's Honeymoon
Bunny's Little Brother
Bunny's Mistake
Bunny's Scheme
Bunny's Suicide
Bunny's Swell Affair
Burnt Cork
Captain Barnacle's Baby
Captain Barnacle's Courtship
Captain Barnacle's Messmate
Captain Jack's Dilemma
Captain Jack's Diplomacy
Change in Baggage, A
Chased by Bloodhounds
Chumps
Cork and Vicinity
Cupid and the Motor Boat
Cupid's Hired Man
Cure for Pokeritis, A
Diamond Cut Diamond
Doctor Bridget
Doctor Cupid -- (debut)
Eventful Elopement, An
Father's Flirtation
Feudists, The
First Violin, The
First Woman Jury in America
Flaming Hearts
Fortune, The
Freckles
Gentleman of Fashion, A
Girl at the Lunch Counter, The
Golf Game and the Bonnet, The
Gossip, The
He Answered the Ad
He Who Laughs Last
Hearts and Diamonds
Her Crowning Glory
Her Hero (the husband)
Her Old Sweetheart
Her Sister's Children
His Honor, the Mayor
His Mother-in-Law
His Tired Uncle
Honeymooners, The
How Cissy Made Good (Bunny's last
    film)
How He Prepared the Room
Hubby Buys a Baby
Hubby's Toothache
Ida's Christmas (Santa Claus)
In the Arctic Night
In the Clutches of a Vapor Bath
Intrepid Davey
Irene's Infatuation

Jack Fat and Jim Slim at Coney
  Island
John Tobin's Sweetheart
Kitty and the Cowboys
Latent Spark, The
Leading Lady, The
Leap Year Proposals
Locked House, The
Locket, The
Love, Luck and Gasoline
Love Sick Maidens of Cuddleton
Love's Old Dream
Love's Quarantine
Madge of the Mountains
Man Higher Up, The
Martha's Rebellion
Ma's Apron Strings
Michael McShane, Matchmaker
Millinery Bomb, A
Misadventures of a Mighty Monarch
Mr. Bolter's Infatuation
Mr. Bolter's Niece
Mr. Bunny in Disguise
Mr. Bunnyhug Buys a Hat for His
  Bride
New Stenographer, The
Old Doll, The
Old Fire Horse and the New Fire
  Chief, The
Old Maid's Baby, The
One Good Joke Deserves Another
One Hundred Dollar Bill, The
Pandora's Box
Persistent Lover, A
Personal Introductions
Pickpocket, The
Pickwick Papers
Pigs Is Pigs
Pirates, The
Polishing Up
Politician's Dream, The
Private Bunny
Pseudo Sultan
Queen for a Day
Red Ink Tragedy
Return of Widow Pogson's Husband
Schemers, The
Seeing Double
Selecting His Hieress
Setting the Style
Slight Mistake, A
Stenographer Troubles
Stenographer Wanted (Jones)
Subduing of Mrs. Nag, The
Such a Hunter
Suing Susan
Suit of Armor, The
Suspicious Henry

Tangled Tangoists
There's Music in the Hair
Those Troublesome Tresses
Thou Shalt Not Covet
Three Black Bags, The
Tired, Absent-Minded Man, The
Train of Incidents, A
Treasure Trove
Troublesome Stepdaughters, The
Two Cinders
Two Overcoats
Umbrellas to Mend, or Mr. Nice-
  man's Umbrella
Unexpected Review, An
Unknown Violinist, The
Ups and Downs
Vanity Fair
Vases of Hymen, The
Ventriloquist's Trunk, The
When the Press Speaks
Which Way Did He Go?
Who Stole Bunny's Umbrella?
Who's to Win?
Widow Visits Springtown, The
Winsor McCay's Drawings
Woes of a Wealthy Widow, The
Wonderful Statue, The
Working for Hubby
Wrong Patient, The
--Bunny in Bunnyland: A Cartoon,
  John Bunny did not appear in it.
Stage:
Aunt Hannah 1900
Cheater, The 1910
Easy Dawson (on tour) 1905-06
Embarrassment of Riches, The 1906
Fluffy Ruffles 1908-09
Grand Opera House (Salt Lake City--
  manager & director) 1897-98
Midsummer Night's Dream, A
  (Bottom) 1906
Old Dutch 1909
Proud Laird, The 1905
Tom Jones (on tour) 1907-08
Way Down East 1903
Weather Hen, The 1900

333
BURKE, Billie (1886-1970)
Arms and the Girl
Eve's Daughter
Gloria's Romance (Gloria) (serial)
Good Gracious, Annabelle
In Pursuit of Polly
Land of Promise, The
Let's Get a Divorce
Make-Believe Wife, The
Marquise, The

Misleading Widow, The
My Wife
Mysterious Miss Terry, The
Peggy
Sadie Love
Truth Game
Stage:
Amazons, The (Lady Thomasin) 1913
Caesar's Wife 1919
Jerry-Jerry 1914
Land of Promise, The 1913
Love Watches (Jacquiline) 1908
Mind-the-Paint Girl, The 1912
Mrs. Dot (Mrs. Worthy) 1910
My Wife 1907
Philosopher in the Apple Orchard, The
  1911
Rescuing Angel, The 1917
Runaway, The 1911
Suzanne 1910

334
BURKE, J. Frank*
Civilization (Luther Rolf)
Hell's Hinges (Zeb Taylor)

335
BURKE, Joseph*
Cecilia of the Pink Roses (Dr.
  McNeil)
Deluxe Annie
Kidnapped

336
BURMASTER, Augusta*
Mary Moreland

337
BURNS, Edmund (1892-)
Love Burglar, The
Male and Female (Treherne)
Ordeal of Rosetta, The

338
BURNS, Fred*
During the Round-up
Fighting Trail, The (serial)
Home Sweet Home (Sheriff)
Indian's Loyalty, An
Vengeance and the Woman (serial)

339
BURNS, Neal (1892-1962)
Be Yourself
Bucking Broadway
Movie Mad
No Parking
Ocean Swells

Ouija Did It, The
Out of the Night
Pair of Sixes, A
Rambling Romeo
Sand Witches
Shuffle the Queen
Wedding Blues

340
BURNS, Robert "Bobby"*
Busted Hearts
Captain of the Gray Horse Troop
Chickens
Counterfeit Trail
Frenzied Finance
Little Yank, The
This Way Out
Tryout, The
Ups and Downs

341
BURRELL, George*
Flashlight, The (Barclay)
Lon of Lone Mountain

342
BURRESS, William*
Heartease
Lord and Lady Algy
Paid in Advance (Regan)
Stage:
After Office Hours 1900
Bird Center 1904
Con and Co. 1910
Dancing Duchess, The 1914
Girl from Rector's, The 1909
Hyphen, The 1915
It Happened in Nordland 1904-05
Land of Nod, The 1907
Little Red Riding Hood 1900
Million, The 1911
Miss Millions (Ephraim Tutt) 1919
Spring Maid, The 1910
Summer Widowers, The 1910
Twiddle-Twaddle 1906
Yankee Girl, The 1910

343
BURT, Nellie*
Bound and Gagged (serial)

344
BURTON, Charlotte*
Diamond from the Sky, The (serial)
Man's Way, A
Sequel to the Diamond from the Sky
  (serial)
Trapped in a Forest Fire

345
BURTON, Clarence (1882-)
Hawthorne of the U. S. A.
Male and Female (Captain of Yacht)
Sporting Life, The

346
BURTON, Ethel*
Frenzied Finance
He Winked and Won

347
BURTON, Frederick (1871-)
Anne of Green Gables
Getting Mary Married (Amos Bussard)
Stage:
College Widow, The 1904
General John Regan 1913
Just a Wife 1910
Man's Friends, A 1913
Modern Girl, A 1914
Nest Egg, The 1910
Oh, Look! 1918
Ringmaster, The 1909
Ruggles of Red Gap 1915
Trap, The 1915
Unwritten Law, The 1913
Wanderer, The 1917

348
BURTON, John*
Forbidden Room, The (Dr. Jarvis)
Menace to Carlotta, The (The
    Vulture)
Tragedy of Whispering Creek, The
    (Prospector)
Stage:
As Ye Sow 1905

349
BURTON, Langhorne (1872-)
Auld Robin Gray
Bootles' Baby
Daddy
Difficult Way, The
God and the Man
Impossible Woman, The
King's Minister, The
Liberty Hall
Profligate, The
Sweet and Twenty
Tom Jones
Treasure of Heaven, The
Turtle Doves

350
BURTON, William H. *
Romeo and Juliet

351
BUSCH, Mae (1897-1946)
Agitator, The
Bath House Blunder
Because He Loved Her
Best of Enemies, The
Better Late Than Never /aka/
    Getting Married
Devil's Passkey, The (La Belle
    Odesa)
Favorite Fool, A
Grim Game
One Night Stand, A
Rascal of Wolfish Ways, A
Rent Jumpers, The
Settled at the Seaside
Wife and Auto Trouble
Worst of Friends, The

352
BUSH, Pauline*
Accusing Evidence (the girl)
Adventures of Francois Villon, The
    (Philippa de Annonay in "The
    Oubliette" and Lady Eleyne in
    "The Higher Law")
All for Peggy (Peggy)
Back to Life (the wife)
Bloodhounds of the North
    (Embezzler's daughter)
Desert Breed, The (Pauline)
Discord and Harmony (the girl)
Embezzler, The (Miss Spencer)
End of the Feud, The (June)
Forbidden Room, The (dual role of
    mother and daughter)
Girl of the Night, The
Grind, The (one of the sisters)
Her Bounty (Ruth Braddon)
Her Chance (Nance)
Her Escape (the girl)
Her Life Story (Carlotta)
Honor of the Mounted, The (Marie
    Laquox)
Hopes of Blind Alley, The
Idyll of the Hills, An (Kate Graham)
Lamb, the Woman, the Wolf (the
    woman)
Lights and Shadows (dual role of
    mother and daughter)
Lion, the Lamb, the Man, The
    (Agnes Duane)
Maid of the Mist (the girl)
Mask of Love, The (the girl)
Measure of a Man, The (Helen
    MacDermott)
Menace to Carlotta, The (Carlotta)
Outside the Gates (Sister Ursula)

Pipes of Pan, The (Marian)
Red Margaret--Moonshiner (Title
  role)
Remember Mary Magdalen (the
  woman)
Richelieu (Julie Mortemar)
Sin of Olga Brandt, The (Olga)
Star of the Sea, The (the fisher girl)
Steady Company (the girl)
Stronger Mind, The (the girl)
Such Is Life (Polly)
Threads of Fate, The (the wife)
Tragedy of Whispering Creek, The
  (the orphan)
Unlawful Trade, The (Amy Partlan)
When the Gods Played a Badger Game
  (the chorus girl)
Where the Forest Ends (Rose)

353
BUSHMAN, Francis X. (Francis
  Xavier Bushman) (1885-1966)
Adopted Son, The
Billy the Bear Tamer
Blood Will Tell
Brass Check, The
Corner in Cotton, A
Cyclone Higgins, D. F.
Daring Hearts
Fate's Funny Frolic
Good Catch, A
Graustark
Great Secret, The (serial)
Ladies' World
Lost Years, The
Magic Wand, The
Master Thief, The
Neptune's Daughter
One Wonderful Night
Pair of Cupids, A
Pennington's Choice
Poor Rich Man, The
Red, White and Blue Blood
Return of Richard Neal
Romeo and Juliet (Romeo)
Rosary, The
Rosemary
Second in Command, The
Silent Voice, The
Social Quicksands
Spy's Defeat, The
Their Compact
Under Royal Patronage
Under Suspicion
Virtue of Rags, The
Voice of Conscience, The
When Soul Meets Soul
With Neatness and Dispatch

Stage:
Queen of the Moulin Rouge, The
  (used name Frank H. Bushman)
  1908

354
BUSKIRK, Bessie*
Macbeth (Donalbain)

355
BUTLER, David (1894-)
Better Times
Bonnie, Bonnie Lassie
Girl Who Stayed at Home, The
  (Johann Kant)
Greatest Thing in Life, The (M.
  LeBebe)
Nugget Nell
Petal on the Current, The
Rush Hour
Unpainted Woman, The
Upstairs and Down

356
BUTLER, Fred*
Little Meena's Romance
Nugget Nell

357
BUTLER, William J. "Daddy"*
Blot on the 'Scutcheon, A
Dan the Dandy
Fighting Blood
Flash of Light, A
Great Secret, The (serial)
Hero of Little Italy, The
In Old Kentucky
Last Drop of Water, The
Man's Genesis (cave man)
Man's Lust for Gold
One Night, and Then--
Purgation, The
Romany Tragedy, A
1776, or the Hessian Renegades
Timely Interception, A
Two Sides, The
Unveiling, The
Usurer, The
Stage:
Great Divide, The (Dr. Newberry)
  1906-07
Pippa Passes 1906
Serio-Comic Governess, The 1904

358
BUTT, W. Lawson*
Danger Trail, The
Miracle Man, The (Richard King)

Romeo and Juliet (Tybalt)
Stage:
Merry Wives of Windsor, The 1917
Twelfth Night 1914
Wanderer, The 1917

359
BUTTERWORTH, F.*
Till I Come Back to You (Hans)

360
BYRAM, Ronald*
Out of the Shadow
Stage:
Indestructible Wife, The 1918
Shirley Kaye 1916
Somebody's Luggage 1916

361
BYTELL, Walter*
Wild and Woolley (Jeff's father)

- C -

362
CABBANE, Christy W. (1888-1950)
Judith of Bethulia
Punishment, The
Under Burning Skies

363
CAHILL, Lily /aka/ Lillian*
Fugitive, The
Stage:
Good Morning, Rosamond 1917
In for the Night 1917
Joseph and His Brethren 1913
Man's Friends, A 1913
Marquis de Priola, The 1919
Melody of Youth, The 1916
Over Here 1918
Purple Mask, The (Laurette de
   Chateaubriand) 1919
Road to Arcady, The 1912
Two Women 1910
Under Cover 1914

364
CAHILL, Marie (1871-)
Glady's Day Dreams
Judy Forgot
Stage:
Boys and Betty, The 1908
H. M. S. Pinafore (Little Buttercup)
   1911
It Happened in Nordland 1904; 1905
Judy Forgot 1910

Just Around the Corner 1919
Marrying Mary 1906
Moonshine 1905
Nancy Brown 1903
90 in the Shade 1915
Opera Ball, The 1912
Sally in Our Alley 1902
Star and Garter 1900
Three Little Lambs 1899
Wild Rose, The 1902

365
CAIN, Robert*
Dawn of Tomorrow, The
Eternal Grind, The
In Mizzoura
Male and Female (Lord Brocklehurst)
My Lady Incog
Stage:
He Comes up Smiling 1914
Misleading Lady, The 1913
Stitch in Time, A 1918
What Money Can't Buy 1915

366
CAINE, Derwent Hall*
Crime and Punishment

367
CALDARA, Orme*
Spreading Dawn, The
Stage:
Her Husband's Wife 1910
Lilac Time 1917

368
CALDWELL, Orville (1896-1967)
A silent color film produced by
   J. Searle Dawley

369
CALDWELL, Virginia*
Lombardi, Ltd.

370
CALHOUN, Alice (1903-1966)
Bride in Bond, A
Dream Lady, The
Everybody's Business
Thirteenth Chair, The

371
CALLAHAN, Joseph*
A La Cabaret
Dollars and Sense /aka/ The Twins
Her Circus Knight
His Last Laugh
Oriental Love
Sultan's Wife, The

372
CALLAM, D. *
Little Lord Fauntleroy

373
CALLIS, Clifford*
Charity Castle

374
CALTHORP, Donald (1888-1940)
Gay Lord Quex, The (debut)
Nelson
Stage:
Wire Entanglement, A (debut) 1906

375
CALVERT, Catherine*
Behind the Mask
Career of Katherine Bush, The
Fires of Faith
Marriage
Marriage of Convenience
Out of the Night
Romance of the Underworld, A
Stage:
Deep Purple, The (Laura Moore)
 1911

376
CALVERT, Charles, Mrs. *
Henry VIII (An old lady)

377
CALVERT, E. H. (1890-)
Affinities
Daughter of the City, A
From the Submerged
Into the North
Is Marriage Sacred?
Last Adventure, The
Love Test, The
Money to Burn
Outer Edge, The
Reaping, The
Tapped Wires
Vultures of Society

378
CALVERT, Louis*
King John (Cardinal Pandulph)
Stage:
Bargain, The 1915
Cottage in the Air, The 1909
Dear Brutus (Matey) 1918
Don (Albert Thompsett) 1909
Earth, The 1916
Major Barbara (Andrew Undershaft)
 1915

Masqueraders, The 1917
Merry Wives of Windsor, The (Sir
 John Falstaff) 1910
Naughty Marietta 1910
Noah's Flood 1911
Old Heidelberg 1910
School for Scandal, A 1909
Strife 1909
Tempest, The (Prospero) 1916
Twelfth Night (Sir Toby Belch) 1910
Vanity Fair 1911
Washington Square Players, The
 1917

379
CAMDEN, Dorothea*
Seven Sisters
Stage:
Happiness 1917

380
CAMERON, Donald*
Kitty Mackay
Stage:
Lady Windermere's Fan 1914

381
CAMERON, Rudolph*
Girl Philippa, The
Stage:
Rich Man, Poor Man 1916

382
CAMPANARI, Giuseppe*
Webb Singing Pictures 1917

383
CAMPBELL, Colin*
Vitagraph player 1914
Stage:
Better 'Ole, The 1918-19
Great Catherine (Sergeant) 1916
Greater Love, The 1906
Heir to the Hoorah, The 1905-06
Inca of Jerusalem, The 1916
Madonna of the Future, The 1918
Once upon a Time 1905
Out There 1917
Overruled 1916-17
Triangle, The 1906

384
CAMPBELL, Eric (1870-1917)
Adventurer, The
Behind the Screen
Between Showers
Caught in a Cabaret
Count, The

Cruel, Cruel Love
Cure, The
Easy Street
Fatal Mallet, The
Fireman, The
Floorwalker, The
Her Friend the Bandit
His New Job
Immigrant, The
Knockout, The
Mabel at the Wheel
Pawnshop, The
Rink, The
Vagabond, The
Stage:
Pom-Pom 1916
Tipping the Winner 1914

385
CAMPBELL, Eva*
Cecilia of the Pink Roses (Dolly
    Vernon)

386
CAMPBELL, Webster*
Clock Struck One, The
Oh, Daddy

387
CAMPEAU, Frank (-1943)
Arizona (Kellar)
Bound in Morocco (Bashe El Harib)
Cheating Cheaters
Down to Earth
He Comes up Smiling (John Bartlett)
Headin' South (Spanish Joe)
His Majesty the American (Grand
    Duke Sarzeau)
Intolerance (a soldier)
Jordan Is a Hard Road
Knickerbocker Buckaroo, The (the
    crooked sheriff)
Light of the Western Stars
Man from Painted Post, The (Bull
    Madden)
Mr. Fixit (Uncle "Hen")
Modern Musketeer, A (Navajo guide)
Reaching for the Moon (Black Boris)
Say, Young Fellow! (the villain)
When the Clouds Roll By (Mark
    Drake)
Stage:
Believe Me, Xantippe (Simp Calloway)
    1913
Ghost Breaker, The 1913
Rio Grande 1916
Virginian, The (Trampas)
    1904-05

388
CANNON, Raymond*
Nobody Home
Nugget Nell
True Heart Susie (Sporty Malone)

389
CAPELLANI, Paul*
La Boheme

390
CAPELLI, Dante*
Macbeth (Macbeth)

391
CAPOZZI, Alberto*
Grandmother's Lamp
Mysterious Piano, The
Perjury

392
CAPRICE, June (1899-1936)
Blue Eyed Mary
Camouflaged Kiss, A
Caprice of the Mountains
Child of the Wild, A
Every Girl's Dream
Heart of Romance
Little Miss Happiness
Love Cheat, The
Miss Innocence
Miss U. S. A.
Modern Cinderella, A
Oh, Boy!
Ragged Princess, The
Small Town Girl, A
Sunshine Maid
Unknown 274

393
CARBASSE, Louise see LOVELY,
    Louise

394
CAREW, Arthur Edmund (1894-   )
World and Its Women, The

395
CAREW, James*
Twelve: Ten
Stage:
Captain Brassbound's Conversion
    (Capt. Brassbound) 1907
Good Hope, The 1907
Sweet Kitty Bellairs 1903-04
Two Little Sailor Boys 1904

396
CAREW, Ora*

A La Cabaret
Dollars and Sense /aka/ The Twins
   (dual role)
Go West, Young Man
Her Circus Knight /aka/ The Circus
   Girl
Her Painted Hero
Little Lady of the Big House, The
Loot
Love Comet
Martyrs of the Alamo
Oriental Love
Reckless Romeo, A
Saved by Wireless
Skidding Hearts
Terror of the Range, The (serial)
Too Many Millions
Under Suspicion
Wings and Wheels

397
CAREWE, Edwin (1883-1940)
Final Judgment, The
Lubin player 1913
Shadow of Suspicion
Snowbird, The
Splendid Sinners, The
Trail to Yesterday
Stage:
O'Neill of Derry 1907

398
CAREY, Harry (1875-1947)
Ace of the Saddle
Adventure in the Autumn Woods, An
Bare Fists
Blue Streak McCoy
Broken Ways
Brothers
Bucking Broadway
Chance of Deception, A
Cheyenne's Pal
Cry for Help, A
Fight for Love, A
Freeze-Out, The
Friends
Graft (serial)
Gun Fightin' Gentleman, A
Heart Beat
Hell Bent
Her Father's Silent Partner
Heredity
Hero of Little Italy, The
Hillbilly, The
In the Aisles of the Wind
Informer, The
Judith of Bethulia
Knight of the Range, A

Left Handed Man, The
Love in an Apartment Hotel
Love's Lariat
Man Who Wouldn't Shoot, The
Marked Man, A
Marked Men
Musketeers of Pig Alley, The
My Hero
Olaf (An Atom)
Outcasts of Poker Flat, The
Phantom Riders, The
Ranchero's Revenge, The
Riders of the Law
Riders of Vengeance
Roped
Scarlet Drop, The
Secret Man, The
Sheriff's Baby, The
Soul Herder, The
Straight Shooting
Struggle, The
Thieves' Gold
Three Mounted Men
Unseen Enemy, An
Unwelcome Guest, The
Wanderer, The
Wild Woman
Woman's Fool, A

399
CARLETON, Henry*
Daughter of Uncle Sam, A (serial)

400
CARLETON, Lloyd*
Fugitive, The
Stage:
L'Aiglon 1900
Little Minister, The (Twaits) 1904
Peter Pan (Great Big Little Panther)
   1905-06
Royal Family, A 1900

401
CARLETON, William T. *
Daughter of Maryland, A
Gloria's Romance (serial)
Madame Butterfly
Pearl of the Army (serial)
Poor Little Peppina
Society Exile
Stage:
Balkan Princess, The 1911
Charm of Isabel, The 1914
Joseph and His Brethren 1913
Lady Teazle (Sir Peter Teazle)
   1904
Medal and the Maid, The 1904

Mlle. Mischief 1908
Prince of Peace, The 1901
Three Little Lambs 1899

402
CARLTON, Barbara*
Man Who Turned White, The

403
CARLTON, William Probert*
Society in Exile, A
Stage:
Broadway and Buttermilk 1916
Cadet Girl, The 1900
Wall Street Girl, The 1912

404
CARLYLE, Francis*
Perils of Pauline, The (serial)
Stage:
Clarice 1906
Flag Lieutenant, The 1909
Gentleman of Leisure, A 1911
Honor of the Family, The (Commandant Max Gilet) 1908
Under Two Flags 1901

405
CARLYLE, Richard (1879-   )
Men Women Marry, The
Spotlight Sadie
Stage:
Alibi Bill 1912
Torches, The 1917

406
CARMEN, Jewel*
American Aristocracy (Miss Jewel
    Hicks)
Bride of Fear, The
Children in the House
Confession
Conqueror, The
Fallen Angel
Flirting with Fate (Gladys Kingsley)
Girl with the Champagne Eyes, The
Half-Breed, The (Nellie Wynn)
Intolerance (slave girl)
Kingdom of Love
Lawless Love
Les Miserables
Manhattan Madness (the girl)
Matrimaniac, The
Tale of Two Cities, A

407
CARMI, Maria*
Homunculus (serial)

408
CARNEY, Augustus*
Alkali Ike's Motorcycle

409
CARPENTER, Billy*
Kaiser, the Beast of Berlin, The
    (a Belgian woman)

410
CARPENTER, Francis*
Children in the House
Jack and the Bean Stalk
Macbeth (a Macduff child)

411
CARPENTER, Horace B. *
Arab, The (the Shiek)
Call of the North, The (Rand)
Carmen (Pastia)
Devil Stone, The
Golden Chance, The (Steve Denby)
Joan, the Woman (Jacques d'Arc)
Man from Home, The (Ivanoff)
Maria Rosa (Pedro)
Terror of the Range, The (serial)
Virginian, The (Spanish Ed)

412
CARPENTER, Merta*
What's His Name (Nellie's friend)

413
CARPENTER, William*
Adventures of Kathlyn, The (serial)

414
CARR, Cameron*
Daughter of Eve, A

415
CARR, Mary (1874-   )
Beloved Rogue
Mrs. Wiggs of the Cabbage Patch

416
CARRIGAN, Thomas J. *
Checkers
Cinderella
Stage:
Copperhead, The (Philip Manning)
    1918
Mother Carey's Chickens 1917

417
CARRINGTON, Murray*
Julius Caesar (Brutus)
Macbeth
Taming of the Shrew, The

418
CARROLL, William A. *
Bill Henry
Black Sheep
Trail of the Octopus (serial)

419
CARTER, Calvin*
Wild and Wooly (hotel keeper)

420
CARTER, Harry*
Gray Ghost, The (serial)
Judge Not
Master Key, The (serial)
Stage:
Excuse Me (the porter) 1911
Walls of Jericho, The 1905; 1906

421
CARTER, Mrs. Leslie (1862-1937)
Heart of Maryland, The
La DuBarry
Stage:
Adrea 1905
DuBarry (La DuBarry) 1901; 1902
Kassa 1909
Second Mrs. Tanqueray, The (Paula)
    1913
Two Women 1910
Zaza (Title role) 1900

422
CARTER, Nan*
Serpent, The (Erma Lachno)

423
CARUSO, Enrico (1873-1921)
My Cousin
Prince Ubaldo
Splendid Romance, The
Webb Singing Pictures
Stage:
Girl of the Golden West, The (Dick
    Johnson) 1910

424
CARVER [Miss]*
Macbeth (Lady Macbeth)
Romeo and Juliet (nurse)

425
CARVER, Louise (Louise Spigler
    Murray) (1875-   )
Mack Sennett comedies
Stage:
Chicago Grand Opera 1892

426
CASE, Anna*
Hidden Truth, The

427
CASE, Helen*
Adventures of Ruth, The (serial)

428
CASELLI, Ernest*
Merchant of Venice, The (Lorenzo)

429
CASEY, Kenneth*
Feudists, The

430
CASHMAN, Harry*
Essanay player 1912

431
CASLER, Herman*
Sparring film

432
CASSADY, James*
Siren of Corsica

433
CASSIDY, Ellen*
Checkers
Other Man's Wife, The
Stage:
Words and Music 1917

434
CASSINELLI, Dolores*
Lafayette, We Come
Soul Adrift, A
Unknown Love
When Souls Meet

435
CASTLE, Irene (Irene Foote) (1893-
    1969)
Arms and the Woman
Convict 993
Firing Line, The
First Law, The
Girl from Bohemia, The
Hillcrest Mystery, The (serial)
Invisible Bond, The
Mark of Cain, The
Mysterious Client, The
Mystery of the Double Cross
Patria (serial)
Short features, several 1914
Stranded in Arcady

Sylvia of the Secret Service
Vengeance Is Mine
Whirl of Life, The
Stage:
Miss 1917
Watch Your Step 1914

436
CASTLE, Vernon (Vernon Blythe)
   (1885-1918)
Short features, several 1914
Whirl of Life, The
Stage:
About Town 1906
Girl behind the Counter, The 1907
Hen-Pecks, The 1911
Lady of the Slipper, The 1912
Midnight Sons, The 1909
Old Dutch 1909
Summer Widowers, The 1910
Sunshine Girl, The 1913
Watch Your Step 1914

437
CASTLETON, Barbara (1896-   )
Americanism
Dangerous Hours
Daughter of the Gods
Empty Pockets
For Freedom of the World
Heart of a Girl, The
Heredity
Just Sylvia
Man Who Turned White, The
On Trial
Peg o' My Heart
Silver King, The
Sins of Ambition
Tower of Ivory, The
Vengeance
War Brides
What Love Forgives

438
CAVALIERI, Lina (1874-   )
Eternal Temptress, The
La Sposa Della Morte
Love's Conquest
Manon Lescaut
Rose of Granada /aka/ The House
   of Granada
Temptress, The
Two Brides
Woman of Impulse, A

439
CAVANAUGH, William*
Great Gamble, The (serial)
Traffic in Souls

440
CAVENDER, Glen*
Because He Loved Her
Dog Catcher's Love, A
Fatty and Mabel Adrift
Fickle Fatty's Fall
Pawnbroker's Heart, The
Submarine Pirate, A
Surf Girl, The (Poppa)
Village Blacksmith, The

441
CECIL, Edward*
Fast Company (Richard Barnaby)

442
CECIL, Nora (1879-   )
Miss Crusoe
Prunella
Woman, Woman

443
CHADWICK, Helene (1897-1940)
Adventure in Hearts, An
Angel Factory, The
Caleb Piper's Girl
Girls
Go Get 'Em Garringer
Heartease
Naulahka

444
CHAGNON, Jack*
Three Musketeers, The (Porthos)

445
CHALLENGER, Percy*
Blind Husbands (man from home)

446
CHAMBERS, Marie*
Fifty-Fifty

447
CHAMIER, Francis*
Henry VIII (Capucius)

448
CHAMPION, George*
Lightning Bryce (serial)

449
CHANEY, Lon (1883-1930)
Accusing Evidence (Lon)
Adventures of Francois Villon, The
   (Chevalier Bertrand de la la Payne
   in "The Oubliette" and Sir Stephen
   in "The Higher Law"
   Alas and Alak (the husband)

All for Peggy (the stable groom)
Almost an Actress (the cameraman)
Anything Once (Waughnt Moore)
Back to Life (the rival)
Bloodhounds of the North (a mountie)
Bobbie of the Ballet (Hook Hoover)
Bondage (a seducer)
Bound on the Wheel (drunken husband)
Broadway Love (Elmer Watkins)
Broadway Scandal, A (Kink Colby)
By the Sun's Ray (discarded suitor)
Chimney's Secret, The (a
  schizophrenic)
Danger--Go Slow (Bud)
Desert Breed, The (Fred)
Discord and Harmony (the sculptor)
Doll's House, A (Nils Krogstadt)
Dolly's Scoop (Dan Fisher)
Elephant on His Hands, An (Eddie)
Embezzler, The (J. Roger Dixon)
Empty Gun, The
End of the Feud, The (Wood Dawson)
False Faces (Karl Eckstrom)
Fascination of the Fleur de Lis
  (Duke of Safoulrug)
Fast Company (Dan McCarty)
Father and the Boys (Tuck
  Bartholomew)
Felix on the Job (Tod)
Fires of Rebellion (the city tempter)
Flashlight, The (dual role of Henry
  and Brixton Norton)
For Cash
Forbidden Room, The (John Morris)
Gilded Spider, The (Giovanni)
Girl in the Checkered Coat, The
  (Hector Maitland)
Girl of the Night, The (reformed
  crook)
Grand Passion, The (Paul Argos)
Grasp of Greed (Jimmie)
Grind, The (old man)
Grip of Jealousy, The (Silas Lacey)
Hell Morgan's Girl (Sleter Noble)
Her Bounty (Fred Howard)
Her Chance (Jerry)
Her Escape (underworld leader)
Her Grave Mistake (Nunez)
Her Life's Story (Don Valesquez)
Honor of the Mounted, The (Jacques
  Laquox)
Hopes of Blind Alley, The (rascally
  dealer)
Idyll of the Hills, An (a mountaineer)
If My Country Should Call (Dr.
  George Ardath)
Kaiser, the Beast of Berlin, The
  (Admiral Von Tirpitz)

Lamb, the Woman, the Wolf, The
  (the Wolf)
Lie, The (Young MacGregor
Lights and Shadows (Bentley)
Lion, the Lamb, the Man, The
  (crafty brother)
Lon of Lone Mountain (Lon Moore)
Maid of the Mist (Postmaster)
Man's Country, A ("Three Card"
  Duncan)
Mark of Cain, The (Dick Temple)
Mask of Love, The (Marino)
Measure of a Man, The (Lt. Jim
  Stuart)
Menace to Carlotta, The (Giovanni)
Millionaire Paupers, The (meddlesome
  villain)
Miner's Romance, A (John Burns)
Miracle Man, The (Frog)
Mother's Atonement, A (the tempter)
Mountain Justice (a mountaineer)
Night of Thrills, A (house visitor)
Old Cobbler, The (Wild Bill)
Outside the Gates (Perez)
Oyster Dredger, The
Paid in Advance (Bateese LeBlanc)
Pay Me (Joe Lawson)
Pine's Revenge, The
Piper's Price, The (Billy Kilmartin)
Pipe's of Pan, The (Arthur Farrell)
Place beyond the Winds (Jerry Jo)
Poor Jake's Demise
Price of Silence, The (Dr. Edmund
  Stafford
Quits (Frenchy)
Ranch Romance, A (Raphael Praz)
Red Margaret--Moonshiner (Lon)
Remember Mary Magdalen (the
  half-wit)
Rescue, The (Thomas Holland)
Richelieu (Baradas)
Riddle Gawne (Hame Bozzam)
Scarlet Car, The (Forbes)
Sea Urchin, The (hunchbacked fisher-
  man)
Sin of Olga Brandt, The (Stephen
  Leslie)
Star of the Sea, The (Tomasco)
Steady Company (factory man)
Stool Pigeon, The (first picture
  directed for Universal)
Stranger Than Death
Stronger Mind, The (crook's pal)
Such Is Life (Tod Wilkes)
Talk of the Town, The (Jack
  Lanchome)
Tangled Hearts (Society husband)
That Devil, Bateese (Louis Courteau)

Threads of Fate, The (the Count)
Tragedy of Whispering Creek, The
(the Greaser)
Trap, The (ne'er-do-well)
Triumph (Paul Niehoff)
Trust, The (the burglar)
Under a Shadow (jealous husband)
Unlawful Trade, The (Cross Blood)
Vengeance of the West
Victory (Ricardo)
Violin Maker, The
Virtue Its Own Reward (Duncan
Bronson)
When Bearcat Went Dry (Kindard
Powers)
When the Gods Played a Badger
Game (property man)
Where the Forest Ends (Paul
Rouchelle)
Wicked Darling, The (Stoop Conners)

450
CHAPIN, Benjamin*
Lincoln Cycle, The (Abraham
Lincoln)
Stage:
Lincoln 1906; 1909

451
CHAPLIN, Charlie (Charles Spencer
Chaplin) (1889-)
Adventurer, The
Bank, The /aka/ Charlie at the Bank
Behind the Screen
Between Showers /aka/ Charlie and
the Umbrella; The Flirts; In the
Wrong
Bond, The
Burlesque on Carmen (Darn Hosiery)
Busy Day, A /aka/ Militant
Suffragette
By the Sea
Caught in a Cabaret /aka/ Faking
with Society; Jazz Waiter; The
Waiter
Caught in the Rain /aka/ At It Again;
In the Park; Who Got Stung?
Champion, The /aka/ Champion
Charlie
Chase Me, Charlie
Count, The
Cruel, Cruel Love /aka/ Lord
Helpus
Cure, The
Day's Pleasure, A
Dog's Life, A
Dough and Dynamite /aka The Cook;
The Doughnut Designer

Essanay--Chaplin Revue of 1916, The
Easy Street
Face on the Barroom Floor, The
/aka/ The Ham Artist
Fatal Mallet, The /aka/ Pile Driver
Film Johnnie, A /aka/ Million
Dollar Job; Movie Nut
Fireman, The
Floorwalker, The
Gentleman of Nerve /aka/ Some
Nerve
Getting Acquainted /aka/ A Fair
Exchange (Mr. Sniffles)
Her Friend the Bandit /aka/ Mabel's
Flirtation
His Favorite Pastime /aka/ The
Bonehead
His Musical Career /aka/ Musical
Tramps; The Piano Movers
His New Profession /aka/ Good-For-
Nothing; Helping Himself
His New Job
His Prehistoric Past /aka/ The
Dream (Weakchin)
His Regeneration (bit part)
His Trysting Place /aka/ The
Family House
Immigrant, The
In the Park
Introducing Charlie Chaplin
Jitney Elopement
Kid Auto Races at Venice
Knockout, The /aka/ Counted Out;
The Pugilist
Laughing Gas /aka/ Down and Out;
Turning His Ivories (dental
assistant)
Mabel at the Wheel /aka/ His Dare-
devil Queen; Hot Finish
Mabel's Busy Day /aka/ Charlie and
the Sausages; Hot Dogs; Love and
Lunch
Mabel's Married Life /aka/ The
Squarehead; When You're Married
Mabel's Strange Predicament /aka/
Hotel Mix-up
Masquerader, The /aka/ The Female
Impersonation; The Picnic; Putting
One Over
New Janitor, The /aka/ The Blunder-
ing Boob; The New Porter
Night in the Show /aka/ Charlie at
the Show (dual role Mr. Pest and
Mr. Rowdy)
Night Out, A
One A. M. (solo performance)
Pawnshop, The
Perils of Patrick, The

Police
Property Man, The /aka/ Getting
  His Goat; The Roustabout
Recreation /aka/ Spring Fever
Rink, The
Rounders, The /aka/ Oh, What a
  Night; Revelry; Two of a Kind
Shanghaied
Shoulder Arms
Star Border, The /aka/ Mash-House
  Hero
Sunnyside
Tango Tangles /aka/ Charlie's
  Recreation; Music Hall
Those Love Pangs /aka/ Busted
  Hearts; The Rival Mashers
Tillie's Punctured Romance (city
  slicker)
Tramp, The
Triple Trouble
Twenty Minutes of Love /aka/ Cops
  and Watches; He Loved Her So;
  Love Friend
Vagabond, The
Woman, A /aka/ Charlie, the Per-
  fect Lady; The Perfect Lady
Work /aka/ The Paperhanger
  (Paperhanger's assistant)
Counterfeit Films (Made by using bits
  of Chaplin films with new material
  shot around them)
Charlie in a Harem
Dishonor System, The
Fall of the Rummy-Nuffs, The
One Law for Both
Son of the Gods, A

452
CHAPLIN, Syd /aka/ Sydney (1885-
  1965)
Better 'Ole, The
Bit of Fluff, A
Dog's Life, A
Fatty's Wine Party (his first Key-
  stone role)
Fortune Hunter, The
Giddy, Gay and Ticklish /aka/ A
  Gay Lothario
Gussle Rivals Jonah
Gussle, the Golfer
Gussle Tied to Trouble
Gussle's Backward Way
Gussle's Day of Rest
Gussle's Wayward Path
Hushing the Scandal /aka/ Friendly
  Enemies
Lover's Lost Control, A /aka/
  Looking Them Over

No One to Guide Him
One Hundred Million
Shoulder Arms
Submarine Pirate, A
That Springtime Feeling

453
CHAPMAN, Charles*
Anthony and Cleopatra (Anthony)
Midsummer Night's Dream, A
  (Quince)
Othello (soldier)
Romeo and Juliet (Montague)
Stage:
Romeo and Juliet 1903

454
CHAPMAN, Edythe (1863-1948)
Alias Ladyfingers
Alias Mike Moran
Bound in Morocco (the mother)
Everywoman
Evil Eye, The
Experimental Marriage
Flame of the Desert
Golden Chance
Hometown Girl, The
Knickerbocker Buckaroo, The (the
  mother)
Little American, The
Little Princess, The
Public Opinion
Rescuing Angel, The
Richelieu (the Queen)
Say, Young Fellow!
Secret Service
Selfish Woman, The (Mrs. Hillary)
Whispering Chorus, The (John
  Trimble's mother)
Winning Girl, The
Stage:
Light Eternal, The 1906

455
CHAPMAN, Ned*
Lass of the Lumberlands (serial)

456
CHARLES, John*
Cecilia of the Pink Roses (George
  Dickson)

457
CHARLESON, Mary (1885-1968)
Country That God Forgot, The
His Robe of Honor
Honeymooners, The
Humdrum Brown

Little Shoes
Long Lane's Turning, A
Prince Chap, The
Road o' Strife, The (serial)
Saint's Adventure, The
Truant Soul, The
Upstairs and Down
With Hoops of Steel

458
CHARLEY, John*
Law of Compensation, The

459
CHASE, Bud*
Father and the Boys

460
CHASE, Charlie (Charles Parrott)
    (1893-1940)
A Keystone Cop 1912
Chased into Love
Cursed by His Beauty
Dash of Courage, A
Dough and Dynamite
Gentleman of Nerve
Hash House Mashers
Hearts and Sparks
Hello Trouble
Her Father's Footsteps
Her Torpedoed Love
His Musical Career
His New Profession
Home Breakers, The
Hunt, The
Knock-Out, The
Long Flib the King
Love in Armor
Love, Loot and Crash
Mabel's New Job
Masquerader, The
Only a Farmer's Daughter
Panic Is On, The
Paste and Waste
Public Ghost No. 1
Rent Jumpers, The
Rounders, The
Settled at the Seaside
Ship Ahoy
Shot in the Excitement
Tillie's Punctured Romance
Versatile Villian, A
Stage:
Stolen Story, The 1906

461
CHATTERTON, Thomas /aka/ Tom*
Father and the Boys
Secret of the Submarine, The (serial)

462
CHAUTARD, Emile (1881-1934)
Eternal Temptress, The
House of Glass
Human Driftwood
Hungry Heart
L'Aiglon
L'Apprentie
Le Poison de L'Humanitie
Magda
Marionettes
Mystery of the Yellow Room, The
Poppy
Sapho
Under the Greenwood Tree

463
CHENE, Dixie*
Great Vacuum Robbery, The
Gussle, The Golfer

464
CHESEBRO, George*
Girl of Hell's Agony, The
Hands Up! (serial)
She Wolf

465
CHESTER, Virginia*
Hash House Mashers

466
CHEVALIER, Maurice (Maurice
    Auguste Chevalier) (1888-1971)
Max Linder comedies 1910
Trop Crédule (an extra)
Stage:
Cirque d'Hiver 1898 (debut)
Tourelles Casino 1901
La Ville Japonaise 1902
Casino de Montmartre 1902
La Fourmi 1902
Concert de l'Univers 1902
Satyre Bouchonné at the Parisiana
    1904
Le Figaro at Follies Bergère 1905
Grand Revue d'Hiver (*)
Folies Bergère 1916
Hullo America 1918-19

467
CHICHESTER, Emily*
Nobody Home
Nugget Nell

468
CHILDERS, Naomi (1892-1964)
Anselo Lee
Blind Man's Eyes

Devil's Price, The
Dust of Egypt
Gay Lord Quex, The
Island of Regeneration
Lord and Lady Algy
Shadows of Suspicion
Yellow Dove, The

469
CHRISMAN, Pat*
Local Color

470
CHRISTIANS, Margarete*
Audrey

471
CHURCH, Frederick /aka/ Fred*
Madame DuBarry (Cosse Brissac)
Shootin' Mad (Bull Martin)
Temple of Terror, The

472
CHURCHILL, Ruth*
Stone Age, The /aka/ Her Cave Man

473
CLAIRE, Gertrude*
Blind Man's Eyes
Boomerang, The
City of Darkness
Civilization
Coward, The (Mrs. Winslow)
Crimson Gardenia, The
Cup of Life, A
Golden Rule Kate
Hard Boiled
His Mother's Boy
Honor Thy Name
Jinx
Latent Spark, The
Little Commrade
Nine O'Clock Town, A
Peggy
Ramona
Romance and Arabella
Stepping Out
Wells of Paradise
Widow by Proxy
Wolf Woman

474
CLAIRE, Ina (Ema Fagan) (1892-)
Puppet Crown, The
Wild Goose Chase, The (Betty
    Wright)
Stage:
Gold Diggers, The (Jerry Lamar)
    1919

Jumping Jupiter 1911
Lady Luxury 1914
Polly with a Past (Polly Shannon)
    1917
Quaker Girl, The (Prudence) 1911
Ziegfeld Follies of 1915
Ziegfeld Follies of 1916

475
CLANCY, George*
Secret of the Submarine, The (serial)

476
CLAPHAM, Leonard*
Lion Man, The (serial)
Lion's Claw, The (serial)

477
CLARGES, Berner*
Face at the Window, The
Flash of Light, A
His Trust Fulfilled
In Old Kentucky
Lesson, The
Little Angels of Luck
1776, or The Hessian Renegades
Was Justice Served?
Stage:
Boys of Company "B", The 1907
Clean Slate, A 1903
Edmund Burke 1905
Lady Margaret 1902
Monkey's Paw, The 1907
Noble Spaniard, The 1909
Olive Latimer's Husband 1910
Sir Anthony 1906
Third Degree, The (Jones) 1909
When Knighthood Was in Flower
    1901

478
CLARK, Andy*
Andy series (child)

479
CLARK, Edwin*
Active Life of Dolly of the Dailies,
    The (serial)
Stage:
Auto Race, The 1907
Ballet of Niagara, The 1910
Earthquake, The 1910
International Cup, The 1910
Society Circus, A 1905
Sporting Days 1908

480
CLARK, Frank*
Spoilers, The (old timer)

Stage:
Captain Barrington 1903

481
CLARK, Jack*
From the Manger to the Cross (a
  disciple)

482
CLARK, Marguerite (1883-1940)
Amazons, The
Bab's Burglar
Bab's Diary
Bab's Matinee Idol
Bluebird, The
Come Out of the Kitchen
Crucible, The
Fortunes of Life
Girls
Golden Bird
Goose Girl, The
Gretna Green
Helene of the North
Honeymoon for Three, A
Let's Elope
Little Lady Eileen
Little Miss Hoover
Luck in Pawn
Mice and Men
Miss George Washington
Molly-Make-Believe
Mrs. Wiggs of the Cabbage Patch
Out of a Clear Sky
Out of the Drifts
Pretty Sister of Jose, The
Prince and the Pauper, The (dual
  role)
Prunella
Rich Man, Poor Man
Seven Sisters
Seven Swans
Silks and Satins
Snow White (Title role)
Still Waters
Three Men and a Girl
Uncle Tom's Cabin (dual role, Topsy
  and Eva)
Valentine Girl, The
Widow by Proxy
Wildflower
Stage:
Affairs of Anatol, The (Hilda) 1912
Are You a Crook? 1913
Baby Mine 1910-11
Beauty Spot, The 1909
Belle of Bohemia, The 1900
Happyland 1905-06
Jim, the Penman 1910

King of Cadonia 1910
Lights O' London, The 1911
Mr. Pickwick 1903
Pied Piper, The 1908
Prunella (Title role) 1913
Snow White and the Seven Dwarfs
  (Snow White) 1912-13
Wild Rose, The 1902

483
CLARKE, George*
Tiger Woman, The (Marion's father)
Vixen, The (Adm. Drummond)

484
CLARKSON, Willie*
Romeo and Juliet

485
CLARY, Charles*
Adventures of Kathlyn, The (serial)
Back to the Primitive
Children of the Sea
Joan, the Woman (La Tremoville)
Madame DuBarry (Louise XV)
Rose of the Blood, The (Prince
  Arabassoff)

486
CLAYTON, Ethel (1884-1966)
College Widow, The
Dormant Power
Easy Money
Essanay player 1909-10
For the Defense
Fortune Hunter, The
Girl Who Came Back, The
Great Divide, The
Husband and Wife
Journey's End
Lion and the Mouse, The
Maggie Pepper
Mazie Puts One Over
Men, Women and Money
Mystery Girl, The
Pettigrew's Girl
Soul without Windows, The
Sporting Chance, A
Stolen Hours
Stolen Paradies, The
Whims of Society
Witch Woman
Woman Beneath, A
Woman Next Door, The
Woman's Way, A
Woman's Weapons, A
Stage:
Bobby Burnit 1910

Brute, The 1912
Fancy Free 1918
His Name on the Door 1909
Nobody Home 1915

487
CLAYTON, Marguerite (1896-   )
Bolshevist Burlesque
Bride Thirteen
Bronco Billy's Capture (Evelyn)
Bronze Man, The
Clock Struck One, The
Cowboy Coward, The
Daughter of the City, A
Hit the Trail Holiday
Inside the Lines
Last Round-Up, The
Long Green Trail, The
New Moon, The
Prince of Graustark
Promised Land, The
When Love and Honor Called

488
CLEAVE, Arthur*
Better 'Ole, The

489
CLEMENT, Eloise*
Burden of Proof, The (Mrs. Durand)

490
CLEMENTE, Steve*
Lightning Bryce (serial)

491
CLERGET, Paul*
Woman
Stage:
Pierrot the Prodigal 1916

492
CLEWING, Carl*
Midsummer Night's Dream, A
   (Lysander)

493
CLIFFE, H. Cooper*
Gold and the Woman (Col. Ernest
   Dent)

494
CLIFFORD, Kathleen*
When the Clouds Roll By (Lucette
   Bancroft)
Who Is Number One? (serial)
Stage:
Belle of London Town, The 1907

Fad and Folly 1902
Fascinating Flora 1907
Gaby 1911
Hell 1911
Man Who Owns Broadway, The 1909
Pair of Queens, A 1916
Tommy Rot 1902
Top O' the World, The 1907-08
Whirl of Society 1912

495
CLIFFORD, Ruth (1900-   )
Cabaret Girl, The
Desire of the Moth
Door Between, The
Game's Up, The
Guilt of Silence, The
Kaiser, the Beast of Berlin, The
   (a Belgian woman)
Kentucky Cinderella, A
Lure of Luxury, The
Midnight Madness
Millionaire Pirate, The
Mothers-in-Law
Mysterious Mr. Tiller, The
Red, Red Heart, The
Savage

496
CLIFFORD, William*
Corner in Cotton, A
Paradise Garden
Pay Me (Hal Curtis)
Rosemary

497
CLIFTON, Elmer (1890-1949)
Birth of a Nation, The (Phil
   Stoneman)
Fall of Babylon, The
Intolerance (the Rhapsode)
Little School Ma'am, The
Missing Links, The
Nobody Home
Sisters, The
Stage:
Deep Purple, The (valet) 1911

498
CLIFTON, Emma*
Between Showers

499
CLINE, Edward*
Knock-Out, The
Stage:
Certain Party, A 1911

500
CLISBEE, Ethel*
Hazards of Helen, The (serial)

501
CLIVE, Henry*
Fighting Odds, The

502
CLONBOUGH, G. Butler*
Dark Star, The (German Spy)
When I Come Back to You (Karl
   VonKrutz)

503
CLOSE, Ivy (1893-   )
Adam Bede
Adventures of Dick Dolan, The
Cophetua
Darby and Joan
Darkest London
Flag Lieutenant, The
Ghosts
Girl from the Sky, The
Haunting of Silas P. Gould
Her Cross
Hon. William's Jonah
House Opposite, The
Irresistible Flapper, The
Ivy's Elopement
La Cigale
Lady of Shallot, The
Legend of the King, The
Lure of London, The
Mifanwy
Missing the Tide
Peep behind the Scenes, A
Pygmalion and Galatea
Sleeping Beauty, The
Terrible Twins, The
Two Elderly Cupids
Ware Case, The

504
COBB, Edmund*
Adventures of Kathlyn, The (serial)
Film for St. Louis Motion Picture
   Co. in 1910

505
COBB, Irvin S. (Irvin Shrewsbury
   Cobb) (1876-1944)
Arab, The (an American tourist)

506
CODY, Lew (Louis Joseph Coté)
   (1884-1934)
Beloved Cheater, The

Branded Soul, A
Broken Butterfly
Comrade John
Demon, The
Don't Change Your Husband
   (Schuyler VanStuphen)
For Husbands Only
Life Line, The
Mating, The (debut)
Mickey (Reggie Drake)
Treasure of the Sea

507
CODY, William ("Buffalo Bill")
   (1891-1948)
Life of Buffalo Bill

508
COGHLAN, Rose /aka/ Rosalind
   (1853-   )
As You Like It (Rosalinda)
Stage:
Admirable Crichton, The 1903
American Lord, The 1906
Cottage in the Air, The 1909
Fine Feathers 1913
Getting a Polish 1910
Jack Straw 1908
Lady of the Camellias, The (Mme.
   Prudence) 1917
Merry Wives of Windsor, The
   (Mistress Page) 1910
Nobel Spaniard, The 1909
Our Betters 1917
Pretty Soft 1919
School for Scandal, The 1909
Silent Call, The 1911
Squaw Man, The 1911
Trilby (Madam Vinard) 1915
Ulysses 1903
Vanity Fair 1911
Whirlwind, The (Mrs. Forest) 1919
Winter's Tale, The 1910
Yvette 1904

509
COGLEY, Nick (1869-   )
A La Cabaret
Bandit, A
Bangville Police, The
Cohen Saves the Flag
Coward, The (Negro servant)
Dizzy Heights and Daring Hearts
Dollars and Sense
Hearts and Sparks
Her Circus Knight
Hide and Seek
Lucky Leap, A

Mabel's Heros
Maid O' the Storm
Mother's Boy
Oriental Love
Peanuts and Bullets
Peeping Pete
Saved by Wireless
Sis Hopkins
Speed Queen, The
Toby's Bow

510
COHAN, George M. (1878-1942)
Broadway Jones
Hit the Trail Holiday
Seven Keys to Baldpate
Stage:
Broadway Jones (Jackson Jones) 1912
45 Minutes from Broadway 1912
George Washington, Jr. 1906; 1907
Governor's Son, The 1901; 1906
Hello Broadway 1914
Honeymooners, The 1907
Little Johnny Jones 1904-05; 1907
   (first starring role)
Little Millionaire, The 1911
Man Who Stole the Castle, The 1903
Out There 1918
Prince There Was, A 1918
Yankee Prince, The 1908

511
COHILL, William*
Life without Soul

512
COHL, Emile (1857-1938)
Pioneer French Cartoonist:
Adventures d'une Bout de Papier
Don Quichotte
Fantasmagorie
Les Allumettes Animees
Les Pieds Nickeles
Monsieur Stop
Snookums series

513
COLDWELL, Goldie*
Adventures of Kathlyn, The (serial)

514
COLE, James*
Almo, The Mighty (serial)

515
COLE, Slim*
Smashing Barriers (serial)

516
COLEMAN, Cherrie*
Crime and Punishment

517
COLEMAN, Frank J. *
Adventurer, The
Bank, The
Behind the Screen
Burlesque on Carmen
Count, The
Cure, The
Easy Street
Fireman, The
Floorwalker, The
His New Job
Immigrant, The
Pawnshop, The
Police!
Rink, The
Vagabond, The

518
COLLIER, Constance (Laura
   Constance Hardie) (1878-1955)
Code of Marcia Gray
Macbeth (Lady Macbeth)
Stage:
Explorer, The 1912
Ideal Husband, An (Mrs. Cheveley)
   1918
Israel 1909
Merry Wives of Windsor, The
   (Mistress Ford) 1916; 1917
Nan 1913
Oliver Twist 1912
Othello 1914
Peter Ibbetson (Mary, Duchess of
   Towers) 1917
Samson (Anne Marie) 1908
Thais 1911
Trelawny of the Wells (Imogen
   Parrott) 1911

519
COLLIER, William, Sr. (1866-1944)
Better Late Than Never /aka/
   Getting Married
Fatty and the Broadway Stars
My Valet
Never Again
No-good Guy, The
Plain Jane
Wife and Auto Trouble
Stage:
Are You the Father? 1903
Bunty, Bulls and Strings 1912
Caught in the Rain 1906

Dictator, The 1904; 1911
Fool and His Money, A 1904
Hello Broadway 1914
H. M. S. Pinafore 1877
Hokey-Pokey 1912
I'll Be Hanged if I Do 1910
Little Water on the Side, A 1914
Lucky Star, A 1910
Man from Mexico, The 1909
Never Say Die 1912
Nothing but Lies 1918
Nothing but the Truth 1916
On the Quiet 1901; 1905
Patriot, The 1908
Personal 1907
Take My Advise 1911
Twirly Whirly 1902
Who's Who? 1913

520
COLLIER, William, Jr. /aka/
   "Buster" (1903-   )
Bugle Call, The (debut)
Servant Question, The
Taking the Count
Stage:
Dictator, The 1911
I'll Be Hanged if I Do 1910
Little Water on the Side, A 1914
Lucky Star, A 1910
Never Say Die 1912
Patriot, The 1908
Take My Advise 1911
Who's Who? 1913

521
COLLINS, José
Light That Failed, The
Stage:
Alone at Last 1915
Merry Countess, The 1912
Passing Show of 1914, The 1914
Suzi 1914
Vera Violetta 1911
Whirl of Society 1912
Ziegfeld Follies of 1913

522
COLMAN, Ronald (1891-1958)
Anna, the Adventuress
Daughter of Eve, A (bit)
Live Wire, The (debut, never
   released)
Snow in the Desert (Rupert Sylvester)
Son of David, A (a pugilist)
Toilers, The (Bob)
Stage:
Damaged Goods (in London) 1918

Lena Ashwell Sketch (blackface;
   Coliseum, London) 1916
Misleading Lady, The (in London)
   1917

523
COMBE, Boyce*
Runaway Romany

524
COMMERFORD, Thomas*
Graustark
String of Victory, The
White Sister, The

525
COMPSON, Betty (1897-   )
All Dressed Up
All over a Stocking
Almost a Bigamist
Almost a Widow
Almost a Scandal
Almost Divorced
As Luck Would Have It
Betty Makes Up
Betty's Adventure
Betty's Big Idea
Bold Bad Knight, A
Brass Buttoned Romance, A
Brother Raiders
Christie comedies (78) 1915-16
Crazy by Proxy
Cupid Trims His Lordship
Cupid's Papa
Cupid's Uppercut
Deacon's Waterloo, The
Devil's Trail, The
Down by the Sea
Eddie's Night Out
He Almost Eloped
Her Celluloid Hero
Her Crooked Career
Her Friend the Chauffeur
Her Friend the Doctor
Her Steady Carfare
He's a Devil
His Baby
His Last Pill
Hist at Six O'Clock
Hubby's Night Out
Janitor's Busy Day, The
Jed's Trip to the Fair
Leap Year Tangle, A
Lem's College Career
Light of Victory
Little Diplomat
Love and a Savage
Love and Locksmiths

Love and Vaccination
Making of a Mother, The
Many a Slip
Mingling Spirits
Miracle Man, The (Rose)
Nearly a Papa
Nestor comedies 1910
Newlywed's Mix Up, The
Out for the Coin
Pott Bungles Again
Prodigal Liar
Quiet Supper for Four, A
Sheriff, The
Small Change
Some Chaperone
Some Kid
Somebody's Baby
Suspended Sentence
Terror of the Range (serial)
Their Quiet Honeymoon
Their Seaside Tangle
Those Wedding Bells
Wanted: a Husband
Wanted: a Leading Lady
When Lizzie Disappeared
When the Losers Win
Where the Heather Blooms
Whose Wife?
Won in a Cabaret
Wooing of Aunt Jamima, The

526
COMPSON, John*
Her First Biscuits
His Wife's Mother
Jones and His New Neighbors (Mr.
  Jones)
Jones and the Lady Book Agent (Mr.
  Jones)
Jones Have Amateur Theatricals, The
  (Mr. Jones)
Mr. Jones at the Ball (Mr. Jones)
Mr. Jones' Burglar (Mr. Jones)
Mr. Jones Has a Card Party (Mr.
  Jones)
Monday Morning in a Coney Island
  Police Court
Mrs. Jones Entertains (Mr. Jones)
Mrs. Jones' Lover or I Want My
  Hat (Mr. Jones)
Smoked Husband, A

527
COMPTON, Fay (1894-)
Labour Leader, The
One Summer's Day
She Stoops to Conquer
Stage:

At Royal Albert Hall, London
  (debut) 1906
At Shubert Theatre 1914
Tonight's the Night 1914

528
CONDON, Jackie*
Daddy Long Legs
Hoodlum, The

529
CONESA, Marie*
Webb Singing Pictures

530
CONKLIN, Charles "Heinie"
  (1880-1959)
Battle Royal
Mack Sennet comedies 1915-1920
Salome vs. Shenandoah

531
CONKLIN, Chester (1888-)
Ambrose's Sour Grapes
Back to Nature Girls
Battle of Ambrose and Walrus, The
Best of Enemies, The
Between Showers (a cop)
Bird's a Bird, A
Bucking Society
Bulldog Yale
Business Is Business
Cannon Ball, The
Caught in a Cabaret
Cinders of Love
Clever Dummy, A (a playful
  property)
Country Chickens
Cruel, Cruel Love
Curses! They Remarked
Dizzy Heights and Daring Hearts
Do-Re-Mi-Fa
Dodging His Doom
Dough and Dynamite
Droppinton's Devilish Dream
Droppington's Family Tree
Face on the Barroom Floor, The
False Alarm
First Heir, The
Gentleman of Nerve
Great Nickel Robbery, The
Ham Artist, The
Hash House Fraud
Hash House Masher
Hearts and Planets
Her Private Husband
His First False Step
His Son's Wife

His Taking Ways
Home Breakers, The
Home Rule
How Heroes Are Made
Hushing the Scandal
Laughing Gas
Love Egg, The
Love, Loot and Crash (Chief)
Love, Speed and Thrills
Love Thief, The
Mabel at the Wheel (Father)
Mabel's Busy Day
Mabel's New Job
Mabel's Strange Predicament
Making a Living (dual role, Cop and
  Bum)
Masquerader, The
One Night Stand, A
Pawnbroker's Heart, The
Perfect Villain
Piper, The
Pullman Bride, The
Rural Cinderella, A
Saved by Wireless
Shot in the Excitement
Soft Boiled Yegg
Step Lively, Please
Tango Tangles
Those Dangerous Eyes
Those Love Pangs
Tillie's Punctured Romance
Tugboat Romeo, A
Twenty Minutes of Love
Uncle Tom's Cabin (a burlesque)
When Ambrose Dared Walrus
Wild West Love
Woman, A

532
CONKLIN, William (1877-1935)
Flare-Up Sal
Hay Foot! Straw Foot!
Joan, the Woman (John of
  Luxembourg)
Love Letters
Neal of the Navy (serial)
Price Mark, The
Red Hot Dollars
Virtuous Thief, The
Stage:
Anna Karenina 1907
Rack, The 1911
Shadowed 1913

533
CONNELLY, Bobby*
Intrigue
Love's Sunset (boy)

Out of a Clear Sky
Prince in a Pawnshop, A
Professional Patient, The
Seal of Silence, The
Unpardonable Sin, The
Youthful Affair, A

534
CONNELLY, Edward*
Fall of the Romanoffs
Good Little Devil, A
Great Secret, The (serial)
Rasputin, the Mad Monk
Toys of Fate
Stage:
Babette 1903
Good Little Devil, A (Old Nick, Sr.)
  1913
Great Adventure, The 1913
Wild Duck, The 1918

535
CONNOLLY, Jack*
Egg-Crate Wallop, The

536
CONVILLE, Robert*
Out of the Drifts
Stage:
Dragon's Claw, The 1914

537
CONWAY, Jack*
Macbeth (Lennox)
Restless Souls
Valley of the Moon

538
COOGAN, Jackie (1915-)
Day's Pleasure, A
Skinner's Baby

539
COOK, Clyde (1891-)
Artist, The
Chauffeur, The
Eskimo, The
Greater Law, The
Lazy Bones
Show Down
Soldiers of Fortune
Southern Justice
Toreador, The
Up or Down?
Stage:
Happy Days 1919

540
COOK, John*
Gray Ghost, The (serial)

541
COOK, Warren*
Great Gamble, The (serial)
Pride of the Clan, The
Stage:
Bachelors and Benedicts 1912

542
COOKSON, S. A. *
Hamlet (Horatio)
Henry VIII (Cardinal Campeius)
Tempest, The (Alonzo)
Stage:
H. B. Irving--Dorothea Baird
    Repertory 1906
Forbes--Robertson Repertory 1913
Light That Failed, The (James
    Vickery) 1913

543
COOLEY, Hallam (1888-   )
Bull's Eye (serial)
Dog Catcher's Love, A
Girl Dodger, The
Girl from Outside, The
Happy though Married
More Deadly Than the Male
One of the Finest
Royal Rogue, A
Upstairs

544
COOLEY, James*
Eternal Sapho, The (Billey)
Reliance player 1913
Tale of Two Nations, A
Stage:
Beethoven 1910
Mademoiselle Marni 1905
Thunderbolt, The 1911

545
COOLEY, Willard*
Burden of Proof, The (Frank
    Raymond)

546
COOMBS, Guy*
Barbara Frietchie
School for Scandal, The
Stage:
Prisoner of Zenda, The 1908
Triangle, The 1906

547
COOPER, Bigelow*
Mary Stuart

548
COOPER, Claude H. *
Country Girl, The
Stage:
American Ace, An 1918
Betrothal, The (drunken ancestor)
    1918
Boys Will Be Boys (Nick Bell) 1919
Burgomaster of Belgium, A 1919
Checkers 1903; 1904
Daddy Dufard 1910
Old Town, The 1910
On with the Dance 1917
Red Mill, The 1906

549
COOPER, Earl*
Teddy Telzlaff and Earl Cooper,
    Speed Kings

550
COOPER, Edna Mae*
Male and Female (Fisher)
Old Wives for New (Bertha)
Whispering Chorus, The (Good Face)

551
COOPER, F. B. *
Dangers of a Bride

552
COOPER, George (1891-   )
Auction Block, The
Dark Star, The (Mr. Brandes)
Find the Woman
Her Secret
Hunted Woman
Night Out, A
Small Town Romance, A
Suspect, The
Tragedy of Whispering Creek, The
    (the kid)
Unlawful Trade, The (Young Tate)
Veiled Mystery, The

553
COOPER, Gladys (1888-   )
Masks and Faces
Real Thing at Last, The
Stage:
Misleading Lady, The (in London)
    1917

554
COOPER, Miriam (1894-   )

Betrayed
Birth of a Nation, The (Margaret)
Confederate Ironclad
Duke's Plan, The
Evangeline
Girl Who Came Back, The
Home Sweet Home (Easterner's fiance)
Honor System, The
Innocent Sinners, The
Intolerance (the Friendless one)
Mother and the Law, The
Odalisque, The
Prussian Cur, The
Should a Husband Forgive?
Silent Lie, The
Their First Acquaintance
When Fate Frowned
Woman and the Law

555
CORBETT, Ben*
Lightning Bryce (serial)

556
CORBETT, James J. (1867-1933)
Corbett-Courtneay Fight
Midnight Man, The (serial)
Stage:
Cashel Byron (Title role) 1906
Doing Our Bit 1917

557
CORBIN, Virginia Lee (1910-)
Ace High
Aladdin and the Wonderful Lamp
Babes in the Woods
Chorus Girl and the Kid, The
Enemies of Children
Fan Fan
Jack and the Beanstalk
Mikado, The
Six Shooter Andy
Treasure Island

558
CORNWALL, Anne (1897-)
Firing Line, The
Hollow of Her Hand, The
Indestructible Wife, The
Knife, The
Prunella
Quest of the Big 'Un
World to Live In, The

559
CORRADO, Gino*
Intolerance (the runner)

560
CORRIGAN, Thomas J. *
Selig player 1912

561
CORTES, Armand*
Yellow Menace, The (serial)

562
COSGRAVE, Jack*
Hearts of the World (Mr. Hamilton)

563
COSSART, Ernest (1876-1951)
Strange Case of Mary Page, The
    (serial)
Stage:
Androcles and the Lion (the Centurion)
    1915
Doctor's Dilemma, The (newspaper
    man) 1915
Love among the Lions 1910
Man Who Married a Dumb Wife, The
    1915
Midsummer Night's Dream, A
    (Bottom) 1915
Mr. Dot (Mr. Rixon) 1910
Sherman Was Right 1915
Typhoon, The 1912

564
COSTELLO, Dolores (1905-)
Captain Jack's Dilemma
Geranium, The /aka/ Mission of
    a Flower
Her Sister's Children
Hindu Charm, The
Ida's Christmas
Misdummer Night's Dream, A (a
    fairy)
Old San Francisco

565
COSTELLO, Helene (1903-1957)
At Scrogginses' Corner
Captain Barnacle's Baby
Captain Barnacle's Messmate
Captain Jack's Dilemma
First Violin, The
Geranium, The /aka/ Mission of a
    Flower
Her Crowning Glory
Her Sister's Children
Matrimonial Maneuvers
Midsummer Night's Dream, A (a
    fairy)
Mr. Bolter's Niece
Night before Christmas, The

Old Doll, The
Rip Van Winkle
Toymaker, The

566
COSTELLO, Maurice (Herbert Blythe)
(1877-1950)
Altar of Love
As You Like It (Orlando)
Aunt's Romance
Cambric Mask, The
Cap'n Abe's Niece
Captain's Captain, The
Crimson Stain Mystery, The (serial)
Crown Prince's Double, The
Dr. LeFleur's Theory
Extremities
First Violin, The
Girl Woman
Her Crowning Glory
Her Sister's Children
Man Who Couldn't Beat God, The
Midsummer Night's Dream, A
(Lysander)
Mr. Barnes of New York
Moonstone of Fez, The
My Old Dutch
Mysterious Lodger, The
New Stenographer, The
Night before Christmas, The
Sale of a Heart, The
Tale of Two Cities, A (Sydney Carton)
Tried for His Own Murder
Tyrant Is Dead, The
Stage:
Cecil Spooner Stock Company (Brooklyn) 1905

567
COTTON, Lucy*
Broken Melody, The
Fugitive, The
Life without Soul
Miracle of Love, The
Prodigal Wife, The
Stage:
Polygamy (Helen Fenton) 1914
Turn to the Right! (Betty Bascom)
1916
Up in Mabel's Room 1919

568
COULTER, Frazer*
Lady Audley's Secret (Lt. Devenant)

569
COURTLEIGH, William (1869-1930)
Eyes of Youth

Neal of the Navy (serial)
Out of the Drifts
Susie Snowflake
Stage:
Blind Youth 1917-18

570
COURTNEAY, Peter*
Corbett-Courtneay Fight

571
COURTNEAY, William F. (1875-1933)
Miss Jerry
Stage:
Ambassador, The 1900
Arsene Lupin 1909
Camille (Armond Duval) 1904
Cappy Ricks 1918
General Post 1917
Girl and the Penant, The 1913
Importance of Being Earnest
(Algernon) 1902
Interrupted Honeymoon, The 1900
Iris 1902
La Belle Marseillaise 1905
Lady Huntworth's Experiment 1900
Light That Lies in Woman's Eyes,
The 1904
Lights o' London, The 1911
Love Letter, The 1906
Maid of the Mountains, The 1918
Making Good 1912
Man of Forty, The 1900
Mrs. Leffingwell's Boots 1905
Pals First 1917
Rector's Garden, The 1908
Ready Money 1912
Richard Mansfield Repertory 1899
Romance (dual role, Bishop and
Thomas Armstrong) 1913
Secret Orchard, The 1907
Trilby (Little Billie) 1905
Under Cover 1914
Under Fire 1915
Wolf, The 1908

572
COURTOT, Marguerite (1897-)
Barefoot Boy, The
Bound and Gagged (serial)
Crime and Punishment
Natural Law, The
Octoroon, The
Perfect Lover, The
Roaring Oaks (serial)
Rolling Stones
Teeth of the Tiger
Unbeliever, The

Vampire, The
Ventures of Marguerite, The (Title
role) (serial)

573
COURTRIGHT, Jennie Lee*
Bill Henry

574
COWARD, Noel (1899-1973)
Hearts of the World (debut as man
with wheelbarrow and a villager)

575
COWIE, Laure*
Anne Boleyn (Anne)
Henry VIII (Anne Boleyn)

576
COWL, Jane (1890-1950)
Garden of Lies, The (debut)
Spreading Dawn, The
Stage:
Common Clay (Ellen Neal) 1915
Crowded Hour, The 1918
Gamblers, The 1910
Grand Army Man, A 1907-08
Is Matrimony a Failure? (Fanny
Perry) 1909
Lilac Time 1917
Music Master, The (Octavie)
1904-05-06
Rose of the Rancho, The 1906; 1907
Smilin' Through (dual role, Kathleen
Dungannon and Moonyean Clare)
1919
Sweet Kitty Bellairs (debut) 1903-04
Upstart, The 1910
Within the Law (Mary Turner) 1912

577
COX, Olive*
Cinderella
Stage:
Babette 1903
Mlle. Modiste 1905; 1906; 1907

578
CRAFT, Virginia*
Elmo, the Mighty (serial)

579
CRAIG, Blanche (1878-)
Behind the Scenes
Cinderella
Come on In
Dawn of Tomorrow, The
Eagle's Nest, The

Hulda of Holland
I Want to Forget

580
CRAIG, Charles*
Englishman and the Girl, The
Rocky Road, The
Serpent, The (Grand Duke Valanoff)
Sporting Life, The
Under Two Flags (Rockingham)
Stage:
As Ye Sow 1905
Bridal Path, The 1913

581
CRAIG, Nell*
In the Palace of the King
Primitive Strain, The
Return of Richard Neal, The

582
CRAMPTON, Howard*
Black Orchids
Gray Ghost, The (serial)
Traffic in Souls
Trail of the Octopus (serial)
Voice on the Wire, The (serial)

583
CRANE, Doc*
Father and the Boys
Tragedy of Whispering Creek, The
(a prospector)

584
CRANE, Frank*
Winter's Tale, A

585
CRANE, Harry F. *
Adventures of Francois Villon, The
(King Louis XI)

586
CRANE, James*
Dark Lantern, A
Misleading Widow, The
Stage:
American Ace, An 1918
Pawn, The 1917

587
CRANE, Ward (-1928)
Dark Star, The (French secret agent)
Soldiers of Fortune

588
CRANE, William H. *

Dark Harum
Stage:
American Lord, The 1906
Business Is Business 1904
David Harum 1900
Father and the Boys 1908
Fool of Fortune, A 1896; 1912
New Henrietta, The (Nicholas Van-
    Alstyne) 1887; 1889; 1913
Peter Stuyvesant 1899
Price of Money, The 1906
Rich Man's Son, A 1899
Senator Keeps House, The 1911
Spenders, The 1903

589
CRANSTON, Mary*
Beatrice Fairfax (serial)

590
CRAVEN, Walter S.*
Unwelcome Mrs. Hatch, The
Stage:
Barbara's Millions 1906
Branded 1917
Jim Bludso of the Prairie Belle 1903
Just Like John 1912
Law of the Land, The 1914
Pierre of the Plains 1908
Princess of Kensington, A 1903
Snobs 1911
Third Degree, The (Mr. Bennington)
    1909

591
CRAWLEY, Constance*
Pelléas and Melésande

592
CREHAM, Joseph*
Under Two Flags (Rake)

593
CREIGHTON, Walter R.*
Henry VIII (Lord Sands)
Stage:
Twelfth Night (Sir Andrew Aguecheeck)
    1914

594
CREWS, Laura Hope (1880-1942)
Lasky Player 1915
Stage:
Blackbirds 1913
Brown of Harvard 1906
Chief, The 1915
Faith Healer, The 1910

Great Divide, The (Polly Jordan)
    1906
Havoc, The 1911
Hedda Gabler (Mrs. Elvsted) 1906
Her First Divorce 1913
Her Husband's Wife 1910; 1917
Honeymoon, The 1913
Joseph Entangled 1904
Merely Mary Ann (Rosie) 1903-04
Much Ado about Nothing (Beatrice)
    1913
On the Hiring Line (Mrs. Sherman
    Feesden) 1919
Pair of Petticoats, A 1918
Peter Ibbetson (Mrs. Deane) 1917
Phantom Rival, The 1914
Rainbow, The (Betsey Sumner) 1912
Romance and Arabella 1917
Saving Grace, The (Mrs. Corbett)
    1918
Tyranny of Tears, The 1913

595
CRISP, Donald (1882-1974)
Battle, The
Battle of the Sexes, The
Believe Me, Xantippe
Birth of a Nation, The (Gen. U. S.
    Grant)
Broken Blossoms (Battling Burrows)
By Man's Law
Countess Charming
Escape, The (McGee)
Eyes of the World
Fate's Turning
Girl of Yesterday, A
Home Sweet Home (son)
Intolerance (a soldier)
It Pays to Advertise
Lost in Transit
Love Insurance
Mountain Rat, The
Mysterious Shot, The
Newer Woman, The
Primal Call, The
Ramona
Tavern of Tragedy, The
Two Paths, The
Under the Top
Very Good Young Man, A
Why Smith Left Home
Yankee Prince, The
Stage:
Little Millionaire, The 1911

596
CRITTENDEN, Dwight*
Hoodlum, The

597
CRITTENDEN, T. D.*
Gray Ghost, The (serial)

598
CROMMIE, Liege*
Dollars and Sense
Her Circus Knight
His Last Laugh

599
CROSMAN, Henrietta (1865-1944)
How Molly Made Good
Unwelcome Mrs. Hatch, The
Stage:
All-of-a-Sudden Peggy 1907
Anti-Matrimony 1910
As You Like It (Rosalind) 1902
Christian Pilgrim, The (Pirgrim)
    1907
Getting Married (Mrs. George) 1916
Joan O' the Shoals 1902
Madeline 1906
Mary, Mary, Quite Contrary 1905-06
Merry Wives of Windsor, The (Mis-
    tress Nell) 1916
Mistress Nell (Nell Gwyne) (first
    star role) 1900
Our Pleasant Sins 1919
Real Thing, The 1911
Sham 1909
Sweet Kitty Bellairs 1903-04
Sword of the King, The 1902
Tongues of Men, The 1913

600
CROSTHWAITE, Ivy*
By Stork Delivery
Fatty and the Broadway Stars
Fickle Fatty's Fall
Surf Girl, The

601
CROWELL, Josephine* (-1929)
Betsy's Burglar
Birth of a Nation, The (Mrs.
    Cameron)
Flames of the Flesh
Greatest Question, The (Mrs. Cain)
Hearts of the World (Mother)
Home, Sweet Home (Mrs. Payne)
House of Intrigue, The
Intolerance (Catherine de Medici)
Joselyn's Wife
Little School Ma'am, The
Old Folks at Home
Painted Lady, The
Penitents, The

Peppy Polly
Pillars of Society
Puppy Love
Rebecca of Sunnybrook Farm
Stella Maris
Three Brothers
Yank from the West, A
Stage:
Captain Molly 1902

602
CRUTE, Sally*
Helen of the Chorus
White the Tide Was Rising

603
CRUZE, James (Jens Cruz Bosen)
    (1884-1942)
Cymbeline (Posthumus Leonatus)
Dr. Jekyll and Mr. Hyde
Joseph in the Land of Egypt
Lucile
Million Dollar Mystery, The (serial)
Zudora (The Twenty Million Dollar
    Mystery) (serial)

604
CUMBERLAND, John*
Baby Mine
Stage:
Double Exposure 1918
Girl in the Limousine, The (Tony
    Hamilton) 1919
Misleading Lady, The 1913
Parlor, Bedroom and Bath 1917
Rich Man's Son, A 1912
Up in Mabel's Room 1919

605
CUMMERFORD, Tom*
Strange Case of Mary Page, The
    (serial)

606
CUMMINGS, Irving (1888-1959)
American Widow, An
Ashes
Bells, The
Better Wife, The
Camille
Diamond from the Sky, The (serial)
Don't Change Your Husband
Everywoman
Faith Healer, The
Fight for the Right
Guilded Cage, The
Her Code of Honor
Interloper, The

Jane Eyre
Ladder of Lies
Last Volunteer, The
Mandarin's Gold
Men, Women and Money
Million Dollar Mystery, The (serial)
Rasputin, The Mad Monk
Round Up, The
Royal Romance, A
Saleslady, The
Secret Service
Uncle Tom's Cabin
Unveiling Hand
What Everywoman Learns
Woman Who Gave, The
Stage:
In the Long Run 1909
Lillian Russell's Company 1909
Object--Matrimony 1916

607
CUMMINGS, Richard*
Blind Husbands (village physician)
Common Property
Reaching for the Moon (Old Bingham)

608
CUMMINGS, Robert*
Romeo and Juliet (Friar Lawrence)
Stage:
Awakening of Helena Richie, The
   1909
Broken Threads 1917
Cameo Kirby 1909
Dark Rosaleen 1919
Gipsy Trail, The 1917-18
Great Divide, The (Lon Anderson)
   1906
His Honor, Abe Potash (Robert
   Stafford) 1919
Kassa 1909
Pippa Passes 1906
Stop Thief! 1912
Trench Fantasy, A 1918
Winterfeast, The 1908

609
CUMPSON, John R.*
Bumptious As Romeo (Title role)
Stage:
Up State New York 1901

610
CUNARD, Grace (1893-1967)
Adventures of Peg o' the Ring (serial)
After the War
Bandit's Wager, The
Born of the People

Brennon o' the Moor
Broken Coin, The (serial)
Campbells Are Coming, The
Elmo, the Mighty (serial)
Favorite Son, The
Her Better Self
Her Western Adventure
Hidden City, The
Lady Raffles Return
Lucille Love, Girl of Mystery (serial)
Lumber Yard Gang, The
Man Hater, The
Mysterious Rose, The
Phantom Violin, The
Princely Bandit, The
Purple Mask, The (serial)
Puzzle Woman, The
Return of the Riddle Rider (serial)
Society's Driftwood
Three Bad Men and a Girl
Unmasked

611
CUNARD, Mina*
Broken Coin, The (serial)

612
CUNEO, Lester (1888-1925)
Big Tremaine
Blue Blazes
Corner in Cotton, A
Grustark
Haunted Pajamas, The
Love Me for Myself Alone
Masked Avenger, The
Master 44
Paradise Garden
Pidgin Island (Donald Smead)
Rosemary
Under Handicap
Under Royal Patronage

613
CUNNINGHAM, Vera*
Love in a Wood (Celia)

614
CUNY, Joe*
Bound and Gagged (serial)

615
CURLEY, James*
Intolerance (Charioteer)

616
CURLEY [Miss]
Girl Philippa, The

617
CURLEY, Pauline*
Bound in Morocco (the girl)
Life without Soul
Range Rider series
Santa Fe Mac
Square Deceiver, The
Turn in the Road, The
Stage:
Polygamy (Rhoda) 1914

618
CURRIER, Frank (1857-1928)
Brat, The
Easy to Make Money
Her Kingdom of Dreams
Hidden Letters, The
It Pays to Advertise
Peggy Does Her Darndest
Quality of Mercy, The
Red Lantern, The
Revelation
Should a Woman Tell?
To Hell with the Kaiser
Toys of Fate
Stage:
Aviator, The 1910
Beethoven 1910
Gay Life, The 1909
Old New Yorker, An 1911
Poor Little Rich Girl, The (Organ
    Grinder) 1913
This Woman and This Man 1909
Twelfth Night (Sir Andrew) 1904
Way Down East 1905
Winter's Tale, The (Autolycus) 1904

619
CURTIS, Jack*
Brute Breaker, The
Little Red Decides
Lydia Gilmore
Man's Desire
Pest, The
Until They Get Me

620
CURTIS, Marie*
Her Greatest Love (Lady Dolly)

621
CUSACK, Cyril (1910-)
Debut as a child in 1917

622
CUSHING, Sidney*
Kreutzer Sonata (G. Belushoff)

- D -

623
DAGMAR, Florence*
Call of the North, The (Elodie)
Chimmie out West (Betty Van
    Courtlandt)
Kindling (Alice)
Man from Home, The (Ivanoff's
    maid)

624
DAGOVER, Lil (Marta Maria Liletta)
    /aka/ Lillitts Daghofer (1897-)
Cabinet of Dr. Caligari, The
Kara (Kiri)
Spinner, Die

625
DAILEY, Joseph*
Romeo and Juliet (Peter)
Stage:
Big Scene, The 1918

626
DALBROOK, Sidney*
Danger's Peril, The
Fatal Fortune, The (serial)
Gilded Cage, The
Heart of the Wilds
Lost Battalion, The
Three Men and a Girl

627
DALTON, Dorothy (1894-)
Back of the Man
Black Is White
Captive God, The
Disciple, The
Extravagance
Flame of the Yukon, The
Flare-Up Sal
Green Eyes
Hard Boiled
Home Breaker, The
Jungle Child, The
Kaiser's Shadow, The
L' Apache
Lady of Red Butte, The
Love Letters, The
Love Me
Market of Souls
Mating of Marcella
Other Men's Wives
Price Mark, The
Quicksands
Taming of the Whirlwind
Ten of Diamonds, The

Tyrant Fear
Unfaithful
Vagabond Prince
Vive La France!
Weaker Sex, The
Wild Winship's Widow
Stage:
Aphrodite (Chrysis) 1919

628
DALY, Arnold (1875-1927)
Exploits of Elaine, The (Craig
  Kennedy) (serial)
New Exploits of Elaine, The (serial)
Romance of Elaine (serial)
Stage:
After the Opera 1907
Angel in the House 1915
Are You a Mason? 1901
Arms and the Man (Capt. Bluntschli)
  1906; 1915
Beau Brummell (Title role) 1916
Bird in the Cage, The 1903
Boys of Company "B", The 1907
Candida (Eugene Marchbanks) 1903-04;
  1905; 1907; 1915
Cynthia 1903
Democracy's King 1918
Flag Station, The 1907
Fool and His Money, A 1903
General John Regan 1913-14
Girl from Dixie, The 1903
Hearts Aflame 1902
His Wife's Family 1908
Hour Glass, The 1907
How He Lied to Her Husband (the
  lover) 1904; 1905; 1906; 1907
John Bull's Other Island (Larry
  Doyle) 1905
Josephine 1918
Kathleen ni Houlihan 1907
Know Thyself 1909
Lady Margaret 1902
Lemonade Boy, The 1907
Major André 1903
Man of Destiny, The (Napoleon
  Bonaparte) 1904; 1905
Master, The 1916-17; 1918
Monkey's Paw, The 1907
Mrs. Warren's Profession (Frank
  Gardner) 1905
Regeneration, The 1908
Return from Jerusalem, The 1912
Self and Lady 1900
Shrikers, The 1907
Steve 1912
Van Dycke, The 1907
Very Minute, The 1917

Washington's First Defeat 1907
You Never Can Tell (Dr. Valentine)
  1905; 1915

629
DALY, Bob*
Imp player 1910

630
DALY, Hazel*
Corner in Smith's, A
Filling His Own Shoes
Gay Lord Quex, The
Little Rowdy, The
Skinner's Bubble
Skinner's Dress Suit
Stop Thief!
Tom Brown of Harvard

631
DANA, Viola (Violet Flugrath)
  (1897-)
Aladdin's Other Lamp
Baby Devil, The
Blind Fiddler, The
Breakers Ahead
Blue Jeans
Diana Ardway
False Evidence
Flower of the Dusk
God's Law and Man's
Gold Cure, The
Jeanne of the Gutter
Lena
Microbe, The
Molly the Drummer Boy
Night Rider, The
Only Road, The
Opportunity
Parisian Tigress
Please Get Married
Poor Little Rich Girl, The
Riders of the Night
Rosie O'Grady
Satan Junior
Some Bride!
Weaver of Dreams, A
Winding Trail, The
Stage:
Poor Little Rich Girl, The
  (Gwendolyn) 1913

632
DANE, Dorothy*
Her Breezy Affair

633
DANE, Karl (Karl Daen) (1886-1934)

My Four Years in Germany
To Hell with the Kaiser
Stage:
In Copenhagen (first appearance) 1900

634
DANGMAN, William*
Freddy Versus Hamlet (Freddy)
Goddess, The (serial)

635
DANIELS, Bebe (Virginia Daniels)
   (1909-1971)
All Aboard
All at Sea
Bashful
Bumping into Broadway
Call for Mr. Cave Man
Captain Kidd's Kids
Common Enemy, A
Everywoman
Floor Below, The
Giving the Bride Away
How Dry I Am
It's a Hard Life
Just Neighbors
Lonesome Luke, Circus King
Lonesome Luke from London to
   Laramie
Lonesome Luke Loses Patients
Lonesome Luke Mechanic
Lonesome Luke Messenger
Lonesome Luke on Tin Can Alley
Lonesome Luke Plumber
Lonesome Luke's Honeymoon
Lonesome Luke's Lively Life
Lonesome Luke's Lively Rifle
Lonesome Luke's Wild Women
Looking for Trouble
Luke and Rural Roughnecks
Luke and the Bang-Tails
Luke and the Bomb Throwers
Luke and the Mermaid
Luke Crystal Gazer
Luke Does the Midway
Luke Foils the Villain
Luke Gladiator
Luke Joins the Navy
Luke Laughs Last
Luke Leans to the Literary
Luke Locates the Lute
Luke Lugs Luggage
Luke Pipes the Pippins
Luke Rides Roughshod
Luke Rolls in Luxury
Luke the Candy Cut-up
Luke the Chauffeur
Luke Wins Ye Ladye Faire

Luke's Busy Days
Luke's Double
Luke's Fatal Fliver
Luke's Fireworks
Luke's Last Liberty
Luke's Late Lunches
Luke's Lost Lamb
Luke's Movie Muddle
Luke's Newsie Knockout
Luke's Patient Provider
Luke's Preparedness Preperation
Luke's Shattered Sleep
Luke's Society Mix-up
Luke's Speedy Club Life
Luke's Trolley Trouble
Luke's Washful Waiting
Male and Female (the King's
   favorite)
Order in Court
Over the Fence
Start Something
Step Lively
Stop! Luke! Listen!
Tough Luck
We Never Sleep
Stage:
Common Enemy, A 1908
Richard III (the Princess Stock
   Company) 1904
Squaw Man, The (Los Angeles) 1906

636
DANIELS, Frank (1860-1935)
Crooky Scruggs
Stage:
Ameer, The 1899
Belle of Brittany, The 1909
Miss Simplicity 1902
Office Boy, The 1903
Roly Poly 1912
Sergeant Brue 1905
Tattooed Man, The 1907
Without the Law 1912

637
DARBY, Rhy*
Male and Female (Lady Eileen
   Duncragie)

638
D'ARCY, Camille*
Daughter of the City, A
White Sister, The

639
D'ARCY, Roy (Roy F. Guisti)
   1894-1969)
Oh, Boy!

640
DARE, Doris*
Mystery of 13, The (serial)

641
DARK CLOUD*
Indian's Loyalty, An
Song of the Wildwood Flute, The
Squaw's Love, The

642
DARKFEATHER, Mona*
Little Dove's Gratitude
Paleface Brave

643
DARLING, Grace (1896-)
Beatrice Fairfax (serial)
False Gods
Virtuous Men

644
DARLING, Ida*
Ghosts of Yesterday
Nightingale, The
Stage:
Children of Destiny 1910
Common Clay (Mrs. Fullerton) 1915
Cupid Outwits Adam 1900
Embassy Ball, The 1906
Full House, A 1915
Her Lord and Master 1902
House of Bondage, The 1914
Land of the Free, The 1917
Please Get Married 1919
Rachel 1913
Ready Money 1912
Spenders, The 1903
Uncle Sam 1911
Vinegar Buyer, The 1903

645
DARLING, Ruth*
Intolerance (slave girl)

646
DARMOND, Grace (1898-1964)
Diplomatic Mission, A
Gentleman of Quality, A
Girl in His House, The
Gulf Between, The
Highest Trump, The
Seal of Silence, The
Selig player 1915
Shielding Shadow, The (serial)
Valley of the Giants
What Every Woman Wants

647
DARNELL, Jean*
Cymbeline (the Quees)

648
DARNTON, Fred*
Smashing Barriers (serial)

649
DARWELL, Jane (Patti Woodward)
    (1880-1967)
Only Son, The
Rose of the Rancho, The (Senora
    Castro Kenton)
Stage:
Wedding Day, The 1909

650
DAVENPORT, Alice (1864-)
Ambrose's Fury
Best Man Wins, The
Caught in a Cabaret (the mother)
Caught in the Rain
Cohen's Outing
Cruel, Cruel Love
Cursed by His Beauty
Drummer's Vacation, The
Fickle Fatty's Fall
Gentlemen of Nerve
His Last Scent
Home Breakers, The /aka/ Other
    People's Wives
Just Brown's Luck
Love Riot, A
Mabel's Lovers
Mabel's New Job
Mabel's Strange Predicament
Maggie's First False Step
Maiden's Trust, A
Making a Living (the mother)
My Valet
Perils in the Park
Pills of Peril
Secrets of a Beauty Parlor
Snow Cure, The
Star Border, The
Stolen Magic
Telltale Light, The
Tillie's Punctured Romance
Wife and Auto Trouble
Worst of Friends, The

651
DAVENPORT, Dorothy (Mrs. Wallace
    Reid) (1895-)
Best Man Wins, The
Breed of the Mountains
Countess Betty's Mine

Cracksman Santa Claus, A
Crackman's Reformation, The
Fires of Conscience
Fires of Fate
Flash in the Dark, A
Fruit of Evil
Fugitive, The
Greater Devotion
Heart of the Hills
Her Indian Hero
His Only Son
Hopi Legend, A
Intruder, The
Lightning Bolt
Man Within, The
Mohawk's Way, A
Squaw Man's Son, The
Way of a Woman, The
Wheel of Life

652
DAVENPORT, Harry (1866-1949)
Father and the Boys
Stage:
Children of Destiny 1910
Country Mouse, A 1902
Dancing Duchess, The 1914
Debut made in 1872
Defender, The 1902
Girl from Kay's, The 1903-04
Girl from Up There, The 1901
In Gay Paree 1899
Inner Man, The 1917
It Happened in Nordland 1904-05
Liberty Belles, The 1902
Lightnin' (Rodney Harper) 1918
Next of Kin, The 1909
On the Eve 1909
Rounders, The 1899
Sari 1914
Squab Farm, The 1918
Three Wise Fools (Dr. Richard
    Gaunt) 1918
Yvette 1904

653
DAVENPORT, Milla*
Brat, The
Daddy Long Legs
In Mizzoura

654
DAVESNES, Edouard*
Cabiria

655
DAVIDSON, Dore*
Intolerance (friendly neighbor)

Stage:
Bluebird, The 1911
Mademoiselle Marni 1905
Stronger Sex, The 1908
To Have and to Hold 1901
What the Butler Saw 1906

656
DAVIDSON, John (1886-   )
Black Circle
Caravan
Danger Signal
Forest Rivals
Genius Pierre, The
Green Cloak, The
Million a Minute, A
Pawn of Fate
Romeo and Juliet (Paris)
Sentimental Lady
Spurs of Sybil, The
Through the Toils
Wall Between, The
Stage:
Excuse Me (Arthur Fosdick) 1911
Madame Sand 1917
Penrod 1918

657
DAVIDSON, Max (1875-1950)
Hoodlums, The
Hun Within, The
Intolerance (a Neighbor)
Love in Armor
Village Vampire, The

658
DAVIDSON, William B. (1888-1947)
Call of Her People, The
Capitol, The
Friend Husband
Greatest Power, The
Impossible Catharine
La Belle Russe
Lure of Ambition, The (Hon. Cyril
    Ralston)
Our Little Wife
Persuasive Peggy
White Raven, The
Why I Would Not Marry
Woman There Was, A (Rev. Winthrop
    Stark

659
DAVIES, Howard*
Heart of Paula, The

660
DAVIES, Marion (Marion Douras)
    (1897-1961)

Beatrice Fairfax (Title role) (serial)
Belle of New York, The (Violet Gray)
Burden of Proof, The (Elaine Brooks)
Cecilia of the Pink Roses (Cecilia)
Cinema Murder, The (Elizabeth
  Dalston)
Dark Star, The (Rue Carew)
Getting Mary Married (Mary)
Runaway Romany (Romany)
Stage:
Betty 1916
Bluebird, The (in the pony line) 1912
Chin Chin 1913 (Broadway debut)
Chu, Chin, Chow 1917
Miss 1917
Oh, Boy (Jane Packard) 1917
Stop! Look! Listen! 1915
Very Good Eddie (small role) 1917
Words and Music 1917
Ziegfeld Follies of 1916 (Miss Chief;
  Jane Seymour in Henry III spoof)

661
DAVIES, Reine*
Sunday

662
DAVIS, Edward*
Deluxe Annie
Invisible Ray, The (serial)
Stage:
Daddies (Michalson Walters)
Miranda of the Balcony

663
DAVIS, Mildred (1903-1969)
All Wrong
His Royal Slyness
Marriage A la Carte
Weaver of Dreams

664
DAW, Marjorie (1902-)
Americano, The
Arizona (Bonita)
Bound in Morocco
Captive, The (bit)
Carmen (bit)
Chorus Lady, The
He Comes up Smiling (Betty)
Headin' South
His Majesty, the American (Felice,
  Countess of Montenac)
House with the Golden Windows, The
Joan, the Woman (Katherine)
Knickerbocker Buckaroo (Mercedes)
Mr. Fix-It (Olive)
Modern Musketeer, A (Dorothy Moran)

Rebecca of Sunnybrook Farm
Say, Young Fellow! (the girl)
Sunset Princess
Unafraid, The (Irenya)
Warren's of Virginia (bit)

665
DAWN, Allan*
American player 1913

666
DAWN, Doris*
Blue Blood and Red

667
DAWN, Hazel (1891-)
Feud Girl, The
Lone Wolf, The
Masqueraders, The
My Lady Incog
Niobe
One of Our Girls
Pink Lady, The
Saleslady, The
Under Cover
Stage:
Century Girl, The 1916
Debutante, The 1914
Little Cafe, The 1913
Pink Lady, The 1911
Up in Mabel's Room 1919

668
DAY, Edith*
Grain of Dust
Romance of the Air, A

669
DAYTON, Frank*
Essanay player 1912

670
DAYTON, Lewis*
Daughter of Uncle Sam, A (serial)

671
DEAN, Hector*
Francesca Da Rimini

672
DEAN, Jack*
Cheat, The (Dick Hardy)
Tennessee's Pardner
Stage:
Other House, The 1907

673
DEAN, Julia (1878-1952)

Black Monk, The
Honorable Cad, An
How Molly Made Good
Judge Not
Matrimony
Ransom, The
Ruling Passions
Stage:
Altar of Friendship, The 1902
Bought and Paid For (Virginia Blaine)
   1911
Her Own Money 1913
Law of the Land, The 1914
Lilly, The (Christiane) 1909
Little Gray Lady, The 1906
Magic Melody, The (dual role Gianina
   and Madame Jessonda) 1919
Marriage of Reason, A 1907
Merely Mary An (Lady Gladys
   Foxwell) 1903-04
On with the Dance 1917
Round Up, The 1907; 1908
Woman on the Index, The 1918

674
DEAN, Louis*
Darling of Paris, The (Grinpoire)
Tiger Woman, The (Baron Kesingl)

675
DEAN, Priscilla*
Beautiful Beggar
Beloved Jim
Brazen Beauty
Exquisite Thief, The
Gray Ghost, The (serial)
Kiss or Kill
Paid in Advance (Marie)
Pretty Smooth
She Hired a Husband
Silk Lined Burglar
Two Souled Woman
Wicked Darling, The (Mary Stevens)
Wildcat of Paris
Witch Woman

676
DEANE, Hazel*
Matrimoniac, The
Monkey Movie Hero
Soft Boiled Yeggs
White Winged Monkey, The

677
DEANE, Sydney*
Arab, The (Dr. Hilbert)
Call of the North, The (McTavish)
Doll's House, A (Dr. Rank)

Girl of the Golden West, The (Sid-
   ney duck)
Gray Ghost, The (serial)
Male and Female (Thomas)
Romance of the Rancho (Espinoza)
Virginian, The (Uncle Hughey)
What's His Name? (Uncle Peter)
Stage:
Florodora (Abercoed) 1900-01-02
Knickerbocker Girl, The 1900
Mocking Bird, The 1902-03
My Lady Molly 1904

678
DEARHOLT, Ashton*
Brass Bullet, The (serial)

679
DeBREY, Claire*
Man and His Money, A

680
DeBRULIER, Nigel (1878-1948)
Boomerang, The
Flames of the Flesh
Ghosts
Intolerance (extra)
Kaiser, the Beast of Berlin, The
   (Capt. VonNeigle)
Mystery of 13, The (serial)
Sahara

681
DeCARLTON, George*
Life without Soul

682
DECOEUR, M. Albert*
Anne Boleyn (Henry VIII)

683
DeCORDOBA, Pedro (1881-1950)
Barbary Sheep
Carmen (Escamillo)
Maria Rose (Ramon)
New Moon, The
Runaway Romany (Zinga)
Temptation (Julian)
Stage:
Anthony and Cleopatra (Diomedes)
   1909
Arrow Maker, The 1911
As You Like It (Orlando) 1914; 1918
Beverly's Balance 1915
Bluebird, The 1910-11
Everyman 1918
Five Frankforters, The 1913
Hamlet 1902; 1903

His Bridal Night 1916
Lady Windemere's Fan 1914
Master of the House, The 1912
Merchant of Venice, The (Bassanio)
    1917
Merry Wives of Windsor, The 1910
Nigger, The 1909
90 in the Shade 1915
Noah's Flood 1911
Old Heidelberg 1910
Othello 1914
Paper Chase, The 1912
Piper, The 1911
Proud Prince, The 1903
Sadie Love 1915-16
Sister Beatrice 1910
Sothern and Marlowe Repertory
    1904; 1905
Strife 1909
Tiger Rose (Pierre LaBey) 1917
Twelfth Night 1910 (played Orsino in
    1914)
Vanity Fair 1911
Wanderer, The 1917
Where Poppies Bloom 1918
Winter's Tale, The 1910

684
DEELEY, Ben*
East Lynne (Arch Carlisle)
Victory (Mr. Jones)

685
DeGARDE, Adele*
Drunkard's Reformation, A
Lonely Villa, The (daughter)
Medicine Bottle, The
Roue's Heart, The
Through the Breakers
Trail of the Books, The
What Drink Did

686
deGRASSE, Sam (1875-1953)
Anything Once (Sir Mortimer Beggs)
Birth of a Nation, The (Senator Sum-
    ner)
Blind Husbands (Dr. Armstrong)
Children of the Feud
Devil's Passkey, The (Warren Good-
    wright)
Diane of the Follies
Empty Gun, The
Good Bad Man, The (Bud Frazer)
Half Breed, The (Sheriff Dunn)
Heart of the Hills
Her Chance (District Attorney)
Her Official Fathers

Hope Chest, The
Innocent Magdalene, An
Intolerance (Jenkins)
Martyrs of the Alamo
Place beyond the Winds (Anton
    Farwell)
Scarlet Car, The (mystery man)
Silk Lined Burglar
Sis
Sis Hopkins
Slippery
Where the Forest Ends (Silent
    Jordan)
Wild and Wolly (Steve)

687
deGRAY, Sidney /aka/ Sydney*
Jane
Stage:
King Highball 1902
Military Maid, The 1900

688
DeGROFF, Etta*
Witching Hour, The

689
DeHAVEN, Carter*
Close to Nature
College Orphan
Entertaining the Boss
From Broadway to a Throne
In a Pinch
Keep 'Em Home
Losing Winner, The
Rice and Old Shoes
That's Me
Timothy Dobbs
Twin Husbands
Waggin' Tale, The
Why Divorce?
Stage:
All Aboard 1913
Girl in the Taxi, The 1910
Hanky Panky 1912
His Little Widows 1917
Miss Dolly Dollars 1905
Queen of the Moulin Rouge, The 1908
Whoop-Dee-Doo 1903-04

690
DeHAVEN, Mrs. Carter (Flora
    Parker)*
Close to Nature
Excess Baggage
Hoodooed
In a Pinch
Mad Cap, The

Teasing the Sail
That's Me
Timothy Dobbs
What Could Be Sweeter?
Why Divorce?
Stage:
All Aboard 1913
His Little Widdows 1917

691
deJARDINS, Silvion*
Almost an Actress (Benny)

692
de la MOTHE, Leon*
Red Glove, The (serial)

693
DE LA MOTTE, Marguerite (1903-
1950)
Arizona (Lena)
For a Woman's Honor
In Wrong
Pagon God, The
Sagebrush Hamlet, A

694
DELANEY, Jerry*
Regular Girl, A

695
DELANEY, Leo*
As You Like It (Jacques deBois)
Bunny and the Bunny Hug
His Tired Uncle
Madge of the Mountains
Unknown Violinist, The
Vanity Fair

696
DELANO, James*
Clever Dummy, A (partner)

697
de la PARELLE, Marion*
Gypsy Joe

698
DELARO, Hattie*
Gold and the Woman (nurse)
Mind-the-Paint Girl, The
Stage:
Babes in Toyland 1903
Mam'selle 'Awkins 1900

699
DELIANE, Helen*
Adventures of Ruth, The (serial)

700
DELMAR, Herbert*
Three Musketeers, The (Athos)

701
DEL RIO, Dolores (Lolita Dolores
Asunsolo de Martinez) (1905-)
Voice of the Child, The

702
DELVAIR, Jeanne*
Macbeth (Lady Macbeth)

703
DEMIDOFF, Mme. *
Children of Edward, The

704
DE MILLE, Cecelia*
What's His Name? (Phoebe)

705
DeMOORE, Harry*
Paid in Advance (Flap Jack)

706
DEMPSTER, Carol (1902-)
Girl Who Stayed at Home, The
(Mlle. Acoline)
Hope Chest
Intolerance (slave girl)
Romance of Happy Valley, A
Scarlet Days (Lady Fair)
True Heart Susie (Bettina's friend)

707
DENNIS, Ruth see Ruth St. Dennis

708
DENNY, Reginald (Reginald Leigh
Daymore) (1891-1967)
Bringing Up Betty
Experience
Leather Pushers, The
Oakdale Affair, The (Arthur
Stockbridge)

709
DE REMER, Ruby*
Auction Block, The
Dust of Desire
Enlighten thy Daughter
Fires of Faith
Great Romance, The
Pals First
Safe for Democracy

710
DE ROCHE, Charles (1880-1952)

La Faute Des Autres
La Fille Du Peuple
La Masque d'Horreur
Le Tango Rouge

711
DeROY, Harry*
Chimmie Fadden (Perkins)

712
deRUE, Baby*
Squaw Man, The (Hal)

713
DESLYS, Gaby*
Infatuation
Stage:
Belle of Bond Street, The 1914
Bluebird, The 1912
Honeymoon Express, The 1913
Revue of Revues, The (first American
   appearance) 1911
Stop! Look! Listen! 1915
Vera Violetta 1911-12

714
DESMOND, Eric*
David Copperfield
Princess in the Tower, The (Reginald
   Sheffield)

715
DESMOND, William (1878-1949)
Bare Fisted Gallagher
Beyond the Shadow
Big Timber
Captain of His Soul, The
Captive God, The
Closin' In
Criminal, The
Dangerous Waters
Dawn Maker, The
Deuce Duncan
Fightin' Mad
Fighting Back
Flying Colors
Hell's End
Her Code of Honor
Honest Man, The
Life's Funny Proposition
Marriage Bubble
Mints of Hell
Muffled Drums
Not My Sister
Old Hartwell's Cub
Paws of the Bear
Peggy
Peer Gynt

Pretender, The
Prodigal Liar, The
Sagebrush Hamlet, A
Sea Panther
Society for Sale
Sudden Gentleman, A
White-Washed Walls
Wild Life
Stage:
Judge and the Jury, The 1906

716
deVARNEY, Emil*
Carmen (Capt. Morales)
Tiger Woman, The (Count Zerstorf)

717
deVAULL, William*
Birth of a Nation, The (Jake)

718
DeVERE, Daisy*
Freddy Versus Hamlet (Mabel)
Stage:
Tattooed Man, The 1907
Winter's Tale, The 1904-05

719
deVOGT, Carl*
Spinner, Die

720
DEVORE, Dorothy (1901-)
Babies Welcome
Fair Enough
45 Minutes from Broadway
Girl Dodger, The
Hazel from Hollywood
Law of the North
Let 'Er Run
Mile-a-Minute Mary

721
DeVRIES, Henri*
Cleopatra (Octavius Caesar)
Stage:
Case of Arson, A (1st American
   appearrance played 7 roles) 1906
Double Life, The

722
DEWHURST, George*
Toilers, The

723
DE WITT, Elizabeth*
Gypsy Joe
Social Club, A

724
DEXTER, Elliot (1870-1941)
Castles for Two
Daphne and the Pirate
Diplomacy
Don't Change Your Husband (James
   Denby Porter)
For Better, for Worse (Dr. Edward
   Meade)
Girl Who Came Back, The
Heart of Nora Flynn, The (Nolan)
Lash, The
Lost and Won
Maggie Pepper
Masqueraders, The
Old Wives for New (Charles Murdock)
Public Opinion
Rise of Jennie Cushing, The
Romance of the Redwoods, A
   ("Black" Brown)
Squaw Man, The (Jim Wynnegate)
Sylvia of the Secret Service
Tides of Barnegat
We Can't Have Everything (Jim
   Dykman)
Whispering Chorus, The (George
   Coggeswell)
Woman and Wife
Stage:
Anna Karenina 1907
Consequences 1914
Just Outside the Door 1915
Love Leash, The 1913
Master Mind, The 1913
Player Maid, The 1905
Siberia 1905

725
DICKENSON, Jennie*
Kathleen Mavourneen (Kathleen's
   mother)

726
DICKSON, Dorothy (1902-   )
Money Mad
Stage:
Girl o' Mine 1918
Rock-a-Bye Baby 1918
Royal Vagabond, The 1919
Ziegfeld Follies of 1917

727
DICKSON: William K. L. *
Figure with Hand on Horse
Violin Player

728
DIEGELMANN, Wilhelm*
Othello

729
DIESTAL, Edith*
King Lear (Regan)

730
DIEU DONNE, Albert*
Folie du Docteur Tube, La

731
DILLON, Edward ("Eddie")*
Almost a Man
As the Bells Rang Out
Banker's Daughter, The
Brahma Diamond, The
Don Quixote
Dutch Gold Mine, The
Embarrassment of Riches, The
Examination Day at School
Faithful to the Finish
Feud and the Turkey, The
Fisher Folks
Fugitive, The
Her Mother's Oath
His Sister-in-Law
Home, Sweet Home (musician)
Indian's Loyalty, An
Intolerance (a crook)
Judith of Bethulia
Lady in Black, The
Little Teacher, The
Look Up
Lonedale Operator, The
Love in an Apartment Hotel
Luck and Pluck
Massacre, The
Miser's Heart, The
Muggsy Becomes a Hero
One Busy Hour
Ostler Joe
Pa Pays
Reconking, The /aka/ After Many
   Years
Salvation Army Lass
Sheriff's Baby, The
Snow Man, The
Sorrows of the Unfaithful, The
Spirit Awakened, The
Sunshine Dad
Sunshine through the Dark
Tender Hearted Boy, A
Those Hicksville Boys
Wanderer, The
Welcome Burglar, The
Would-Be Shriner, The
Stage:
Francesca da Rimini 1901
Prince Otto 1900
Ranger, The 1907

School for Scandal, The 1905
Taming of the Shrew, The 1905

732
DILLON, Jack (John Dillon)*
Captain Maclean
Decree of Destiny, A
Greaser's Gauntlet, The
Iconoclast, The
Love in an Apartment Hotel
New Janitor, The
Sheriff's Baby, The
Stage:
Salvation Nell (Al McGovern) 1908

733
DILLON, John Webb*
Darling of Paris, The (Clopin)
Heart and Soul (Pedro)
Romeo and Juliet (Tybalt)
Tiger Woman, The (Stevan)
Stage:
Winter's Tale, The 1904; 1905

734
DILLON, Paul*
House of Hate, The (serial)

735
diMARZIO, Matilde*
Anthony and Cleopatra (Charmian)

736
diNAPOLI, Raffele*
Cibiria

737
DION, Hector*
King Lear (Edmund)
Othello (The Iago)
Stage:
Hearts Courageous 1903
Old Homestead, The (Rueben
    Whitcomb) 1904
Twomen and That Man 1909

738
DIONE, Rose*
World and Its Women, The

739
DIX, Richard (Ernest Carlton
    Brimmer) (1894-1949)
A Goldwyn player 1919
Stage:
First Is Last (Phil) 1919
Hawk, The 1914
I Love You 1919
Little Brother, The 1918

740
DIXEY, Henry E. (1859-1943)
Seven Ages
Stage:
Becky Sharp (Marquis of Steyne)
    1911
Burgomaster, The 1900
Chu Chin Chow (Ali Baba) 1917-18
David Garrick 1905
David Garrick on the Art of Acting
    1904
Deluge, The 1917
Devil, The (Dr. Miller) (Chicago and
    New York) 1908
Facing the Music 1903
H. M. S. Pinafore (Sir Joseph
    Porter) 1911
Little Mary 1904
Long Dash, The 1918
Man on the Box, The 1905
Mary Jane's Pa 1908-09
Mr. Buttles 1910
Mr. Lazarus 1916
Modern Magdalen, A 1902
Mrs. Bumpstead-Leigh (Peter Swallow)
    1911
Oliver Goldsmith (David Garrick)
    1900
Over a Welsh Rarebit 1903; 1904
Papa Leonard 1908
Prince Consort, The 1905
Thousand Years Ago, A 1914
Twelfth Night (Malvolio) 1914

741
DIXON, Charles*
American Widow, An

742
DIXON, Florence*
Independence B'Gosh

743
DOLLY, Roziska /aka/ Rose
    (1892-)
Million Dollar Dollies, The
Stage:
Echo, The 1910
Hello Broadway 1914
His Bridal Night 1916
Lieber Augustin 1913
Merry Countess, The 1912
Whirl of the World, The 1914
Winsome Widow, The 1912
Ziegfeld Follies of 1911

744
DOLLY, Yancsi /aka/ Jennie
    (1892-1941)

Million Dollar Dollies, The
Stage:
Echo, The 1910
His Bridal Night 1916
Honeymoon Express, The 1913
Maid in America 1915
Merry Countess, The 1912
Winsome Widow, The 1912
Ziegfeld Follies of 1911

745
DOMINICUS, Evelyn*
Deerslayer, The

746
DONDONI, Cesare*
Othello (The Iago)

747
DONNELLY, Dorothy (Dorothy Agnes
  Donnelly) (1880-)
Madame X
Stage:
Bargain, The 1915
Candida (Title role) 1903-04; 1915
Daughters of Men, The 1906
Disengaged 1909
Friquet 1905
Granny Maumee 1914
Kathleen ni Houlihan 1903
Little Gray Lady, The 1906
Madame X (Jacqueline) 1910
Man of Destiny, The (the lady) 1904
Maria Rosa 1914
Mrs. Battle's Bath 1905
New England Folks 1901
Proud Laird, The 1905
Right to Be Happy, The 1912
Soldiers of Fortune (Madame Alvarez)
  1902
Song of Songs, The 1914
When We Dead Awake (Mrs. Maia
  Rubek) 1905

748
DONNELLY, James*
Bubbles of Trouble
Clever Dummy, A (the father)
She Needed a Doctor
Snow Cure, The
Stage:
Marta of the Lowlands 1903

749
DONOHUE, Joe*
Within the Law

750
DOOLEY, Billy (1893-)

Campus Cuties
Dizzy Diver, The
Gallant Gob, A
Gobs of Love
Happy Heels
Oriental Rugs
Sea Food
She-Going Sailor, A

751
DOOLEY, Johnny (1887-)
Beauty's Worth
Bobby, the Office Boy
Johnny Dooley comedies
Pep
Private Preserves
When Knighthood Was in Flower
Stage:
Listen Lester 1918

752
DORALINDA, Mlle.*
Castles for Two
Diplomacy
Heart of Nora Flynn, The
Heart's Desire
Lash, The
Lost and Won
Morals of Marcus
Mysterious Princess, The
Naulahka
Oliver Twist
Twelve Ten
White Pearl, The
Wood Nymph, The
Stage:
Red Dawn, The (Miss Vera Devere)
  1919
Step This Way 1916

753
DORETTO, Roberta*
Chinese Laundry

754
DORIA, Vera*
Salome (Naomi)
Stage:
So Long, Letty 1916

755
DORIAN, Charles*
Society for Sale

756
DORO, Marie (Marie Stewart)
  (1881-1956)
Castles for Two
Common Ground

Diplomacy
Heart of Nora Flynn, The (Nora)
Lash, The
Morals of Marcus, The
Mysterious Princess, The
Oliver Twist (Oliver)
Twelve Ten
White Pearl, The
Wood Nymph, The
Stage:
Barbara 1917
Billionaire, The 1902
Clarice 1906
Diplomacy 1914
Electricity 1910
Friquet 1905
Girl from Kay's, The 1903
Granny 1904
Little Mary 1904
Morals of Marcus, The 1907
New Secretary, The 1913
Oliver Twist (Oliver) 1912
Patience 1912
Richest Girl, The 1909

757
D'ORSAY, Lawrence*
Ruggles of Red Gap
Stage:
All Aboard 1913
Belle of Bond Street, The 1914
Earl of Pawtucket, The (Lord
    Cardington) 1903
Embassy Ball, The 1906
Lancers, The 1907
Lights o' London, The 1911
Miss Innocence 1908
Rented Earl, The 1915
Robinson Crusoe, Jr. 1916
Royal Family, A 1900
Sinbad 1918
Whirl of Society 1912
Zebra, The 1911

758
DOSCHER, Doris (1882-1970)
Birth of a Nation, The (Eve)

759
DOUCET, Paul*
Devil's Daughter, The (Lucio Settlea)

760
DOUGLAS, Leal*
Beetle, The

761
DOVEY, Alice*

Commanding Officer, The
Stage:
Hands Up! 1915
Nobody Home 1915
Old Dutch 1909
Papa's Darling 1914
Pink Lady, The 1911
Queen of the Movies, The 1914
Stubborn Cinderella, A 1909
Summer Widowers, The 1910
Very Good Eddie 1915-16

762
DOWLAN, William C. *
All for Peggy (Will Jordan)
Desert Breed, The (Fred's Partner)
Embezzler, The (Arthur Bronson)
End of the Feud, The (Joel)
Her Escape (the lover)
Measure of a Man, The (Bob Brandt)
Menace to Carlotta, The (Tony)
Outside the Gates (Manuel)
Richelieu (Adrien deMauprat)
Sin of Olga Brandt, The (Rev. John
    Armstrong
Star of the Sea, The (Mario Brisoni)
Such Is Life (Will Deming)
Threads of Fate, The (the lover)
Tragedy of Whispering Creek, The
    (Bashful Bill)
Under the Crescent (serial)
Unlawful Trade, The (Neut Date)
Where the Forest Ends (Jack Norton)

763
DOWLING, Joseph S. (1850-   )
Bells, The
Carmen of the Klondike
Deserter, The (Col. Taylor)
Girl Who Came Back, The
Home
Intelligence
Joyous Liar, The
Law unto Himself, A
Maid o' the Storm
Man's Country, A (Marshall Leland)
Midnight Stage, The
Miracle Man, The (The Patriarch)
More Trouble
Pinch Hitter, The
Riders of the Dawn
Shoal Light, The
Sudden Jim
Tidebrook

764
DRAKE, Dorothy*
Cleopatra (Charmian)

Lure of Ambition, The (Murial
    Ralston)
Madame DuBarry (Henriette)
Stage:
Double Life, The 1906

765
DRESSLER, Marie (Leila Kerber)
    (1869-1934)
Agonies of Agnes, The
Cross Red Nurse, The
Scrub Lady, The
Tillie Wakes Up (Tillie)
Tillie's Punctured Romance (Tillie)
    (debut)
Tillie's Tomatoe Surprise (Tillie)
Stage:
Boy and the Girl, The 1909
Hall of Fame, The 1902
Higgledy-Piggledy 1904-05
King Highball 1902
King's Carnival, The 1901
Marie Dressler's All Star Gambol
    1913
Miss Prinnt 1900
Mix-up, A 1914
Robber on the Rhine 1892
Roly Poly 1912
Tillie's Nightmare (Tillie) 1910
Twiddle-Twaddle 1906
Under Two Flags (Cigarette) (Stock
    1886)
Within the Law 1912

766
DREW, John (1853-1927)
Essanay player 1912
Stage:
Caliban of the Yellow Sands 1916
Captain Dieppe 1903
Chief, The 1915
DeLancey 1905
Duke of Killicrankie, The (Title role)
    1904
Gay Lord Quex, The 1917
His House in Order 1906
Inconstant George 1909
Jack Straw 1908
Liars, The (Col. Sir Christopher
    Deering) 1898
Major Pendennis 1916
Much Ado about Nothing (Benedick)
    1913
Mummy and the Humming Bird, The
    1902; 1903
My Wife 1907
Perplexed Husband, The 1912
Prodigal Husband, The 1914

Richard Carvel 1900
Rosemary (Sir Jasper Thorndyke)
    1896; 1915
Scrap of Paper, A (Prosper
    Couramant) 1914
Second in Command, The 1901
Single Man, A 1911
Smith (Thomas Freeman) 1910
Tyranny of Tears, The (Mr.
    Parbury) 1899; 1913
Will, The 1913

767
DREW, Lillian*
One Wonderful Night

768
DREW, Sidney (1864-1920)
Amateur Liar, The
As Others See Us
At a Premium
At the Count of Ten
Auntie's Portrait
Awakening of Helen Minor
Before and after Taking
Blackmail
Booble's Baby
Borrowing Trouble
Bunkered
Case of Eugenics, A
Cave Man's Bluff
Childhood's Happy Days
Close Resemblance
Dentist, The
Double Life
Duplicity
Feudists, The
Following the Scent
Fox Trot Finesse
Gas Logic
Good Gracious! or Movies as They
    Shouldn't Be
Handy Henry
Harold, the Last of the Saxons
Help!
Henry's Ancestors
Her Anniversaries
Her Economic Independence
Her First Game
Her Lesson
High Cost of Living, The
His Curiosity
His Deadly Calm
His Ear for Music
His First Game
His First Love
His Obsession
His Perfect Day

His Rival
Hist ... Spies!
Home Cue, The
Honeymoon Baby, The
Hypochondriac, The
Jerry's Uncle's Namesake (Jerry)
Joy of Freedom, The
Lady in the Library, A
Lest We Forget
Locked Out
Matchmakers, The
Mr. Parker, Hero
Miss Sticky Moufit Kiss
Model Young Man, A
Music Hath Charm
Mysterious Mr. Davey, The
Never Again
Nobody Home
Nothing to Wear
Number One
Once a Man
Once a Mason
One of the Family
Patriot, The
Pest, The
Professional Patient, The (Buxton)
Putting It over on Henry
Rebellion of Mr. Minor, The
Regiment of Two, A
Reliable Henry
Romance and Kings
Romantic Peggy
Royal Wild West, The
Rubbing It In
Safe Investment (Charley Sharp)
Shadowing Henry
Sisterly Scheme, A
Special Today
Spirit of Merry Christmas
Squared
Story of a Glove, The (Mr. Huggins)
Taking a Rest
Their First
Too Many Husbands
Too Much Henry
Tootsie
Twelve Good Hens and True
Unmarried Look, The
Wager No Object
Wanted: a Nurse
When Two Hearts Won (debut)
Why Henry Left Home
Youthful Affair, A
Stage:
Billy 1909
Keep Her Smiling 1918
She Stoops to Conquer (Tony Lampkin)
   1905
Sweet and Twenty 1901-02

769
DREW, S. Rankin*
Girl Philippa, The
His Tired Uncle
Mr. Barnes of New York

770
DRISCOLL, Tex*
Girl of the Golden West, The (Nick,
   the bartender)
Virginian, The (Shorty)

771
DU BREY, Claire (1893-)
Anything Once (the mysterious
   Senorita)
Border Raiders
Dangerous Hours
Devil's Trail, The
Man in the Open
Modern Husbands
Old Maid's Baby, The
Pay Me (Nita)
Peggy
Piper's Price, The (the maid)
Rescue, The
Sawdust Doll, The
Spite Bride
Triumph (Lillian DuPont)
What Every Woman Wants
When Fate Divides
Wishing Ring Man, The
World Aflame

772
DU CELLO, Countess*
Baseball Madness

773
DUDLEY, Charles*
Bell Boy, The

774
DUFFY, John*
Purple Mask, The (serial)

775
DUFORT, Alphonse*
Hearts of the World (a Poilu)

776
DUKE, Ivy (1895-)
Double Life of Mr. Alfred Burton
Fancy Dress
Garden of Resurrection, The
I Will
March Hare, The

777
DU MAURIER, Gerald (1873-)
Justice
Masks and Faces
Stage:
Old Jew, An (Garrick Theatre,
   London) 1894

778
DUMERCIER, Jean*
Hearts of the World (a Poilu)

779
DUMONT, J. M.*
Miracle Man, The (the Dope)

780
DUMONT, Montague*
Midnight Romance, A

781
DUNBAR, Helen*
Essanay player 1912-1914
Fighting Through
Graustark
Great Secret, The (serial)
Romeo and Juliet (Lady Capulet)
Shuttle, The
Squaw Man, The (Dowager Countess)

782
DUNCAN, A. E.*
Seaside Romeos (Bud)

783
DUNCAN, Dell*
Cleopatra (Iras)

784
DUNCAN, Ted*
Intolerance (bocyguard)

785
DUNCAN, William (1878-1961)
Aladdin from Broadway
Bill's Birthday
Buck's Romance
Cattle Thief's Escape, The
Dead Shot Baker
Dynamiters, The
Embarrassed Bridegroom, An
Fight for Millions, A (serial)
Fighting Trail, The (serial)
Galloping Romeo
Good Indian, The
Hawlin' Jones
His Father's Deputy
How Betty Made Good

Jealousy of Miguel and Isabella
Juggling with Fate
Last Man, The
Law and the Outlaw
Made a Coward
Man of Might (serial)
Marian the Holy Terror
Marrying Gretchen
Marshall's Capture, The
Matrimonial Deluge, A
Money Magic
Peggy
Range Law
Rejected Lover's Luck, The
Religion and Gun Practice
Romance of the Forest Reserve
Rough Ride with Nitroglycerine, A
Sallie's Sure Shot
Saved from the Vigilantes
Senorita's Repentance, The
Servant Question out West, The
Silver Grindstone, The
Smashing Barriers (serial)
Stolen Moccasins
Suffrogette, The
Taming of a Tenderfoot
Taming of Texas Pete, The
Tenderfoot, The
Vengeance and the Woman (serial)
Waifs
Wolfville

786
DUNKINSON, Harry*
Brass Bullet, The (serial)
Dash of Courage, A
Strange Case of Mary Page, The (serial)

787
DUNN, Bobby*
Bubbles of Trouble
By Stork Delivery
His Auto Ruination
His Bread and Butter
His Busted Trust
His Pride and Shame
Hogan's Romance Upset
Secrets of a Beauty Parlor
Villa of the Movies
Winning Punch, The

788
DUNN, J. E. *
Iron Claw, The (serial)

789
DUNN, John J.*
Seven Pearls, The (serial)

790
DUNN, William R. *
Cure for Pokeritus
Gossip, The
Secret Kingdom, The (serial)
Vanity Fair
Stage:
Passing Show of 1916, The 1916

791
DURFEE, Minta (1897-   )
Bright Lights, The
Cabaret, The
Caught in a Cabaret (dancer)
Court House Crooks
Cruel, Cruel Love
Dirty Work in a Laundry /aka/
    Desperate Scoundrel, A
Fatty and Minnie He-Haw
Fatty's Jonah Day
Fickle Fatty's Fall
Fickle Fatty's Romance
Film Johnnie, A
Gentlemen of Nerve
Great Pearl Tangle, The
Hearts and Planets
His New Profession
His Trysting Place
His Wife's Mistakes
Home Breakers, The
Knock-Out, The
Leading Lizzie Astray
Love, Speed and Thrills
Mabel, Fatty and the Law
Making a Living
Masquerader, The
Mickey (Elsie Drake)
Misplaced Foot, A
New Janitor, The
Other Man, The
Our Daredevil Chief
Rounders, The
Sheriff, The
Tillie's Punctured Romance
Twenty Minutes of Love
Stage:
Climbers, The (Clara Hunter) 1901

792
DURNING, Bernard*
When Bearcat Went Dry (Turner
    Stacy)

793
DUSE, Elenora (1859-1924)
Cenere 1916 (only firm appearance)
Stage:
Camille (first New York Appearance)
    1893

Elenora Duse Repertory 1902
Francesca da Rimini (farewell
    appearance--Metropolitan Opera
    House) 1903

794
DUVALLE, William*
Blind Husbands

795
DUVOISIN, Yvette, Mlle. *
Hearts of the World (refugee)

796
DWIGGENS, Jay*
Dangers of a Bride
His Majesty, the American (Emile
    Mertz)
His Uncle Dudley
Secrets of a Beuty Parlor
Whose Baby?

797
DWYER, Ruth*
Lurking Peril, The (serial)

798
DYER, Madge*
Macbeth (a Macduff child)

799
DYER, William J. *
Trail of the Octopus (serial)
Triumph (Stage Manager)

- E -

800
EAGLE, Chief Black*
Gold and the Woman (Chief Duskara)

801
EAGLES, Jeanne (1894-1929)
Under False Colors
World and the Woman, The (debut)
Stage:
Daddies (Ruth Atkins) 1918
Disraeli 1917
Great Pursuit, The 1916
Hamilton (Mrs. Reynolds) 1917
Jumping Jupiter (Miss Renault) 1911
Midsummer Night's Dream, A
    (Puck) 1901
Mind-the-Paint Girl, The 1912
Professor's Love Story, The (Lucy
    White) 1917
Young Man's Fancy, A (Mary
    Darling and Mary's Image) 1919

802
EAGLESHIRT, William*
Heart of an Indian, The

803
EARLE, Arthur*
Butcher Boy, The
Dark Star, The (Mr. Stull)
His Wife's Mistakes 1916

804
EARLE, Edward (1884-   )
Blind Adventure, The
For France
Gates of Eden, The
His Bridal Night
Innocence of Ruth, The
Miracle of Love, The
$1,000
Ransom's Folly
Transients in Arcadia
Stage:
Triumph of Love, The 1904

805
EARLE, Josephine*
Scarlet Runner, The (serial)

806
EATON, Elwin /aka/ Elwyn*
Romeo and Juliet (Montague)
Stage:
Betrothal, The (the Great Mendicant)
   1918-19
Explorers, The 1912
Gamblers All 1917
Hamlet (Polonius) 1912-13
Merchant of Venice, The 1913
Monsieur Beaucaire 1912
Oedipus 1913
Panthea 1914
Sherlock Holmes (Thomas Leary) 1899
Taking Chances 1915

807
EBERT, Carl*
Golem, Der

808
EDDY, Helen Jerome (1897-   )
Pasquale
Rebecca of Sunnybrook Farm
Strange Unknown, The
Turn in the Road, The

809
EDESON, Robert (1868-1931)
Absentees, The

Big Jim Garrity
Call of the North, The (dual role
   Graehame and Ned Stewart)
Cave Man, The
Extravagance
How Molly Made Good
Light That Failed, The
Man's Prerogative
Mortmain
On the Night Stage
Public Defender, The
Sealed Hearts
Where the Trail Divides
Stage:
Call of the North, The 1908
Cave Man, The 1911
Classmates 1907
Climbers, The (Edward Warden) 1901
Fine Feathers
Good Bad Woman, The 1919
Husband and Wife 1915
Knife, The 1917
Little Minister, The (Davin Dishart)
   1897
Long Dash, The 1912
Mistress Nel (King Charles II) 1900
Moment of Death, The 1900
Noble Spaniard, The 1909
Offenders, The 1908
Ransom's Folly 1904
Riddle: Woman, The 1918
Sinners 1915
Soldiers of Fortune (Robert Clary)
   1902
Strong Heart 1905

810
EDMUNDSON, Harry*
Secret of the Submarine, The (serial)

811
EDWARDS, Harry*
Little Lord Fauntleroy

812
EDWARDS, Henry (1883-1952)
Alone in London
Bachelor's Love Story, A
Broken in the Wars
Broken Threads
City of Beautiful Nonsense, The
Clamcarty
Cobweb, The
Dick Carson Wins Through
Doorsteps
East Is East
Far from the Madding Crowd
Film Tags series

Grim Justice
Hanging Judge, The
His Dearest Possession
Kinsman, The
Lost and Won
Man Who Stayed at Home, The
Merely Mrs. Stubs
My Old Dutch
Nearer My God to Thee
Possession
Refugee, The
Tares
Touch of a Child, The
Towards the Light
Welsh Singer, A

813
EDWARDS, Neely*
Hall Room Boys series

814
EDWARDS, Thornton*
False Faces, The (Lt. Thackeray)

815
EDWARDS, Vivian*
Dough and Dynamite
Face on the Barroom Floor, The
From Patches to Plenty
His Busted Trust
His Lying Heart
His Wilk Oats
Masquerader, The
Modern Enoch Arden, A
One Night Stand, A
Only a Farmer's Daughter
Those Love Pangs
Village Blacksmith, The
When Ambrose Dared Walrus

816
EGAN, Gladys*
As It Is in Life
Broken Doll, The
Child's Faith, A
Child's Impulse, A
Child's Remorse, A
Child's Strategem, A
Christmas Burglars, The
Convict's Sacrifice, A (child)
Crooked Road, The
In the Watches of the Night
Lonely Villa, The
Romany Tragedy, A /aka/ The Two
    Sides
Ruling Passion, The
Salutary Lesson, A
Stolen Jewels, The

Trap for Santa Claus
Unexpected Help

817
EKMAN, John*
Outlaw and His Wife, The

818
ELDRIDGE, Charles*
As You Like It (Corin)
Bunny as a Reporter
Bunny Backslides
Bunny for the Cause
Bunny's Honeymoon
Captain Jack's Dilemma
Captain Jack's Diplomacy
Cure for Pokeritus
Doctor Bridget
First Violin, The
Hearts and Diamonds
His Honor, the Mayor
Locket, The
Love Sick Maidens of Cuddleton
Pickpocket, The
Pirates, The
Private Bunny
Stenographer Wanter (Brown)
Sporting Life, The
Ventriloquist's Trunk, The
When the Press Speaks
Who's to Win?

819
ELINE, Marie*
Uncle Tom's Cabin (Little Eva)

820
ELKUS, Edward*
When Men Desire (Professor Lohr)

821
ELLINGFORD, William*
Wilderness Trail

822
ELLIOTT, Gertrude*
Hamlet (Ophelia)
Stage:
Caesar and Cleopatra (Cleopatra)
    1906; 1913
Forbes-Robertson Repertory 1913
Hamlet (Ophelia) 1904
Light That Failed, The 1903; 1913
Preserving Mr. Panmure 1912
Rebellion 1911
White Magic 1912

823
ELLIOTT, Maxine (1871-1940)

Eternal Magdalene, The
Fighting Odds
Stage:
Altar of Friendship, The 1902
Bludgeon, The 1914
Chaperon, The 1908
Cowboy and the Lady, The 1899
Her Great Match (Jo Sheldon) 1905
Her Own Way (Georgiana Carley) 1903
Inferior Sex, The 1910
Lord and Lady Algy 1917
Merchant of Venice, The (Portia) 1901
Myself (Bettina) 1908
Professor's Love Story, The (Lady
   Gilding) 1892
Under the Greenwood Tree 1907

824
ELLIOTT, Robert*
Checkers
L'Apache
Mary Moreland
Resurrection
Spirit of Lafayette, The
Unknown Love
Woman There Was, A (Pulke)
Stage:
Ben Hur (Arrius) 1900
Country Girl, A 1911

825
ELLIOTT, William*
Comrade John
Fortune Hunter, The
Hearts of the World
Stage:
Charley's Aunt (Charley Wykerman)
   1906
Experience 1914-15
Grand Army Man, A 1907-08
Greatest Nation, The 1916
Madame X (Raymond Florist) 1910
Pink Lady, The 1911
Richard Mansfield Repertory 1905
Robert Emmet 1904
That Man and I 1904
Wanderer, The 1917

826
ELLIS, Robert (1892-   )
Louisiana
Upstairs and Down
Stage:
Baxter's Partner 1911

827
ELLISON, Margorie*
Dolly's Scoop

Gilded Spider, The
Tangled Hearts

828
ELMER, Billy*
Arab, The (Meshur)
Captive, The (bit)
Carmen (Morales)
Girl of the Golden West, The
   (Ashby)
Joan, the Woman (Guy Townes)
Kindling (Rafferty)
Rose of the Rancho (halfbreed)
Squaw Man, The (Cash Hawkins)
Unafraid, The (Jack McCarty)
Virginian, The (Trampas)
We Can't Have Everything (Props)
Stage:
Cashel Byron 1900

829
ELMER, Clarence Jay*
Hamlet Made Over /aka/ Hamlet-
   up-to-Date (The King)

830
ELMORE, Pearl*
Intolerance (Uplifter)

831
ELSOM, Isobel (Isobel Reed)
   (1893-   )
Debt of Honor, A
Edge o' Beyond
Elder Miss Blossom, The
God Bless Our Red White and Blue
In Bondage
Linked by Fate
Man Who Won, The
Member of the Tattersalls
Milestones
Mrs. Thompson
Onward Christian Soldiers
Prehistoric Love, A
Quinneys
Tinker, Tailor, Soldier, Sailor
Way of an Eagle, The

832
ELTINGE, Julian (William Julian
   Dalton) (1882-1941)
Adventuress, An
Clever Mrs. Carfax, The
Countess Charming, The
Cousin Lucy
Crinoline Girl
Her Grace the Vampire
How Molly Made Good

Isle of Love
Over the Rhine
War Relief (Propaganda film)
Stage:
Cohan and Harris Minstrels 1908
Cousin Lucy 1915
Crinoline Girl 1914
Fascinating Widow, The 1911
Mr. Wix of Wickham (debut) 1904

833
ELTON, Edmund*
Romeo and Juliet (Lord Capulet)
Stage:
Penrod 1918

834
ELVEY, Maurice (William Folkard)
    (1887-1967)
Adam Bede
Beautiful Jim
Bells of Rheims, The
Black-Eyed Susan
Bleak House
Bridegrooms Beware
Charity Ann
Comradeship
Cup Final Mystery, The
Dombey and Son
Esther Driven
Fallen Idol, The
Fine Feathers
Flames
Florence Nightingale
From Shopgirl to Duchess
Gay Lord Quex, The
Gilbert Dying to Die
Gilbert Gets Tiger-itis
God's Good Man
Goodbye
Great Gold Robbery, The
Grip Home
Grit of a Jew, The
Her Luck in London
Her Nameless Child
Hindle Wakes
Honeymoon for Three, A
Idol of Paris, The
Inquisitive Ike
It's a Long Way to Tipperary
Justice
Keeper of the Door
King's Daughter, The
Lest We Forget
Life Story of David Lloyd George, The
London's Yellow Peril
Loss of the Birkenhead
Love in a Wood

Maria Marten
Mary Girl
Meg the Lady
Midshipman Easy
Money for Nothing
Motherlove
Mr. Wu
Nelson
Popsy Wopsy
Princess of Happy Chance, The
Rocks of Valpre
Smith
Sound of Her Voice, The
Suicide Club, The
Swindler, The
There's Good in Everyone
Trouble for Nothing
Vice Versa
Victory Leaders, The
When Knights Were Bold
White Feather, The
Will of Her Own, A
Woman Who Was Nothing, The

835
ELVIDGE, June (1893-)
Appearance of Evil
Bluffer, The
Broken Ties
Call of the Yukon, The
Coax Me
His Father's Wife
Joan of the Woods
La Boheme
Love and the Woman
Love Defender
Lure of a Woman, The
Marriage Market, The
Moral Deadline
Mrs. Reynolds
Oldest Law, The
Poison Pen
Power and the Glory, The
Quickening Flame, The
Rack, The
Rasputin
Shall We Forgive Her?
Social Pirate
Steel King, The
Stolen Orders
Strong Way, The
Tenth Case, The
Three Green Eyes
Way Out, The
Woman of Lies
Woman of Redemption
Zero Hour
Stage:
Passing Show of 1914, The 1914

836
ELY, G. A. *
Bright Lights, The

837
EMERSON, John (1874-   )
Conspiracy, The
Stage:
Are You a Mason? 1904
Big Jim Garrity 1914
Blue Mouse, The 1908-09
Conspiracy, The 1912
Eyes of the Heart, The 1906
Mary and John 1905
Military Mad 1904
Tit for Tat 1904
Watcher, The 1910
Whirlwind, The 1910

838
EMMONS, M. *
Hearts of the World (Doug's Brother)

839
EMORY, Maude*
Liberty, a Daughter of the U. S. A.
   (serial)

840
EMORY, May*
Ambrose's Cup of Woe
By Stork Delivery
Fickle Fatty's Fall
Fido's Fate
Hunt, The
Madcap Ambrose
Stars and Bars
Teddy at the Throttle (guardian's
   sister)
Thirst
Vampire Ambrose

841
EMPEY, Guy*
Over the Top

842
EMPRESS, Marie*
Old Dutch
Stage:
Little Cafe, The 1913

843
ENNIS, Patrick*
Ireland, a Nation

844
ERASTOFF, Edith*
Outlaw and His Wife, The

845
ESMELTON, Fred*
Avalanche, The

846
ESTABROOK, Howard (1894-   )
Mysteries of Myra, The (serial)
Who's Guilty? (serial)
Stage:
Boss, The 1911
Boys of Company "B", The 1907
Brown of Harvard 1906
Divorcons (M. Gratignan) 1913
Honeymoon, The 1913
Little Women (Laurie) 1912
Miss Information 1915
Point of View, The 1912
Search Me 1915
Straight Road, The 1907
Things That Count, The

847
ETHIER, Alphonse*
Forbidden Path
Oh, Johnny!
Sandy Burke of the U-Bar-U
Thelma
Stage:
April 1918
Argyle Case, The 1912
Barrier, The 1910
Eternal Magdalene, The 1915
Greatest Thing in the World, The 1900
Keep It to Yourself 1918
Land of Heart's Desire, The 1900
Marie (Odile) 1915
Moment of Death, The 1900
Our Children 1915
Seremonda 1917
Steve 1912
Strange Woman, The 1913
What Happened to Jones? 1917

848
EUSTACE, Fred*
Little Lord Fauntleroy

849
EVANS, Dame Edith (1888-   )
East Is East
Welsh Singer, A

850
EVANS, Frank*
Death Disc, The
Destruction (Bonner)
Gibson Goddess, The
Vaquero's Vow, The
Woman Scorned, A

851
EVANS, Fred (1889-1951)
Charley Smiler Joins the Boy Scouts
   (Charley)
How Lt. Pimple Captured the Kaiser
   (Pimple)
Lieutenant Pimple on Secret Service
   (Pimple)
Pimple as Hamlet (Pimple)
Pimple Does the Turkey Trot
   (Pimple)
Pimple's Battle of Waterloo (Pimple)
Pimple's Clutching Hand (Pimple)
Pimple's Better 'Ole (Pimple)
Pimple's Ivanhoe (Pimple)
Pimple's Midsummer Night's Dream
   (Pimple)
Pimple's Million Dollar Mystery
   (Pimple)
Pimple's Royal Divorce (Pimple)
Pimple's Three Weeks (Pimple)
Sexton Pimple (Pimple)

852
EVANS, Joe (1891-1967)
Battle of Gettysownback
Charley Smiler Joins the Boy Scouts
House of Distemperley
How Lt. Pimple Captured the Kaiser
   (Joey)
Last of the Dandy, The
Lieutenant Pimple on Secret Service
Mile-a-Minute Kendall
Pimple as Hamlet
Pimple Does the Turkey Trot
Pimple's Battle of Waterloo
Pimple's Clutching Hand
Pimple's Better 'Ole
Pimple's Ivanhoe
Pimple's Midsummer Night's Dream
Pimple's Million Dollar Mystery
Pimple's Royal Divorce
Pimple's Three Weeks
Rations
Sexton Pimple

853
EVANS, Madge (1909-)
Adventures of Carol, The
Beloved Adventuress, The
Burglar, The
Corner Grocer, The
Gates of Gladdness, The
Golden Wall, The
Hilda
Home Wanted
Husband and Wife
Little Dutchess, The

Little Patriot, The
Love Defenders, The
Love Nest
Maternity
Neighbors
Power and the Glory, The
Seven Sisters
Seventeen
Sign of the Cross, The
Stolen Orders
Sudden Riches
True Blue
Volunteer, The
Wanted: a Mother
Web of Desire
Woman and Wife
Zaza

854
EVERS, Arthur*
Camille

855
EVERTON, Paul*
Eagle's Eye, The (serial)
Stage:
Dragon's Claw, The 1914
Five o'Clock (Dr. Gould) 1919
Garrett O'Magh 1901; 1902
Kick In ("Whip" Fogarty) 1914
Lucky Miss Dean 1906
Macbeth 1916
My Lady's Garter 1915
Rich Man's Son, A
Romance of Athlone, A 1899; 1901
Sign on the Door, The (Inspector
   Treffy) 1919
Silent Witness, The 1916
Taps 1904

856
EVILLE, William*
Virtuous Vampire, A
Stage:
Ambassador, The 1900
Cheer Up 1912
Humpty Dumpty 1918
Indiscretion of Truth, The 1912
Manoeuvres of Jane, The 1899
Prunella (Third Gardener) 1913
Squaw Man, The (Rt. Rev. Bishop
   of Exeter) 1905; 1907

857
EYTON, Bessie (1890-)
Alone in the Jungle
Beware of Strangers
City of Purple Dreams

Crisis, The
Cycle of Fate, The
Fifth Man, The
God of Gold, The
Heart of Texas Ryan, The
Law North of 65, The
Long Ago, The
Love of Madge O'Mara, The
Man of Honor
Prince Chap, The
Salvation of Nance O'Shaughnessy
Smouldering Flame, The
Sole Survivor, The
Spoilers, The
Steel Alarm, The
Story of Lavinia, The
Three Wise Men
Twisted Trails
Usurper, The
Victor of the Plot, The
Way of a Man with a Maid, The
Who Shall Take My Life?
Wild Ride, A

- F -

856
FAIR, Elinor (1902-   )
Be a Little Sport
End of the Trail
Love Is Love
Married in Haste
Miracle Man, The (Claire King)
Vagabond Luck
Words and Music

857
FAIRBANKS, Douglas, Sr. (Julius
    Ullman) (1883-1939)
American Aristocracy (Cassius Lee)
Americano, The (Title role)
Arizona (Lt. Danton)
Bound in Morocco (the boy)
Double Trouble (Mr. Amidon)
Down to Earth (Bill Gaynor
Fire the Kaiser
Flames of '49, The
Flirting with Fate (Augy Holliday)
Good Bad Man, The (a Passin' Thru')
Habit of Happiness, The ("Sunny"
    Wiggins)
Half-Breed, The (Lo Dorman)
He Comes Up Smiling (Jerry Martin)
Headin' South ("Headin'" South-outlaw)
His Majesty, the American (William
    Brooks)
His Picture in the Papers (Pete

Prindle)
In Again--Out Again (Teddy Rutherford)
Intolerance (a soldier)
Knickerbocker Buckaroo (Teddy
    Drake)
Lamb, The (Gerald) (debut)
Man from Painted Post, The (Francis
    Jim Sherwood)
Manhattan Madness (Steve O'Dare)
Matrimaniac, The (Jimmy Conroy)
Modern Musketeer, A (Ned Thacker)
Mr. Fix-It (Title role)
Mystery of the Leaping Fish, The
    (Coke Enneyday)
Reaching for the Moon (Alexis
    Caesar Napoleon Brown)
Reggie Mixes In (Reginald Morton)
Say, Young Fellow! (Newspaper
    reporter)
Sic 'Em Sam
Social Secretary, The
War Relief (propaganda film)
When the Clouds Roll By (Daniel
    Boone Brown)
Wild and Woolly (Jeff Hillington)
Stage:
All for a Girl 1908
As Ye Sow 1905
Case of Frenzied Finance, A 1905
Clothes 1906
Cub, The (Steve Oldham) 1910
Fantana 1905
Gentleman from Mississippi, A 1908
Gentleman of Leisure, A 1911
Hawthorne of the U. S. A. 1912
Her Lord and Master 1902
He Comes up Smiling 1914
Julius Caesar (Young Cato) (Holly-
    wood Stadium) 1916
Lights o' London, The 1911
Man of the Hour, The (Perry Carter
    Wainwright) 1906
New Henrietta, The (Bertie) 1913
Pit, The 1904
Rose o' Plymouth Town, A 1902
Show Shop, The 1914
Two Little Sailor Boys 1904

858
FAIRBANKS, Gladys*
Poor Little Rich Girl, The
Stage:
Poor Little Rich Girl, The (Nurse
    Jane) 1913
Redemption (a nurse) 1918
Road to Happiness, The 1915

859
FAIRBANKS TWINS

(Madeleine and Marion)*
Thanhouser players 1917
Stage:
Snow White and the Seven Dwarfs
    1912-13
Ziegfeld Follies of 1917
Ziegfeld Follies of 1918

860
FAIRBROTHER, Sydney (Sydney
    Tapping) (1873-1941)
Iron Justice (debut)
Stage:
Squire, The 1890

861
FALKENSTEIN, Julius*
Othello

862
FANG, Charles*
Great Secret, The (serial)

863
FARLEY, Dot (Dorothy Farley)
    (1894-   )
Fatty Joins the Force
Life in the Balance, A
Murphy's I. O. U.
Peril of the Plains
Raiders on the Mexican Border
Romantic Redskins
Rural Romeos
Wife Wanted, A
Stage:
Farley Stock Company 1897

865
FARLEY, James (1882-   )
Bride's Silence, The
Brute Force
For the Family Name
Nugget Nell
Sue of the South

866
FARNUM, Dustin (1874-1929)
Ben Blair
Cameo Kirby
Captain Courtesy
Corsican Brothers, The (dual role)
David Garrick
Davy Crockett
Durand of the Bad Lands
Gentleman from Indiana, A
Girl of the Golden West, The
Intrigue
Iron Strain, The

Light of the Western Stars
Man in the Open, A
Man's Fight, A
Modern Taming of the Shrew, A
North of '53
Parson of Panamint, The
Rose of the Rancho
Scarlet Pimpernel, The
Soldiers of Fortune
Son of Erin, A
Spy, The
Squaw Man, The (Capt. James
    Wynnegate)
Virginian, The (title role)
Stage:
Arizona 1913
Cameo Kirby 1909
Littlest Rebel, The 1911
Marcelle 1900
More Than Queen 1900
Ranger, The 1907
Rector's Garden, The 1908
Silent Call, The 1911
Squaw Man, The 1911
Virginian, The (Title role) 1904;
    1905

867
FARNUM, Franklyn /aka/ "Smiling
    Frank" (1876-1961)
Anything Once (Theodore Crosby)
Clock, The
Fast Company (Laurence Percival
    VanHuyler)
Fighting Grin, The
In Judgment Of
Scarlet Car, The (Billy Winthrop)
Stage:
Somewhere Else 1913

868
FARNUM, William (1876-1953)
American Methods
Battle of the Hearts, The
Conqueror, The
End of the Trail, The
For Freedom
Heart of a Lion, The
Jungle Trail
Last of the Duanes
Les Miserables
Lone Star Ranger, The
Man Hunter, The
Man of Sorrow, A
Men from Bitter Roots, The
Nigger, The
Plunderers, The
Rainbow Trail, The

Riders of the Purple Sage
Rough and Ready
Sign of the Cross, The
Spoilers, The (Roy Glennister)
Tale of Two Cities, A
True Blue
When a Man Sees Red
Wolves of the Night
Stage:
Arizona 1913
Battle Cry, The 1914
Ben-Hur (Title role) 1900
Edward Ferry Shakespeare Company
  1892
Julius Caesar (Anthony) (Hollywood
  Stadium) 1916
Littlest Rebel, The 1911
Midsummer Night's Dream, A
  (Demetrius) 1903
Prince of Indice, The 1906
Society and the Bulldog 1908
White Sister, The 1909

869
FARRAR, Geraldine (1882-1967)
Carmen (Title role)
Devil Stone, The (Marcia Manot)
Flame of the Desert, The
Hell Cat, The
Jaguar's Claws, The
Joan, the Woman (Title role)
Maria Rosa (Title role)
Riddle: Woman, The
Shadows
Stronger Vow, The
Temptation (René Duprée)
Turn of the Wheel, The
Woman God Forgot, The (Tecza)
World and Its Women, The

870
FARRINGTON, Adele*
Country Mouse, The
If My Country Should Call (Mrs.
  Landon)
Stage:
Cadet Girl, The 1900
Miss Prinnt 1900
Modern Magdalene, A 1902

871
FARRINGTON, Frank*
Million Dollar Mystery, The (serial)
Mistake Slight, A
Stage:
Belle of London Town, The 1907
Cupid Outwits Adam 1900
Girl in the Taxi, The 1910

Lieber Augustin 1913
Merry Countess, The 1912
Miss Dolly Dollars 1906
Mlle. Mischief 1908
New Yorkers, The 1901
Riviera Girl, The 1917
Sapho (Mephistophles) 1900

872
FATIMA*
Danse du Ventre
Fatima
Fatima at Coney Island

873
FAUST, Martin*
Winter's Tale, A (King of Sicilia)

874
FAVERSHAM, William (1868-1940)
Julius Caesar
Metro player 1915
Silver King, The
Stage:
Barber of New Orleans, The 1909
Brother Officers (Lt. John Hinds)
  1900; 1901
Diplomacy (Henry Beauclere) 1901
Faun, The 1911
Getting Married 1916
Hawk, The 1914
Herod (Title role) 1909
Importance of Being Earnest, The
  (Algernon) 1895
Imprudence 1902
Julius Caesar 1912
Letty 1904
Lord and Lady Algy 1899; 1903; 1917
Man and His Wife, A 1897; 1900
Miss Elizabeth's Prisoners 1903
My Lady's Lord 1899
Old Country, The 1917
Othello (Iago) 1914
Royal Rival, A (first starring role)
  1901
Squaw Man, The (Capt. James
  Wynnegate) 1905; 1907

875
FAWCETT, George (1860-1939)
Cinderella Man, The
Country That God Forgot, The
Crisis, The
Girl Who Stayed at Home, The
  (Edward Gray)
Great Love, The (Rev. Josephus
  Broadplains)
Greatest Question, The (Mr. Hilton)

Habit of Happiness, The (Jonathan
  Pepper)
Hearts of the World (Village
  Carpenter)
Hope Chest, The
Hun Within, The
I'll Get Him Yet
Intolerance (Judge)
Little Miss Rebellion
Nobody Home
Out of Luck
Panthea
Prince Chap, The
Railroaders, The
Romance of Happy Valley, A (John
  Logan, Sr.)
Scarlet Days (the sheriff)
Such a Little Queen
Talk of the Town, The (Major
  French)
True Heart Tessie (the stranger)
Turning the Tables
Stage:
Are You a Crook? 1913
Caleb West 1900
Gentleman of Leisure, A 1911
Getting a Polish 1910
Governor's Boss, The 1914
Great John Ganton, The 1909
Last Resort, The 1914
Law of the Land, The 1914
Man of the House, The (James
  Phelen) 1906
Man's Friends, A 1913
Peter Stuyvesant 1899
Silent Call, The 1911
Silver Girl, The 1907
Son of the People, A 1910
Squaw Man, The (Big Bill) 1905;
  1907; 1911
Unleavened Bread 1901
What Money Can't Buy 1915
Woman in the Case, The 1905

876
FAY, Hugh*
Bath Tub Perils
Crooked to the End
Maiden's Trust, A
Oily Scoundrel, An
Secrets of a Beauty Parlor
She Loved a Sailor
Stars and Bars

877
FAYE, Julia (1894-1966)
Don Quixote
Don't Change Your Husband

His Auto Ruination
His Last Laugh
Lover's Might /aka/ The Fire Chief
Male and Female (Susan)
Mrs. Leffingwell's Boots
Old Wives for New (Jessie)
Squaw Man, The (Lady Mabel)
Stepping Out
Surf Girl, The (daughter)
Till I Come Back to You (Susette)
Whispering Chorus, The (girl in
  waterfront dive)
Woman God Forgot, The (Tecza's
  handmaiden)

878
FAZENDA, Louise (1895-1962)
A La Cabaret
Almost an Actress (Susie)
Ambrose's Fury
Ambrose's Little Hatchet
Ambrose's Lofty Perch
Astray from Steerage
Back to the Kitchen
Bear Affair, A
Betrayal of Maggie, The
Bombs
Crossed Love and Swords
Fatty's Tin Type Tangle
Feathered Nest, The /aka/ Girl
  Guardian /aka/ Only a Farmer's
  Daughter
Fireside Brewer
Game Old Knight, A
Great Vacuum Robbery, The
Hash House Fraud, A
Her Fame and Shame
Her First Mistake
Her Marble Heart
Her Screen Idol
Her Torpedoed Love
His Hereafter /aka/ Murray's
  Mix-up
His Precious Life
Hubby's Cure
It's a Boy
Judge, The
Kitchen Lady, The
Love Riot, A
Maggie's First False Step
Maid Mad /aka/ The Fortune Teller
Mike and Jake at the Beach
Pills of Peril, The
Summer Girls, The
That Little Band of Gold /aka/ For
  Better or Worse
Treatin' 'Em Rough
Versatile Villain, A

Village Chestnut, The
Village Smithy, The
Wedding Bells out of Tune
Wilful Ambrose

879
FEARNLEY, Jane*
Reliance player 1911

880
FEATHERSTONE, John*
Purple Mask, The (serial)

881
FEDER, I. *
Seven Sisters

882
FEHER, Friedrich*
Cabinet of Dr. Caligari (Francis)

883
FELIX, George*
Felix on the Job (Felix)
Haystacks and Steeples

884
FELLOWES, Rockliffe (1885-1950)
Bondage of Fear, The
Cup of Fury
Easiest Way, The
Friendly Husband
House Cat, The
Regeneration
Web of Desire, The
Stage:
Eve's Daughter 1917
Her Sister 1907

885
FENTON, Marc*
Adventures of Peg o' the Ring, The
    (serial)
Baseball Madness
Black Box, The (serial)
Mark of Cain, The (Mr. Temple)
Stage:
Francesca da Rimini 1901
Helena Modjeska Repertory 1900

886
FENWICK, Irene (1887-1936)
Coney Island Princess, A
Stage:
Along Came Ruth 1914
Bosom Friends 1917
Co-respondent, The 1916
Curiosity 1919

Family Cupboard, The 1913
Guilty Man, The 1916
Hawthorne of the U. S. A. 1912
Lord and Lady Algy 1917
Mary's Ankle 1917
Pay-day 1916
Song of Songs, The 1914
Stitch in Time, A 1918

887
FERGUSON, Casson (1891-)
Alias Mary Brown
Flame of the Desert
How Could You, Jean?
Jane Goes a-wooing
Johnny Get Your Gun
Merely Mary Ann
Only Road, The
Secret Service
Shuttle, The
Stage:
Robert B. Mantell Repertory 1911

888
FERGUSON, Elsie (1883-1961)
Avalanche, The (dual role, mother
    and daughter)
Barbary Sheep
Counterfeit, The
Danger Mark, The
Doll's House, A
Eyes of the Soul
Heart of the Wilds
His House in Order
His Parisian Wife
Lie, The
Marriage Price, The
Rise of Jennie Cushing, The
Rose of the World
Society Exile, A
Song of Songs, The
Under the Greenwood Tree
Witness for the Defense
Stage:
Arizona 1913
Battle, The 1908
Brigadier Guard 1906
Caste 1910
First Lady in the Land, The 1911
Girl from Kay's, The 1903-04
Julie Bonbon 1906
Liberty Belles, The 1901
Margaret Schiller 1916
Merchant of Venice, The (Portia)
    1916
Miss Dolly Dollars 1905
New Clown, The 1902
Outcast 1914

Pierre of the Plains 1908
Rosedale 1913
Second Fiddle, The 1904
Shirley Kaye 1916
Strange Woman, The 1913
Such a Little Queen (Anna Victoria)
   1909
Two Schools, The 1902
Wild Rose, The 1902

889
FERGUSON, Helen (1901-   )
Gamblers, The
Gift o' Gab, The
Stage:
Is Matrimony a Failure? (Carrie)
   1909

890
FERGUSON, Mattie*
Fatal Ring, The (serial)
Stage:
Captain Jinks of the Horse Marines
   (Mrs. Greenborough) 1907

891
FERNANDEZ, E. L.*
Eye for Eye
Two Orphans, The (Jacques)
Stage:
Maria Rosa 1914

892
FIELD, George*
Derelict, The
Tiger's Trail, The (serial)

893
FIELD, Grace*
Avalanche, The
Stage:
Babes in Toyland 1903
It Happened in Nordland 1904-05
Kiss Burglar, The 1918
Lieber Augustin 1913
Little Cherub, The 1906; 1907
Little Miss Fix-it 1911
Molly O' 1916
Night of the Fourth, The 1901
Red Petticoat, The 1912

894
FIELDING, Romaine*
Lubin player 1913

895
FIELDS, Lew (Lewis Fields)
   (1867-1941)

Best of Enemies, The
Corner Grocer, The
Fatty and the Broadway Stars
Old Dutch
Worst of Friends, The
Stage:
About Town 1906
All Aboard 1913
Bosom Friends 1917
Bunty, Bulls and Strings 1912
Fiddle-dee-dee 1900
Girl behind the Counter, The 1907
Hen-Pecks, The 1911
High Cost of Living, The 1914
Hoity Toity 1901
Hokey-Pokey 1912
It Happened in Nordland 1904-05
Lonely Romeo, A 1919
Miss 1917 1917
Old Dutch 1909
Roly Poly 1912
Step This Way 1916
Summer Widowers, The 1910
Twirly-Whirly 1902-03
Whirl-i-gig 1899
Whoop-Dee-Doo 1903
Without the Law 1912

896
FIELDS, W. C. (William Claude
   Dukinfield) (1879-1946)
His Lordship's Dilemma
Pool Sharks (debut)
Stage:
Ham Tree, The 1905
Ziegfeld Follies of 1915
Ziegfeld Follies of 1916
Ziegfeld Follies of 1917
Ziegfeld Follies of 1918
Ziegfeld Follies of 1919

897
FIGMAN, Max*
Adventures of Wallingford, The
Lasky player 1914
What's His Name? (Harvey)
Stage:
Divorcons, The 1902
Doll's House, A (Torvald) 1902
Fine Feathers 1913
Gretna Green 1903
Little Nell and the Marchioness 1900
Mary of Magdala 1902-03
Miranda of the Balcony 1901
Strength of the Weak, The 1906
Truth Wagon, The 1912
Unwelcome Mrs. Hatch, The 1901

898
FILLMORE, Clyde (1876-1948)
Devil's Passkey, The (Rex Strong)
Fire Flingers
Millionaire Pirate, The

899
FILSON, Mrs. Al W. *
Squaw Man, The (Dowager Lady
   Kerhill)
String Beans
Widow by Proxy

900
FILSON, Al W. *
Scarlet Car, The (editor)

901
FINCH, Flora (1869-1940)
And His Wife Came Back
Autocrat of Flapjack Junction, The
Awakening of Jones, The
Bunce Bill's Visit
Bunny and the Twins
Bunny as a Reporter
Bunny Backslides
Bunny Buys a Harem
Bunny for the Cause
Bunny's Birthday
Bunny's Dilemma
Bunny's Little Brother
Bunny's Mistake
Bunny's Scheme
Bunny's Suicide
Bunny's Swell Affair
Change in Baggage, A
Cupid's Hired Man
Cure for Pokeritis
Dawn
Diamond Cut Diamond
Doctor Bridget
Father's Flirtation
Feudists, The
First Woman Jury in America
Fortune, The
Freckles
Gentleman of Fashion, A
Girl at the Lunch Counter, The
Golf Game and the Bonnet, The
Gossip, The
He Answered the Ad
Hearts and Diamonds
Her Crowning Glory (old maid)
Her Hero
Her Old Sweetheart
His Better Half
His Honor, the Mayor
How Cissy Made Good

How He Prepared the Room
Hubby Buys a Baby
Hubby's Toothache
Intrepid Davy
Irene's Infatuation
John Tobin's Sweetheart
Jones and the Lady Book Agent
Lady of Shalott, The
Leap Year Proposals
Locked House, The
Locket, The
Love's Old Dream
Love's Quarantine
Martha's Rebellion
Millinery Bomb, A
Misadventures of a Mighty Monarch,
   The
Mr. Bolter's Niece
Mr. Bullington Ran the House
Mr. Bunny in Disguise
Mr. Bunnyhug Buys a Hat for His
   Bride
Mrs. Jones Entertains
Muggsy's First Sweetheart
New Secretary, The
New Stenographer, The
Night Out, A
Oh, Boy!
Old Fire Horse and the New Fire
   Chief, The
Old Maid's Baby, The
One Good Joke Deserves Another
Pandora's Box
Persistent Love, A
Pickpocket, The
Polishing Up
Politician's Dream, The
Private Bunny
Prudence, the Pirate
Pseudo Sultan, The
Red Ink Tragedy, The
Schemers, The
Selecting His Heiress
Starring Flora Finchurch
Stenographer Trouble
Stenographer Wanted
Strategy of Anne, The
Subduing of Mrs. Nag, The
Such a Hunter
Suing Susan
Suit of Armour, The
Suspicious Henry
Tangled Tangoists
There's Music in the Hair
Those Troublesome Tresses
Thou Shalt Not Covet
Three Black Bags, The
Tired, Absent-minded Man, The

Train of Incidents, A
Two Overcoats
Umbrellas to Mend or Mr.
   Niceman's Umbrella
Unwelcome Guest, The
Vases of Hymen, The
Ventriloquist's Trunk, The
War Brides
When the Press Speaks
Which Way Did He Go?
Woes of a Wealthy Widow, The
Women Go on the War Path
Wonderful Statue, The

902
FINLAY, Bob*
Winning Punch, The

903
FINLAYSON, James /aka/ Jimmy
   (1887-1953)
Mack Sennett comedies 1916-1919
Stage:
Bunty Pulls the Strings (U. S. Tour)
   1916
Rob Roy (Edinburgh, Scotland)
   (debut)*

904
FINLEY, Ned*
Goddess, The (serial)
Goddness Gracious! or Movies as
   They Shouldn't Be
Hubby's Toothache
Secret Kingdom, The (serial)

905
FISCHER, Margarita [dropped "C"
   from name in 1918] (1893-   )
Ann's Finish
Charge It to Me
Devil's Assistant, The
Dragon, The
Girl Who Couldn't Grow Up, The
Impossible Susan
In Slavery Days
Jilted Jane
Mantle of Charity
Miracle of Life, The
Miss Jackie of the Navy
Modern Othello, A
Molly Go Get 'Em
Molly of the Follies
Money Isn't Everything
Peacock Feather Fan, The
Pearl of Paradise
Primeval Test, The
Primitive Woman

Put Your Hands Up!
Quest, The
Square Deal, A
Susie's New Shoes
Tiger Lily
Trixie from Broadway
Uncle Tom's Cabin (Topsy)

906
FISHER, George*
Civilization (The Christus)
Environment
Man Who Went Out, The

907
FISKE, Mrs. (Minnie Maddern Fiske)
   (1865-1932)
Tess of the D'Urbervilles
Vanity Fair
Stage:
Beck Sharp (Title role) 1899; 1904;
   1911
Divorcons, The (Cyprienne) 1897;
   1902
Dolce 1906
Doll's House, A (Nora) 1894; 1902
Erstwhile Susan (Juliet Miller) 1916
Hannele 1910
Hedda Gabler (Title role) 1903; 1904
High Road, The (Mary Page) 1912
Lady Patricia (Lady Patricia
   Cosway) 1912
Leah Kleschna (Title role) 1904
Light from St. Agnes, The 1896
Little Italy 1899; 1902
Madame Sand 1917
Mary of Magdla 1902-03
Miranda of the Balcony 1901
Mis' Nellie of N'Orleans (Nelly
   Daventry) 1919
Mrs. Bumpstead-Leigh (Title role)
   1911
New York Idea, The (Mrs. Cynthia
   Carslake) 1906
Pillars of Society (Lona Hessel) 1910
Rosmersholm (Rebecca West) 1907
Salvation Nell (Nell Sanders) 1908
Service 1918
Tess of the D'Urbervilles (Tess)
   1897; 1902
Unwelcome Mrs. Hatch, The 1901

908
FITZGERALD, Cissy (1894-1941)
Accomplished Mrs. Thompson, The
Cissy and Bertie
Cissy's Funnymoon
Cissy's Innocent Wink

Curing Cissy
How Cissy Made Good
Winsome Widow, The /aka/ The
    Win(k)some Widow

909
FITZPATRICK, Charlotte*
Kid Auto Races at Venice

910
FITZROY, Emily*
East Lynne (Cornelia)
Stage:
I. O. U. 1918
Just to Get Married 1912
Lady Patricia (Mrs. O'Farrell) 1912
Never Say Die 1912
Rich Man, Poor Man 1916

911
FITZROY, Louis
Blind Husbands (Village priest)
Stage:
Sergeant Burce 1905

912
FITZSIMMONS, Robert*
First Championship Fight Film

913
FLAGG, James Montgomery (1877-
    1960)
Beresford and the Baboons
Good Sport, The
One Every Minute
Perfectly Fiendish Flanagan
Spoiled Girl, The
Tell That to the Marines

914
FLEMING, Robert*
Man from Home, The (Ribiere)
Nugget Nell

915
FLETCHER, Cecil*
Song of Songs, The
Stage:
General Past 1917

916
FLIMM, Florence*
Little Women

917
FLUGRATH, Edna*
Edison player 1913

918
FOLEY, George*
Life of William Shakespeare, The
    (Sir Thomas Lucy)

919
FONSS, Olaf*
Homunculus (serial)

920
FOOTE, Courtenay*
Captain Courtesy
Cross Currents
False Colors
His Parisian Wife
Home, Sweet Home (husband)
International Marriage, An
Love's Law
Reincarnation of Karma, The
Two Brides, The
Wonderful Statue, The
Stage:
Actors' and Authors' Theatre, Inc.,
    The 1918
Adam and Eva (Lord Andrew
    Gordon) 1919
Debtors, The 1909
Fires of Fate, The 1909
Oliver Twist 1912
Upstairs and Down 1916

921
FORBES, Mary Elizabeth (1880-1964)
Zudora (The Twenty Million Dollar
    Mystery) (serial)
Stage:
Duke of Killicrankie, The 1915
House of a Thousand Candles, The
    1908
Just Boys 1915
Romance (Miss Snyder) 1913
Thais 1911
Walls of Jericho, The 1905-06

922
FORBES, Norman*
Real Thing at Last, The

923
FORBES-ROBERTSON, Johnston
    (1853-1937)
Hamlet (Title role)
Masks and Faces
Passing of the Third Floor Back,
    The (Walter Walturdow)
Stage:
Caesar and Cleopatra (Caesar) 1906;
    1913

Forbes-Robertson Repertory 1913
Hamlet (Title role) 1904; 1905
Light That Failed, The (Dick Heldar)
    1913
Love and the Man (on tour) 1903-04
Passing of the Third Floor Back,
    The (Title role) 1909

924
FORD, Arthur*
Mysterious Mrs. Musslewhite, The

925
FORD, Eugenie*
Diamond from the Sky, The (serial)

926
FORD, Francis (Francis Feeney)
    (1883-1953)
Adventures of Peg o' the Ring, The
    (serial)
Bandit's Wager, The
Be Neutral
Black Box, The (serial)
Brennon o' the Moor
Broken Coin, The (serial)
Chicken-Hearted Jim
Doorway of Destruction, The
Favorite Son
Four from Nowhere
Hidden City, The
Isle of Intrigue, The
John Ermine of Yellowstone
Lady Raffles Returns
Lucille Love, Girl of Mystery
    (serial)
Lumber Yard Gang, The
Mysterious Rose, The
Mystery of 13, The (serial)
Phantom Ship, The
Phantom Violin, The
Purple Mask, The (serial)
Puzzle Woman, The
Silent Mystery, The (serial)
Three Bad Men and a Girl
Thunderbolt Jack
Unmasked
Who Was the Other Man?

927
FORD, Harrison (1892-1959)
Cruise of the Make-Believe, The
Experimental Marriage
Girls
Goodnight, Paul
Gray Chiffon Veil, The
Happiness a la Mode
Hawthorne of the U. S. A.

Lady's Name, A
Lottery Man, The
Molly Entangled
Mrs. Leffingwell's Boots
Mysterious Mrs. Musslewhite, The
Pair of Stockings, A
Romance and Arabella
Sauce for the Goose
Such a Little Pirate
Third Kiss, The
Tides of Barnegat
Unclaimed Goods
Veiled Adventure, The
Who Cares?
Stage:
Bubble, The 1915
Fight, The 1912
Princess Players, The 1913
Rolling Stones 1915
Strongheart 1905

928
FORD, John (Sean O'Fearna)
    (1895-1973)
Broken Coin, The (serial)
Scrapper, The (Buck)
Tornado, The
Stage:
King's Carnival 1901
Tumble In 1919

929
FORD, Phil*
Mystery of 13, The (serial)

930
FORDE, Eugene (1898-   )
Diamond from the Sky, The (serial)
Fair Enough
Sis Hopkins
Strictly Confidential

931
FORDE, Hal*
Mayblossom
Stage:
Actors' and Authors' Theatre, Inc.,
    The 1918
Adele 1913
Enchantress, The 1911
Girl from Brazil, The 1916
Greatest Nation, The 1916
Maid in America 1915
Oh, Boy! 1917

932
FORDE, Victoria*
Local Color
Pedro's Dilemma

933
FOREST, Alan*
Master Key, The (serial)

934
FORESTELLE, W. H.*
La Tosca

935
FORMAN, Tom (1893-1938)
American Consul, The
Chimmie Fadden (Antoine)
Chimmie Fadden out West (Antoine)
Evil Eye, The
For Better, for Worse (Richard
  Burton)
Forbidden Paths
Girl Who Came Back, The
Governor's Lady, The
Hashimura to Go
Heart of Youth, The
Her Strange Wedding
Jaguar's Claws, The
Kindling (Dr. Taylor)
Kiss for Susie, A
Louisana
Public Opinion
Puppet Crown, A
Ragamuffin, The
Silent Partner
Sweet Kitty Bellairs
Those without Sin
Thousand Dollar Husband, The
Tides of Barnegat
Told in the Hills
Trouble Buster
Unprotected, The
Virtue Its Own Reward (Seadley
  Swaine)
Wild Goose Chase, The (Bob Randall)
Yellow Pawn, The
Young Romance

936
FORMBY, George (1904-1961)
By the Shortest of Heads

937
FORMES, Carl, Jr.*
Macbeth (Bishop)

938
FORREST, Alan (1889-   )
Bachelor's Wife, A
Captivating Mary Carstairs
Discord and Harmony (the artist)
Rosemary Climbs the Heights

FORREST, Ann (1897-   )
Birth of Patriotism, The
Grim Game, The
Midnight Man, The
Tar Heel Warrior, The

940
FORSHAY, Harold*
Scarlet Runner, The (serial)

941
FORSTER, Ralph*
Daughter of Eve, A

942
FOSS, Darrell*
Her Decision
You Can't Believe Everything

943
FOSS, Kenelm (1885-1963)
Arsene Lupin
Damages for Breach
Double Life of Mr. Alfred Burton,
  The
Fine Feathers
Love in a Wood (Oliver)
Marked Man, A
Not Guilty
Odd Charges
Persecution of Bob Pretty, The
Skipper of the Osprey, The
Till Our Ship Comes In (series)
Top Dog, The
Wages of Sin, The
Whosoever Shall Offend

944
FOSTER, Edna*
Adventures of Billy, The
Baby and the Stork, The

945
FOSTER, J. Morris*
Gray Ghost, The (serial)

946
FOX, Harry*
Beatrice Fairfax (serial)
Stage:
Honeymoon Express, The 1913
Oh, Look 1918
Passing Show of 1912, The 1912
Stop! Look! Listen! 1915

947
FOXE, Earle (1891-   )
Alien Souls

Ashes of Embers
Dream Girl, The (Tom Merton)
Fatal Ring, The (serial)
Floor Above, The
From Two to Six
Home, Sweet Home
Honeymoon, The
Love Mask, The
Outwitted
Panthea
Public Opinion
Peck's Bad Girl
Studio Girl, The
Trail of the Lonesome Pine, The
  (Dave Tolliver)

948
FOY, Eddie (1854-1928)
Favorite Fool, A
Stage:
Earl and the Girl, The 1905
Mr. Bluebeard 1903
Mr. Hamlet of Broadway 1908
Orchid, The 1907
Over the River 1912
Piff! Paff! Pauf! 1904
Strollers, The 1901
Up and Down Broadway 1910
Wild Rose, The 1902

949
FOYS, Seven Little, The*
Favorite Fool, A

950
FRANCIS, Alec B. (1857-1934)
Ballet Girl, The
Cinderella Man, The
City of Comrades
Crimson Cross, The
Crimson Gardenia, The
Day Dreams
Face in the Dark, The
Flame of the Desert
Gilded Cage, The
Glorious Adventure
Heartease
Her Code of Honor
Hungry Heart, A
In the Clutches of a Vapor Bath
Kitty and the Cowboys
Lola
Lord and Lady Algy
Man of the Hour
Marionettes, The
Old Doll, The
Probation Wife
Robin Hood

Spectre Bridegroom, The
Vanity Fair
Venus Model, The
Vitagraph films debut 1910
World and Its Women, The

951
FRANEY, William*
Honest Man, An

952
FRANK, Herbert*
Destruction (Dave)
Secret of the Storm, The
Social Secretary, The

953
FRANKMAN, Charles*
Panthea

954
FRASER, Harry*
Iron Claw, The (serial)
Mystery of the Double Cross, The
  (serial)

955
FRASER, Robert* (-1944)
Ballet Girl, The
Bolshevism of Trial
Feast of Life
Her Code of Honor
Robin Hood
Without Limit

956
FRAWLEY, William (1887-1966)
American Beauty Comedy, An

957
FREDERICK, Pauline (1883-1938)
Ashes of Embers
Audrey (Title role)
Bella Donna
Bonds of Love
Daughter of the Old South, A
Double Crossed
Eternal City, The
Fear Women
Fedora
Her Final Reckoning
Hungry Heart, The
La Tosca
Love That Lies
Lydia Gilmore
Madame Jealousy
Madame X
Moment Before, The

Mrs. Dave's Defense
Nanette of the Wilds
On Trial
One Week of Life
Paid in Full
Peace of Roaring River, The
Resurrection
Sacred Flame
Slave Island
Slave Market
Sleeping Fires
Smouldering Fires
Sold
Spider, The
Woman in the Case, The
Woman on the Index, The
World's Great Snare, The
Zaza
Stage:
Innocent 1914
It Happened in Nordland 1904-05
Joseph and His Brethren 1913
Paper Chase, The 1912
Princess of Kensington, A 1903
Rogers Brothers in Harvard, The
    (debut in chorus) 1902
Samson (Elsie Vernette) 1908
Toddles 1908
Twenty Days in the Shade 1908
When Knight's Were Bold 1907

958
FREEMEN, William*
Birth of a Nation, The (sentry)
Mirandy Smiles

959
FREMONT, Alfred*
Salome (Galla)
Siren's Song, The (Jules Bernais)
When a Woman Sins (Augustus
    VanBrooks)

960
FRENCH, Charles K. *
At the Crossroads of Life
Civilization (Prime Minister)
Clodhopper, The
Corner in Colleen's A
Coward, The (Confederate
    Commander)
Fisherman's Romance, A
Hearts United (Davey Crockett)
Hermit Doctor of Garja
Hired Man
His Own Home Town
Honorable Clergy, The
Law of the North, The

Lifted Veil, The
Modern Taming of the Shrew, A
Playing the Game
Sheriff's Son, The
Son of His Father
That Hero Stuff
Tiger Man
True Indian's Heart, A
Weaker Sex, The
Stage:
Nancy Stair 1905

961
FRENCH, George B. (1883-   )
Back to Nature
Back to the Woods
Doctor and the Woman, The
Five Hundred or Bust
His Pajama Girl
In and Out
Sally's Blighted Career
Tarzan of the Apes

962
FRENYEAR, Mabel*
Fool There Was, A (the fool's wife)

963
FRIEBUS, Theodore*
Mystery of the Double Cross (serial)
Pearl of the Army (serial)
Stage:
Brown of Harvard 1906
Children of Destiny 1910
Faith Healer, The 1910
Press Agent, The 1905
Tailor Made Man, A (Dr. Gustavus
    Sonntag) 1917

964
FUJITA, Toyo*
Dragon Painter, The

965
FULLER, Charles*
Henry VIII (Cranmer)
Stage:
Mother Goose 1903

966
FULLER, Dale (1897-   )
Bath Tub Perils
Dodging His Doom
Oily Scoundrel, An
Scoundrel's Tale, The
Surf Girl, The (Mama)
Village Vampire, The /aka/ The
    Great Leap

967
FULLER, Haidee*
Squaw Man, The (Lady Mabel
  Wynnegate)

968
FULLER, Mary (1893-)
Active Life of Dolly of the Dailies,
  The (serial)
Aida
Convict's Parole, The
Elektra
Harbinger of Peace
It's Never Too Late to Mend
Long Trail, The
Martin Chuzzlewit
Mary Stuart
Mercy Merrick
Three Musketeers, The
  (Constance)
What Happened to Mary? (serial)
With Eyes of the Blind

969
FULLER, Olive Gordon (1896-)
Devil's Own, The
Knight of the Range, A
Love's Lariat
Tess of the Storm Country
Woman's Eyes, A

970
FURNEY, James A. *
Destruction (Jerome Froment)
Stage:
Darling of the Gallery Gods, The
  1903
Dress Parade, The 1903
Jersey Lily, The 1903
New Yorkers, The 1901
Sally in Our Alley 1902
Sergeant Kitty 1904
Strollers, The 1901

971
FURNSTMAN, Georgia*
Seven Sisters

- G -

972
GADEN, Alexander*
Leah Kleschna

973
GAIL, Jane*
Dr. Jekyll and Mr. Hyde

Twenty Thousand Leagues under the
  Sea
Universal player 1914

974
GAILLARD, Robert*
As You Like It

975
GALE, Alice*
Camille (Madame Prudence)
Darling of Paris, The (Gypsy Queen)
Heart and Soul (Dulce)
Her Greatest Love (Nurse)
Romeo and Juliet (Nurse)
Stage:
Silver Wedding, The 1913

976
GALE, Margaret*
Yellow Menace, The (serial)

977
GALLAGHER, Ray (1889-1953)
Her Life's Story (Don Manuel)
His Divorced Wife
Maid of the Mist (the boy)

978
GALLAHER, Donald*
Eye for Eye

979
GAMBLE, Fred*
Oh, Daddy!

980
GAMBLE, Warburton*
La Belle Russe (Phillip Sackton)
Silver King, The
Society Exile, A
Unforseen, The
Stage:
Milestones 1912

981
GARCIA, Al Ernest*
Unafraid, The (Joseph)

982
GARDEN, Mary (1875-1967)
Splendid Sinner, The
Thais

983
GARDINER, Reece*
Village Blacksmith, The

984
GARDNER, Amelia*
Lure of Ambition, The (Lady
  Constance Bromey)

985
GARDNER, Helen*
Cleopatra
Helen Gardner Picture Corp. (first
  star to form her own company)
  1912
Princess of Bagdad, A
Sister to Carmen, A
Vanity Fair (Becky Sharp)

986
GARDNER, Jack*
Gift o' Gab
Stage:
Belle of Mayfair, The 1906
Madame Sherry 1910

987
GARON, Pauline (1901-1967)
Good for Nothing

988
GARVIN, Anita (1907-   )
Old Wives for New
Sport Girl, The

989
GARWOOD, William*
Business vs. People
Carmen
Man's Way, A

990
GASTON, Mae*
Dolly's Scoop
Silent Mystery, The (serial)

991
GASTROCK, Phail*
Man's Country, A (Connell)

992
GAUNTIER, Gene (1891-   )
Collen Bawn
Became the KALEM GIRL in 1909
Daughter of the Confederacy
Down through the Ages
From the Manger to the Cross
Girl Spy, The (series)
Heart's Desire
In the Form of a Hypnotist
Prisoner of the Harem, A
Tragedy of the Desert
Winning a Widow

993
GAYE, Howard*
Birth of a Nation, The (Gen. Robert
  E. Lee)
Flirting with Fate (Ronald Dabney)
Intolerance (the Nazarene)

994
GEBHARDT, Frank*
At the Altar
Balked at the Altar
Cord of Life, The
Devil, The
Fatal Hour, The
Feud and the Turkey, The
Greaser's Gauntlet, The
Man and the Woman, The
Mr. Jones at the Ball
One Touch of Nature
Romance of a Jewess
Song of the Shirt, The
Tavern Keeper's Daughter, The

995
GEBHARDT, Mrs. Frank*
Adventures of Dollie, The (Gypsy's
  wife)
Tavern Keeper's Daughter

996
GELDART, Clarence (1867-1936)
Fall of a Nation, The
Intolerance
Squaw Man, The (Solicitor)
Till I Come back to You (U. S.
  Colonel)

997
GEORGE, Gladys (Gladys Clare)
  (1902- 1954)
Red Hot Dollars
Woman in the Suitcase, The

998
GEORGE, Maud (1890-   )
Blue Blazes Rawden
Devil's Pass Key, The
Even as You and I
Idle Wives
Lamb and the Lion, The
Marriage Ring, The
Midnight Stage, The
Piper's Price, The (Jessica)
Rogue's Romance, A
Shadows of Suspicion

999
GEORGE, Peggy*
Heart of Nora Flynn, The (Anne Stone)

1000
GERALD, Peter*
Adventures of Peg o' the Ring, The
    (serial)
Purple Mask, The (serial)

1001
GERARD, Ambassador*
My Four Years in Germany

1002
GERARD, Carl*
Crime and Punishment
Vixen, The (Charlie Drummond)

1003
GERARD, Charles*
Isle of Conquest, The
New Moon, The

1004
GERBER, Neva*
Awakening, The
Caught in the Act
Fight for Love, A
Great Secret, The
Hell Bent
Like Wildfire
Mystery Ship, The (serial)
Phantom Ship, The
Prodigal Widow, The
Roped
Spindle of Life, The
Three Mounted Men
Trail of the Octopus (serial)
Voice on the Wire, The (serial)

1005
GERMONPREZ, Valerie*
Blind Husbands (a honeymooner)

1006
GERRARD, Charles (1887-   )
Counterfeit
Double Standard
Down to Earth (a society fop)
Hun Within, The
Isle of Conquest, The
Little Miss Optimist
New Moon, The
Pettigrew's Girl
Something to Do
Teeth of the Tiger

1007
GERRARD, Douglas (1888-   )
Commanding Officer
Dumb Girl of Portici, The

Lord and Lady Algy
Merchant of Venice, The

1008
GERTIE, the Dinosaur
First important animated cartoon
    created by Winsor McCay

1009
GIBBS, Raton*
Lure of Ambition, The (Miguel
    Lopez)

1010
GIBSON, Helen (Rose August Wenger)
    (1892-   )
Border Watch Dogs
Fighting Mad
Ghost of Canyon Diablo, The
Girl of Gopher City, The
Gun Law, The
Hazards of Helen, The (started in
    Chapter 49) (serial)
Peril of the Rails
Robber of the Golden Star, The
Rustlers, The
Trail of the Rails
Trapped Wires
When Seconds Count

1011
GIBSON, Hoot (Edward Gibson)
    (1892-1962)
By Indian Post
Cactus Kid, The
Cheyenne's Pal
Crow, The
Daughter of Daring, A (serial)
Double Holdup, The
Fighting Brothers
Gun Law
Gun Packer, The
Hazards of Helen, The (serial)
His Only Son
Jay Bird, The
Knight of the Range, A
Marked Man, A
Rustlers, The
Soul Herder, The
Straight Shooting
Trail of the Holdup
Voice on the Wire, The (serial)

1012
GIBSON, Margaret*
Coward, The (Amy)

1013
GILBERT, Billy (1894-   )
Bubbles of Trouble

1014
GILBERT, Edwin J.*
Safety Curtain, The

1015
GILBERT, Jack*
Widow by Proxy

1016
GILBERT, John (John Pringle)
   (1895-1936)
Apostle of Vengeance
Busher, The
Devil Dodger, The
Golden Rule Kate
Heart of the Hills
Hell's Hinges (a townsperson)
Millionaire Vagrant, The
Mother Instinct, The
Princess of the Dark
Should a Woman Tell?
White Heather

1017
GILFETHER, Daniel*
Who Pays?

1018
GILL, Basil (1877-1955)
Adventures of Dick Dolan
Chains of Bondage
God's Good Man
Henry VIII
Irresistible Flapper, The
Keeper of the Door
Missing the Tide
On the Banks of Allan Water
Rocks of Valpre, The
Soul's Crucifixion, A
Spinner o' Dreams
What's the Use of Grumbling?

1019
GILLESPIE, Albert T.*
Surf Girl, The

1020
GILLESPIE, William (1894-   )
Immigrant, The

1021
GILLET, Florence*
Lucky Dog

1022
GILLETTE, William (1855-1937)
Secret Service
Sherlock Holmes (Title role)
Stage:
Admirable Crichton, The 1903
Clarice 1906
Dear Brutus 1918
Diplomacy 1914
Held by the Enemy 1910
Private Secretary, The 1910
Samson 1908
Secret Service 1910; 1915
Sherlock Holmes (Title role) 1900;
   1910; 1915
Successful Calamity, A 1917
Too Much Johnson 1910

1023
GILMOUR, John*
House of Hate, The (serial)

1024
GIRACCI, May*
Till I Come Back to You (Rosa)

1025
GIRARD, Joseph W. (1871-1949)
Bare Fists
Brass Bullet, The (serial)
Danger-Go Slow (Judge Cotton)
Hell Morgan's Girl (Oliver Curwell)
Kaiser, the Beast of Berlin, The
   (Ambassador Gerard)
Loot
Midnight Man, The
Paid in Advance (John Gray)
Sign of the Rat
Twenty Thousand Leagues under the
   Sea
Two Souled Woman
Voice on the Wire, The (serial)

1026
GIRARD, Pete*
Mystery of 13, The (serial)

1027
GIRARDOT, Etienne (1856-1939)
Belle of New York, The (William
   Bronson)
Goodness Gracious! or Movies as
   They Shouldn't Be
New Secretary, The
Violin of Monsieur, The
Stage:
Leah Kleschna (Valentin Favre) 1904

1028
GISH, Dorothy (Dorothy de Guiche)
    (1898-1968)
Adopted Brother, The
Almost a Wild Man
Arms and the Gringo
Atta-Boy's Last Race
Availing Prayer, The
Back to the Kitchen
Battling Jane
Best Bet
Better Way, The
Betty of Graystone
Boots
Bred in the Bone
Children of the Feud
City Beautiful, The
Cry for Help, A
Down the Road to Creditville
Fair Rebel, A
Floor Above, The
Gold and Glitter
Granny
Gretchen, the Greenhorn
Hearts of the World (Little Disturber)
Her Father's Silent Partner
Her Grandparents
Her Mother's Daughter
Her Mother's Necklace
Her Mother's Oath
Her Official Fathers
Her Old Teacher
Home Sweet Home (sister)
Hope Chest, The
House of Discord, The
How Hazel Got Even
Hun Within, The
I'll Get Him Yet!
Jordan Is a Hard Road
Judith of Bethulia
Just Gold
Katie Bauer
Lady and the Mouse, The
Lady in Black, The
Lesson in Mechanics, A
Liberty Belles, The
Little Catamount
Little Meena's Romance
Little School Ma'am
Little Yank, The
Lost Lord Lowell, The
Minerva's Mission
Mountain Girl, The
Mountain Rat, The
Musketeers of Pig Alley, The
My Hero
Mysterious Shot, The
New York Hat, The

Newer Woman, The
Nobody Home
Nugget Nell
Nun, The
Oil and Water
Old-Fashioned Girl, An
Old Heidelberg
Old Man, The
Out of Bondage
Out of Luck
Pa Pays
Painted Lady, The
Peppy Polly
Perfidy of Mary
Rebellion of Kitty Belle, The
Sands of Fate
Saving Grace, The
Silent Sandy
Sisters, The
Stage Struck
Suffragette's Battle, The
Susan Rocks the Boat
Tavern of Tragedy, The
That Colby Girl
Their First Acquaintance
Those Little Flowers
Turning the Tables
Unseen Enemy, An (debut)
Vengeance of Galora, The
Victorine
Warning, The
Widow's Kids, The
Wife, The

1029
GISH, Lillian (Lillian de Guiche)
    (1896-)
Angel of Contention
Battle of Elderbush Gulch, The
Battle of the Sexes, The (Jane
    Andrews)
Birth of a Nation, The (Elsie
    Stoneman)
Broken Blossoms (Lucy)
Burglar's Dilemma, The
Captain Macklin
Children Pay
Conscience of Hassan Bey, The
Cry for Help, A
Daphne and the Pirate
Diane of the Follies
During the Roundup
Enoch Arden
Escape, The
Flirting with Faith
Folly of Anne, The
Great Love, The (Susie Broadplains)
Greatest Question, The

Greatest Thing in Life, The (Jeanette
  Peret)
Green-Eyed Devil, The
Hearts of the World (Marie Stephen-
  son)
Home, Sweet Home (John's sweet-
  heart)
House Built upon Sand, The
House of Darkness, The
Hunchback, The
In the Aisles of the Wild
Indian's Loyalty, An
Innocent Magdalene, An
Intolerance (Woman who rocks the
  cradle)
Judith of Bethulia
Just Gold
Lady and the Mouse, The
Left-Handed Man, The
Liberty Bond
Life's Pathways
Lily and the Rose, The
Lord Chumley
Lost House, The
Madonna and Her Child, The
Man's Enemy
Men and Muslin
Men and Women
Misunderstood Boy, A
Modest Hero, A
Mothering Heart, The
Mountain Rat, The
Musketeers of Pig Alley, The
My Baby
New York Hat, The
Oil and Water
One She Loved, The
Quicksands
Rebellion of Kitty Belle, The
Remodeling Her Husband (Directed)
Romance of Happy Valley, A
  (Jennie Timberlake)
Silent Sandy
Sisters, The
So Runs the Way
Sold for Marriage
Soul's Triumph
Tear That Burned, The
Test, The
Timely Interception, A
True Heart Susie (Susie)
Two Daughters of Eve
Unseen Enemy, An
Unwelcome Guest, The
Wife, The
Woman in Ultimate, A
Stage:
Good Little Devil, The 1913

1030
GISH, Mary*
Hearts of the World (Refugee mother)

1031
GLASS, Gaston (1899-1965)
Behind Closed Doors
Open Your Eyes

1032
GLAUM, Louise (1894-   )
Alien Enemy, An
Aryan, The
Between Men
Boomerang
City of the Dead
Conversion of Frosty Blake, The
Cup of Life, The
Goddess of Lost Lake, The
Golden Rule Kate
Hell's Hinges (Dolly)
Home
Honor Thy Name
Idolators, The
Ike Gets a Goat
Iron Strain, The
Keno Bates, Liar (Anita)
Lass unto Herself, A
Lone Wolf's Daughter, The
Love and Justice
Lure of Woman, The
Quakeress, The
Renegade, The
Return of Draw Egan
Sahara
Sweetheart of the Doomed, The
Transgressor, The
Weaker Sex, The
Wedlock
Wolf Woman, The

1033
GLEASON, Ada*
Ramona (Title role)
That Devil, Bateese (Kathleen St.
  John)
Voice in the Fog, The

1034
GLENDON, J. Frank*
Third Judgment, The
Woman in the Web, A (serial)
Wooing of Princess Pat, The

1035
GLYNNE, Marg (1898-1954)
Cry of Justice, The

1036
GOLDEN, Marta*
Janitor's Wife's Temptation, A
Woman, A
Work

1037
GOLDEN, Olive*
Such Is Life (Olive Trent)
Tess of the Storm Country

1038
GOLDSMITH, Frank*
Clemenceau Case, The (Duke Sergius)
Two Orphans, The (Marquis de
   Presies)

1039
GONZALES, Myrtle*
Captain Alvarez

1040
GOODRICH, Edna*
Daughter of Maryland, A
Stage:
Evangeline 1913
Genius, The 1906
That Rollicking Girl 1905

1041
GOODRICH, Katherine*
Lass of the Lumberlands (serial)

1042
GOODWIN, Harold (1902-   )
Dad's Out-Laws
Heart o' the Hills
Old Heidelberg

1043
GOODWIN, Nat C. (1859-1919)
Master Hand, The
Oliver Twist
Stage:
Altar of Friendship, The 1902
Celebrated Case, A 1915
Genius, The 1906
Merchant of Venice, The 1901
Midsummer Night's Dream, A
   (Bottom) 1903
Oliver Twist (Fagin) 1912
When We Were Twenty-One 1900
Why Marry? 1917

1044
GOODWIN, Rom*
Bound and Gagged (serial)

1045
GOODWINS, Fred*
Bank, The
Jitney Elopement, A
Night in the Show, A
Night Out, A
Police
Shanghaied
Tramp, The

1046
GORDON, Huntley (1897-1956)
Common Cause, The
Glorious Lady, The
Million Dollar Dollies, The
Our Mrs. McChesney
Out Younder
Too Many Crooks
Unknown Quantity, The

1047
GORDON, Julia Swayne (-1933)
Beau Brummel
Bid, A
Captain's Captain, The
Cardinal Wolsey
Girl Problem, The
Hamlet
Her Right to Live
Hidden Letters, The
Hillman, The
Lady Godiva
Lady of the Lake, The
Love Watches
Message of the Mouse, The
Miss Dulcie from Dixie
Moonshine Trail, The
Napoleon
Over the Top
Red and White Roses
Soap Girl, The
Soldiers of Chance
Song of the Hills, A
Soul Master, The
Stenographer Wanted (Mrs. Jones)
Tiger Lady, The
Troublesome Step-Daughters, The
Twelfth Night
Two Women
Uncle Bill
Victoria Cross, The

1048
GORDON, Kitty (1870-   )
Adele
As in a Looking Glass
Belgian, The
Diamonds and Pearls

Divine Sacrifice
Her Hour
Interloper, The
Mandarin's Gold, The
Merely Players
Playthings of Passion
Purple Lily, The
Scar, The
Tinsel
Unveiling Hand, The
Wasp, The
Stage:
Alma, Where Do You Live? 1910
Enchantress, The 1911
Girl and the Wizard, The 1909
La Belle Paree 1911
Veronique 1905
World of Pleasure, A 1915

1049
GORDON, Maude Turner (1870-)
Bringing up Betty
Danger Mark, The
Home
Honeymoon, The
Kreutzer Sonata (Rebecca
    Friedlander)
Making Her His Wife
Oakdale Affair, The

1050
GORDON, Robert*
Captain Kidd, Jr.
Five films for Blackton-Pathé 1919
Huck and Tom
Missing
My Husband's Other Wife
Pair of Silk Stockings, A
Tom Sawyer
Varmit, The

1051
GORDON, Ruth (Ruth Jones) (1896-)
Camille
Wheel of Life, The
Stage:
Peter Pan 1915
Seventeen 1918

1052
GOWDOWSKY, Dagmar*
Lord and Lady Algy
Trap, The

1053
GOWLAND, Gibson (1882-)
Birth of a Nation, The
Blind Husbands (the mountain guide)

Hawk, The
Macbeth
White Heather

1054
GRAHAM, Charles*
Master Mystery, The (serial)

1055
GRAN, Albert*
Out of the Drifts

1056
GRANBY, Joseph*
Jealousy

1057
GRANDIN, Elmer*
Getting Mary Married (John Bussard)

1058
GRANDIN, Ethel (1896-)
Across the Plains
Crimson Stain Mystery, The
    (Florence Montrose) (serial)
Dawn of a Romance, The
Jane Eyre
Traffic in Souls

1059
GRANDIN, Francis*
Ramona

1060
GRANDON, Frank*
Chief's Daughter, The
Duke's Plan, The
Enoch Arden, Part I and Part II
In Old California
Lonedale Operator, The
Primal Call, The
Swords and Hearts

1061
GRANT, Corrine*
Neglected Wife, The

1062
GRANT, Lawrence (1898-1952)
To Hell with the Kaiser!

1063
GRANT, Sydney*
Jane
Stage:
Pretty Mrs. Smith 1914

1064
GRANT, Valentine*

Belgian, The
Brute, The
Daughter of MacGregor, The
Innocent Life, The
Melting Pot, The
Mother of Men, A

1065
GRASSBY, Bertram (1880-   )
Battling Jane
For the Defense
Hope Chest, The
Liberty, a Daughter of the U. S. A.
    (serial)
Lone Wolf's Daughter, The
Romance of Happy Valley, A (Judas)
Salome (Prince David)

1066
GRAUER, Ben*
Mad Woman, The

1067
GRAVES, Ralph (1900-   )
Greatest Question, The (John Hilton)
Home Town, Girl, The
I'll Get Him Yet!
Nobody Home
Out of Luck
Scarlet Days
Sporting Life
Tinsel
White Heather

1068
GRAVINA, Caesare (1858-   )
Fatal Ring, The (serial)
Fricot e le Uova
Less Than Dust
Madame Butterfly

1069
GRAY, Betty*
His Wife's Mistakes

1070
GRAY, Gilda (Marianna Michalska)
    (1899-1959)
Virtuous Vamp, A
Stage:
Hello, Alexander 1919

1071
GRAY, Nadia (Nadia Kujnir-Herescu)
    (1923-   )
Silver King, The

1072
GRAY, Stella see LaRUE, Grace

1073
GRAY, Stephen*
Joan, the Woman (Pierre)

1074
GRAYBILL, Joseph*
Bobby, the Coward
Decree of Destiny, A
Italian Barber, The
Italian Blood
Last Drop of Water, The
Light That Came, The
Lonedale Operator, The
Love in the Hills
Making of a Man, The
Painted Lady, The
Purgation, The
Romany Tragedy, A
Saved from Himself
Through Darkened Vales
Victim of Jealousy, A

1075
GREELEY, Evelyn*
Oakdale Affair, The (Gail Prim)
Road to France, The

1076
GREEN, Dorothy*
Dark Star, The
Patria (serial)

1077
GREEN, Helen*
Amazons, The
Perils of Our Girl Reporters (serial)

1078
GREENE, Kempton (1890-   )
Brown of Harvard
Carter Case, The (The Craig
    Kennedy Serial) (serial)
Crook of Dreams
Fool's Gold
Forest Rivals
Fortune's Child
My Little Sister
Our Little Wife

1079
GREENWOOD, Charlotte (1893-   )
Jane
Stage:
Linger Longer, Letty 1919
Passing Show of 1912, The 1912
So Long, Letty 1916
Ziegfeld Follies of 1913

1080
GREENWOOD, Winifred*
Come Again Smith
Crystal Gazer, The
Deciding Kiss, The
Derelict, The
Dust
Lottery Man, The
Lying Lips
Maggie Pepper
Men, Women and Money
Profligate, The
Reclamation
Two Orphans, The

1081
GRETILLAT*
Man with the White Gloves, The

1082
GREY, Jane (1883-1944)
Waifs
Stage:
DeLuxe Annie 1917
Kick In 1914
Nearly Married 1913
Tempest, The 1916

1083
GREY, Olga*
Birth of a Nation, The (Laura Keene)
Double Trouble
Intolerance (Mary Magdalene)
Woman God Forgot, The (Aztec
    woman)

1084
GREY, Ray*
Movie Star, A

1085
GRIBBON, Eddie (1892-1965)
Keystone Kop comedies 1919

1086
GRIBBON, Harry (1888-1960)
Ambrose's Sour Grapes
Dash of Courage, A
Great Pearl Tangle, The
His Auto Ruination
His Wild Oats
Janitor's Wife's Temptation, A
Ladies First
Love Will Conquer
Lover's Might, A
Mabel, Fatty and the Law
Maiden's Trust, A
Perils of the Park
Pinched in the Finish

Social Club, A
Stars and Bars
Two Crooks
Worst of Friends, The

1087
GRIFFIN, Gerald*
Yellow Menace, The (serial)

1088
GRIFFITH, Corinne (1898-)
Adventure Shop
Bramble Bush, The
Climbers, The
Clutch of Circumstances, The
Girl at Bay, A
Girl of Today
Girl Problem
I Will Repay
Last Man, The
Love Doctor, The
Love Watches
Menace, The
Miss Ambition
Thin Ice
Unknown Quantity
Who Goes There?

1089
GRIFFITH, David Wark /aka/
    Lawrence (1875-1948)
Actor:
Adventures of Dolly, The
At the Crossroads of Life
For Love of Gold
Music Master, The
Old Isaac, the Pawnbroker
Rescued from an Eagle's Nest
When Knights Were Bold
Director:
Adventure in the Autumn Woods, An
Adventures of Billy, The
Adventures of Dollie, The
Affair of Hearts, An
After Many Years
And a Little Child Shall Lead
    Them
Arcadian Maid, An
As in a Looking Glass
As It Is in Life
As the Bells Ring Out
At the Altar
Awakening, The
Awful Moment, An
Baby and the Stork, The
Baby's Shoe, A
Balked at the Altar
Bandit's Waterloo, The
Banker's Daughters, The

Barbarian, Ingomar, The
Battle, The
Battle at Elderbush Gulch
Beast at Bay, A
Behind the Scenes
Betrayed by a Hand Print
Better Way, The
Billy's Strategem
Birth of a Nation, The
Black Sheep
Blind Love
Blind Princess and the Poet, The
Blot on the 'Scutcheon, A
Bobby the Coward
Boy Detective, The
Brahma Diamond, The
Broken Blossoms
Broken Cross, The
Broken Doll, The
Broken Locket, The
Broken Ways
Brothers
Brutality
Burglar's Dilemma, The
Burglar's Mistake, A
Calamitous Elopement, A
Call, The
Call of the Wild, The
Call to Arms, The
Cardinal's Conspiracy, The
Chance Deception, A
Change of Heart, A
Change of Spirit, A
Chief's Daughter, The
Child of the Ghetto, A
Child's Faith, A
Child's Impulse, A
Child's Remorse, A
Child's Strategem, A
Children's Friend, The
Choosing a Husband
Christmas Burglars, The
Cloister's Touch, The
Clubman and the Tramp, The
Comata, the Sioux
Coming of Angelo, The
Concealing a Burglar
Confidence
Conscience
Converts, The
Convict's Sacrifice, A
Cord of Life, The
Corner in Wheat, A
Corporal's Daughter, The
Country Cupid, A
Country Doctor, The
Cricket on the Hearth, The
Criminal Hypnotist

Crooked Road, The
Crossing the American Plains in the
    Early Fifties
Cry for Help, A
Crutain Pole, The
Dan the Dandy
Dancing Girl of Butte, The
Dash through the Clouds, A
Day After, The
Death Disc, The
Death's Marathon
Deception, The
Decree of Destiny, A
Devil, The
Diamond Star, The
Drink's Lure
Drive for Life, The
Drunkard's Reformation, A
Duke's Plan, The
During the Roundup
Eavesdropper, The
Edgar Allan Poe
Eloping with Auntie
Englishman and the Girl, The
Enoch Arden, Part I and Part II
Eradicating Auntie
Escape
Eternal Mother, The
Examination Day at School
Expiation, The
Face at the Window, The
Faded Lilies, The
Failure, The
Fair Exchange, A
Faithful
Fall of Babylon, The
Fascinating Mrs. Frances, The
Fatal Hour, The
Fatal Marriage, The
Fate
Fate's Interception
Fate's Turning
Father Gets in the Game
Female of the Species, The
Feud and the Turkey, The
Feud in the Kentucky Hills, A
Fighting Blood
Final Settlement, The
Fisher Folks
Flash of Light, A
Fools of Fate
Fool's Revenge, A
For a Wife's Honor
For His Son
For Love of Gold
French Duel, The
Friend of the Family, The
Friends

Fugitive, The
Getting Even
Gibson Goddess, The
Girl and Her Trust, The
Girl and the Outlaw, The
Girl Who Stayed at Home, The
Girls and Daddy, The
Girl's Strategem, A
God Within, The
Goddess of Sagebrush Gulch, The
Gold and Glitter
Gold Is Not All
Gold Seekers, The
Golden Louis, The
Golden Supper, The
Greaser's Gauntlet, The
Great Love, The
Greatest Question, The
Greatest Thing in Life, The
Guerrilla, The
Heart Beats of Long Ago
Heart of Oyama, The
Hearts of the World
Heaven Avenges
Helping Hand, The
Her Awakening
Her Father's Pride
Her First Biscuits
Her Mother's Oath
Her Sacrifice
Her Terrible Ordeal
Heredity
Hero of Little Italy, The
Hindoo Dagger, The
His Daughter
His Duty
His Last Burglary
His Lesson
His Lost Love
His Mother's Scarf
His Mother's Son
His Sister-in-Law
His Trust
His Trust Fulfilled
His Ward's Love
His Wife's Mother
His Wife's Visitor
Home Folks
Honor of His Family, The
Honor of Thieves, The
Hoodoo Ann
House of Darkness, The
House with the Closed Shutters, The
How She Triumphed
I Did It, Mama
Iconoclast, The
If We Only Knew
Impalement, The

In a Hempen Bag
In Life's Cycle
In Little Italy
In Old California
In Old Kentucky
In the Aisles of the Wild
In the Border States
In the Days of '49
In the Season of Buds
In the Watches of the Night
In the Window Recess
Indian Brothers, The
Indian Runner's Romance, The
Indian Summer, An
Indian's Loyalty, An
Informer, The
Ingrate, The
Inner Circle, The
Innocent Magdalene, An
Intolerance
Iola's Promise
Italian Barber, The
Italian Blood
Jealous Husband, The
Jealousy and the Man
Jilt, The
Jones and His New Neighbors
Jones and the Lady Book Agent
Jones Have Amateur Theatricals, The
Judith of Bethulia
Just Gold
Just Like a Woman
Knight of the Road, A
Lady and the Mouse, The
Lady Helen's Escapade
Last Deal, The
Last Drop of Water, The
La Tosca
Leather Stockings
Lena and the Geese
Lesser Evil, The
Lesson, The
Life of Villa
Light That Came, The
Lily and the Rose, The
Lily of the Tenements, The
Lines of White on the Sullen Sea
Little Angels of Luck
Little Darling, The
Little Teacher, The
Little Tease, The
Lodging for the Night, A
Lonedale Operator, The
Lonely Villa, The
Long Road, The
Love among the Roses
Love Finds a Way
Love in an Apartment Hotel

Love in the Hills
Lucky Jim
Lure of the Gown, The
Macbeth
Madame Rex
Making of a Man, The
Man, The
Man and the Woman, The
Man's Genesis
Man's Lust for Gold
Maniac Cook, The
Marked Time-table, The
Marriage of Molly O', The
Martyrs of the Alamo, The
Massacre, The
Medicine Bottle, The
Mended Lute, The
Mender of the Nets, The
Message, The
Message of the Violin, The
Mexican Sweethearts, The
Midnight Adventure, A
Midnight Cupid, A
Mills of the Gods, The
Misappropiated Turkey, A
Miser's Heart, The
Mistake, The
Mr. Jones at the Ball
Mr. Jones' Burglar
Mr. Jones Has a Card Party
Misunderstood Boy, A
Modern Prodigal, The
Mohawk's Way, A
Monday Morning in a Coney Island
    Police Court
Money Mad
Mother and the Law
Mothering Heart, The
Mountaineer's Honor, The
Mrs. Jones Entertains
Mrs. Jones' Lover or I Want My Hat
Muggsy's First Sweetheart
Music Master, The
Musketeers of Pig Alley, The
My Baby
My Hero
Narrow Road, The
Near to Earth
Necklace, The
New Dress, The
New Trick, A
New York Hat, The
Newlyweds, The
Note in the Shoe, The
Nursing a Viper
Oath and the Man, The
Oh, Uncle!
Oil and Water

Olaf--an Atom
Old Actor, The
Old Bookkeeper, The
Old Confectioner's Mistake, The
Old Folks at Home
Old Isaac, the Pawnbroker
On the Reef
One Busy Hour
One Is Business, the Other Crime
One Night, and Then--
One She Loved, The
One Touch of Nature
Open Gate, The
Ostler Joe
Outcast among Outcasts, An
Over Silent Paths
Painted Lady, The
Peach Basket Hat, The
Penitents, The
Perfidy of Mary, The
Pippa Passes
Pirate Gold
Pirate's Gold, The
Plain Song, A
Planter's Wife, The
Politician's Love Story
Pranks
Prehistoric Days, In /aka/ Wars of
    the Primal Tribes; Brute Force
Primal Call, The
Princess in the Vase, The
Prussian Spy, The
Pueblo Legend, A
Punishment, The
Purgation, The
Ramona
Ranchero's Revenge, The
Reckoning, The
Red Girl, The
Redman and the Child, The
Redman's View, The
Reformers, The or The Lost Art of
    Minding One's Business
Renunciation, The
Restoration, The
Resurrection
Revenue Man and the Girl, The
Rich Revenge, A
Road to the Heart, The
Rocky Road, The
Romance of a Jewess
Romance of Happy Valley, A
Romance of the Western Hills, A
Romany Tragedy, A
Root of Evil, The
Rose o' Salem Town
Rose of Kentucky, The
Roue's Heart, The

Rude Hostess, A
Ruling Passion, The
Rural Elopement, A
Sacrifice, The
Salutary Lesson, A
Salvation Army Lass, The
Sands of Dee, The
Saved from Himself
Scarlet Days
Schneider's Anti-noise Crusade
School Teacher and the Waif, The
Sculptor's Nightmare, The
Sealed Room, The
Serious Sixteen
1776, or The Hessian Renegades
Seventh Day, The
Shadows of Doubt
Sheriff's Baby, The
Simple Charity
Siren of Impulse, A
Sister of Six, A
Sister's Love, A
Slave, The
Smile of a Child, A
Smoked Husband, A
So Near, Yet So Far
Sold for Marriage
Song of the Shirt, The
Song of the Wildwood Flute, The
Son's Return, The
Sorrowful Example, The
Sorrowful Shore, The
Sorrows of the Unfaithful, The
Souls Triumphant
Sound Stuper, A
Spanish Gypsy, The
Spirit Awakened, The
Squaw's Love, The
Stage Rustler, The
Stolen Bride, The
Stolen Jewels, The
Strange Meeting, A
String of Pearls, A
Stuff Heros Are Made Of, The
Suicide Club, The
Summer Idyll, A
Sunbeam, The
Sunshine Sue
Sunshine through the Dark
Sweet and Twenty
Sweet Revenge
Swords and Hearts
Tale of the Wilderness, A
Taming a Husband
Taming of the Shrew
Tavern Keeper's Daughter, The
Teaching Dad to Like Her
Telephone Girl and the Lady, The

Temporary Truce, A
Tender Hearted Boy, The
Tender Hearts
Terrible Discovery, A
Test, The
Test of Friendship, The
That Chink at Golden Gulch
They Would Elope
Thief and the Girl, The
Those Awful Hats
Those Boys
Thou Shalt Not
Thread of Destiny, The
Three Friends
Three King Fishers, The
Three Sisters
Through Darkened Vales
Through the Breakers
Timely Interception, A
'Tis an Ill Wind That Blows No Good
To Save Her Soul
Tragic Love
Trail of the Books, The
Transformation of Mike, The
Trap for Santa Claus, A
Trick That Failed, The
Troublesome Satchel, A
True Heart Susie
Trying to Get Arrested
Twin Brothers
Twisted Trail, The
Two Brothers, The
Two Daughters of Eve
Two Little Waifs
Two Memories
Two Men of the Desert
Two Paths, The
Two Sides, The
Two Women and a Man
Unchanging Sea, The
Under Burning Skies
Unexpected Help
Unseen Enemy, An
Unveiling, The
Unwelcome Guest, The
Usurer, The
Vaquero's Vow, The
Victim of Jealousy, A
Violin Maker of Cremona, The
Voice of the Child, The
Voice of the Violin, The
Waiter No. 5
Wanderer, The
Wanted, A Child
Was He a Coward?
Was Justice Served?
Way of a Man, The
Way of the World, The

Welcome Burglar, The
Welcome Intruder, A
What Drink Did
What Shall We Do with Our Old?
What the Daisy Said
What's Your Hurry?
When a Man Loves
When Kings Were the Law
When Knights Were Bold
Where the Breakers Roar
White Rose of the Wilds, The
White Roses
Wild Girl of the Sierra
Wilful Peggy
Winning Back His Love
Winning Coat, The
With Her Card
Woman from Mellon's, The
Woman Scorned, A
Woman's Way, A
Wooden Leg, The
Wreath in Time, A
Wreath of Orange Blossoms, A
Yaqui Cur, The
Zulu's Heart, The
Supervisor:
American Aristocracy
Americano, The
Double Trouble
Flirting with Fate
For Her Father's Sins
For Those Unborn
Good Bad Man, The
Habit of Happiness
Half-Breed, The
His Picture in the Papers
Lamb, The
Little Country Mouse, The
Manhattan Madness
Matrimaniac
Men and Women
Mystery of the Leaping Fish
Odalisque, The
Old Maid, The
Reggie Mixes In
Second Mrs. Roebuck, The
Soul of Honor, The
Strong Heart
Stage:
East Lynne 1904
Elizabeth the Queen of England
    (Francis Drake; San Francisco)
    1905
Ensign, The (Abe Lincoln; Chicago)
    1904
Fedora (Oregon) 1905
Financier (San Francisco) 1905
Fool and the Girl, The (Washington,
    D. C.) 1907

Grismonda (spear carrier) 1896
Julia Marlowe Touring Company 1896
La Dame aux Camélias 1896
Magda (Boston) 1907
Meffert Stock Company (Louisville,
    Kentucky) 1896-1899:
All the Comforts of Home (walk on)
    1896
Count of Monte Cristo, The (a
    villain 1898
Held by the Enemy (Capt. Woodford)
    1897
Jim the Penman (Lord Drelincourt)
    1898
Lady Windermere's Fan (Parker
    Serrant) 1897
Lights o' London, The (Marks) 1896
Little Lord Fauntleroy (Thomas)
    1898
Shenandoah (Frank Bedloe) 1898
Three Musketeers, The (Athos)
    1899
Wages of Sin, The (servant) 1896
Wife, The (Mr. Randolph) 1897
Miss Petticoats (San Francisco) 1905
One Woman, The (road tryout) 1906
Ramona (Alessandro) (Los Angeles)
    1905
Ramona (Alessandro) (San Francisco)
    1905
Rosmersholm (Boston) 1905
Salome (Astor Theatre) 1907

1090
GRIFFITH, Gordon*
Caught in a Cabaret (kid)
Kid Auto Races at Venice (the kid)
Star Border, The (kid)
Tarzan of the Apes (the boy Tarzan)
Tillie's Punctured Romance (child)
Twenty Minutes of Love (child)

1091
GRIFFITH, Katherine (1858-1934)
Fast Company (Mrs. Van Huyler)
Little Princess, A

1092
GRIFFITH, Raymond (1896-1957)
Follies Girl, The
Royal Rogue, A
Scoundrel's Tale, The
Surf Girl, The (Captain's Assistant)

1093
GRIFFO*
Griffo-Barnett Fight

1094
GRIMWOOD, Herbert*
When the Clouds Roll By (Dr.
  Ulrich Metz)

1095
GRIPP, Harry*
Kathleen Mavourneen (Denis
  O'Rourke)

1096
GRISWOLD, James*
Girl of the Golden West, The
Virginian, The (stage driver)

1097
GRÖNROOS, Georg*
Ingeborg Holm

1098
GUILHENE, Jacques*
Jesus

1099
GUINAN, Texas (Mary Louise
  Guinan) (1891-1933)
Desert Vulture, The
Fuel of Life, The
Girl of Hell's Agony, The
Girl of the Rancho
Gun Woman, The
Letters of Fire
Little Miss Deputy
Love Brokers
My Lady Robin Hood
Night Raider, The
She Wolf
Stainless Barrier, The
Stage:
Hop o' My Thumb 1913

1100
GUISE, Thomas*
Bugle Call, The
Twenty-three and a Half Hours'
  Leave

1101
GUNN, Charles*
Firefly of Tough Luck, The

1102
GUY, Alice*
Misadventures of a Piece of Veal

1103
GWENN, Edmund (1875-1959)
Real Thing at Last, The

Stage:
Jealous Mistake, A (Globe Theatre;
  debut) 1899

- H -

1104
HACKATHORNE, George (1896-1940)
Armarilly of Clothesline Alley
Heart of Humanity
Huck and Tom
Shepherd of the Hills
Sue of the South
Tom Sawyer

1105
HACKETT, Albert*
Anne of Green Gables
Come out of the Kitchen
Ginger
Mickey

1106
HACKETT, Florence*
Beloved Adventurer, The (serial)
Siren of Corsica

1107
HACKETT, James K. (1869-1926)
Prisoner of Zenda, The
Stage:
Better 'Ole, The (Old Bill) 1918
Crisis, The 1902
Crown Prince, The 1904
Don Caesar's Return 1901
Grain of Dust, The 1912
Macbeth 1916
Out There 1918
Pride of Jennico, The
Prisoner of Zenda, The
Rise of Silas Lapham, The 1919
Walls of Jericho, The 1905

1108
HACKETT, Jeanette*
Beloved Adventurer, The (serial)

1109
HACKETT, Raymond (1903-1958)
Cruise of the Make-Believe, The

1110
HADFIELD, Harry*
Chimmie Fadden out West (Preston)

1111
HAGART, Dorothy*

Home Breaking Hound, A
Hunt, The

1112
HAGGERTY, Charles*
Zuzu, the Band Leader

1113
HA HA, Minnie*
Mickey

1114
HAINES, Ella*
His Bitter Pill (the mother)
His Wild Oats

1115
HAINES, Horace J. *
Moonshiners, The
Other Man, The

1116
HAINES, Robert T. (1870-1943)
Capitol, The
Victim, The
Stage:
Clothes 1906
Darling of the Gods, The 1902
In the Palace of the King 1900
Little Eylof 1910
Silver Box, The 1907
Writing on the Wall, The 1909

1117
HALE, Alan (Rufus Alan McKahan)
   (1892-1950)
By Man's Law
Cowboy and the Lady, The (debut)
Cricket on the Hearth, The
Jane Eyre
Lone Thief, The
Martin Chuzzlewit
Masks and Faces
Men and Women
Moral Suicide
One Hour
Price She Paid, The
Prisoner of Zenda, The
Puddin' Head Wilson
Scarlet Oath, The
Scrap of Paper, A
Strongheart
Trap, The
Whirlpool, The
Woman in the Case, The

1118
HALE, Creighton (Patric Fitzgerald)
   (1882-1965)

Cavell Case, The
Charity
Damsel in Distress
Exploits of Elaine, The (serial)
Honor of His House, The
Iron Claw, The (serial)
Love Cheat, The
Million Dollar Mystery, The (serial)
New Exploits of Elaine, The (serial)
Oh, Boy!
Romance of Elaine, The (serial)
Seven Pearls, The (serial)
Thirteenth Chair, The
Three of Us, The
Why Germany Must Pay
Wilson or the Kaiser
Woman the Germans Shot, The
Stage:
Moloch 1915

1119
HALL, Donald*
Anselo Lee
Carter Case, The (The Craig Kennedy
   Serial)
Christian, The
Moth, The
Mr. Barnes of New York

1120
HALL, Ella (1896-   )
Beauty in Chairs
Bitter Sweet
Bugler of Algiers, The
Charmer, The
Gates of Doom, The (serial)
Green Magic
Heart of Rachel, The
Jewell in Pawn, A
Little Orphan, The
Master Key, The (serial)
My Little Boy
New Love for Old
Spotted Lily, The
Three Mounted Men
Under the Top
We Are French
Which Woman?

1121
HALL, George*
Mystery of the Leaping Fish, The
   (Japanese accomplice)

1122
HALL, J. A. *
Yellow Menace, The (serial)

1123
HALL, J. Robinson*
Beloved Adventurer, The (serial)

1124
HALL, Lillian*
Little Women
Safety Curtain, The

1125
HALL, Thurston (1883-1959)
Cleopatra (Mark Anthony)
Squaw Man, The (Henry)
Tyrant Fear
Unpainted Woman, The
We Can't Have Everything (Peter
   Cheever)
Weaker Vessel, The
Stage:
Civilian Clothes 1919
Mrs. Wiggs of the Cabbage Patch
   1904
Only Girl, The 1914

1126
HALL, Winter (1878-   )
Captain Kidd, Jr.
City of Dim Faces
For Better, for Worse, (the doctor)
House of Silence, The
Money Corral, The
Primrose Ring, The
Red Lantern, The
Romance of the Redwoods (John
   Lawrence)
Squaw Man, The (Fletcher)
Till I Come Back to You (King
   Albert of Belgium)
Turn in the Road, The
When Bearcat Went Dry (Lone Stacey
   Macauley)
Why Smith Left Home

1127
HALL DAVIS, Lilian (1901-1933)
Admirable Crichton, The
Better 'Ole, The

1128
HALLAM, Henry*
God's Law and Man's
Kathleen Mavourneen (Sir John
   Clancarthy)
Mystery of the Sleeping Death, The

1129
HALLERAN, Edith*
Troublesome Step-daughters, The

1130
HALLOR, Ray (1900-   )
Amateur Orphan

1131
HALLWARD, M. *
Squaw Man, The (Lord Tommy)

1132
HAM, Harry*
Crazy by Proxy
Down by the Sea
Father and the Boys
Gay Deceiver, A
He Fell on the Beach
His Wedded Wife
Honeymooners, The
Kissing Sister
Seminary Scandal, A
Tramp, Tramp, Tramp

1133
HAMIL, Lucille*
Battle Cry of Peace, The

1134
HAMILTON, Hale (Hale Rice
   Hamilton) (1883-1942)
After His Own Heart
Five Thousand an Hour
Four-Flusher, The
Full of Pep
Her Painted Hero
In His Brother's Place
Johnny on the Spot
That's Good
Winning of Beatrice, The
Stage:
Get-Rich-Quick Wallingford 1910
Pair of Sixes, A 1914
Pit, The 1904

1135
HAMILTON, Jack "Shorty"*
Bucking Society
Gypsy Joe
His Busted Trust
Rough Knight, A
She Loved a Sailor

1136
HAMILTON, Lloyd V. (1891-1935)
Gentlemen's Ball
Ham and Bud series
Ham and the Garbage
Ham and the Piano Mover

1137
HAMILTON, Mahlon (1885-1960)
Daddy Long Legs
Danger Mark, The
Death Dance, The
Eternal Question, The
Her Kingdom of Dreams
Hidden Hand, The (serial)
In Old Kentucky

1138
HAMLISH, Joseph*
Gold and the Woman (Murray)

1139
HAMMERSTEIN, Elaine (1897-1948)
Accidental Honeymoon
Argyle Case, The
Beatrice Fairfax (serial)
Co-Respondent, The
Country Cousin, The
Her Man
Love or Fame
Mad Love
Wanted for Murder
Stage:
Hi Jinks 1913

1140
HAMMON, William*
Children of the Sea

1141
HAMMOND, Gilmore*
Bobbie of the Ballet
Gilded Spider, The
Mark of Cain, The (Jake)

1142
HAMMOND, Virginia*
Battler, The
Discard, The (debut)
Hand Invisible, The
Miss Crusoe
World to Live In, The

1143
HAMPDEN, Walter (Walter Hampden
    Dougherty) (1879-1955)
Dragon's Claw, The
Stage:
Be Calm Camilla 1918
Good Gracious Annabelle 1916
Master Builder, The 1907
Servant in the House, The 1908
Tempest, The 1916

1144
HAMPER, Genevieve*

Spider and the Fly, The
Wife's Sacrifice, A
Stage:
Oedipus Rex 1911
Shakespearean repertory 1918

1145
HANAWAY, Frank*
Great Train Robbery, The

1146
HANDFORTH, Ruth*
Intolerance (Brown Eye's Mother)
Siren's Song, The (Aunt Caroline)

1147
HANDWORTH, Octavia*
Lubin player 1913

1148
HANDYSIDE, Clarence*
His Picture in the Paper (Proteus
    Prindle)

1149
HANFORD, Roy*
Bull's Eye (serial)
Lion's Claw, The (serial)
Trey o' Hearts, The (serial)

1150
HANLON, Alma*
Gold and the Woman (Hester)
Weakness of Man, The

1151
HANNA, Franklyn*
Her Double Life (the doctor)

1152
HANNAN, Patricia*
Lombardi, Ltd.

1153
HANSEN, Juanita (1897-1961)
Black Eyes and Blue
Brass Bullet, The (serial)
Broadway Love (Cherry Blow)
Clever Dummy, A (a leading lady)
Dangers of a Bride
Fast Company (Alice Vandervelt)
Finishing Touch, The
Glory
His Pride and Shame
Lombardi, Ltd.
Mack Sennett comedies 1917
Martyrs of the Alamo
Mating of Marcella, The
Midnight Romance, A

Poppy Girl's Husband, The
Rough Lover, The
Rough Riding Romance
Royal Rogue, A
Sea Flower, The
Secret of the Submarine, The (serial)
Whose Baby?

1154
HANSON, Gladys (1887-   )
Havoc, The
Straight Road, The
Stage:
Builder of Bridges, The 1909
Governor's Lady, The 1912
Our American Cousin 1908

1155
HANSON, Lars (1887-1965)
Dolken
Erotikon
Engeborg Holm (debut)
Stroke of Midnight, The

1156
HANSON, Spook*
Busted Hearts
Chickens
Frenzied Finance
This Way Out
Try Out, The
Ups and Downs

1157
HARBAUGH, Carl*
Carmen (Escamillo)
Serpent, The (Prince Valanoff)

1158
HARDIN, Neil*
Neglected Wife, The (serial)

1159
HARDING, Ben*
Busher, The

1160
HARDWICKE, Sir Cedric (Cedric
    Webster Hardwicke) (1893-1964)
Riches and Rogues 1913
Stage:
Monk and the Woman, The (debut)
    (Lyceum Theatre) 1912

1161
HARDY, Oliver (Oliver Norville
    Hardy) (1892-1957)
Aerial Joyride, An

All for a Girl
Ambitious Ethel
Artist, The
Artistic Atmosphere
Artists and Models
Aunt Bill
Avenging Bill
Babe's School Days
Baby
Baby Doll
Back Stage
Back to the Farm
Bandmaster, The
Barber, The
Battle Royal, A
Better Halves
Billy West comedies 1918
Boycotted Baby
Brave Ones, The
Bright and Early
Bungalow Bungle, A
Bungles' Elopement
Bungles Enforces the Law
Bungles Lands a Job
Bungles' Rainy Day
Bungs and Bunglers
Busted Hearts
Candy Kid, The
Candy Trail, The
Cannibal King, The
Charley's Aunt
Chickens
Chief Cook, The
Cleaning Time
Clothes Make the Man
Cupid's Rival
Cupid's Target
Day at School, A
Dead Letter, The
Dough-Nuts
Dreamy Knights
Edison Bugg's Invention
Ethel's Romeos
Expensive Visit, An
Fat and Fickle
Fatty's Fatal Fun
Female Cop, The
Flips and Flops
Fly Cop, The
Freckled Fish
Free lanced for Pathé, Gaumont
    Wharton, Edison, and Vitagraph
    1917-1918
Frenzied Finance, A
Genius, The
Goat, The
Guilty One, The
Guns and the Anarchists

Handy Man, The
Haunted Hat, The
He Winked and Won
Healthy and Happy
Her Choice
Hero, The
Heroes, The
Hired and Fired
His Day Out
Hobo, The
Hop the Bellhop
Human Hounds
Hungry Hearts
It Happened in Pikersville
Janitor's Joyful Job, A
Jimmy Aubrey (one reelers) 1917
King Solomon
Life Savers
Love and Duty
Love Bugs, The
Lucky Dog (a robber; his first film
   with Stan Laurel)
Lucky Strike, A
Maid to Order, A
Mama's Boys
Mates and Models
Matilda's Legacy
Messenger, The
Millionaire, The
Mixed Flats
Mix-up in Hearts, A
Modiste, The
Mother's Child
Mules and Mortgages
Nerve and Gasoline
Never Again
New Butler, The
One Too Many
Orderly, The
Other Girl, The
Outwitting Dad (debut)
Paper Hanger's Helper, The
Pest, The
Pins Are Lucky
Pipe Dreams
Playmates
Plump and Runt (Plumb) (a series)
   1916-1917
Pokes and Jabs series 1914-1915
Precious Parcel, A
Prize Baby
Prize Winners
Prospector, The
Reformer, The
Rheumatic Joint, A
Rogue, The
Royal Blood
Safety Worst

Schemers, The
Scholar, The
Sea Dogs
Serenade, The
Shoddy the Tailor
Side-Tracked
Simp and the Sophomores, The
Slave, The
Smuggler's Daughter, The
Something in Her Eye
Soubrette and the Simp, The
Spaghetti
Spaghetti a la Mode
Spaghetti and Lottery
Squabs and Squabbles
Star Boarder, The
Station Master, The
Stickey Affair, A
Straight and Narrow, The
Stranded
Stranger, The
Switches and Sweeties
Terrible Tragedy, A
Their Honeymoon
Their Vacation
Thirty Days
This Way Out
Three Rings and a Goat
Tootsies and Tamales
Tramps, The
Try-Out, The
Twin Flats
Twin Sisters
Ups and Downs
Villain, The
Wanted: a Bad Man
Warm Reception, A
Water Cure, The
What a Cinch!
What He Forgot
What's Sauce for the Goose
Who Stole the Dogies?
Yaps and Yokels

1162
HARDY, Sam*
Woman's Experience, A

1163
HARE, Lumsden (1875-1964)
Arms and the Woman
As in a Looking Glass (debut)
Avalanche, The
Barbary Sheep
Country Cousin, The
Love's Crucible

1164
HARKNESS, Carter B. *
Gold and the Woman (Leelo Duskara)

1165
HARLAM, Macey*
Flame of the Desert

1166
HARLAN, Kenneth (1895-1967)
Betsy's Burglars (debut)
Bread
Cheerful Givers
Girl Who Came Back, The
Hoodlum, The
Lash of Power
Man's Man, A
Midnight Madness
Model's Confession, The
Turning Point, The
Whim, The
Wine Girl, The
Stage:
More Than Queen 1902

1167
HARLAN, Otis (1865-1940)
Chronicles of Bloom Center
Stage:
Little Boy Blue 1911

1168
HARLEY, Ed*
Girl of the Golden West, The (Old
    Minstrel)

1169
HARMON, Henry*
Out of the Fog

1170
HARMON, Pat (1890-   )
Busher, The
Speed Maniac, The

1171
HARRIS, Caroline*
Madame Butterfly

1172
HARRIS, Joseph*
Oh, Daddy!

1173
HARRIS, Lenore*
Betty of Graystone
Stage:
Lights o' London, The 1911

Our Betters 1917
Whip, The 1912

1174
HARRIS, Marcia*
Anne of Green Gables
Foundling, The
Kathleen Mavourneen (Lady Clancarthy)
Poor Little Rich Girl, The
Prunelia

1175
HARRIS, Mildred (1905-1944)
Bad Boy
Borrowed Clothes
Doctor and the Woman, The
Enoch Arden
For Husbands Only
Home
Hoodoo Anne
Intolerance (a harem girl)
Old Fashioned Young Man, An
Old Folks at Home
Price of a Good Time, The
Quest of the Holy Grail
Warrens of Virginia, The (bit)
When a Girl Loves
Wizard of Oz, The

1176
HARRIS, Winifred*
Panthea

1177
HARRISON, Jimmy*
Bad Boy
Christie comedies (14) 1917
Kids and Kidlets
Madame Bo-Beep
Nearly Newlyweds
Reno, All Change

1178
HARRON, Jessie*
Hearts of the World (refugee)

1179
HARRON, Johnny (1903-   )
Hearts of the World (Baywith Barrell)

1180
HARRON [Mrs.]*
Hearts of the World (the mother)

1181
HARRON, Mary*
Hearts of the World (wounded girl)

1189
HARTE, Betty*
Pride of Jennico, The
Roman, The

1190
HARTFORD, David*
Shootin' Mad (John Cowan)
Tess of the Storm Country

1191
HARTMAN, Gretchen (1897-)
Bandbox
Fantine
House without Children
Les Miserables
Mary Jane's Pa
Painted Madonna
Stage:
Mary Jane's Pa 1908

1192
HARVE, M.*
Shylock

1193
HARVEY, Fletcher*
Melting Pot, The

1194
HARVEY, Jack*
Imp player 1910

1195
HASSELL, George*
Old Dutch

1196
HASTINGS, Carey L.*
Country Girl, The

1197
HASTINGS, Seymour*
Her Grave Mistake (Isabel's Father)
Miner's Romance, A (Dave Williams)
Ranch Romance, A (John Preston)

1198
HATCH, William Riley*
Hazel Kirke
Lady Audley's Secret (Luke Martin)

1199
HATHAWAY, Jean*
Adventures of Peg o' the Ring, The
   (serial)
Bobbie of the Ballet
Master Key, The (serial)
Purple Mask, The (serial)

1200
HATHAWAY, Lillian*
Serpent, The (Martsa Lazar)

1201
HATTON, Raymond (1892-)
Arab, The (mysterious messenger)
Arizona (Tom)
Chimmie Fadden (Larry)
Circus Man, The
Dub, The
Everywoman
Experimental Marriage
Firefly of France, The
For Better, for Worse (Bud)
Girl of the Golden West, The (Castro)
Golden Chance, The (Jimmy)
Honorable Friend, The
Joan, the Woman (Charles VIII, King
   of France)
Kindling (Steve)
Little American, The (Count Jules
   de Destin)
Love Burglar, The
Love Mask, The
Male and Female (Ernest Wooley)
Nan of Music Mountain
Oliver Twist
Public Opinion
Romance of the Redwoods (Dick
   Rowland)
Source, The
Sowers, The
Temptation (Baron Cheurial)
Unafraid, The (Russian valet)
We Can't Have Everything (Marquis
   of Strathdene)
Whispering Chorus, The (John
   Trimble)
Wild Goose Chase, The (Betty's
   Father)
Woman God Forgot, The (Montezuma)
You're Fired!

1202
HAUBER, Billy*
Lion and the Girl, The

1203
HAVER, Phyllis (1899-1960)
Sultan's Wife, The

1204
HAWLEY, Dudley*
American Widow, An
Stage:
Up in Mabel's Room 1919

1205
HAWLEY, Ormi (1890-1942)
Antics of Ann, The
Insurrection
Prince Ubaldo
Ragged Earl, The
Road Called Straight, The
Runaway Romany (Anitra St. Clair)
Splendid Romance, The
Temptation
Where Love Leads

1206
HAWLEY, Wanda (1897-)
Derelict, The
Everywoman
For Better, for Worse (Betty Hoyt)
Greased Lightning
Gypsy Trail, The
Lottery Man, The
Mr. Fix-It (Mary)
Old Wives for New (Sophy)
Pair of Silk Stockings, A
Peg o' My Heart (never released)
Pirates of the Sky
Secret Service
Virtuous Sinners
Way of a Man with a Maid, The
We Can't Have Everything (Kedzie
    Thropp)
You're Fired!

1207
HAY, Mary (1901-1957)
Hearts of the World (dancer)

1208
HAYAKAWA, Sessue (1889-1973)
After Five Years
Alien Souls
Ambassador's Envoy, The
Vanzai
Bonds of Honor
Bottle Imp, The
Bravest Way, The
Call of the East
Cheat, The (Tori)
City of Dim Faces
Clue, The
Courageous Coward, The
Daughter of the Dragon
Debt, The
Dragon Painter, The
Each to His Own Kind
Forbidden Paths
Gray Horizon
Hashimura to Go
Hidden Pearls, The

His Birthright
His Highness, the Beggar
Honor of His House
Honorable Friend, The
Jaguar's Claws, The
Last of the Line (Tiah)
Loyalty
Man Beneath, The
Man Who Laughed Last, The
Mysterious Prince, The
Only a Nigger
Scarlet Sin, A
Secret Game, A
Secret Sin
Temple of Dusk
Temptation (an opera admirer)
Tong Man, The
Typhoon
White Man's Law
Wrath of the Gods

1209
HAYDEL, Dorothy*
Great Secret, The (serial)

1210
HAYES, Alice*
Tale of Two Nations, A

1211
HAYES, Frank* (-1924)
Bath House Blunder, A
Fatty and Mabel Adrift
Fatty and Mabel at the San Diego
    Exposition
Fido's Fate
Her Marble Heart
His Uncle Dudley
Hoosier Romance, A
Mabel, Fatty and the Law
Madcap Ambrose
Stolen Magic

1212
HAYES, Helen (Helen Hayes Brown)
    (1900-)
Jean and the Calico Doll
Weavers of Life, The
Stage:
Clarence 1919
Dear Brutus 1918
Never Homes, The 1911
Old Dutch 1909
Penrod 1914
Pollyanna (on tour) 1918-19
Prodigal Husband, The 1914
Royal Family, The 1905 (debut)
Stock in Washington, D. C. 1913-16
Summer Widowers, The 1910

1213
HAYWOOD, Doris*
Devil's Daughter, The (Franceska
  Silvia)

1214
HAZELTONE [Miss]*
Jane Eyre

1215
HEADRICK, Richard (1917-)
Should a Woman Tell?

1216
HEARN, Edward (1888-)
Her Bitter Cup
Idle Wives
Into the Night
Last of His People, The
Lost Express, The (serial)
Lure of Luxury, The
Seekers, The
Treason
Undercurrent
White Scar

1217
HEARN, Fred*
Bruden of Proof, The (William Kemp)
Getting Mary Married (William
  Carew)

1218
HEDLUND, Guy*
Bobby, the Coward
Modern Prodigal, The

1219
HELD, Anna (1873-1918)
Madame la Presidente
Stage:
Follow Me 1916
Higgledy Piggledy 1904
Little Duchess, The 1901
Mam'selle Napoleon 1903
Miss Innocence 1908
Papa's Wife 1900
Parisian Model, The 1906

1220
HEMING, Violet (1893-)
Almost Married
Circumstances
Danger Trail
Everywoman
Judgment House
Turn of the Wheel
Stage:

Fluffy Ruffles 1908
Lie, The 1914
Three Faces East 1918
Under Fire 1915

1221
HEMPHILL, F. L.*
Lass of the Lumberlands (serial)
Railroad Raiders, The (serial)

1222
HENABERRY, Joseph*
Birth of a Nation, The (Abraham
  Lincoln)
Intolerance (Adm. Coligny)

1223
HENDERSON, Del (1877-1956)
Battle at Elderbush Gulch, The
Beautiful Adventure
Child's Impulse, A
Comrades (Marmaduke Bracegirdle)
Courage for Two
Crooked Road, The
Imposter, The
In the Days of '49
Intolerance
Last Drop of Water, The
Lines of White on a Sullen Sea
Lonedale Operator, The
Making of a Man, The
Massacre, The
My Wife
Outcast, The
Please Help Emily
Purgation, The
Road to France, The
Runaway, The
String of Pearls, A
Teaching Dad to Like Her
That Chink at Golden Gulch
Those Hickville Boys
When a Man Loves

1224
HENDERSON, Grace*
Comrades
Corner in Wheat, A
Enoch Arden, Part I
Her Sacrifice
His Trust Fulfilled
Lucky Jim
Marked Time-Table, The
Midnight Cupid, A
Old Confectioner's Mistake, The
Purgation, The
String of Pearls, A
Sunshine through the Dark

Unseen Enemy, An
Unveiling, The
Usurer, The

1225
HENDERSON, Jack*
Bubbles of Trouble
Bucking Society
Charlie Chaplin's Burlesque on
    Carmen
Dog Catcher's Love, A
Royal Rogue, A

1226
HENDRICKS, Ben*
Galley Slave, The (Mr. Blaine)
Temperamental Wife, A

1227
HENDRY, Anita*
Peach Basket Hat, The
Road to the Heart, The

1228
HENLEY, Hobart*
Graft (serial)

1229
HENLEY, Rosina*
Sign of the Cross, The

1230
HENRY, Gale (1893-   )
One reel comedies 1919

1231
HENSON, Leslie (1891-1958)
Lifeguardsman, The
Real Thing at Last, The
Wanted, A Widow

1232
HEPWORTH, Baby*
Rescued by Rover

1233
HEPWORTH, Cecil (1874-1953)
Blind Fate
Coming Thro' the Rye
Rescued by Rover

1234
HEPWORTH, Mrs. Cecil*
Rescued by Rover

1235
HERBERT, Gwynne*
Toilers, The

1236
HERBERT, Henry J. (1879-1942)
Ghosts of Yesterday

1237
HERBERT, Holmes (Edward Singer)
    (1882-1956)
Doll's House, A
Whirlpool, The
White Heather

1238
HERBERT, Jack*
Squaw Man, The (Nick)

1239
HERNANDEZ, George*
Mary Regan

1240
HERNDON, Anita*
Imp player 1910

1241
HERRING, Aggie (-1938)
Cupid Forecloses
Home
Honor Thy Name
Hoodlum, The
Man's Fight, A
Millionaire Vagrant, The
Within the Cup
Yankee Princess, A

1242
HERSHOLT, Jean (1886-1956)
Hell's Hinges (a townsperson)
Soul Herder, The

1243
HEWITT, Russell*
Anne of Green Gables

1244
HEYES, Herbert (1889-1958)
Adventures of Ruth, The (serial)
Darling of Paris, The (Capt. Phoebus)
Deliverance
Heart of Rachel, The
Heart of the Sunset
Salome (Sejanus)
Tiger Woman, The (Mark Harris)
Under Two Flags (Bertie Cecil)
    (debut)
Vixen, The (Knowles Murray)

1245
HICKMAN, Alfred*

Fall of the Romanoff's, The
Here Comes the Bride
Mad Woman, The
Master Key, The (serial)

1246
HICKMAN, Howard (1880-1949)
Alias Jimmy Valentine
Civilization (Count Ferdinaud)
First Command, The
Jane
Matrimony
Social Ambition
Society Sinners

1247
HICKS, Sir Seymour (1871-1949)
Always Tell Your Wife
David Garrick
Prehistoric Love Story, A
Scrooge
Seymour Hicks and Ellaline Terriss

1248
HIERS, Walter (1893-1933)
Bill Henry
Experimental Marriage, An
Fear Woman, The
Hard Boiled
It Pays to Advertise
Leave It to Susan
Lesson, The
Seventeen
Spotlight Sadie
Turning Point, The
When Doctors Disagree
Why Smith Left Home

1249
HIGBY, Wilbur*
Nugget Nell
True Heart Susie (William's Father)

1250
HILL, Bonnie*
Brat, The

1251
HILL, Lee*
Station Content

1252
HILL, Maud*
When Men Desire (Lola Santez)

1253
HILLIARD, Harry*
Cheating Herself

Destiny
Every Girl's Dream
Heart and Soul (John Niehl)
Her Greatest Love (Lucas Coresze)
Little Rowdy, The
Little White Savage, The
Romance of Rome, A
Romeo and Juliet (Romeo)
Sneak, The
Successful Adventure, The

1254
HINCKLEY, William L. *
Martha's Vindication
Out of Bondage
Reputation

1255
HINES, Johnny (1895-)
As Ye Sow
Dancer's Peril, The
Eastward Ho!
Heart of Gold
Just Sylvia
Little Intruder, The
Man of the House, The
Miss Petticoats
Neighbors
Three Green Eyes
Tillie Wakes Up

1256
HITCHCOCK, Charles*
Essanay player 1912

1257
HITCHCOCK, Raymond (1865-1929)
My Valet
Stolen Magic
Village Scandal, The
Stage:
Beauty Shop, The 1914
Betty 1916
Easy Dawson 1905
Gallop, The 1906
Hitchy-Koo 1917
King Dodo 1902
Man Who Owns Broadway, The 1909
Red Widow, The 1911
Three Little Lambs 1900
Yankee Consul, The 1904
Yankee Tourist, A 1907

1258
HOBBS, Jack (1893-)
Lady Clare, The
Love's Legacy
Tom Brown's Schooldays

Hodge

1259
HODGE, Runa*
Fool There Was, A (the child)

1260
HOFFMAN, H. F.*
East Lynne (Otway Bethel)

1261
HOFFMAN, Otto (1879-)
Busher, The
City of Comrades
Egg Crate Wallop, The
Family Skeleton, The
Greased Lightning
His Own Home Town
Home Town Girl
Nine o'Clock Town, A
Playing the Game
Sheriff's Son, The
String Beans
Twenty-Three and a Half Hours'
  Leave

1262
HOFFMAN, Ruby*
Fatal Ring, The (serial)
Mistress Nell

1263
HOIER, Esther W.*
Destruction (Josine)

1264
HOLDEN, Harry*
Kaiser, the Beast of Berlin, The
  (General Joffre)

1265
HOLDERNESS, Fay*
Blind Husbands (vamp waitress)
Hearts of the World (Innkeeper)

1266
HOLDING, Thomas*
Beckoning Roads
Danger Zone, The
Daughters of Destiny
Eternal City, The
Lady of Red Butte, The
Lone Wolf's Daughter, The
Magda
Moment Before, The
Peace of Roaring River, The
Redeeming Love
Tangled Threads
Vanity Pool
White Pearl, The

1267
HOLLAND, Edward*
Almost an Actress (the heavy)

1268
HOLLINGSWORTH, Alfred*
Hell's Hinges (Silk Miller)
Leave It to Susan
Man's Country, A (Oliver Kemp)

1269
HOLLIS, Hylda*
Secret of the Submarine, The (serial)

1270
HOLLISTER, Alice (1890-)
Brand, The
Destroyer, The
Don Caesar de Bazan
From the Manger to the Cross
Her Better Self
Kerry Gow, The
Knife, The
Lotus Woman
Sister's Burden, A
Vampire
Vampire's Trail, The
Yellow Sunbonnet, The

1271
HOLLOWAY, Carol*
Fighting Trail, The (serial)
Iron Test, The (serial)
Perils of Thunder Mountain (serial)
Tenderfoot, The
Vengeance and the Woman (serial)

1272
HOLMES, Gerda*
Robin Hood

1273
HOLMES, Helen (1892-1950)
Danger Trail
Desperate Deed, A
Fatal Fortune, The (serial)
Girl and the Game, The (Helen)
  (serial)
Hazard's of Helen, The (title role)
  (serial)
Hide and Seek
Lass of the Lumberlands (serial)
Lost Express, The (serial)
Medicine Bend
Railroad Raiders, The (serial)
Whispering Smith

1274
HOLMES, Lois*
Cinders of Love

1275
HOLMES, Stuart (1887-)
Clemenceau Case, The (Constantin)
Daughter of the Gods, A
Dust of Desire
East Lynne (Capt. Levison)
Galley Slave, The (Antoine)
Ghosts of Yesterday
Her Double Life (Lloyd Stanley)
How Mrs. Murray Saved the Army
In the Stretch
Isle of Jewels
Life's Shop Window
Little Intruder, The
New Moon, The
Other Man's Wife, The
Poor Rich Man
Scarlet Letter, The
Sins of Men, The
Sins of the Children
Treason
Way of a Woman, The
When Men Betray
Wild Girl, The

1276
HOLMES, Taylor (1872-1959)
Efficiency Edgar's Courtship
Fools for Luck
It's a Bear
Pair of Sixes, A
Regular Fellow, A
Ruggles of Red Gap (title role)
Small Town Guy, The
Taxi
Three Black Eyes
Twenty Dollars a Week
Two-Bit Seats
Uneasy Money
Upside Down
Stage:
His Majesty Bunker Bean 1916
Million, The 1911
Third Party, The 1914
Trilby 1915

1277
HOLT, Edwart*
Tiger Woman, The (Mr. Harris)

1278
HOLT, Edwin*
Heart and Soul (Silas Croft)
Romeo and Juliet (Capulet)

1279
HOLT, George*
Fighting Trail, The (serial)
Vengeance and the Woman (serial)

1280
HOLT, Jack (1888-1951)
Broken Coin, The (serial)
Cheating Cheaters
Cigarette, That's All, A
Claw, The
Desert Wooing, A
For Better, for Worse (Crusader)
Held by the Enemy
Honor of His House, The
Joan, the Woman
Kitty Kelly, M. D.
Liberty, a Daughter of the U. S. A.
   (serial)
Life Line, The
Little American, The (Karl
   VonAustreim)
Lone Wolf, The
Marriage Ring, The
Midnight Romance, A
Sporting Chance, A
Squaw Man, The (Cash Hawkins)
Victory (Axel Heyst)
Woman Thou Gavest Me, The

1281
HOLUBAR, Alan*
Twenty Thousand Leagues under the
   Sea

1282
HOOPS, Arthur*
Esmeralda
Gretna Green
Mistress Nell
Such a Little Queen
Stage:
Alice of Old Vincennes 1901
Prisoner of Zenda, The 1908

1283
HOPE, Gloria (1901-)
Burglar by Proxy
Day She Paid, The
Gay Lord Quex, The
Great Love, The (Jessie Lovewell)
Heart of Rachel, The
Hushed Hour
Law of the North, The
Naughty! Naughty!
Outcasts of Poker Flats, The
Riders of the Law, The

1284
HOPKINS, Clyde*
Intolerance (Jenkin's secretary)
Prince of Power, The

1285
HOPKINS, Mae*
Beatrice Fairfax (serial)

1286
HOPPER, DeWolfe (DeWolfe Casey
   Hopper) (1858-1935)
Casey at the Bat
DonQuixote
Girl and the Mummy, The
Intolerance (a soldier)
Mr. Goode, Samaritan
Poor Papa
Puppets
Rough Knight, A
Sunshine Dad
Stage:
Better 'Ole, The (Old Bill) 1918
Fiddle-dee-dee 1900
Happyland 1905
H. M. S. Pinafore 1911
Hop o' My Thumb 1913
Mr. Pickwick 1903
Passing Show of 1917, The 1917
Patience 1912
Wang 1904
Yeomen of the Guard 1915

1287
HOPPER, DeWolfe, Jr. (DeWolfe
   Casey Hopper, Jr.)*
Sunshine Dad

1288
HOPPER, Hedda (Elda Furry)
   (1891-1966)
Battle of Hearts, The
By Right of Purchase
Her Excellency, the Governor
Isle of Conquest
Men Women Marry, The
Moriarity
Nearly Married
Seven Keys to Baldpate
Third Degree
Virtuous Wives
Stage:
Be Calm, Camilla 1918

1289
HOPSON, Violet*
Adventures of Dick Dolan, The
American Heiress, The

Baby on the Barge, The
Barnaby Rudge
Blindness of Fortune, The
Bunch of Violets, A
Canker of Jealousy, The
Chimes, The
Cobweb, The
Comin' Thro' the Rye
Cry of the Captive, The
Curtain's Secret, The
Daughter of Eve, A
Drake's Love Story
Eternal Triangle, The
Exploits of Tubby, The (series) 1916
Fortune at Stake, A
Gamble for Love, A
Gentleman Rider, The
Girl Who Played the Game, The
Grand Babylon Hotel
Heart of Midlothian, The
Her Marriage Lines
House of Fortescue, The
House Opposite, The
In the Gloaming
Irresistible Flapper, The
Jewel Thieves Outwitted, The
Life's Dark Road
Love in a Laundry
Man from India, The
Man Who Stayed at Home, The
Marriage of William Ashe, The
Missing the Tide
Molly Bawn
Munition Girl's Romance, A
Nightbirds of London, The
Outrage, The
Quarry Mystery, The
Ragged Messenger, The
Recalling of John Grey, The
Schemers, The
Second String, The
Shepherd of Sould, The
Sisters in Arms
Snare, The
Snow in the Desert
Soul's Crucifixion, A
Sowing the Wind
Stress of Circumstances
Terror of the Air, The
Time, the Great Healer
Tragedy of Basil Grieve, The
Trelawney of the Wells
Turf Conspiracy, A
Umbrellas They Could Not Lose, The
Unfit
Vicar of Wakefield, The
Ware Case, The
White Boys, The

White Hope, The
Woman Wins, The

1290
HORNE, W.*
Graft (serial)

1291
HORNER, Violet*
Marble Heart, The

1292
HORTON, Clara (1904-   )
Eclair player 1914
Everywoman
Girl from Outside, The
Huck and Tom
In Wrong
Tom Sawyer

1293
HOSFORD, Maud*
Mrs. Wiggs of the Cabbage Patch

1294
HOTELY, Mae*
Lubin comedy series with Oliver
    Hardy) 1914
New Butler, The

1295
HOUDINI, Harry (Ehrich Weiss)
    (1874-1926)
Grim Game, The
Master Mystery, The (serial)
Stage:
Vaudeville 1913

1296
HOUSE, Marguerite*
Warrens of Virginia, The (Betty
    Warren)

1297
HOUSMAN, Arthur (1890-1937)
All Woman
Back to the Woods
Bondage of Barbara, The
Brown of Harvard
Gay Lord Quex, The
Red, White and Blue Blood
Toby's Bow

1298
HOWARD, Arthur*
Broken Blossoms (Burrow's manager)

1299
HOWARD, Helen*
Brass Buttons

1300
HOWARD, Leslie (Howard Stainer)
    (1893-1943)
Happy Warriors, The
Lackey and the Lady, The

1301
HOWARD, Vincente*
Vengeance and the Woman (serial)

1302
HOWARD, Wanda*
Raven, The

1303
HOWE, Betty*
Beatrice Fairfax (serial)
Scarlet Runner, The (serial)

1304
HOWELL, Alice (1892-   )
Caught in a Cabaret
Caught in the Rain
His Musical Career
Knock-Out, The
Laughing Gas (the wife)
Mabel's Married Life
Shot in the Excitement
Tillie's Punctured Romance

1305
HOWLAND, Jobyna (1880-1936)
Her Only Way
Way of a Woman, The
What Might Have Been
Stage:
Little Journey, A 1918
Passing Show of 1912, The 1912
Third Party, The 1914

1306
HOWLAND, Olin*
Independence b' Gosh

1307
HOXIE, Jack (Jack Hartford Hoxie)
    (1885-1965)
Blue Blazes Rawden
Dumb Girl of Portici, The
Gallopin' Through
Hazards of Helen, The (serial)
Joan, the Woman
Lightning Bryce (title role) (serial)
Nan of Music Mountain

Riders of the Law, The
Valley of the Giants, The

1308
HOYT, Arthur*
Bringing Home Father
Broadway Arizona
Lash, The
Little Partner, The
Man Who Took a Chance, The
Polly Ann
Show-Down, The

1309
HUFF, Louise*
Bunker Bean
Caprice
Crook of Dreams, The
Freckles
Ghost House, The
Great Expectations
Heart of Gold
In the Bishop's Carriage
Jack and Jill
Little Intruder, The
Oh, You Women!
Sea Waif
Seventeen
Spirit of 17, The
T' Other Dear Charmer
Tom Sawyer
Varmint, The
What Money Can't Buy
Wild Youth

1310
HUGHES, Gareth (1894-1965)
And the Children Pay
Eyes of Youth, The
Ginger
Mrs. Wiggs of the Cabbage Patch
Red Viper, The
Woman under Oath
Stage:
Guilty Man, The 1916
Moloch 1915

1311
HUGHES, Lloyd (1897-1960)
Haunted Bedroom, The
Heart of Humanity, The
Impossible Susan
Indestructible Wife, The
Satan, Jr.
Turn in the Road, The
Virtuous Thief, The

1312
HULETTE, Gladys*

Active Life of Dolly of the Dailies,
    The (serial)
Annexing Bill
Candy Girl, The
Cigarette Girl, The
Crooked Romance, A
For Sale
Her New York
Hiawatha
Last of the Carnabys, The
Miss Nobody
Mrs. Slacker
Over the Hill
Pots and Pans Peggy
Streets of Illusion, The
Stuff Dreams Are Made Of, The
Thanhouser player 1914
Waifs
Stage:
Bluebird, The 1910
Little Women 1912

1313
HULING, Lorraine*
King Lear
Unwelcome Mrs. Hatch, The

1314
HULL, Henry (1890-)
Volunteer, The
Stage:
Man Who Came Back, The 1916
39 East 1919

1315
HUMAN, William*
Adventures of Ruth, The (serial)

1316
HUMPHREY, Ola*
Under the Crescent (serial)

1317
HUMPHREY, Orral*
Diamond from the Sky, The (serial)
Midnight Man, The (serial)
Sequel to the Diamond from the Sky,
    The (serial)

1318
HUMPHREY, William (1874-)
Napoleon
Vitagraph player 1911

1319
HUNTER, Edna*
Deluxe Annie
Prince in a Pawn Shop, A

1320
HUNTER, George*
Lightning Bryce (serial)

1321
HUNTLEY, Fred*
Everywoman
For Better, for Worse (Colonial
    soldier)
Heart o' the Hills
Heart of the Wetona, The
Johanna Enlists

1322
HUNTLEY, Luray*
Intolerance (Uplifter)

1323
HURLEY, Julia*
Gold and the Woman (Duskara's
    Squaw)

1324
HURST, Brandon (1866-1947)
Via Wireless
Stage:
Two Women 1910

1325
HURST, Paul C. (1889-1953)
Champion of the Law, A
Lass of the Lumberlands (serial)
Lightning Bryce (serial)
Railroad Raiders, The (serial)

1326
HUTCHINSON, Charles*
Golden God, The
Great Gamble, The (serial)
Hawk, The
Hidden Aces
Mystic Hour, The
Wolves of Kultur, The (serial)

1327
HUTTON, Lucille*
Miracle Man, The (Ruth Higgins)

1328
HYDE, Harry*
Her Awakening
Narrow Road, The
Punishment, The
Root of Evil, The
String of Pearls, A

1329
HYLAND, Peggy (Gladys Hutchinson)*

Angel of Mons
Bonnie Annie Laurie
Caste
Caught in the Act
Chattel, The
Cheating Herself
Cowardice Court
Debt of Honor, A
Enemy, The
Fetters of Fear
Girl with No Rights, The
In the Ranks
Infelice
Infidelity
Intrigue
John Halifax, Gentleman
Lochinvar
Marriages Are Made
Miss Adventure
Official Chaperone
Other Men's Daughters
Other Woman, The
Pair of Spectacles, A
Peg of the Pirates
Persuasive Peggy
Price of Silence, The
Rebellious Bride, The
Rose of the South
Sally Bishop
Sir James Mortimer's Wager
Twixt Cup and Lip

- I -

1330
ILLINGTON, Margaret (1881-1934)
Inner Shrine, The (debut)
Sacrifice
Stage:
His House in Order 1906
Kindling 1911
Lie, The 1914
Mrs. Leffingwell's Boots 1905
Our Little Wife 1916
Thief, The 1907
Two Orphans, The 1904

1331
INCE, John Edwards*
Madame Sphinx

1332
INCE, Ralph (1887-1937)
Battle Hymn of the Republic
Darkening Trail, The
He Danced Himself to Death
Lady and the Lake, The

Lincoln's Gettysburg Address
One Flag at Last
Perfect Lover, The
Regiment of Two
Serpents, The
Seventh Son, The
Shadow of the Past
Virtuous Men

1333
INCE, Thomas (1882-1924)
Anthony and Cleopatra
Julius Caesar
Imp Player 1910
Merchant of Venice, The
Richard III
Seven Ages

1334
INGRAHAM, Lloyd*
Intolerance (Judge)

1335
INGRAM, Rex (Rex Fitchcock)
     (1892-1950)
Artist's Madonna, The

1336
INSLEE, Charles*
Adventures of Dolly, The
After Many Years
Bank, The
Burglar's Mistake, A
Call of the Wild, The
Confidence
Cord of Life, The
Cricket on the Hearth, The
For a Wife's Honor
For Love of Gold
Girl and the Outlaw, The
Girls and Daddy, The
Her First Biscuits
His New Job
His Wife's Mother
Lure of the Gown, The
Mr. Jones at the Ball
Money Mad
One Touch of Nature
Red Girl, The
Redman and the Child, The
Romance of a Jewess
Where the Breakers Roar
Woman, A
Work

1337
IRVING, Mary Jane*
Brand, The

1338
IRVING, W. J.*
Till I Come Back to You (Stroheim)

1339
IRWIN, May (1862-1938)
First Kiss, The
Mrs. Black Is Back
Stage:
Getting a Polish 1910
Mrs. Black Is Back 1904
Mrs. Peckam's Carouse 1908
No. 33 Washington Square 1915
Sister Mary 1900
Widow by Proxy 1913

1340
IVES, Charlotte*
Prince in a Pawn Shop, A
Stage:
Princess Players (series of one-act
     plays) 1913

- J -

1341
JACKSON, Charles*
Cecilia of the Pink Roses (Young
     Johnny)

1342
JACKSON, Joe "Shoeless" (1875-1942)
Bath House Blunder, A
Fatty and the Broadway Stars
Gypsy Joe
Lion and the Girl, The
Modern Enoch Arden, A

1343
JACKSON, Peaches*
Greatest Thing in Life, The (Mlle.
     Peaches)

1344
JACOBS, Billy*
Heart of Nora Flynn, The (Tommy
     Stone)
Kid Auto Races at Venice

1345
JACOBS, Paul*
Ambrose's Cup of Woe
Back Yard Theater, A
Cactus Nell
His Lying Heart
Little Billy's City Cousin
Little Billy's Strategy

Little Billy's Triumph
Lost, a Crook
Teddy Telzlaff and Earl Cooper,
  Speed Kings
Thirst

1346
JAMES, Gladden*
Babbling Tongues
Heart of the Wetona, The
Hearts of Love
Mystery of the Double Cross, The
  (serial)
Runaway Romance
Runaway Romany ("Inky" Ames)
Scandal
Social Secretary, The
Who's Your Brother?

1347
JAMISON, William "Bud"
  (1894-1943)
By the Sea
Champion, The
Charlie Chaplin's Burlesque on
  Carmen
Dog's Life, A
Floorwalker, The
In the Park
Night in the Show, A
Night Out, A
Police
Shanghaied
Tramp, The
Triple Trouble

1348
JANIS, Elsie (Elsie Bierbauer)
  (1889-1956)
Betty in Search of a Thrill
Nearly a Lady
Regular Girl, A
Stage:
Century Girl, The 1916
Fair Co-ed, The 1909
Hoyden, The 1907
Lady of the Slipper, The 1912
Miss Information 1915
Slim Princess, The 1911
Vaudeville 1906

1349
JANNINGS, Emil (1886-1950)
Bruder Karamazoff
Das Leben ein Traum, Die Augen
  der Mumie Ma
Der Steir von Oliviera
Eyes of the Mummy, The

Frau Eva; Die Ehe der Luise
  Rohrbach
Im Banne der Leidenschaft
Madame Dubarry/Passion (Louis XV)
Passionels Tagebuch
Rose Bernd
Bendetta
Wen Vier Dasselbe Tun

1350
JEAN [Collie dog, first dog star of
  films]
Bachelor Buttons 1911

1351
JEANS, Isabel (1891-)
Profligate, The

1352
JEFFERSON, Joseph (1829-1905)
Rip Van Winkle
Stage:
Cricket on the Hearth, The 1902
Rip Van Winkle 1902

1353
JEFFERSON, Thomas (1859-1923)
Beloved Liar, The
Fencing Master, The
Hands Up!
Hoosier Romance, A
Judith of Bethulia
Lombardi, Ltd.
Missing Links, The
Paid to Love
Poor Gentleman, The
Romance of Tarzan, The
Sable Lorcha
Stage:
Rip Van Winkle 1905

1354
JEFFERSON, William*
He Did and He Didn't
His Wife's Mistake
Other Man, The

1355
JEFFRIES, James J.*
Jeffries-Sharkey Fight

1356
JENNINGS, Al (Alphonso J. Jennings)
  (1864-1962)
Wolfville Tales

1357
JENNINGS, DeWitt (DeWitt Clarke
  Jennings) (1879-1937)

At Bay
Hillcrest Mystery, The
Warrens of Virginia, The

1358
JENNINGS, Gladys (1902-   )
Face at the Window, The
Lady Clare, The

1359
JENNINGS, S. E. *
Vengeance and the Woman (serial)

1360
JENSEN, Eulalie*
Beating the Odds
Captain's Captain, The
Cinema Murder, The (Mrs. Pawer)
Girl Problem, The
Mary Jane's Pa
Salvation Joan
Song of the Ghetto, A
Strength of the Weak, The
Tangled Lives
Tarantula, The
Temperamental Wife, A
Wild Primrose

1361
JESSEL, George (1898-   )
Other Man's Wife, The

1362
JEWETT, Ethel*
Edison player 1911

1363
JOHNSON, Arthur V. (1876-1916)
Adventures of Dollie, The
After Many Years
All on Account of Milk
Amateur Iceman
At the Altar
Awakening, The
Balked at the Altar
Bandit's Waterloo, The
Beloved Adventurer, The (serial)
Cloister's Touch, The
Concealing a Burglar
Confidence
Converts, The
Corner in Wheat, A
Day After, The
Drive for Life, The
Drunkard's Reformation, A
Eradicating Auntie
Expiation, The
Faithful, The

Final Settlement
Gibson Goddess, The
Girls and Daddy, The
Greaser's Gauntlet, The
Helping Hand, The
Her Awakening
Her First Biscuits
Her Two Sons
In Old California
Indian Runner's Romance, The
Ingrate, The
Iola's Promise
Light That Came, The
Lily of the Tenements, The
Little Darling, The
Little Teacher, The
Midnight Adventure, A
Mills of the Gods, The
Mountaineer's Honor, The
Necklace, The
Newlyweds, The
Nursing a Viper
Pippa Passes
Planter's Wife, The
Politician's Love Story, The
Pranks
Red Girl, The
Resurrection
Rich Revenge, A
Romance of the Western Hills, A
Rose o' Salem Town
Rude Hostess, A
Sealed Room, The
Song of the Shirt, The
Sound Sleeper, A
Strange Meeting, A
Taming a Husband
Taming of the Shrew, The
Test of Friendship, The
Thread of Destiny, The
'Tis an Ill Wind That Blows No Good
To Save Her Soul
Tragic Love
Trick That Failed, The
Two Memories
Unchanging Sea, The
Unexpected Help
Usurer, The
Valet's Wife, The
Vaquero's Vow, The
Voice of the Violin, The
Way of a Man, The

1364
JOHNSON, Edith (1895-   )
Behind the Lines
Cycle of Fate, The
Fight for Millions, A (serial)

Fighting Fate (serial)
For Love and Gold
Franc Piece, The
Giant Powder
In the Talons of the Eagle
Love and Honor (serial)
Man of Might (serial)
Scarlet Car, The (Beatrice Forbes)
Scarlet Crystal, The
Silent Avenger, The
Smashing Barriers (serial)
Steelheart (serial)
Wolves of the North, The

1365
JOHNSON, Emory*
Gray Ghost, The (serial)
Johanna Enlists
Kentucky Cinderella, A
Woman Next Door, The

1366
JOHNSON, Martin (1884-1937)
Borderland of Civilization
Canibals of the South Seas
Captured by Canibals
East of Suez
Jack London's Adventures in the
   South Seas
Martin Johnson's Voyage

1367
JOHNSON, Noble*
Bull's Eye, The (serial)
Midnight Man, The (serial)
Red Ace, The (serial)

1368
JOHNSON, Tefft*
Cardinal Wolsey
Vanity Fair

1369
JOHNSTON, J. W.*
Fifty-Fifty
Man from Home, The (Prefect of
   Italian Police)
Rose of the Rancho (Kearney)
Runaway June (serial)
Virginian, The (Steve)
Where the Trail Divides

1370
JOHNSTON, Julanne (1906-   )
Better Times
Youth

1371
JOHNSTONE, Lamar*

Secret of the Submarine, The (serial)
That Devil Bateese (Martin Stuart)

1372
JOLIVET, Rita (1894-   )
Cuore Edarte
Fata Morgana
International Marriage, An
La Mano Di Fatima
Lest We Forget
L'onore Di Morire
Monna Vanna
One Law for Both
Quello Che Videro I Mici Occhi
Unafraid, The (Delight Warren)
Zavni
Stage:
Kismet 1911
Thousand Years Ago, A 1914

1373
JONASSON, Frank*
Midnight Man, The (serial)

1374
JONES, Buck (Charles Jones)
   (1889-1942)
Rainbow Trail
Riders of the Purple Sage, The
Speed Maniac
True Blue
Western Blood

1375
JONES, Edgar*
Lubin player 1913

1376
JONES, Fred*
Eagle's Eye, The (serial)

1377
JONES, J. Parke*
Arab, The (Ibrahim)
Old Wives for New (Charley Murdock)
Whispering Chorus, The (Tom Burns)

1378
JONES, J. W.*
Wild and Wooly (the lawyer)

1379
JONES, Johnny*
Barrier, The
Edgar series 1918
Salomy Jane
Shepherd of the Hills
Shuttle, The
Walls of Jericho, The

1380
JONES, Park*
Dog's Life, A
Shoulder Arms
Sunnyside

1381
JORDAN, Sid*
Local Color
Roman Cowboy, The

1382
JORGENS, Alice*
Safety First Ambrose /aka/ Sheriff
    Ambrose

1383
JOSE, Edward*
Fool There Was, A (the fool, John
    Schuyler)
Perils of Pauline, The (serial)

1384
JOSLIN, Margaret*
Alkali Ike's Motorcycle
Snakeville comedies 1915

1385
JOUBE, M.*
Shylock

1386
JOY, Ernest*
Chimmie Fadden (Van Cortlandt)
Chimmie Fadden out West (Van
    Cortlandt)
Devil Stone, The
Golden Chance, The (Mr. Hillary)
Heart of Nora Flynn, The (Brantley
    Stone)
Joan, the Woman (Jean de Metz)
Maria Rosa (Carlos)
We Can't Have Everything
    (the heavy)
Wild Goose Chase, The
    (Mr. Randall)

1387
JOY, Leatrice (Leatrice Joy
    Zeidler) (1899-)
For Better, for Worse
Girl's Folly, A
Man Hunter, A

1388
JOYCE, Alice (1889-1955)
Alabaster Box, The
American Princess, An

Bell of Penance, A
Brand, The
Business of Life, The
Cabaret Dancer, The
Cambric Mask, The
Captain Abe's Niece
Captain's Captain, The
Celebrated Case, A
Courage of Silence, The
Engineer's Sweetheart, The
Everybody's Girl
Fettered Woman, The
Find the Woman
Lion and the Mouse, The
Mystery of the Sleeping Death
Nina of the Theatre (serial)
Riddle of the Green Umbrella
School for Scandal, The
Shadow, The
Song of the Soul, The
Spark Divine, The
Third Degree, The
To the Highest Bidder
Triumph of the Weak, The
Unseen Terror, An
Vampire's Trail, The
Winchester Woman, The
Within the Law
Woman between Friends, A
Womanhood

1389
JOYNER, Francis*
Brass Check, The
Daybreak
Less Than the Dust

1390
JUDELS, Charles*
Old Dutch
Stage:
Summer Widowers, The 1910
Twin Beds 1914
Ziegfeld Follies of 1912

1391
JULIAN, Rupert (1886-)
Bugler of Algiers, The
Dumb Girl of Portici, The
Kaiser, the Beast of Berlin, The
    (Title role)
Kentucky Cinderella, A
Merchant of Venice, The
    (Antonio)

1392
JUNIOR, John*
Daughter of the City, A

- K -

1393
KAELRED, Katharine*
Enlighten Thy Daughter
Stage:
Fool There Was, A 1909

1394
KALICH, Bertha (1874-1939)
Ambition
Marta of the Lowlands
Scandal
Slander
Stage:
Feodora 1905
Kreutzer Sonata, The 1906
Monna Vanna 1905
Rachel 1913
Riddle: Woman, The 1918

1395
KALIZ, Armand*
Temperamental Wife, A

1396
KANE, Gail*
Paying the Price
Serpent's Tooth, The
Stage:
Affairs of Anatol, The 1912
Famous Mrs. Fair, The 1919
Harp of Life, The 1916
Miracle Man, The 1914
Seven Keys to Baldpate 1913
Vanity Fair 1911

1397
KARLOFF, Boris (William Henry
    Pratt) (1887-1969)
Dumb Girl of Portici, The [Karloff
    denied being in this film;
    research claims he was]
His Majesty, the American (spy)
Lightning Raider, The (serial)
Masked Raider, The (serial)

1398
KARNES, Roscoe (1893-1970)
Poor Relations

1399
KARR, Darwin*
Vitagraph player 1914

1400
KAY, Marjorie*
Sherlock Holmes

1401
KEATON, Buster (Joseph Francis
    Keaton) (1895-1966)
Bell Boy, The
Butcher Boy, The
Cook, The
Country Hero, A
Fatty at Coney Island
Garage, The
Goodnight Nurse
Hayseed, The
His Wedding Night
Moonshine
Oh, Doctor!
Out West
Reckless Romeo, A
Rough House

1402
KEEFE, Zena (1896-   )
Challenge Accepted
Enlighten Thy Daughter
Hero of Submarine D-2
La Boheme
Oh, Boy!
One Hour
Perils of Our Girl Reporters (serial)
Scarlet Runner, The (serial)
Shame
Woman That God Sent, The

1403
KEELING, Robert Lee*
La Belle Russe (Sir James Sackton)

1404
KEENAN, Frank (1858-1929)
Bells, The
Coward, The (Col. Jefferson
    Beverly Winslow)
Gates of Brass
Honor Thy Name
Loaded Dice
Master Man
Midnight Stage, The
More Trouble
Ruler of the Road, The
Silver Girl, The
Stepping Stone, The
Throughbred, The
Todd of the Times
Stage:
Girl of the Golden West, The 1905
Julius Caesar 1912
Warrens of Virginia, The 1907

1405
KELCEY, Herbert (1857-1917)
After the Ball
Stage:
Children of Earth 1915
Her Lord and Master 1902
Moth and the Flame, The 1900
Years of Discretion 1912

1406
KELLAR, Gertrude*
Unafraid, The (Countess Novna)

1407
KELLARD, Ralph*
Hillcrest Mystery, The
Pearl of the Army (serial)
Shielding Shadow, The (serial)
Stage:
Eyes of Youth 1917
Rebecca of Sunnybrook Farm 1910
Warrens of Virginia, The 1907

1408
KELLER, E. *
Ranch Romance, A (Don Jose Praz)

1409
KELLER, Kate Adams*
Deliverance 1919

1410
KELLER, Phillip Brooks*
Deliverance

1411
KELLERMAN, Anette (1888-   )
Art of Diving, The
Daughter of the Gods, A
Diving Displays
Honor System, The
Isle of Love, The
Neptune's Daughter
Queen of the Sea
Stage:
Undine 1911

1412
KELLEY, Pat*
His Hereafter /aka/ Murray's Mixup

1413
KELLY, Dorothy*
Secret Kingdom, The (serial)
Troublesome Stepdaughters, The

1414
KELLY, James T. *

Behind the Screen
Count, The
Cure, The
Dog's Life, A
Easy Street
Fireman, The
Floorwalker, The
Immigrant, The
Night in the Show, A
Pawnshop, The
Police
Rink, The
Triple Trouble
Vagabond, The

1415
KELLY, Paul (Paul Michael Kelly)
    (1899-1956)
Anne of Green Gables
Buddy's Downfall
Buddy's First Call
Fit to Fight
Good Little Devil, A
Jarr Family series 1914
Knights of the Square Table
Star Spangled Banner, The
Vitagraph player 1911
Stage:
Penrod 1918
Seventeen 1918

1416
KELSEY, Fred (1884-1961)
Arms and the Gringo
Light of Victory, The
Silent Sands

1417
KELSO, Mayme*
Cheating Cheaters
Daughter of the World
His Birthright
Male and Female (Lady Brocklehurst)
Men, Women and Money
Mirandy Smiles
Old Wives for New (housekeeper)
Peg o' My Heart
Samson
Why Smith Left Home

1418
KELSON, George*
Little Women

1419
KENDAL, Leo*
Lion and the Girl, The

1420
KENDRICK, Ruby*
Blind Husbands (a village blossom)

1421
KENNARD, Victor*
Soul of Buddha, The (Ysora)

1422
KENNEDY, Edgar (1890-1948)
Ambrose's Cup of Woe
Bombs
Caught in a Cabret
Dough and Dynamite
Fatty's Tin Type Tangle
Game Old Knight, A
Getting Acquainted
Great Vacuum Robbery, The
Her Fame and Shame
Her Torpedoed Love
His Bitter Pill
His Hereafter
Keystone Cop (one of the original)
Knock-Out, The
Lost Lady, The
Madcap Ambrose
Noise of Bombs, The (Chief)
Oriental Love
Scoundrel's Tale, The
Star Boarder, The
Those Love Pangs
Tillie's Punctured Romance
Toreador, The
Twenty Minutes of Love
Village Scandal, The

1423
KENNEDY, Madge (1892-   )
Baby Mine
Danger Game, The
Daughter of Mine
Day Dreams
Fair Pretender, The
Friend Husband
Kingdom of Youth, The
Leave It to Susan
Nearly Married
Our Little Wife
Perfect Lady, A
Service Star, The
Strictly Confidential
Through the Wrong Door
Venus Model
Wild Primrose
Stage:
Fair and Warmer 1915
Twin Beds 1914

1424
KENNEDY, Tom (1885-1965)
Ambrose's Rapid Rise
Double Trouble (Judge Blodgett)
Hearts and Sparks
Mickey (Tom Rawlings)
Nick-of-Time Baby
One Round Hogan (debut)
Village Blacksmith, The

1425
KENNY, Colin*
Toby's Bow

1426
KENT, Charles (1852-   )
Daniel
Dixie Mother, A
Dreams
Duplicity of Hargraves, The
Enemy, The
Examination Day at School
Gamblers, The
Kennedy Square
Love's Way
Miss Dulcie from Dixie
Old Flute Player, The
On Her Wedding Night
Price for Folly, The
Rose of the South
Scarlet Runner, The
Soldiers of Chance
Supreme Temptation, The
Tarantula, The
Twelfth Night
Uncle Tom's Cabin
White Lie, The
Whom the Gods Destroy

1427
KENT, Crawford (1881-1953)
Better Half, The
Broadway Jones
Career of Katherine Bush, The
Come out of the Kitchen
Danger Mark, The
Deep Purple, The
Dollars and the Women
Good Gracious, Annabelle
Kildare of the Storm
Knife, The
Ordeal of Rosetta, The
Prince Cosmo
Song of Songs, The
Thais
Thou Shalt Not
Trap, The

1428
KENT, Leon*
Riddle Gawne (Jess Cass)

1429
KENYON, Doris (1897-)
Band Box, The
Girl's Folly, A
Great White Trail, The
Hidden Hand, The (serial)
Inn of the Blue Moon, The
Ocean Waif, The
On Trial
Pawn of Fate, The
Rack, The
Street of Seven Stars, The
Strictly Business
Twilight
Traveling Salesman, The
Wild Honey
Stage:
Girl in the Limousine, The 1919

1430
KERBY, Marion*
Two Daughters of Eve

1431
KERRIGAN, J. Warren (Jack Warren
    Kerrigan) (1880-1947)
Adventures of Jacques, The
Adventures of Terence O'Rourke, The
Agitator, The
Best Man, The
Burglar for a Night
Calamity Anne, Detective
Come Again Smith
Drifters, The
Eastern Flower
End of the Game
For Cash
For the Flag
Hand of Uncle Sam, The
Her Big Story
His Heart, His Hand, and His Sword
    (serial)
In the Days of the Trojan
Landon's Legacy
Man's Man, A
One Dollar Bid
Oyster Dredger, The
Poisoned Flume, The
Prisoner of the Pines
Samson
Sheriff's Sister, The
Stool Pigeon, The
Stranger at Coyote, The
Three X Gordon

Truth in the Wilderness
Turn of a Card, The
Voice from the Fireplace, A
White Man's Chance, A
Wishing Seat, The

1432
KERRY, Norman (Arnold Kaiser)
    (1889-1956)
Amarilly of Clothesline Alley
Black Butterfly, The
Dark Star, The (Jim Nieland)
Getting Mary Married (James
    Winthrop)
Goodnight, Paul
Little American, The
Little Princess, The
Manhattan Madness
Rose of Paradise
Soldiers of Fortune
Soul Market, The
Such a Little Princess
Talk of the Town, The
Up the Road with Sally
Virtuous Sinners

1433
KERSHAW, Willette*
Cecilia of the Pink Roses (Mary)
Sporting Life
Stage:
Brown of Harvard 1906
Country Boy, The 1910
Crowded Hour, The 1918
King Henry VIII 1916
Princess Players 1913
Snobs 1911
Unchastened Woman, The
Yes or No

1434
KEYSTONE KIDS, The (Helen
    Badgley, Marie Eline, Paul Jacobs,
    Carmen LaRue, Betty Marsh)
Back Yard Theatre, A
Horse Thief, The
Our Children (the first kiddie comedy)

1435
KEYSTONE PETS, The
Teddy a Great Dane
Pepper a Cat

1436
KIERNAN, Baby Marie*
By Stork Delivery

1437
KILGOUR, Joseph (1863-1933)
Battle Cry for Peace, The
Divorcee, The
Easiest Way, The
My Lady's Slipper
Runaway Romany (Theodore True)
Secret Kingdom, The (serial)
Thou Art the Man
Writing on the Wall, The
Stage:
Easiest Way, The 1909

1438
KIMBALL, Edward M. *
Lola
Marionettes, The

1439
KING, Anita (1889-1963)
Carmen (a gypsy girl)
Chimmie Fadden (Fanny)
Girl Angle, The
Girl of the Golden West, The
  (Wowkle)
Man from Home, The (Helene
Maria Rosa (Ana)
Mistaken Identity
One Against Many
Rose, The
Snobs
Virginian, The (Mrs. Ogden)
Whatever the Cost

1440
KING, Emmett*
Fear Women, The
In His Brother's Place
Please Get Married
Reckoning Roads

1441
KING, Henry (1892-   )
Joy and the Dragon
Sporting Chance, A
Who Pays?

1442
KING, Joe*
Everywoman's Husband
Her Bounty (David Hale)
Pipes of Pan, The (Stephen Arnold)
Rose of Blood, The (Prime Minister)
Secret Code
Shifting Sands

1443
KING, Leslie*
Fatal Fortune, The (serial)

1444
KING, Mollie (1898-   )
Blind Man's Luck
Human Clay
Kick In (serial)
Mystery of the Double Cross, The
  (serial)
On-the-Square Girl
Seven Pearls, The (serial)
Summer Girl, The
Suspense
Woman's Power, A
Stage:
Goodmorning, Judge 1919
Ziegfeld Follies of 1913

1445
KINGSLEY, Florida (1879-   )
Boy-Girl, The
Iron Heart, The
Made in America
Mrs. Slacker
Sealed Hearts
Thou Shalt Not
Turmoil, The
Woman under Oath

1446
KINGSTON, Winifred (d. 1967)
Call of the North, The (Virginia)
Corsican Brothers, The
David Garrick
Davy Crockett
Lifted Veil, The
Light of the Western Stars
Parson of Panamint, The
Scarlet Pimpernel, The
Squaw Man, The (Lady Diana)
Virginian, The (Molly Wood)
Where the Trail Divides

1447
KIRKBY, Ollie*
Social Pirates, The

1448
KIRKHAM, Kathleen (1895-   )
Arizona (Estrella)
Beauty Market, The
Beloved Cheater, The
He Comes up Smiling
Master of Men, The
Modern Musketeer, A (Mrs. Moran)
Tarzan of the Apes
Third Kiss, The
Upstairs and Down

1449
KIRKLAND, Hardee*

Galley Slave, The (Baron le Bois)
Peace of Roaring River, The

1450
KIRKWOOD, James (1883-1963)
At the Altar
Back to God's Country
Beating Back
Behind the Scenes
Better Way, The
Comata, the Sioux
Convict's Sacrifice, The
Corner in Wheat, A
Death Disc, The
Eagle's Mate, The
Final Settlement
Fools of Fate
Foundling, The
Gibson Goddess, The
Home, Sweet Home (the son)
Honor of His Family, The
House of Discord, The
Indian Runner's Romance, The
Last Deal, The
Light That Came, The
Lonely Villa, The (burglar)
Lost Bridegroom, The
Marriage of the Underworld
Mended Lute, The
Message, The
Modern Prodigal, The
Mountain Rat, The
Pippa Passes
Prince Charming
Rags
Redman's View, The
Restoration, The
Road to the Heart, The
Rocky Road, The
1776 or The Hessian Renegades
   (Colonial farmer)
Seventh Day, The
Sioux, The
Struggle of the Everlasting
Through the Breakers
Victim of Jealousy, A
Was Justice Served?
Winning Back His Love

1451
KIRTLEY, Virginia*
Film Johnnie, A
Making a Living (the girl)
Oh, Daddy!

1452
KLINTBERT, Walter*
Saved by Wireless

1453
KNIGHT, James (1891-)
Big Money
Deception
Gates of Duty
Happy Warrior, The
Man Who Forgot, The
Nature's Gentleman
Power of Right, The
Romany Lass, The
Silver Greyhound, The
Splendid Coward, The

1454
KNOTT, Lydia (1873-)
Clodhopper, The
Crime and Punishment
Danger-Go Slow (Jimmy's mother)
Heart of Youth, The
His Mother's Boy
Home
In Wrong
Pointing Finger, The
Should Women Tell?
Sudden Jim
What Everywoman Learns

1455
KNOWLAND, Alice (1879-)
Delicious Little Devil
Rustling a Bride
Satan, Jr.

1456
KNOX, Foster*
Squaw Man, The (Sir John)

1457
KOCH, Hugo B.*
Joan, the Woman (Duke of Burgundy)

1458
KOHLER, Fred (1889-1938)
Soldiers of Fortune
Tiger's Trail, The (Bull Shotwell)
   (serial)

1459
KOLB and DILL*
Glory

1460
KOLKER, Henry (1874-1947)
Blackie's Redemption
Gloria's Romance (serial)
Her Purchase Price
How Molly Made Good
Red Lantern, The

Stage:
Great Name, The 1911
Greyhound, The 1912
Help Wanted 1914
Three of Us, The 1906
Winter's Tale, The 1910

1461
KORTMAN, Robert*
Ambrose's Rapid Rise
Cactus Nell
Great Radium Mystery, The (serial)
Hell's Hinges (henchman)
His Naughty Thought
Safety First Ambrose /aka/
    Sheriff Ambrose

1462
KOSLOFF, Theodore (1882-1956)
Woman God Forgot, The (Guatemoco)

1463
KRAUSS, Henri*
Les Miserables

1464
KRAUSS, Werner (1884-1959)
Cabinet of Dr. Caligari, The

1465
KROMAN, Ann*
Her Decision

1466
KUWA, George K.*
Toby's Bow

1467
KYLE, Alex*
Scarlet Runner, The (serial)

- L -

1468
LA BADIE, Florence (1893-1917)
Blind Princess and the Poet, The
Broken Cross, The
Country Girl, The
Cymbeline
Enoch Arden, Part I and II
Fighting Blood
How She Triumphed
Lucille
Merchant of Venice, The
Million Dollar Mystery, The (serial)
Primal Call, The
Snare of Fate, The

Star of Bethlehem
Thief and the Girl, The
Undine
War and the Woman

1469
LACKAYE, James*
Battle Cry of Peace, The
Goodness Gracious! or Movies as
    They Shouldn't Be (Father)

1470
LACKAYE, Wilton (1862-1932)
Trilby

1471
LACKTEEN, Frank (1894-)
Woman
Yellow Menace, The

1472
LAFAYETTE, Ruby (1844-)
Big Bob
Dragnet, The
In His Brother's Place
Kaiser, the Beast of Berlin, The
    (Belgian woman)
Miracle Man, The
Mother o' Mine
My Mother
Toby's Bow

1473
LAFFEY, James*
Dark Star, The (Ship's Captain)

1474
LAIDLAW, Roy*
Back to God's Country
His Robe of Honor
Honor's Cross
With Hoops of Steel

1475
LAIRCE, Margaret*
Heart and Soul (Jess in prologue)

1476
LAKE, Alice (1896-1967)
Back Stage
Bell Boy, The
Chicago Sal
Come Through
Cook, The
Country Hero, A
Deserted Hero, A
Garage, The
Goodnight Nurse!

Her Nature Dance
Her Picture Idol
His Wedding Night
Late Lamented, The
Matrimony
Moonshine
Moonshiners, The
Oh, Doctor!
Out West
Reckless Romeo, A /aka/ A
    Creampuff Romance /aka/ His
    Alibi
Red Lights
Should a Woman Tell?
Waiter's Ball, The

1477
LAKE, Arthur (Arthur Silverlake)
    (1905-)
Jack and the Beanstalk
Stage:
Vaudeville 1908-1918
Uncle Tom's Cabin 1905

1478
LAMBERT, Albert*
Assassination of the Duc de Guise

1479
LAMON, Isabel*
Little Women

1480
LAMPTON, Dee*
Night in the Show, A

1481
LANCASTER, John*
Katzenjammer Kids (Uncle Heine)
Sweeney series 1913

1482
LANDICUTT, Philip*
Unbeliever, The

1483
LANDIS, Cullen (1895-)
Almost a Husband
Beware of Blondes
Girl from Outside, The
Jinx
Outcast of Poker Flats, The
Upstairs
Where the West Begins
Who Is Number One? (serial)

1484
LANDOWSKA, Yona*
Father and the Boys

1485
LANE, Adele*
Selig player 1913

1486
LANE, Charles (1899-)
Mrs. Black Is Back
Wanted: a Husband

1487
LANE, Lupino (Henry Lane)
    (1892-1957)
Clarence Crooks and Chivalry
Dreamland Frolic, A
Dummy, The
Hello, Who's Your Lady Friend?
His Busy Day
His Cooling Courtship
His Salad Days
Love and Lobster
Man in Possession, The
Missing Link, The
Nipper and the Curate
Nipper's Bank Holiday
Nipper's Busy Bee Time
Nipper's Busy Holiday
Splash Me Nicely
Trips and Tribunals
Unexpected Treasure
Wife in a Hurry, A

1488
LANG, Matheson (1879-1948)
Everybody's Business
House Opposite, The
Masks and Faces
Merchant of Venice, The
Mr. Wu
Victory and Peace
Ware Case, The

1489
LANG, Peter*
Peter's Pledge

1490
LANGDON, Lillian*
Americano, The
Diane of the Follies
Everywoman's Husband
Flirting with Fate (Mrs. Kingsley)
His Majesty, the American
    (Marguerita)
Intolerance (Mary the Mother)
Kindling (Mrs. Burke-Smith)
Lamb, The
Prudence on Broadway
Regular Fellow, A
Shifting Sands

Society for Sale
Usurper, The

1491
LANGTRY, Lily (Lillian Langtry)
    (1856-1929)
His Neighbor's Wife
Stage:
Cross-Ways, The 1902
Mrs. Deering's Divorce 1903
Mrs. Thompson 1915

1492
LANNING, Frank*
Bull's Eye (serial)
Lion's Claw, The (serial)

1493
la RENO, Richard*
Cameo Kirby
Fires of Rebellion
Gray Ghost, The (serial)
Man from Home, The (old man
    Simpson)
Rose of the Rancho (Esra Kincaid)
Squaw Man, The (Big Bill)
Virginian, The (Balaam)
Warrens of Virginia, The (General
    Griffin)

1494
LARKIN, George (1889-)
Border Raiders
Coming of the Law, The
Devil's Trail, The
Eclair player 1912
Hands Up! (serial)
Lurking Peril, The (serial)
Terror of the Range (serial)
Tiger's Trail, The (serial)
Trey o' Hearts, The (serial)
Unfortunate Sex, The
While Father Telephoned
Zongar

1495
LA ROCQUE, Rod (Roderick la
    Rocque de la Rour) (1898-1969)
Efficiency Edgar's Courtship
Essanay player 1914
Hidden Fires
Kaiser's Bride, The
Perfect 36, A
Venus Model, The

1496
LARRIMORE, Francine*
Devil's Darling, The

Max Wants a Divorce (bit)
Princess from the Poorhouse, The
Resurrection
Royal Pauper
Somewhere in America
Stage:
Any Night 1913
Here Comes the Bride 1917
Scandal 1919
Some Baby 1915
Sometime 1918

1497
LARSSON, William
Ingeborg Holm

1498
LA RUE, Fontaine*
Boots
Lifted Veil, The
Wildcat of Paris, The
Woman under Cover, The

1499
LA RUE, Grace /aka/ Stella Gray*
That's Good

1500
LA STRANGE, Dick*
Girl of the Golden West, The (Senor
    Slim)
Squaw Man, The (Grouchy)
What's His Name? (Best man)

1501
LAUGHLIN, Anna (1885-1937)
Crooky Scruggs

1502
LAUREL, Stan (Arthur Stanley
    Jefferson) (1890-1965)
Bears and Bad Men
Do You Love Your Wife?
Evolution of Fashion, The
Frauds and Frenzies
Hickory Hiram
Hoot Man
Huns and Hyphens
Hustling for Health
It's Great to be Crazy
Just Rambling Along
Lucky Dog, A (young man; first film
    with Oliver Hardy)
Mixed Nuts
Mud and Sand
No Place Like Jail
Nuts in May
Phoney Photos

Scars and Strings
When Knights Were Cold
Whose Zoo?
Stage:
Fred Karno's Company 1910
Juvenile Pantomime Company 1903
Understudied Charlie Chaplin with
    Karno's Company 1913

1503
LAURELL, Kay*
Brand, The
Stage:
Ziegfeld Follies of 1914

1504
LAVARNE, Laura*
Mickey (Mrs. Geoffrey Drake
    "Mickey")

1505
LA VERNE, Lucille (1872-1945)
Polly of the Circus
Stage:
Romeo and Juliet (Juliet) 1873
Seven Days 1909

1506
LAW, Walter*
Camille (Count de Varville)
Darling of Paris, The (Claude
    Frollo)
Frobidden Path, The (Mr. Lynde)
Heart and Soul (Martin Drummond)
Her Double Life (Longshoreman)
Romeo and Juliet (Friar Laurence)
Unwelcome Mother, The

1507
LAWLER, Jerome*
Slander

1508
LAWLOR, Robert*
Intolerance (Judge)

1509
LAWRENCE, Dakota (1902-   )
Across the Line
Code of the North, The
Danger Patrol
Fate's Chessboard
Heart of Big Dan, The
Hidden Pit, The
When Big Dan Rides
Where Peril Lurkes

1510
LAWRENCE, E. W.*
Common Clay

1511
LAWRENCE, Florence (1888-1938)
Angel of the Studio, The
At the Altar
Awful Moment, An
Barbarian, The
Barbarian, Ingomar, The
Behind the Scenes
Betrayed by a Hand Print
Biograph Girl (became 1909)
Biograph player (47 films) 1908-09
Brahma Diamond, The
Broken Bath, The
Calamitous Elopment, A
Call of the Wild, The
Cardinal's Conspiracy, The
Christmas Burglars, The
Comata, the Sioux
Concealing a Burglar
Confidence
Deception, The
Devil, The
Dispatch Bearers, The
Eloping with Auntie
Flo's Discipline
Girl and the Outlaw, The
Girls and Daddy, The
Good Turn, A
Heart of Oyama, The
Helping Hand, The
Her First Biscuits
Her Two Sons
His Wife's Mother
In Swift Waters
Ingrate, The
Jones and His New Neighbor (Mrs.
    Jones)
Jones and the Lady Book Agent
    (Mrs. Jones)
Jones Have Amateur Theatricals,
    The (Mrs. Jones)
Lady Helen's Escapade
Look Up
Lure of the Gown, The
Mended Lute, The
Mr. Jones at the Ball (Mrs. Jones)
Mr. Jones' Burglar (Mrs. Jones)
Mr. Jones Entertains (Mrs. Jones)
Mr. Jones Has a Card Party (Mrs.
    Jones)
Mrs. Jones' Lover or I Want My
    Hat (Mrs. Jones)
Necklace, The
Note in the Shoe, The

Peach Basket Hat, The
Planter's Wife, The
Redemption
Resurrection
Road to the Heart, The
Romance of a Jewess
Romeo and Juliet (Juliet)
St. Elmo
Salvation Army Lass, The
Singular Cynic, A
Slave, The
Smoked Husband, A
Song of the Shirt, The
Taming of the Shrew, The
Test of Friendship, The
Vaquero's Vow, The
Valet's Wife, The
Way of Man, The
Where the Breakers Roar
Winning Coat, The
Woman's Way, A
Zulu's Heart, The

1512
LAWRENCE, Lillian*
Galley Slave, The (Mrs. Blaine)
Stage:
Ben Hur 1911

1513
LAWRENCE, Marjory*
Anything Once (Theodore's cousin)

1514
LAWRENCE, W. E. *
Children in the House, The
Flirting with Fate (Augy's friend)
Intolerance (Henry of Navrre)

1515
LAWSON, Elsie*
Amazons, The

1516
LAWTON, Jack*
Mystery of 13, The (serial)

1517
LEARN, Bessie*
Edison player 1912

1518
LEDERER, Gretchen (1891-1955)
Bobbie of the Ballet
Chimney's Secret, The
Cruise of the Jolly Roger
Grasp of Greed
Greater Law, The

Green Magic
House of Gloom
If My Country Should Call (Mrs. Ardath)
Kaiser, the Beast of Berlin, The (Belgian woman)
Kentucky Cinderella, A
Little Orphan, The
Mark of Cain, The (Mrs. Wilson)
Millionaire Paupers, The
Model's Confession, The
Pointing Finger, The
Red, Red Heart
Rescue, The (Nell Jerold)
Riddle Gawne (Blanche Dillon)
Silent Lady
Under a Shadow (the wife)
Violin Maker, The (the wife)
Wife or Country

1519
LEDERER, Otto (1886-   )
By Right of Possession
Captain of the Gray Horse Troop
Cupid Forecloses
Dead Shot Baker
Diplomat of Wolfville
Follow Me
Flaming Omen, The
Lady Sheriff, The
Mr. Aladdin of Broadway
Over the Garden Wall
Red Prince, The
Woman in the Web, The

1520
LEE, Alberta*
Intolerance (Neighbor's wife)

1521
LEE, Carey*
Darling of Paris, The (Paquette)
Her Double Life (Longshoreman's wife)
Three Musketeers, The (Cardinal's spy)

1522
LEE, Dixie (1911-1952)
Law of Nature, The
Where Bonds Are Loosed

1523
LEE, Frankie (1912-   )
Bonds of Love
Ching
Daddy Long Legs
Durand of the Bad Lands
Field of Honor

Miracle Man, The
Sheriff's Son, The
Vive La France
Westerners, The
Woman Who Dared, The

1524
LEE, Jane (1912-1957) and Katharine*
  [both unless stated]:
American Buds
Clemenceau Case, The
Circus Imps
Dicksville Terrors, The
Dixie Madcaps
Daughter of the Gods, A
Doing Our Bit
Double Trouble
Her Double Life (Longshoreman's
  daughter) (Katharine only)
Kids and Skids
Love and Hate
Master Hand, The (Katharine only)
Pair of Aces, A
Patsy, The
Smiles
Soul of Broadway, The (Jane only)
Spider and the Fly, The
Swat the Spy
Tell It to the Marines
Troublemakers
Two Little Imps
We Should Worry

1525
LEE, Janet*
Clemenceau Case, The (Janet)
Galley Slave, The (Dolores)
Her Double Life (naughty girl)

1526
LEE, Jennie*
Birth of a Nation, The (Cindy)
Her Mother's Oath
His Mother's Son
Man's Genesis (cave woman)

1527
LEE, Joe*
By Stork Delivery

1528
LEE, Lila (Augusta Appel)
  (1905-1973)
Cock o' the Walk
Cruise of the Make-Believe, The
  (debut)
Daughter of the Wolf, A
Hawthorne of the U. S. A.

Lottery Man, The
Male and Female (Tweeny)
Puppy Love
Rose of the River
Rustling a Bride
Secret Garden, The
Such a Little Pirate
Stage:
Ten years in vaudeville as
  "Cuddles"

1529
LEE, Raymond (1910-   )
Day's Pleasure, A

1530
LEE, Roberta*
Martha's Vindication

1531
LeGUERE, George*
Cecilia of the Pink Roses (Johnny
  as a boy)
Seven Deadly Sins ("Envy" and
  "Pride" segments)
Soul of a Woman, The
Way of a Woman, The
Stage:
Auctioneer, The 1913
Woman of No Importance, A 1916

1532
LEHR, Anna*
For Freedom
Home Wanted
Jungle Trail, The
Laughing Bill Hyde
Men
My Own United States
Open Door, The
Thunderbolts of Fate
Upside Down
Yellow Ticket, The

1533
LEHRMAN, Henry*
As the Bells Rang Out
Beast at Bay, A
Her Sacrifice
Iconoclast, The
Kid Auto Races at Venice
Making a Living

1534
LEIBER, Fritz (1883-1949)
Cleopatra (Caesar)
Stage:

Ben Greet Company 1902; 1907
Robert B. Mantell Co. 1911; 1918

1535
LEIGH, Frank*
Common Property
Feodora
Lord and Lady Algy

1536
LEIGH, Leslie*
Forbidden Path, The

1537
LEIGHTON, Lillian*
Cinderella
Devil Stone, The
Freckles
Joan, the Woman (Isambeau)
Katzenjammer Kids, The (Mrs.
    Katzenjammer)
Lady's Name, A
Little American, The
Louisiana
Male and Female (Mrs. Perkins)
Old Wives for New (maid)
Other People's Money
Poor Relations
Secret Service
Sweeney series 1913
Till I Come Back to You (Margot)
Two Orphans, The
Witchcraft

1538
LEMONTIER, Jules*
Hearts of the World (a stretcher
    bearer)

1539
LENOR, Jacque*
Bobby, the Coward
Italian Blood
Lena and the Geese
Long Road, The
Spirit Awakened, The

1540
LENOX, Fred*
Burden of Proof, The (butler)

1541
LEO [a lion]
Sunshine Dad

1542
LEONARD, Marion (1881-1956)
As It Is in Life

At the Altar
At the Crossroads of Life
Awful Moment, An
Burglar's Mistake, A
Card of Life, The
Carmen (Title role)
Christmas Burglars, The
Comata, the Sioux
Converts, The
Criminal Hypnotist, The
Day After, The
Dragon's Claw, The
Eavesdropper, The
Expiation, The
Fatal Hour, The
Father Gets in the Game
Fools of Fate
Gibson Goddess, The
Gold Is Not All
Golden Louis, The
Hindu Dagger, The
His Lost Love
In Little Italy
In Old California
Light That Came, The
Love among the Roses
Lonely Villa, The
Maniac Cook, The
Mills of the Gods, The
Nursing a Viper
On the Reef
Over Silent Paths
Pippa Passes
Pranks
Restoration, The
Roue's Heart, The
Rude Hostess, A
Salutary Lesson, A
Sealed Room, The
Shadows of Doubt
Sorrows of the Unfaithful, The
Test of Friendship, The
Through the Breakers
Trap for Santa Claus, A
Two Brothers, The
Two Memories
Two Paths, The
Voice of the Violin, The
Welcome Burglar, The
With Her Card
Wreath in Time, A
Stage:
Billy the Kid (road show) 1907

1543
LEONARD, Mary*
Lonely Villa, The

1544
LEONARD, Robert Z. *
Code of Honor, The
Master Key, The (serial)
Primeval Test, The
Robinson Crusoe
Sea Urchin, The

1545
LEONE, Henri*
My Cousin
Sin (Giovanni)

1546
LEPANTO, Victoria*
Carmen

1547
LESLIE, Gladys (1899-   )
Beloved Imposter, The
Fortune's Child
Girl Woman, The
His Own People
Little Miss No Account
Mating, The
Miss Dulcie of Dixie
Nymph of the Woods
Soap Girl, The
Stitch in Time, A
Too Many Crooks
Vicar of Wakefield, The
Wild Primrose
Wooing of Princess Pat, The

1548
LESLIE, Helen*
If My Country Should Call (Patricia
    London)

1549
LESLIE, Lilie*
Siren of Corsica, The

1550
LESTER, Kate*
Adventures of Carol, The
Bonds of Love
Coney Island Princess, A
Little Women
Man and His Money, A
Unbeliever, The

1551
LESTER, Louise*
Calamity Ann, Detective

1552
LESTINA, Adolphe*

Cord of Life, The
Girl Who Stayed at Home, The
    (Monsieur France)
Greatest Thing in Life, The (Leo
    Peret)
Hearts of the World (Grandfather)
Inner Circle, The
Romance of Happy Valley, A (Vinegar
    Watkins)
Two Paths, The
What Shall We Do with Our Old?
Woman Scorned, A

1553
L'ESTRANGE, Julian*
Bella Donna
Quest of Life, The
Stage:
Lady of Dreams, The 1912
Yellow Ticket, The 1914

1554
LEUBAS, Louis*
Vampires, The

1555
LEVERING, Lieutenant Jack*
Fatal Fortune, The (serial)

1556
LEVESQUE, Marcel*
Vampires, The

1557
LEWIS, Edgar P. *
Wives of Men, The

1558
LEWIS, Ida*
Bells, The
Dangerous Waters
Heart of Rachel, The
Maid o' the Storm
Man's Man, A
Whither Thou Goest

1559
LEWIS, Jay*
Janitor's Wife's Temptations, A

1560
LEWIS, Jeffrey, Mrs. *
Regular Girl, A

1561
LEWIS, Joy*
Shootin' Mad (the girl)

1562
LEWIS, Mitchell (1880-1956)
Bar Sinister
Barrier, The
Children of Banishment
Code of the Yukon
Fool's Gold
Jacques of the Silver North
Life's Greatest Problem
Million Dollar Mystery, The (serial)
Nine-Tenths of the Law
Safe for Democracy
Sign Invisible
Stage:
Touring with Willie Collier 1902

1563
LEWIS, Ralph (-1937)
Avenging Conscience, The (detective)
Big James' Heart
Birth of a Nation, The (Austin
    Stoneman)
Cheating the Public
Dub, The
Escape, The (Senator)
Eyes of Youth, The
Faith Healer, The
Floor Above, The
Flying Torpedo, The
Gangsters of New York
Going Straight
Gretchen the Greenhorn
Her Awakening
Home, Sweet Home
Hoodlum, The
Intolerance (Governor)
Jack and the Beanstalk
Jordan Is a Hard Road
Little Catamount, The
Martha's Vindication
Mountain Girl, The
Nectorine
Tale of Two Cities, A
Talk of the Town, The
Valley of the Giants, The
When the Clouds Roll By (Curtis
    Brown)

1564
LEWIS, Sheldon (1868-1958)
Affair of Three Nations, An
Bishop's Emeralds, The
Braga's Double
Charity
Clutching Hand, The (serial)
Coward, The
Dr. Jekyll and Mr. Hyde (Title role)
Exploits of Elaine, The (lawyer)
    (serial)

Hidden Hand, The (serial)
Iron Claw, The (serial)
King's Game, The
Warfare of the Flesh
Wolves of Kultur (serial)
Stage:
Lady from the Sea, The 1911
Thousand Years Ago, A 1914

1565
LEWIS, Vera (-1958)
As the Sun Went Down
Intolerance (Mary Jenkins)
Lombardi, Ltd.
Lost in Transit
Mother and the Law, The
Still Small Voice, A

1566
LEWIS, Walter (1871-)
Man Who Might Have Been, The
My Hero
Woman under Oath, A

1567
LIGON, Grover G. *
Maiden's Trust, A
Tillie's Punctured Romance

1568
LIKES, Don*
Bath House Blunder, A

1569
LINCOLN, E. K. *
Desert Gold
Fighting Through
For Freedom of the World
Jimmy Dale, Alias the Grey Seal
    (serial)
Lafayette, We Come
Littlest Rebel, The
Stars of Glory
Virtuous Men

1570
LINCOLN, Elmo (Otto Elmo Linken-
    helter) (1889-1952)
Betsy's Burglar
Birth of a Nation, The (White Arm
    Joe)
Children of the Feud
Desperation
Elmo, the Mighty (Title role) (serial)
Greatest Thing in Life, The (an
    American soldier)
Intolerance (Mighty Man of Valor)
Kaiser, the Beast of Berlin, The
    (Marcus)

Romance of Tarzan, The (Tarzan)
Tarzan of the Apes (Tarzan)
Treasure Island

1571
LIND, Jenny*
Deliverance

1572
LIND, Myrtle*
Danger Girl, The /aka/ Love on
  Skates
His Hereafter /aka/ Murray's
  Mixup
Maiden's Trust, A
Pills of Peril
Pinched in the Finish

1573
LIND, Sarah*
Deliverance

1574
LINDEN, Einar*
Carmen (Jose)
Eternal Sapho, The (Mr. Drummond)
Romeo and Juliet (Paris)

1575
LINDER, Max (Gabriel Levielle)
  (1883-1925)
All's Well That Ends Well
American Marriage, An
Before and after the Wedding
Billet Doux, The
Boxing Match on Skates
Collegian's First Cigar, The
Collegian's First Outing, The (debut)
Contrabanders, The
Cross Country Original, The
Death of a Toreador, The
Duel of Monsieur Myope, The
Entente Cordiale
Escape of Gas, An
Evening at the Cinema, An
Flying by Hydroplane
Graduation Celebration, A
How Max Went Around the World
I Want a Baby
Legend of Polichinelle, The
Little Cafe, The /aka/ The Miracle
  of the Wolves
Little Roman, The
Mabel's Dramatic Moment
Marriage by Telephone
Marriage Is a Puzzle
Max--Aeronaut
Max and His Mother-in-Law's False
  Teeth

Max and His Taxi
Max and Jane Go to the Theatre
Max and Jane Make a Dessert
Max and the Clutching Hand
Max and the Statue
Max Attends an Inauguration
Max between Two Women /aka/ Max
  between Two Fires
Max Comes Across
Max Creates a Fashion
Max Does Not like Cats
Max Does Not Speak English
Max Embarrassed
Max Gets the Reward
Max--Heartbreaker
Max Hypnotized
Max in a Dilemma
Max in a Museum
Max in the Alps
Max in the Arms of His Family
Max in the Movies
Max Is Absent-Minded
Max Is Almost Married
Max Is Decorated
Max Is Distraught
Max Is Forced to Work
Max Is Jealous
Max Is Stuck Up
Max, Jockey for Love
Max--Magician
Max Makes a Conquest
Max Makes Music
Max on Skis
Max--Pedicurist
Max--Photographer
Max Plays Detective
Max Plays in Drama
Max Searches for a Sweetheart
Max Takes a Bath
Max Takes up Boxing
Max Teaches the Tango /aka/ Too
  Much Mustard
Max--Toreador
Max, Victim of Quinquina
Max--Virtuoso
Max Wants a Divorce
Max Wears Tight Shoes
Max's Astigmatism
Max's Double
Max's Duel
Max's Hanging
Max's Hat
Max's Honeymoon
Max's Marriage
Max's Mother-in-Law
Max's Neighborly Neighbors
Max-s New Landlord
Max's Vacation

My Dog Dick
Never Kiss the Maid
One Exciting Night
Painter for Love
Paris Original, A
Pathé player in 360 comedies
     1907-1914
Poison
Second of August, The
Skater's Debut, The
Unexpected Meeting, An
Whim of an Apache, The
Who Killed Max?
Stage:
Ciné Max Linder (Paris) 1917
King, The 1906
Miquette and Her Mother 1906
Rome Opera House 1915
Theatre des Varities (Paris) 1906

1576
LINDGREN, Aron*
Ingeborg Holm

1577
LINDHOLM, Eric*
Ingeborg Holm

1578
LINDRITH, Nellie*
Fatal Fortune, The (serial)

1579
LINGHAM, Thomas*
Adventures of Ruth, The (serial)
Lass of the Lumberlands (serial)
Lion's Claw, The (serial)
Lost Express, The (serial)
Railroad Raiders, The (serial)
Red Glove, The (serial)

1580
LITTLE, Ann (1891-   )
Alias Mike Moran
Bear Trap, The
Believe Me, Zantippe
Black Box, The (serial)
Damon and Pythias
Firefly of France, The
For the Wearing of the Green
Heart of an Indian, The
House of Bondage, The
House of Silence, The
Less Than Kin
Lightning Bryce (serial)
Man from Funeral Range, The
Nan of Music Mountain
Past Redemption

Paths of Genius
Rimrock Jones
Roaring Road, The
Service Stripes
Silent Master, The
Source, The
Square Deal Sanderson
Squaw Man, The (Naturich)
That Girl of Burke's
Told in the Hills

1581
LITTLEFIELD, Lucien (1895-1959)
Blacklist
Everywoman
Golden Fetter, The
Gutter Magdalene, The
Hostage, The
Joan of Arc
Miser, The
Squaw Man's Son, The
Wild Goose Chase, The (The "Grind")

1582
LIVINGSTON, Jack*
Captivating Mary Carstairs, The
Everywoman's Husband
Stronger Love, The
Wooden Shoes

1583
LIVINGSTON, Margaret (1902-   )
All Wrong
Billie's Fortune
Busher, The
Leather Pushers
Social Buccaneer
When Johnny Comes Marching Home
Within the Cup

1584
LLOYD, Ethel*
Love's Old Dream

1585
LLOYD, Frank*
Black Box, The (serial)
Test, The

1586
LLOYD, Harold (1893-1971)
All Aboard
Are Crooks Dishonest?
Ask Father
At the Stage Door
Awful Romance, An
Back to the Woods
Bashful
Be My Wife

Beat It!
Bees in the Bonnet
Before Breakfast
Big Idea, The
Billy Blazes, Esq.
Bliss
Braver Than Bravest
Bride and Groom
Bughouse Bell Hops
Bumping into Broadway
Busting the Beanery
By the Sad Sea Waves
Captain Kidd's Kiddies
Caught in a Jam
Chop Suey and Company
City Slicker, The
Clubs Are Trump
Count the Votes
Count Your Change
Crack up Your Heels
Don't Shove!
Drama's Dreadful Deal
Dutiful Dub, The
Fireman, Save My Child!
Flirt, The
Follow the Crowd
Fozzle at a Tea Party, A
Fresh from the Farm
From Hand to Mouth
From Italy's Shore
Gasoline Wedding, A
Giving Them Fits
Going! Going! Gone!
Great While It Lasted (Bearskin)
He Leads, Others Follow
Heap Big Chief
Hear 'Em Rave
Here Come the Girls
Hey There!
His Royal Slyness
Hit Him Again
Ice
I'm on My Way
It's a Wild Life
Jailed
Jazzed Honeymoon, A
Just Dropped In
Just Neighbors
Just Nuts
Kicked Out
Kicking the Germ out of Germany!
Lamb, The
Let's Go!
Lonesome Luke, Circus King (Luke)
Lonesome Luke from London to
    Laramie
Lonesome Luke in Tin Pan Alley
Lonesome Luke, Lawyer

Lonesome Luke Loses Patients
Lonesome Luke, Mechanic
Lonesome Luke, Messenger
Lonesome Luke, Plumber
Lonesome Luke, Social Gangster
Lonesome Luke's Honeymoon
Lonesome Luke's Lively Life
Lonesome Luke's Lively Rifle
Lonesome Luke's Wild Women
Look out Below
Look Pleasant Please
Loves, Laughs and Lather
Luke and the Bang-Tails
Luke and the Bomb Throwers
Luke and the Mermaids
Luke and the Rural Roughnecks
Luke, Crystal Gazer
Luke Does the Midway
Luke Foils the Villain
Luke, Gladiator
Luke Joins the Navy
Luke Laughs Last
Luke Leans to the Literary
Luke Locates the Loot
Luke Lugs Luggage
Luke, Patient Provider
Luke Pipes the Pippins
Luke Rides Roughshod
Luke Rolls in Luxury
Luke the Candy Cut-up
Luke, the Chauffeur
Luke Wins Ye Ladye Faire
Luke's Busy Days
Luke's Double
Luke's Fatal Flivver
Luke's Fireworks Fizzle
Luke's Last Liberty
Luke's Late Lunches
Luke's Lost Lamb
Luke's Movie Muddle
Luke's Newsie Knockout
Luke's Preparedness Preparation
Luke's Shattered Sleep
Luke's Society Mixup
Luke's Speedy Club Life
Luke's Trolley Trouble
Luke's Wishful Waiting
Marathon, The
Matrimonial Mixup, A
Mixup for Mazie, A
Naked Yaqui (bit)
Next Aisle Over
Never Touched Me
Non-Stop Kid, The
Nothing but Trouble
Off the Trolley
On the Fire
On the Jump

Once Every Ten Minutes
Over the Fence (first film in which
   he wore horn rimmed glasses)
Ozark Romance, An
Pay Your Dues
Peculiar Patients' Pranks
Phunphilms
Pinched
Pipe the Whiskers
Pistols for Breakfast
Pressing His Suit
Ragtime Snapshots
Rainbow Island
Rajah, The
Reckless Wrestlers
Ring up the Curtain
Ruses, Rhymes, Roughnecks
Sammy in Siberia, A
Samson (extra)
She Looses Me
She Loves Me Not
Si, Senor
Sic 'em Towser!
Skylight Sleep
Soaking the Clothes
Social Gangster
Soft Money
Some Baby
Somewhere in Turkey
Spit Ball Sadie
Spring Fever
Step Lively
Stop! Luke! Listen!
Swat the Crook
Swing Your Partner
Take a Chance
Terribly Stuck Up
That's Him!
Them Was the Happy Days
Tinkering with Trouble
Tip, The
Too Scrambled
Trouble Enough
Two Gun-Gussie
Unfriendly Fruit
Wanted--$5,000
We Never Sleep
Why Pick on Me?
Willie Work comedies (none released)
Young Mr. Jazz
Stage:
Macbeth (Felance)
Tess of the D'Urbervilles 1905

1587
LLOYD, William*
Bloodhounds of the North, The
   (embezzler)

Embezzler, The (William Perkins)
End of the Feud, The (Jed Putnam)
Lie, The (Mac's brother)
Richelieu (Joseph)
Tragedy of Whispering Creek, The
Unlawful Trade, The (Ol' Tate)

1588
LOCKNEY, J. P.*
Egg-Crate Wallop, The
Hey Foot, Straw Foot
Greased Lightning
String Beans

1589
LOCKWOOD, Harold (1887-1919)
Avenging Trail, The
Big Tremaine
Broadway Bill
Child of the Sea
Comeback, The
Conspiracy
County Chairman, The
Great Romance, The
Harbor Island
Haunted Pajamas, The
Hearts Adrift
Landloper, The
Lend Me Your Name
Life's Blind Alley
Man of Honor, A
Mansion of Misery, A
Pals First
Paradise Green
Pidgin Island
Promise, The
River of Romance, The
Secret Wire, The
Shadows of Suspicion
Shopgirls
Square Deceiver, The
Such a Little Queen
Tess of the Storm Country
Under the Handicap
Unwelcome Mrs. Hatch, The
Wildflower
Yankee Doodle in Berlin

1590
LOFTUS, Cecilia /aka/ Cissie (Ce-
   cilia Marie Loftus) (1876-1943)
Lady of Quality
Stage:
If I Were King 1901
Othello 1914
Shakesperean Company (Hollywood)
   1895
Vaudeville 1913

1591
LONG, Walter (1882-1952)
Birth of a Nation, The (Gus)
Chasing Rainbows
Desert Gold
Evil Eye, The
Golden Fetter, The
Hashimura to Go
Her Greatest Love (Zouroff)
Intolerance (Musketeer of the slums)
Joan, the Woman (the executioner)
Jordan Is a Hard Road
Little American, The (German
    Captain)
Mother and the Law, The
Nectorine
Out of Bondage
Poppy Girl's Husband, The
Queen of the Sea
Romance of the Redwoods, A (the
    sheriff)
Scarlet Days (Bagley)
Unprotected
Woman God Forgot, The (Taloc)
Year of the Locust

1592
LONGFELLOW, Malvina*
Adam Bede
Betta the Gypsy
For All Eternity
Holy Orders
Nelson
Romance of Lady Hamilton, The
Thelma
Will of the People, The

1593
LONGFELLOW, Stephanie*
As the Bells Rang Out
Better Way, The
Chief's Daughter, The
Convict's Sacrifice, A
Crooked Road, The
Eradicating Auntie
Impalement, The
In Life's Cycle
Lesson, The
Love among the Roses
Madame Rex
Message of the Violin, The
Necklace, The
Rocky Road, The
Strange Meeting, A
Thou Shalt Not
Two Women and a Man
Winning back His Love

1594
LONGWORTH, Josephine*
Beloved Adventurer, The (serial)

1595
LONSDALE, Harry*
Garden of Allah, The
Ne'er Do-Well, The

1596
LOOMIS, Margaret*
Bottle Imp, The
Everywoman
Told in the Hills
Why Smith Left Home

1597
LORING, Eva*
Felix on the Job (Felix's wife)

1598
LORRAINE, Lillian (1892-1955)
Neal of the Navy (serial)
Playing the Game
Stage:
Little Blue Devil 1919
Whirl of the World, The 1914
Ziegfeld Follies of 1909
Ziegfeld Follies of 1910
Ziegfeld Follies of 1911
Ziegfeld Follies of 1912
Ziegfeld Follies of 1918

1599
LORRAINE, Louise (1901-   )
Should a Wife Forgive?

1600
LOSEE, Frank* (d. 1937)
Ashes of Embers
Bab's series 1917
Eternal City, The
Firing Line, The
Good Gracious, Annabelle
Helene of the North
Here Comes the Bride
His Parisian Wife
Hulda from Holland
In Pursuit of Polly
La Tosca
Marie Limited
Masqueraders, The
Old Homestead, The
Paid in Full
Song of Songs, The
Spider, The
Uncle Tom's Cabin
Valentine Girl, The

Stage:
Dorothy Vernon of Haddon Hall 1903

1601
LOUIS, Willard (1886-1926)
Letty
Madame DuBarry (Guillaume
   DuBarry)

1602
LOVE, Bessie (Juanita Horton)
   (1898-   )
Acquitted
Aryan, The
Birth of a Nation, The (Piedmont
   girl)
Carolyn of the Corners
Cheerful Givers, The
Cupid Forecloses
Dawn of Understanding, The
Enchanted Bard, The
Flying Torpedo, The
Good Bad Man, The (Amy)
Great Adventure, The
Hell-to-Pay Austin
How Could You, Caroline?
Intolerance (Bride of Cana)
Little Boss, The
Little Reformer, The
Little Sister of Everybody, The
Mystery of the Leaping Fish, The
   (Little Fish blower)
Nina the Flower Girl
Over the Garden Wall
Persnickety Polly Ann
Quest of the Holy Grail
Reggie Mixes In (Agnes Shannon)
Sawdust Ring, The
Sister of Six, A
Stranded
Wee Lady Betty
Yankee Princess, The

1603
LOVE, Montagu (1877-1943)
Awakening, The
Bought and Paid For
Brand of Satan, The
Broadway Saint, A
Cross Bearer, The
Gilded Cage, The
Good for Nothing, The
Grouch, The
Hand Invisible, The
Hands Up!
Night of Love
One Hour of Love
Quickening Flame, The

Rasputin, the Black Monk
Rough Neck, The
Social Highwayman, The
Steel King, The
Stolen Orders
Three Green Eyes
Through Toils
To Him That Hath
Vengeance
Woman's Way, A
Stage:
Grumpy 1914

1604
LOVELY, Louise /aka/ Louise
   Carbasse (Louise Welch) (1896-   )
Bobbie of the Ballet
Dolly's Scoop
Father and the Boys
Gilded Spider, The (dual role,
   Leonita and Elisa)
Girl Who Wouldn't Quit, The
Grasp of Greed (Alice Gordon)
Grip of Jealousy, The
Last of the Duanes, The
Nobody's Wife
Painted Lips
Rich Man's Darling, A
Sirens of the Sea
Stronger Than Death
Tangled Hearts
Wings of the Morning
Wolf and His Mate, The
Wolves of the Night

1605
LOVERIDGE, Margaret*
Runaway June (serial)

1606
LOWE, Edmund (1892-1971)
Eyes on Youth
Spreading the Dawn
Vive La France!
Stage:
Brat, The 1917
Roads of Destiny 1918
Son-Daughter, The 1919

1607
LOWE, Maude*
Burden of Proof, The (maid)

1608
LOWERY, W. E. *
Reggie Mixes In (Tony Bernard)

1609
LOWRY, L. *

Hearts of the World (deaf and
  blind musician)

1610
LOYER, Georges*
Hearts of the World (a Poilu)

1611
LUCAS, Sam*
Uncle Tom's Cabin (Uncle Tom)

1612
LUCAS, Slim*
Lightning Bryce (serial)

1613
LUCAS, Wilfred (d. 1940)
Acquitted
As in a Looking Glass
Barbarian, Ingomar, The
Billy's Strategem
Cohen's Outing
Dan the Dandy
Desert's Sting, The
Diamond Star, The
Enoch Arden, Part I and II
Failure, The
Fate's Interception
Fisher Folks
Food Gamblers
Girl and Her Trust, A
Girl from Nowhere, The
Girls and Daddy, The
Golden Louis, The
Hands Up!
Heart Beats of Long Ago
Hell-to-Pay Austin
His Excellency, the Governor
His Mother's Scarf
His Trust
His Trust Fulfilled
Home Folks
Hushed Hours, The
Indian Brothers, The
Intolerance (a soldier)
Italian Blood
Judgment House
Just Like a Woman
Lily and the Rose, The
Lonedale Operator, The (railway man)
Macbeth
Man's Genesis
Massacre, The
Microscope Mystery, The
Miser's Heart, The
New Dress, The
Old Confectioner's Mistake, The
Primal Call, The

Primitive Man, The
Pueblo Legend, A
Red, Red Heart
Return of Mary, The
Rock Road, The
Rose of Kentucky, The
Sailor's Heart, A
1776 or The Hessian Renegades
Sins of Ambition
Soldiers of Fortune
Sorrowful Example, The
Spanish Gypsy, The
Swords and Hearts
Terrible Discovery, A
Thief and the Girl, The
Transformation of Mike, The
Under Burning Skies
Was He a Coward?
Westerners, The
When Kings Were the Law
White Rose of the Wild, The
Wild Cat, The
Wild Girl of the Sierras
Winning Back His Love
Woman of Pleasure, A
Wood Nymph, The

1614
LUGOSI, Bela (Arisztid Olt or Bela
  Lugosi Blasko) (1882-1956)
Alarcosbal
Az Elet Koralya
Az Ezredes
Casanova
Der Tanz auf den Vulken
Hamlet
Kuz delem a Letert
Leopard, A
Nachenschnur des Tot
Ninety Nine
Sklaven Frem der Willens
Tavaszi Vihar
Vad Izalmabogy
Stage:
Hungarian Players (New York)*

1615
LUKAS, Paul (Pal Lugacs) (1895-   )
Sphynx, The
Stage:
Liliom (title role; debut) 1916

1616
LUKE
Paramount dog
Butcher Boy, The

1617
LUMIERE, Auguste (1862-1954)
Baby's Breakfast

1618
LUND, O. A. C.*
Firelight
When Broadway Was a Trail

1619
LUND, Richard*
Ingeborg Holm
Sir Arne's Treasure

1620
LUPI, Ignazio*
Cabiria

1621
LUPINO, Wallace (1897-   )
Mr. Butterburn
Stage:
Babes in the Woods 1904

1622
LUTHER, Anna (1894-   )
Beast, The
Crooked to the End
Great Gamble, The (serial)
Her Moment
Jungle Trail, The
Lurking Peril, The (serial)
Marriage Bubble, The
Moral Suicide
Village Vampire, The /aka/ The
   Great Leap
Woman, Woman
Stage:
L. A. Mason Opera House 1917
   (sold programs)

1623
LUTRELL, Helen*
Gretna Green

1624
LYLE, Edythe*
Deliverance

1625
LYNCH, Walter*
Whispering Chorus, The (Evil Face)

1626
LYNDON, Clarence*
Lion and the Girl, The

1627
LYNDON, Larry*

His Naughty Thought
Nick of Time Baby, The
Thirst

1628
LYNTON, Mayme*
Seven Sisters, The

1629
LYON, Ben (1901-   )
Open Your Eyes

1630
LYONS, Edward (1886-   )
By the Sun's Rays
Eddie's Little Love Affair
Mrs. Plumb's Pudding
Some Runner
Wanted: a Husband
Wanted, a Leading Lady
War Bridegrooms

1631
LYTELL, Bert (1888-1954)
Blackie's Redemption
Blindman's Eyes
Boston Blackie's Little Pal
Easy to Make Money
Empty Pockets
Faith
Hitting the High Spots
Lion's Den, The
Lone Wolf, The (debut)
No Man's Land
One-Thing-at-a-Time o' Day
Spender, The
To Have and to Hold
Trail to Yesterday, The
Stage:
Cumberland '61 1902
First appearance 1891
Mary's Ankle 1917
Mixup, A 1914

1632
LYTELL, Wilfred (1892-1954)
Combat, The
Conflict, The
Destroyer, The
Lily and the Rose, The
Ninety and Nine, The
Our Mrs. McChesney

1633
LYTON, Robert*
Regular Girl, A

1634
LYTTON, L. Rogers*

Battle Cry of Peace, The
Belle of New York, The (Amos
   Gray)
Burden of Proof, The (George Blair)
Fates and Flora Fourflush (The Ten
   Billion Dollar Vitagraph Mystery
   Serial) (serial)
Forbidden City, The
Jerry's Uncle's Namesake (the
   uncle)
Panthea
Win(k)some Widow, The
Stage:
Madame X 1910

- M -

1635
MAC, Nila*
War Brides
Stage:
Hedda Gabler 1918

1636
McALLISTER, Mary*
Borrowed Sunshine
Bride of Fancy, The
Do Children Count?
Essanay child player 1916
Kill Joy, The
Little Missionary, The
Little Shoes
Little White Savage, The
On Trial
Pants
Sadie Goes to Heaven
Sins of Ambition
Uneven Road, The
Where Is My Mother?
Whosoever Shall Offend
Young Mother Hubbard

1637
McALLISTER, Paul (1875-   )
Hearts in Exile
Scales of Justice
Via Wireless
Stage:
Devil, The 1908

1638
McALPIN, Edith*
Spreading Dawn, The

1639
McALPINE, Jane*
Winning Stroke, The

1640
McAVOY, May (1901-   )
Hate
Hit or Miss
I'll Say
Mrs. Wiggs of the Cabbage Patch
My Husband's Other Wife
Perfect Lady, A
To Hell with the Kaiser
Way of a Woman, The
Woman under Oath

1641
McBRIDE, Donald*
Professional Patient, The

1642
MacBRIDE, Donald (1894-1957)
Sidney Drew comedies for Vitagraph

1643
McCALL, William*
Smashing Barriers (serial)

1644
McCARTHY, J. P.*
Intolerance (prison guard)

1645
McCLURE, A. W., Rev.*
Intolerance (Father Farley)

1646
McCOMAS, Carroll*
Paramount player 1919
Stage:
Inside the Lines 1915
Scrap of Paper, The 1917
Seven Chances 1916

1647
McCONNELL, Mollie*
Who Pays?

1648
McCORD, Mrs. Lewis*
Chimmie Fadden (Mother Fadden)
Chimmie Fadden out West (Mother
   Fadden)
Dream Girl, The (character woman)
Heart of Nora Flynn, The (Maggie,
   the cook)
Kindling (Mrs. Bates)
Virginian, The (Mrs. Balaam)

1649
McCOY, Gertrude (1896-1967)
Auction Mart, The

Blue Bird, The
Chips
Christine Johnstone
Edison player 1912
Friend Wilson's Daughter
Greater Than Art
June Friday
On the Stroke of Twelve
Through Turbulent Waters
What Could She Do?

1650
McCOY, Hansen*
His Last Laugh

1651
McCOY, Harry (1894-   )
Because He Loved Her
Bubbles of Trouble
Caught in a Cabaret (the boyfriend)
Cinders of Love
Fair Enough
False Roomers
For Better--but Worse
Garage, The
Getting Acquainted
Great Pearl Tangle, The
High and Dry
His Auto Ruination
His Last Laugh
His New Profession
Hoosier Romance
How Heroes Are Made
Human Hound's Triumph, A
In Again--out Again
Joker Comedies 1911
Keystone Comedies 1912
Love Will Conquer
Mabel at the Wheel (the boyfriend)
Mabel's Busy Day
Mabel's Married Life
Mabel's Strange Predicament
Masquerader, The
Merely a Married Man
Mike and Jake at the Beach
Movie Star, A
One Night Stand, A
Perils in the Park
Property Man, The
Saved by Wireless
She Loved a Sailor
Those Bitter Sweets
Those Love Pangs
Tillie's Punctured Romance
Twilight Baby
Village Scandal, A

1652
McCULLOUGH, Philo (1893-   )

Daughter Angele
Grip of Evil, The (serial)
Neglected Wife, The (serial)
Red Circle, The (serial)
Soldiers of Fortune

1653
McCUTCHEON, Wallace*
Black Secret, The (serial)

1654
McDANIEL, George A.*
Girl and the Game, The (serial)
She-Devil, The

1655
McDERMOTT, Joseph*
Mothering Heart, The
Sheriff's Baby, The
Timely Interception, A

1656
McDERMOTT, Marc (1880-1929)
Aida
Alabaster Box, An
Buchanan's Wife
Colonel of the Red Hussars
Convict's Parole, The
Gauntlet of Washington, The
Girl of Today, The
Green God, The
Intrigue
Kathleen Mavourneen (Squire of Traise)
Lady Clare
Man Who Disappeared, The (serial)
Martin Chuzzlewit
Mary Stuart
New Moon, The
Old Appointment, An
Ranson's Folly
Thirteenth Chair, The
Three Musketeers, The (Cardinal
   Richelieu)
Tony America
What Happened to Mary? (serial)
While John Bolt Slept
With the Eyes of the Blind

1657
MacDONALD, Donald*
String Beans

1658
McDONALD, Francis (1891-1968)
Black Orchids, The
Bold Impersonation, A
Gun Woman, The
Madame Sphinx
Mansard Mystery, The

MacDonald, J. Farrell   168

O' Connor's Mag
Prudence on Broadway
Voice on the Wire, The

1659
MacDONALD, J. Farrell (1875-1952)
Fight for Love, A
Heart of Maryland, The
Imp player 1910
Last Egyptian, The
Marked Men
Outcasts of Poker Flat, The
Oz features 1915
Rags
Roped Tides of Retribution

1660
MacDONALD, Mrs. J. Farrell*
Imp player 1910

1661
MacDONALD, Katherine (1891-1956)
Battling Jane
Beauty Market, The
Headin' South (the lady)
His Own Home Town
Mr. Fixit (Georgina Burroughs)
Riddle Gawne (Kathleen Harkness)
Shark Malone
Squaw Man, The (Diana)
Woman Thou Gavest Me, The

1662
MacDONALD, Wallace (1891-)
Caught in a Cabaret
Dough and Dynamite
Leave It to Susan
Mabel's Busy Day
Mabel's Married Life
Madame Sphinx
Rounders, The
Spotlight Sadie
Tillie's Punctured Romance

1663
McDOUGALL, Rex*
Please Help Emily

1664
MacDOUGALL, Robin*
Blue Bird, The

1665
McDOWELL, Claire (Mrs. Charles
    Mailes) (1887-1967)
As in a Looking Glass
Billy's Strategem
Blot on the 'Scutcheon

Cry for Help, A
Empty Gun, The
Everlasting Mercy
Female of the Species
Fighting Back
Follies Girl, The
Gates of Doom, The
God Within, The
Golden Supper, The
Heart of the Hills
Her Father's Silent Partner
His Last Burglary
His Trust Fulfilled
House of Darkness, The
In the Aisles of the Wild
In the Days of '49
Lena and the Geese
Massacre, The
Men and Women
Mohawk's Way, A
Olaf--an Atom
Primal Call, The
Ranchero's Revenge, The
Romany Tragedy, A
Sands of Dee, The
Ship of Doom, The
Sorrowful Example, The
Storm Woman, The
Sunbeam, The
Swords and Hearts
Telephone Girl and the Lady, The
Temporary Truce, A
Two Daughters of Eve, The
Unwelcome Guest, The
Wanderer, The
Welcome Intruder, A
Wilful Peggy
Woman Scorned, A
You Can't Believe Everything

1666
MACE, Fred*
Algy on the Force
Ambitious Butler, The
At It Again
At Twelve o'Clock
Bangville Police, The
Bath Tub Perils
Battle of Who Run, The
Bear Escape, A
Beating He Needed, The
Chief's Predicament, The
Cohen Collects a Debt
Crooked to the End
Cupid in a Dental Parlor
Cure That Failed, The
Darktown Belle, The
Deaf Burglar, A

Deacan's Trouble, The
Desperate Lover, A
Double Wedding, A
Drummer's Vacation
Elite Ball, The
Family Mix-Up, A
Firebugs, The
Foreman of the Jury, The
Gangsters, The
Heinze's Resurrection
Her Birthday Present
Her New Beau
His Last Scent
Hoffmeyer's Legacy
Hubby's Job
Janitor's Wife's Temptation, The
Jealous Waiter, The
Jenny's Pearls
Just Brown's Luck
Love and Pain
Love Will Conquer
Lover's Might, A
Mabel's Adventures
Mabel's Heroes
Mabel's Lovers
Mabel's Strategem
Man Next Door, The
Mr. Fix-It
Murphy's I. O. U.
My Valet
New Neighbor, The
Oily Scoundrel, An
Pat's Day Off
Pedro's Dilemma
Professor's Daughter, The
Red Hot Romance, A
Riley and Schultz
Rube and the Baron, The
Rural Third Degree, The
Saving Mabel's Day
Sleuths at the Floral Parade, The
Sleuth's Last Stand, The
Stolen Glory
Stolen Purse, The
Tale of a Black Eye, The
Temperamental Husband, A
Toplitsky and Company
Village Vampire, The
Water Nymph, The

1667
McEWEN, Walter*
Probation Wife, The

1668
McFADDEN, Ivor*
Elmo, the Mighty (serial)

1669
McGARRY, Vera*
Call of the North, The (Julie)

1670
McGLYNN, Frank (1867-1951)
Edison player 1907
Gloria's Romance (serial)
Poor Little Rich Girl, The
Stage:
Abraham Lincoln 1919
Gold Bug, The (Casino Theatre,
    New York) 1896

1671
McGOWAN, Bob*
Bold Bad Knight, A

1672
McGOWAN, J. P. (1880-1952)
From the Manger to the Cross
Girl and the Game, The (serial)
Hazards of Helen, The (serial)
Kalem player 1911
Railroad Raiders, The (serial)

1673
McGRAIL, Walter (1889-1970)
Black Secret, The (serial)
Business of Life, The
Country Cousin
Miss Ambition
Perils of Pauline, The (serial)
Scarlet Runner, The (serial)
Song of the Soul, The
Trumpet of the Weak, The
Within the Law
Womanhood

1674
McGRANE, Thomas J.*
Crimson Stain Mystery, The (serial)

1675
McGRAW, John J.*
One Touch of Nature

1676
McGUIRE, Paddy*
Bank, The
Jitney Elopement, A
Night in the Show, A
Shanghaied
Tramp, The
Work

1677
MACHAREN, Mary*
Mysterious Mrs. M., The

1678
MACHIN, Will*
Lad and the Lion, The (William
  Bankinston)

1679
McINTOSH, Burr (1862-1942)
Adventures of Wallingford, The
  (serial)
My Partner
Stage:
Out There 1918
Trilby 1895; 1905; 1915

1680
McINTYRE, Frank*
Too Fat to Fight
Traveling Salesman, The
Stage:
Classmates 1907
Oh! Oh! Delphine 1912
Rose of China, The 1919
Snobs 1911
Traveling Salesman, The 1908

1681
MACISTE*
Warrior, The

1682
MACK, Bobby*
Red Ace, The (serial)

1683
MACK, Hayward*
Dolly's Scoop
Father and the Boys
Gilded Spider, The
Graft (serial)
Grip of Jealousy, The
Jane and the Stranger
Tangled Hearts

1684
MACK, Hughie (1887-1952)
Desert of Egypt, The
Fellow Romans
Make It Snappy
New Secretary, The
Open Another Bottle
Rush Orders
Some Widow
Too Many Husbands
Wink, The
Win(k)some Widow, The

1685
MACK, Willard (1873-1934)

Aloha-Oe
Conqueror, The
Corner, The
Devil Decides, The
Hell Cat
Shadows
Stage:
Tiger Rose 1917

1686
McKAY, Fred*
Lie, The (the father)

1687
McKEE, Lafayette*
Adventures of Kathlyn, The (serial)

1688
McKEE, Raymond*
Captain Kidd, Jr.
Edison player 1916
Heart of the Hills
Kathleen Mavourneen (Terrence
  O'Moore)
Kidnapped
Spirit of the Red Cross, The
Unbeliever, The

1689
MacKENZIE, Donald*
Perils of Pauline, The (serial)
  (Blinky Bill)

1690
McKIM, Robert (1887-)
Brand, The
Claws of the Hun
Disciple, The
Edge of the Abyss, The
Greased Lightning
Green Eyes
Hell's Hinges (clergyman)
Her Kingdom of Dreams
Law of the Land, The
Law of the North, The
Love Me
Marriage Ring, The
Playing the Game
Primal Lure, The
Return of Draw Egan, The
Silent Man, The
Son of His Father
Stepping Stone, The
Vamp, The
Weaker Sex, The
Westerners, The

1691
McKINNON, Al*
Dangers of a Bride

1692
McKINNON, John*
Lost Express, The (serial)

1693
MACKLEY, Mrs. Arthur*
Intolerance (an Uplifter)

1694
MacLAREN, Mary (1896-   )
Amazing Wife, The
Bonnie, Bonnie Lassie
Brand, The
Bread
Creaking Stairs
Idle Wives
Model's Confession, The
Mysterious Mrs. Musslewhite, The
Petal on the Current, A
Pointing Finger, The
Saving the Family Name
Secret Marriage, The
Shoes
Unpainted Woman, The
Vanity Pool
Weaker Vessels

1695
McLAUGHLIN, Ed*
Beloved Adventurer, The (serial)

1696
McLAUGHLIN, J. B.*
Bondage

1697
MacLEAN, Douglas (1890-1967)
As Ye Sow
Captain Kidd, Jr.
Fuss and Feathers
Happy though Married
Home Breaker, The
Hun Within, The
Johanna Enlists
Mirandy Smiles
Souls in Pawn
23 1/2 Hours Leave
When Johnny Comes Marching Home

1698
MacLEOD, Elsie*
Carmen (Michaela)

1699
McLEOD, Elsie*
Edison player 1911

1700
MacMILLAN, Violet*
Mrs. Plumb's Pudding

1701
MacPHERSON, Jeannie*
Captive, The
Carmen (a gypsy girl)
Corner in Wheat, A
Death Disc, The
Desert's Sting, The
Enoch Arden, Part I
Fisher Folks
Girl of the Golden West, The (Nina)
Heart Beats of Long Ago
Last Drop of Water, The
Mr. Jones at the Ball (maid)
Mr. Jones Entertains (maid)
Rose of the Rancho, The (Isabelita
    Espinoza's daughter)
Sea Urchin, The
Vaquero's Vow, The
Winning Back His Love

1702
MacQUARRIE, Albert*
He Comes up Smiling (Batchelor)
Knickerbocker Buckaroo, The
    (Manuel Lopez)

1703
MacQUARRIE, Frank*
Black Box, The (serial)

1704
MacQUARRIE, George*
Betsy Ross

1705
MacQUARRIE, Murdoch /aka/ M. J.
    MacQuarrie*
Bloodhounds of the North (a mountie)
By the Sun's Rays
Discord and Harmony (the composer)
Embezzler, The (John Spencer)
End of the Feud, The (Hen Dawson)
Forbidden Room, The (Dr. Gibson)
Her Grave Mistake (Roger Grant)
Honor of the Mounted, The (a
    mountie)
Lamb, the Woman, the Wolf, The
    (the lamb)
Lie, The (Auld MacGregor)
Menace to Carlotta, The (Tony's
    Father)

Miner's Romance, A Bob Jenkins
Old Cobbler, The (Title role)
Panthea
Poppy
Ranch Romance, A (Jack Deering)
Red Margaret--Moonshiner (a
  government agent)
Remember Mary Magdalen (the
  minister)
Richelieu (the Cardinal
Stronger Mind, The (a crook)
Unlawful Trade, The (the Revenue
  man)

1706
McRAE, Bruce
Hazel Kirke
Star Over Night, A

1707
McVEY, Lucille (Mrs. John Drew)
  (1895-   )
Amateur Liar, The
As Others See Us
At a Premium
At the Count of Ten
Auntie's Portrait
Awakening of Helen Minor
Before and after Taking
Blackmail
Borrowing Trouble
Bunkered
Cave Man's Bluff
Childhood's Happy Days
Close Resemblance
Dentist, The
Double Life
Suplicity
Gas Logic
Handy Henry
Harold, the Last of the Saxons
Help!
Henry's Ancestors
Her Anniversaries
Her Economic Independence
Her First Game
Her Lesson
Her Obsession
High Cost of Living, The
His Curiosity
His Deadly Calm
His Ear for Music
His First Love
His Perfect Day
His Rival
Hist ... Spies!
Hypochondriac, The
Joy of Freedom, The

Kalem player 1911
Lady in the Library, A
Lest We Forget
Locked Out
Matchmakers, The
Mr. Parker, Hero
Music Hath Charm
Nobody Home
Nothing to Wear
Number One
Once a Man
Once a Mason
One of the Family
Patriot, The
Pest, The
Professional Patient, The (woman
  in a waiting room)
Putting it Over on Henry
Rebellion of Mr. Minor, The
Regiment of Two, A
Reliable Henry
Romance and Kings
Rubbing It In
Shadowing Henry
Sisterly Scheme, A
Special Today
Spirit of Merry Christmas
Squared
Story of a Glove, The (Mrs. Huggins)
Taking a Rest
Their First
Too Much Henry
Tootsie
Twelve Good Hens and True
Unmarried Look, The
Wages No Object
Why Henry Left Home
Youthful Affair, A

1708
MACY, Ann Sullivan*
Deliverance

1708
MACY, Carlton*
Destruction (Charles Froment)
Gold and the Woman (Dugald
  Chandos)

1710
MADDEN, Golda (1894-   )
Branded (serial)
Fires of Rebellion
Flying Colors
Girl of My Dreams
Jilted Janet
Lombardi, Ltd.
Turn in the Road, The

1711
MADISON, Cleo (1882-1964)
Alas and Alack
Black Orchids, The
Chalice of Sorrow, The
Cross Purposes
Damon and Pythias
Fascination of the Fleur de Lis
    (Lisette)
Great Radium Mystery, The (serial)
Heart of a Cracksman, The
Mother's Atonement, A (dual role,
    mother and daughter)
Pine's Revenge, The (the girl)
Romance of Tarzan, The
Severed Hand, The
Trap, The
Trey o' Hearts, The (dual role)
    (serial)

1712
MADISON, Ethel*
From Patches to Plenty
That Little Band of Gold

1713
MAHARONI, George*
Patria (serial)

1714
MAILES, Charles Hill (1870-1937)
Adopted Brothers
Adventure in the Autumn Woods, An
At the Altar
Battle at Elderbush Gulch
Beast at Bay, A
Beloved Jim
Bittersweet
Blot on the 'Scutcheon
Brass Bullet, The (serial)
By Man's Law
Change of Spirit, A
Coming of Angelo, The
Dynast, The
Friends
Full of Pep
Girl and Her Trust, The
Girl Who Won Out, The
Her Mother's Oath
Hero of Little Italy, The
Home Folks
House of Darkness, The
Iola's Promise
Judith of Bethulia
Just Gold
Just Like a Woman
Lair of the Wolf, The
Lena and the Geese

Liberty Bells
Lonely Villa, The (Father)
Man's Genesis (Monkeywalk)
Massacre, The
Miser's Heart, The
Misunderstood Boy, A
My Hero
Narrow Road, The
New York Hat, The
Oil and Water
Olaf--an Atom
Out Better Selves
Outcasts of Poker Flat, The
Painted Lady, The
Power, The
Primitive Man
Red Hot Dollars
Reformers, The or The Lost Art
    of Minding One's Business
Sands of Dee, The
So Near, Yet So Far
Speed Maniac, The
Spotted Lily, The
Tale of the Wilderness, A
Talk of the Town, The
Temporary Truce, A
Terrible Discovery, A
Those Hicksville Boys
Unwelcome Guest, The
Wanderer, The
Welcome Intruder, A
Woman Scorned, A
Young Patriot, A

1715
MAINHALL, Harry*
Essanay player 1912

1716
MAISON, Edna*
Richelieu (Marion de Lormer)

1717
MALATESTA, Fred M. (1889-)
Demon, The
Devil's Trail, The
Four-Flusher, The
Full of Pep
Greatest Thing in Life, The
Legion of Death, The
Other Side of Eden, The
Terror of the Range, The (serial)
Wolf-Face Man, The (serial)

1718
MALONE, Florence*
Yellow Menace, The (serial)

1719
MALONE, Molly (1895-   )
Bucking Broadway
Desert Hero, A
Garage, The
Hayseed, The
Hill Billy, The
Marked Man, A
Phantom Riders, The
Pullman Mystery, The
Red Stain, The
Rescue, The (Betty Jerold)
Scarlet Drop, The
Soul Herder, The
Straight Shooting
Thieves' Gold
Wild Women
Woman's Fool, A

1720
MALONEY, Leo D. (-1929)
Horse: Senator and Flash
Dog: Bullet
Fight for Millions, A
Girl and the Game, The (serial)
Lass of the Lumberlands (serial)
Lost Express, The (serial)
Outlaw Express
Partners Three
Railroad Raiders, The (serial)
Range Rider series
Santa Fe Mac
Spitfire of Seville, The
Wolverine, The

1721
MAMRICK, Burwell*
Devil Stone, The

1722
MANDER, Miles /aka/ Luther
   Miles (Lionel Mander)
   (1888-1946)
Once upon a Time

1723
MANLEY, Marie*
Perils of the Park
Snow Cure
Tugboat Romeo, A

1724
MANN, Alice*
His Wedding Night

1725
MANN, Frankie*
Sporting Duchess, The

1726
MANN, Hank (1888-   )
Caught in a Cabaret
Fatal Mallet, The
Hearts and Sparks
His Bread and Butter (a waiter)
In the Clutches of a Gang
Knockout, The
Mabel's Married Life
Mabel's Strange Predicament
Modern Enoch Arden, A
Tillie's Punctured Romance (a
   Keystone Cop)
Village Blacksmith, The

1727
MANN, Harry*
Broken Coin, The (serial)

1728
MANN, Margaret (1868-   )
Heart of Humanity, The
Once to Every Woman
Right to Happiness, The

1729
MANNERS, Lady Diana*
Great Love, The (herself)

1730
MANNING, Joseph*
Rags

1731
MANNING, Mildred*
Enemy to the King, An
Third Judgement, The
Westerners, The

1732
MANON, Marcia (Camille Ankewich)*
Old Wives for New (Viola)
Stella Maris
Test of Honor

1733
MANSFIELD, Martha (1899-1923)
Broadway Bill
Max Comes Across
Max in a Taxi
Max Wants a Divorce
Stage:
Ziegfeld Midnight Frolic 1919

1734
MANTELL, Robert B. *
Spider and the Fly, The
Wife's Sacrifice, A

Stage:
Dagger and the Cross, The 1900
Hamlet (Title role) 1911
King John (Title role) 1909
Oedipus Rex 1911
Repertory 1905; 1909; 1911; 1915;
   1917; 1918
Richard III 1904
Richelieu 1907

1735
MANZINE, Italia Almirante*
Cabiria

1736
MARBA, Joseph*
Carter Case, The (The Craig
   Kennedy Serial) (serial)

1737
MARBURGH, Bertram*
Eagle's Eye, The (serial)

1738
MARCEAU, Emilie*
Open Your Eyes

1739
MARCUS, James A.*
Carmen (Dancaire)
Serpent, The (Ivan Lazar)

1740
MARDIJANIAN, Aurora*
Auction of Souls

1741
MARINOFF, Fania*
McTeague
Stage:
House Next Door, The 1909
Tempest, The 1916
Thousand Years Ago, A 1914

1742
MARION, F.*
Hearts of the World (Doug's
   Brother)

1743
MARION, Frances*
Girl of Yesterday, A

1744
MARION, George (1860-   )
Film debut 1914

1745
MARKEY, Enid (1895-   )

Aloha-Oe
Aztec God, The
Between Men
Captive God, The
Card Sharp
Cheating the Public
City of Darkness
Civilization (Katheryn Haldermann)
Cup of Life, A
Curse of Eve, The
Darkening Trail
Devil's Double, The
Fortunes of War, The
Friend, The
In the Cow Country
In the Tennessee Hills
Iron Strain, The
Jim Greenberg's Boy
Mother, I Need You
Not of the Flock
Responsibility
Romance of Tarzan, The (Jane)
Shell 43
Spirit of the Bell, The
Taking of Luke McVane, The /aka/
   The Fugitive (Mercedes)
Tarzan of the Apes (Jane)
War's Women
Yankee Way, The
Zeppelin's Last Raid, The
Stage:
Up in Mabel's Room 1919

1746
MARKS, Willis*
Greased Lightning

1747
MARLBOROUGH, Helen*
Wild Goose Chase, The (Betty's
   Mother)

1748
MARMONT, Percy (1883-   )
Climbers, The
In the Hollow of Her Hand
Indestructible Wife, The
Lie, The
Pride
Rose of the World
Three Men and a Girl
Turn of the Wheel
Vengeance of Durand
Winchester Woman, The

1749
MARSH, Betty*
Gypsy Joe

Janitor's Wife's Temptations, The
Modern Enoch Arden, A

1750
MARSH, Gene*
His Prehistoric Past /aka/ The
    Hula Hula Dance

1751
MARSH, Mae (Mary Warne Marsh)
    (1895-1968)
Adventure in the Autumn Woods, An
All Woman
Avenging Conscience (the maid)
Battle at Elderbush Gulch
Battle of the Hearts, The
Beloved Traitor
Big James' Heart
Birth of a Nation, The (Flora
    Cameron)
Bondage of Barbara
Broken Ways
Brothers
Brutality
Brute Force
By Man's Law
Child of the Paris Streets, A
Cinderella Man, The
Down by the Sounding Sea
Escape, The (Jennie Joyce)
Face in the Dark, The
Fields of Honor
Fighting Blood
Glorious Adventure, A
Her Mother's Oath
Hidden Fires
His Mother's Son
Home Folks
Home, Sweet Home (Apple Pie Mary)
Hoodoo Ann
In Prehistoric Days
Indian Uprising at Sante Fe
Influence of the Unknown
Intolerance (Dear One)
Judith of Bethulia
Kentucky Girl, The
Lady and the Mouse, The
Lena and the Geese
Lesser Evil, The
Little Tease, The
Love in an Apartment Hotel
Man's Genesis (Lilywhite)
Marriage of Molly O', The
Money Mad
Mother and the Law
Near to Earth
New York Hat, The
One Exciting Night

One Is Business, the Other Crime
Parante, The
Perfidy of Mary, The
Polly of the Circus
Primitive Man
Quest of the Holy Grail
Racing Strain, The
Reformers, The or The Lost Art of
    Minding One's Business
Sands of Dee, The
Spirit Awakened, The
Spotlight Sadie
Sunshine Alley
Telephone Girl and the Lady, The
Temporary Truce, A
Tender Hearted Boy, The
Wanderer, The
Wharf Rat, The
Wild Girl of the Sierra
Yaqui Cur, The

1752
MARSH, Margaret*
Exploits of Elaine, The (serial)

1753
MARSH, Marguerite (1892-   )
Carter Case, The (The Craig
    Kennedy Serial) (serial)
Conquered Hearts
Devil's Needle, The
Eternal Magdelene, The
Fair Enough
Fields of Honor
Goldwyn player 1917
Intolerance (debutante)
Little Meena's Romance
Master Mystery, The (serial)
Mender of the Nets, The
Mr. Goode, the Samaritan
Royal Democrat

1754
MARSHALL, Boyd*
King Lear

1755
MARSHALL, Jack*
Whom the Gods Destroy

1756
MARSHALL, Tully (T. M. Phillips)
    (1864-1943)
Arizona
Birth of a Nation, The
Bound in Morocco
Cheating Cheaters
Child of the Paris Streets, A

Countess Charming
Crimson Gardenia, The
Daughter of Mine
Devil Stone, The (Silas Martin)
Devil's Needle, The
Everywoman
Fall of Babylon, The
Girl Who Stayed at Home, The
  (man about town)
Golden Fetter, The
Grim Game, The
Hawthorne of the U. S. A.
Her Kingdom of Dreams
Intolerance (High Priest of Bel)
Joan, the Woman (L'Oiseleur, the
  Man Monk)
Lady of Red Butte, The
Let Katy Do It
Life Line
Lottery Man, The
M' Liss
Maggie Pepper
Man from Funeral Range, The
Martha's Vindication
Modern Musketeer, A (Phillip
  Marden)
Old Wives for New (Simcox)
Oliver Twist (Fagin)
Paid in Full
Romance of the Redwoods, A (Sam
  Sparks)
Sable Lorcha
Squaw Man, The (Sir John Applegate)
Thing We Love, The
Too Many Millions
Unconquered
We Can't Have Everything (the
  director)
Whispering Chorus, The (F. P.
  Chumley)
Stage:
City, The 1909
Paid in Full 1908
Talker, The 1912

1757
MARSTINI, Rosita*
Madame DuBarry (Mother Savord)

1758
MARTEN, Helen*
Lubin player 1913

1759
MARTIN, Chris-Pin (Ysabel
  Ponciana Chris-Pin Martin Piaz)
  /aka/ "El Comico"*
Began film career with a troup of

Indians 1911
Extra and bits up to 1919

1760
MARTIN, Florence*
Forbidden Path, The (Barbara
  Reynolds)
Light, The (Jeanette)
Soul of Buddah, The (Mrs. M.
  Romaine)
Tiger Woman, The (Marion Harding)
When Men Desire (Elsie Henner)

1761
MARTIN, Glenn*
Girl of Yesterday, A

1762
MARTIN, Marvin*
Railroad Raiders, The (serial)

1763
MARTIN, Mary*
Eternal Sapho, The (Mrs. Drummond)
Scarlet Letter, The
Tiger Woman, The (Mrs. Mark
  Jarris)
Vixen, The (Helen Drummond)

1764
MARTIN, Vivian (1893-   )
Butterfly on the Wheel
Fair Barrier
Forbidden Paths
Girl at Home, The
Her Country First
Her Father's Son
Home Town Girl, The
Innocent Adventuress, An
Jane Goes a-Wooing
Little Comrade, The
Little Miss Optimist
Little Scrub Lady, The
Louisana
Mary Gusta
Merely Mary Ann
Mirandy Smiles
Modern Thelma, A
Molly Entangled
Molly Shawn
Old Dutch
Petticoat Pilot
Stronger Love, The
Sunset Trail, The
Third Kiss, The
Trouble Buster, The
Unclaimed Goods
Vivette

Wishing Hour, The
You Never Saw Such a Girl
Stage:
High Cost of Loving, The 1914
Marriage Game, The 1913
Officer 666 1912
Stop Thief! 1912

1765
MARTINDEL, Edward*
Foundling, The
Stage:
Wedding Trip, The 1911

1766
MASON, Ann*
Deliverance

1767
MASON, Smilin' Billy*
Baseball Bill
Baseball Bill series
Baseball Madness
Black Nine, The
Box of Tricks
Flirting with Marriage
Her Breezy Affair
Strike One!

1768
MASON, Charles*
Runaway June (serial)

1769
MASON, Dan*
Lure of Ambition, The (Sylvester
    Dolan)
Yellow Ticket, The

1770
MASON, Edna*
Under the Crescent (serial)

1771
MASON, James*
Squaw Man, The (Grouchy)

1772
MASON, John*
Jim, the Penman
Stage:
As a Man Thinks 1911
Attack, The 1912
Big Change, The 1918
Common Clay 1915
Ghost Breaker, The 1913
Leah Kleschna 1904
Mice and Men 1903

Nurse Marjorie 1906
Son of the People, A 1910
Song of Songs, The 1914
Witching Hour, The 1907
Yellow Ticket, The 1914

1773
MASON, Le Roy (1903-1947)
Fox player 1919

1774
MASON, Shirley (Leona Flugarth)
    (1900-   )
Apple Tree Girl, The
Awakening of Ruth, The
Come on In
Cy Whittaker's Ward
Final Close-Up, The
Goodbye, Bill
Gosh Darn the Kaiser
Rescuing Angel, The
Seven Deadly Sins, The ("Passion")
Tell-Tale Step, The
Unwritten Code, The
Vanity Fair
Wall Invisible, The
Winning Girl, The
Stage:
Passers By (*)
Poor Little Rich Girl (*)
Rip Van Winkle (*)

1775
MASON, Sidney /aka/ Sydney*
Forbidden Path, The (Felix
    Benavente)
His Neighbor's Wife
Seven Sisters

1776
MASON, William*
Cinders of Love
Dash of Courage, A
Dizzy Heights and Daring Hearts

1777
MASSIMER, Howard*
Gold and the Woman (Finlay)

1778
MASTERS, Mary*
Snow in the Desert

1779
MATHÉ, Edouard*
Vampires, The

1780
MATIESEN, Otto (1893-   )
Floor Below, The

1781
MATTHISON, Edith Wynne*
Lasky player 1915
Stage:
Everyman (American debut) 1902;
   1913
King Henry VIII 1916
Piper, The 1911
Servant in the House, The 1908
Twelfth Night (Viola) 1904
Winter's Tale, The 1910

1782
MATTOX, Martha (-1938)
Eve in Exile
Polly Put the Kettle On
Scarlet Drop, The
Scarlet Shadow, The
Thieves' Gold
Wild Women

1783
MAUDE, Arthur*
Pelléas and Melésande

1784
MAUDE, Cyril (1862-1951)
Beauty and the Barge
House of Temperley, The
Peer Gynt
Stage:
Grumpy 1913
Saving Grace, The 1918
Second in Command, The (American
   debut) 1913

1785
MAUREICE, Ruth*
Mystery of 13, The (serial)

1786
MAURICE, "Mother" Mary
   (1844-1918)
Battle Cry of Peace, The
For France
Saving an Audience

1787
MAWSON, Edward*
Return of Eve

1788
MAXAM, Louella*
Ambrose's Rapid Rise

Bucking Society
Deuce Duncan
His Bitter Pill (Sheriff's girl)
His Lying Heart
Movie Star, A
Oily Scoundrel, An

1789
MAXWELL, Edwin*
Law of Compensation, The

1790
MAY, Ann*
Lombardi, Ltd.

1791
MAY, Doris*
Hired Man, The
Let's Be Fashionable
Little American, The (doubled for
   Mary Pickford)
Playing the Game
23 1/2 Hours Leave
What's Your Husband Doing?

1792
MAY, Edna*
Vitagraph player 1916
Stage:
Belle of New York, The 1888
Catch of the Season, The 1905
Girl from up There, The 1901
School Girl, The 1904

1793
MAY, Lola*
Beggar of Cawpore, The
Civilization (Queen Eugenie)
Heart of Nora Flynn, The (Mrs.
   Stone)
Stage:
Gentleman from Mississippi, The 1908

1794
MAYALL, Herschel*
Card Sharp
Carmen of the Klondike
City of Darkness
City of the Dead
Civilization (King of Wredpryd)
Cleopatra (messenger)
Heart of Rachel, The
Keno Bates, Liar--Wind River /aka/
   The Last Card
Kismet
Madame DuBarry (Jean DuBarry)
Money Corporal, The
Renegade, The

Rose of the Blood, The (Koliensky)
Seal of Death, The
Spirit of the Bell, The
Wings of the Morning

1795
MAYO, Edna (1893-   )
Blindness of Virtue, The
Chaperon, The
Hearts of Love
Key to Yesterday, The
Little Straw Wife, The
Misleading Lady, The
Prince of Graustark, The
Return of Eve
Salvation Joan
Strange Case of Mary Page, The
  (serial)
Woman Hater, The

1796
MAYO, Frank (1886-1963)
Betsy Rose
Brute Breaker, The
Evil of the Rich
Glory
Hot Head, The
Interloper, The
Little Brother of the Rich, A
Mary Regan
Red Circle, The (serial)
Trap, The
Who Wins? /aka/ The Price of
  Folly

1797
MAZZATO, Umberto*
Cabiria

1798
MEEKS, Kate*
David Harum

1799
MEI, Lady Tsen*
For Freedom of the East

1800
MEIGHAN, Thomas (1879-1936)
Arms and the Girl
Dupe, The
Fighting Hope, The
For Better, for Worse
Forbidden City (U. S. Consul
  assistant)
Frontier of the Stars
Heart of the Hills
Heart of the Wilds

Heart of Wetona, The (Indian Agent)
In Pursuit of Polly
Kindling ("Honest" Heine Schultz)
Land of Promise, The
M' Liss
Male and Female (Crichton the
  butler)
Miracle Man, The (Tom Burke)
Missing
Mysterious Miss Terry, The
Out of a Clear Sky
Prince Chap, The
Probation Wife, The
Puddin' Head Wilson
Secret Sin, The
Silent Partner, The
Sowers, The
Storm, The
Trail of the Lonesome Pine, The
  (Jack Hale)
Stage:
Dictator, The 1904
Return of Peter Grimm, The 1911

1801
MELFORD, George*
Kalem player 1911

1802
MELIES, Georges (1861-1938)
Artist's Dream, The
Baron Munchausen
Cinderella
Conquest of the Pole (Professor
  Mahaul)
Dreyfus Affair, The
Impossible Voyage, The
Indianrubber Head, The
Kingdom of the Fairies
Twenty Thousand Leagues under the
  Sea
Une Partie de Cartes (debut)
Voyage to the Moon

1803
MELLININA, Ardita*
Deliverance

1804
MELLISH, Fuller*
Esmeralda

1805
MELVILLE, Rose*
She Came, She Saw, She Conquered
  (Sis Hopkins)
Stage:
Sis Hopkins 1900

1806
MENJOU, Adolphe (Adolphe Jean
    Menjou) (1890-1963)
Amazons, The
Bella Donna
Blue Envelope, The
Moth, The
Parisian Romance, A
Rupert of Hentzau
Valentine Girl, The

1807
MEREDITH, Charles (1890-1964)
Family Honor, The
Luck in Pawn

1808
MEREDITH, Lois*
Conspiracy, The
Stage:
Help Wanted 1914

1809
MEREDYTH, Bess*
Desert's Sting, The

1810
MERKYL, John*
Burden of Proof, The (Robert Ames)

1811
MERKYL, Wilmuth*
Gretna Green
Kalem player 1915

1812
MERLOW, Anthony*
Soul of Buddah, The (M. Romaine)

1813
MERSEREAU, Claire*
Nestor player 1911
Universal player 1918

1814
MERSEREAU, Violet (1894-)
Cricket on the Hearth, The
Girl by the Roadside, The
Little Miss Nobody
Nature Girl, The
Nestor player 1911
Princess Tatters
Ragged Queen, The
Souls United
Test of Friendship
Together
Universal player 1918
Wild Cat, The

1815
MERSON, Billy (William Thompson)
    (1881-1947)
Billy Strikes Oil
Billy the Truthful
Billy's Spanish Love Spasm
Billy's Stormy Courtship
Man in Possession, The
Only Man, The
Perils of Pork Pie, The
Tale of a Shirt, The
Terrible Tec, The

1816
MESSINGER, Buddy /aka/ Buddie
    (1909-)
Aladdin and His Wonderful Lamp
Hoodlum, The

1817
MESSINGER, Gertrude (1911-)
Aladdin and His Wonderful Lamp
Ali Baba and the Forty Thieves

1818
MESTAYER, Harry*
Atom, The
Gold Ship, The
High Tide
House of a Thousand Candles, The
Wife or Country
Stage:
Princess Players 1913

1819
METCALFE, Earle (1889-1928)
Battler, The
Coax Me
Insurrection
Lubin player 1913
Perils of Our Girl Reporters
    (serial)
Phantom Happiness, The
Poison Pen
Woman of Lies
World to Live In, A

1820
MICHELENA, Beatriz*
Alco player 1914
Mignon
Salomy Jane

1821
MIDGELY, Fannie*
Civilization (bit)
Lottery Man, The

1822
MILES, David*
Imp player 1910
Violin Maker of Cremona, The

1823
MILES, Herbert*
Eavesdropper, The
Feud and the Turkey, The
Helping Hand, The
Lady Helen's Escapade
Test of Friendship, The
Tragic Love
Violin Maker of Cremona, The

1824
MILES, Mrs. Herbert*
Her First Biscuits
His Wife's Mother
Peach Basket Hat, The

1825
MILFORD, Bliss*
Edison player 1912

1826
MILLARDE, Harry*
Don Caesar de Bazan

1827
MILLER, Carl*
Mary Regan

1828
MILLER, Josephine*
Cinderella

1829
MILLER, Patsy Ruth (1905-)
Camille
Judgment

1830
MILLER, Rube*
High Spots on Broadway /aka/
   Having a Good Time
In the Clutches of a Gang
Muddy Romance, A

1831
MILLER, W. Christy /aka/ W.
   Christie Miller (1892-1940)
Battle at Elderbush Gulch
Examination Day at School
Her Father's Pride
His Mother's Son
In Old California
In the Days of '49

Indian Summer, An
Informer, The
Last Drop of Water, The
Lesson, The
Little Tease, The
Man's Genesis
Newlyweds, The
Old Actor, The
Old Bookkeeper, The
Plain Song, A
Redman's View, The
Reformers, The or The Lost Art
   of Minding One's Business
Rocky Road, The
Sands of Dee, The
Struggle, The
Swords and Hearts
Thread of Destiny, The
Timely Interception, A
Two Brothers, The
Unwelcome Guest, The
Way of the World, The

1832
MILLER, Walter*
Adopted Brother
Adventure in the Autumn Woods, An
Brutality
Change of Heart, A
Coming of Angelo, The
Cry for Help, A
Death's Marathon
Draft 258
Eleventh Commandment, The
Feud in the Kentucky Hills, A
Friendly Call, The
Girl at Bay, A
His Mother's Son
Love in an Apartment Hotel
Manhattan Nights
Marble Heart, The
Miss Robinson Crusoe
Mothering Heart, The
Musketeers of Pig Alley, The (the
   husband)
Near to Earth
Oil and Water
Open Door, The
Perfidy of Mary, The
Slacker, The
So Near, Yet So Far
Thin Ice
Two Daughters of Eve, The
Two Men of the Desert
Wanderer, The
Yaqui Cur, The
You Can't Win (serial)

1833
MILLETT, Arthur*
Shifting Sands
Station Content

1834
MILLEY, Jane*
Devil's Daughter, The (Franceska)

1835
MILLIKEN, Robert*
Dangers of a Bride
Whose Baby?

1836
MILLS, Frank*
Deluxe Annie
Misleading Widow, The
Moral Fabric, The
Wives of Men
Stage:
Way of the World, The 1901

1837
MILLS, Thomas R. *
Crown Prince's Double, The
Scarlet Runner, The (serial)

1838
MILLY, Louise, Mlle. *
Bedtime for the Bride

1839
MILTON, Ernest (1890-   )
Wisp in the Woods, A

1840
MINEAU, Charlotte*
Behind the Screen
Count, The
Easy Street
Floorwalker, The
His New Job
Rink, The
Vagabond, The

1841
MINTER, Mary Miles (1902-   )
Amazing Imposter, The
Anne of Green Gables
Annie for Spite
Bachelor's Wife, The
Barbara Frietchie
Beauty and the Rogue
Bit of Jade, A
Charity Castle
Dimples
Environment

Eyes of Julia Deep, The
Fairy and the Waif, The
Ghost of Rosy Taylor, The
Her Country Calls
Her Country's Call
Homespun
Intrusion of Isabel, The
Mate of Sally Ann, The
Nurse, The
Peggy Leads the Way
Peggy Rebels
Rosemary Climbs the Heights
Social Briars
Wives and Other Wives
Yvonne from Paris
Stage:
Littlest Rebel, The 1911

1842
MISSIMER, Howard*
Essanay player 1912

1843
MITCHELL, Bruce*
Captivating Mary Carstairs

1844
MITCHELL, Dodson*
Conspiracy, The
Stage:
John Bull's Other Island 1905

1845
MITCHELL, Doris*
Jimmy Dale Alias the Grey Seal
   (serial)

1846
MITCHELL, Howard M. *
Beloved Adventurer, The (serial)
Road of Strife, The (serial)

1847
MITCHELL, Rhea (1894-1957)
Goat, The
Hawk's Trail, The (serial)
Honor's Cross
Money Corporal, The
Mutual player 1916
On the Night Stage
Sequel to the Diamond from the Sky,
   The (serial)
Unexpected Places

1848
MITCHELL, Yvette*
Red Ace, The (serial)

1849
MIX, Tom (Thomas Hallen Mix)
 (1880-1940) Horse: Tony from
 1917; Old Blue (1897-1919)
Ace High
Along the Border
Arizona Wooing, An
Back to the Primitive
Bear of a Story, A
Brave Deserve the Fair, The
Briton and Boer
Cactus Jim
Catus Jim's Shop Girl
Canby Hill Outlaws, The
Child of the Prairie, The
Chip of the Flying U
Close Call, A
Coming of the Law
Corner in Water, A
Cowpuncher's Peril, The
Crooked Trails /aka/ Twisted
 Trails
Cupid's Roundup
Days of Daring
Do and Dare
Durand of the Badlands
Escape of Jim Dolan
Fame and Fortune
Fighting for Gold
$5000 Elopement, A
Foreman of the Bar Z
Forked Trails
Getting a Start in Life
Going West to Make Good
Heart of a Sheriff, The
Heart of Texas Ryan, The
Hearts and Saddles
Hell Roarin' Reform
In Defense of the Law
In the Days of the Thundering Herd
Indian Wife's Devotion, An
Law and the Outlaw
Legal Advice
Local Color
Long Trail, The
Lucky Deal, A
Making an Impression
Making Good
Man from Texas, The
Man from the East, The
Militant Schoolman, A
Millionaire Cowboy
Mistake in Rustlers, A
Mr. Haygood Producer
Mixup in the Movies, A
Moving Picture Cowboy
Mrs. Murphy's Cook
On the Eagle's Trail

Outlaw's Bride, The
Pals in Blue
Parson Who Fled West, The
Passing of Pete, The
Pony Express, The
Pony Express Rider
Raiders, The
Ranch Life in the Great Southwest
 (debut)
Range Girl and the Cowboy, The
Range Law, The
Range Rider, The
Ranger's Romance, The
Riders of the Purple Sage
Rival Stage Lines, The
Roman Cowboy, The
Roping a Sweetheart
Sagebrush Tom
Saved by a Watch
Saved by Her Horse
Scapegoat, The
Sheriff's Blunder, The
Sheriff's Duty, The
Sheriff's Girl, The
Sheriff's Reward, The
Shooting up the Movies
Single Shot Parker
Six Cylinder Love
Six Shooter Andy
Slim Higgins
Soft Tenderfoot, A
Some Duel
Speed Maniac, The
Stage Coach Driver, The
Stagecoach Guard, The
Taking a Chance
Taming of Grouchy Bill
Tom and Jerry Mix
Tom's Sacrifice
Tom's Strategy
Treat 'Em Rough
Up San Juan Hill
Wagon Trail, The
Way of the Redman, The
Weary Goes Wooing
Western Blood
Western Masquerade, A
When the Cook Fell In
Why the Sheriff Is a Bachelor
Wilderness Mail, The
Wilderness Trail, The

1850
MODJESKA, Felix*
Intolerance (bodyguard to the
 Princess)

1851
MOLANDER, Karin*
Thomas Graal's First Child

1852
MONACO, Princess of*
Great Love, The (herself)

1853
MONG, William V. (1875-1940)
Hopper, The
Man Who Woke Up, The
Severed Hand, The
Turning Point, The

1854
MONTAGUE, Fred*
Call of the North, The (Jack Wilson)
Cameo Kirby
Fast Company (Peter Van Huyler)
Man from Home, The (Earl of
    Hawcastle)
Squaw Man, The (Mr. Petrie)
What's His Name? (Fairfax)

1855
MONTANA, Bull (1887-1950)
Brass Buttons
Down to Earth
Go and Get It
He Comes up Smiling (Baron Bean)
In Again-out Again (the burglar)
Treasure Island
Unpardonable Sin, The
Victory (Pedro)
When the Clouds Roll By (man in
    the nightmare)

1856
MONTI, Palola*
Kiss of Glory, The

1857
MOODY, Harry*
Tiger's Trail, The (Tiger Face)
    (serial)

1858
MOONEY, Margaret*
Intolerance (slave girl)

1859
MOORE, Colleen (Kathleen Morrison)
    (1900-   )
Bad Boy, The
Busher, The
Common Property
Egg-Crate Wallop, The

Hands Up!
Hearts of the World (bit cut out)
Hoosier Romance, A
Intolerance (credited in this but did
    NOT appear)
Little American, The
Little Orphant Annie
Man in the Moonlight, The
Old Fashioned Young Man, An
Savage, The
That's a Bad Girl
Wilderness Trail, The

1860
MOORE, Joe*
Universal player 1914

1861
MOORE, Lucia*
Her Double Life (Lady Clifford)

1862
MOORE, Marcia*
Grip of Jealousy, The
Lon of Lone Mountain
Millionaire Paupers, The

1863
MOORE, Mary*
Lola (the maid)
Stage:
David Garrick 1904

1864
MOORE, Matt (1888-1960)
Dark Star, The (Prince Alik)
Getting Mary Married (Ted Barnacle)
Glorious Lady
Heart of the Hills
Heart of the Wilds
Pride of the Clan, The
Regular Fellow, A
Regular Girl, A
Runaway Romany (Bud Haskell)
Sahara
Singular Cynic, A
Sport of Kings, The
Traffic in Souls
Twenty Thousand Leagues under the
    Sea
Unpardonable Sin, The
Victor player 1913

1865
MOORE, Owen (1886-1939)
Baby's Shoe, A
Battle of the Sexes, The (Frank
    Andrews)

Betty of Graystone
Burglar's Mistake, A
Caprice
Change of Heart, A
Cinderella
Coney Island Princess, A
Courting of Mary, The
Cricket on the Hearth, The
Crimson Gardenia, The
Dancing Girl of Butte, The
Enoch Arden, Part I and II
Escape, The (Dr. Von Eiden)
Expiation, The
First Misunderstanding, The
Flo's Discipline
Girl Like That, A
Golden Louis, The
Her Terrible Ordeal
His Lost Love
Home, Sweet Home (Tempter)
Honor of Thieves, The
Iconoclast, The
Imp player 1910
In Old Kentucky
In Swift Waters
Intolerance (a soldier)
Jordan Is a Hard Road
Last Deal, The
Leather Stockings
Lesser Evil, The
Light That Came, The
Little Boy Scout, The
Little Meena's Romance
Little Teacher, The /aka/ A Small
    Town Bully
Lonely Villa, The
Mabel Lost and Won
Mended Lute, The
Mistress Nell
My Valet
Nearly a Lady
Open Gate, The
Pippa Passes
Pretty Mrs. Smith
Restoration, The
Resurrection
Salvation Army Lass, The
Selznick player 1919
1776, or The Hessian Renegades
Shadows of Doubt
Stolen Love
Susan Rocks the Boat
Thing, The
Two Memories
Under Cover
Valet's Wife, The
Violin Maker of Cremona, The
Winning Coat, The

1866
MOORE, Pat*
Fires of Faith, The
Sahara
Squaw Man, The (Little Hal)

1867
MOORE, Tom (1884-1955)
American Princess, An
Barefoot Boy, The
Brand, The
Brown of Harvard
Cinderella Man, The
City of Comrades
Floor Below, The
Go West Young Man
Heartease
Jaguar's Claw, The
Just for Tonight
Kingdom of Youth, The
Lesson, The
Lord and Lady Algy
Man and His Money, A
Mystery of the Sleeping Death
Nina of the Theatre
One of the Finest
Thirty a Week
Toby's Bow
Unseen Terror, An
Vampire's Trail, The
Who's Guilty? (serial)

1868
MOORE, Victor (1876-1962)
Best Man, The
Bungalowing
Camping
Chimmie Fadden (Title role)
Chimmie Fadden out West (Title
    role)
Cinderella Husbands, The
Clown, The
Flivvering
Home Defense
Moneyless Honeymoon, The
Moving
Race, The
Snobs
Stage:
Debut 1893
Forty-Five Minutes from Broadway
    1906

1869
MOORE, Vin*
By Stork Delivery

1870
MOORE, W. Scott*

Cinema Murder, The (Douglas
   Romilly)

1871
MORAN, Billy*
Great Gamble, The (serial)

1872
MORAN, Lee (1899-1960)
Apartment Wanted
Bullsheviks
Camping Out
Dog Gone Shame
Ducks out of Water
Hello, Judge
Lyons and Moran comedies 1909
P. D. Q.
Robinson's Trousseau
Some Family
Straphanger, The
Ten Seconds
Three Weeks Off
Touch Down, The
Upper and Lower
War Bridegrooms
Whose Wife Is Kate?

1873
MORAN, Percy (1886-1952)
At the Torrent's Mercy
Belle of Bettys-y-Coed
Britain's Naval Secret
Dick Trupin series (4) 1912
Favourite for the Jamaica Cup, The
Gaumont chase comedies 1904
Great Anarchist Mystery
Houseboat Mystery, The
How Men Love Women
It Is for England
Jack, Sam and Pete
Lt. Daring and the Dancing Girl
Lt. Daring and the Plans of the
   Minefield
Lt. Daring and the Secret Service
   Agents
Live Wire, The
London Nighthawks
London's Enemies
Mountaineer's Romance, The
Nurse and the Martyr, The
O. H. M. S., Our Helpless
   Millions Saved
Parted by the Sword
Redemption of His Name, The
Slavers of the Thames
Tom Cringle in Jamaica
Stage:
Chicago 1898

Orpheum Theatre in Los Angeles
   1915

1874
MORAN, Polly (Pauline Theresa
   Moran) (1885-1952)
Bath House Blunder
By Stork Delivery
Cactus Nell
Favorite Fool, A
Her Fame and Shame
Her Painted Hero
High and Dry
His Hereafter
His Naughty Thought
His Uncle Dudley
His Wild Oats
Hunt, The (in black-face)
In Again--out Again
Janitor, The (debut)
Love Will Conquer
Madcap Ambrose
Pullman Bride, The
Roping Her Romeo
She Needed a Doctor
Sheriff Nell's Come Back
Their Social Splash
Those College Girls /aka/ His
   Bitter Half
Vampire Ambrose
Village Blacksmith, The

1875
MORDANT, Edwin*
Poor Little Peppina
Seven Sisters

1876
MORENO, Antonio (1886-1967)
Accomplished Mrs. Thompson, The
Aladdin from Broadway
Angel Factory, The
Anselo Lee
Birth of a Nation, The
By Man's Law
By Right of Possession
Captain of the Gray Horse Troop,
   The
Dust of Egypt
First Law, The
Fogg's Millions
Goodbye Summer
Gypsy Trail, The
Her Right to Live
Hidden Letters, The
His Father's House
House of a Thousand Candles, The
House of Discord

House of Hate, The (serial)
In the Latin Quarter
Invisible Man, The
Iron Test, The (serial)
Island of Regeneration, The
John Rance--Gentleman
Judith of Bethulia
Kennedy Square
Latin Quarter, The
Loan Shark King, The
Love's Way
Magnificent Meddler, The
Mark of Cain, The
Memories in Men's Souls
Model Wife, A
Money Magic
Musketeers of Pig Alley, The
Naulahka, The /aka/ The Jeweled
  Girdle
No Place for Father
Old Flute Player, The
On Her Wedding Night
Our Mutual Girl
Park Honeymooners, The
Peacemaker, The
Perils of Thunder Mountain, The
  (serial)
Persistent Mr. Prince, The
Politics and the Press
Price for Folly, The
Quality of Mercy, The
Rose of the South
777
She Won the Prize
So Near, Yet So Far
Son of the Hills, A
Song of the Ghetto
Strongheart
Sunshine and Shadows
Supreme Temptation, The
Susie, the Sleuth
Too Many Husbands
Two Daughters of Eve, The
Under False Colors
Voice of the Million
Youth

1877
MOREY, Harry T. (1879-1936)
All Man
As You Like It
Aunty's Romance
Bachelor's Children
Battle of the Weak, The
Beating the Odds
Beauty Proof
Casey at the Bat
Courage of Silence, The

Deerslayer, The
Desired Woman, A
Fighting Destiny
Gamble, The
Game with Fate, A
Golden Goal, The
Green God, The
His Own People
Hoarded Assets
Indian Romeo and Juliet
King of Diamonds
Lady of the Lake, The
Man Who Won, The
Million Bid, A
My Official Wife
Other Man, The
Playing with Fate
Price for Folly, The
Salvation Joan
Shadow of the Past
Silent Strength
Tangled Lives
Who Goes There?
Within the Law
Wreck, The

1878
MORGAN, Frank (Francis
  Wupperman) (1890-1949)
At the Mercy of Men
Baby Mine
Child of the Wild, A
Daring of Diana, The
Golden Shower, The
Gray Towers of Mystery, The
Knife, The
Light in Darkness
Modern Cinderella, A
Raffles, the Amateur Cracksman
Sight in Darkness
Suspect
That Girl Philippa
Who's Your Neighbor?
Stage:
Mr. Wu (juvenile lead) 1914
My Lady Friends 1919
Rock-a-Bye Baby 1918
Stock in Northampton, Mass (*)
Woman Killed with Kindness, A (*)

1879
MORGAN, Joan /aka/ Joan Went-
  worth Wood; Iris North (1905-)
Because
Cup Final Mystery, The
Drink
Frailty
Great Spy Raid, The

Her Greatest Performance
Iron Justice
Light
Queenie of the Circus
Woman Who Did, The
World's Desire, The

1880
MORHANGE, Marcel*
Serpent, The (Gregoire)

1881
MORLAY, Gaby (Blanche Fumoleau)
    (1897-1964)
La Scandle Rouge

1882
MORRIS, Chester (John Chester
    Brooks Morris) (1901-1970)
Beloved Traitor, The

1883
MORRIS, Gladys*
Star over Night, A

1884
MORRIS, Lee*
Almost an Actress (Moran)
Baseball at Mudville
Bush Leaguer, The
His First False Step
Property Man, The

1885
MORRIS, Mildred*
Foundling, The

1886
MORRIS, Reggie*
Haystacks and Steeples
Social Club, A

1887
MORRISON, Arthur*
Destruction (Lang)

1888
MORRISON, James (1888-   )
As You Like It
Babbling Tongues
Bad Boy, The
Battle Cry of Peace, The
Enemy, The
Hero of Submarine D-2, The
Life against Honor
Moral Suicide
Over the Top
Redemption of Dave Darcey

Sacred Silence
Saving an Audience
Tale of Two Cities, A
Womanhood

1889
MORRISON, Louis*
Gypsy Joe
Lion and the Girl, The
Lover's Might, A /aka/ The Fire
    Chief
Madcap Ambrose

1890
MOSJOUKINE, Ivan (1889-1939)
Defence of Sevastapol, The

1891
MOSS, George*
Les Miserables

1892
MOSZATO, Umberto*
Cabiria

1893
MOUNET-SULLY*
Oedipus

1894
MOWER, Jack (1890-1965)
Beloved Cheater, The
Island of Intrigue
Mantle of Charity, The
Molly of the Follies
Money Isn't Everything
Primitive Woman, The

1895
MUIR, Helen*
Strictly Confidential

1896
MULHALL, Jack (1891-   )
Brass Bullet, The (serial)
Cold Cash
Danger-Go Slow (Jimmy)
Grand Passion, The (Jack Ripley)
House of Discord (debut)
Madam Spy
Mickey
Midnight Man, The (serial)
Place beyond the Winds (Dick
    Travers
Price of Silence, The (Ralph Kelton)
Sirens of the Sea
Solitary Sin, The
Tides of Retribution

Universal player 1917
Whom the Gods Destroy
Wild Youth

1897
MULLALY, Jode*
Call of the North, The (Picard)
Man from Home, The (Horace
   Granger Simpson)

1898
MULLEN, Gordon*
Keno Bates, Liar (Jim Maitland)
   /aka/ The Last Card

1899
MUNN, Charles*
Adventures of Peg o' the Ring
   (serial)

1900
MUNSON, Audrey*
Purity

1901
MURATORE, Lucian*
House of Granada, The
Manon Lescaut

1902
MURDOCK, Ann (1890-   )
Beautiful Adventure, The
Captain Jinks of the Horse Marines
My Wife
Outcast, The
Please Help Emily
Richest Girl, The
Seven Deadly Sins ("Envy")
Stage:
Beautiful Adventure, The 1914
Celebrated Case, A 1915
Excuse Me 1911
Noble Spaniard, The 1909
Pair of Sixes, A 1914
Please Help Emily 1916

1903
MURDOCK, Frank*
Regular Girl, A

1904
MURNANE, Allen*
Mysteries of Myra, The (serial)
Patria (serial)

1905
MURPHY, John Daly*
Kreutzer Sonata (Sam Friedlander)

Our Mrs. McChesney
Two Orphans, The (Picard)

1906
MURRAY, Charlie (1872-1941)
Almost a Man
Anglers, The
Beauty Bunglers, The
Bedroom Blunder, A
Betrayal of Maggie
Bombs
Cursed by His Beauty
Fatal Flirtation, A
Feathered Nest, The /aka/ Girl
   Guardian /aka/ Only a Farmer's
   Daughter
Fido's Fate
From Patches to Plenty
Game Old Knight, A
Great Vacuum Robbery, The
Her Fame and Shame
Her Friend the Bandit
Her Marble Heart
Her Painted Hero
His Hereafter /aka/ Murray's
   Mixup
His Halted Career
His Precious Life
His Second Childhood
His Talented Wife
Hogan out West
Hogan the Parter
Hogan's Annual Spree
Hogan's Mussy Job
Hogan's Romance Upset
Hogan's Wild Oats
Judge, The
Love and Bullets /aka/ The
   Trouble Mender
Love Riot, A
Mabel's Married Life /aka/ The
   Squarehead
Maggie's First False Step
Maid Mad /aka/ The Fortune Teller
Masquerader, The
Never Too Old
Noise of Bombs, The
Passing of Izzy, The
Pills of Peril
Plumber, The (Hogan)
Reilly's Wash Day
Soldiers of Misfortune
Speak-Easy, The
Stout Heart, but Weak Knees
Such a Cook /aka/ The Bungling
   Burglars
Their Social Splash
Those College Girls /aka/ His

Bitter Half
Tillie's Punctured Romance
Trying to Get Along
Up in Alf's Place
Watch Your Neighbor

1907
MURRAY, Mae (Marie Adrienne
    Koenig) (1889-1965)
At First Sight
Big Little Person, The
Big Sister
Bride's Awakening, The
Danger-Go Slow (Muggsy Mulane)
Delicious Little Devil, The
Dream Girl, The (Meg Dugan)
Face Value
Gilded Lady, The
Girl for Sale
Her Body in Bond
High Stakes
Modern Love
Plow Girl, The
Primrose Ring, The
Princess Virtue
Scarlet Shadow, The
Sweet Kitty Bellairs
To Have and to Hold
Twin Pawns
What Am I Bid?
Stage:
About Town 1906
Los Angeles Mason Opera House
    1917
Ziegfeld Follies of 1908
Ziegfeld Follies of 1909
Ziegfeld Follies of 1915

1908
MURRAY, Marie*
Great Train Robbery, The

1909
MURRAY, Walter*
Reformers, The or The Lost Art
    of Minding One's Business

1910
MUSIDORA /aka/ Irama Vep*
Vampires, The

1911
MYERS, Carmel (1899-1966)
All Night
Birth of a Nation, The
Broadway Scandal, A (Ninette Bison)
City of Tears
Girl in the Dark

Haunted Pajamas, The
Heart of a Jewess, The
Intolerance
Little White Savage
Marriage Lie, The
Matrimaniac
Might and the Man
My Dream Lady
My Unmarried Wife
Sirens of the Sea
Society Sensation, A
Stage Struck
Who Will Marry Me?
Wife He Brought Back, The
Wine Girl, The
Stage:
Magic Melody, The 1919

1912
MYERS, Harry C. (1882-1938)
Baby
Gurellia, The
Her First Biscuits
Her Two Sons
Housekeeping
Jones and His New Neighbors
Jones and the Lady Book Agent
Jones Have Amateur Theatricals,
    The
Masked Rider, The (serial)

1913
MYERS, Ray*
Across the Plains

- N -

1914
NAGEL, Conrad (1896-1970)
Little Women
Redhead
Stage:
Forever After 1918

1915
NALDI, Nita (Anita Donna Dooley)
    (1889-1961)
Paramount player 1919
Stage:
Passing Show of 1918, The 1918

1916
NANSEN, Betty*
Fox player 1915

1917
NAPIERKOWSKA*
Wild Ass' Skin, The

1918
NARES, Owen (Owen N. Ramsey)
   (1888-1943)
Dandy Donovan
Edge o' Beyond
Elder Miss Blossom, The
Flames
Gamblers All
God Bless the Red, White and Blue
Just a Girl
Labour Leader, The
Man Who Won, The
Milestones
One Summer's Night
Onward Christian Soldiers
Real Thing at Last, The
Tinker, Tailor, Soldier, Sailor
Stage:
Debut in London 1908
Romance (Bishop Armstrong)
   (London) 1913

1919
NAZIMOVA, Alla (1879-1945)
Brat, The
Eye for Eye
Out of the Fog
Red Lantern
Revelation
Toys of Fate
Stage:
Bella Donna 1912
'Ception Shoals 1917
Comet, The 1908
Comtesse Coquette 1907
Doll's House, A 1907; 1918
Hedda Gabler 1918
Little Eyolf (first New York
   production) 1910
Marionettes, The 1911
Master Builder, The 1907
Paul Orlenoff Company 1906
That Sort 1914
War Brides 1915
Wild Duck, The 1918

1920 no entry

1921
NEDELL, Bernard (1898-1972)
Serpent, The

1922
NEGRI, Pola (Appolonia Chalupec)
   (1894-   )
Arabella
Carmen
Carmen /aka/ Gypsy Blood

Czarma Ksiazka /aka/ Zolty
   Paszport
Der Gelbe Schein
Die Auger der Mumie Ma (Eyes
   of the Mummy, The) (Temple
   Dancer)
Die Beastie
Die Toten Augen
DuBarry
Jego Ostatni Czyn
Karussell des Lebens
Montesse Doddy
Kreuzigt Sie
Küsse die Man Stiehlt in Dunkeln
Love and Passion
Manja
Nicht Lange Tauschte mich des
   Glück
Niewolnica Zomyslow
Pojkoj Nr 13 /aka/ Tajemnica
   Hotelu
Rosen die der Sturm Entblättert
Studenci
Wenn das Herz in Hass Erglüht
Zona
Stage:
Hannele (debut in Warsaw) 1913
Sumurun (Warsaw) 1916

1923
NEIL, Richard*
Active Life of Dolly of the Dailies,
   The (serial)
Great Gamble, The (serial)

1924
NEILAN, Marshal /aka/ Steve
   Neilan /aka/ Horace Peyton
   (1891-1958)
American Pictures player (50 films)
   1912-1913
Billionaire, The
Classmates
Commanding Officer, The
Country Boy, The
Crisis, The
Daddy Long Legs
Don't Monkey with a Buzz Saw
Father's Favorite
Fired Cook, The
Girl of Yesterday, A
Greaser and the Weakling, The
Ham and the Villain Factory
Hash-House Count, The
Her Sentimental System
House of Discord
How Jim Proposed
Judith of Bethulia

Laskey player 1916
Little Pal
Madame Butterfly (Lt. Pinkerton)
Manicurist and the Mutt, The
May Blossom
Men and Women
Mice and Men
Nell of the Pampas
Pasadena Peach, The
Prince Chap, The
Reformation of Sierra Smith, The
Reward of Valor, The
Romance of a Dry Town, The
Rube and the Boob
Sis's Wonderful Mineral Spring
Stranger at Coyote, The
Tattered Duke, The
Two Men of the Desert
Wanderer, The
Wedding Gown, The
When Women Are Police
Stage:
Barney Bernard Stock Company
   (San Francisco) 1905
Belasco Stock Company (Los
   Angeles) 1903
Financier, The (juvenile lead; on
   tour) 1905-06

1925
NEILL, James*
Bloodhounds of the North (the
   refugee)
Bottle Imp, The
Cheat, The (Jones)
Country That God Forgot, The
Devil Stone, The
Discord and Harmony (the symphony
   conductor)
Don't Change Your Husband (the
   butler)
Dream Girl, The (Benjamin Merton)
Everywoman
Girl at Home, The
Girl Who Came Back, The
His Official Financee
Honor of the Mounted, The (Post
   Commandant)
Joan, the Woman (Laxart)
Lie, The (the gambler)
Little American, The
Little Shepherd of Kingdom Come,
   The
Man from Home, The (Officer of
   Gendarmes)
Maria Rosa (the priest)
Men, Women and Money
Red Margaret--Moonshiner (the
   sheriff)

Rescuing Angel, The
Richelieu (the king)
Romance and Arabella
Rose of the Rancho, The (Padre
   Antonio)
Say! Young Fellow
Warrens of Virginia, The (General
   Warren)
We Can't Have Everything (detective)
Whispering Chorus, The (Channing)

1926
NEILSON, Agnes*
Butcher Boy, The

1927
NELSON, Frances*
Metro player 1917

1928
NELSON, Jack (1882-   )
Flash of Fate, The
Girl Dodger, The
If My Country Should Call (Donald)
Long Chance, The
Man Trap, The
Pasquale
Rose of the West
Rough Riding Romance
23 1/2 Hour's Leave
Wilderness Trail, The
Winner Takes All

1928a
NeMOYER, Francis*
Gold and the Woman (Murray's
   daughter)

1929
NESBIT, Evelyn (1885-1967)
Fox player 1918
Her Mistake
I Want to Forget
Judge Not
My Little Sister
Redemption
Threads of Destiny
Thou Shalt Not
Woman Who Gave, The
Woman, Woman

1930
NESBITT, Miriam*
Aida
Foreman's Treachery, The
Man Who Disappeared, The (serial)
Three Musketeers, The (the queen)

1931
NEWALL, Guy (1885-1937)
Comradeship
Driven
Esther
Fancy Dress
Garden of Resurrection, The
Heart of Sister Anne, The
I Will
Manxman, The
March Hare, The
Money for Nothing
Motherlove
Smith
Trouble for Nothing
Vice Versa
Stage:
Sam Lodge (debut in London) 1911

1932
NEWBERG, Frank*
Saving an Audience

1933
NICHOLS, George (1864-   )
As It Is in Life
As the Bells Ring Out
Battling Jane
Behind the Scenes
Bill Apperson's Boy
Child of the Ghetto, A
Child's Faith, A
Cloister's Touch, The
Death Disc, The
Fighting Blood
Flash of Light, A
Gibson Goddess, The
Greatest Question, The (Martin
    Cain)
Hearts of the World (a German
    Sergeant)
Her Terrible Ordeal
Heredity
His Last Burglary
In Little Italy
In the Watches of the Night
Jilt, The
Keys of the Righteous
Lily of the Tenements, The
Lines of White on the Sullen Sea
Mickey (Joe Meadows)
Midnight Cupid, A
Rocky Road, The
Romance of Happy Valley, A (Mr.
    Timberlake)
1776, or The Hessian Renegades
Son of His Father
Turn in the Road, The

Two Daughters of Eve, The
Usurer, The
Victory (Capt. Davison)
What Shall We Do with Our Old?
When Doctors Disagree
Woman from Mellon's, The

1934
NICHOLS, Norma*
Dough and Dynamite
Those Love Pangs

1935
NIELSEN, Asta (1883-   )
Der Abgrund
Engelein

1936
NIGH, William*
Salomy Jane

1937
NILLSON, Alex*
Sir Arne's Treasure
Thomas Graal's First Child

1938
NILLSON, Carlotta*
Leah Kleschna
Stage:
Letty 1904
Three of Us, The 1906

1939
NILSSON, Anna Q. (1893-   )
Goldwyn player 1918
Heart of the Sunset
Her Kingdom of Dreams
In Judgment Of
Kalem player 1909
Love Burglar, The
No Man's Land
Over There
Seven Keys to Baldpate
Siege of Petersburg
Silent Master, The
Sister's Burden, A
Soldier of Fortune
Trail of Yesterday
Under a Flag of Truce
Way of the Strong, The
Who's Guilty? (serial)

1940
NORMAN, Gertrude*
Strictly Confidential
Unwelcome Mrs. Hatch, The
Widow by Proxy

1941
NORMAND, Mabel (Mabel Fortescue
  (1894-1930) [Biograph circa 1911
  refused to release names of their
  stars, therefore, Miss Normand's
  name appeared on some posters as
  Muriel Fortescue]
Alarm, The
Ambitious Butler, The
At Coney Island /aka/ Cohen at
  Coney Island
At It Again
At the San Diego Exposition
At Twelve o'Clock
Baby Day
Back to the Woods
Bangville Police, The
Barney Oldfield's Race for a Life
Battle of Who Run, The
Betty in the Lion's Den
Bowling Match, The
Bright Lights /aka/ The Lure of
  Broadway
Brothers
Brown's Séance
Caught in a Cabaret (society girl)
Champion, The
Cohen Collects a Debt
Cohen Saves the Flag
Cure That Failed, The
Dash through the Clouds, A
Deacon Outwitted, The
Deacon's Trouble, The
Desperate Lover, A
Diving Girl, The
Doctored Affair, A
Dodgin' a Million
Duel, The
Eternal Mother, The
Faithful Taxicab, The
Family Mix-up, A
Fatal Mallet, The
Father's Choice
Fatty and Mabel
Fatty and Mabel Adrift
Fatty and Mabel at the San Diego
  Exposition
Fatty and Mabel's Married Life
Fatty and Mabel's Simple Life
Fatty's Flirtation
Fatty's Jonah Day
Fatty's Wine Party
Flirting Husband, The
Floor Below, The
Foiling Fickle Father
For the Love of Mabel
Foreman of the Jury, The
Gentlemen of Nerve

Getting Acquainted
Glimpse of Los Angeles, A
Goldwyn player 1916
Grocery Clerk's Romance, The
Gusher, The
Gypsy Queen, The
Hansom Driver, The
He Did and He Didn't /aka/ Love
  and Lobster
Heinze's Resurrection
Hello, Mabel
Her Awakening
Her Friend the Bandit
Her New Beau
Hide and Seek
His Luckless Love
His Trysting Place
How Heroes Are Made
Hubby's Job
Joan of Plattsburg
Just Brown's Luck
Little Hero, A
Little Teacher, The /aka/ A
  Small Town Bully
Love and Courage
Love and Gasoline /aka/ The
  Skidding Joy Riders
Love Sickness at Sea
Lover's Post Office
Mabel and Fatty's Viewing the
  World's Fair at San Francisco
Mabel and Fatty's Wash Day
Mabel at the Wheel /aka/ His Dare-
  devil Queen
Mabel, Fatty and the Law
Mabel Lost and Won
Mabel's Adventures
Mabel's Awful Mistake /aka/ Her
  Deceitful Lover
Mabel's Bare Escape
Mabel's Blunder
Mabel's Busy Day
Mabel's Dramatic Career /aka/ Her
  Dramatic Debut
Mabel's Greatest Moment
Mabel's Heroes
Mabel's Latest Prank /aka/ A
  Touch of Rheumatism
Mabel's Lovers
Mabel's Married Life /aka/ The
  Squarehead
Mabel's Nerve
Mable's New Job
Mabel's New Hero
Mabel's Stormy Love Affair
Mabel's Strange Predicament
Mabel's Strategem
Mabel's Wilful Way

Mack at It Again
Making a Living
Mender of the Nets, The
Mickey
Mickey Gets Ready
Midnight Elopment, A
Misplaced Foot, A
Mistaken Masher, The
Mr. Fix-It
Mrs. Nag
Mud Bath, A
Muddy Romance, A /aka/ Muddled
    in Mud
My Valet
Near to Earth
New Neighbor, The
Noise from the Deep, A
Pedro's Dilemma
Perfect 36, A
Pest, The
Professor Bean's Removal
Professor's Daughter, The
Ragtime Band, The /aka/ The
    Jazz Band
Red Hot Romance, A
Riley and Schultz
Riot, The
Rivals, The
Rube and the Baron, The
Rural Third Degree, The
Saved from Himself
Saving Mabel's Day
Sea Nymphs, The /aka/ His
    Diving Beauty
Sis (Title role)
Sis Hopkins (Title role)
Sleuths at the Floral Parade, The
Sleuths' Last Stand, The
Speed Queen
Squaw's Love, The
Stolen Glory
Stolen Magic
Strong Revenge, A
Subduing of Mrs. Nag, The
Tangled Affair, A
Teddy Telzlaff and Earl Cooper,
    Speed Kings
Telltale Light, A
Temperamental Husband, A
That Little Band of Gold /aka/
    For Better or Worse
Their Social Splash
Those Country Kids
Those Good Old Days
Tillie's Punctured Romance
Troublesome Stepdaughters, The
Unveiling, The
Upstairs

Venus Model, The
Vitagraph player 1909
Waiter's Picnic, The
Water Nymph, The
When Doctors Disagree
Wished on Mabel
Won in a Closet
Zuzu, the Band Leader

1942
NORRIS, William*
Good Little Devil, A
Stage:
Babes in Toyland 1903
In the Palace of the King 1900
Maytime 1917

1943
NORTHRUP, Harry S. *
Battle Cry of Peace, The
Christian, The

1944
NORTON, Betty*
Child star in several Mabel
    Normand films

1945
NORWOOD, Eille (1841-1948)
Adventures of Sherlock Holmes,
    The (series)
Charlatan, The
Frailty
Further Adventures of Sherlock
    Holmes, The (series)
Last Adventures of Sherlock Holmes,
    The (series)
Princess Clementina

1946
NOVA, Hedda*
Bar Sinister
Barrier, The
Crimson Gardenia, The
Mask, The
Spitfire of Seville, The
Woman in the Web, A (serial)

1947
NOVAK, Eva (1899-)
Speed Maniac, The

1948
NOVAK, Jane (1896-)
Claws of the Hun
Eyes of the World
From Italy's Shore
Graft (serial)

His Debt
Just Nuts
Money Corporal, The
Nine o'Clock Town
Selfish Yates
String Beans
Temple of Dusk, The
Tiger Man, The
Wagon Tracks

1949
NOVARRO, Ramon (Ramon
  Samaniegoes) (1899-1968)
Goat, The
Hostage, The
Joan, the Woman (starving peasant)
Little American, The (extra)
Little Princess, The
Stage:
Marion Morgan dance troup 1919

1950
NOVELLI, Anthony*
Julius Caesar

1951
NOWELL, Wedgewood (1878-1957)
Deserter, The

1952
NYE, G. Raymond*
Adventures of Peg o' the Ring, The
  (serial)
Liberty, a Daughter of the U. S. A.
  (serial)
Salome (King Herod)
Under the Yoke (Diabolo Ramierez)
When Men Desire (Von Rohn)

- O -

1953
OAKER, John*
Joan, the Woman (Jean de Metz)

1954
OAKLAND, Ethel Mary*
Dummy, The (child)

1955
OAKLEY, Annie*
Buffalo Bill

1956
OAKLEY, Laura*
Black Box, The (serial)
Her Life's Story (Sister Agnes)
Star of the Sea, The (Janice)

1957
OAKMAN, Wheeler (1890-1949)
Cycle of Fate, The
Face Value
Hell's Hinges
Long Ago, The (evil medicine man)
Mickey (Herbert Thornhill)
Ne'er-Do-Well, The
Salvation of Nance O'Shaughnessy
Son of the Wolf
Spoilers, The (Broncho)
Story of the Blood Red Rose
Three Wise Men
When the Cook Fell In

1958
O'BRIEN, Barry*
Ireland, a Nation

1959
O'BRIEN, Eugene (1882-1966)
Broken Melody, The
Brown of Harvard
By Right of Purchase
Chaperon, The
Come out of the Kitchen
Deluxe Annie
Fires of Faith, The
Ghosts of Yesterday, The
Her Only Way
Little Miss Hoover
Moonstone, The
Moth, The
Perfect Lover, The
Poor Little Peppina
Poppy
Rebecca of Sunnybrook Farm
Return of Eve
Romance of the Underworld, A
Safety Curtain, The
Scarlet Woman, The
Sealed Hearts
Under the Greenwood Tree
Stage:
Builder of Bridges, The 1909
Celebrated Case, A 1915
Country Cousin, The 1917
Kitty MacKay 1914
Million, The 1911
That Rollicking Girl 1905
Trelwaney of the Wells 1911

1960
O'BURRELL, James*
Two Orphans, The

1961
O'CONNOR, Edward*
Cecilia of the Pink Roses (Jeremiah

Madden)
Edison player 1911
Kathleen Mavourneen (Kathleen's
    father)

1962
O'CONNOR, James*
East Lynne (Old Hellejohn)

1963
O'CONNOR, Kathleen*
Lion Man, The (serial)

1964
O'CONNOR, Loyola*
Intolerance (slave)
True Heart Susie (Susie's aunt)

1965
O'CONNOR, Robert Emmett
    (1885-   )
Bit player 1909-1919

1966
O'DARE, Peggy*
In the Balance

1967
ODELL, George*
Vixen, The (butler)

1968
ODETTE, Mary (Odette Giombault)
    (1901-   )
As He Was Born
Castle of Dreams
Cynthia in the Wilderness
Combey and Son
Greatest Wish in the World, The
Lackey and the Lady, The
Lady Clare, The
Mr. Gilfil's Love Story
Peace, Perfect Peace
Spinner o' Dreams
Top Dog
Wages of Sin, The
Way of an Eagle, The
Whosoever Shall Offend
With All Her Heart

1969
OGDEN, Vivia*
Mrs. Wiggs of the Cabbage Patch

1970
OGLE, Charles (1875-   )
Active Life of Dolly of the Dailies,
    The (serial)

Alias Mike Moran
Believe Me, Xantippe
Captain Hawthorne of the U. S. A.
Dub, The
Edison player 1907
Firefly of France
Frankenstein
Hard Cash
How Mrs. Murray Saved the Army
Less Than Kin
Lottery Man, The
M'Liss
Martin Chuzzlewit
Rebecca of Sunnybrook Farm
Romance of the Redwoods, A (Jim
    Lyn)
Source, The
Squaw Man, The (Bull Cowan)
Thing We Love, The
Those without Sin
Told in the Hills
Too Many Millions
Valley of the Giants
We Can't Have Everything (Kedzie's
    father)
What Happened to Mary (serial)

1971
OLAND, Warner (1880-1938)
Avalanche, The
Cigarette Girl, The
Convict 993
Destruction (Delaveau)
Eternal Question, The
Eternal Sapho (Coudal)
Fatal Ring, The (serial) (Carslake)
Fool's Revenge, A
Lightning Raider, The (serial) Wu
    Fang
Mad Talon, The
Mandrin's Gold, The
Mysterious Client, The
Naulahka, The /aka/ The Life of
    John Bunyan (dual role)
Reapers, The
Roaring Oaks
Serpent, The
Sin (Pietro)
Twin Pawns
Witness for the Defense
Yellow Ticket, The

1972
OLANOVA, Olga*
Crimson Stain Mystery, The

1973
OLCOTT, Sidney (John S. Alcott)
    (1873-1949)

Kalem player 1915
Kleine player 1907

1974
OLDFIELD, Barney*
Barney Oldfield's Race for a Life

1975
OLIVER, Guy (1875-   )
Debut 1908
Golden Fetter, The
Hawthorne of the U. S. A.
Heart of Youth
Hidden Pearls, The
It Pays to Advertise
Less Than Kin
Little American, The
Little Princess, The
Lottery Man, The
Male and Female (pilot of Lord
   Loam's yacht)
Nan of Music Mountain
Raven, The
Rimrock Jones
Roaring Road, The
Robin Hood
Secret Service
Squaw Man, The (Kid Clarke)
Told in the Hills
Under the Top
Valley of the Giants
Whispering Chorus, The (Chief
   McFarland)

1976
O'MALLEY, J. Patrick (Patrick H.
   O'Malley, Jr.) (1891-1966)
Edison player 1907
False Evidence
Kalem player 1915
Papered Door, The
Red Glove, The (serial)
Universal player 1918

1977
O'MOORE, Barry /aka/ Herbert
   Yost*
Edison player 1914
Every Rose Has It's Stem
Man Who Disappeared, The (serial)
What Happened to Mary? (serial)
Stage:
Over Night (as Herbert Yost) 1911
Polly with a Past (as Herbert Yost)
   1917

1978
O'Neil, Nance (1875-1965)

Fall of the Romanoffs, The
Hedda Gabler
Kreutzer Sonata, The (Miriam
   Friedlander)
Mad Woman, The
Seven Deadly Sins, The ("Greed")
Witch, The
Stage:
Camille (in repertory West Coast
   1900
Debut in San Francisco 1893
Fires of St. John, The 1904
Hedda Gabler 1904
Judith of Bethulia 1904
Lily, The 1909
Magda (in repertory West Coast)
   1900
Magda in San Francisco 1893
Wanderer, The 1917

1979
O'NEILL, James (1847-1920)
Count of Monte Cristo, The (Title
   role)
Stage:
Joseph and His Brethren 1913
Monte Cristo (Title role) 1900
Two Orphans, The 1904
Wanderer, The 1917
White Sister, The 1909

1980
ONG, Dana*
Cheat, The (the District Attorney)

1981
OPPERMAN, Frank*
Best of Enemies, The
Better Late Than Never /aka/
   Getting Married
Dash of Courage, A
Hash House Mashers
Her Fame and Shame
Hunt, The
My Valet
Old Actor, The
Rent Jumpers, The

1982
ORDYSNKE, Richard*
Rose of the Blood, (Vassea)
Stage:
Sumurun 1915

1983
ORILO, V. *
Mystery of 13, The (serial)

1984
ORMONDE, Eugene*
Dancing Girl, The
Light, The (Chabin)
Modern Musketeer, A (Raymond
    Peters)
Reaching for the Moon (Minister of
    Vulgaris)

1985
ORTEGO, Art*
Girl of the Golden West, The
    (Antonio)
Great Secret, The (serial)

1986
ORTEGO, John*
Girl of the Golden West, The
    (stage coach driver)

1987
ORTH, Louise*
L-KO (Lehrman-Knock Out) player
    1915
Mr. Shoestring in the Hole
Three Black Eyes

1988
OSBORNE, Baby Marie (1911-)
Baby Pulls the String
Baby's Diplomacy
Child of M'sieur
Cupid by Proxy
Daddy's Girl
Daughter of the West, A
Dolly Does Her Bit
Dolly's Vacation
Evidence, The
Joy and the Dragon
Little Diplomat, The
Little Mary Sunshine
Little Patriot, A
Milady o' the Beanstalk
Old Maid's Baby, The
Sawdust Doll
Tears and Smiles
Voice of Destiny
When Baby Forgot
Winning Grandma

1989
OSBORNE, Miles "Bud" (1888-)
Range Rider series
Santa Fe Mac

1990
OSMOND, V. (Miss)
Little Lord Fauntleroy

1991
OSTRICHE, Muriel (1897-)
Betty Sets the Pace
Betty's Green-Eyed Monster
Bluffer, The
By Whose Hand?
Circus Romance, A
Daughter of the Sea, A
Dormant Power, The
Hand Invisible, The
Kennedy Square
Leap to Fame
Man She Married, The
Moral Courage
Moral Deadline
Mortmain
Sacred Flame, The
Square Deal
Thanhouser player 1914
Tinsel
What Love Forgives

1992
O'SULLIVAN, Anthony "Tony"*
Convict's Sacrifice, A
Final Settlement, The
Getting Even
Her Terrible Ordeal
Honor of His Family, The
In the Watches of the Night
Mrs. Jones Entertains
Newlyweds, The
Pirate's Gold, The
Red Girl, The
Strange Meeting, A
'Tis an Ill Wind That Blows No
    Good
What Drink Did

1993
OTIS, Elita Proctor*
Oliver Twist (Nancy Sykes)
Stage:
Celebrated Case, A 1915
Greyhound, The 1912
Two Orphans, The 1904

1994
OTT, Fred*
Fred Ott's Sneeze

1995
OUSPENSKAYA, Maria (1876-1949)
Nichtozhniye (Worthless)
Sverchok Na Pechi (The Cricket
    on the Hearth)
Tsveti Zapozdaliye (Belated Flowers
    /aka/ Doktor Toporkov)

Zazhivo Pogrebenni (Burried Alive)
Stage:
Moscow Art Theatre 1911-1921
    (150 roles)
Russian stock company 1911

1996
OVERTON, Evart*
Enemy, The

1997
OVEY, George*
Cub player 1918
Horsley's Cub comedies (Jerry)

1998
OWEN, Seena (Signe Auen)
    (1895-1966)
Branding Broadway
Breed of Men
Bred in the Bone
City of Comrades
Craven, The
Fall of Babylon, The
Fox Woman, The
Intolerance (Princess Beloved)
Lamb, The (Mary)
Life Line, The
Madame Bo-Peep
Man and His Money, A
Martha's Vindication
Old Fashioned Girl, An
One of the Finest
Out of the Air
Penitents, The
Sheriff's Son, The
Triangle player 1918
Victory (Alma)
Yankee from the West, A

- P -

1999
PAGANI, Ernesto*
Cabiria
Warrior, The

2000
PAGET, Alfred*
Aladdin and His Wonderful Lamp
Banker's Daughters, The
Battle at Elderbush Gulch, The
Beast at Bay, A
Big Timber
Call to Arms, The
Dash through the Clouds, A
Enoch Arden Part I and II

Girl and Her Trust, The
Goddess of Sagebrush Gulch, The
Heredity
Inner Circle, The
Intolerance (Belshazzar)
Iola's Promise
Just Gold
Lesser Evil, The
Man's Genesis
Misunderstood Boy, A
Mohawk's Way, A
Musketeers of Pig Alley, The
Newlyweds, The
Nina the Flower Girl
Oath and the Man, The
Oil and Water
Old Bookkeeper, The
One Is Business, the Other Crime
Out from the Shadow
Primal Call, The
Primitive Man
Romance of the Western Hills, A
Sheriff's Baby, The
Spanish Gypsy, The
Spirit Awakened, The
Temporary Truce, A
Terrible Discovery, A
Timely Interception, A
When Kings Were the Law

2001
PAIL, Edward*
Boots

2002
PALLETTE, Eugene (1889-1954)
After Twenty Years
Amateur Adventuress
Birth of a Nation, The (Union
    soldier)
Bond Between, The
Breakers Ahead
Broken Nose Bailey
Burden, The
Children in the House
Death Doll, The
Debut 1910
Diamond in the Rough, A
Each to His Kind
Emerald Broach, The
Ever Living Isles, The
Fair and Warmer
Ghost House, The
Going Straight
Gretchen and the Greenhorn
Handsome Chap, The
Heir of the Ages, The
Hell-to-Pay Austin

Highbinders, The
His Guardian Angel
His Robe of Honor
Horse Wranglers, The
How Hazel Got Even
Intolerance (Prosper Latour)
Isle of Content
Madame Who?
Man's Man, A
Marcellini Millions, The
Monroe
No Man's Land
On the Border
Peach Brand, The
Penalty, The
Purple Scar, The
Runaway Freight
Scarlet Lady, The
Sheriff's Prisoner, The
Spell of the Poppy, The
Story of a Story, The
Sunshine Dad
Tarzan of the Apes
Tattered Arm, The
Turn of a Card, A
Undersea Loot
Victim, The
Vivette
When Jim Returned
When Love Is Mocked
Winning of Sally Temple, The
Words and Music By ...
World Apart
Stage:
Appearances 1907-1913

2003
PANZER, Paul W. (1872-1958)
Cheapest Way, The
Clutching Hand, The (serial)
Curious Dream, A
Governor's Double, The
Jimmy Dale Alias the Grey Seal
    (serial)
Last Volunteer, The
Life of Buffalo Bill, The
Masked Rider, The (serial)
Perils of Pauline, The (serial)
    (Raymond Owen)
Romeo and Juliet (Romeo)
Sunshine in Poverty Row

2004
PARKER, Albert*
American Aristocracy
In Again--out Again (Jerry)

2005
PARQUET, Corinne*
Waiter's Ball, The

2006
PARR, Peggy*
Lure of Ambition, The (Minna Dolan)

2007
PARROTT, Charles see CHASE,
    Charley

2008
PARRY, Peggy*
Cinema Murder, The (the fiancée)

2009
PARSONS, Billy /aka/ "Smiling
    Bill"*
Dad's Knockout
Matching Billy

2010
PARSONS, Harriet "Baby"*
Magic Wand, The

2011
PASQUE, Ernest*
False Faces, The (Blensop)

2012
PATRICK, Jerome*
Three Men and a Girl
Stage:
Little Lady in Blue 1916
Marie (Odile) 1915
Thousand Years Ago, A 1914

2013
PATTERSON, Walter*
Lightning Bryce (serial)

2014
PAULAS*
Film to accompany his singing
    (Méliés) 1897

2015
PAVIS, Marie*
Trail of the Octopus (serial)

2016
PAVLOWA, Anna (1885-1931)
Dumb Girl of Portici, The (debut
    as Fenella)
Stage:
Big Show, The 1916

2017
PAWLE, Lennox (1872-1936)
Admirable Crichton, The

2018
PAWN, Doris (1896-   )
Blue Blood and Red
Book Agent, The
City of Dim Faces, The
Kid Is Clever, The
Some Boy
Toby's Bow
Trey o' Hearts, The (serial)

2019
PAYNE, Edna*
Lubin player 1910

2020
PAYSON, Blanche*
A La Cabaret
Bath House Blunder, A
Dollars and Sense /aka/ The Twins
Her Circus Knight /aka/ The Circus
   Girl
Oriental Love
Wife and Auto Trouble

2021
PAYTON, Claude*
Woman There Was, A (high priest)

2022
PEARCE, George*
Everywoman's Husband

2023
PEARCE, Peggy /aka/ Viola Barry*
Bubbles of Trouble
Dog Catcher's Love, A
His Bread and Butter (the waiter's
   wife)
His Busted Trust
His Favorite Pastime
Mothering Heart, The
Pawnbroker's Heart, The
Villa of the Movies
Winning Punch, The

2024
PEARSON, Virginia (1888-1958)
All for a Husband
Bishop's Emerald, The
Bitter Truth, The
Blazing Love
Buchanan's Wife
Daughter of France, A
Firebrand, The

Her Price
Hypocrisy
Liar, The
Love Auction
Queen of Hearts
Royal Romance, A
Stain, The
Stolen Honor
Thou Shalt Not
Tortured Heart, The
Vital Question, The
When False Tongues Speak
Stage:
Nearly Married 1913

2025
PEGGY, Baby*
Little Patriot, A

2026
PEIL, Edward (1888-1958)
Broken Blossoms (Evil Eye)
Eyes of the World
Greatest Thing in Life, (German
   Officer)
I'll Get Him Yet
Peppy Polly
Stronger Love, The
Up the Road
You Can't Believe Everything

2027
PEMBROOK, P. S. *
Hazards of Helen, The (serial)

2028
PENNINGTON, Ann (1895-   )
Antics of Ann, The
Little Boy Scout, The
Rainbow Princess, The
Sunshine Nan
Susie Snowflake (debut)
Stage:
Miss 1917
Scandals Of 1919
Ziegfeld Follies of 1914, The 1914
Ziegfeld Follies of 1915, The 1915
Ziegfeld Follies of 1916, The 1916
Ziegfeld Follies of 1918, The 1918

2029
PEPA, Bonafe*
Shylock

2030
PEPPER*
Keystone cat

2031
PERCY, Eileen*
Beloved Cheater, The
Brass Buttons
Desperate Gold
Down to Earth (Ethel Forsythe)
Empty Cab, The
Gray Horizon, The
In Mizzoura
Man from Painted Post, The
  (school teacher)
Reaching for the Moon (Elsie)
Some Liar
Where the West Begins
Wild and Wolly (Nell Larrabe)

2032
PERIOLAT, George (-1960)
Adventures of Terrence O'Rourke
American player 1911
Diamond from the Sky, The (serial)
Ghost of Rosy Taylor, The
Landon's Legacy
Mate of the Sally Ann
Stool Pigeon, The
Tiger Lily

2033
PERKINS, Walter*
Bill Henry

2034
PERRIN, Jack (Jack Perrin Rayart)
  (1896-1968)
Blind Husbands (a honeymooner)
Cyclone Smith Plays Trumpet
Cyclone Smith's Comeback
Cyclone Smith's Partner
Cyclone Smith's Vow
Double Crossed
Lion Man, The (serial)
Toton, the Apache
With the Keystone Cops

2035
PETERS, House (1888-1967)
Brute, The
Captive, The (Mahmud)
Forfeit
Girl of the Golden West, The
  (Ramerrez)
Great Divide, The
Hour before the Dawn, An
Lady of Quality, A
Leah Kleschna
Mignon
Port of Doom
Pride of Jennico, The

Salomy Jane
Stolen Goods
Thunderbolts
Unafraid, The (Stefan Balsic)
Warrens of Virginia, The (Ned
  Burton)
Winged Idol, The
You Never Know Your Luck

2036
PETERS, Page*
Captive, The (Marko)
Madame La Presidente
Unafraid, The (Michael Balsic)
Warrens of Virginia, The (Arthur
  Warren)

2037
PETROVA, Olga (Muriel Harding) (1886-)
Black Butterfly
Daughter of Destiny, A
Eternal Question, The
Exile
Law of the Land
Life Mask, The
Light Within, The
Metro player 1915
More Truth Than Poetry
Orchid Lady, The
Panther Woman, The
Patience Sparhawk
Petrova film company 1919
Silence Sellers, The
Soul of a Magdalen, The
Soul Market, The
Tempered Steel
Tigress, The
Undying Flame, The
Vampire, The (debut)
Stage:
Quaker Girl, The 1911
Panthea 1914

2038
PEYTON, Lawrence "Larry"*
Joan, the Woman (Gaspard)
Red Ace, The (serial)
Unafraid, The (Danilo Lesendra)

2039
PHILLIPS, Augustus*
Edison player 1912
God's Law and Man's
Toby's Bow

2040
PHILLIPS, Blanche*
Teddy at the Throttle (the mercenary
  aunt)

2041
PHILLIPS, Carmen (1895-   )
Chased into Love
Pipes of Pan, The (Caprice)
Under the Crescent (serial)

2042
PHILLIPS, Dorothy (1892-   )
Ambition
Bondage (Elinor Crawford)
Broadway Love (Midge O'Hara)
Destiny
Doll's House, A (Nora Helmer)
Fate's Funny Frolic
Fires of Rebellion
Flashlight, The (Delice Brixton)
Girl in the Checkered Coat, The
   (dual role, Mary Graham and
   Flash Fan)
Grand Passion, The (Viola)
Heart of Humanity, The
Hell Morgan's Girl (Lola)
If My Country Should Call (Margaret
   Ardrath)
Imp player 1914
Into the North
Mark of Cain, The (Doris)
Mortgaged Wife
Paid in Advance (Joan)
Pay Me (Maria)
Piper's Price, The (Amy Hadley)
Place beyond the Winds (Priscilla
   Glenn)
Price of Silence, The (Helen Urmy)
Rescue, The (Anne Wetherall)
Right to Happiness, The
Risky Road, The
Rosary, The
Soul for Sale, A
Talk of the Town, The (Ginevera
   French)
Triumph (Nell Baxter)

2043
PHILLIPS, E. R. *
New Stenographer, The

2044
PHILLIPS, Norma (1893-1931)
Became the Mutual Girl in 1913
Runaway June (serial)

2045
PICKFORD, Jack (Jack Smith)
   (1896-1933)
All on Account of the Milk
Bill Apperson's Boy
Burglar by Proxy

Child's Strategem, A
Dash through the Clouds, A
Dummy, The
Examination Day at School
Fanchon the Cricket
Freckles
Ghost House, The
Girl at Home, The
Girl of Yesterday, A
Great Expectations
Heredity
His Majesty Bunker Bean
Home, Sweet Home
Huck and Tom
Iconoclast, The
In Wrong
Jack and Jill
Liberty Bells
Massacre, The
Mile-a-Minute Kendall
Modern Prodigal, The
Musketeers of Pig Alley, The
Mysterious Shot, The
New York Hat, The
Poor Little Peppina
Pretty Sister of Jose, The
Sandy
Seventeen
Speed Demon, The
Spirit of '17, The
Tom Sawyer
Unwelcome Guest, The
Varmint, The
What Money Can't Buy
White Roses
Wildflower
With the Enemy's Help
Would-Be Shriner, The
Stage:
Edmund Burke (billed as Edith
   Smith) 1905
Los Angeles Mason Opera House 1917

2046
PICKFORD, Lottie (Lottie Smith)
   (1895-1936)
Diamond from the Sky, The (serial)
Fanchon the Cricket
Flying A (serial)
Imp player 1910
Little Darling, The
Man from Funeral Range, The
Mile-a-Minute Kendall
Summer Idyll, A
Two Memories
Stage:
Edmund Burke (billed as Lottie
   Smith) 1905

Los Angeles Mason House 1917
   (sold programs)

2047
PICKFORD, Mary (Gladys Smith)
   [Miss Pickford was born on April
   8, 1893 in Toronto, Canada;
   blonde hair, hazel eyes, height, 5'.
   Marriages: Owen Moore--divorced
   1920; Douglas Fairbanks, married
   March 1920--divorced 1935;
   Charles "Buddy" Rogers, married
   1937. Vice-President of Mary
   Pickford Famous Players Company
   1915. Mary Pickford Company
   organized 1916. Prominent organ-
   izer of United Artists Corp. 1919.
   Became known as "America's
   Sweetheart" 1914.]
All on Account of the Milk
Amarilly of Clothesline Alley
Arcadian Maid, An
Artful Kate
As Is Is in Life
At a Quarter of Two
At the Duke's Command
Awakening, The
Back to the Soil
Beast at Bay, A
Behind the Scenes
Better Way, The
Broken Locket, The
Caddy's Dream, The
Call of the Song, The
Call to Arms, The
Caprice
Captain Kid, Jr.
Cardinal's Conspiracy, The
Child's Impulse, A
Cinderella
Country Doctor, The
Courting of Mary, The
Daddy Long Legs
Dawn of Tomorrow, A
Decree of Destiny, A
Dream, The
Eagle's Mate, The
Englishman and the Girl, The
Esmeralda
Eternal Grind, The
Examination Day at School
Face at the Window, The
Faded Lilies, The
Fair Dentist, The
Fanchon the Cricket
Fate's Interception
Female of the Species, The
Feud in the Kentucky Hills, A

Fisher-Maid, The
For Her Brother's Sake
For the Queen's Honor
Foundling, The
Friends
From the Bottom of the Sea
Gasoline Engagement, A
Getting Even
Gibson Goddess, The
Girl of Yesterday, A
Going Straight
Gold Necklace, A
Good Little Devil, A
Gypsy Girl, The
Heart of the Hills
Hearts Adrift
Her Darkest Hour
Her First Biscuits
His Dress Shirt
His Lost Love
His Wife's Visitor
Home Folks
Honor Thy Father
Hoodlum, The
How Could You, Jean?
Hulda from Holland
In Old Kentucky
In Old Madrid
In the Bishop's Carriage
In the Season of Buds
In the Sultan's Garden
In the Watches of the Night
Indian Runner's Romance, The
Indian Summer, An
Informer, The
Inner Circle, The
Iola's Promise
Italian Barber, The
Johanna Enlists
Jonsey
Just Like a Woman
Lena and the Geese
Less Than the Dust
Light That Came, The
Lighthouse Keeper, The
Little American, The
Little Darling, The
Little Pal
Little Princess, The
Little Red Riding Hood
Little Teacher, The
Lodging for the Night, A
Lonely Villa, The
Love among the Roses
Love Heeds Not the Showers
Lover's Tryst
Lucky Toothache, A
M'Liss

Madame Butterfly (Cho-Cho San)
Maid or Man
Manly Man, A
Masher, The
Master and the Man
May and December
May to December
Mender of the Nets, The
Message in the Bottle, The
Mexican Sweethearts, The
Midnight Adventure, A
Mirror, The
Mistress Nell (Nell Gwynn)
Molly Entangled
Mountaineer's Honor, The
Muggsy becomes a Hero
Muggsy's First Sweetheart
My Baby
Narrow Road, The
Necklace, The
Never Again
New York Hat, The
Newlyweds, The
Oh, Uncle!
Old Actor, The
100% American (Propaganda film)
One She Loved, The
Paris Hat, The
Pippa Passes
Plain Song, A
Poor Little Peppina
Poor Little Rich Girl, The
Pride of the Clan, The
Pueblo Legend, A
Rags
Ramona: a Story of the White Man's
    Injustice to the Indian
Rebecca of Sunnybrook Farm
Renunciation, The
Restoration, The
Retrospect /aka/ Sweet Memories
Rich Revenge: a Comedy of the
    California Oil Fields
Romance of the Redwoods, A (Jenny
    Lawrence)
Romance of the Western Hills, A
Rose's Story, The
Savage Princess, The
School Teacher and the Waif, The
Science
Scraps
Sealed Room, The
Second Sight
Sentinel Asleep, The
1776, or The Hessian Renegades
Shadows of Doubt
Simple Charity
Skating Bug, The

Slave, The
Smoker, The
So Near, Yet So Far
Son's Return, The
Song of the Wildwood Flute, The
Sorrows of the Unfaithful, The
Stampede, The
Stella Maris
Strange Meeting, A
Such a Little Queen
Sweet and Twenty
Tess of the Storm Country
Test, The
Their First Misunderstanding
They Would Elope
Thread of Destiny: a Story of the
    Old Southwest
Three Friends
Three Sisters
To Save Her Soul
Toss of a Coin, The
Trick That Failed, The
'Tween Two Loves
Twisted Trail: a Story of Fate
    in the Mountain Wilds
Two Brothers, The "In the Days
    of the Padres"
Two Memories
Unchanging Sea, The
Unwelcome Guest, The
Victim of Jealousy, A
Violin Maker of Cremona, The
    (first star role)
Waiter No. 5
War Relief (Propaganda film)
Way of a Man, The
Wedded but No Wife
What Drink Did
What the Daisy Said
What's Your Hurry?
When a Man Loves
When the Cat's Away
When We Were in Our 'Teens
White Roses
Wilful Peggy
With the Enemy's Help
Woman from Mellon's, The
Won by a Fish
Stage:
Edmund Burke (billed as Gladys
    Smith) 1905
Fatal Wedding (billed as Gladys
    Smith) (Toronto Stock) 1902
Good Little Devil, A (Juliet) 1913
Little Red School House (billed as
    Gladys Smith) (Toronto Stock) 1897
Los Angeles Mason Opera House
    1917

Uncle Tom's Cabin (billed as
   Gladys Smith) (Toronto Stock)
   1897
Valentine Stock Company (billed as
   Gladys Smith) (Toronto) 1898
Warrens of Virginia, The (Betty)
   (first time billed as Mary
   Pickford) 1907-08

2048
PIERCE, George*
Three Weeks

2049
PIKE, William*
Carter Case, The (The Craig
   Kennedy Serial) (serial)
Master Mystery, The (serial)

2050
PILCER, Harry*
Her Triumph

2051
PITTS, Zasu (1898-1963)
As the Sun Went Down
Better Times
For the Defense (debut)
How Could You, Jean?
Little American, The
Little Princess, The
Men, Women and Money
Modern Musketeer, A
Other Half, The
Poor Relations
Rebecca of Sunnybrook Farm

2052
PLAYTER, Wellington (1883-   )
Back to God's Country
Eagle's Eye (serial)
Fool's Gold
In Search of Arcady
Marta of the Lowlands
Wicked Darling, The (Kent
   Mortimer)

2053
POFF, Lon (1870-   )
Light of the Western Stars, The
Shepherd of the Hills, The

2054
POLLARD, Harry*
Peacock Feather Fan, The
Susie's New Shoes
Uncle Tom's Cabin (Uncle Tom)

2055
POLLARD, "Snub" (Harold Fraser)
   (1886-1962)
All Aboard
Bashful
Big Idea, The
Birds of a Feather
Bliss
Bumping into Broadway
By the Sad Sea Waves
Call for Mr. Cave Man
Captain Kidd's Kiddies
Chop Suey and Company
Clubs Are Trump
Flirt, The
Floor Below, The
Gasoline Wedding, A
Giving the Bride Away
Great While It Lasted
Heap Big Chief
His Only Father
His Royal Slyness
How Dry I Am
It's a Hard Way to Die
Lamb, The
Lonesome Luke in Tin Can Alley
Lonesome Luke, Social Gangster
Lonesome Luke's Double
Lonesome Luke's Lively Life
Look out Below
Looking for Trouble
Loves, Laughs and Lather
Luke and the Mermaids
Luke, Crystal Gazer
Luke Does the Midway
Luke Foils the Villain
Luke Joins the Navy
Luke Laughs Last
Luke Leans to the Literary
Luke Lugs Luggage
Luke Pipes the Pippins
Luke Rides Roughshod
Luke Rolls in Luxury
Luke the Candy Cut-up
Luke's Fatal Flivver
Luke's Lost Lamb
Luke's Society Mixup
Luke's Speedy Club Life
Luke's Wishful Waiting
Marathon, The
Move On
Non-Stop Kid, The
Nothing but Trouble
On the Fire
Order in the Court
Over the Fence
Peculiar Patients' Pranks
Pistols for Breakfast

Punch the Clock
Rainbow Island
Rajah, The
Rural Roughnecks
She Loves Me Not
Soft Money
Spring Fever
Start Something
Tip, The
Tough Luck
We Never Sleep

2056
POLO, Eddie (1875-1961)
Adventures of Peg o' the Ring, The
   (serial)
Broken Coin, The (serial)
Bull's Eye (serial)
Captain Kidd
Cyclone Smith Plays Trumpet
Cyclone Smith's Comeback
Cyclone Smith's Partner
Cyclone Smith's Vow
For Liberty (serial)
Gray Ghost, The (serial)
Heritage of Hate
Hidden City, The
Liberty, a Daughter of the U. S. A.
   (serial)
Lure of the Circus (serial)
Money Madness
Ouda of the Orient
Ride for a Rancho, A
Thirteenth Hour, The (serial)
Verdict, The
White Messenger
Yellow Streak, The

2057
POLO, Sam*
Midnight Man, The (serial)

2058
POTEL, Victor (1889-1947)
Amateur Adventuress
Billy Fortune series
Captain Kidd, Jr.
Full of Pep
His Last Scent
In Mizzoura
Joyriding
Keystone player 1917
Mustang Pete comedy series
   (Slippery Slim)
One a Minute
Outcasts of Poker Flat
Petal on the Current, A
Slippery Slim series (Title role)

Snakeville comedy series
Three Slims, The

2059
POUYET, Eugene*
Hearts of the World (a Poilu)

2060
POWELL, Baden*
Crooked Road, The
Inner Circle, The
Smile of a Child
Sorrowful Example, The
Thief and the Girl, The

2061
POWELL, David (1887-1923)
Beautiful Adventure, The
Better Half, The
Counterfeit, The
Dawn of Tomorrow, A
Firing Line, The
Gloria's Romance (serial)
Great Chances, The
His Parisian Wife
Less Than the Dust
Lie, The
Make-Believe Wife, The
Maternity
Romance of the Underworld, A
Teeth of the Tiger
Under the Greenwood Tree
Unforeseen, The
Woman under Oath
Stage:
Captain Brassbound's Conversion 1907
Good Hope, The 1907

2062
POWELL, Frank*
Broken Locket, The
Cardinal's Conspiracy, The
Corner in Wheat, A (the Wheat
   King)
Country Doctor, The
Faithful
Fool There Was, A (the doctor)
Fools of Fate
His Duty
His Wife's Visitor
Honor of Thieves, The
Impalement, The
Knight of the Road, A
Necklace, The
Politician's Love Story
Rocky Road, The
1776, or The Hessian Renegades
Seventh Day, The

Two Women and a Man
Was Justice Served?
With Her Card

2063
POWELL, William (William Horatio
     Powell) (1892-   )
Avalanche, The
Society Exile, A
Stage:
King, The 1917
Ne'er Do Well, The (debut) 1912
Within the Law 1913

2064
POWER, Jules*
Gloria's Romance (serial)

2065
POWER, Tyrone, Sr. (F. Tyrone
     Power) (1869-1931)
John Needham's Double
Lorelei, Siren of the Sea, The
Planter, The
Texas Steer, A
Where Are My Children?
Stage:
Chu Chin Chow 1917
Julius Caesar 1912
Mary of Magdala 1902
Servant in the House, The 1908
Thais 1911
Ulysses 1903

2066
POWERS, Tom (1890-1955)
Auction Block, The
Debut at Vitagraph 1910
Saving an Audience
Stage:
On, Boy! 1917

2067
PRESCOTT, Vivian*
Binks series
Comrades
Flash of Night, A
Her Sacrifice
How She Triumphed
Italian Blood
Primal Call, The
Salutary Lesson, A
Teaching Dad How to Like Her
Three Sisters
Winning Back His Love
Woman Scorned, A

2068
PRETTY, Arline (1893-   )

Challenge of Chance, The
Crossed Currents
Dawn of Freedom, The
Hidden Hand, The (serial)
In Again--out Again (the Sheriff's
     daughter)
Old Guard, The
Scarlet Shadow, The
Secret Kingdom, The (Princess
     Julia) (serial)
Surprises of an Empty Hotel, The
Thirteenth Girl, The
Where the Devil Drives
Woman in Gray, The (serial)

2069
PREVOST, Marie (Marie Bickford
     Dunn) (1898-1937)
Dentist, The
East Lynne with Variations
Her Nature Dance
His Hidden Purpose
Love's False Faces
Mack Sennett Bathing Beauty 1917
Never Too Old
Ol' Swimmin' Hole, The
Reilly's Wash Day
Salome vs. Shenandoah
Secrets of a Beauty Parlor
Sleuths
Speak-Easy, The
Two Crooks /aka/ A Noble Crook
Uncle Tom's Cabin (burlesque)
When Love Is Blind
Yankee Doodle in Berlin

2070
PRICE, Kate (1873-1943)
Amarilly of Clothesline Alley
Arizona (Mrs. Canby)
As You Like It
Casey at the Bat
Dangerous Game, A
Fat and Fickle
Fisherman Kate
Goodness Gracious, or Movies as
     They Shouldn't Be
How Mr. Billington Ran the House
Jack Fat and Jim Slim
Lady and Her Maid, The
Mother's Child
Night Out, A
Officer Kate
O'Hara Helps Cupid
Oracles and Omens
Perils of Thunder Mountain, The
     (serial)
Put up Your Hands!
Sleuthing

Spaghetti a la Mode
Stenographer Wanted (Mrs. Brown)
Tin Pan Alley
Vanity Fair
Vitagraph player 1911
Waiter's Ball, The
Week End Shopping

2071
PRICE, Mark*
Daughter of the Gods, A

2072
PRINGLE, Aileen (Aileen Bisbee)
   (1895-)
Redhead
Stage:
Bracelet, The (London debut) 1915

2073
PRINGLE, Della*
Haystacks and Steeples

2074
PRIOR, Herbert*
Burglar for a Night, A
Cricket on the Hearth, The
Edison player 1907
Great Expectations
Model's Confession, The
Mrs. George Washington
On the Lazy Line
Poor Little Rich Girl
Society for Sale
'Tis an Ill Wind That Blows No
   Good

2075
PROUT, Eva*
Little Red Riding Hood

2076
PURDON, Richard*
Adventures of Marguerite, The
   (serial)

2077
PURVIANCE, Edna (1894-1958)
Adventurer, The
Bank, The
Behind the Screen
Between Showers
Bond, The
By the Sea
Champion, The
Charlie Chaplin's Burlesque on
   Carmen
Count, The

Cruel, Cruel Love
Cure, The
Day's Pleasure, A
Dog's Life, A
Easy Street
Fireman, The
Floorwalker, The
His New Job
Immigrant, The
In the Park
Jitney Elopement, A
Night in the Show, A
Night Out, A
Pawnshop, The
Perfect Lady, A
Police
Rink, The
Shanghaied
Shoulder Arms
Sunnyside
Tramp, The
Triple Trouble
Vagabond, The
Woman, A
Work
Stage:
Los Angeles Mason Opera House 1917
   (sold programs)

- Q -

2078
QUARANTA, Lydia*
Cabiria

2079
QUINN, Allen*
Sporting Duchess, The

2080
QUINN, William*
Trust, The

2081
QUIRK, Billy (William Quirk)
   (1888-)
Bertisi Strategem
Billy the Bear Tamer
Billy's Troubles
Billy's Wager
Blood Stain, The
Boarding House Feud
Corner in Wheat, A
Egyptian Mummy, The
Evolution of Percival, The
Father's Time Piece
Forcing Dad's Consent

Fra Diavolo
Franks
Getting Even
Gibson Goddess, The
Green Cat, The
His Wife's Visitor
Hubby Does the Washing
In Bridal Attire
Little Darling, The
Little Teacher, The
Master of His House
Mended Lute, The
Midnight Adventure, A
Muggsy's First Sweetheart
Oh, Uncle!
Pathé player 1913
Renunciation, The
Rich Revenge, A
1776, of The Hessian Renegades
Son's Return, The
Sound Sleeper, A
Spades Are Trumps
Stamp in Tramps, A
Sweet and Twenty
They Would Elope
Two Brothers, The
Vanishing Vault, The
Woman from Mellon's, The
Young Man Who Figered, The

- R -

2082
RADCLIFFE, Violet*
Aladdin and His Wonderful Lamp
Children in the House

2083
RAE, Isabel*
Universal player 1918

2084
RAE, Zoe*
Kaiser, the Beast of Berlin, The
    (Belgian woman)

2085
RAINEY, Paul J.*
Rainey's African Hunt

2086
RALE, M. W.*
Mysteries of Myra, The (serial)

2087
RALEIGH, Cecil*
Clemenceau Case, The (Countess
    Dobronowska)

2088
RAMBEAU, Marjorie (1889-   )
Dazzling Miss Davison, The
Debt, The
Greater Woman, The
Mary Moreland
Stage:
Cheating Cheaters 1916
Eyes of Youth 1917
Sadie Love 1915
Where Poppies Bloom 1918

2089
RAMBOVA, Natacha (1897-1966)
Woman in Chains

2090
RAND, John*
Bank, The (salesman)
Behind the Screen
Charlie Chaplin's Burlesque on Carmen
Count, The
Cure, The
Easy Street
Fireman, The
Immigrant, The
Night in the Show, A
Pawnshop, The
Police (a policeman)
Rink, The
Shanghaied
Vagabond, The

2091
RANDOLF, Anders /aka/ Anders
    Randolph (1875-1930)
Belgian, The
Black Beach, The
Cinema Murder, The (Sulvanus
    Power)
Erstwhile Susan
Her Man
Hero of Submarine D-2
Lion and the Mouse, The
Price of Virtue, The
Safety Curtain, The
Splendid Sinner
Uncle Bill
Who's Your Neighbor?
Within the Law

2092
RANKIN, Caroline*
Lottery Man, The
Pawnbroker's Heart, The

2093
RATTENBURY, Harry*
Lucille Love, Girl of Mystery (serial)

2094
RAUCOURT, Jules (1890-   )
Frou-Frou
La Tosca
Prunella

2095
RAWLINSON, Herbert (1885-1953)
Back to the Woods
Black Box, The (serial)
Blind Fools
Brace Up
Carter Case, The (The Craig
    Kennedy Serial) (serial)
Charge It
Chief Flynn, Secret Service series
Come Through
Common Cause, The
Count of Monte Cristo, The
Damon and Pythias
Dangerous Affair, A
Don't Shoot!
Exploits of Elaine, The (serial)
Flesh of Fate
Flirting with Death
God of Gold
Good Gracious, Annabelle!
High Sign, The
Kid Regan's Hands
Kill or Be Killed
Man Trap, The
Novice, The
Old Clerk, The
On the Verge of War
Sea Wolf, The
Selig Western 1910
Smashing Through
Sun Shinning Through, The
Turn of the Wheel
Won in the Clouds

2096
RAY, Charles (1891-1943)
Ace of Hearts
Back of the Man
Bill Henry
Bondsman, The
Boomerang, The
Bread Cast upon the Waters
Busher, The
Card Sharp, The
City, The
City of Darkness
Claws of the Hun
Clodhopper, The
Conversion of Frosty Blake, The
Corner in Coleen's Home, A
Coward, The (Frank Winslow)

Crooked Straight, The
Cup of Life, A
Curse of Humanity, The
Desert Gold
Deserter, The (Lt. Parker)
Dividend, The
Egg-Crate Wallop, The
Eileen of Erin
Exoneration, The
Family Skeleton
Favorite Son
For Her Brother's Sake
For the Wearing of the Green
Fortunes of War, The
Friend, The
Gangsters and the Girl, The
Girl Dodger, The
Greased Lightning
Grey Sentinel, The
Hay Foot, Straw Foot!
Hired Man, The
His Mother's Boy
His Own Home Town
Home
Honor Thy Name
Honorable Algy
House of Bondage
In the Cow Country
In the Tennessee Hills
Kay-Bee player 1914
Latent Spark
Law of the North, The
Lost Dispatch
Lure of a Woman, The (Broncho)
Military Judas, A
Millionaire Vagrant, The
Nine o'Clock Town, A
Not of the Flock
One of the Discard
Open Door, The
Paddy O'Hara
Painted Soul, The
Path of Genius
Peggy
Pinch Hitter, The
Plain Jane
Playing the Game
Quakeress, The
Red Hot Dollars
Red Mask, The
Renegade, The
Repaid
Rightful Heir, The
Sharpshooter
Sheriff's Son, The
Shoal Light, The
Shorty's Sacrifice
Sinews of War

Slave's Devotion, A
Son of His Father
Soul of the South
Spirit of the Bell, The
String Beans
Sudden Jim
Transgressor, The
Weaker Sex, The
Wells of Paradise
Witch of Salem, The
Wolf Woman, The
Word of His People, The

2097
RAYMOND, Whitney*
Essanay player 1912-1914

2098
RAYMOND, William*
Francesca Da Rimini

2099
RAZETO, Stella*
Selig player 1916

2100
REA, Isabel*
Imp player 1919

2101
REAL, Louise*
Sin (Maria)

2102
REARDON, Mildred*
Male and Female (Lady Agatha
    Lasenby)

2103
RED WING, Princess (Lillian St.
    Cyr)*
Apache Father's Revenge, An
Back to the Prairie
Falling Arrow, The
Flight of Red Wing, The
In the Days of the Thundering Herd
Mended Lute, The
Ramona
Red Wing's Gratitude
Squaw Man, The (Nat-U-Rich)
White Squaw, The
Stage:
Pioneer Days (New York
    Hippodrome)*

2104
REDMAN, Frank*
Bound and Gagged (serial)

2105
REED, Florence (1863-1967)
Call of the Heart
Cowardly Way, The
Dancing Girl, The
Eternal Mother, The
Eternal Sin, The
Her Code of Honor
Lucretia Borgia
New York
Struggle Everlasting, The
Today
Wives of Men
Woman under Oath
Woman's Law, The
Stage:
Celebrated Case, A 1915
Chu Chin Chow 1917
Girl and the Pennant, The 1913
Parlor, Bedroom and Bath 1917
Roads of Destiny 1918
Seven Days 1909
Typhoon, The 1912
Wanderer, The 1917
Yellow Ticket, The 1914

2106
REED, Vivian*
Bull's Eye (serial)
Nakhla

2107
REEL, Edward*
Girl Who Stayed at Home, The
    (Herr Turnverein)

2108
REEVES, Billie*
New Butler, The
Stage:
Ziegfeld Follies of 1909, The 1909

2109
REEVES, Robert*
Great Radium Mystery, The (serial)

2110
REICHERT, Kittens*
Eternal Sapho, The (the Drummond
    child)
Heart and Soul (Bess in the
    prologue)
Scarlet Letter, The (the child)
Tiger Woman, The (the Harris
    child)

2111
REID, Hal*

Cardinal Wolsey
Deerslayer, The

2112
REID, Wallace (1890-1923)
Across the Mexican Line
Alias Mike Moran
Animal, The
Another Chance
Arms and the Gringo
At Cripple Creek
At Dawn
Baby's Ride
Before the White Man Came
Believe Me, Xantippe
Big Timber
Birth of a Nation, The (Jeff, the
    blacksmith)
Breed of the Mountains, A
Brothers
Carmen (Don Jose)
Chorus Lady, The
Chumps
City Beautiful, The
Countess Betty's Mine, The
Cracksman Santa Claus, A
Cracksman's Reformation, The
Craven, The
Cross Purposes
Cupid Incognito
Curfew Shall Not Ring Tonight, The
Dead Man's Shoes
Deerslayer, The
Den of Thieves, A
Devil Stone, The (Guy Sterling)
Diamond Cut Diamond
Down by the Sounding Sea
Down the Road to Creditville
Dub, The
Enoch Arden
Every Inch a Man
Firefly of Franch
Fires of Conscience
Fires of Fate, The
Flash in the Dark, A
For Her Father's Sins
Foreign Spy, A
Fruit of Evil, The
Golden Chance, The
Golden Fetter, The
Gratitude of Wanda
Greater Devotion, The
Gypsy Romance, A
Harvest of Flame, The
Hawthorne of the U. S. A.
Heart of a Cracksman, The
Heart of the Hills
Hearts and Horses

Her Awakening
Her Innocent Marriage
Hieroglyphic, The
His Mother's Son
His Only Son
Hopi Legend, A
Hostage, The
House of Silence
Illumination, The
Indian Raiders
Indian Romeo and Juliet
Intolerance
Intruder, The
Jean Intervenes
Joan, the Woman (Eric Trent)
Kaintuck
Kiss, The
Leading Lady, The
Leather Stocking Tales
Less Than Kin
Lightning Bolt, The
Little Country Mouse, The
Lost House, The
Lottery Man, The
Love and the Law
Love Burglar, The
Love Mask, The
Love's Western Flight
Making Good
Man from Funeral Range, The
Man Within, The
Man's Duty, A
Maria Rosa (Andreas)
Mental Suicide
Modern Snare, A
Moonshine Molly
Mother's Influence, A
Mountaineer, The
Mystery of the Yellow Aster Mine
Nan of Music Mountain
Niggard, The
Odalisque, The
Old Heidelberg
Over the Ledge
Passing of the Beast
Pathfinder, The
Phoenix, The
Picket Guard
Picture of Dorian Gray, The
Powder Flash of Death, The
Pride of Lonesome
Prison without Walls, The
Quack, The
Regeneration
Reporter, The
Retribution
Rimrock Jones
Roaring Road, The

Rose of Old Mexico, A
Second Mrs. Roebuck, The
Secret Service Man, The
Seepore Rebellion, The
Selfish Woman, The
Seventh Son, The
Sierra Jim's Reformation
Siren, The
Skeleton, The
Source, The
Spark of Manhood, The
Spider and Her Web, The
Spirit of the Flag, The
Squaw Man's Son, The
Station Content
Tattooed Arm, The
Telephone Girl, The
Test, The
Thing We Love, The
Three Brothers, The
To Have and to Hold (Capt. Ralph
  Percy)
Too Many Millions
Tribal Law, The
Valley of the Giants
Via Cabaret
Victoria Cross /aka/ Charge of
  the Light Brigade
Voice of Viola, The
Wall of Money, The
Way of a Woman, The
Ways of Fate, The
Wheel of Life, The
When Jim Returned
When Luck Changes
Whoso Diggeth a Pit
Wife on a Wager, A
Woman God Forgot, The
Women and Roses
World Apart
Yankee from the West, A
Yellow Pawn, The
You're Fired!
Youth and Jealousy
Stage:
Los Angeles Mason Opera House 1917

2113
REIGER, Margie*
By the Sea
Woman, A (a flirt)

2114
REILLY, Dominick*
Ireland, a Nation

2115
REINHARD, John*
Bound and Gagged (serial)

2116
REISNER, Charles*
Dog's Life, A
Her First False Step
His Lying Heart

2117
REJANE, Gabrielle (1857-1920)
Madame Sans-Gene
Stage:
Appeared in 1895
Repertory 1904

2118
RENEVANT, George*
Erstwhile Susan
Light, The (Auchat)
Stage:
Mis' Nelly of N'Orleans 1919

2119
RENFELD, C.*
Till I Come Back to You (Rosa's
  father)

2120
REVELLE, Hamilton*
Metro player 1917
Star over Night, A
Thais
Stage:
Carmen 1905
Devil, The 1908
DuBarry 1901
Fair and Warmer 1915
Mis' Nelly of N'Orleans 1919
Sapho 1900; 1905

2121
RHODES, Billie (1906-   )
Beware of Blondes
Blue Bonnet
Dad's Knockout
Girl of My Dreams
Her Hero
Hoop-La of the Circus
In Search of Aready
Lion and the Lamb, The
Love Call, The
Mutual player 1914
Perils of the Sea
Seminary Scandal, A
Some Nurse
Two Cylinder Courtship, A

2122
RIAVME, Helen*
Where Are My Children?

2123
RICE, John C. *
First Kiss, The (from The Widow
   Jones)

2124
RICH, Irene (Irene Luther) (1894-   )
Blue Bonnet
Law unto Herself, A
Michael O'Halloran
Ropin' Fool
Stella Maris
Street Called Straight, A
Tale of Two Worlds
Todd of the Times
Trap, The
Wolves of the Night

2125
RICH, Lillian (1902-1954)
Dead Man's Shoes
Foreign Spy, A
Hearts and Horses
Her Innocent Marriage
Modern Snare, A
Tattooed Arm, The
Ways of Fate, The
When Jim Returned
When Luck Changes
Youth and Jealousy

2126
RICH, Vivian*
Business vs. Love
Enchantment, The

2127
RICHARDS, Mary*
Burden of Proof, The (Mrs. Brooks)

2128
RICHARDSON, Jack (1883-   )
American player 1911-1914
Dangerous Hours
Desert Law
Girl of Hell's Agony, The
His Enemy, the Law
Man above the Law
Mayor of Filbert, The
Painted Lily, The
Selig western 1910
She Wolf
Wife or Country

2129
RICHMAN, Charles (1879-1940)
Battle Cry of Peace, The
Echo of Youth, The

Everybody's Business
Hero of Submarine D-2
Hidden Truth, The
Lasky player 1914
More Excellent Way, The
Over There
Public Be Damned, The
Secret Kingdom, The (serial) (Phil
   Barr)
Stage:
Bought and Paid For 1911
Diplomacy 1900; 1910
Help Wanted 1914
Importance of Being Earnest, The
   1902
Jim, the Penman 1910
Lights o' London, The 1911
Man's World, A 1910
Rose of the Rancho, The 1906
Royal Family, A 1900
Sinners 1915

2130
RICHMOND, Warner P. (1895-1948)
As a Man Thinks
Betty of Graystone
Eyes of Youth
Gray Towers of Mystery, The
Lady Audley's Secret (Sir Michael
   Audley)
Little Miss Brown
Manhattan Madness (Jack Osborne)
Misleading Lady
Sporting Life
Test of a Code, The

2131
RICKETTS, Tom (-1939)
Daughter of the Well Dressed
   Poor, A
Other Side of the Door
Single Code, The

2132
RIDGELY, Cleo (1893-1962)
Chorus Lady, The
Golden Chance, The (Mary Denby)
House with the Golden Windows, The
Joan, the Woman (the King's
   favorite)
Love Mask, The
Secret Orchard
Selfish Woman, The
Stolen Goods
Yellow Pawn, The

2133
RIDGEWAY, Fritzie (1898-1960)

Danger Zone, The
Fire Flingers
Petal on the Current, A
Ranger of Pike's Peak
Soul Herder, The
Up or Down
Winning of a Bride

2134
RIDGWAY, Jack*
Soul of Buddha, The (M. Romaine's
    father-in-law)

2135
RING, Blanche*
Yankee Girl, The
Stage:
Defender, The 1902
Gay White Way, The 1907
His Honor, the Mayor 1906
Passing Show of 1919, The 1919
Wall Street Girl, The 1912
When Claudia Smiles 1914
Yankee Girl, The 1910

2136
RING, Sutherland*
His Last Laugh

2137
RIPLEY, Charles*
Great Secret, The (serial)

2138
RISDON, Elizabeth (1887-1958)
Another Man's Wife
Beautiful Jim
Bells of Rheims, The
Black-eyed Susan
Bridegrooms Beware
Charity Ann
Christian, The
Courage of a Coward, The
Cup Final Mystery, The
Driven
Esther
Fine Feathers
Finger of Destiny
Florence Nightingale
From Shopgirl to Duchess
Gilbert Gets Tiger-itis
Grip
Her Luck in London
Her Nameless Child
Home
Honeymoon for Three
Idol of Paris
Inquisitive Ike

It's a Long, Long Way to Tipperary
London's Yellow Peril
Loss of the Birkenhead, The
Love in a Wood
Manxman, The
Maria Marten
Meg, the Lady
Midshipman Easy
Morals of Weybury, The
Mother
Mother of Dartmoor, A
Mother's Influence, A
Motherlove
Princess of Happy Chance, The
Smith
Sound of Her Voice, The
Star over Night, A
Suicide Club, The
There's Good in Everyone
Will of Her Own, A
Stage:
Fanny's First Play (debut) 1912
Seven Day's Leave 1918

2139
RITCHIE, "Billie"*
Universal player 1914

2140
RITCHIE, Franklin*
Biograph player 1915

2141
RITZ, Al (Al Joachin)*
Avenging Trail, The (an extra)

2142
RIVIERE, Gaston*
Hearts of the World (stretcher
    bearer)

2143
ROACH, Bert (1891-)
Cactus and Kate
Dirty's Daring Dash
Fatty's Magic Pants /aka/ Fatty's
    Suitless Day
Soapsuds and Sirens
Yankee Doodle in Berlin

2144
ROBBINNE*
Assassination of the Duc de Guise

2145
ROBBINS, Edwina*
Crooky Scruggs

2146
ROBBINS, Jesse*
Lucky Dog, A

2147
ROBERTS, Edith (1901-1935)
Beans
Bill Henry
Brazen Beauty, The
Burglar by Request, A
Cherries Are Ripe
Deciding Kiss, The
Five Little Widows
Her City Beau
Jilted in Jail
Lasca
Lost Appetite, The
Love Swindle, The
Madame Spy
O'Connor's Mag
Seeing Things
Set Free
Sue of the South
Taste of Life, A

2148
ROBERTS, Florence*
Shappo
Stage:
Jim, the Penman 1910

2149
ROBERTS, Theodore (1861-1928)
Arab, The (Turkish Governor)
Arizona (Canby)
Believe Me, Xantippe
Call of the North, The (Galem
    Albert)
Captive, The (Turkish Officer)
Case of Becky, The
Circus Man, The
Don't Change Your Husband (the
    Bishop)
Dream Girl, The (Jim Dugan)
Everywoman
For Better, for Worse (Head of
    Hospital)
Girl of the Golden West, The
    (Rance)
Ghost Breaker, The
Hawthorne of the U. S. A.
Joan, the Woman (Cauchon)
Little Princess, The
Lottery Man, The
M'Liss
Male and Female (Earl of Loam)
Man from Home, The (Grand Duke
    Vasill)

Nan of Music Mountain
Old Wives for New (Berkeley)
Only Way, The
Puddin' Head Wilson
Ready Money
Roaring Road, The
Say! Young Fellow
Secret Orchard, The
Secret Service
Source, The
Sowers, The
Squaw Man, The (Big Bill)
Stolen Goods
Storm, The
Temptation (Otto Mueller)
Trail of the Lonesome Pine, The
    (Judd Tolliver)
Unafraid, The (Secret Agent of
    Dual Empire)
Uncle Tom
Unprotected, The
War Relief (Propaganda film)
We Can't Have Everything (The
    Sultan)
What's His Name? (a character man)
Where the Trail Divides
Wild Goose Chase, The (Horatio
    Brutus Bangs)
Wild Youth
Woman Thou Gavest Me, The
You're Fired!
Stage:
Arizona 1900
Much Ado about Nothing 1904

2150
ROBERTSHAW, Jerrold (1866-1941)
Dombey and Son

2151
ROBERTSON, Lolita*
Adventures of Wallingford (serial)
What's His Name? (Nellie)
Stage:
Fine Feathers 1913

2152
ROBEY, Sir George (Sir George Wade)
    (1869-1954)
Blood Tells
Doing His Bit
George Robey Turns Anarchist
George Robey's Day Off
£66.13.9 3/4 for Every Man Woman
    and Child

2153
ROBINSON, Arthur*
Scarlet Runner, The (serial)

2154
ROBINSON, Daisy*
When the Clouds Roll By (Bobbie
DeVere)

2155
ROBINSON, Forest*
Dawn of Tomorrow, A

2156
ROBINSON, Gertrude*
Arab, The (Mary)
Death Disc, The
Examination Day at School
Gold Is Not All
Judith of Bethulia
Open Gate, The
Pippa Passes
Purgation, The
Reliance player 1911
Summer Idyll, A
What the Daisy Said

2157
ROBINSON, "Spike"*
Struggle, The

2158
ROBINSON, W. C. *
Musketeers of Pig Alley, The

2159
ROBSON, Andrew*
Broadway Scandal, A (Armand
Bison)
That Devil Bateese (Father Pierre)
Upstairs and Down

2160
ROBSON, May (Mary Robison)
(1865-1942)
Broadway Saint, A
His Bridal Night
How Molly Made Good
Lost Battalion, The
Night Out, A
Vitagraph player 1916
Stage:
Billionaire, The 1902
Cousin Billy 1905
Dorothy Vernon of Haddon Hall
(Queen Elizabeth) 1903
It Happened in Nordland 1904
Messenger Boy, The 1901
Rejuvenation of Aunt Mary, The 1907

2161
ROCCARDI, Albert*
New Secretary, The

2162
ROCK, Charles*
Better 'Ole, The

2163
RODGERS, Walter*
Fight for Millions, A (serial)
Fighting Trail, The (serial)
Smashing Barriers (serial)
Vengeance and the Woman (serial)

2164
RODNEY, Earl*
Biggest Show on Earth
City of Tears
Crooked to the End
Keys of the Righteous
Naughty! Naughty!
Nick of Time Baby, The
Oily Scoundrel, An
Paramount player 1919
Secrets of a Beauty Parlor
Village Vampire, The /aka/ The
Great Leap

2165
ROGERS, Dora*
Battle of Ambrose and Walrus, The
Bucking Society
Dodging His Doom
Gypsy Joe
His First False Step
His Naughty Thought
His Precious Life
Love, Loot and Crash
Love Riot, A
Modern Enoch Arden, A

2166
ROGERS, Gene*
Pinched in the Finish
Scoundrel's Tale, A
Stars and Bars

2167
ROGERS, Rene*
Where Are My Children?

2168
ROGERS, Will (William Penn Adair
Rogers) (1879-1935)
Almost a Husband
Jubilo
Laughing Bill Hyde (debut)
Water, Water Everywhere
Stage:
Hammerstein's Roof Garden (*)
Hands Up! 1915
Keith's Union Square 1905

Madison Square Garden Horse Fair
  1905
Passing Show of 1917, The 1917
St. Louis World's Fair 1904
Wall Street Girl, The 1912
Ziegfeld Follies of 1917
Ziegfeld Follies of 1918
Ziegfeld Midnight Frolic (*)

2169
ROLAND, Ruth (1893-1937)
Adventures of Ruth, The (serial)
Comrade John
Fringe of Society
Girl Detective, The (serial)
Ham at the Garbage Gentleman's
  Ball
Ham, the Piano Mover
Hands Up! (serial)
Haunted Queen, The
Hypnotic Nell
Neglected Wife, The (serial)
Price of Folly, The (serial)
Ranch Girls on a Rampage
Red Circle, The (serial)
Tiger's Trail, The (Belle) (serial)
While Father Telephoned
Who Pays? (serial)
Who Wins? (serial)

2170
ROLLINS, Jack*
When a Woman Sins (Reggie West)

2171
ROME, Stewart (Septimus Wernham
  Ryott) (1886-1965)
American Heiress, The
Annie Laurie
As the Sun Went Down
Baby on the Barge, The
Barnaby Rudge
Bottle, The
Bronze Idol, The
Brothers
Canker of Jealousy, The
Chimes, The
Cobweb, The
Comin' thro' the Rye
Court Martialled
Creatures of Clay
Cry of the Captive, The
Curtain's Secret, The
Daughter of Eve, A
Eternal Triangle, The
Face to Face
Gentleman Rider, A
Girl Who Lived in Straight Street,
  The

Girl Who Played the Game, The
Golden Pavement, The
Grain of Sand, A
Grand Babylon Hotel
Great Coup, A
Grip of Ambition, The
Guest of the Evening, The
Heart of Midlothian, The
Her Marriage Lines
His Country's Bidding
House of Fortescue, The
Incorruptible Crown, The
Iris
John Linworth's Atonement
Justice
Lancashire Lass, A
Life's Dark Road
Man behind the Times, The
Man from India, The
Marriage of William Ashe
Molly Bawn
Nightbirds of London, The
Partners
Recalling of John Grey, The
Schemers, The
Second String, The
Shepherd of Souls, The
Snow in the Desert
Sowing the Wind
Stress of Circumstances
Sweater, The
Sweet Lavender
Terror of the Air, The
Thou Shalt Not Steal
Throw of the Dice, A
Time, The Great Healer
Touch of a Child, The
Tragedy of Basil Grieve
Trelawney of the Wells
Unfit
Whirr of the Spinning Wheel, The
White Boys, The
White Hope, The

2172
ROOSEVELT, Buddy (Kent Sanderson)
  (1898-   )
Hell's Hinges

2173
RORKE, J. E. Lieutenant*
Unbeliever, The

2174
ROSAMONDE, Miss*
Thelma
Winter's Tale, A

2175
ROSCOE, Albert (1887-1931)
Camille (Armand Duval)
City of Comrades
Cleopatra (Phaeon)
Evangeline
Her Purchase Price
Last Card, The
Man's Country, A (Ralph Bowen)
Salome (John the Baptist)
She-Devil, The (Maurice Taylor)
Shuttle, The
Siren's Song, A (Gaspard Prevost)
Under the Yoke (Capt. Paul Winter)
When a Woman Sins (Michael West)

2176
ROSELLE, William*
Avalanche, The
Gloria's Romance (serial)

2177
ROSEMAN, Edward F.*
Barrier, The
Tiger Woman, The (Prince
    Petrovich)
Adventures of Marguerite, The
    (serial)

2178
ROSEMOND, Anna*
Actor's Children, The

2179
ROSMER, Milton (Arthur Milton
    Lunt) (1881-)
Chinese Puzzle, The
Cynthia in the Wilderness
Greater Need, The
Lady Windermere's Fan
Little Women
Man without a Soul, The
Mystery of a Hansom Cab, The
Odds against Her
Still Waters Run Deep
Whoso Is without Sin

2180
ROSS, Edna*
Deliverance

2181
ROSS, James B.*
School for Scandal, The

2182
ROSS, Mary*
Brand, The

2183
ROSS, Milton*
False Faces, The (Ralph Crane)
Riddle Gawne (Reb Butler)

2184
ROSS, Thomas W.*
Only Son, The
Stage:
Checkers 1903
Soldiers of Fortune 1902

2185
ROSSON, Arthur*
Lie, The

2186
ROSSON, Helene*
American player 1914
Grind, The (one of three sisters)

2187
ROSSON, Queenie*
Grind, The (one of three sisters)

2188
ROSSON, Richard*
Embezzler, The (the Penman)
Her Escape (dope fiend)
Lie, The
Old Cobbler, The (Cobbler's son)
Panthea
Richelieu (Francois)

2189
ROTH, Lillian (1911-)
A child actress 1916

2190
ROTHGARDT, Wanda*
Sir Arne's Treasure

2191
ROTHIER, Leon*
Webb Singing Pictures

2192
ROUBERT, Matty*
Universal child player 1916

2193
RUB, Christian (1887-1956)
Belle of New York, The

2194
RUBENS, Alma (Alma Smith)
    (1897-1931)
Americano, The (the President's
    daughter

Answer, The
Blue Blood
Diana of the Green Van
False Ambition
Firefly of Tough Luck, The
Ghost Flower, The
Gown of Destiny
Half-Breed, The (Teresa)
I Love You
Intolerance (a slave girl)
Judith of the Cumberlands
Love Brokers, The
Madame Sphinx
Man's Country, A (Kate Carewe)
Master of His House
Mystery of the Leaping Fish
    (female accomplice)
Old Fashioned Young Man, An
Painted Lily, The
Regenerates
Reggie Mixes In
Restless Souls
Truthful Tolliver

2195
RUBY, Mary*
Graft (serial)
Tragedy of Whispering Creek, The

2196
RUGGLES, Charles (1890-)
Peer Gynt
Stage:
Canary Cottage 1917
Girl in the Limousine, The 1919
Help Wanted 1914
Passing Show of 1918, The 1918
Rolling Stones 1915
Tumble In 1919

2197
RUGGLES, Wesley*
Bank, The
Police
Shanghaied
Submarine Pirate, A
Triple Trouble

2198
RUSSELL, Lilian (Helen Louise
    Leonard) (1861-1922)
Wildfire
Stage:
Genius, The 1906
Hokey-Pokey 1912
Lady Teazle 1904
Lilian Russell Company 1909
Twirly Whirly 1902

Vaudeville 1913
Weber and Fields' Music Hall
    1900-03
Whirl-I-Gig 1900
Whoop-Dee-Doo 1903
Widow's Might, The 1909
Wildfire 1908

2199
RUSSELL, Martha*
Essanay player 1912

2299
RUSSELL, Ray*
Royal Rogue, A

2201
RUSSELL, William (1884-1929)
All the World to Nothing
Brass Buttons
Cricket on the Hearth, The
Cymbeline
Diamond from the Sky, The (serial)
Garden of Lies, The
Hearts or Diamonds?
Hobbs in a Hurry
In Bad
Lucile
Merchant of Venice, The
Midnight Trail, The
New York Luck
Pride and the Man
Robin Hood
Sands of Sacrifice
Sea Master, The
Sequel to the Diamond from the
    Sky, The (serial)
Signet of Sheba
Six Feet Four
Slave, The
Snap Judgment
Some Liar
Sporting Chance, A
Star of Bethlehem, The
Straight Road, The
This Hero Stuff
Undine
Up Romance Road
When a Man Rides Alone
Where the West Begins

2202
RYAN, Joe*
Fight for Millions, A (serial)
Fighting Trail, The (serial)
Man of Might, A (serial)

2203
RYAN, Sam*
Perils of Pauline, The (serial)

- S -

2204
SACK, Nathaniel*
Social Secretary, The

2205
SACKVILLE, Gordon*
Best Man Wins, The
Red Circle, The (serial)

2206
ST. CLAIR, Mal*
A la Cabaret
Dollars and Sense /aka/ The Twins
Her Circus Knight /aka/ The
  Circus Girl
Lost--a Cook
Three Slims, The

2207
ST. DENNIS, Ruth (1877-   )
Dance
Intolerance
Stage:
Auctioneer, The (Mandy) 1901
DuBarry (Mlle. LeGrand) 1901-02
Vaudeville 1916
Zaza (Adele) 1900

2208
ST. JOHN, Al /aka/ "Fuzzy"
  (1893-1963)
Back Stage
Bell Boy, The
Bright Lights /aka/ The Lure of
  Broadway
Butcher Boy, The
Camping Out
Cook, The
Crossed Love and Swords
Deserted Hero, A
Dirty Work in a Laundry /aka/
  A Desperate Scoundrel
Fatty and Mabel Adrift
Fatty and the Broadway Stars
Fatty in Coney Island
Fickle Fatty's Fall
Fool Days
Garage, The
Good Night Nurse!
He Did and He Didn't /aka/ Love
  and Lobsters

High Sign, The
His Prehistoric Past /aka/ The
  Hula Hula Dance
His Wedding Night
His Wife's Mistake
In the Clutches of a Gang
Knockout, The /aka/ The Pugilist
Love
Mabel at the Wheel /aka/ His
  Daredevil Queen
Mabel's Strange Predicament
Moonshine
Moonshiners, The
New Janitor, The /aka/ The New
  Porter
Oh, Doctor!
Other Man, The
Our Dare Devil Chief
Pullman Porter, The
Reckless Romeo, A
Rough House, The
Rounders, The
Sheriff, The /aka/ Out West
Stone Age, The /aka/ Her Cave Man
Tillie's Punctured Romance
Village Scandal, A
Waiter's Ball, The

2209
ST. POLIS, John (1887-1942)
Mark of Cain, The

2210
SAIS, Marin (1888-   )
Bonds of Honor
City of Dim Faces, The
His Birthright
Manya
Social Pirates, The
Thunderbolt Jack
Twelfth Night
Vanity Pool

2211
SALISBURY, Monroe (1879-1935)
Blinding Trail, The
Devil Between, The
Double Trouble
Eagle, The
Eyes of the World
Goose Girl, The
Guilt of Silence, The
Hands Down
Hugo, the Mighty
Lamb, The
Man from Home, The (Hon. Almerc
  St. Aubyn)
Man in the Moonlight

Millionaire Pirate
Ramona (Alessandro)
Red, Red Heart, The
Rose of the Rancho (Don Luise
    del Torre)
Savage, The
Sleeping Lion, The
Squaw Man, The (Henry, Earl of
    Kerkill)
Sundown Trail, The
That Devil Bateese (Bateese Latour)
Virginian, The (Mr. Ogden)
Winner Takes All
Zollenstein

2212
SALTER, Harry*
At the Altar
Balked at the Altar
Barbarian, Ingomar, The
Burglar's Mistake, A
Calamitous Elopement, A
Cardinal's Conspiracy, The
Criminal Hypnotist, The
Devil, The
Eavesdropper, The
Father Gets in the Game
For a Wife's Honor
For Love of Gold
Girls and Daddy, The
Guerrilla, The
Helping Hand, The
Iconoclast, The
Mr. Jones at the Ball
Reckoning, The
Redman and the Child, The
Renunciation, The
Roue's Heart, The
Slave, The
Song of the Shirt, The
Sunday Morning in a Coney Island
    Police Court
Taming of the Shrew
Test of Friendship
Vaquero's Vow, The
Was Justice Served?
Welcome Burglar, The
What Drink Did
When Knights Were Bold
Winning Coat, The

2213
SALTER, Thelma*
Kid Auto Races at Venice
Matrimony

2214
SALTIKOW, N. *

American Millionaire Perishes on
    the Lusitania (Vanderbilt)

2215
SALVINI, Alexander*
Twelve Ten

2216
SAMSON, Teddy (1895-)
Fighting for Gold
Her American Husband
Our Little Wife
Triangle player 1916
Stage:
Los Angeles Mason Opera House 1917
    (sold programs)

2217
SANDERSON, Julia*
Runaway, The
Stage:
Arcadians, The 1910
Dairymaids, The 1907
Fantana 1905
Girl from Utah, The 1914
Kitty Grey 1909
Rambler Rose 1917
Siren, The 1911
Sunshine Girl, The 1913
Sybil 1916
Tourists, The 1906
Winsome Winnie (minor role) 1903

2218
SANDOW, Eugene*
Strong Man Poses

2219
SANFORD, Stanley*
Count, The
Floorwalker, The
Immigrant, The

2220
SANTLEY, Frederic*
Kalem player 1911
Stage:
Cohan Revue of 1916, The 1916
Cohan Revue of 1918, The 1918
Debut at age of 4 as a girl in
    The Silver King (*)
Royal Vagabond, The 1919

2221
SANTSCHI, Thomas /aka/ Tom
    (1882-1931)
Adventures of Kathlyn, The (serial)
Alone in the Jungle
Beware of Strangers

City of Purple Dreams
Count of Monte Cristo, The
Country That God Forgot, The
Crisis, The
Garden of Allah, The
God of Gold
Guilty Cause, A
Helgon, the Mighty
Hell Cat, The
Her Kingdom of Dreams
In the Long Ago
King of the Forest
Little Orphant Annie
Lorraine of the Timberlands
Millionaire Baby, The
Mother McGuire
Mother o' Dreams
Scarlet Shadow, The
Selig Western 1910
Shadows
Spirit of the Lake
Spoilers, The (MacNamara)
Still Alarm
Stronger Vow, The
Sultan's Power, The
Test, The
Thor, Lord of the Jungle
Three Wise Men
Who Shall Take My Life?
Wild Ride, A

2222
SARGENT, Lewis (1904-   )
Soul of Youth, The

2223
SARLE, Regina*
Nugget Nell

2224
SARNO, Hector*
Madame DuBarry (Lebel)
Rose of Blood, The (a revolutionist)

2225
SAUERMAN, Carl*
Beautiful Adventure, The

2226
SAUM, Grace*
Her Greatest Love (the maid)

2227
SAUNDERS, Jackie (1893-   )
Bab, the Fixer
Betty Be Good
Bit of Kindling, A
Checkmate, The

Grip of Evil, The (serial)
Miracle of Love
Muggsy
Shrine of Happiness

2228
SAUNDERS, John see SAUNDERS,
   Jackie

2229
SAUTER, William*
Midnight Man, The (serial)

2230
SAVILLE, Jack*
Mystery of 13, The (serial)

2231
SAWYER, Laura (1885-1970)
Lighthouse Keeper's Daughter, The

2232
SAXE, Temple*
At the Barn
Dangerous Paradise, A
Fates and Flora Fourflush, The
   (The Ten Billion Dollar Vitagraph
   Mystery Serial) (serial)
Intrigue
Lion and the Mouse, The
Mind-the-Paint Girl, The
Miss Ambition
Pride
Strength of the Weak
Teeth of the Tiger

2233
SCARDON, Paul*
Goddess, The (serial)
Majestic player 1912

2334[1]
SCHABLE, Robert*
Test of Honor

2335
SCHADE, Betty*
Bonds of Love
Deliverance
Girl in Bohemia, A
Happiness a la Mode
Through the Wrong Door

2336
SCHADE, Fritz*
Dangers of a Bride
Dough and Dynamite /aka/ The
   Doughnut Designer

1. No entries are missing. The break in numbering is an inadvertent
error.

Face on the Barroom Floor, The
/aka/ The Ham Artist
Fido's Fate
Hash House Fraud, A
Hash House Mashers
Her Nature Dance
His Last Scent
His Musical Career
His Prehistoric Past /aka/ The
Hula Hula Dancer (Cleo)
Human Hound's Triumph
Hunt, The
Laughing Gas (dentist)
Love, Loot and Crash
Masquerader, The
New Janitor, The
Only a Farmer's Daughter
Property Man, The /aka/ The
Roustabout
Rascal of Wolfish Ways, A /aka/
A Polished Villain
Rent Jumpers, The
Rounders, The
Snow Cure, The
Surf Girl, The (the Captain)
Whose Baby?

2337
SCHAEFER, Anne*
Johanna Enlists
Little Princess, A

2338
SCHEFF, Fritzi (1879-1954)
Pretty Mrs. Smith
Stage:
Babette 1903 (first Broadway role
after 16 leading roles with
Metropolitan Opera Company)
Boccaccio 1905-07; 1913
Duchess, The 1911
Mikado, The 1910
Mlle. Modiste 1905
Pretty Mrs. Smith 1914
Prima Donna, The 1908
Two Roses, The 1904

2339
SCHENCK, Earl*
Kaiser's Finish, The

2340
SCHILDKRAUT, Rudolph
(1862-1930)
Country Doctor, The
Ramon und Mensch
Es Werde Licht
Ivan Koschula
Lache Bajazzo

2341
SCHRAM, Violet (1898-   )
Desert of Wheat
Graft (serial)
Saving the Family Name
Shoes
Toby's Bow
Two Rebels

2342
SCHRAMM, Karla*
Broken Blossoms
His Majesty, the American

2343
SCHUMM, Harry*
Broken Coin, The (serial)
Doorway of Destruction
Girl of Mystery, The
Mysterious Rose, The

2344
SCOTT, Cyril (1866-1945)
How Molly Made Good
Stage:
Patience 1912
Polly with a Past 1917
Prince Chap, The 1905; 1909
Tell Me, Pretty Maiden 1900

2345
SCOTT, Estelle*
Romance of an American Duchess,
The

2346
SCOTT, Howard*
Intolerance (a Babylonian dandy)

2347
SCOTT, Mabel Juliene*
Barrier, The
Beach player 1919

2348
SCOTT, Wallace*
Barbara Frietchie

2349
SCOTT, William*
Amarilly of Clothes Line Alley

2350
SEABURY, Forest*
Wild and Wolly (banker)

2351
SEARLE, Sam*
Male and Female

2352
SEARS, A. D. *
Intolerance (a mercernary)
Mystery of the Leaping Fish, The
   (a gent rolling in wealth)

2353
SEASTROM, Victor see
   SJÖSTRÖM, Victor

2354
SEDGWICK, Eileen (1897-   )
Dropped from the Clouds
Great Radium Mystery, The (serial)
Lure of the Circus (serial)
Man and Beast
Number 10 Westbound
Temple of Terror

2355
SEDGWICK, Josie (1900-   )
Boss of the Lazy Y
Camouflaged
Jubilo
Lure of the Circus (serial)
Maternal Spark, The
One Shot Rose
Wild Life
Wolves of the Border

2356
SEIGMANN, George (1884-1928)
Angel of Contention
At Dawn
Avenging Conscience, The (an
   Italian)
Birth of a Nation, The (Silas
   Lynch)
Grafters, The
Great Love, The (Mr. Seymour)
Hearts of the World (Von Strohm)
Home, Sweet Home
Intolerance (Cyrus)
Little Yank, The
Man's Duty, A
My Unmarried Wife
Saving Grace
Spitfire of Seville
Tell Tale Heart, The
Trembling Hour, The
War of the Primal Tribes
Woman under Cover
Yankee from the West, A

2357
SEITER, Bill*
Mabel at the Wheel /aka/ His
   Dare Devil Queen

2358
SEITZ, George B. *
Astra player 1919
Black Secret, The (serial)
Bound and Gagged (serial)

2359
SELANDER, Concordia*
Sir Arne's Treasure

2360
SELANDER, Hjalmar*
Sir Arne's Treasure

2361
SELBIE, Evelyn*
Bronco Billy Outwitted
Bronco Billy's Heart
Bronco Billy's Love Affair
Bronco Billy's Promise
Bronco Billy's Wife
Grand Passion, The (Boston Kate)
Hand That Rocks the Cradle, The
Mysterious Mrs. M., The
Pay Me (Hilda Hendricks)
People vs. John Doe, The
Price of Silence, The (Jenny Cupps)
Red Glove, The (serial)

2362
SELBY, Norman /aka/ "Kid
   McCoy"*
Broken Blossoms (a prizefighter)

2363
SELL, Henry, G. *
Fatal Ring, The (serial)
Lightning Raider, The (serial)
Seven Pearls, The (serial)

2364
SELWYN, Clarissa*
Bride's Awakening, The
Home
Smashing Through
Talk of the Town, The (Aunt Harriet)
Tower of Ivory

2365
SELWYN, Edgar*
Arab, The (Jamil)
Stage:
Arab, The 1911
Gentleman of France, A 1901
Nearly Married 1912
Pierre of the Plains 1908
Pretty Sister of Jose 1903
Strongheart 1907

2366
SEMELE, Harry*
Bound and Gagged (serial)

2367
SEMON, Larry (1889-1928)
Babes and Boobs
Bathing Beauties and Big Boobs
Battler, The
Bears and Bad Men
Between the Acts
Big Bluffs and Bowling Balls
Boasts and Boldness
Bombs and Blunders
Boodle and Bandits
Bullies and Bullets
Chumps and Chances
Cops and Cussedness
Dew Drop Inn
Duds and Drygoods
Dull Care
Dunces and Danger
Footlights and Fakers
Frauds and Frenzies
Gall and Gold
Guff and Gunplay
Guns and Greasers
Hash and Havoc
Hazards and Home Runs
He Never Touched Me
Headwaiter, The
Help! Help! Help!
Hindoos and Hazards
His Conscious Conscience
His Home, Sweet Home
Humbus and Husbands
Huns and Hyphens
Jealous Guy, A
Jolts and Jewelry
Jumps and Jealousy
Loot and Love
Losing Weight
Man from Egypt, The
Meddlers and Moonshine
More Money Than Manners
Mutts and Motors
Noisy Naggers and Nosey Neighbors
Passing the Buck
Pests and Promises
Plagues and Puppy Love
Plans and Pajamas
Pluck and Plotters
Rah! Rah! Rah!
Rips and Rushes
Risks and Roughnecks
Romance and Rough House
Romans and Rascals
Rooms and Rumors

Rough Toughs and Rooftops
Rummies and Razors
Sands Scamps and Strategy
Scamps and Scandals
She Who Laughs Last
Shells and Shivers
Simple Life, The
Skids and Scalawags
Slips and Slackers
Soapsuds and Sapheads
Spies and Spills
Spooks and Spasms
Sports and Splashes
Star Boarder, The
Stripes and Stumbles
There and Back
Tough Luck and Tin Lizzies
Traps and Tangles
Tubby Turns the Tables
Villainous Villain, A
Worries and Wobbles
Well, I'll Be ...
Whistles and Widows

2368
SENNETT, Mack (Michael Sinnott)
   (1880-1960) (As an Actor)
Alarm, The
Ambitious Butler, The
Arcadian Maid, An
At Coney Island /aka/ Cohen at
   Coney Island
At the Altar
At Twelve o'Clock
Awakening, The
Awful Moment, An
Balked at the Altar
Bangville Police, The
Barney Oldfield's Race for a Life
Battle of Who Run, The
Bear Escape, A
Better Way, The
Burglar's Mistake, A
Caught in the Rain /aka/ At It Again
Cohen Collects a Debt
Cohen Saves the Flag
Comrades
Convict's Sacrifice, A
Cord of Life
Corner in Wheat, A
Curtain Pole, The
Dancing Girl of Butte, The
Decree of Destiny, A
Desperate Lover, A
Duel, The
Dutch Gold Mine, The
Elite Ball, The
Examination Day at School

Faithful
False Beauty, A /aka/ Faded
  Vampire, A
Family Mix-up, A
Fatal Flirt, A
Fatal Mallet, The /aka/ The Pile
  Driver
Father Gets in the Game
Fatty and the Broadway Stars
Fickle Spaniard, The
For the Love of Mabel
Getting Even
Gibson Goddess, The
Girls and Daddy, The
Golden Louis, The
Hansom Driver, The
Hearts and Planets
Helping Hand, The
Her New Beau
His Crooked Career
His Talented Wife
Hoffmeyer's Legacy
Home Folks
In a Hamper Bag
In the Clutches of a Gang
In the Watches of the Night
Jealous Waiter, The
Jilt, The
Jones and the Lady Book Agent
Judge, The
Knockout, The /aka/ The Pugilist
Light That Came, The
Little Darling, The
Little Teacher, The /aka/ A Small
  Town Bully
Lonely Villa, The
Love Sickness at Sea
Lucky Jim
Lure of the Gown, The
Mabel at the Wheel /aka/ His
  Daredevil Queen
Mabel's Awful Mistake /aka/ Her
  Deceitful Lover
Mabel's Dramatic Career /aka/ Her
  Dramatic Debut
Mabel's Heroes
Mabel's Lovers
Mack at It Again
Man's Genesis
Midnight Adventure, A
Midnight Cupid, A
Mistaken Masher, The
Mr. Fix-It
Mr. Jones at the Ball
Mr. Jones Has a Card Party
Mohawk's Way, A
Murphy's I. O. U.
My Valet

New York Girl, A
New York Hat, The
Newlyweds, The
One Busy Hour
Pat's Day Off
Pedro's Dilemma
Peeping Pete
Politician's Love Story, The
Property Man, The /aka/ The
  Roustabout
Rivals, The
Rube and the Baron, The
Salvation Army Lass, The
Sculptor's Nightmare, The
1776 or The Hessian Renegades
Seventh Day, The
Sleuths at the Floral Parade, The
Sleuths' Last Stand, The
Song of the Shirt, The
Sound Sleeper, A
Stolen Glory
Stolen Magic
Stolen Purse, The
Strong Revenge, A
Test of Friendship
Their First Divorce Case
Their First Execution
Those Hicksville Boys
Three Sisters
Trick That Failed, The
Two Memories
Water Nymph, The
Wreath in Time, A

2369
SERRANO, Vincent*
Eyes of Youth
Stage:
Arizona 1900; 1913
Deluxe Annie 1917
Lure, The 1913
Merchant of Venice, The 1901

2370
SEYMOUR, Clarine (1900-1920)
Girl Who Stayed at Home, The
  (Cutie Beautiful)
Scarlet Days (Chiquita)
True Heart Susie (Bettina)

2371
SHADE, Betty*
Dumb Girl of Portici

2372
SHAFFNER, Lillian*
Other Man, The

2373
SHANNON, Alex K. *
Doll's House, A (Nils Krogstad)

2374
SHANNON, Effie (1867-1954)
After the Ball
Manon Lescaut
Stage:
Children of Earth 1915
Daughters of Men, The 1906
Her Lord and Master 1902
Moth and the Flame, The 1900
Under Orders 1918
Years of Discretion 1912

2375
SHANNON, Ethel*
Easy to Make Money
John Petticoats

2376
SHANOR, Peggy*
House of Hate, The (serial)
Lurking Peril, The (serial)

2377
SHARKEY, Jack*
Jeffries-Sharkey Fight

2378
SHAW, Brinsley*
Arsene Lupin
Broncho Billy and the Rustler's
    Child
Enemy to the King, An
Mary Regan

2379
SHAW, Harold*
Martin Chuzzlewit
Three Musketeers, The (Aramis)

2380
SHAWN, Ted*
Don't Change Your Husband (Faun)

2381
SHAY, William E. *
Clemenceau Case, The (Pierre
    Clemenceau)
Eternal Sin, The
Heart of Maryland, The
Imp player 1910
Kreutzer Sonata (Gregor Randor)
Neptune's Daughter
Sin (Luigi)
Two Orphans, The (Chevalier de
    Vaudrey)

2382
SHAYNE, Edith*
Poor Little Peppina

2383
SHEA, William J. *
Chumps
Imp Player 1910

2384
SHELBY, Miriam*
Red Ace, The (serial)

2385
SHELLEY, Miriam*
Doll's House, A (Christina Linder)

2386
SHEP, the Vitagraph
    Collie*
Violin of Monsieur, The

2387
SHEPARD, Iva*
Romance of an Actor
Selig Western, A 1910

2388
SHEPHERD, Ivy*
Uncle Tom's Cabin (Tessie)

2389
SHERMAN, Lowell (1885-1934)
Behind the Scenes
Stage:
Heart of Wetona, The 1916
Judith of Bethulia 1904
Our Little Wife 1916
Sign on the Door, The 1919

2390
SHERMAN, Paula*
Adventures of Margeurite, The
    (serial)

2391
SHERRILL, Jack*
Invisible Ray, The
Witching Hour, The

2392
SHERRY, J. Barney (1874-   )
Back of the Man
Civilization (the blacksmith)
Cup of Life, A
Eileen of Erin
Evidence, The
Fuel of Life
Flying Colors

For Her Brother's Sake
Heart of an Indian, The
Her Decision
High Stakes
Latent Spark
Lion Man, The (serial)
Little Brother of the Rich, A
Made 12 series of Westerns 1909
Mayor of Filbert
Millionaire Vagrant, The
Raffles, Amateur Cracksman
Recording Day
Secret Code
Soul of the South
Weaker Sex, The
Who Killed Walton?
Word of His People, The

2393
SHIELDS, Ernest*
Broken Coin, The (serial)
Lucille Love, Girl of Mystery
    (serial)
Voice on the Wire, The (serial)

2394
SHIELDS, Sidney*
Clemenceau Case, The (Madame
    Ritz)
Stage:
Parlor, Bedroom and Bath 1917

2395
SHINE, John L. *
Little Lady Eileen

2396
SHIPMAN, Gertrude*
Camille

2397
SHIPMAN, Nell (1892-1970)
Back to God's Country
Baree, Son of Kazan
Cavanaugh of the Forest Range
Eighth Great Grandparent, The
Gentleman's Agreement, A
Girl from Beyond, The
God's Country and the Woman
Home Trail, The
Through the Wall
Tiger of the Sea
Wild Strain, The

2398
SHIRLEY, Arthur*
Alas and Alack (a hapless lover)
Bound on the Wheel

Fall of a Nation, The
Fascination of the Fleur de Lis,
    The (Antone Gerome)
Lon of Lone Mountain
Millionaire Paupers, The
Mother's Atonement, A
Mountain Justice
Pine's Revenge, The
Quits (the sheriff)
Stronger Than Death
Under a Shadow

2399
SHORT, Antrim*
Jewel in Pawn
Please Get Married
Poor Girl, Rich Girl?
Pride and the Man
Romance and Arabella
Tom Sawyer
Yellow Dog, The

2400
SHORT, Florence*
Eagle's Eye, The (serial)

2401
SHORT, Gertrude*
Blackie's Redemption
Heart of Youth
Hostage, The
In Mizzoura
Little Angel of Canon Creek
Little Princess, A
Riddle Gawne (Jane)
Uncle Tom's Cabin (Little Eva)

2402
SHORT, Hassard*
Stronger Vow, The
Turn of the Wheel, The
Way of a Woman, The
Stage:
Man from Home, The 1908
Second in Command, The 1901
Unchastened Woman, The 1915

2403
SHORT, Lou*
Gray Ghost, The (serial)

2404
SHOTWELL, Marie*
Thirteenth Chair, The
Witching Hour, The

2405
SHUMWAY, Lee C. /aka/ L. C.
    Shumway (1884-   )

Bird of Prey
Bride of Fear
Eve in Exile
Girl in Bohemia, A
Helen Grayson's Strategy
Love Hunger, The
Phantom's Secret, The
Scarlet Road, The
Siren's Song, A (Raoul Nieppe)

2406
SIEGEL, Bernard*
Cambric Mask, The
Green God, The
Malestrom

2407
SIEGLER, Al*
Mysterious Mrs. Musslewhite, The

2408
SIEGMANN, George (1884-1928)
Avenging Conscience, The (the
    Italian)
Birth of a Nation, The (Silas
    Lynch, mulatto Lt. Governor)
Fall of Babylon, The
Great Love, The (Mr. Seymour of
    Brazil)
Hearts of the World (VonStrohm)
In Prehistoric Days
Intolerance (Cyrus, the Persian)
Sealed Room, The

2409
SIGNORET, Gabriel*
Mothers of France

2410
SILLS, Milton (1882-1930)
Claw, The
Deep Purple, The
Eyes of Youth
Fear Woman, The
Fringe of Society
Hellcat, The
Honor System
Hushed Hour, The
Married in Name Only
Mysterious Client, The
Other Woman, The
Patria (serial)
Pit, The
Rack, The
Savage Woman, The
Shadows
Souls Adrift
Street Called Straight, A

Stronger Vow, The
Struggle Everlasting, The
What Every Woman Learns
Woman Thou Gavest Me, The
Yellow Ticket, The
Stage:
Diplomacy 1910
Governor's Lady, The 1912
Law of the Land, The 1914
Panthea 1914

2411
SIMPSON, Ivan (1875-   )
Dictator, The (debut)
Out of the Drifts

2412
SIMPSON, Russell (1880-1959)
Barrier, The
Bill Apperson's Boy
Blue Jeans
Brand, The
Fate's Boomerang
Fighting Cressy
Our Teddy

2413
SINDELAR, Pearl*
Pathé player 1913

2414
SINGLETON, Joe E. *
Squaw Man, The (Tabywana)

2415
SINGLETON, Joseph*
Good Bad Man, The (Amy's father
    /aka/ "The Weasel")
Midnight Man, The (serial)
Reggie Mixes In (Reggie's valet)
Wild and Wooly (Hillington's butler)

2416
SISSON, Vera (1895-   )
Blackmailers, The
Experimental Marriage
Heart of Youth
His Official Fianceé
Iron Woman, The
Landon's Legacy
Laurel of Tears, The
Marriage Blunder, The
Oyster Dredger, The
Paradise Garden
Trail of the Serpent
Veiled Adventure, The

2417
SJÖSTRÖM, Victor (1879-1960)

Ingeborg Holm
Outlaw and His Wife, The
Terje Vigen
Thomas Graal's First Child

2418
SKINNER, Otis (1858-1942)
Kismet
Stage:
Celebrated Case, A 1915
Cock o' the Walk 1915
Duel, The 1906
Francesca Da Rimini 1902
Honor of the Family, The 1908;
    1919
Kismet 1911
Merchant of Venice, The (Petruchio
    and Shylock) 1904
Mister Antonio 1916
Silent Voice, The 1914
Your Humble Servant 1910

2419
SLOMAN, Edward*
Trey o' Hearts, The (serial)
Under the Crescent (serial)

2420
SLOMEN, Hilda*
Girl of the Night, The

2421
SLOUGHTON, Mabel*
Biograph player 1908

2422
SMALLEY, Phillips (1870-   )
Cigarette--That's All
Dumb Girl of Portici
False Colors
Fatal Warning, The (serial)
Merchant of Venice, The (Shylock)
Picture of Dorian Grey, The
Rex player 1909
Spider and Her Web, The

2423
SMILEY, Joseph W. *
Imp player 1910
Isle of Conquest

2424
SMITH, C. Aubrey (Sir Charles
    Aubrey Smith) (1863-1948)
Builders of Bridges (American
    debut)
Red Pottage
Witching Hour, The

World Player, 1917
Stage:
American tour 1896
Debut (touring British provinces)
    1892
Legend of Leonora, The 1914
Morals of Marcus, The 1907

2425
SMITH, Cliff (Clifford S. Smith*)
Taking of Luke McVane, The
    (Sheriff Stark)

2426
SMITH, Cyril (1892-1963)
Made over 500 films 1908-1919
    (all British)

2427
SMITH, Florence*
Wild Goose Chase, The (Bob
    Randall's mother)

2428
SMITH, Sid*
His Uncle Dudley
Oriental Love

2429
SMITH, Viola*
Price of Silence, The (Alice)

2430
SNOW, Marguerite (1888-1958)
Broadway Jones
Carmen
Dr. Jekyll and Mr. Hyde
Dora Thorne
Eagle's Eye, The (Dixie Mason)
    (serial)
East Lynne
First Law, The
Half Million Bride, The
Her Great Triumph
Her Marble Heart
Hunting of the Hawk
In His Brother's Place
Joseph in the Land of Egypt
Lucile
Million Dollar Mystery, The (serial)
Notorious Gallagher
Second in Command, The
She
Silent Voice, The
Undine
Zudora (The Twenty Million Dollar
    Mystery) (serial)

2431
SNYDER, Matt*
Crisis, The

2432
SORELLE, William*
Daughter of Uncle Sam, A (serial)

2433
SOTHERN, E. H. (Edward H.
    Sothern) (1859-1933)
Chattle, The
Enemy to the King, An
Stage:
Anthony and Cleopatra (Anthony)
    1909
David Garrick 1916
Debut 1880
Hamlet (first New York appearance
    as Hamlet) 1900
If I Were King 1901; 1916
Jeanne D'Arc 1907
John the Baptist 1907
Our American Cousin 1908
Romeo and Juliet (Romeo) 1904
Shakesperean repertory 1905; 1910;
    1911; 1912; 1919
Sunken Bell 1907
Two Virtues, The 1915

2434
SOTHERN, Eve (1898-   )
Intolerance (slave girl)

2435
SOTHERN, Jean*
Mysteries of Myra, The (serial)
Two Orphans, The (Louise)

2436
SOUTHERN, Sam*
Eyes of Youth
His Majesty, the American (Philippe
    the Fourth)
Two Orphans, The

2437
SPARKS, Ned (Ned A. Sparks)
    (1883-1957)
Virtuous Vamp, A
Stage:
Nothing but the Truth 1916

2438
SPENCER, George Soule*
Fortune Hunter, The
Sporting Duchess, The

2439
SPOONER, Cecil, Miss*
Dancer and the King, The
Prince and the Pauper, The (dual
    role)
Stage:
My Lady Peggy Goes to Town 1903

2440
STAHL, Rose*
Debut 1912
Stage:
Chorus Lady, The 1906
Maggie Pepper 1910
Moonlight Mary 1916
Our Mrs. McChesney 1915
Out There 1918
Perfect Lady, A 1914
Vaudeville 1904-05

2441
STANDING, Herbert*
Almost a Husband
Amarilly of Clothesline Alley
He Comes up Smiling (Mike, a hobo)
How Could You, Jean?
Man from Painted Post, The (Mr.
    Brandon)
Squaw Man, The (Dean of Trentham)
Strictly Confidential
Through the Wrong Door
Stage:
Candida 1903

2442
STANDING, Jack*
Fanchon the Cricket
Good Turn, A
Hell's Hinges (Rev. Robert Henly)
Lubin player 1914
Road of Strike, The (serial)

2443
STANDING, Percy Darnell*
Fall of a Nation, The
Life without Soul

2444
STANDING, Wyndham (1880-   )
Ave Maria
Eyes of the Soul
Hushed Hour, The
Hypocrisy
Isle of Conquest
Journey's End
Marriage Price, The
Miracle of Love
Out of the Shadow

Paid in Full
Port of Missing Girls
Rose of the World
Struggle Everlasting, The
Temperamental Wife, A
Witness for the Defense
Wolf Woman, The

2445
STANLEY, Forest (1889-   )
Code of Marcia Gray, The
Heart of Paula, The
His Official Financeé
Jane
Kilkeny
Madame la Presidente
Making of Madalena, The
Reform Candidate, The
Rug Maker's Daughter, The
Thunderbolt, The
Under Suspicion
Yankee Girl, The

2446
STANLEY, George*
Smashing Barriers (serial)

2447
STANLEY, Henry*
Neal of the Navy (serial)

2448
STANLEY, Maxfield*
Birth of a Nation, The (Duke
   Cameron)
Great Love, The (John Broadplains)
Intolerance (Duc d'Anjou)
23 1/2 Hours Leave

2449
STANTON, Fred R. *
Deluxe Annie
Great Secret, The (serial)

2450
STANTON, Richard*
Graft (serial)

2451
STANWOOD, Rita*
Deserter, The (Barbara Taylor)

2452
STARK, Leighton*
Two Orphans, The

2453
STARKE, Pauline (1900-   )

Alias Mary Brown
Atom, The
Daughter of Angele
Eyes of Youth
Innocents' Progress
Intolerance (Harem girl)
Irish Eyes
Judith
Life Line, The
Little Shepherd of Kingdom Come,
   The
Man Who Woke Up, The
Shoes That Danced, The
Soldiers of Fortune
Untamed, The
Until They Get Me
Wharf Rat
Whom the Gods Destroy

2454
STARR, Fred*
Elmo, the Mighty (serial)

2455
STATHER, Frank*
Little Lord Fauntleroy

2456
STEADMAN, Vera (1900-1966)
Hula Hula Land

2457
STEARNS, Louis*
Safety Curtain, The

2458
STEDMAN, Myrtle (1888-1938)
American Beauty, The
Hollow of Her Hand, The
In Honor's Web
It's No Laughing Matter
Out of the Night
Peer Gynt
Prison without Walls, The
Selig player 1913
Soul of Kura San
Teeth of the Tiger
Valley of the Moon
World Apart, The

2459
STEELE, R. V. *
Firing Line, The

2460
STEELE, Vernon*
For the Defense
Goldwyn player 1917

Hearts in Exile
Little Lady Eileen
Polly of the Circus
Witness for the Defense

2461
STEELMAN, Hosea*
Trail of the Lonesome Pine, The
  (one of the Tolliver men)
Virginian, The (Lin McLean)

2462
STEERS, Larry (1881-1951)
City of Dim Faces
Heartease
Little Comrade, The
Pair of Silk Stockings, A

2463
STEPHENSON, Henry (1871-1956)
Spreading Dawn, The
Stage:
Crowded Hour, The 1918
Justice 1916
Lilac Time 1917
Message from Mars, A 1901

2464
STEPPLING, John*
Essanay player 1912

2465
STERLING, Ford (George Ford
  Stitch) (1885-1939)
Abe Gets Even with Father
Ambitious Butler, The
Ambrose's Little Hatchet
At Coney Island /aka/ Cohen at
  Coney Island
At It Again
Baby Day
Bad Game, A
Baffles, Gentleman Burglar
Barney Oldfield's Race for a Life
Battle of Who Run, The
Bear Escape, A
Beating He Needed, The
Between Showers
Beware of Boarders
Bowling Match, The
Cohen Collects a Debt
Cohen Saves the Flag
Cohen's Outing
Court House Crooks
Cure That Failed, The
Deacon Outwitted, The
Deacon's Trouble, The
Dirty Work in a Laundry /aka/ A
  Desperate Scoundrel

Dollar Did It, A
Double Crossed
Double Wedding, A
Dramatic Mistake, A
Elite Ball, The
Faithful Taxicab, The
False Beauty, A /aka/ Faded
  Vampire
Father's Choice
Fatty and the Broadway Stars
Firebugs, The
Fishy Affair, A
Flirting Husband, The
Forced Bravery
Game of Poker, A
Game of Pool, A
Gentlemen of Nerve /aka/ Some
  Nerve
Grocery Clerk's Romance, The
Gusher, The
Hansom Driver, The
He Wouldn't Stay Down
Healthy Neighbor, A
Hearts and Flowers
Heinze's Ressurection
Her Screen Idol
Her Torpedoed Love
Hide and Seek
His Chum the Baron
His Crooked Career
His Father's Footsteps
His Lying Heart
His Pride and Shame
His Ups and Downs
His Wild Oats
Hoffmeyer's Legacy
How Hiram Won Out
Hunt, The
In the Clutches of a Gang
Jealous Waiter, The
Just Brown's Luck
Kaiser's Last Squeal, The
Land Salesman, The
Landlord's Trouble, A
Life in the Balance, A
Love and Dynamite
Love and Pain
Love and Rubbish
Love Sickness at Sea
Mabel's Adventures
Mabel's Dramatic Career /aka/
  Her Dramatic Debut
Maiden's Trust, A
Man Next Door, The
Midnight Elopement, A
Mistaken Masher, The
Mr. Fix-It
Muddy Romance, A /aka/ Muddled
  in Mud

Murphy's I. O. U.
New Conductor, The
New Neighbors, The
On His Wedding Day
Only a Messenger Boy
Our Dare Devil Chief
Out and In
Pat's Day Off
Peddler, The
Pedro's Dilemma
Peeping Pete
Pinched in the Finish
Professor Bean's Removal
Professor's Daughter, The
Ragtime Band, The /aka/ The
    Jazz Band
Red Hot Romance, A
Riely and Schultz
Riot, The
Rivals, The
Rube and the Baron, The
Safe in Jail
Schnitz, the Tailor
Sleuths at the Floral Parade, The
Small Time Act, A
Snow Cure, The
Speed Queen, The
Stars and Bars
Stolen Glory
Stolen Purse, The
Strong Revenge, A
Tango Tangles
Teddy Telzlaff and Earl Cooper,
    Speed Kings
Temperamental Husband, A
That Little Band of Gold /aka/
    For Better but Worse
That Minstrel Man
Too Many Brides /aka/ The Love
    Chase
Toplitsky and Company
Trying to Get Along
Two Widows, The
Waiter's Picnic, The
Water Nymph, The
When Dreams Come True
Zuzu, the Band Leader

2466
STERRETT, Thomas Captain*
Unbeliever, The

2467
STEVENS, Charles (1893-1964)
Americano, The
Birth of a Nation, The (a volunteer)
Mystery of the Leaping Fish
    (Japanese accomplice)
Wild and Wooly (Pedro)

2468
STEVENS, Edwin*
Cheating Cheaters
Crimson Gardenia
Devil's Toy
Faith
Hawthorne of the U. S. A.
Home Breaker
Lottery Man, The
Lone Wolf's Daughter, The
Profiteers
Sahara
Squaw Man, The (Bud Hardy)
Unpardonable Sin, The
Upstairs
Yellow Menace, The (Ali Singh)
    (serial)
Stage:
Geisha, The 1913
L'Aiglon 1900
Royal Rival, A 1901

2469
STEVENS, Emily (Emily A. Stevens)
    (1882-1928)
Slacker, The
Soul of a Woman, The
Stage:
Boss, The 1911
Fugitive, The 1917
Mary of Magdla 1902
Today 1913
Unchastened Woman, The 1915

2470
STEVENS, George*
Fates and Flora Fourflush (The
    Ten Billion Dollar Vitagraph
    Mystery Serial) (serial)

2471
STEVENS, Josephine*
Butcher Boy, The

2472
STEWART, Anita (Anna May Stewart)
    (1895-1961)
Awakening, The
Back to Broadway
Classmates' Frolic, The
Clover's Rebellion
Combat, The
Count 'Em /aka/ The Counts
Daring of Diana, The
Diana's Dress Reform
Fighting Chance, A
Forgotten Latchkey, The
From Headquarters
Girl from Prosperity, The

Girl Philippa, The
Glory of Yolanda, The
Goddess, The (serial)
Godmother, The
He Never Knew
Her Choice
Her Kingdom of Dreams
His Last Fight
His Phantom Sweetheart
His Second Wife
In Old Kentucky
Lincoln, the Lover
Lost Millionaire, The
Love Finds a Way /aka/ Love
    Laughs at Blacksmiths
Lucky Elopement, The
Mary Regan
Message of the Mouse, The
Midnight Romance, A
'Midst Woodland Shadows
Million Bid, A
Mind-the-Paint Girl, The
More Excellent Way, The
Moulding, The
My Lady's Slipper
Painted World, The
Prince of Evil, The
Regiment of Two, A
Right and Wrong of It, The
Right Girl, The
Shadow of the Past
Sins of the Mothers
Song Bird of the North, The
Song of the Shell, The
Sort of a Girl Who Came from
    Heaven, The
Suspect, The
Swan Girl, The
Tiger, The
Treasure of Desert Island, The
Two Women
Two's Company, Three's a Crowd
Uncle Bill
Virtuous Wives
Web, The
Why Am I Here?
Wife Wanted
Wood Violet, The
Wreck, The

2473
STEWART, Eldean*
East Lynne (Little Willie)

2474
STEWART, Jean*
Seven Sisters

2475
STEWART, Julia*
Eclair Player 1913

2476
STEWART, Leslie*
Secret Code

2477
STEWART, Lock*
East Lynne (Little Isabel)

2478
STEWART, Lucille Lee (1894-   )
Conflict
Eleventh Commandment, The
Five Thousand an Hour
His Wife's Good Name
Ninety and Nine, The
Our Mrs. McChesney
Perfect Lover, The
Sealed Hearts

2479
STEWART, Roy (1884-1933)
Bond of Fear
Boss of the Lazy Y
By Proxy
Cactus Crandell
Come Through
Daughter of the Poor, A
Desert of Wheat
Devil Dodger, The
Doll Shop, The
Faith Endurin'
Fly God, The
House Built upon Sand, The
Just Nuts
Keith of the Border
Law's Outlaw, The
Learnin' of Jim Benson, The
Liberty, a Daughter of the U. S. A.
    (serial)
Medicine Man, The
One Shot Ross
Paying His Debt
Red-Haired Cupid, A
Silent Rider, The
Taking of Luke McVane, The /aka/
    The Fugitive
Untamed, The
Westerners, The
Wolves of the Border

2480
STOCKDALE, Carl (1874-1942)
Americano, The
Atta Boy's Last Race

Bank, The
Crash, The
Fatal Thirty, The (serial)
Greatest Question, The
Intolerance (King Nabonidus)
Lady of the Dugout, The
Night in New York, A
Peggy Leads the Way
Trembling Hour, The
Wanted, a Home

2481
STOCKLASSA, Erik*
Sir Arne's Treasure

2482
STONE, Fred (1873-1959)
Debut 1917
Goat, The
Johnny Get Your Gun
Under the Top
Stage:
Chin Chin 1914
Girl from up There, The 1901
Jack O'Lantern (first solo vehicle
    after death of David C.
    Montgomery) 1917
Lady of the Slipper, The 1912
Montgomery and Stone (a team)
    1894-1917
Old Town, The 1910
Red Mill, The 1906
Wizard of Oz, The 1903

2483
STONE, George E. (George Stein)
    (1903-1967)
Children of the Feud
Going Straight
Gretchen, the Greenhorn
Little School Ma'am, The
Martha's Vindication
Sudden Jim
Till I Come Back to You (Jacques)

2484
STONE, Harry*
Bound and Gagged (serial)

2485
STONE, Lewis (Lewis S. Stone)
    (1879-1953)
Havoc, The
Honour's Altar (debut)
Inside the Lines
Johnny Get Your Gun
Man of Bronze, The
Man's Desire

Two Brides
Stage:
Bird of Paradise 1912
Brat, The 1917
Inside the Lines 1915
Misleading Lady, The 1913
Where Poppies Blossom 1918

2486
STONEHOUSE, Ruth (1894-1941)
Adventures of Peg o' the Ring, The
    (serial)
Blood Will Tell
Daredevil Dan
Dorothy Dares
Edge of the Law, The
Follow the Girl
Four-Flusher, The
From the Submerged
Heart of Mary Ann, The
In Convict Garb
Limb of Satan, A
Mary Ann in Society
Masked Rider, The (serial)
Master Mystery, The (serial)
Papered Door, The
Phantom Husband, The
Puppy Love
Romance of an American Duchess,
    The
Spy's Defeat, The
Stolen Actress, The
Tacky Sue's Romance

2487
STOREY, Edith (1892-   )
Aladdin from Broadway
As the Sun Went Down
Billy the Kid
Captain of the Gray Horse Troop,
    The
Christian, The
Claim, The
Demon, The
Dust of Egypt
Enemy to the King, An
Eyes of Mystery
In the Latin Quarter
Island of Regeneration, The
Lady of the Lake, The
Legion of Death, The
Love's Way
Money Magic
Old Flute Player, The
On Her Wedding Night
Price for Folly, The
Quality of Mercy, The
Regiment of Two, A

Revenge
Scarlet Runner, The (serial)
Serpents, The
Silent Woman, The
Susie, the Sleuth
Tarantula, The
Telephone Girl, The
Treasure of the Sea
Troublesome Stepdaughters, The
True till Death
Victoria Cross, The /aka/ Charge
   of the Light Brigade
Winifred, the Shop Girl
Stage:
Little Princess, The 1903

2488
STORM, Jerome*
Civilization (the blacksmith's son)

2489
STOWE, Leslie*
Carter Case, The (The Craig
   Kennedy Serial) (serial)
La Boheme

2490
STOWELL, William*
Bondage (Evan Kilvert)
Broadway Love (Henry Rockwell)
Doll's House, A (Torvald Helmer)
Essanay player 1913
Flashlight, The (Jack Lane)
Girl in the Checkered Coat, The
   (David Norman)
Grand Passion, The (Dick Evans)
Heart of Humanity, The
Hell Morgan's Girl (Roger Curwell)
Man in the Moonlight, The
Mutual player 1916
Paid in Advance (Jim Blood)
Pay Me (Bill, the boss)
Piper's Price, The (Ralph Hadley)
Rescue, The (Kent Wetherall)
Selig player 1913
Talk of the Town, The (Laurence
   Tabor)
Triumph (Dudley Weyman)

2491
STRADLING, Walter*
M'Liss

2492
STRONG, Eugene*
Border Legion, The
Crimson Stain Mystery, The
   (serial)

2493
STRONG, Mark*
Tiger's Trail, The (Jim Gordon)
   (serial)

2494
STRONG, Porter*
Romance of Happy Valley, A (the
   Negro farmhand)

2495
STUART, Jean*
Scarlet Runner, The (serial)

2496
STUART, Ralph*
Mystery of the Double Cross, The
   (serial)
Stage:
Under Southern Skies 1902

2497
STULL, Walter*
Busted Hearts
Chickens
Frenzied Finance
Play Ball
Pokes and Jabbs series (Pokes)
   1914-15
This Way Out
Try Out, The
Ups and Downs

2498
SULLIVAN, David L. *
Cecilia of the Pink Roses (Father
   McGowan)

2499
SULLY, Janet Miller*
Adventurer, The
Cure, The
Dog's Life, A
Easy Street

2500
SUMMERVILLE, Amelia (1862-1934)
Getting Mary Married (Mrs.
   Bussard)
Probation Wife, The

2501
SUMMERVILLE, Slim (George J.
   Summerville) (1892-1946)
Are Waitresses Safe?
Cinders of Love
Cursed by His Beauty
Dog Catcher's Love, A

Dough and Dynamite /aka/ The
  Doughnut Designer
Essanay player 1913
Game Old Knight, A
Gentlemen of Nerve /aka/ Some
  Nerve
Great Vacuum Robbery, The
Gussle's Day of Rest
Her Fame and Shame
Her Painted Hero
Her Winning Punch
High Diver's Last Kiss, The
His Bread and Butter
His Busted Trust
His Precious Life
Hold the Line
Home Breakers, The /aka/ Other
  People's Wives
It Pays to Exercise
Kitchen Lady, The
Knockout, The /aka/ The Pugilist
Laughing Gas /aka/ The Dentist
Mabel's Busy Day
Mary's Little Lobster
Roping Her Romeo
Their Social Splash
Ten Nights without a Barroom
Those Bitter Sweets
Those College Girls /aka/ His
  Bitter Half
Three Slims, The
Tillie's Punctured Romance
Villa of the Movies
Winning Punch, The

2502
SUNSHINE, Marion*
Dan the Dandy
Decree of Destiny, A
Her First Biscuits
Heredity
In the Season of Buds
Red Girl, The
Rose of Kentucky, The
Stuff Heroes Are Made Of, The
Sunshine Sue
Tavern Keeper's Daughter, The
Three Sisters

2503
SURATT, Valeska (1882-   )
Immigrant, The
Jealousy
Stage:
Belle of Mayfair, The 1906
Red Rose, The 1911
Vaudeville 1913

2504
SUTCH, Herbert*
Comrades (a tramp)
Hearts of the World (a French
  Major)
Scarlet Days

2505
SUTHERLAND, Anne*
Kreutzer Sonata (Olga Belushoff)

2506
SUTHERLAND, Eddie*
Tillie's Punctured Romance (a
  Keystone cop)
Veiled Adventure, The

2507
SUTHERLAND, John*
Silver King, The

2508
SUTHERLAND, Joseph*
Laughing Gas /aka/ The Dentist

2509
SUTHERLAND, Victor*
Dancer and the King, The

2510
SWAIN, Mack (1876-1935)
Ambrose and the Lion Hearted
Ambrose's Cup of Woe
Ambrose's Day Off
Ambrose's First Falsehood /aka/
  In Loving Memory
Ambrose's Fury
Ambrose's Little Hatchet
Ambrose's Lofty Perch
Ambrose's Nasty Temper
Ambrose's Rapid Rise
Ambrose's Sour Grapes
Battle of Ambrose and Walrus, The
Best of Enemies, The
Busy Day, A /aka/ Militant
  Suffragette
By Stork Delivery
Caught in a Cabaret /aka/ The
  Jazz Waiter
Caught in the Rain /aka/ At It
  Again
Danger Girl
False Beauty, A /aka/ A Faded
  Vampire
Fatal Mallet, The /aka/ The Pile
  Driver
From Patches to Plenty
Gentlemen of Nerve /aka/ Some
  Nerve

Getting Acquainted /aka/ Fair
  Exchange, A
Gussle, the Golfer
His Auto Ruination
His Bitter Pill /aka/ Big-Hearted
  Sheriff
His Musical Career /aka/ Musical
  Tramps
His Naughty Thought
His Prehistoric Past /aka/ The
  Hula Hula Dance
His Trysting Place /aka/ Family
  House
His Wild Oats
Home Breakers, The /aka/ Other
  People's Wives
Home Run Ambrose
Human Hound's Triumph, A
Knockout, The /aka/ The Pugilist
Laughing Gas /aka/ The Dentist
Leading Lizzie Astray
Lost--a Cook
Love, Speed and Thrills
Love Will Conquer
Mabel Lost and Won
Mabel's Married Life /aka/ The
  Squarehead
Madcap Ambrose
Modern Enoch Arden, A
Movie Star, A
Muddy Romance, A /aka/ Muddled
  in Mud
Our Dare Devil Chief
Pullman Bride, A
Safety First Ambrose /aka/
  Sheriff Ambrose
Saved by Wireless
Schemers, The
Sea Nymphs, The /aka/ His
  Diving Beauty
That Little Band of Gold /aka/
  For Better but Worse
Thirst
Tillie's Punctured Romance
Vampire Ambrose
When Ambrose Dared Walrus
Wilful Ambrose
Ye Olden Grafter

2511
SWAN, Paul*
Diana the Huntress

2512
SWANSON, Gloria (Gloria Josephine
  May Swanson) (1898-   )
Ambition of the Baron (bit)
At the End of a Perfect Day (bit)

Broken Pledge, The (bit) (billed as
  Gloria Mae)
Danger Girl /aka/ Love on Skates
Dangers of a Bride
Dash of Courage, A (bit)
Don't Change Your Husband (Leila
  Porter)
Everywoman's Husband (Edith
  Emerson)
Fable of Elvira and Farina and
  the Meal Ticket (debut)
For Better, for Worse (Sylvia
  Norcross)
Haystacks and Steeples (bit)
Hearts and Sparks (bit)
Her Decision (Phyllis Dunbar)
His New Job (bit)
Male and Female (Lady Mary
  Lasenby)
Nick of Time Baby, The (bit)
Pullman Bride, A
Romance of an American Duchess,
  The (bit)
Secret Code, The (Sally Carter
  Rand)
Shifting Sands (Marcia Grey)
Social Club, A (bit)
Society for Sale (Phyllis Clyne)
Station Content (Kitty Manning)
Sultan's Wife, The
Sweedie Goes to College (bit)
Teddy at the Throttle
Whose Baby?
Wife or Country (Sylvia Hamilton)
You Can't Believe Everything
  (Patricia Reynolds)

2513
SWEET, Blanche (Sarah Blanche
  Sweet) (1896-   )
All on Account of the Milk
Ashes of the Past
Avenging Conscience (the nephew's
  sweetheart)
Battle, The
Battle at Elderbush Gulch, The
Blacklist, The
Blind Love
Blind Princess and the Poet, The
Broken Ways
Captive, The (Sonya)
Chance Deception, A
Change of Spirit, A
Chief's Blanket, The
Chosing a Husband
Cinderella Jane
Classmates
Clue, The

Coming of Angelo, The
Corner in Wheat, A
Country Cupid, A
Country Lovers
Day after Day
Death's Marathon
Dupe, The
Escape, The (May Joyce)
Eternal Mother, The
Evil Eye, The
Fighting Blood
Fighting Cressy
For Her Father's Sins
For His Son
For Those Unborn
God Within, The
Goddess of Sagebrush Gulch, The
Her Awakening
Her Wedding Bell
Hero of Little Italy, The
Home Folks
Home, Sweet Home (the wife)
House of Discord
How She Triumphed
Hushed Hour
If We Only Knew
Inner Circle, The
Judith of Bethulia
Last Drop of Water, The
Lesser Evil, The
Little Country Mouse, The
Lonedale Operator, The
Long Road, The
Love in an Apartment Hotel
Love in the Hills
Making of a Man, The
Man with Three Wives, A
Man's Lust for Gold
Massacre, The
Men and Women
Mistake, The
Near to Earth
Odalisque, The
Oil and Water
Old Maid, The
One Is Business, the Other Crime
Out from the Shadows
Outcast among Outcasts, An
Painted Lady, The
Pirate Gold
Primal Call, The
Public Opinion
Punishment, The
Ragamuffin, The
Rocky Road, The
Romance of the Western Hills, A
Sailor's Heart, A
Second Mrs. Roebuck, The

Secret Orchard, The
Secret Sin, The (dual role)
Sentimental Sister, The
Silent Partner, The
Sister's Love, A
Smile of a Child
Soul of Honor, The
Sowers, The
Spirit Awakened, The
Stolen Bride, The
Stolen Goods
Storm, The
Strongheart
Stuff Heroes Are Made Of, The
Tear That Burned, The
Temporary Truce, A
Those without Sin
Thousand Dollar Husband, The
Three Friends
Through Darkened Vales
Tides of Barnegat, The
Transformation of Mike, The
Two Men of the Desert
Under Burning Skies
Unpardonable Sin, The
Unprotected, The
Vengeance of Galora, The
Virtuous Wives
Voice of the Child, The
Warrens of Virginia, The (Agatha
    Warren)
Was He a Coward?
White Rose of the Wilds, The
With the Enemy's Help
Woman of Pleasure, A
Woman Scorned, A
Stage:
Old Limerick Town 1902

2514
SWICKARD, Joseph (1867-1940)
Ambrose's Cup of Woe
Best of Enemies, The
Caught in a Cabaret /aka/ The
    Jazz Waiter
Haystacks and Steeples
His Wild Oats
Home Breaking Hound, A
Keys of the Righteous
Last of His People
Laughing Gas /aka/ The Dentist
Love, Loot and Crash
Love Will Conquer
Plumber, The
Social Club, A
Tale of Two Cities, A
Trick of Fate, A
Twenty Minutes of Love /aka/
    Cops and Watches

Village Vampire, The /aka/ The
  Great Leap
When a Woman Sins (Mortimer
  West)
Woman of Pleasure, A

2515
SYLVA, Vesta*
Daughter of Eve, A

2516
SYNDECONDE*
Girl Who Stayed at Home, The
  (Count de Brissac)

- T -

2517
TAAFE, Alice see TERRY,
  Alice

2518
TABER, Richard*
Caught
Eyes That See Not
Miss Crusoe
When My Lady Smiles

2519
TALIAFERRO, Edith*
Lasky player 1915
Stage:
Captain Kidd, Jr. 1916
Mother Carey's Chickens 1917
Polly of the Circus (road company)
  1907
Rebecca of Sunnybrook Farm 1910
Young Wisdom 1914

2520
TALIAFERRO, Mabel (1887-)
Barricade, The
Battle for Billions, The
Cinderella
Dawn of Love
Draft 258
Great Price, The
Jury of Fate, The
Magdalene of the Hills, A
Peggy Leads the Way
Snowbird, The
Sunbeam, The
Three of Us, The
Wife by Proxy, A
Stage:
Little Princess, The 1903
Polly of the Circus 1907

Springtime 1909
Young Wisdom 1914

2521
TALMADGE, Constance (1900-1973)
Beached and Bleached
Bertie's Stratagem
Betsey's Burglar
Billy the Bear Tamer
Billy's Wager
Birth of a Nation, The
Boarding House Feud
Buddy's Call
Buddy's Downfall
Can You Beat It?
Captivating Mrs. Carstairs
Egyptian Mummy, The
Evolution of Percival, The
Experimental Marriage
Fall of Babylon, The
Father's Time Piece
Forcing Dad's Consent
Girl of the Timber Claims
Good Night, Paul
Green Cat, The
Grey Chiffon Veil, The
Happiness a la Mode
Honeymoon, The
In Bridal Attire
In the Latin Quarter
Intolerance (a mountain girl and
  Margurite deValois)
Lady of Shalott, The
Lady's Name, The
Lesson, The
Master of His House
Matrimaniac (Marna Lewis)
Microscope Mystery, The
Missing Bank Notes, The
Missing Links, The
Moonstone of Fez, The
Mrs. Leffingwell's Boots
Mysterious Lodger, The
Our Fairy Play
Pair of Silk Stockings, A
Peacemaker, The
Romance and Arabella
Sauce for the Goose
Scandal
Shuttle, The
Spades Are Trumps
Studio Girl, The
Study in Tramps, A
Temperamental Wife, A
Uncle Bill
Up the Road with Sally
Vanishing Vault, The
Veiled Adventure, The

Virtuous Vamp, The
Who Cares?
Young Man Who Figered, The

2522
TALMADGE, Natalie (1898-1969)
Bell Boy, The
Birth of a Nation, The
Civilization
Intolerance (slave girl)
Isle of Conquest, The
Temperamental Wife, A

2523
TALMADGE, Norma (1896-1957)
'Arriet's Baby
Barrier of Faith, The
Battle Cry of Peace, The
Blue Rose, The
Broken Spell, A
By Right of Purchase
Captain Barnacles' Messmate
Captain Barnacles--Reformer
Captain Barnacles' Waif
Captivating Mary Carstairs
Casey at the Bat
Child Crusoes, The
Children in the House
Convict's Child, The
Counsel for the Defense
Country Barber
Crown Prince's Double, The
Cupid Versus Money
Curing of Myra May, The
Daughter of Israel, A
Daughter's Strange Inheritance
Deluxe Annie
Devil's Needle, The
Dixie Mother, The
Doctor's Secret, The
Dorothy Danesbridge (Militant)
Elopement at Home, An
Elsa's Brother
Etta of the Footlights
Extension Table, The
Extremities
Fanny's Conspiracy
Father's Hatband
Fifty-Fifty
First Violin, The
Fogg's Millions
Forbidden City
Forgotten
Fortunes of a Composer
General's Daughter, The
Ghosts of Yesterday, The
Going Straight /aka/ Corruption
Goodbye Summer

He Fell in Love with His Mother-
  in-Law
Heart o' the Hills
Heart of Wetona, The
Helpful Sisterhood, The
Her Hero
Her Only Way
Her Sister's Children
Hero, The
Hidden Letters, The
His Little Page
His Official Appointment
His Silver Bachelorhood
Honorable Algernon, The
Household Pest, The (debut)
In Neighboring Kingdoms
Isle of Conquest
Janet of the Chorus
John Rance--Gentleman
Just Show People
Lady and Her Maid, The
Law of Compensation, The
Loan Shark King, A
Love of Chrysanthemus
Lovesick Maidens of Cuddleton, The
Martha's Vindication
Memories in Men's Souls
Midget's Revenge, The
Mill of Life, The
Miser Murphy's Wedding Present
Missing Links, The
Mr. Bolter's Sweetheart
Mr. Butler Butles
Moth, The
Mother by Proxy
Mrs. Carter's Necklace
Mrs. 'Enery 'Awkins
Nellie, the Model
New Moon, The
Officer John Donovan
O'Hara as Guardian Angel
O'Hara Helps Cupid
O'Hara, Squatter and Philosopher
O'Hara's Godchild
Old Man's Love Story, An
Old Reliable
Omens and Oracles
Other Woman, The
Panthea
Paola and Francesca
Peacemaker, The
Plot and Counterplot
Politics and the Press
Poppy
Probation Wife, The
Question of Clothes, A
Right of Way, The
Sacrifice of Kathleen, The

Safety Curtain, The
Sawdust and Salome
Secret of the Storm Country, The
Silver Cigarette Case, The
Sky Pilot
Sleuthing
Social Secretary, The
Solitaries
Sunshine and Shadows
Tables Turned, The
Tale of Two Cities, A
Thumb Print, The
Troublesome Stepdaughters, The
Under False Colors
Under the Daisies
Vavasour Ball, The
Wanted--a Strong Hand
Way of a Woman, The
Wayward Daughter, A
Wild Cat, The

2524
TALMADGE, Richard (Ricardo
  Metzetti) (1896-)
Double for Douglas Fairbanks,
  Harold Lloyd and others

2525
TANGUAY, Eva*
Selznick player 1917
Recording:
I Don't Care (Veritas Records
  "Ziegfeld Follies" VM107)
Stage:
Vaudeville 1913
Ziegfeld Follies of 1909, The 1909

2526
TANSEY, Johnny*
Redman and the Child, The (child)

2527
TAPLEY, Rose (1883-)
As You Like It
Christian, The
Money Kings
Rose of the South
Susie, the Sleuth
Vanity Fair
Victoria Cross, The /aka/ Charge
  of the Light Brigade
Wanted, a Wife

2528
TARLARNI, Mme. *
Grandmother's Lamb
Mysterious Piano, The
Perjury

2529
TARVERS, Jim*
Jack and the Beanstalk

2530
TAUROG, Norman (1899-)
A child actor 1917

2531
TAYLOR, Alma (1896-)
Adrift on Life's Tide
American Heiress, The
Annie Laurie
Baby on the Barge, The
Basilisk, The
Blind Faith
Bottle, The
Boundary House
Broken in the Wars
Burglar and Little Phyllis, The
By Whose Hand?
Canker of Jealousy, The
Cobweb, The
Comin' thro' the Rye
Court Martialled
Curfew Must Not Ring Tonight
Dear Little Teacher, The
Evicted
Fight with Fire, A
Film Tag series
For a Baby's Sake
Forest on the Hill, The
Girl at Lancing Mill, The
Girl Who Lived in Straight Street,
  The
Golden Pavement, The
Grand Babylon Hotel
Heart of Midlothian, The
Hills Are Calling, The
His Country's Bidding
In the Shadow of Big Ben
Iris
Justice
King Robert of Sicily
Lancashire Lass, A
Little Milliner and the Thief, The
Little Widow Is a Dangerous Thing,
  A
Man Who Stayed at Home, The
Marriage of William Ashe
Merely Mrs. Stubbs
Mill Girl, The
Molly Bawn
Morphis, the Death Drug
Nature of the Beast, The
Nearer My God to Thee
Old Curiosity Shop, The
Oliver Twist

Outrage, The
Quality of Mercy, The
Refugee, The
Schemers, The
Sheba
Smuggler's Stepdaughter, The
Sowing the Wind
Story of a Picture, The
Sunken Rocks
Sweet Lavender
Tares
Tilly the Tomboy Goes Boating
Time, the Great Healer
Touch of a Child, The
Trelawney of the Wells
Tried in the Fire
Veteran's Pension, The
Whirr of the Spinning Wheel, The

2532
TAYLOR, William Desmond (-1921)
Captain Alvarez

2533
TAYLOR, Wilton*
Girl from Outside, The

2534
TEARE, Ethel*
International Sneak, An
Lost--a Cook
Thirst

2535
TEARLE, Conway (Frederick
    Levy) (1882-1938)
Common Law, The
Fall of the Romanoffs, The
Heart of the Hills
Helene of the North
Her Game
Mind-the-Paint Girl, The
Nightingale, The
Reason Why, The
Seven Sisters
Stella Maris
Virtuous Sinners
Virtuous Vamp, A
Virtuous Wives
Way of a Woman, The
Stage:
Debut 1892
Grace George Company repertory
    1915-16
Hawk, The 1914
Lady of the Camellias, The
    1917
Truth, The 1914

2536
TEARLE, Godfrey, Sir (1884-1953)
Fancy Dress
Fool, The
Lachinvar
March Hare, The
Nobody's Child
Queen's Evidence
Real Thing at Last, The
Romeo and Juliet
Sinless Summer, A
Sir James Mortimer's Wager
Stage:
Debut at Burnley, England 1893

2537
TEDDY, the Keystone Dog*
Nick of Time Baby, The
Sultan's Wife, The
Teddy at the Throttle

2538
TEDMARSH, W. J.*
Diamond from the Sky, The (serial)
Secret of the Submarine, The (serial)
Sequel to the Diamond from the Sky,
    The (serial)

2539
TELL, Alma (1892-1937)
Smugglers, The

2540
TELL, Olive (1894-1951)
Girl and the Judge, The
Her Sister
Secret Strings
Silent Master, The
Smuggler, The
To Hell with the Kaiser!
Trap, The
Unforseen, The
Stage:
Civilian Clothes 1919
King of Nowhere, A 1916

2541
TELLEGEN, Lou (1881-1934)
Adirenne Lecouvreur
Explorer, The
Flame of the Desert
La Dame aux Camelias
Lasky player 1915
Long Trail, The
Maria Rose
Queen Elizabeth
Thing We Love, The
Unknown, The

Victory Cross, The
Victory of Conscience, The
What Money Can't Buy
World and Its Woman, The
Stage:
Blind Youth 1917
King of Nowhere, A 1916
Maria Rosa 1914
Sara Bernhardt farewell tour (his
    American debut) 1910
Taking Chances 1915
Ware Case, The 1915

2542
TELZLAFF, Teddy*
Teddy Telzlaff and Earl Cooper,
    Speed Kings

2543
TEMPEST, Marie*
Universal player 1915
Stage:
American debut 1890
Caste 1910
Her Husband's Wife 1917
Lady's Name, A 1916
Marriage of Kitty 1903; 1914
Penelope 1909
Rosalind 1915

2544
TENNANT, Barbara*
Closed Road, The
Firelight
Price of Malice, The
Robin Hood
When Broadway Was a Trail

2545
TENNYSON, Gladys*
Broadway Love (Mrs. Watkins)

2546
TERRIS, Tom*
Keystone player 1915
My Country First

2547
TERRY, Alice (Alice Taafe)
    (1896-)
Bottom of the Well
Bugle Call, The
Clarion Call, The
Corner in Colleen's Home, A
Love Burglar, The
Love Watches
Not My Sister
Old Wives for New (a saleslady)

Strictly Business
Thin Ice
Valley of the Giants

2548
TERRY, Ellen*
British film released through
    Triangle 1919
Stage:
British stage 1856-1906
Captain Brassbound's Conversion
    1907
Good Hope, The 1907
Readings and lectures 1910; 1915

2549
TERRY, Ethel Grey (1898-)
Arsene Lupin
Carter Case, The (The Craig
    Kennedy Serial) (serial)
Denny from Ireland
Intolerance
Mystery of the Yellow Room
Phil for Short
Sign of the Cross
Snail, The

2550
THATCHER, Eva*
Haystacks and Steeples
Her Nature Dance
His Naughty Thought
She Needed a Doctor
Thirst

2551
THATCHER, Heather*
Altar Chains
First Men in the Moon, The
Green Terror, The
Key of the World
Little Hour of Peter Wells, The
Pallard the Punter
Prisoner of Zenda, The

2552
THAW, Evelyn Nesbit*
Threads of Destiny

2553
THAW, Russell*
Redemption

2554
THEBY, Rosemary (1885-)
Are You Legally Married?
As You Like It
Ashes

Baby
Boston Blackie's Little Pal
Bright and Early
Fight for the Right
Great Love, The (Mademoiselle
    Corintee)
Heartease
House of a Thousand Relations
Housekeeping
Hushed Hour
Illumination, The
Kismet
Love's Pay Day
Mystery of 13, The (serial)
Reincarnation of Karma
Shooting of Sadie Rose, The
Silent Mystery, The (serial)
Too Much Woman
Unexpected Places
Upstairs and Down
Wager, The
War Bridegrooms
Web, The
When a Woman Strikes
When the Earth Trembled /aka/
    The Strength of Love
Winged Mystery, The

2555
THEW, Manora*
Toilers, The

2556
THOMAE, R. L. Mr.*
Execution of Mary Queen of Scots
    (Mary)

2557
THOMAS, Olive (Oline Duffy)
    (1898-1920)
Beatrice Fairfax (serial)
Betty Takes a Hand
Broadway Arizona
Even Break, An
Follies Girl
Frankly Chaste
Girl Like That, A
Glorious Lady
Heiress for a Day, An
Indiscreet Corinne
Limousine Life
Love's Prisoner
Madcap Madge
Prudence on Broadway
Spite Bride, The
Toto
Upstairs and Down
Stage:
Ziegfeld Follies of 1915, The 1915

2558
THOMAS, Queenie (1900-   )
Angels of Mons, The
Chance of a Lifetime, The
Frills
It's Happiness That Counts
John Halifax, Gentleman
Little Child Shall Lead Them, A
Man the Army Made, A
Meg o' the Woods
Rock of Ages
Vengeance of Allah, The
What Could a Gentleman Do?
Won by Losing
Ye Wooing of Peggy

2559
THOMPSON, Grace*
Grip of Jealousy, The
Millionaire Paupers, The
Mountain Justice

2560
THOMPSON, Hugh*
Forbidden Path, The (Robert Sinclair)
Primitive Strain, The
Queen of the Sea
Soul of Buddha, The (Sir John Drake)

2561
THOMPSON, Margaret*
Keno Bates, Liar /aka/ The Last
    Card (Doris Maitland)
Man Who Went Out, The
Triangle player 1916

2562
THOMPSON, William*
Peggy

2563
THORPE, Morgan*
Kathleen Mavourneen (Father O'Flynn)

2564
THURMAN, Mary (1894-1925)
Bedroom Blunder, A
Betrayal of Maggie, The
Bombs
Bombs and Brides
Danger Girl
Haystacks and Steeples
His First False Step
His Last Laugh
House of Betty, The
Late Lamented, The
Maggie's First Flase Step
Pinched in the Finish
Scoundrel's Tale, A

Spotlight Sadie
Stone Age, The /aka/ Her Cave
  Man
Sunshine Dad
This Hero Stuff
Watch Your Neighbor

2565
TIDMARSH, Ferdinand*
Sporting Duchess, The

2566
TILBURY, Zeffie*
Avalanche, The

2567
TILTON, Edwin B. *
Riddle Gawne (Col. Harkness)
Under the Yoke (Don Ramon
  Valverde)

2568
TINCHER, Fay*
Battle of the Sexes (the siren)
Bedelia's Bluff
Don Quixote
Faithful to the Finish
French Milliner, The
Home, Sweet Home (a worldly
  woman)
Lady Drummer, The
Laundry Liz
Rough Knight, A
Skirts
Two o'Clock Train, The

2569
TINLEY, Ned*
Good Gracious! or Movies as
  They Shouldn't Be

2570
TITUS, Lydia Yeamans (1874-1929)
Aladdin
All Night
Bound on the Wheel
Edge of the Law, The
Felix on the Job (Tod's wife)
Gun Fightin' Gentleman, A
Happy though Married
Little Marian's Triumph
Mark of Cain, The (Dick's mother)
Peace of Roaring River
Romance of Happy Valley, A (Old
  Lady Smiles)
Strictly Confidential
World and Its Woman, The
Yankee Princess

2571
TODD, Harry*
Shootin' Mad (the father)
Snakeville comedy series

2572
TOKONAGA, Frank*
Voice on the Wire, The (serial)

2573
TONCRAY, Kate*
Battling Jane
Boots
Change of Spirit, A
Double Trouble
Fisher Folks
Going Straight /aka/ Corruption
Hero of Little Italy, The
Hope Chest, The
Lady and the Mouse, The
Lamb, The
Liberty Bells
Little Meena's Romance
Little Yank, The
Long Road, The
Love in an Apartment Hotel
New Dress, The
Old Heidelberg
Out of Luck
Peppy Polly
Rebecca of Sunnybrook Farm
Stage Struck
Those Little Flowers
Turning the Tables

2574
TOOKER, William (1875-)
East Lynne (Judge Hare)
Fool's Revenge, A
Woman the Germans Shot

2575
TORRENCE, David (1880-1942)
Prisoner of Zenda, The
Tess of the D'Ubervilles
Stage:
What Every Woman Knows 1908

2576
TORRES, Cathie*
Her Greatest Love (J. D. Jeanne
  de Fannaz)

2577
TOTO*
Pathé player 1918

2578
TOWNLEY, Robin*
Beatrice Fairfax (serial)

2579
TRACY, Helen*
Romeo and Juliet (Lady Capulet)

2580
TRASK, Wayland*
Bombs
Bombs and Brides
Cactus Nell
Dodging His Doom
Fatty and Mabel Adrift
Feathered Nest, The /aka/ Only
   a Farmer's Daughter
Great Vacuum Robbery, The
Her Marble Heart
Her Tropedoed Love
His Hereafter /aka/ Murray's
   Mixup
His Precious Life
Judge, The
Love Riot, The
Maid Mad /aka/ The Fortune
   Teller
Maiden's Trust, A
Pills of Peril

2580a
TRAVERS, Jim*
Jack and the Beanstalk

2581
TRAVERS, Madalaine (1875-1964)
Caillaux Case
Danger Zone, The
Gambling in Souls
Leah Kleschna
Love That Dares, The
Pathé player 1916
Poor Little Rich Girl, The
Rose of the West
Shielding Shadow, The (serial)
Sins of Ambition
Splendid Sin, The
Three Weeks
When Fate Decides

2582
TRAVERS, Richard (1890-   )
Borrowed Sunshine
Captain Jinks of the Horse Marines
House with Children
In the Palace of the King
Lost--24 Hours
Love Nest, The

Phantom Buccaneer
Romance of an American Duchess,
   The
White Sister, The

2583
TREADOR, Marie*
Yellow Menace, The (serial)

2584
TREE, Herbert Beerbohm, Sir*
Intolerance (a soldier)
Macbeth
Triangle player 1915
Stage:
Colonel Newcome 1917
King Henry VIII 1916
Merchant of Venice, The 1916

2585
TRENT, Tom*
Hazards of Helen, The (serial)

2586
TRENTON, Pell*
Metro player 1919

2587
TREVOR, Norman (1877-1929)
Runaway, The
Stage:
Caesar's Wife 1919
Ideal Husband, An 1918
Kiss for Cinderella, A 1916
Toby's Bow 1919

2588
TRICK, Martha*
Black Eyes and Blue
Dangers of a Bride
Royal Rogue, A
Tugboat Romeo, A
Whose Baby?

2589
TRIMBLE, Larry*
Imp player 1910
Vitagraph player 1911

2590
TROJANO, John*
New Stenographer, The

2591
TROTSKY, Leon (Lev Davidovich
   Bronstein) (1879-1940)
My Official Wife

2592
TROWBRIDGE, Charles*
Thais
Stage:
Come out of the Kitchen 1916
Marriage Game, The 1913

2593
TRUBETZSKOY, Youcca (1905-   )
Hawk

2594
TRUESDELL, Fred C. *
Eclair player 1915

2595
TRUEX, Ernest (1890-1973)
American Citizen, An
Bashful Lover, The
Bond Boy, The
Come on In
Good Little Devil, A
Goodbye, Bill
Little, but Oh, My!
Oh, You Women!
Stick Around
Too Good to Be True
Stage:
Debut 1896
Dummy, The 1914
Good Little Devil, A 1913
Rebecca of Sunnybrook Farm 1910
Very Good Eddie 1915
Wildfire 1908

2596
TRUFANOFF, Sergios*
Fall of the Romanoffs

2597
TRUNNELLE, Mabel*
Edison player 1913
Ranson's Folly

2598
TSCHERNICHIN-LARSSON, Jenny*
Outlaw and His Wife, The
Thomas Graal's First Child

2599
TSINGH, Hurri*
Adventures of Kathlyn, The (serial)

2600
TUCKER, Lillian*
World player 1917

2601
TUCKER, Richard (1869-1942)

Vanity Fair
While the Tide Was Rising

2602
TUNIS, Fay*
Carmen (Carlotta)

2603
TURNER, Bert*
Rose of the Blood (Princess
    Arbassoff)

2604
TURNER, Florence (1887-1946)
    (First film star to be known by
    name)
Alone in London
Angel of the Studio
As Ye Repent
Auld Robin Grey
Aunty's Romance
Became The Vitagraph Girl in 1907
Creatures of Habit
Daisy's Doodad's Dial
Deerslayer, The
Dixie Mother, The
Doorsteps
East Is East
Far from the Madding Crowd
Film Favorites
Flotilla the Flirt
Fool's Gold
For Her People
Francesca Da Rimini
Harper Mystery, The
Grim Justice
How Championships Are Won and
    Lost
How Mr. Bullington Ran the House
Jean's Evidence
Lost and Won
Lucky Stone, The
Murdock Trial, The
My Old Dutch
New Stenographer, The
One Thing after Another
Polly's Progress
Prejudice of Pierre Marie, The
Rose of Surrey
St. Elmo
Shepherd Lassie of Argyle, The
Shop Girls
Snobs
Tale of Two Cities, A (Lucy)
Through the Valley of Shadows
Welsh Singer, A

2605
TURNER, Fred A. *

Escape, The (father)
Intolerance (Dear One's father)
Miracle Man, The (Mr. Higgins)

2606
TURNER, Wedgwood*
Deserter, The (Captain Turner)

2607
TURNER, William*
Perils of Our Girl Reporters
    (serial)

2608
TURPIN, Ben (1874-1940)
Are Waitresses Safe?
Battle Royal, The
Bucking the Tiger
Butcher's Nightmare, The
By the Sea
Caught in the End
Charlie Chaplin's Burlesque on
    Carmen
Circus Cyclone, A
Clever Dummy, A
Cupid's Day Off
Deep Sea Liar, A /aka/ The
    Landlubber
Delinquent Bridegroom, The
Doctoring a Leak /aka/ a Total
    Loss
Ducking a Discord
East Lynne with Variations
For Ten Thousand Bucks
Frightened Flirts
Hide and Seek, Detectives
Hired and Fired /aka/ The Leading
    Man
His Blowout /aka/ The Plumber
His Bogus Boast /aka/ A Cheerful
    Liar
His New Job
Iron Mitt, The
Jealous Jolts
Lost--a Cook
Masked Mirth
Midnight Disturbance
Musical Marvels, The
Night Out, A
No Mother to Guide Him
Pawnbroker's Heart, The
Picture Pirates
Poultry a la Mode /aka/ The
    Harem
Roping Her Romeo
Salome vs. Shenandoah
Saucy Madeline
She Loved Him Plenty

Sheriff Nell's Tussle
Shot in the Fracas
Sleuths
Some Liars
Stolen Booking, The
Studio Stampede, A
Taming Target Center
Two Tough Tenderfeet
Uncle Tom without the Cabin
When Love Is Blind
When Papa Died
Whose Little Wife Are You?
Why Ben Bolted /aka/ He Looked
    Crooked
Wicked City, The
Yankee Doodle in Berlin

- U -

2609
ULLMAN, Ethel*
Civilization (the blacksmith's
    daughter)

2610
ULRIC, Lenore (1892-1970)
Better Woman, The
Capital Punishment
Essanay player 1912
Heart of Paula, The
Heart of Wetona, The
Her Own People
Intrigue
Kilmeny
Morosco player 1915
Road to Love, The

2611
UNDERWOOD, Loyal*
Adventurer, The
Cure, The
Day's Pleasure, A
Dog's Life, A
Easy Street
Immigrant, The
Shoulder Arms
Sunnyside

- V -

2612
VALE, Louise*
Jane Eyre

2613
VALE, Vola*

Adventures of the Last Cigarette,
 The
Balboa player 1917
Bloodhound, The
Each to His Kind
Eagle's Wings, The
Happy though Married
Hearts Asleep
Hearts in Pawn
Hornet's Nest, The
Price of Silence, The
Secret of Black Mountain, The
Silent Man, The
Six Feet Four
Son of His Father
Wolves of the Rail

2614
VALENTINE, Grace (1890-)
Babbling Tongues
Brand of Cowardice, A
Dorian's Divorce
New Adam and Eve
Unchastened Woman
Stage:
Help Wanted 1914
Lombardi, Ltd. 1917
Yellow Jacket, The 1912

2615
VALENTINE, Vangie*
When Bearcat Went Dry (Blossom
 Fulkerson)

2616
VALENTINO, Rudolph (Rudolpho
 Alfonzo Raffaelo Pierre Filibert
 Guglielmi di Valentina d'Anton-
 guolla) (1895-1926)
Alimony (a dancer)
All Night /aka/ The Marriage
 Virgin (dancer)
Ambition
Big Little Person, The (bit)
Delicious Little Devil, The (bit)
Eyes of Youth
Greatest Thing in Life
Home Breaker, The
Isle of Love
My Official Wife
Out of Luck
Patria (serial)
Rogue's Romance, A (an Apache
 dancer)
Society Sensation, A (bit)
Virtuous Sinners

2617
VALKYRIEN*

Fox player 1917
Hidden Valley

2618
VALLI, Valli (1882-1927)
Turmoil, The
Stage:
Cohan Revue of 1916, The 1916
Dollar Princess, The 1909
Purple Road, The 1913
Queen of the Movies 1914
Veronique 1905

2619
VALLI, Virginia (Virginia McSweeney)
 1898-1968)
Efficiency Edgar's Courtship
Fibbers, The
Girl Next Door, The
Golden Idiot, The
Skinner's Dress Suit
Uneasy Money

2620
VAN, Beatrice*
Black Box, The (serial)
Her Bounty (Bessie Clay)
Her Life's Story (the wife)

2621
VAN, Wally*
New Secretary, The
Win(k)some Widow, The

2622
VAN BUREN, A. H.*
Vixen, The (Martin Stevens)
Stage:
Ben Hur 1916
Man Who Stayed at Home, The 1918

2623
VAN BUREN, Mabel*
Charmed Arrow, The
Countess Charming
Devil Stone, The
Girl of the Golden West, The (the
 girl)
Hashimuro To Go
Hearts of Men
House with the Golden Windows, The
Jaguar's Claws, The
Man from Home, The (Ethel Granger
 Simpson)
Money Master, The
Selig player 1913
Silent Partner, The
Sowers, The
Squaw Man's Son, The

Unconquered
Victoria Cross, The
Warrens of Virginia, The (Mrs.
    Warren)

2624
VANCE, Jane*
Daughter of Uncle Sam, A (serial)

2625
VAN DYKE, Truman (1897-   )
Lady's Name, The
Over the Garden Wall
Peddler, The
Red Glove, The (serial)
Wishing Ring Man

2626
VAN DYKE, W. S. *
Intolerance (a wedding guest)

2627
VAN METER, Harry*
Beachcombers
Beloved Rogues
Broadway Love (Jack Chalvey)
Day She Paid, The
Kaiser, the Beast of Berlin, The
    (Capt. VonHancke)
Man's Fight, A
Man's Man, A
Out of the Ashes
Princess Virtue

2628
VAN NAME, Elsie*
Silent Mystery, The (serial)

2629
VAN OLE, Rhea*
Kreutzer Sonata (maid)

2630
VAN TRUMP, Jessalyn*
Back to Live (the charmer)
Mutual player 1916

2631
VAUGHAN, Vivian*
Life of an American Fireman

2632
VEIDT, Conrad (1893-1943)
Cabinet of Dr. Caligari, The
    (Sesare, the somnambulist)
Das Rasel Von Bangalore
Das Tagebuch einer Verlorenen
Es Werde Licht

Prostitution
Satanas
Stage:
Berlin debut 1913

2633
VENESS, Amy (Amy Springett)*
Brat, The

2634
VEP, Irma see MUSIDORA

2635
VERNON, Agnes*
By the Sun's Ray
Her Grave Mistake (Isabel Norris)
Miner's Romance, A (Lucy Williams)
Old Cobbler, The (Jess)
Ranch Romance, A (Kate Preston)
Tangled Hearts

2636
VERNON, Bobby (1895-1939)
Christie player 1918
Danger Girl, The /aka/ Love on
    Skates
Dangers of a Bride
Dash of Courage, A
Fickle Fatty's Fall
Haystacks and Steeples
Hearts and Sparks
His Pride and Shame
Hunt, The
Mike and Jake at the Beach
Nick of Time Baby, The
Our Dare Devil Chief
Papa by Proxy
Save the Pieces
Social Club, A
Sultan's Wife, The
Teddy at the Throttle (a ficklehearted
    young man)
Whose Baby?

2637
VICTOR, Henry (1898-1945)
Call of the Sea
Heart of a Rose
Lass o' the Looms
Ora Pro Nobis
Picture of Dorian Gray, The
Revolution
Secret Woman, The
She

2638
VIDOR, Florence (Florence Arto)
    (1895-   )

American Methods
Better Times
Bravest Way, The
Countess Charming
Honor of His House, The
Old Wives for New (Juliet Raeburn)
Other Half, The
Poor Relations
Tale of Two Cities, A
Till I Come Back to You (Yvonne)
Tong War
Turn in the Road, The
White Man's Law
Widow's Might, The
Yellow Girl, The

2639
VIDOR, King*
Intrigue (an extra)

2640
VIGNOLA, Robert C. (1882-1953)
Kalem player 1910

2641
VINER, Edward*
Little Lord Fauntleroy

2642
VIVIAN, Robert (1885-1944)
La Belle Russe (butler)

2643
VOLARE, Lorna*
Moth, The
Secret of the Storm Country, The

2644
VON ELTZ, Theodore (1889-1964)
Way of the Strong, The

2645
VON METER, Harry*
Lion's Claw, The (serial)

2646
VON RITZAU, Gunther*
Intolerance (First Pharisee)

2647
VON SCHILLER, Carl*
Sins of the Parents

2648
VON SEYFFERTITZ, Gustav B.
   (1863-1943)
Countess Charming
Devil Stone, The

Down to Earth (Dr. Jollyem)
Less Than Kin
Little Princess, A
Old Wives for New (Bladgen)
Rimrock Jones
Whispering Chorus, The (Mocking
   Face)

2649
VON STROHEIM, Erich (Hans Erich
   Maria Stroheim von Nordenwall)
   (1885-1957)
Birth of a Nation, The (man who
   falls from roof)
Blind Husbands (the other man)
Bold Impersonation, A
Captain Machlin (bit)
Failure, The
For France
Front for a Hotel
Ghosts
Heart of Humanity
Hearts of the World (a Hun)
His Picture in the Papers (bit)
Hun Within, The
In Again-Out Again (bit)
Intolerance (Second Pharisee)
Less Than the Dust (bit)
Macbeth
Old Heidelberg (Lutz, the Prussian
   Officer)
Panthea (bit)
Reaching for the Moon
Social Secretary, The (bit)
Sylvia of the Secret Service
Unbeliever, The

2650
VON TWARDOWSKI, Hans*
Cabinet of Dr. Caligari, The (Alan)

2651
VOSBURGH, Alfred see WHITMAN,
   Alfred

2652
VOSBURGH, Harold*
Selig player 1913
Smugglers, The
Stage:
Woman, The 1911

- W -

2653
WADE, John P. *
Eagle's Eye, The (serial)

2654
WADSWORTH, William*
Andy series 1914
What Happened to Mary? (serial)

2655
WALBURN, Ray*
Scarlet Runner, The (serial)

2656
WALCAMP, Marie (1894-)
Dragon's Net, The
Flirt, The
For Liberty (serial)
Hop, the Devil's Brew
Indian's Lament, The
John Needham's Double
Jungle Master, The
Liberty, a Daughter of the U. S. A.
  (title role) (serial)
Lion's Claw, The (serial)
Onda of the Orient
Patria (serial)
Quest of Virginia, The
Red Ace, The (serial)
Red Glove, The (serial)
Red Robe, The (serial)
Silent Terror, The
Tempest Cody's Manhunt
Tongues of Flame (serial)

2657
WALDRON, Andrew*
Red Glove, The (serial)

2658
WALDRON, Charles D. (1874-1946)
Esmeralda
Stage:
Warrens of Virginia, The 1907

2659
WALKER, Allan, Mrs. *
Clemenceau Case, The (Marie)

2660
WALKER, Antoinette*
Sting of Victory, The
Stage:
Yellow Jacket, The 1912

2661
WALKER, Charlotte (1878-1958)
Eve in Exile
Every Mother's Son
Just a Woman
Kindling (Maggie Schultz)
Lone Wolf, The

Men
Out of the Darkness
Pardners
Seven Deadly Sins ("Sloth")
Trail of the Lonesome Pine, The
  (June Tolliver)
Stage:
Crisis, The 1902
Gentleman of France, A 1901
Trail of the Lonesome Pine, The
  1912
Warrens of Virginia, The 1907

2662
WALKER, Johnnie (1894-1949)
Knife, The

2663
WALKER, Lillian (1888-)
Accomplished Mrs. Thompson, The
Artist's Madonna, The
Better Wife, The
Blue Envelope, The
Carpenter, The
Embarrassment of Riches
Grain of Dust, The
How Mr. Bullington Ran the House
Joyous Liar, A
Kitty McKay
Love, Luck and Gasoline
Lust of the Ages, The
Model Wife, A
New Secretary, The
Persistent Mr. Prince, The
Princess of Park Row
Reincarnation of Karma
Star Gazer, The
Stenographer Wanted (the blonde
  applicant)
Tale of Two Cities, A
Troublesome Stepdaughters, The
Unseen Enemy, The
White Man's Chance, The

2664
WALKER, Robert*
Kalem player 1915
Light, The (Etienne Desechette)
Lion Man, The (serial)

2665
WALLACE, Dorothy*
Secret Code, The (Mrs. Walker)

2666
WALLACE, Irene*
Other Man, The

2667
WALLER, Lewis*
Universal player 1915
Stage:
Discovering America 1912
Explorer, The 1912
Garden of Allah, The 1911
Henry V 1912
Monsieur Beaucaire 1912

2668
WALLOCK, Edwin*
War o' Dreams

2669
WALSH, Blanche (1873-1915)
Ressurection (Maslova)
Stage:
Kreutzer Sonata, The 1906
Ressurection 1903
Vaudeville 1913

2670
WALSH, Felix*
Her Life's Story (the child)

2671
WALSH, George (1892-)
Beast, The
Blue Blood and Red
Book Agent, The
Brave and Bold
Don Quixote
Gold and the Woman (Lee Duskara)
Help! Help! Police!
Honor System
I'll Say So
Intolerance (bridegroom)
Island of Desire, The
Jack Spurlock--Prodigal
Kid Is Clever, The
Luck and Pluck
Never Say Quit
On the Jump
Pride of New York, The
Putting One Over
Seventh Person, The
Some Boy
This Is the Life
Winning Stroke, The
Yankee Way, The

2672
WALSH, Raoul (1889-)
Availing Prayer, The
Birth of a Nation, The (John
    Wilkes Booth)
Dishonored Medal, The

Double Knot, The
Final Verdict, The
For His Master
Greaser, The
Great Leap, The
Man for All of That, A
Mystery of the Hindu Image
Sands of Fate
Sierra Jim's Reformation
Smuggler, The

2673
WALSH, Tom*
Trey o' Hearts, The (serial)

2674
WALTEMEYER, Jack*
Perils of Thunder Mountain, The
    (serial)

2675
WALTERS, Easter*
Hands Up! (serial)
Tiger's Trail, The (serial)

2676
WALTERS, John*
Sting of Victory, The

2677
WALTERS, May*
Station Content (Mrs. Rathfield)

2678
WALTERS, William*
Essanay player 1912

2679
WALTHALL, Anna Mae*
Hearts of the World (a French
    peasant)
Intolerance (a slave girl)

2680
WALTHALL, Henry B. (1880-1936)
And a Still Small Voice
Avenging Conscience (the nephew)
Banker's Daughters, The
Battle at Elderbush Gulch, The
Beating Back
Birth of a Nation, The (Col. Ben
    Cameron)
Boomerang, The
Broken Ways
Burglar's Dilemma, The
Call, The
Change of Spirit, A
Chosing a Husband

Classmates
Cloister's Touch, The
Comeback, The
Confession, The
Converts, The
Convict's Sacrifice, A
Corner in Wheat, A
Death's Marathon
During the Roundup
Face at the Window, The
False Faces, The (the Lone Wolf)
Feud in the Kentucky Hills, A
Floor Above, The
Fools of Fate
Friends
Gangsters of New York
Ghosts
God Within, The
Gold Is Not All
Gold Seekers, The
Great Love, The (Sir Roger
    Brighton)
His Last Burglary
His Robe of Honor
His Mother's Oath
Home Folks
Home, Sweet Home (John Howard
    Payne)
Honor of His Family, The
House with the Closed Shutters, The
Humdrum Brown
If We Only Knew
In Life's Cycle
In Little Italy
In Old California
In Old Kentucky
In the Aisles of the Wild
Influence of the Unknown
Informer, The
Inner Circle, The
Judith of Bethulia
Lady and the Mouse, The
Leather Stockings
Little Child, A
Little Tease, The
Long Arm of Mannister, The
Long Lane's Turning, A
Love in an Apartment Hotel
Mistake, The
Misunderstood
Modern Husbands
Mountain Rat, The
My Baby
My Hero
Mysterious Shot, The
Odalisque, The
Oil and Water
Old Man, The

On the Reef
One She Loved, The
Parted Curtains
Perfidy of Mary, The
Phantom of the House
Pippa Passes
Pranks
Ramona: a Story of the White Man's
    Injustice to the Indian
Raven, The
Sealed Room, The
1776, or The Hessian Renegades
Sheriff's Baby, The
Sorrows of the Unfaithful, The
Soul of Honor, The
Sting of Victory, The
Strange Case of Mary Page, The
Strongheart
Summer Idyll, A
Thou Shalt Not
Three Friends
Two Daughters of Eve, The
Two Men of the Desert
Usurer, The
Vengeance of Galora, The
Wanderer, The
Wilful Peggy
With Hoops of Steel
Stage:
Great Divide, The 1906

2681
WALTON, Florence*
Quest of Life, The
Stage:
Broadway to Paris 1912
Ziegfeld Follies of 1908, The 1908

2682
WARD, Carrie Clarke*
Bank, The
Night in the Show, A
Siren's Song, A (Paulette Remey)
Under the Yoke (Duenna)
Why Smith Left Home

2683
WARD, Fannie (1872-1952)
Betty to the Rescue
Cheat, The (Edith Hardy)
Common Clay
Cry of the Weak
Crystal Gazer, The
Each Hour a Pearl
For the Defense
Gutter Magdalene, A
Her Strange Wedding
Innocent

Japanese Nightingale, A
La Rafale
Marriage of Kitty, The
Narrow Path, The
On the Level
Only Way, The
Our Better Selves
Profiteers, The
School for Husbands, The
Secret of the Lone Star, The
Sunset Trail, The
Tennessee's Partner
Winning of Sally Temple, The
Years of the Locust, The
Yellow Ticket, The
Stage:
Madame President 1913
New Lady Bantock, The 1909

2684
WARD, Fleming*
When Men Desire (Robert Stedman)

2685
WARD, Gerald*
Captive, The (Milos)

2686
WARD, Jerold*
Clown, The (little boy)

2687
WARD, Mrs. *
Mickey

2688
WARD, Warwick (Mannon Ward)
   (1890-1967)
Silver Lining, The

2689
WARDE, Frederick*
King Lear
Richard III
Under False Colors

2690
WARE, Helen (1877-1939)
Cross Currents
Deep Purple, The
Escape, The
Garden of Allah, The
Price, The
Revolt, The
Third Degree
Stage:
Celebrated Case, A 1915
Out There 1918

Price, The 1910
Third Degree, The 1909

2691
WARFIELD, Irene*
Essanay player 1916

2692
WARFIELD, Theodora*
War Brides

2693
WARNER, H. B. (Henry Byron
   Charles Stewart Warner)
   (1876-1958)
Beggar of Cawnpore, The
Danger Trail, The
Ghost Breaker, The
God's Man
House of a Thousand Candles
Lost Paradise
Man Who Turned White, The
Market of Vain Desire, The
Pagan God, The
Raiders, The
Seven Deadly Sins ("Envy")
Vagabond Prince, The
Your Girl and Mine
Stage:
Alias Jimmy Valentine 1910
Battle, The 1908
Clothes 1906
England debut 1883
Ghost Breaker, The 1913
Out There 1918
Salomy Jane 1907
Sleeping Partners 1918

2694
WARNER, J. Wesley*
Scarlet Days

2695
WARREN, Fred*
Matrimaniac, The (Rev. Tobias Tubbs)

2696
WARRENTON, Lule*
Bobbie of the Ballet
Gilded Spider, The

2697
WARWICK, Henry*
Soul of Buddha, The (stage manager)

2698
WARWICK, Robert (Robert Taylor
   Bien) (1881-1964)

Accidental Honeymoon, An
Argyle Case, The
Dollar Mark, The
Face in the Moonlight, The
Human Driftwood
In Mizzoura
Mad Lover, The
Man of the Hour
Modern Othello, A
Secret Service
Silent Master, The
Told in the Hills
Stage:
Anna Karenina 1907
Balkan Princess, The 1911
Celebrated Case, A 1915
Glad of It (an understudy) 1903
Grace George repertory 1916
Kiss Waltz, The 1911
Miss Princess 1912
Secret, The 1913
Two Women 1910

2699
WASHBURN, Alice*
Edison player 1913

2700
WASHBURN, Bryant (1889-1963)
All Wrong
At the End of a Perfect Day
Blindness of Virtue, The
Destiny
Fibbers, The
Final Fraud, The
Ghost of the Rancho
Golden Idiot, The
Gypsy Trail, The
Havoc, The
It Pays to Advertise
Kidder & Company
Little Straw Wife, The
Love Insurance
Man Who Was Afraid, The
Marriage a la Carte
Masked Wrestler, The
Old, Old Song, An
One Wonderful Night
Our People
Poor Snob, The
Prince of Graustark, The
Promised Land, The
Putting It Over
Skinner's Baby
Skinner's Bubble
Skinner's Dress Suit
Something to Do
Sparks of Fate

Tides That Meet
Till I Come Back to You (Capt.
   Jefferson Strong)
Try and Get It
Twenty One
Under Royal Patronage
Venus in the East
Very Young Man, A
Voice of Conscience
Way of a Man with a Maid, The
Why Smith Left Home

2701
WATERMAN, Ida*
Amarilly of Clothesline Alley
Behind the Scenes
Eagle's Mate, The
Esmeralda
Lure of Ambition, The (Duchess)
Stella Maris

2702
WATSON, Henry, Jr. *
Mishaps of Musty Suffer, The

2703
WATSON, Roy*
Hazards of Helen, The (serial)

2704
WAYNE, Marie*
Pearl of the Army (serial)

2705
WAYNE, Maude*
Hula Hula Land
Shanghaied Jonah, A

2706
WEAVER, Henry*
Gloria's Romance (serial)

2707
WEBB, George*
Secret of the Submarine, The (serial)
Triangle player 1917

2708
WEBB, Millard*
Reaching for the Moon (Mr. Mann)

2709
WEBB, Percy Sergeant*
Unbeliever, The

2710
WEBER, Joe (1867-1942)
Best of Enemies, The

Fatty and the Broadway Stars
Worst of Friends, The
Stage:
Higgledy-Piggledy 1904
Hoity Toity 1901
Hokey-Pokey 1912
Merry Widow Burlesque, The 1908
Twiddle-Twaddle 1906
Twirly Whirly 1902
Weber and Field Music Hall 1900;
    1901
Whoop-Dee-Doo 1903

2711
WEBER, Lois*
Became first important woman
    producer at Universal 1916
Dumb Girl of Portici, The
False Colors
Merchant of Venice, The
Midnight Romance, A

2712
WEBSTER, Ben (1864-1947)
Because
Bootle's Baby
Cynthia in the Wilderness
Enoch Arden
Garret in Bohemia, A
Gay Lord Quex, The
His Daughter's Dilemma
House of Temperley, The
If Thou Wert Blind
In the Blood
Liberty Hall
Lil o' London
Masks and Faces
Nobody's Child
Profligate, The
Twelve-Ten
Two Roads
V. C.
Vicar of Wakefield, The
Stage:
London debut 1887
Marriage of William Ashe, The 1905

2713
WEED, Frank*
Cinderella

2714
WEER, Helen*
Social Secretary, The

2715
WEGENER, Paul (1874-1948)
Golem, The
Student Von Prag

2716
WEHLEN, Emmy*
Metro player 1917
Who's Guilty? (serial)
Stage:
Girl in the Film, The 1913
Marriage a la Carte 1911
Rose Maid, The 1912
Tonight's the Night 1914
Winsome Widow, The 1912

2717
WEIGEL, Paul*
Beachcombers, The
DuBarry
Kismet
Light, The
Luck in Pawn
Siren's Song, A (Hector Remey)
She-Devil, The
Smiles

2718
WEIR, Helen*
Incorrigible Dukane, The

2719
WELCH, Niles (1888-   )
Beckoning Roads
Gulf Between, The
Her Boy
Jane Goes A-Wooing
Law of Men
Metro player 1915
Miss George Washington
One of Many
Reclaimed
Secret of the Storm Country, The
Stepping Out
Virtuous Thief, The

2720
WELLESLEY, Charles*
Poor Little Rich Girl, The
Secret Kingdom, The (serial)

2721
WELLMAN, William (1896-   )
Knickerbocker Buckaroo, The
    (Merecedes' brother)

2722
WELLS, Jane*
Little Lord Fauntleroy

2723
WELLS, L. M. *
Graft (serial)
Liberty, a Daughter of the U. S. A.

(serial)
Red Ace, The (serial)

2724
WELLS, May*
Cactus Nell
Fatty and Mabel Adrift
Her Busted Trust
His Auto Ruination
His First False Step
Lion and the Girl, The
Madcap Ambrose
Movie Star, A
Safety First Ambrose /aka/
    Sheriff Ambrose

2725
WELLS, Raymond*
Old Heidelberg

2726
WELSH, William*
Bull's Eye (serial)

2727
WEST, Billie*
King-Bee player 1917

2728
WEST, Charles (1886-   )
As the Bells Ring Out
Battle, The
Black Sheep
Blind Love
Broken Cross, The
Burglar's Dilemma, The
Child's Impulse, A
Dan the Dandy
Dream Girl, The ("English" Hal)
Fair Rebel, A
Fate's Interception
Fate's Turning
Flash of Fate, The
Flash of Light, A
From out the Shadows
Girl and Her Trust, The
Girl Who Came Back, The
Goddess of Sagebrush Gulch, The
Golden Supper, The
Heart of Nora Flynn, The (Jack
    Murray)
Her Sacrifice
Hero of Little Italy, The
His Divorced Wife
His Mother's Scarf
In Life's Cycle
In Old California
In the Days of '49

Italian Barber, The
Just Gold
Last Drop of Water, The
Left Handed Man, The
Lesser Evil, The
Lines of White on the Sullen Sea
Lodging for the Night, A
Long Road, The
Love in the Hills
Massacre, The
Mender of the Nets, The
Old Actor, The
One Is Business, the Other Crime
Outcast among Outcasts, An
Romance of the Western Hills, A
Siren of Impulse, A
Sunshine Sue
Tale of the Wilderness, A
Temporary Truce, A
Through Darkened Vales
Two Paths, The
Welcome Intruder, A
What Shall We Do with Our Old?
White Man's Law
Wife or Country (Jack Holiday)
Would-Be Shriner, The

2729
WEST, Dorothy*
Biograph player 1908
Child of the Ghetto, A
Deception, The
Eternal Grind, The
Fugitive, The
Girls and Daddy, The
Golden Supper, The
Habit of Happiness, The (Elsie
    Pepper)
His Last Burglary
His Mother's Scarf
House with the Closed Shutters, The
Italian Barber, The
Knight of the Road, A
Lily of the Tenements, The
Lines of White on the Sullen Sea
New Dress, The
Revenue Man and the Girl, The
Rose o' Salem Town
Salutary Lesson, A
Squaw's Love, The
Swords and Hearts

2730
WEST, Henry*
Sporting Life

2731
WEST, Lillian*

Everywoman's Husband (Delia
    Marshall)
Society for Sale (Vi Challoner)

2732
WEST, Olive*
Madame Butterfly

2733
WEST, William H. /aka/ Billy
    West (1888-)
Active Life of Dolly of the Dailies,
    The (serial)
Back Stage
Best Man Wins, The
Billy West comedies 1918
Bright and Early
Candy Kid, The
Cupid's Rival
Dough-Nuts
He Loves Her Still
Hero, The
His Lordship's Dilemma
In Again
Kentucky Girl, The
Messenger, The
Millionaire, The
Parasite, The
Pest, The
Playmates
Rogue, The
Sap, The
Scrapper, The
Service Stripes
Slave, The
Stolen Love
Straight and Narrow
Stranger, The
Sweethearts
Why Marry?
Wife Wanted

2734
WESTON, Maggie*
Foundling, The

2735
WESTON, Mildred*
Essanay player 1912

2736
WESTOVER, Winifred (1890-)
Gift of the Desert
Hobbs in a Hurry
Intolerance (a harem favorite)
John Petticoats
Marked Men
Matrimaniac, The (the maid)

Microscope Mystery, The
This Hero Stuff
Watch Out, William

2737
WHARTON, Bessie*
Mysteries of Myra, The (serial)

2738
WHEATCROFT, Stanhope (1888-)
Amazing Wife, The
Blue Bonnet
Destiny
East Lynne (Richard Hare)
Modern Cinderella, A
Old Town Girl, The
Right to Happiness, The
Under Two Flags (Berkeley Cecil)
Veiled Adventure, The

2739
WHIFFEN, Thomas, Mrs. (1845-1936)
Barbara Frietchie

2740
WHITE, Arthur*
Life of an American Fireman

2741
WHITE, Billy*
Dog's Life, A

2742
WHITE, Blanche*
Dawn Maker, The

2743
WHITE, Carolina*
My Cousin

2744
WHITE, Chrissie (1895-)
As the Sun Went Down
At the Foot of the Scaffold
Barnaby Rudge
Basilisk, The
Blindness of Fortune, The
Blood and Bosh
Broken in the Wars
Broken Threads
Bunch of Violets, A
Cabman's Good Fairy, The
Captain Jack
Carrots
City of Beautiful Nonsense, The
Cloister and the Heart, The
Comin' thro' the Rye
Curate's Love Story, A

Curtain's Secret, The
David Garrick
Dick Carson Wins Through
Dr. Fenton's Ordeal
Drake's Love Story
Eternal Triangle, The
Exploits of Tubby Series
Face to Face
Film Tags series
Fireman's Daughter, The
For the Little Lady's Sake
Gipsy Man
Girl Who Joined the Bushrangers
Girl Who Lived in Straight Street,
  The
Grain of Sand, A
Hanging Judge, The
Held for Ransom
Her Crowning Glory
Her Marriage Lines
His Dearest Possession
Kissing Cup
Lt. Pie's Love Story
Lieutenant's Bride, The
Man behind the Times, The
Man Who Stayed at Home, The
Mermaid, The
Nightbirds of London, The
Partners
Plot and Pash
Recalling of John Grey, The
Refugee, The
Second String, The
Shadows of a Great City
Sheriff's Daughter, The
Sowing the Wind
Sweater, The
Sweet Lavender
Tilly the Tomboy Goes Boating
Time, the Great Healer
Towards the Light
Trelawney of the Wells
V. C.
Vicar of Wakefield, The
White Boys, The

2745
WHITE, Glen*
Camille (Gaston Rieux)
Darling of Paris, The (Quasmodo)
Graft (serial)
Heart and Soul (Jantze)
Her Greatest Love (Lord Jura)
Love and the Law
Romeo and Juliet (Mercutio)
Sporting Blood
Tiger Woman, The (Edwin Harris)

2746
WHITE, Leo (1887-1948)
Bank, The
Behind the Screen
Champion, The
Charlie Chaplin's Burlesque on
  Carmen
Count, The
Easy Street
Fireman, The
Floorwalker, The
His New Job
In the Park
Jitney Elopement, A
Night in the Show, A
Night Out, A
Police
Shanghaied
Tramp, The
Triple Trouble
Vagabond, The
Woman, A
Work

2747
WHITE, May*
Charlie Chaplin's Burlesque on
  Carmen
Night in the Show, A

2748
WHITE, Pearl (Pearl Fay White)
  (1889-1938)
Angel of the Slums, The
Bella's Beau
Black Secret, The (serial)
Blossom and the Bee, The (serial)
Chorus Girl, The
Dip into Society, A
Exploits of Elaine, The (serial)
  (Elaine)
Fatal Ring, The (serial)
Floating Coffin, The
For Honor of the Name
Girl in the Next Room, The
Girl Reporter, The
Gypsy Flirt, The
Hazel Kirk
Heroic Harold
Hidden Voice, The
Hooded Helper, The
House of Hate, The (serial)
Iron Claw, The (serial)
King's Game, The
Lightning Raider, The (serial)
Lizzie and the Iceman
Mayblossom
Mind Cure, The

Necklace, The
New Exploits of Elaine, The (serial)
  (Elaine)
New Magdalene, The
New York Lights
Oh, You Pearl
Pearl and the Poet
Pearl and the Tramp
Pearl as a Detective
Pearl of the Army (serial) (Pearl)
Pearl's Hero
Pearl's Mistake
Perils of Paris, The (serial)
Perils of Pauline, The (serial)
  (Pauline)
Ring, The
Romance of Elaine, The (serial)
  (Elaine)
That Other Girl
Where Charity Begins

2749
WHITEHORSE*
Range Rider series
Sante Fe Mac

2750
WHITESIDE, Walker (1869-1942)
Belgian, The
Melting Pot, The
Stage:
Little Brother, The 1918
Melting Pot, The 1909
Mr. Wu 1914
Typhoon, The 1912

2751
WHITFORD, Annabelle*
Annabelle's Butterfly Dance
Tambourine Dance
Stage:
Ziegfeld Follies of 1908, The 1908

2752
WHITING A. E., Mrs.*
Girl in the Checkered Coat, The
  (Ann Maitland)

2753
WHITLOCK, Lloyd (1900-1962)
Boomerang, The
Edge of the Law, The
Gentle Ill Wind, A
Lasca
Love Call, The
Rose Marie
Rouge and Riches

2754
WHITMAN, Alfred (Alfred Vosburgh)
  (1890-)
Baree, the Son of Kazan
Best Man, The
Cavanaugh of the Forest Range
Days of '49
Eighth Grandparent, The
Enchantment, The
End of the Game
Flaming Omen, The
Gentleman's Agreement, A
Girl from Beyond, The
Her Father's Son
Home Trail, The
My Country First
Princess in the Dark
Serpent's Tooth, The
Souls in Pawn
Sunlight's Last Raid
Tongues of Flame, The (serial)
Trick of Fate, A
When Men Are Tempted
Wild Strain, The

2755
WHITMAN, Walt*
When Bear Cat Went Dry (Joel
  Fulkerson)

2756
WHITNEY, Claire*
Better 'Ole, The
Camille (Celeste Duval)
Career of Katherine Bush
East Lynne (Barbara Hare)
Galley Slave, The (Cicely Blaine)
Heart and Soul (Bess)
Isle of Conquest
Kaiser's Finish, The
Life's Shop Window
Man Who Stayed at Home, The
New York Peacock, The
Nigger, The
Romance of Old Bill, The
Ruling Passions
Shirley Kane
Solax player 1914
Thou Shalt Not
Under Two Flags (Venetia)
Victim, The
When False Tongues Speak

2757
WHITSON, Frank*
Gold and the Woman (Montrevor)
If My Country Should Call (Robert
  Ogden)

Mark of Cain, The (John Graham)
Price of Silence, The (Oliver Urmy)

2758
WHITTY, May, Dame (1865-1948)
Film debut 1914
Stage:
London debut 1882
St. James Theatre (as understudy)
1883-1885
Touring stock company (England)
1885

2759
WHITWORTH, Robert*
War Brides

2760
WILBUR, Crane (1889-)
All Love Excelling
Blood of His Fathers, The
Breezy Jim
Compact, The
Corsair, The
Devil M' Care
Eye of Envy, The
Finger of Justice
For Massa's Sake
Heirs of Hate
Morals of Men, The
Nation's Peril, A
Painted Lie, The
Perils of Pauline, The (serial)
  (Harry Marvin)
Road of Strife, The (serial)
Spite Husband, The
Stripped for a Million
Unlucky Jim

2761
WILDER, Marshall P. *
Chumps

2762
WILKEY, Violet*
Birth of a Nation, The (Flora
  as a child)

2763
WILLARD, Jess*
Challenge of Chance, The
Heart Punch, The

2764
WILLIAMS, Bert*
Natural Born Gambler, A
Stage:
In Dahomey 1903

Ziegfeld Follies of 1910, The 1910
Ziegfeld Follies of 1911, The 1911
Ziegfeld Follies of 1912, The 1912
Ziegfeld Follies of 1914, The 1914
Ziegfeld Follies of 1915, The 1915
Ziegfeld Follies of 1916, The 1916

2765
WILLIAMS, Clara*
Carmen of the Klondyke (serial)
Hell's Hinges (Faith Henly)
Paws of the Bear
Selig player 1910

2766
WILLIAMS, Cora*
His Parisian Wife

2767
WILLIAMS, Earle (1880-1927)
American Live Wire, An
Arsene Lupin
Artist's Madonna, The
Awakening, The
Carpenter, The
Christian, The
Diplomatic Mission, A
Gentleman of Quality, A
Girl in His House, The
Goddess, The (serial)
Grell Mystery, The
Happy-Go-Lucky
Highest Trump, The (dual role)
In the Balance
Juggernaut, The
Lady of the Lake, The
Love Doctor, The
Man Who Wouldn't Tell, The
Mother's Sin, A
My Lady's Slipper
My Official Wife
Rogue's Romance, A
Saving an Audience
Scarlet Runner, The (serial)
Seal of Silence, The
Seventh Son, The
Souls in Bondage
Stolen Treaty, The
Tiger Lady, The
Two Women
Usurper, The
Wager, The
War
Wolf, The

2768
WILLIAMS, G. A. *
Hazards of Helen, The (serial)

2769
WILLIAMS, Guinn "Big Boy"
   (1907-1962)
Almost a Husband

2770
WILLIAMS, Kathlyn (1888-1960)
Adventures of Kathlyn, The (serial)
   (Kathlyn)
Back to the Primitive
Better Wife, The
Big Timber
Child of the Sea, A
Chip of the Flying U
Coming of Columbus, The
Fire Chief's Daughter, The
Harbor Island
Highway of Hope, The
Juggernaut, The
Last Dance, The
Leopard's Foundling, The
Lost in the Jungle (serial)
Mansion of Misery, A
Maude Miller
Mezeppa
Ne'er-Do-Well, The
Out of the Wreck
Redeeming Love
Spoilers, The (Cherry Malotte)
Story of the Blood Red Rose
Sweet Lady Peggy
Ten Nights in a Bar Room
Thing We Love, The
Two Orphans, The
We Can't Have Everything (Charity
   Coe Cheever)
Whispering Chorus, The (Jane
   Trimble)
Wise Old Elephant

2771
WILLIS, Nat*
Webb Singing Pictures

2772
WILLIS, Paul*
Trouble Buster, The

2773
WILSON, Alice*
La Belle Russe (Lady Sackton)

2774
WILSON, Ben (1885-)
Brass Bullet, The (serial)
Her Brother's Crime
Mystery Ship, The (serial)
Screaming Shadow, The (serial)

Trail of the Octopus (serial)
Voice on the Wire, The (serial)
What Happened to Mary? (serial)
When the Cartridges Failed
While the Tide Was Rising
Who Will Marry Mary? (serial)

2775
WILSON, Edna May*
Man's Country, A (Ruth Kemp)

2776
WILSON, Elsie Jane*
Bound on the Wheel
Mountain Justice
Oliver Twist
Temptation (Madame Maroff)

2777
WILSON, Georgia*
Cinderella

2778
WILSON, Jack*
Shoulder Arms

2779
WILSON, Lois (1896-)
Alimony
Bells, The
Dumb Girl of Portici, The
End of the Game
His Robe of Honor
It Pays to Advertise
Love Insurance
Man's Man, A
One Dollar Bid
Turn of a Card, A
Why Smith Left Home

2780
WILSON, Margery*
Bearing Her Cross
Bred in the Bone
Clodhopper, The
Corner in Colleen's Home, A
Crooked Straight, The
Desert Gold
Desert Man, The
Double Trouble
Eye of the Night
Flames of Chance, The
Hand at the Window, The
Hard Rock Breed, The
Honorable Algy
Intolerance (Brown Eyes)
Kentucky School Master, The
Law of the Great Northwest, The

Lupin Gal
Mother Instinct, The
Mountain Dew
Primal Lure, The
Return of Draw Egan
Toll Gate, The
Upholding the Law
Wild Sumac
Without Honor
Wolf Lowry

2781
WILSON, Millard K. *
Fascination of the Fleur de Lis
   (the king)
Idyll of the Hills, An (Dick Massey)
Lion, the Lamb, the Man, The
   (the brother)
Millionaire Paupers, The
Mother's Atonement, A
Pine's Revenge, The
Stronger Than Death
Under a Shadow
When Bear Cat Went Dry (Jerry
   Henderson)

2782
WILSON, Tom (1880-1965)
Amarilly of Clothesline Alley
Americano, The
Atta Boy's Last Race
Birth of a Nation, The
Day's Pleasure, A
Dog's Life, A
Greatest Question, The (Zeke)
Intolerance (the policeman)
Shoulder Arms
Sunnyside
Wild and Woolly (engineer)

2783
WINANT, Forrest*
New York
Stage:
Country Boy, The 1910
East Is West 1918
Family Cupboard, The 1913
Kick In 1914
Turn to the Right 1916

2784
WINDSOR, Claire (1897-   )
Heart of a Fool
Luck of the Irish

2785
WINGE, Torsten*
Thomas Graal's First Child

2786
WINNINGER, Charles (1884-1969)
Film debut at Universal 1915
Stage:
Cohan Revue of 1916, The 1916
Cohan Revue of 1918, The 1918
Passing Show of 1919, The 1919
Winninger Family Novelty Company
   to 1909
Yankee Girl 1909

2787
WINSTON, Laura*
Victory (Mrs. Shomberg)

2788
WOLFE, Jane*
Men, Women and Money
Woman Next Door, The

2789
WOLHEIM, Louis R. (1880-1931)
Carter Case, The (The Craig
   Kennedy Serial) (serial)

2790
WONG, Anna May (Wong Liu Tsong)
   (1907-1960)
Red Lantern

2791
WONTNER, Arthur (1875-1960)
Bigamist, The
Frailty
Lady Windermere's Fan

2792
WOOD, Peggy*
Almost a Husband
Stage:
Buddies 1919
Maytime 1917
Mlle. Modiste 1913
Old Town, The (debut) 1910
Young America 1914

2793
WOOD, Sam*
Little American, The

2794
WOODRUFF, Bert (1856-   )
Bill Henry
Busher, The
Greased Lightning
Jim Bludson
Love Sublime, A
Men of the Desert

2795
WOODRUFF, Eleanor*
Hero of Submarine D-2, The
Perils of Pauline, The (serial)
Weakness of Man, The

2796
WOODRUFF, Henry*
Triangle player 1915
Stage:
Alice Nielsen Comic Opera Co.
   1900
Ben Hur 1903
Brown of Harvard 1906
Mary of Magdala 1902
Olympe 1904
Orlando 1902
Vaudeville 1913

2797
WOODTHORPE, Georgia*
Midnight Man, The (serial)

2798
WOODWARD, Eugenie*
East Lynne (Mrs. Hare)

2799
WOODWARD, Guy*
Best of Enemies, The
Dash of Courage, A
Dodging His Doom
Fickle Fatty's Fall
His Pride and Shame
His Wild Oats
Hula Hula Land
Hunt, The
Shanghaied Jonah, A
Tugboat Romeo, A

2800
WOODWARD, Henry*
Male and Female (McGuire)

2801
WOODWARD, Jill*
My Country First

2802
WORNE, Duke*
Mystery Ship, The (serial)

2803
WORTHINGTON, William (-1941)
Back to Life (the gambler)
Black Box, The (serial)
Damon and Pythias
Devil's Pay Day, The

Grail, The
In Search of a Wife
On the Level

2804
WRIGHT, Helen*
Black Box, The (serial)
Brass Bullet, The (serial)
Doll's House, A (Anna)
Under the Crescent (serial)

2805
WRIGHT, Hugh E. (1879-)
Better 'Ole, The
Stage:
Romantic Knights, The (debut at
   Portsmouth) 1902

2806
WRIGHT, Mack*
Lion Man, The

2807
WRIGHT, Nannie*
Graft (serial)

2808
WULF, Fred*
Essanay player 1912

2809
WUNDERLEE, Frank*
Carter Case, The (The Craig
   Kennedy Serial) (serial)
Fatal Fortune, The (serial)

2810
WYNDHAM, Poppy*
Snow in the Desert

- Y -

2810a
YOST, Herbert see O'MOORE,
   Barry

2811
YOUNG, Clara Kimball (1890-1960)
Anne Boleyn
Beau Brummel
Better Wife
Camille
Cardinal Wolsey
Charge It
Cheating Cheaters
Claw, The
Common Law, The

Deep Purple, The
Easiest Way, The
Eyes of Youth
Fates and Flora Fourflush, The
  (The Ten Billion Dollar Vitagraph
  Mystery Serial) (serial)
Feast of Life
Foolish Virgin, The
Good Gracious! or Movies as
  They Shouldn't Be
Hamlet
Happy-Go-Lucky (debut)
Heart of the Blueridge
Hearts in Exile
La Rubia
Little Minister, The
Lola
Love's Sunset
Magda
Marionettes, The
My Official Wife
Reason Why, The
Rise of Susan
Road through the Dark
Savage Woman, The
She Paid the Price
Shirley Kane
Trilby
Violin of Monsieur, The
Women Go on the Warpath
Yellow Passport

2812
YOUNG, James*
Anne Boleyn
As You Like It
Beau Brummel
Little Minister, The
Violin of Monsieur, The
World player 1915
Stage:
Winter's Tale, The 1904

2813
YOUNG, Loretta (Gretchen Young)
  (1913-)
Only Way, The

2814
YOUNG, Tammany (-1935)
Amazons, The
Checkers
Great Secret, The (serial)
Intolerance (a soldier)
Racing Strain, The
Regular Girl, A
Service Star, The
Woman on the Index, The

2815
YVONNE, Mimi*
Littlest Rebel, The

- Z -

2816
ZABELLE, Flora*
Red Widow, The
Village Scandal, A
Stage:
Kiss Waltz, The 1911
Man Who Owns Broadway, The
  1909
Yankee Consul, The 1904
Yankee Tourist, The 1907

2817
THE KEYSTONE KOPS
Arbuckle, Roscoe "Fatty"
Avery, Charles
Bletcher, Billy
Cavender, Glenn
Chase, Charley
Cline, Eddie
Clyde, Andy
Colvig, Pinto
Conklin, Chester
Conklin, Heinie
Dant, Vernon
Dillon, George
Dunn, Bobby
Finlayson, James
Gilbert, Billy
Gray, George
Gribbon, Eddie
Gribbon, Harry
Hauber, Billy
Henderson, Del
Hunt, Rea M.
Jamison, Bud
Jesky, George
Keaton, Buster
Kennedy, Edgar
Kennedy, Tom
Lebeck, George "Fats"
Ligen, Grover G.
McCoy, Horace
Mann, Hank
Miller, Rube
Moran, Kewpie
Murphy, Joe J.
Murray, Charlie
Pasha, Kalla
Pickett, Ingram
Potel, Victor

Riley, Mack
Ruggles, Wesley
St. John, Al
Sterling, Ford
Summerville, Slim
Sutherland, Eddie
Thompson, Al
Turpin, Ben
Vernon, Bobby

2818
MACK SENNETT BATHING
BEAUTIES
Anderson, Claire Amthes
Banvard, Fifi
Bird, Violet
Crosthwaite, Ivy (Rice Barrett)
Eilers, Sally
Evans, Cecile
Faye, Julia
Fazenda, Louise
Fox, Virginia
Fuller, Dale
Hammond, Harriet
Hansen, Phyllis
Hurlock, Madeline
Kingston, Natalie
Lentz, Irene
Logan, Jacqueline
Lombard, Carole (Jane Peters)
Lynn, Evelyn
Miller, Lucille
Prevost, Marie
Steadman, Vera
Swanson, Gloria [Although she ap-
    peared in Sennett films, and
    posed with the Bathing Beauties,
    Miss Swanson claims she was
    never actually a Sennett Bathing
    Beauty]
Thurman, Mary

A NOTE ON THE INDEX

Holland Brothers' Kinetoscope Parlor, 1155 Broadway, New York City held the first public showing of a motion picture on April 14, 1894. The first eighteen years of film making saw more than 10,000 pictures produced. This index covers not only films referred to in the first section, but many other titles released during this period for which no credits could be unearthed. Research of "The Formidable Years" discovered numerous deficiencies in titles such as article omissions, inconsistencies of articles, and word and name misspellings and/or omissions.

Dates following titles refer to either release or production dates. A great many inconsistencies also exist in this area of reference. Wherever reliable, release date is given in preference to that of production. Films bearing identical titles are listed according to date. Following the date is the production and/or releasing company. Numbers after the company refer to players in the first section, enabling the researcher to locate players in a specific film. In as many instances as possible, complete casts may be determined. It must be remembered that in these early years players' names were not given, as film makers felt the identification of artists to be unimportant. Later, many times only stars' names were given. Where obtainable, chapter titles of serials are listed under the title.

To use this index, simply look up the film title, then refer to the numbers for cast list:

Romance of the Redwoods 1917 (Art/Par) 724, 1126, 1201, 1591, 1756, 1970, 2047

Produced by Artcraft Pictures Corporation
Released by Paramount Pictures Corporation

724--Elliott Dexter	"Black" Brown
1126--Winter Hall	John Lawrence
1201--Raymond Hatton	Dick Rowland
1591--Walter Long	the Sheriff

1756--Tully Marshall	Sam Sparks
1970--Charles Ogle	Jim Lyn
2047--Mary Pickford	Jenny Lawrence

This volume covers the period of 1893-1919. It may be that some of the films listed were produced in 1919, but not released until 1920; however, the date used is the one this author found most reliable. Therefore, should you not find a film you feel, or know, was produced in 1919, check Volume II. British and other foreign players and films are included either because of their importance to the industry or because the player later became an American artist.

It is understandably impossible to list every film made from 1893-1919. The author will appreciate corrections and/or additions for a revised edition. Write care of publisher.

ABBREVIATIONS OF

PRODUCTION AND RELEASING COMPANIES

Am	American Film Mfg. Co.
AMB	American Mutoscope & Biograph
Art	Artcraft
B&C	British & Colonial Kinematograph
Bio	Biograph Company
Bo	Bosworth
Br	British--company unknown
Bw	Broadwest
CFC	Capital Film Co.
Ed	Edison
Es	Essanay Film Mfg. Co.
F	Fox Film Co.
FA	Fine Arts
FdA	Film d'Art
FN	First National
FP	Famous Players
GB	Gaumont British (Also Gaumont)
Go	Goldwyn
Hep	Hepworth
K	Kleine
Kal	Kalem
Key	Keystone
Las	Lasky
LFC	London Film Co.
L-KO	Lehrman-Knock Out
M	Metro
Mu	Mutual
P	Pathé
Pal	Pallas
Par	Paramount
SB	Svenske-Biograph
Sel	Selznick
T	Thanhouser
Tri	Triangle
UA	United Artists
Un	Universal
UP	United Pictures
V	Vitagraph
W	World
WB	Warner Brothers (Also Warner)
WS	World-Selznick

INDEX

- A -

A la Cabaret 1916 (Tri/Key) 179, 371,
    396, 509, 878, 2020, 2206
Abductors, The 1905 (AMB)
Abe Gets Even with Father 1911 (Bio)
    2465
Absent-Minded Cupid, An 1909 (Ed)
Absentees, The 1914 ( ) 809
Absinthe 1913 (Imp) 108, 111
Acadian Elopement, An 1907 (AMB)
Accidental Honeymoon, An 1918 ( ) 1139,
    2698
Accidents Will Happen 1903 (AMB)
Accidents Will Happen 1910 (Ed)
Accommodating Cow, The 1902 (AMB)
Accomplished Mrs. Thompson, The 1914
    (V) 908, 1876, 2663
Accusing Evidence 1916 (Un) 352, 449
Ace High 1918 (F) 557, 1849
Ace of Hearts 1915 ( ) 2096
Ace of the Saddle 1919 (Un) 398
Acquitted 1916 (Tri) 27, 1602, 1613
Acrobatic Burglars, The 1906 (V)
Acrobatic Monkey 1898 (Ed)
Acrobatic Pills 1908 (Lubin)
Across the Atlantic 1914 ( ) 108
Across the Line * ( ) 1509
Across the Mexican Line 1914 ( ) 2112
Across the Plains 1911 (Es) 50, 1058,
    1913
Across the Wires 1915 (Br) 150
Active Life of Dolly of the Dailies, The--
    serial 1914 (Ed) 159, 257, 479, 968,
    1312, 1923, 1970, 2733
    1. The Perfect Truth
    2. The Ghost of Mother Eve
    3. An Affair of Dress
    4. Putting One Over
    5. The Chinese Fan
    6. On the Heights
    7. The End of the Umbrella
    8. A Tight Squeeze
    9. A Terror of the Night
    10. Dolly Plays Detective
    11. Dolly at the Helm
    12. The Last Assignment
Actor Annoys the Boarders, The 1907
    (Lubin)
Actor's Children, The 1910 (T) 2178
Adam Bede 1918 (Br) 43, 503, 834, 1592
Adele 1919 ( ) 1048
Admirable Crichton, The 1918 (GB) 1127,
    2017

Admiral Cigarette 1897 (Ed)
Adopted Brother 1913 (Bio) 1028, 1182,
    1714, 1832
Adopted Son, The 1918 (M) 156, 353
Adoption, The 1910 (Ed)
Adrienne Lecouvreur 1913 ( ) 212, 2541
Adrift 1912 (Un)
Adrift on Life's Tide 1913 (Hep) 2531
Adventure in Hearts 1919 (Go) 443
Adventure in the Autumn Woods, An 1912
    (Bio) 141, 398, 1714, 1751, 1832
Adventure Shop 1919 (V) 1088
Adventurer, The 1917 (Mu) 97, 175, 204,
    384, 451, 517, 2077, 2499, 2611
Adventures d'une Bout de Papier--cartoon
    1911 (French) 512
Adventures of a Baby, The 1911 (Ed)
Adventures of a Drummer Boy 1909 (V)
Adventures of an Old Flirt 1909 (Ed)
Adventures of Billy, The 1911 (Bio) 944
Adventures of Carol, The 1918 ( ) 853,
    1550
Adventures of Dick Dolan, The 1917 (Br)
    503, 1018, 1289
Adventures of Dollie, The--serial (AMB)
    23, 79, 995, 1089, 1336, 1363
Adventures of Fifine, The 1909 (V)
Adventures of François Villon, The 1914
    (101-Bison/Univ) 352, 449, 585
Adventures of Jacques, The 1913 ( )
    1431
Adventures of Kathlyn, The--serial 1913
    (Selig) 413, 485, 504, 513, 1687,
    2221, 2599, 2770
    1. The Unwelcome Throne
    2. The Two Ordeals
    3. In the Temple of the Lion
    4. The Royal Slave
    5. A Colonel in Chains
    6. Three Bags of Silver
    7. The Garden of Brides
    8. The Cruel Crown
    9. The Spellbound Multitude
    10. The Warrior Maid
    11. The Forged Parchment
    12. The King's Will
    13. The Court of Death
Adventures of Marguerite, The see Ven-
    tures of Marguerite
Adventures of Mr. Troubles 1908 (Lubin)
Adventures of Peg o' the Ring, The--
    serial 1916 (Un) 610, 885, 926, 1000,
    1199, 1899, 1952, 2056, 2486
    1. The Leopard's Mark
    2. A Strange Inheritance

*Asterisk indicates date is unknown.

3. In the Lion's Den
4. The Circus Mongrels
5. The House of Mystery
6. The Cry for Help or Cry of
the Ring
7. The Wreck
8. Outwitted
9. The Leap
10. In the Hands of the Enemy
11. The Stampede
12. On the High Seas
13. The Clown Act
14. The Will
15. Retribution
Adventures of Ruth, The--serial 1919 (P)
188, 427, 699, 1315, 1244, 1579, 2169
1. The Wrong Countess
2. The Celestial Maiden
3. The Bewitching Spy
4. The Stolen Picture
5. The Bank Robbery
6. The Border Fury
7. The Substitute Messenger
8. The Harem Model
9. The Cellar Gangsters
10. The Forged Check
11. The Trap
12. The Vault of Terror
13. The Fighting Chance
14. [Unknown]
15. The Key to Victory
Adventures of Sherlock Holmes; or Held
for Ransom 1905 (V)
Adventures of Sherlock Holmes, The--
series 1915 (Br) 1945
Adventures of Terrence O'Rourke 1915
(Un) 1431, 2032
Adventures of the Last Cigarette, The
1916 ( ) 2613
Adventures of Wallingford, The--serial
1915 (P) 897, 1679, 2151
Adventuress, An 1914 ( ) 832
Aerial Joyride, An 1916 (Vim) 1161
Affair of Hearts, An 1910 (Bio)
Affair of Honor, An 1902 (AMB)
Affair of Honor, An 1901 (Lubin)
Affair of Three Nations, An 1915 ( )
1564
Affinities 1915 ( ) 377
After Five Years 1915 ( ) 1208
After His Own Heart 1919 ( ) 1134
After Launching 1898 (Ed)
After Many Years 1908 (AMB) 1336, 1363
After Many Years 1912 (Imp)
After the Bachelors' Ball 1909 (Lubin)
After the Ball 1911 (Bio)
After the Ball 1914 (Photo Drama) 1405,
2374
After the Explosion 1904 (AMB)
After the First Snow 1903 (AMB)
After the War 1919 ( ) 610
After Twenty Years 1915 ( ) 2002
Agitator, The 1912 ( ) 351, 1431
Agonies of Agnes, The 1918 (Go) 765
Aida 1911 (Ed) 968, 1656, 1930
Airy Fairy Lillian Tries on Her New
Corsets 1905 (AMB)
Alabaster Box, An 1917 (V) 1388, 1656
Aladdin 1917 ( ) 2570

Aladdin and His Wonderful Lamp 1917
(F) 557, 1816, 1817, 2000, 2082
Aladdin from Broadway 1917 (V) 785,
1876, 2487
Aladdin Up-to-Date 1912 (Ed)
Alladin's Other Lamp 1917 (M) 631
Alarcosbal 1917 ( ) 1614
Alarm, The 1914 (Key) 65, 1941, 2368
Alas and Alack 1915 (Rex/Un) 449, 1711,
2398
Algy on the Force 1913 (Key) 1666
Algy the Watchman 1912 (Bio)
Algy's Glorious Fourth of July 1902 (AMB)
Ali Baba and the Forty Thieves 1918 (F)
1817
Alias Jimmy Valentine 1918 ( ) 1246
Alias Ladyfingers 1918 (Par) 454
Alias Mary Brown 1918 ( ) 887, 2453
Alias Mike Moran 1919 (Par) 454, 1580,
1970, 2112
Alice's Adventures in Wonderland 1910 (Ed)
Alien, The 1915 (Ince) 160
Alien Enemy, An 1918 ( ) 1032
Alien Souls 1916 (Las) 60, 947, 1208
Alimony 1917 (FN) 2616, 2779
Alkali Ike in Joyville 1913 (Es) 50
Alkali Ike Plays the Devil 1912 (Es) 50
Alkali Ike Stung! 1912 (Es) 50
Alkali Ike's Auto 1913 (Es) 50
Alkali Ike's Boarding House 1912 (Es) 50
Alkali Ike's Close Shave 1912 (Es) 50
Alkali Ike's Homecoming 1913 (Es) 50
Alkali Ike's Misfortune 1913 (Es) 50
Alkali Ike's Motorcycle 1912 (Es) 50, 408,
1384
Alkali Ike's Pants 1912 (Es) 50
All a Mistake 1912 (Imp)
All Aboard 1917 (P) 635, 1586, 2055
All at Sea 1919 (P) 635
All Dressed Up 1915 (Christie) 525
All for a Girl 1916 (Vim) 1161
All for a Husband 1918 (F) 2024
All for Her 1912 (Imp)
All for Peggy 1915 (Rex/Un) 352, 449,
762
All for the Love of a Lady 1911 (Ed)
All Love Excelling 1914 ( ) 2760
All Man 1918 ( ) 243, 1877
All Night /aka/ Marriage Virgin, The
1918 (Un) 1911, 2570, 2616
All of a Sudden Norman 1919 ( ) 134
All on Account of a Butterfly 1908 (Lubin)
All on Account of a Laundry 1910 (Ed)
All on Account of the Milk 1910 (Bio)
1363, 2045, 2047, 2513
All Over a Stocking 1915 (Christie) 525
All the World to Nothing 1918 (Mu) 2201
All Woman 1918 (Go) 153, 1297, 1751
All Wrong 1919 (Par/Art) 1583, 2700
All Wrong 1919 (P) 663
Allabad; the Arabian Wizard 1902 (AMB)
All's Fair in Love 1909 (Ed)
All's Fair in Love and War 1910 (CFC)
All's Well That Ends Well 1910 (P) 1575
Almost a Bigamist 1915 (Christie) 525
Almost a Hero 1910 (Ed)
Almost a Husband 1919 (Go) 274, 1483,
2168, 2441, 2769, 2792
Almost a King 1903 (AMB)

Almost a Man 1913 ( ) 731, 1906
Almost a Scandal 1915 (Christie) 525
Almost a Widow 1915 (Christie) 525
Almost a Wild Man 1913 (Bio) 1028
Almost an Actor 1913 (Joker/Un) 81
Almost an Actress 1913 (Joker/Un) 449,
 691, 878, 1267, 1884
Almost Divorced 1915 (Christie) 525
Almost Married 1919 (M) 41, 1220
Aloha-Oe 1915 (Tri) 1685, 1745
Alone 1904 (AMB)
Alone in London 1915 (GB) 812, 2604
Alone in New York 1912 (Ed)
Alone in the Jungle 1913 (Selig) 857, 2221
Along the Border 1916 (Selig Polyscope)
 1849
Alphonse and Gaston 1903 (AMB)
Altar Chains 1916 (LFC) 2551
Altar of Love 1915 (V) 566
Always Room for One More 1905 (AMB)
Always Tell Your Wife 1914 (Br) 1247
Amarilly of Clothesline Alley 1917 (FP)
 138, 1104, 1432, 2047, 2070, 2349,
 2441, 2701, 2782
Amateur Adventuress 1919 (Un) 2002, 2058
Amateur Champion 1907 (Lubin)
Amateur Hypnotist, The 1908 (Lubin)
Amateur Iceman 1912 (Bio) 1363
Amateur Liar, The 1919 (M) 768, 1707
Amateur Night; or Get the Hook 1907 (V)
Amateur Night 1910 (Ed)
Amateur Orphan 1917 ( ) 1130
Amateur William Tell, The 1909 (Ed)
Amazing Imposter, The 1919 ( ) 1841
Amazing Wife, The 1919 ( ) 1694, 2738
Amazons, The 1917 (Select) 482, 1077,
 1515, 1806, 2814
Ambassador's Envoy, The 1914 ( ) 1208
Ambition 1916 (F) 1394, 2042, 2616
Ambition of the Baron 1915 (Es) 2512
Ambitious Butler, The 1912 (Key) 1666,
 1941, 2368, 2465
Ambitious Ethel 1916 (Vim) 1161
Ambrose and the Lion Hearted 1919 (Tri/
 Key) 2510
Ambrose's Cup of Woe 1916 (Tri/Key)
 840, 1345, 1422, 2510, 2514
Ambrose's Day Off 1919 (Tri/Key) 2510
Ambrose's First Falsehood /aka/ In
 Loving Memory 1914 (Key) 2510
Ambrose's Fury 1915 (Key) 650, 878,
 2510
Ambrose's Little Hatchet 1915 (Key) 118,
 878, 2465, 2510
Ambrose's Lofty Perch 1915 (Key) 118,
 878, 2510
Ambrose's Nasty Temper 1915 (Key) 2510
Ambrose's Rapid Rise 1916 (Tri/Key)
 1424, 1461, 1788, 2510
Ambrose's Sour Grapes 1915 (Key) 531,
 1086, 2510
Ambulance at the Accident 1897 (Ed)
Ambulance Call 1897 (Ed)
American Aristocracy 1916 (FA/Tri) 406,
 857, 2004
American Beauty, The 1916 ( ) 2458
American Beauty comedies 1915 (Mu)
 256, 956
American Buds 1918 (F) 1524

American Citizen, An 1913 (FP) 140, 2595
American Consul, The 1917 (Art/Par) 935
American Heiress, The 1917 (Hep) 1289,
 2171, 2531
American Live Wire, An 1918 (V) 2767
American Marriage, An 1911 (P) 1575
American Methods 1917 (F) 868, 2638
American Millionaire Perishes on the
 Lusitania 1915 (Russian) 2214
American Princess, An 1913 (Kal) 1388,
 1867
American Soldier in Love and War, The
 1903 (AMB)
American Widow, An 1917 (M) 139, 606,
 741, 1204
Americanism 1919 ( ) 437
Americano, The 1916 (FA/Tri) 25, 664,
 857, 1490, 2194, 2467, 2480, 2782
Ameta 1903 (AMB)
Amorous Militiman, The 1904 (AMB)
And a Little Child Shall Lead Them 1908
 (Lubin)
And a Little Child Shall Lead Them 1909
 (AMB)
And a Still Small Voice 1919 ( ) 2680
And His Coat Came Back 1909 (V)
And His Wife Came Back 1913 (V) 332,
 901
And Pat Took Him at His Word 1904 (AMB)
And the Children Pay 1919 ( ) 1310
And the Dog Came Back 1907 (Lubin)
And the Law Says 1915 ( ) 193
And the Villain Still Pursued Her; or The
 Author's Dream 1906 (V)
Andy series 1914 (Ed) 478, 2654
Angel and the Stranded Troupe, The 1912
 (Ed)
Angel Child, The 1908 (Ed)
Angel Factory, The 1917 (V) 443, 1876
Angel of Contention 1914 ( ) 1029, 2356
Angel of Mons, The 1915 (Br) 1329, 2558
Angel of the Slums, The 1911 ( ) 2748
Angel of the Studio 1910 (V) 1511, 2604
Angelic Servant, An 1907 (Melies)
Anglers, The 1914 (Key) 1906
Angler's Nightmare 1905 (Melies)
Animal, The 1913 ( ) 2112
Animated Costumes, The 1904 (Melies)
Animated Dummy, An 1900 (Lubin)
Animated Luncheon, An 1900 (Ed)
Animated Painting 1904 (Ed)
Animated Picture Studio 1903 (AMB)
Animated Poster, The 1903 (Ed)
Animated Snowballs 1908 (Ed)
Anna Held 1901 (AMB)
Anna, the Adventuress 1919 (Bw) 522
Annabelle in Flag Dance 1896 (AMB)
Annabelle's Butterfly Dance 1897 (Ed)
 2751
Anne Boleyn 1912 (V) 2811, 2812
Anne Boleyn 1913 (Eclipse) 575, 682
Anne of Green Gables 1919 (Realart) 347,
 1105, 1174, 1243, 1415, 1841
Annexing Bill 1918 ( ) 1312
Annie for Spite 1918 ( ) 1841
Annie Laurie 1916 (Hep) 2171, 2531
Ann's Finish 1918 ( ) 905
Another Chance 1914 ( ) 2112
Another Glance 1914 ( ) 27

Another Job for the Undertaker 1901 (Ed)

Another Man's Wife 1915 (Br) 2138

Another Name Was Maude 1906 (AMB)

Another Story with a New Ending 1910
(Bio) 1182

Anselo Lee 1915 (V) 468, 1119, 1876

Answer, The 1918 (Tri) 2194

Answering the Call 1914 (Br) 150

Anthony and Cleopatra 1908 (V) 453, 1333

Anthony and Cleopatra 1913 (K) 735

Antics of Ann, The 1917 (Art/Par) 1205,
2028

Anything Once 1917 (Un) 449, 686, 771,
867, 1513

Apache Father's Revenge, An * (101-Bison)
2103

Apartment Wanted 1917 ( ) 1872

Apostle of Vengeance, The 1917 ( ) 1016,
1188

Apparition, The 1903 (Melies)

Appearance of Evil 1919 ( ) 835

Apple Tree Girl, The 1917 (Ed) 1774

April Fool 1911 (Ed)

April Fool Joke, An 1903 (AMB)

Aquarium 1897 (American Mutoscope)

Arab, The 1915 (Par) 306, 411, 505, 677,
828, 1201, 1377, 2149, 2156, 2365

Arabella 1916 ( ) 1922

Arabian Gun Twirler 1899 (Ed)

Arbitrator, The 1904 (AMB)

Arcadian Maid, An 1910 (Bio) 2047, 2368

Archibald Chubbs and the Widow 1912 (Ed)

Are Crooks Dishonest? 1918 (P) 1586

Are Waitresses Safe? 1917 (Key/Tri)
2501, 2608

Are You a Mason? 1913 (FP) 140

Are You Legally Married? 1919 ( ) 2554

Are You the Man? 1909 (Lubin)

Argyle Case, The 1917 ( ) 27, 1139,
2698

Arizona 1918 (Art/Par) 387, 664, 693,
857, 1201, 1448, 1756, 2070, 2149

Arizona Wooing, An 1915 (Selig Polyscope)
1849

Arms and the Girl 1917 (Art/Par) 333,
1800

Arms and the Gringo 1914 ( ) 1028,
1416, 2112

Arms and the Woman 1910 (Ed)

Arms and the Woman 1916 ( ) 435, 1163

Army of Two, The 1908 (Ed)

'Arriet's Baby 1913 (V) 2523

Arsene Lupin 1916 (Br) 43, 943

Arsene Lupin 1917 (V) 223, 2378, 2549,
2767

Art of Diving, The 1916 ( ) 1411

Artful Kate 1910 (Imp) 2047

Artist, The 1918 (King-Bee) 539, 1161

Artist and the Brain Specialist, The 1912
(Ed)

Aftistic Atmosphere 1916 (Vim) 1161

Artists and Models 1915 (Lubin) 1161

Artist's Dilemma, The 1901 (Ed)

Artist's Dream, The 1898 (Melies) 1802

Artist's Dream, The 1900 (Ed)

Artist's Dream, The 1903 (AMB)

Artist's Joke, The 1912 (Ed)

Artist's Madonna, The 1913 (V) 1335,
2663, 2767

Artist's Model Wanted, An 1908 (Lubin)

Artist's Point 1903 (AMB)

Artist's Revenge, The 1909 (V)

Aryan, The 1916 (Tri) 189, 1032, 1188,
1602

As a Man Thinks 1919 ( ) 111, 2130

As He Was Born 1919 (Br) 1968

As in a Looking Glass 1903 (AMB)

As in a Looking Glass 1911 (Bio) 1613,
1665

As in a Looking Glass 1916 (W) 1048,
1163

As It Is in Life 1910 (Bio) 315, 816, 1542,
1933

As Luck Would Have It 1915 (Christie) 525

As Others See Us 1917 (M) 768, 1707

As Seen on the Curtain 1904 (AMB)

As the Bells Rang Out 1910 (Bio) 731,
1533, 1593, 1933, 2728

As the Sun Went Down 1915 (Hep) 2171,
2744

As the Sun Went Down 1919 (M) 1565,
2051, 2487

As Ye Repent 1915 (GB) 2604

As Ye Sow 1918 ( ) 273, 1255, 1697

As You Like It 1912 (V) 508, 566, 695,
818, 974, 1877, 1888, 2070, 2527,
2554, 2812

Ashes 1910 (Ed)

Ashes 1913 ( ) 606, 2554

Ashes of Desire 1919 ( ) 60

Ashes of Embers 1916 (Par) 947, 957,
1600

Ashes of Hope 1918 ( ) 186

Ashes of the Past 1914 (Mu) 2513

Ask Father 1919 (P) 1586

Assassination of the Duc de Guise 1908 (FdA)
1478, 2144

Astor Tramp, The 1899 (Ed)

Astray from Steerage 1918 ( ) 878

At a Premium 1916 (M) 768, 1707

At a Quarter of Two 1911 (Imp) 2047

At Bay 1915 ( ) 1357

At Coney Island /aka/ Cohen at Coney
Island 1912 (Key) 1941, 2368, 2465

At Cripple Creek 1912 ( ) 2112

At Dawn 1914 ( ) 2112, 2356

At First Sight 1917 ( ) 1907

At It Again 1912 (Key) 2465

At It Again see Caught in the Rain 1914
(Key)

At Jones' Ferry 1911 (Ed)

At Scrogginses' Corner 1912 (V) 332, 565

At the Altar 1909 (AMB) 315, 994, 1363,
1450, 1511, 1542, 1714, 2212, 2368

At the Barn 1919 ( ) 2232

At the Cottage Door 1904 (AMB)

At the Count of Ten 1916 (M) 768, 1707

At the Crossroads of Life 1908 (Bio) 960,
1089, 1542

At the Dentist 1909 (Lubin)

At the Dressmaker's 1903 (AMB)

At the Duke's Command 1911 (Imp) 2047

At the End of a Perfect Day 1915 (Es)
2512, 2700

At the Foot of the Flatiron 1903 (AMB)

At the Foot of the Scaffold 1913 (Hep)
2744

At the Fountain 1902 (AMB)

At the French Ball 1908 (AMB)
At the Hotel Mix-Up 1908 (Melies)
At the Hour of Three 1912 (Br) 177
At the Mercy of Man 1918 ( ) 273, 1878
At the Point of the Sword 1912 (Ed)
At the San Diego Exposition 1915 (Key)
    65, 1941
At the Stage Door; or Bridget's Romance
    1908 (V)
At the Stage Door 1919 (P) 1586
At the Threshold of Life 1911 (Ed)
At the Torrent's Mercy 1915 (Br) 1873
At Twelve o'Clock 1913 (Key) 1666, 1941,
    2368
Athletic Girl and the Burglar, The 1905
    (AMB)
Atlantic City Bathers 1896 (American
    Mutoscope)
Atom, The 1918 (Tri) 186, 1818, 2453
Atta Boy's Last Race 1916 ( ) 1028,
    2480, 2782
Attack on the Mill, The 1910 (Ed)
Attempt to Escape That Led to Misfortune
    1903 (AMB)
Au Clair de la Lune 1904 (Melies)
Auction Block, The 1917 (Go) 552, 709,
    2066
Auction Mart, The 1915 ( ) 1649
Auction of Souls 1919 (FN) 218, 1740
Audrey 1916 (FP) 470, 957
Auld Lang Syne 1917 (Br) 324
Auld Robin Gray 1917 (Br) 349
Auld Robin Grey 1910 (V) 2604
Aunt Bill 1916 (Vim) 1161
Aunt Emmy's Scrap Book 1908 (Lubin)
Aunt Jane and the Tobasco Sauce 1902
    (AMB)
Aunt Jane's Experience with Tobasco
    Sauce 1903 (AMB)
Aunt Miranda's Cat 1912 (Ed)
Aunt Sallie's Wonderful Bustle 1901 (Ed)
Auntie Takes the Children to the Country
    1908 (Lubin)
Auntie's Portrait 1914 ( ) 768, 1707
Aunty's Romance 1912 (V) 566, 1877,
    2604
Auto Heroine, An; or The Race for the
    Vitagraph Cup and How It Was Won
    1908 (V)
Auto Maniac, The 1909 (V)
Autocrat of Flapjack Junction, The 1913
    (V) 332, 901
Automobile Chase, An 1905 (Melies)
    1. In the Mountains
    2. The Town--Due at Dijon
    3. The Garage
    4. In the Country
    5. Monte Carlo
Automobile Thieves, The 1906 (V)
Automobiling among the Clouds 1904 (AMB)
Availing Prayer, The 1914 ( ) 1028,
    2672
Avalanche, The 1919 (Art/Par) 845, 893,
    888, 1163, 1971, 2063, 2176, 2566
Ave Maria 1919 (Par) 2444
Avenged; or The Two Sisters 1908 (V)
Avenging a Crime; or Burned at the Stake
    1904 (Paley & Steiner)
Avenging Bill 1915 (Lubin) 1161

Avenging Conscience 1914 (Mu) 25, 1563,
    1751, 2356, 2408, 2513, 2680
Avenging Hand, The 1915 (Br) 177
Avenging Trail, The 1918 (M) 1589, 2141
Aviator and the Journalist's Wife, The
    1911 (Ingvald C. Oes)
Aviator's Generosity, The 1912 (Ingvald
    C. Oes)
Awakening, The 1909 (Bio) 271, 1363,
    2047, 2368
Awakening, The 1915 (V) 1004, 1603,
    2472, 2767
Awakening of John Bond, The 1911 (Ed)
Awakening of Helen Minor 1917 (M) 768,
    1707
Awakening of Helena Ritchie 1917 (M) 139
Awakening of Jones, The 1912 (V) 332,
    901
Awakening of Mr. Coon, The 1909 (Lubin)
Awakening of Rip, The 1897 (American
    Mutoscope)
Awakening of Rip, The 1902 (AMB)
Awakening of Ruth, The 1917 (Ed) 1774
Away Out West 1910 (Es) 50
Awful Moment, An 1908 (AMB) 79, 209,
    315, 1511, 1542, 2368
Awful Romance, An 1916 (P) 1586
Awful Skate, An 1907 (Es) 50
Awkward Man, The; or Oh! So Clumsy
    1907 (V)
Awkward Waiter, The; or Waiter: Waiter
    Waiting 1904 (AMB)
Az Elet Koralya 1917 ( ) 1614
Az Ezredes 1917 ( ) 1614
Aztec God, The 1916 ( ) 1745

                    - B -

Bab, the Fixer 1917 (Par) 2227
Babbling Tongues 1917 ( ) 1346, 1888,
    2614
Babes and Boobs 1918 (V) 2367
Babes in the Wood 1903 (Lubin)
Babes in the Woods 1918 (F) 557
Babe's School Days 1915 (Lubin) 1161
Babies Welcome 1918 ( ) 720
Bab's Burglar 1917 (Par) 143, 482
Bab's Diary 1917 (Par) 143, 482
Bab's Matinee Idol 1917 (Par) 482
Bab's series 1917 (Par) 1600
Baby, The 1903 (AMB)
Baby, The 1912 (Ed)
Baby, The 1914 (Victor/Un) 1161, 1912,
    2554
Baby and the Stork, The 1912 (Bio) 944
Baby Day 1913 (Key) 1941, 2465
Baby Devil, The 1918 (M) 631
Baby Doll 1916 (Vim) 1161
Baby Mine 1917 (Go) 13, 604, 1423, 2878
Baby of the Boarding House, The 1911 (Ed)
Baby on the Barge, The 1915 (Hep) 1289,
    2171, 2531
Baby Pulls the String 1917 (P) 1988
Baby's Breakfast 1895 (Lumiere) 1617
Baby's Diplomacy 1917 (P) 1988
Baby's Ride 1914 ( ) 2112
Baby's Shoe, A 1909 (AMB) 1865
Baby's Tooth 1902 (AMB)

Bachelor Buttons 1912 (V) 332, 1350
Bachelor's Baby, A; or A General Mis-
understanding 1908 (V)
Bachelor's Children 1918 ( ) 1877
Bachelor's Love Story, A 1914 (Br) 22,
812
Bachelor's Supper, A 1909 (Ed)
Bachelor's Waterloo, The 1912 (Ed)
Bachelor's Wedding Bells 1908 (Lubin)
Bachelor's Wife, The 1919 ( ) 938, 1841
Back of the Man 1917 (Tri) 627, 2096,
2392
Back Stage 1917 (King-Bee) 1161, 2733
Back Stage 1919 (FP/Las) 65, 1476, 2208
Back to Broadway 1914 ( ) 2472
Back to God's Country 1919 (FN) 1450,
1474, 2052, 2397
Back to His Own Home Town 1912
(Independent Motion Picture Co.)
Back to Life 1913 (Victor/Un) 352, 449,
2630, 2803
Back to Nature 1918 ( ) 961
Back to Nature Girls 1914 (Key) 531
Back to the Farm 1914 (Lubin) 1161
Back to the Kitchen 1918 (Key) 878, 1028
Back to the Prairie * (P) 9, 2103
Back to the Primitive 1911 (Selig Poly-
scope) 485, 1849, 2770
Back to the Soil 1911 (Imp) 2047
Back to the Woods 1919 (P) 961, 1297,
1586, 1941, 2095
Back Yard Theater, A 1914 (Key) 1345,
1434
Backward, Turn Backward O Time, in
Your Flight 1909 (Ed)
Bad Boy, The 1917 (FA/Tri) 1175, 1177,
1182, 1859
Bad Boy and the Grocery Man 1905 (AMB)
Bad Boy's Joke on the Nurse 1901 (Ed)
Bad Boy's Joke on the Nurse 1904 (Ed)
Bad Game, A 1913 (Key) 2465
Bad (K)night, A 1902 (AMB)
Bad Luck of Santa Ynez, The 1915 ( )
1188
Bad Man, The: A Tale of the West 1907
(V)
Bad Man from Riley's Gulch, The 1910
(Ed)
Bad Man's Christmas, The 1910 (Es) 50
Bad Man's Downfall, The 1910 (Es) 50
Badger Game, The 1905 (AMB)
Baffles, Gentleman Burglar 1914 (Key)
2465
Bake That Chicken Pie 1909 (Lubin)
Bakers in Trouble 1907 (Melies)
Balked at the Altar 1908 (AMB) 79, 994,
1363, 2212, 2368
Ball Game, The 1898 (Ed)
Ballet Girl, The 1916 (W) 239, 273, 950,
955
Ballet Master's Dream, The 1903 (Melies)
Balloon Ascension, Marionettes 1898 (Ed)
Ballroom Tragedy, A 1905 (AMB)
Bamboo Slide, The 1904 (AMB)
Bandbox, The 1919 ( ) 1191, 1429
Bandit, A 1913 (Key) 65, 509
Bandit and the Preacher, The see On
the Night Stage
Bandit King, The 1907 (Selig)

Bandits, The; or A Story of Sunny Italy
1907 (V)
Bandit's Wager, The 1916 ( ) 610, 926
Bandit's Waterloo, The 1908 (AMB) 363
Bandit's Wife, The 1910 (Es) 50
Bandmaster, The 1918 (King-Bee) 1161
Bangville Police, The 1913 (Key) 509,
1666, 1941, 2368
Bank, The /aka/ Charlie at the Bank
1915 (Es) 71, 106, 451, 517, 1045,
1336, 1676, 2077, 2090, 2197, 2480,
2682, 2746
Bank Defaulter, The 1906 (Lubin)
Bank Messenger, The 1908 (Lubin)
Bank President's Son, The 1912 (Ed)
Bank Robbery, The 1908 (Oklahoma
Natural Mutoscene Co.)
Banker's Daughters, The 1910 (Bio) 731,
1182, 2000, 2680
Banzi 1918 ( ) 1208
Bar Sinister 1917 (Go) 1562, 1946
Barbara Frietchie 1908 (V)
Barbara Frietchie 1915 (M) 546, 1841,
2348, 2739
Barbarian, The 1909 ( ) 1511
Barbarian, Ingomar, The 1908 (AMB) 79,
1511, 1613, 2212
Barbary Sheep 1917 (Art/Par) 683, 888,
1163
Barber, The 1918 (King-Bee) 1161
Barber of Sevilla 1904 (Melies)
The Entrance to the Church
The Square
The Drawing Room
The Kitchen
Barber's Dee-Light, The 1905 (AMB)
Barber's Pretty Patient, The 1905 (AMB)
Barber's Queer Customer, The 1902 (AMB)
Bare-Fisted Gallagher 1919 (CFC) 715,
1186
Bare Fists 1919 (Un) 398, 1025
Bare-Knuckles Gallagher see Bare-Fisted
Gallagher
Baree, Son of Kazan 1918 ( ) 2397, 2754
Barefoot Boy, The 1914 (Kal) 572, 1867
Bargain, The 1914 (Mu) 1188
Bargain Fiend; or Shopping a la Mode
1907 (V)
Barnaby Rudge 1915 (Hep) 1289, 2171,
2744
Barney Oldfield's Race for a Life 1913
(Key) 1941, 1974, 2368, 2465
Barnstormers, The 1905 (AMB)
Barnyard Flirtations 1914 (Key) 65
Baron Munchausen 1911 (Melies) 1802
Barricade, The 1917 ( ) 2520
Barrier, The 1917 (Go) 1379, 1562, 1946,
2177, 2347, 2412
Barrier of Faith, The 1914 (V) 297, 2523
Baseball at Mudville 1917 (Selig) 1884
Baseball Bill series 1916-17 ( ) 1767
Baseball Bill
Black Nine, The
Box of Tricks
Flirting with Marriage
Strike One!
Baseball Madness 1917 (Victor/Un) 772,
885, 1767
Bashful 1917 (P) 635, 1586, 2055

Bashful Lover, The 1919 ( ) 2595
Basilisk, The 1914 (Hep) 2531, 2744
Bath House Beauty, A 1914 (Key) 65
Bath House Blunder 1916 (Key/Tri) 179,
    351, 1211, 1342, 1568, 1874, 2020
Bath Tub Perils 1916 (Key/Tri) 46, 876,
    966, 1666
Bathing; or Charlie and Mary in the
    Country 1908 (V)
Bathing Beauties and Big Boobs 1918 (V)
    2367
Battle, The 1911 (Bio) 25, 141, 595,
    1182, 2513, 2728
Battle at Elderbush Gulch, The 1914 (Bio)
    315, 1029, 1182, 1223, 1714, 1751,
    1831, 2000, 2513, 2680
Battle Cry of Peach, The 1915 (V) 157,
    1133, 1437, 1469, 1786, 1888, 1915,
    1943, 2129, 2523
Battle for Billions, The 1919 ( ) 2520
Battle for Freedom 1913 ( ) 231
Battle Hymn of the Republic 1911 (V)
    1332
Battle of Ambrose and Walrus, The 1915
    (Key) 210, 531, 2165, 2510
Battle of Gettysownback 1914 (Br) 852
Battle of the Hearts, The 1916 (F) 868,
    1208, 1751
Battle of the Red Men, The 1912 (New
    York Motion Picture Co.)
Battle of the Sexes, The 1914 (Mu) 27,
    595, 1029, 1182, 1865, 2568
Battle of the Weak, The 1914 ( ) 1877
Battle of the Wills, The 1911 (Indepen-
    dent Moving Picture Co.)
Battle of Who Run, The 1913 (Key) 1666,
    1941, 2368, 2465
Battle of Youth 1919 ( ) 28
Battle Royal, A 1916 (Vim) 1161
Battle Royal, The 1918 (Key/Tri) 530,
    2608
Battler, The 1916 (V) 2367
Battler, The 1919 ( ) 1142, 1819
Battling Jane 1918 (Art) 1028, 1065,
    1661, 1933, 2573
Baxter's Brain Storm 1907 (Lubin)
Be a Little Sport 1919 ( ) 856
Be Good 1903 (AMB)
Be My Wife 1919 (P) 1586
Be Neutral 1914 ( ) 926
Be Yourself 1917 ( ) 339
Beachcombers, The 1916 ( ) 2627, 2717
Beached and Bleached 1915 ( ) 2521
Beans 1919 ( ) 2147
Bear Affair, A 1915 (Key) 1666, 2368,
    2465
Bear Hunt, The 1919 ( ) 35
Bear of a Story, A * (Selig Polyscope)
    1849
Bear Trap, The 1918 ( ) 1580
Bearded Bandit, The 1910 (Es) 50
Bearing Her Cross 1917 ( ) 2780
Bears and Bad Men 1918 (V) 1502, 2367
Beast, The 1916 (F) 1622, 2671
Beast at Bay, A 1912 (Bio) 1533, 1714,
    2000, 2047
Beat at His Own Game 1912 (Imp)
Beat It! 1918 (P) 1586
Beating Back 1914 ( ) 1450, 2680

Beating He Needed, The 1912 (Key) 1666,
    2465
Beating the Odds 1919 ( ) 1360, 1877
Beatrice Fairfax--serial 1918 (P) 132, 589,
    643, 660, 946, 1139, 1285, 1303,
    2557, 2578
    1. The Missing Watchman
    2. Adventures of the Jealous
        Wife
    3. Billie's Romance
    4. The Stone God
    5. Momosa San
    6. The Forbidden Room
    7. A Name for the Baby
    8. At the Ainsley Ball
    9. Outside the Law
    10. Play Ball
    11. The Wages of Sin
    12. Curiosity
    13. The Ringer
    14. The Hidden Menace
    15. Wrist Watches
Beau Brummel 1913 (V) 1032, 2811, 2812
Beautiful Adventure, The 1917 (Mu) 1223,
    1902, 2061, 2225
Beautiful Beggar 1918 (Un) 675
Beautiful Jim 1914 (Br) 834, 2138
Beauty and the Barge 1914 ( ) 1784
Beauty and the Beast 1903 (Lubin)
Beauty and the Rogue 1918 ( ) 1841
Beauty Bunglers, The 1915 (Key) 1906
Beauty in Chains 1918 ( ) 1120
Beauty Market, The 1919 (FN) 264, 1448,
    1661
Beauty Proof 1919 ( ) 1877
Beauty's Worth * ( ) 751
Because 1918 (Br) 1879, 2712
Because He Loved Her 1916 (Key/Tri)
    211, 351, 440, 1651
Because of a Woman 1918 ( ) 186
Beckoning Roads 1919 ( ) 134, 1266,
    2719
Bedelia's Bluff 1916 (Tri) 2568
Bedroom Blunder, A 1917 ( ) 1906, 2564
Bedtime for the Bride * (Léar) 1838
Bees in the Bonnet 1918 (P) 1586
Beetle, The 1919 (Barker) 760
Before and after Taking 1918 (M) 768,
    1707
Before and after the Wedding 1907 (P)
    1575
Before Breadfast 1919 (P) 1586
Before the Ball 1906 (Winthrop Press)
Before the White Man Came 1912 ( )
    2112
Beg Pardon 1908 (Lubin)
Beggar of Cawnpore, The 1916 (Tri) 1793,
    2693
Behind Closed Doors 1916 ( ) 1031
Behind the Door 1919 ( ) 258
Behind the Lines 1916 ( ) 1364
Behind the Mask 1917 ( ) 375
Behind the Scenes 1908 (AMB) 1511, 1933
Behind the Scenes 1913 (Br) 177, 204
Behind the Scenes 1914 (FP) 146, 579,
    1450, 2047, 2389, 2701
Behind the Screen 1904 (AMB)
Behind the Screen 1916 (Mu) 97, 106, 384,
    451, 517, 1414, 1840, 2077, 2090,
    2746

Belated Meal, A 1909 (V)

Belgian, The 1917 (V) 2091, 2750

Belgian, The 1917 (W) 1048, 1064

Believe Me 1909 (Lubin)

Believe Me if All Those Endearing
Young Charms 1912 (Ed)

Believe Me, Xantippe 1918 (Par) 165, 595,
1580, 1970, 2112, 2149

Bell Boy, The 1918 (FP/Las) 65, 773,
1401, 1476, 2208, 2522

Bell of Penance, A 1912 (Kal) 231, 1388

Bella Donna 1915 (FP) 957, 1553

Bella Donna 1918 ( ) 1806

Bella's Beau 1912 ( ) 2748

Belle of Bettys-y-Coed 1912 (Br) 1873

Belle of New York, The 1919 (Cosmopolitan) 241, 660, 1027, 1634, 2193

Belle of the Ball, The 1907 (V)

Bellringer's Daughter, The 1910 (Ed)

Bells, The 1913 ( ) 606

Bells, The 1918 (P) 763, 1404, 1558,
2779

Bells of Rheims, The 1914 (Br) 834,
2138

Beloved Adventurer, The--serial 1914
(Lubin) 198, 291, 320, 853, 1106,
1108, 1123, 1363, 1695, 1846
   1. Lord Cecil Intervenes
   2. An Untarnished Shield
   3. An Affair of Honor
   4. An American Heiress
   5. The Girl from the West
   6. The Golden Hope
   7. The Holdup
   8. A Partner to Providence
   9. Lord Cecil Plays a Part
  10. Lord Cecil Keeps His Word
  11. The Serpent Comes to Eden
  12. Fate's Tangled Threads
  13. Through Desperate Hazards
  14. A Perilous Passage
  15. In Port o'Dreams

Beloved Blackmailer, The 1918 ( ) 231

Beloved Cheater, The 1919 ( ) 506, 1448,
1894, 2031

Beloved Imposter, The 1919 ( ) 1547

Beloved Jim, 1917 (Un) 675, 1714

Beloved Liar, The 1915 ( ) 1353

Beloved Rogues 1918 ( ) 415, 2627

Beloved Traitor 1915 (Go) 1751, 1882

Beloved Vampire, The 1917 ( )

Ben Blair 1916 (Pal) 866

Beresford and the Baboons 1919 ( ) 1913

Bertha Claiche 1905 (AMB)

Bertie's Stratagem 1917 (V) 2081, 2521

Best Bet, The 1916 ( ) 1028

Best Man, The 1915 ( ) 1431, 1868,
2754

Best Man Wins 1909 (Es) 50

Best Man Wins, The 1911 (N) 146, 650,
651, 2205, 2733

Best of Enemies, The 1915 (Key/Tri)
187, 351, 531, 895, 1981, 2510, 2514,
2710, 2799

Betrayal of Maggie 1917 (Key/Tri) 878,
1906, 2564

Betrayed 1917 ( ) 242, 554

Betrayed by a Hand Print 1908 (AMB) 1511

Betsy Ross 1917 (W) 265, 273, 1704, 1796

Betsy's Burglar 1917 (Select) 242, 315,
601, 1166, 1570, 2521

Betta, the Gypsy 1918 (Br) 1592

Better Half, The 1918 (M) 273, 1427,
2061

Better Halves 1916 (Vim) 1161

Better Late Than Never /aka/ Getting
Married 1916 (Key/Tri) 179, 351,
519, 1981

Better 'Ole, The 1918 (Br) 1127

Better 'Ole, The 1919 (W) 452, 488, 2162,
2756, 2805

Better Times 1919 (Brentwood) 355, 1370,
2051, 2638

Better Way, The 1909 (Bio) 315, 1450,
1593, 2047, 2368

Better Way, The 1911 (Independent Moving
Picture Co.)

Better Wife 1919 ( ) 28, 132, 606, 2663,
2770, 2811

Better Woman, The 1915 (Equitable) 2610

Betty Be Good 1916 ( ) 2227

Betty in Search of a Thrill * ( ) 1348

Betty in the Lion's Den 1913 (Key) 1941

Betty Makes Up 1918 (Christie) 525

Betty of Grayston 1916 (Tri) 315, 1028,
1173, 1865, 2130

Betty Sets the Pace 1919 ( ) 1991

Betty Takes a Hand 1919 ( ) 2557

Betty to the Rescue 1917 ( ) 2683

Betty's Adventure 1918 (Christie) 525

Betty's Big Idea 1915 (Christie) 525

Betty's Buttons 1911 (Ed)

Betty's Choice 1909 (V)

Betty's Green-Eyed Monster 1919 ( ) 1991

Between Men 1915 (Tri) 1032, 1188, 1745

Between Showers /aka/ Charlie and the
Umbrella; The Flirts; In Wrong 1914
(Key) 384, 451, 498, 531, 2077, 2465

Between the Acts 1919 (V) 2367

Between Two Fires 1911 (Ed)

Beulah Binford's Own Story 1911 (Special
Feature Film Co.)

Beware of Blondes 1918 (Mu) 1483, 2121

Beware of Boarders 1918 ( ) 2465

Beware of Strangers 1918 ( ) 318, 857,
2221

Bewildering Cabinet, The 1907 (Melies)

Bewitched Traveller, The 1904 (AMB)

Beyond the Shadow 1915 ( ) 715

Bid, A 1914 (V) 1047

Biddy 1904 (AMB)

Big Bluffs and Bowling Balls 1917 (V)
2367

Big Bob 1919 ( ) 1472

Big-Hearted Jim 1912 (Un)

Big Hearted Sheriff see His Bitter Pill

Big Idea, The 1918 (P) 1586, 2055

Big James' Heart 1914 (Mu) 25, 27, 1182,
1563, 1751

Big Jim Garrity 1916 (P) 809

Big John Garrity 1916 (Tri) 246

Big Little Person, The 1919 ( ) 1907,
2616

Big Money 1918 (Br) 1453

Big Scoop, The 1910 (Ed)

Big Sister 1916 ( ) 1907

Big Timber 1918 (Art/Par) 715, 2000,
2112, 2770

Big Tremaine 1917 (M) 41, 612, 1589
Bigamist, The 1905 (Paley & Steiner)
Bigamist, The 1916 (Br) 2791
Bigamist's Trial 1905 (AMB)
Biggest Show on Earth 1918 ( ) 189, 2164
Bill Apperson's Boy 1919 (FN) 1933, 2045, 2412
Bill Henry 1919 (Ince) 418, 573, 1248, 2033, 2096, 2147, 2794
Bill, the Bill Poster 1909 (Ed)
Bill, the Bill Poster, and Pete, the Paperhanger 1909 (Ed)
Billet Doux, The * (P) 1575
Billie 1912 (Ed)
Billie's Fortune 1916 ( ) 1583
Billionaire, The 1914 (Bio) 1924
Bill's Birthday Present 1913 ( ) 785
Billy Blazes, Esq. 1919 (P) 1586
Billy Fortune series 1919 (Un) 2058
Billy Seance 1911 (Independent Moving Picture Co.)
Billy Strikes Oil 1917 (Br) 1815
Billy the Bear Tamer 1915 (V) 156, 353, 2081, 2521
Billy the Kid 1911 (Melies) 2487
Billy the Truthful 1917 (Br) 1815
Billy West comedies 1918 (V) 1161
Billy's Burglar 1912 (V) 297
Billy's Spanish Love Spasm 1915 (Br) 1815
Billy's Stormy Courtship 1916 (Br) 1815
Billy's Stratagem 1912 (Bio) 1182, 1613, 1665
Billy's Troubles 1913 (Imp) 2081
Billy's Wager 1915 (V) 2081, 2521
Binks series 1914 (Crystal) 2067
Bird in a Gilded Cage, A 1909 (Ed)
Bird of Prey 1918 ( ) 295, 2405
Bird's a Bird, A 1915 (Key) 531
Birds of a Feather 1917 (P) 2055
Birth of a Nation, The 1915 (Epoch) 25, 27, 200, 242, 497, 554, 595, 601, 686, 717, 758, 958, 993, 1029, 1053, 1083, 1182, 1222, 1526, 1563, 1570, 1591, 1602, 1751, 1756, 1876, 1911, 2002, 2112, 2356, 2408, 2448, 2467, 2521, 2522, 2649, 2672, 2680, 2762, 2782
Birth of Patriotism, The 1917 ( ) 939
Bishop's Emeralds, The 1919 (P) 1564, 2024
Bit of Fluff, A (Key/Tri) 452
Bit of Jade, A 1918 ( ) 1841
Bit of Kindling, A 1917 ( ) 2227
Biting Business, A 1911 (Independent Moving Picture Co.)
Bitter Lesson, A 1908 (Lubin)
Bitter Sweet 1917 ( ) 1120
Bitter Truth, The 1917 (F) 2024
Bittersweet 1912 (Bio) 1714
Black and White; or The Mystery of a Brooklyn Baby Carriage 1905 (V)
Black Arrow, The 1911 (Ed)
Black Beach, The 1918 (Select) 2091
Black Bordered Letter, The 1911 (Ed)
Black Box, The--serial 1915 (Un) 885, 926, 1580, 1585, 1703, 1956, 2095, 2620, 2803, 2804
    1. An Apartment House Mystery

    2. The Hidden Hands
    3. The Pocket Wireless
    4. An Old Grudge
    5. On the Rack
    6. The Unseen Terror
    7. The House of Mystery
    8. The Inherited Sin
    9. Lost in London
    10. The Ship of Horror
    11. A Desert Vengeance
    12. Neath Iron Wheels
    13. Tongues of Flame
    14. A Bolt from the Blue
    15. The Black Box
Black Butterfly, The 1916 (M) 1432, 2037
Black Chancellor, The 1912 (Ingvald C. Oes)
Black Circle 1919 ( ) 656
Black Diamond Express, The 1897 (Ed)
Black-Eyed Susan 1914 (Br) 834, 2138
Black Eyes and Blue 1916 (Key/Tri) 1153, 2588
Black Hand, The 1906 (AMB)
Black Imp, The 1905 (Melies)
Black Is White 1919 (Par) 627
Black Mine, The * ( ) 1767
Black Monk, The 1917 (W) 673
Black Orchids 1917 (Bluebird-Un) 582, 1658, 1711
Black Secret, The--serial 1919 (P) 1653, 1673, 2358, 2748
    1. The Great Secret
    2. Marked for Death
    3. The Gas Chamber
    4. Below the Waterline
    5. The Acid Bath
    6. The Unknown
    7. The Betrayal
    8. A Crippled Hand
    9. Woes of Deceit
    10. Inn of Dread
    11. The Death Studio
    12. The Chance Trail
    13. Wings of Mystery
    14. The Hidden Way
    15. The Secret Host
Black Sheep, The 1909 (Es) 50
Black Sheep, 1912 (Bio) 418, 2728
Black Sheep, The 1919 (Art) 1186
Black Spot, The 1914 (Br) 43
Black Storm, A 1903 (AMB)
Black Viper, The 1908 (AMB)
Blackie's Redemption 1919 ( ) 1460, 1631, 2401
Blacklist 1916 ( ) 1581, 2513
Blackmail 1905 (AMB)
Blackmail 1917 (M) 768, 1707
Blackmailers, The 1917 ( ) 2416
Blacksmith's Daughter, The 1907 (Lubin)
Blank Check, A 1909 (Lubin)
Blarney Stone, The 1913 (V) 332
Blazing Love 1916 (V) 151, 2024
Blazing the Trail 1912 (New York Motion Picture Co.)
Bleak House 1919 (Br) 834
Blessed Is the Peacemaker 1903 (AMB)
Blessing from Above, A 1904 (AMB)
Blind Adventure, The 1918 ( ) 804
Blind Boy, The 1908 (Lubin)

Blind Faith 1914 (Hep) 2531
Blind Fate 1912 (Hep) 1233
Blind Fiddler, The 1915 (Ed) 631
Blind Fools 1918 ( ) 2095
Blind Husbands 1918 (Un) 225, 445, 607,
    686, 911, 1005, 1053, 1265, 1420,
    2034, 2649
Blind Love 1912 (Bio) 2513, 2728
Blind Man's Buff 1904 (AMB)
Blind Man's Eyes 1919 ( ) 468, 473
Blind Man's Luck 1917 (P) 1444
Blind Musician, The 1909 (Lubin)
Blind Princess and the Poet, The 1911
    (Bio) 1468, 2513
Blindfolded 1918 ( ) 134
Blinding Trail, The 1919 ( ) 2211
Blindman's Eyes 1919 ( ) 1631
Blindness of Fortune, The 1917 (Hep)
    1289, 2744
Blindness of Virtue, The 1915 (Es) 1795,
    2700
Blinks and Jinks, Attorneys at Law 1912
    (Ed)
Bliss 1917 (P) 1586, 2055
Blizzard, The 1902 (AMB)
Blood and Bosh 1913 (Hep) 2744
Blood Is Thicker Than Water 1912 (Un)
Blood of His Fathers, The 1917 (Mu) 2760
Blood Stain, The 1912 (Solax) 2081
Blood Tells 1916 (Br) 2152
Blood Will Tell 1914 (Es) 353, 2486
Bloodhound, The 1918 ( ) 2613
Bloodhounds of the North 1913 (Gold Seal/
    Un) 352, 449, 1587, 1705, 1925
Bloodstone, The 1908 (Lubin)
Blossom and the Bee, The--serial 1916
    (P)2748
Blot on the 'Scutcheon, A 1912 (Bio) 95,
    209, 357, 1665, 1714
Blue and the Gray, The; or The Days
    of '61 1908 (Ed)
Blue Bird, The 1918 (Art) 176, 482,
    1649, 1664
Blue Blazes 1918 ( ) 612
Blue Blazes Rawden 1918 (Art) 998, 1188,
    1307
Blue Blood * (Tri) 2194
Blue Blood and Red 1916 ( ) 666, 2018,
    2671
Blue Bonnet 1919 ( ) 2121, 2124, 2738
Blue Envelope, The 1916 (V) 1806, 2663
Blue Eyed Mary 1918 (F) 392
Blue Jeans 1918 (M) 631, 2412
Blue Rose, The 1913 (V) 2523
Blue Streak McCoy * (Un) 398
Bluebeard 1909 (Ed)
Bluff from a Tenderfoot, A 1903 (AMB)
Bluffer, The 1919 (WS) 835, 1991
Blundering Boob, The see New Janitor,
    The
Boarding House Bathroom, The 1905 (AMB)
Boarding House Feud 1917 (V) 2084, 2521
Boarding School Girls 1905 (Ed)
Boarding School Prank, A 1903 (AMB)
Boasts and Baldness 1917 (V) 2367
Bob and Rowdy 1911 (Ed)
Bob Kick, l'Enfant Terrible 1903 (Melies)
Bob Kick, the Mischievous Kid 1903
    (Melies)

Bobbie of the Ballet 1916 (Bluebird/Un)
    170, 449, 1141, 1199, 1518, 1604,
    2696
Bobby, the Coward 1911 (Bio) 1074, 1182,
    1218, 1539
Bobby, the Office Boy * ( ) 751
Bobby's Kodak 1908 (AMB)
Bogus Lord, The 1907 (Lubin)
Bold Bad Knight, A 1915 (Christie) 525,
    1671
Bold Bank Robbery 1904 (Lubin)
Bold Impersonation, A 1915 ( ) 1658,
    2649
Bold Soger Boy, The 1904 (AMB)
Bolshevism of Trial 1916 ( ) 955
Bolshevist Burlesque 1918 ( ) 487
Bombs 1916 (Key/Tri) 250, 878, 1422,
    1906, 2564
Bombs and Blunders 1917 (V) 2367
Bombs and Brides 1917 (Key/Tri) 2564,
    2580
Bond, The 1918 (FN/for Liberty Loan
    Committee) 97, 451, 2077
Bond Between, The 1917 ( ) 2002
Bond Boy, The 1914 ( ) 2595
Bond of Fear 1918 (Tri) 186, 2479
Bondage 1917 (Bluebird/Un) 88, 449,
    1696, 2042, 2490
Bondage of Barbara 1919 (Go) 1297, 1751
Bondage of Fear, The 1917 ( ) 884
Bonds of Honor 1919 (Par) 60, 1208, 2210
Bonds of Love 1919 (Par) 957, 1523, 1550,
    2335
Bondsman, The 1913 ( ) 2096
Bondwoman 1915 ( ) 95
Bonehead, The see His Favorite Pastime
Bonnie Annie Laurie 1919 ( ) 1329
Bonnie, Bonnie Lassie 1919 ( ) 355,
    1694
Booble's Baby 1915 (V) 768
Boodle and Bandits 1918 (V) 2367
Book Agent, The 1917 ( ) 2018, 2671
Book Worm, The 1907 (Selig Polyscope)
Boomerang, A 1903 (AMB)
Boomerang, The 1913 ( ) 473, 1032,
    2096
Boomerang, The 1919 ( ) 680, 2680,
    2753
Bootles' Baby 1910 (Ed)
Bootles' Baby 1914 (Br) 349, 2712
Boots 1919 (Art) 1028, 1498, 2001, 2573
Boots He Couldn't Lose 1909 (Ed)
Border Legion, The 1919 ( ) 148, 258,
    2492
Border Raiders 1918 ( ) 771, 1494
Border Ranger, The 1910 (Es) 50
Border Watch Dogs 1917 ( ) 1010
Border Wireless * (Tri) 1188
Borderland of Civilization 1912 ( ) 1366
Born of the People 1916 ( ) 610
Borrowed Clothes; or Fine Feathers Make
    Fine Birds 1909 (V)
Borrowed Clothes 1919 ( ) 1175
Borrowed Sunshine 1917 (Es) 1636, 2582
Borrowing Girl, The 1904 (AMB)
Borrowing Girl and the Atomizer 1904
    (AMB)
Borrowing Trouble 1916 (M) 768, 1707
Boss, The 1914 (W) 239, 273

Boss of Lumber Camp No. 4, The 1912
    (Ed)
Boss of the Katy Mine, The 1912 (Es)
    50
Boss of the Lazy Y 1917 (Tri) 2355,
    2479
Boston Blackie's Little Pal 1918 ( )
    1631, 2554
Boston Tea Party, The 1908 (Ed)
Bo'sun's Watch, The 1911 (Ed)
Bottle, The 1915 (Hep) 2171, 2531
Bottle Imp, The 1917 (Art/Par) 1208,
    1596, 1925
Bottom of the Well, The 1918 ( ) 102,
    2547
Bought and Paid For 1916 ( ) 273, 1603
Bound and Gagged--serial 1919 (P) 343,
    572, 614 1044, 2104, 2115, 2358,
    2366, 2484
        1. The Wager
        2. Overboard
        3. Help! Help!
        4. An Unwilling Princess
        5. Held for Ransom
        6. Out Again, in Again
        7. The Fatal Error
        8. Arrested
        9. A Harmless Princess
       10. Hopley Takes the Liberty
Bound in Morocco 1918 (Art/Par) 387,
    454, 617, 664, 857, 1756
Bound on the Wheel 1915 (Rex/Un) 449,
    2398, 2570, 2776
Boundary House 1919 (Hep) 43, 2531
Bowery Kiss, The 1902 (AMB)
Bowery Waltz 1897 (Ed)
Bowling Match, The 1913 (Key) 1941,
    2465
Box of Tricks * ( ) 1767
Boxing Match on Skates 1912 (P) 1575
Boy and the Girl, The 1912 (Ed)
Boy Detective, The 1908 (AMB) 1182
Boy-Girl, The 1917 ( ) 1445
Boy in the Barrel 1903 (AMB)
Boy, the Bust and the Bath, The 1907
    (V)
Boy under the Table, The 1904 (AMB)
Boycotted Baby 1917 (Vim) 1161
Boyhood Dreams 1909 (Ed)
Boy's Best Friend, A 1911 (Independent
    Moving Picture Co.)
Boys Help Themselves to Foxy Grandpa's
    Cigars 1902 (AMB)
Boys of the Old Brigade 1916 (Br) 150
Boys, Still Determined, Try It again on
    Foxy Grandpa, with the Same Result,
    The 1902 (AMB)
Boys Think They Have One on Foxy
    Grandpa, but He Fools Them, The
    1902 (AMB)
Boys Try to Put One up on Foxy Grand-
    pa, The 1902 (AMB)
Boys Will be Boys 1909 (Lubin)
Boys Will be Boys--Hat Trick 1897
    (American Mutoscope)
Brace Up 1918 ( ) 2095
Bradford's Claim 1910 (Ed)
Braga's Double 1915 ( ) 1564
Braggart, The; or What He Said He

Would Do and What He Really Did,
    The 1908 (V)
Brahma Diamond, The 1909 (AMB) 731,
    1511
Brain-Serum 1909 (Lubin)
Bramble Bush, The 1919 ( ) 1088
Brand, The 1914 (Kal) 1270, 1388, 1867,
    2182
Brand, The 1919 (Go) 1337, 1503, 1690,
    1694, 2412
Brand New Hero, A 1914 (Key) 65
Brand of Cowardice, A 1916 (M) 141,
    2614
Brand of Satan, The 1917 ( ) 1603
Branded--serial 1918 ( ) 1710
Branded Soul, A 1917 ( ) 295, 506
Branding Broadway 1918 (CFC) 1186, 1888,
    1998
Brannigan Sets Off the Blast 1906 (AMB)
Brass Bullet, The--serial 1918 (Un) 678,
    786, 1025, 1153, 1714, 1896, 2774,
    2804
        1. A Flying Start
        2. The Muffled Man
        3. The Mysterious Murder or
            Locked in the Tower
        4. Smoked Out
        5. The Mock Bride
        6. A Dangerous Honeymoon
        7. Pleasure Island or The
            Depth Bomb
        8. The Magnetic Rug
        9. The Room of Flame
       10. A New Peril
       11. Evil Waters
       12. Caught by Wireless
       13. $500.00 Reward
       14. On Trial for His Life
       15. In the Shadow
       16. The Noose
       17. The Avenger
       18. The Amazing Confession
Brass Buttoned Romance, A 1915 (Christie)
    525
Brass Buttons 1919 (Art/Par) 312, 1299,
    1855, 2031, 2201
Brass Check, The 1918 (M) 156, 353,
    1389
Brat, The 1919 (M) 321, 618, 653, 1250,
    1919, 2633
Brave and Bold 1912 (Bio)
Brave and Bold 1918 ( ) 2671
Brave Deserve the Fair, The 1915 (Selig
    Polyscope) 1849
Brave Hunter, The 1912 (Bio)
Brave Irish Lass, A 1909 (V)
Brave Ones, The 1916 (Vim) 1161
Braver Than Bravest 1916 (P) 1586
Bravest Way, The 1918 (Par) 1208, 2638
Brazen Beauty, The 1918 (Un) 675, 2147
Breach of Discipline, The 1910 (Ed)
Breach of Promise 1912 (Imp)
Bread 1918 ( ) 1166, 1694
Bread Cast upon the Waters 1913 ( )
    2096
Break for Freedom, A 1905 (AMB)
Breakdown, The 1912 (Imp)
Breakers Ahead 1918 (M) 631, 2002
Breaking the Seventh Commandment 1911
    (Independent Moving Picture Co.)

Bred in the Bone 1915 ( ) 27, 1028, 1998, 2780
Breed of Men, A 1919 ( ) 1188, 1998
Breed of the Mountains, A 1914 ( ) 651, 2112
Breeze from the West, A 1907 (Lubin)
Breezy Jim 1919 ( ) 2760
Brennon o' the Moor 1916 (Un) 610, 926
Brewster's Millions 1914 (Las) 5, 134
Bridal Chamber, The 1905 (AMB)
Bride and Groom 1918 (P) 1586
Bride in Bond, A 1919 ( ) 370
Bride of Fancy, The 1917 (Es) 1636
Bride of Fear 1918 (F) 406, 2405
Bride of Lammermoor, The 1908 (V)
Bride of Tabaiva, The 1908 (V)
Bride Thirteen 1919 ( ) 487
Bride Won by Bravery, A 1909 (Lubin)
Bridegrooms Beware 1913 (Br) 834, 2138
Bridegroom's Dilemma, The 1909 (Ed)
Bride's Awakening, The 1918 ( ) 1907, 2364
Bride's Dream, The 1908 (Lubin)
Bride's Silence, The 1917 ( ) 865
Bridge of Sighs, The 1908 (Ed)
Bridget on Strike 1909 (V)
Bridget's Sudden Wealth 1912 (Ed)
Bridget's Troubles 1905 (Paley & Steiner)
Bright and Early 1918 (King-Bee) 1161, 2554, 2733
Bright Lights /aka/ The Lure of Broadway 1916 (Key) 65, 322, 791, 836, 1941, 2208
Bringing Home Father 1917 ( ) 1308
Bringing up a Girl in the Way She Should Go 1905 (AMB)
Bringing up Betty 1919 ( ) 708, 1049
Britain's Naval Secret 1915 (Br) 1873
Briton and Boer 1910 (Selig Polyscope) 1849
Broadway Arizona 1917 (Tri) 1308, 2557
Broadway Bill 1918 (M) 162, 1589, 1733
Broadway Jones 1917 (Art/Par) 510, 1427, 2430
Broadway Love 1918 (Bluebird/Un) 449, 1153, 2042, 2490, 2545, 2627
Broadway Saint, A 1919 ( ) 1603, 2160
Broadway Scandal, A 1918 (Bluebird/Un) 95, 449, 1911, 2159
Broke; or How Timothy Escaped 1911 (Independent Moving Picture Co.)
Broken Bath, The 1910 (Imp) 1511
Broken Blossoms 1919 (Griffith/UA) 143, 201, 595, 1029, 1298, 2026, 2342, 2362
Broken Butterfly, The 1919 ( ) 27, 506
Broken Coin, The--serial 1915 (Un) 610, 611, 926, 928, 1280, 1727, 2056, 2343, 2393
   1. The Broken Coin
   2. The Satan of the Sands
   3. When the Throne Rocked
   4. The Face at the Window
   5. The Underground Foe
   6. A Startling Discovery
   7. Between Two Fires
   8. The Prison in the Palace
   9. Room 22
  10. Cornered

  11. The Clash of Arms
  12. A Cry in the Dark
  13. War
  14. On the Battlefield
  15. The Deluge
  16. Kitty in Danger
  17. The Castaways
  18. The Underground City
  19. The Sacred Fire
  20. Between Two Fires
  21. A Timely Rescue
  22. An American Queen
Broken Commandments 1919 (F) 25, 295
Broken Cross, The 1911 (Bio) 1468, 2728
Broken Doll, The 1910 (Bio) 816
Broken Heart, A 1908 (Lubin)
Broken in the Wars 1919 (Hep) 812, 2531, 2744
Broken Lease 1912 (Imp)
Broken Locket, The 1909 (Bio) 2047, 2062
Broken Melody, The 1919 ( ) 567, 1959
Broken Nose Baily 1913 ( ) 2002
Broken Pledge, The 1916 (Key/Tri) 166, 2512
Broken Spell, A 1911 (V) 2523
Broken Threads 1917 (Hep) 812, 2744
Broken Ties 1918 (WS) 835
Broken Violin, The 1908 (Melies)
Broken Ways 1913 (Bio) 398, 1182, 1751, 2513, 2680
Bronco Billy and the Baby 1909 (Es) 50
Bronco Billy and the Bad Man 1914 (Es) 50
Bronco Billy and the Card Sharp 1915 (Es) 50
Bronco Billy and the Claim Jumpers 1914 (Es) 50
Bronco Billy and the Escaped Bandit 1914 (Es) 50
Bronco Billy and the False Note 1915 (Es) 50
Bronco Billy and the Land Grabber 1915 (Es) 50
Bronco Billy and the Lumber King 1915 (Es) 50
Bronco Billy and the Maid 1913 (Es) 50
Bronco Billy and the Mine Shark 1914 (Es) 50
Bronco Billy and the Outlaw's Mother 1913 (Es) 50
Bronco Billy and the Posse 1915 (Es) 50
Bronco Billy and the Rattler 1914 (Es) 50
Bronco Billy and the Red Hand 1914 (Es) 50
Bronco Billy and the Rustler's Child 1913 (Es) 50 2378
Bronco Billy and the Settler's Daughter 1914 (Es) 50
Bronco Billy and the Sheriff 1914 (Es) 50
Bronco Billy and the Sheriff's Kid 1913 (Es) 50
Bronco Billy and the Squatter's Daughter 1913 (Es) 50
Bronco Billy and the Step-Sisters 1913 (Es) 50
Bronco Billy and the Vigilante 1914 (Es) 50
Bronco Billy Begins Life Anew 1915 (Es) 50

Bronco Billy Evens Matters 1915 (Es) 50
Bronco Billy--Guardian 1914 (Es) 50
Bronco Billy--Gun Man 1914 (Es) 50
Bronco Billy Misled 1915 (Es) 50
Bronco Billy Outwitted 1912 (Ed) 50 2361
Bronco Billy Sheepman 1915 (Es) 50
Bronco Billy Steps In 1915 (Es) 50
Bronco Billy Well Repaid 1915 (Es) 50
Bronco Billy's Adventure 1911 (Es) 50
Bronco Billy's Bible 1914 (Es) 50
Bronco Billy's Brother 1913 (Es) 50
Bronco Billy's Capture 1913 (Es) 50 487
Bronco Billy's Christmas Deed 1913 (Es)
    50
Bronco Billy's Close Call 1914 (Es) 50
Bronco Billy's Cowardly Brother 1915 (Es)
    50
Bronco Billy's Cunning 1914 (Es) 50
Bronco Billy's Duty 1914 (Es) 50
Bronco Billy's First Arrest 1913 (Es) 50
Bronco Billy's Gratefulness 1913 (Es) 50
Bronco Billy's Greaser Deputy 1915 (Es)
    50
Bronco Billy's Gunplay 1913 (Es) 50
Bronco Billy's Heart 1912 (Es) 50, 2361
Bronco Billy's Jealousy 1914 (Es) 50
Bronco Billy's Last Deed 1913 (Es) 50
Bronco Billy's Leap 1914 (Es) 50
Bronco Billy's Love Affair 1912 (Es) 50,
    2361
Bronco Billy's Marriage 1915 (Es) 50
Bronco Billy's Mexican Wife 1912 (Es)
    50, 2361
Bronco Billy's Outlaw 1914 (Es) 50
Bronco Billy's Parents 1915 (Es) 50
Bronco Billy's Promise 1912 (Es) 50,
    2361
Bronco Billy's Protege 1915 (Es) 50
Bronco Billy's Punishment 1914 (Es) 50
Bronco Billy's Redemption 1910 (Es) 50
Bronco Billy's Secret 1913 (Es) 50
Bronco Billy's Sentence 1915 (Es) 50
Bronco Billy's Sermon 1914 (Es) 50
Bronco Billy's Sister 1913 (Es) 50
Bronco Billy's Squareness 1913 (Es) 50
Bronco Billy's Teachings 1915 (Es) 50
Bronco Billy's True Love 1914 (Es) 50
Bronco Billy's Vengeance 1915 (Es) 50
Bronco Billy's Ward 1913 (Es) 50
Bronco Billy's Way 1913 (Es) 50
Bronco Billy's Word of Honor 1915 (Es)
    50
Bronco's Surrender 1915 (Es) 50
Bronze Idol, The 1914 (Br) 50
Bronze Man, The 1918 ( ) 487
Brother Officers 1915 (Br) 22, 43
Brother Raiders * (Christie) 525
Brothers, The 1911 (Independent Moving
    Picture Co.)
Brothers, The 1913 (Bio) 398, 1751, 1941,
    2112
Brothers, The 1914 (Br) 2171
Brothers in Arms 1909 (Ed)
Brothers of the Misericordia, Rome 1903
    (AMB)
Brown Moves to Town 1912 (Imp)
Brown of Harvard 1917 (Go) 630, 1078,
    1297, 1867, 1959
Brown's Séance 1912 (Key) 1941

Bruder Karamazoff 1918 ( ) 1349
Brush between Cowboys and Indians 1904
    (Ed)
Brutality 1912 (Bio) 141, 1182, 1751, 1832
Brute, The 1915 (Kal) 1064, 2035
Brute Breaker, The 1919 (P) 619, 1796
Brute Force 1913 (Bio) 1751
Brute Force 1917 ( ) 865
Bubbles 1904 (AMB)
Bubbles of Trouble 1916 (Key/Tri) 748,
    787, 1013, 1225, 1651, 2023
Buchanan's Wife 1918 (F) 1656, 2024
Buck Dance 1898 (Ed)
Buck Parvin series 1915 ( ) 9
Bucking Broadway 1917 (Un) 339, 398,
    1719
Bucking Society 1916 (Key/Tri) 531, 1135,
    1225, 1788, 2165
Bucking the Blizzard 1902 (AMB)
Bucking the Tiger 1917 (Vogue) 2608
Buck's Romance 1913 ( ) 785
Buckskin Jack, the Earl of Glenmore 1911
    (Ed)
Buddy's Call 1914 (V) 2521
Buddy's First Call 1914 (V) 1415
Buddy's Downfall 1914 (V) 1415, 2521
Buffalo Bill 1893 (Ed) 1955
Buffalo Bill and Escort 1897 (Ed)
Buffalo Bill's Wild West and Pawnee Bill's
    Far East 1910 (Buffalo Bill & Pawnee
    Bill Film Co.)
Bughouse Bell Hops 1915 (P) 1586
Bugle Call, The 1915 (Tri) 520, 1100,
    2547
Bugler of Algiers, The 1916 (Un) 181,
    1120, 1391
Builder of Bridges 1915 ( ) 2424
Bulldog Yale 1915 (Key) 531
Bullies and Bullets 1916 (V) 2367
Bull's Eye--serial 1918 (Un) 543, 1149,
    1367, 1492, 2056, 2106, 2726
    1.   First Blood
    2.   The Fearless One
    3.   Desperate Odds
    4.   Still in the Ring
    5.   The Swing of Death
    6.   On the Brink
    7.   Riding Wild
    8.   Dynamite
    9.   The Flaming Crisis
    10. Coyotes of the Desert
    11. Fired
    12. Burning Sands
    13. Sold at Auction
    14. The Firing Squad
    15. The Stained Face
    16. Running Wild
    17. In Irons
    18. The Runaway
Bullsheniks 1917 ( ) 1872
Bumping into Broadway 1919 (P) 635,
    1586, 2055
Bumptious as a Fireman 1910 (Ed)
Bumptious as an Aviator 1910 (Ed)
Bumptious as Romeo 1911 (Ed) 609
Bumptious Plays Baseball 1910 (Ed)
Bumptious Takes up Automobiling 1910
    (Ed)
Bunch of Violets, A 1916 (Hep) 1289, 2744

Bunco Bill's Visit 1914 (V) 332, 901
Buncoed Stage Johnnie 1908 (Melies)
Bungalow Bungle, A 1915 (P) 1161
Bungalow Burglars 1911 (Independent
    Moving Picture Co.)
Bungalowing 1917 (Par) 1868
Bungles' Elopement 1916 (Vim) 1161
Bungles Enforces the Law 1916 (Vim)
    1161
Bungles Lands a Job 1916 (Vim) 1161
Bungles' Rainy Day 1916 (Vim) 1161
Bungs and Bunglers 1919 (V) 1161
Bunker Bean 1917 ( ) 1309
Bunkered 1919 (M) 768, 1707
Bunny All at Sea 1912 (V) 332
Bunny and the Bunny Hug 1913 (V) 111,
    332, 695
Bunny and the Dogs 1912 (V) 332
Bunny and the Twins 1912 (V) 332, 901
Bunny as a Reporter 1913 (V) 332, 818,
    901
Bunny at the Derby 1912 (V) 332
Bunny Attempts Suicide 1914 (V) 332
Bunny Backslides 1914 (V) 332, 818, 901
Bunny Buys a Harem 1914 (V) 332, 901
Bunny for the Cause 1913 (V) 332, 818,
    901
Bunny in Bunnyland 1914 (V) 332
Bunny vs. Cutey 1913 (V) 332
Bunny's Birthday 1914 (V) 332
Bunny's Birthday Surprise 1913 (V) 332,
    901
Bunny's Dilemma 1913 (V) 332, 901
Bunny's Honeymoon 1913 (V) 332, 818
Bunny's Little Brother 1914 (V) 332, 901
Bunny's Mistake 1914 (V) 157, 332, 901
Bunny's Scheme 1914 (V) 332, 901
Bunny's Suicide 1912 (V) 332, 901
Bunny's Swell Affair 1914 (V) 332, 901
Burden, The 1914 ( ) 2002
Burden of Proof, The 1918 (Cosmopolitan)
    489, 545, 660, 1217, 1540, 1607,
    1634, 1810, 2127
Burglar, The 1898 (Ed)
Burglar, The 1903 (AMB)
Burglar, The 1917 (W) 231, 853
Burglar, The; or A Midnight Surprise
    1907 (V)
Burglar and Little Phyllis, The 1910 (Hep)
    2531
Burglar and the Baby, The 1907 (V)
Burglar and the Bundle, The 1903 (AMB)
Burglar by Proxy 1919 (FN) 1283, 2045
Burglar by Request 1919 ( ) 2147
Burglar for a Night, A 1918 (Tri) 1431,
    2074
Burglar in the Bed Chamber, The 1898
    (Ed)
Burglar on the Roof, The 1898 (Ed)
Burglar-Proof Bed, The 1902 (AMB)
Burglar's Ball, The 1908 (Lubin)
Burglar's Child, The 1908 (Lubin)
Burglar's Dilemma, The 1912 (Bio) 141,
    1029, 1182, 2680, 2728
Burglar's Mistake, A 1909 (Bio) 1182,
    1336, 1542, 1865, 2212, 2368
Burglar's Slide for Life, The 1905 (Ed)
Buried Past, A 1911 (Ed)
Burlesque Suicide 1902 (Ed)

Burlesque Tramp Burglars 1905 (Paley &
    Steiner)
Burning Stable, The 1896 (Ed)
Burnt Cork 1912 (V) 332
Bush Leaguer, The 1917 (Selig) 1884
Busher, The 1919 (Ince/Par) 1016, 1159,
    1170, 1261, 1583, 1859, 2096, 2794
Business Is Business 1914 (Key) 531
Business of Life, The 1918 (V) 1388, 1673
Business vs. Love 1915 (Mu) 2126
Business vs. People 1915 (Mu) 989
Busted Hearts see Those Love Pangs
    1914 (Key)
Busted Hearts 1916 (Vim) 340, 1156, 1161,
    2497
Busted Johnny, A see Making a Living
Buster and His Dog: Be a Good Boy 1904
    (AMB)
Buster and His Dog: Buster Quiet 1904
    (AMB)
Buster and His Dog: Good Dog 1904 (AMB)
Buster and His Dog: The Instructions
    1904 (AMB)
Buster Brown series 1904 (Ed)
Buster's Joke on Papa 1903 (Ed)
Busting the Beanery 1916 (P) 1586
Busy Day, A /aka/ Militant Suffragette
    1914 (Key) 451, 2510
Butcher Boy, The 1917 (FP/Las) 65, 803,
    1401, 1616, 1926, 2208, 2471
Butcher's Nightmare, The 1917 (Vogue)
    2608
Butler and the Maid, The 1912 (Ed)
Butterfly on the Wheel 1914 (W) 239, 1764
Button, Button, Where Is the Button? 1908
    (Lubin)
Buying a Title 1908 (Ed)
Buying Manhattan 1909 (Ed)
By a Woman's Wit 1908 (V)
By Hook or Crook 1919 ( ) 231
By Indian Post 1919 ( ) 1011
By Man's Law 1913 (Bio) 595, 1117, 1182,
    1714, 1751, 1876
By Proxy 1918 (Tri) 2479
By Registered Mail 1911 (Independent
    Moving Picture Co.)
By Right of Possession 1917 (V) 27, 1519,
    1876
By Right of Purchase 1918 (Select) 1288,
    1959, 2523
By Stork Delivery 1916 (Key/Tri) 600,
    787, 840, 1436, 1527, 1869, 1874,
    2510
By the House That Jack Built 1911 (In-
    dependent Moving Picture Co.)
By the Sad Sea Waves 1917 (P) 1586, 2055
By the Sea 1915 (Es) 71, 451, 1347, 2077,
    2113, 2608
By the Shorest of Heads 1915 (Br) 936
By the Sun's Rays 1914 (Nestor/Un) 449,
    1630, 1705, 2635
By Whose Hand? 1914 (Hep) 2531
By Whose Hand? 1916 (V) 1991

- C -

Cabaret, The 1918 ( ) 231, 791
Cabaret Dancer, The 1914 ( ) 1388

Cabaret Girl, The 1918 ( ) 495
Cabinet of Dr. Caligari, The 1919
    (Decla-Bioskop) 624, 882, 1464,
    2632, 2650
Cabiria 1914 (K) 654, 736, 1620, 1735,
    1797, 1892, 1999, 2078
Cabman's Good Fairy, The 1909 (Hep)
    2744
Cactus and Kate 1917 (Key) 2143
Cactus Crandell 1918 (Tri) 2479
Cactus Jim 1915 (Selig Polyscope) 1849
Cactus Jim's Shop Girl * (Selig Poly-
    scope) 1849
Cactus Kid, The 1916 ( ) 1011
Cactus Nell 1917 (Key/Tri) 166, 266,
    1345, 1461, 1874, 2580, 2724
Caddy's Dream, The 1911 (Majestic)
    2047
Cage, The 1914 (Br) 43
Caillaux Case, The 1918 ( ) 2581
Calamitous Elopement, A 1908 (Bio)
    1511, 2212
Calamity Anne, Detective 1913 (Am)
    1431, 1551
Caleb Piper's Girl 1919 (Go) 443
Call, The 1910 (Bio) 122, 2680
Call for Mr. Cave Man 1919 (P) 635,
    2055
Call of a Woman 1912 (Ingvald C. Oses)
Call of Her People 1917 (M) 139, 658
Call of the Drum 1912 (Imp)
Call of the East, The 1916 ( ) 60, 1208
Call of the Heart 1909 (Lubin)
Call of the Heart 1918 ( ) 2151
Call of the North, The 1914 (Las) 306,
    411, 623, 677, 809, 1446, 1669,
    1854, 1897, 2149
Call of the Sea 1919 (Br) 2637
Call of the Song, The 1911 (Imp) 2047
Call of the Soul 1919 (F) 295
Call of the Wild, The 1908 (AMB) 1336,
    1511
Call of the Yukon, The 1919 ( ) 835
Call to Arms, The 1910 (Bio) 2000, 2047
Called Back 1914 (Br) 22
Calling of Jim Barton 1914 (Es) 50
Cambric Mask, The 1919 (V) 566, 1388,
    2406
Cameo Kirby 1915 (Las) 866, 1493, 1854
Camille 1912 (Champion) 606, 854, 2396
Camille 1915 (W) 1051, 1829, 2811
Camille 1917 (F) 116, 975, 1506, 2175,
    2745, 2756
Camouflaged 1919 ( ) 2355
Camouflaged Kiss, A 1918 (F) 392
Campbells Are Coming, The 1915 ( ) 610
Camping 1916 (Par) 1868
Camping Out 1918 (FP/Las) 65, 1872,
    2208
Campus Cuties * ( ) 750
Can You Beat It? 1915 (V) 2521
Canby Hill Outlaws, The 1916 (Selig
    Polyscope) 1849
Candy Girl, The 1917 ( ) 1312
Candy Kid, The 1917 (King-Bee) 1161,
    2733
Candy Trail, The 1916 (Vim) 1161
Canker of Jealousy, The 1915 (Hep)
    1289, 2171, 2531

Cannibal King, The 1915 (Lubin) 1161
Cannibals of the South Seas 1912 (Martin
    Johnson Prods.) 1366
Cannon Ball, The /aka/ The Dynamiter
    1915 (Key) 531
Cap of Fortune, The 1909 (Ed)
Capital Joke, but Why Didn't He Laugh?
    1907 (Lubin)
Capital Punishment 1915 ( ) 2610
Capitol, The 1919 ( ) 658, 1116
Cap'n Abe's Niece 1918 (V) 566, 1388
Caprice 1913 (FP) 1309, 1865, 2047
Caprice of the Mountains 1916 (F) 392
Captain Abe's Niece 1918 (V) 566, 1388
Captain Alvarez 1917 (V) 1039, 2532
Captain Barnacles' Baby 1911 (V) 297, 332,
    565
Captain Barnacles' Courtship 1911 (V) 297,
    332
Captain Barnacles' Messmate 1912 (V) 231,
    332, 565, 2523
Captain Barnacles--Reformer 1912 (V)
    2523
Captain Barnacles' Waif 1912 (V) 2523
Captain Courtesy 1915 (Bosworth) 866, 920
Captain Hawthorne of the U. S. A. see
    Hawthorne of the U. S. A.
Captain Jack 1913 (Hep) 2744
Captain Jack's Dilemma 1912 (V) 332, 564,
    565, 818
Captain Jack's Diplomacy 1912 (V) 332,
    818
Captain Jinks of the Horse Marines 1916
    (Es) 1902, 2582
Captain Kidd 1916 (Un) 2056
Captain Kidd, Jr. 1917 (Art/Par) 25, 1050,
    1126, 1688, 1697, 2047, 2058
Captain Kidd's Kiddies 1919 (P) 635, 1586,
    2055
Captain Maclean see Captain Machlin
Captain Machlin 1915 (Tri) 25, 732, 1029,
    2649
Captain Molly 1908 (Lubin)
Captain Nell 1911 (Ed)
Captain of His Soul 1918 ( ) 715
Captain of the Gray Horse Troop, The
    1917 (V) 340, 1519, 1876, 2487
Captain's Bride, The 1910 (Ed)
Captain's Captain, The 1918 (V) 566, 1047,
    1360, 1388
Captivating Mary Carstairs 1915 (National)
    938, 1582, 1843, 2521, 2523
Captive, The 1915 (Par) 664, 828, 1701,
    2035, 2036, 2149, 2513, 2685
Captive God, The 1916 (Tri) 627, 715,
    1188, 1745
Capture of Fort Ticonderoga, The 1911
    (Ed)
Capture of the Biddle Brothers 1902 (Ed)
Capture of the Burglar, The 1910 (Ed)
Capture of Yegg Bank Burglars 1904 (Ed)
Captured by Telephone 1911 (V)
Captured by Cannibals 1912 (Martin
    Johnson Prods.) 1366
Caravan 1915 (M) 116, 656
Card of Introduction, A 1911 (Ed)
Card of Life, The 1909 ( ) 1542
Card Sharp, The 1914 (King-Bee) 1745,
    1794, 2096

Cardinal Wolsey 1912 (V) 1047, 1368,
    2111, 2811
Cardinal's Conspiracy, The 1909 (Bio)
    20, 47, 1511, 2062, 2212
Career of Crime, A 1902 (AMB)
Career of Katherine Bush 1919 ( ) 375,
    1427, 2756
Carmen 1909 (P) 1546
Carmen 1912 (Feature Films Sales Co.)
Carmen 1913 (Monopol) 1542
Carmen 1913 (T) 989, 2430
Carmen 1913 (F) 116, 716, 1157, 1574,
    1698, 1701, 1739, 2112, 2602
Carmen 1915 (Par) 411, 664, 683, 828,
    869, 1439
Carmen 1918 ( ) 1922
Carmen /aka/ Gypsy Blood 1919 ( ) 1922
Carmen of the Klondike--serial 1916 ( )
    189, 763, 1794, 2765
Carmencita, the Faithful 1911 (Es) 50
Carminella 1910 (Ed)
Carnival of Venice, The 1909 (Lubin)
Carolyn of the Corners 1919 (P) 1602
Carpenter, The 1913 (V) 2663, 2767
Carpet from Bagdad 1916 ( ) 218
Carrie De Mar 1910 (Ed)
Carrie Nation Smashing a Saloon 1902
    (AMB)
Carrots 1917 (Hep) 2744
Carter Case, The (The Craig Kennedy
    Serial)--serial 1919 (Oliver Films)
    26, 112, 1078, 1119, 1736, 1753,
    2049, 2095, 2489, 2549, 2789, 2809
    1.   The Phosgene Bullet
    2.   The Vacuum Room
    3.   The Air Terror
    4.   The Dungeon
    5.   *
    6.   The Wireless Detective
    7.   The Nervagraph
    8.   The Silent Shot
    9.   The Camera Trap
    10. The Moonshiners
    11. The White Damp
    12. The X-Ray Detective
    13. The Ruse
    14. *
    15. *
Casanova 1918 ( ) 1614
Case of Becky, The 1915 ( ) 231, 2149
Case of Dynamite, A 1912 (Un)
Case of Eugenics, A 1915 (V) 768
Case of High Treason, A 1911 (Ed)
Case of Identity, A 1910 (Ed)
Case of Spirits; or All's Well That Ends
    Well 1908 (V)
Casey and His Neighbor's Goat 1903 (Ed)
Casey at the Bat 1899 (Ed)
Casey at the Bat 1913 (V) 1286, 1877,
    2070, 2523
Casey's Christening 1905 (AMB)
Casey's Frightful Dream 1904 (Ed)
Casey's Jumping Toothache 1909 (Ed)
Cash Parrish's Pal 1915 ( ) 1188
Cast-Off 1919 ( ) 134
Cast up by the Sea 1907 (V)
Castaways, The 1908 (V)
Caste 1915 ( ) 1329
Castle of Dreams 1919 (Br) 1968

Castles for Two 1917 (Art/Par) 724, 752,
    756
Castles in the Air 1919 (M) 41
Cattle Thief's Escape, The 1913 ( ) 785
Caught 1907 (V)
Caught 1915 ( ) 2518
Caught at Last 1909 (V)
Caught by Wireless 1908 (AMB)
Caught in a Cabaret /aka/ The Jazz
    Waiter; Faking with Society; The
    Waiter 1914 (Key) 37, 65, 384, 451,
    531, 650, 791, 1090, 1304, 1422,
    1651, 1662, 1726, 1941, 2510, 2514
Caught in a Flash 1912 (Un)
Caught in a Jam 1916 (P) 1586
Caught in the Act 1918 ( ) 1004, 1329
Caught in the Act: Is Anyone Looking?
    1904 (AMB)
Caught in the End 1917 (Vogue) 2608
Caught in the Rain /aka/ At It Again;
    In the Park; Who Got Stung? 1914
    (Key) 451, 650, 1304, 1666, 1941,
    2368, 2510
Caught with the Goods 1907 (Lubin)
Caught with the Goods 1911 (Bio)
Cause of All the Trouble, The 1908 (Lubin)
Cavalier's Dream, The 1898 (Ed)
Cavanaugh of the Forest Range 1918 ( )
    2397, 2754
Cave Man, The 1915 (Las) 809
Cave Man's Bluff 1917 (M) 768, 1707
Cave Man's Wooing, A 1912 (Imp)
Cavell Case, The 1919 ( ) 1118
Cecilia of the Pink Roses 1918 (Cosmo-
    politan) 184, 335, 385, 456, 660,
    1341, 1433, 1531, 1961, 2498
Celebrated Case, A 1914 ( ) 1388
Cell No. 13, The 1912 (New York Motion
    Picture Co.)
Cenere 1916 (Ambrosio-Caesar) 793
Ceneri e Vampe 1916 (Italian)
Central American Romance, A 1019 (Ed)
Chains of Bondage 1916 (Br) 1018
Chains of Evidence 1919 ( ) 283
Chalice of Sorrow, The 1916 ( ) 1711
Challenge Accepted 1919 ( ) 1402
Challenge of Chance, The 1919 (Un) 2068,
    2763
Champion, The /aka/ Champion Charlie
    1915 (Es) 50, 451, 1347, 1941, 2077,
    2746
Champion Charlie see Champion, The
Champion of the Law, A 1917 ( ) 1325
Chance Deception, A 1913 (Bio) 398, 2513
Chance of a Lifetime, The 1916 ( ) 2558
Change in Baggage, A 1914 (V) 51, 332,
    901
Change of Heart, A 1909 (Bio) 1832, 1865
Change of Spirit, A 1912 (Bio) 1714, 2513,
    2573, 2680
Change of Stripes, A 1912 (Imp)
Chaperon, The 1916 (Es) 1795, 1959
Chaplin Revue of 1916, The 1916 (Es) 451
Chappie and Ben Bolt 1902 (AMB)
Charge It 1919 (Equity) 132, 243, 2095,
    2811
Charge It to Me 1919 ( ) 905
Charge of the Light Brigade see
    Victoria Cross, The 1912 (V)

Chariot Race, The 1907 (Kal)
Charity 1916 (Bio) 79, 1118, 1564
Charity Ann 1915 (Br) 834, 2138
Charity begins at Home 1908 (V)
Charity Castle 1917 (Mu) 20, 373, 1841
Charlatan, The 1916 (Br) 1945
Charles Peace, King of Criminals 1914
    (Br) 150
Charley Smiles Joins the Boy Scouts 1911
    (Br) 851, 852
Charley's Aunt 1915 (Lubin) 1161
Charley's Ma-in-Law 1908 (Lubin)
Charlie and the Perfect Lady see
    Woman, A
Charlie and the Sausages see Mabel's
    Busy Day
Charlie and the Umbrella see Between
    Showers
Charlie at the Bank see Bank, The
Charlie at the Show see Night in the
    Show, A
Charlie Chaplin's Burlesque on Carmen
    1916 (Es) 267, 451, 517, 1225, 1347,
    2090, 2476, 2608, 2747
Charlie's Recreation see Tango Tangles
Charlie's Reform 1912 (Ed)
Charmed Arrow, The 1914 ( ) 2623
Charmer, The 1917 ( ) 186, 1120
Chase Me, Charlie 1918 (K) 451
Chased by Bloodhounds 1912 (V) 332
Chased into Love 1917 ( ) 460, 2041
Chasing Rainbows 1919 (F) 295, 2591
Chasms; or Woman Always Pays 1911
    (Independent Moving Picture Co.)
Chattle, The 1916 (V) 1329, 2433
Chauffeur, The 1919 ( ) 539
Chauldron Infernal, Le 1903 (Melies)
Chauncey Explains 1915 (AMB)
Cheapest Way, The 1913 ( ) 2003
Cheat, The 1915 (Par) 4, 672, 1208,
    1925, 1980, 2683
Cheating Cheaters 1919 ( ) 387, 1280,
    1417, 1756, 2468, 2811
Cheating Herself 1918 ( ) 1253, 1329
Cheating the Public 1918 ( ) 1563, 1745
Checkers 1919 (M) 7, 416, 433, 824,
    2814
Checkmate, The 1917 ( ) 2227
Cheerful Givers 1917 (Tri) 1166, 1602
Cheerful Liar, A see His Bogus Boast
Cheese Special, The 1913 (Un) 81
Chef's Downfall, The 1912 (Imp)
Cherries Are Ripe 1918 (Un) 2147
Cheyenne's Pal 1917 (Un) 88, 398, 1011
Chicago Sal 1919 ( ) 1476
Chicken Chaser, The 1914 (Key) 65
Chicken-Hearted Jim 1917 ( ) 926
Chicken Thieves 1897 (Ed)
Chickens 1916 (Vim) 340, 1156, 1161,
    2497
Chief Cook, The 1917 (King-Bee) 1161
Chief Flynn, Secret Service series 1919
    ( ) 2095
Chief's Blanket, The 1912 (Bio) 141, 2513
Chief's Daughter, The 1911 (Bio) 1060,
    1593
Chief's Predicament, The 1913 (Key) 1666
Chieftain's Revenge, The 1908 (V)
Child and the Tramp, The 1911 (Ed)

Child Crusoes, The 1911 (V) 2523
Child Mother, The 1913 (Br) 149, 150
Child of M'sieur 1919 (P) 1988
Child of the Forest, A 1909 (Ed)
Child of the Ghetto, A 1910 (Bio) 1933,
    2729
Child of the Prairie, The 1913 (Selig
    Polyscope) 1849
Child of the Paris Streets, A 1916 ( )
    1751, 1756
Child of the Sea, A 1913 (Selig Polyscope)
    1589, 2770
Child of the Wild, A 1918 (F) 392, 1878
Child Stealers, The 1904 (AMB)
Childhood's Happy Days 1916 (M) 768,
    1707
Children in the House 1916 (FA/Tri) 406,
    410, 1514, 2002, 2082, 2523
Children of Banishment 1919 ( ) 1562
Children of Edward, The 1910 (FdA) 703
Children of the Feud 1916 ( ) 686, 1028,
    1570, 2483
Children of the Plains 1909 (V)
Children of the Sea 1909 (Lubin)
Children of the Sea 1915 (Mu) 225, 485,
    1140
Children Pay 1917 ( ) 1029
Children's Friend, The 1909 (Bio)
Children's Toilet 1897 (Ed)
Child's Faith, A 1910 (Bio) 815, 1933
Child's Impulse, A 1910 (Bio) 95, 816,
    1182, 1223, 2047, 2728
Child's Influence, A 1912 (Un)
Child's Prayer; or The Good Samaritans
    1908 (V)
Child's Prayer, The 1909 (Ed)
Child's Remorse, A 1912 (Bio) 816
Child's Stratagem, A 1910 (Bio) 816, 2045
Child's Strategy, A 1912 (Br) 149, 150
Chimes, The 1914 (Br) 1289
Chimmie Fadden 1915 (Par) 87, 711, 935,
    1201, 1386, 1439, 1648, 1868
Chimmie Fadden out West 1915 (Par) 87,
    623, 935, 1110, 1201, 1386, 1648,
    1868
Chimmie Hicks at the Races 1902 (AMB)
Chimney Sweep 1906 (Melies)
Chimney Sweep and the Miller 1902 (AMB)
Chimney's Secret, The 1915 (Victor/Un)
    449, 1518
Chinese Cruiser "Hai Chi" 1911 (Inde-
    pendent Moving Picture Co.)
Chinese Laundry 1894 (Edison Kintescope)
    753
Chinese Laundry: At Work 1904 (AMB)
Chinese Puzzle, The 1919 (Br) 2179
Chinese Revolution, The 1912 (Oriental
    Film Co.)
Chinese Rubbernecks, The 1903 (AMB)
Ching 1919 ( ) 1523
Ching Ling Foo Outdone 1900 (Ed)
Chip of the Flying U 1914 (Selig Polyscope)
    1849, 2770
Chips 1915 ( ) 1649
Chloroform Fiends, The 1905 (Melies)
Choosing a Husband 1909 (Bio) 122, 315,
    2513, 2680
Chop Suey and Company 1919 (P) 1586,
    2055

Chopin's Funeral March 1907 (Melies)
Chorus Girl, The 1908 (V)
Chorus Girl, The 1912 ( ) 2748
Chorus Girl and the Kid, The 1916 (F)
557
Chorus Girl and the Salvation Army Lass
1903 (AMB)
Chorus Lady, The 1915 (Las) 664, 2112,
2132
Christian, The 1914 (V) 1119, 1943,
2487, 2527, 2767
Christian, The 1915 (Br) 43, 2138
Christine Johnstone 1915 ( ) 1649
Christmas Angel 1904 (Melies)
    The Wretched Garret
    The Porch on the Church
    The Cook-shop
    Upon the Bridges
Christmas Burglars, The 1908 (AMB)
815, 1511, 1542
Christmas Carol, A 1910 (Ed)
Christmas in Paradise Alley 1908 (V)
Christmas Morning 1902 (AMB)
Christmas Party, The 1902 (AMB)
Christmas without Daddy 1914 (Br) 149, 150
Chronicles of Bloom Center 1915 ( )
1167
Chums 1903 (AMB)
Chumps 1912 (V) 111, 332, 2112, 2383,
2761
Chumps and Chances 1917 (V) 2367
Cigarette Girl, The 1917 ( ) 1312, 1971
Cigarette Maker of Seville, The 1910 (Ed)
Cigarette--That's All, A 1915 (Un) 1280,
2422
Cinderella 1900 (Melies) 1802
Cinderella 1911 (Selig) 416, 577, 1537,
1828, 2520, 2713
Cinderella 1914 (FO) 579, 1865, 2047,
2777
Cinderella Husbands, The 1916 (Par)
1868
Cinderella Jane 1913 (Bio) 2513
Cinderella Man, The 1917 (Go) 875, 950,
1751, 1867
Cinderella up-to-Date 1909 (Melies)
Cinders of Love 1916 (Key/Tri) 46, 187,
531, 1274, 1651, 1776, 2501
Cinema Murder, The 1919 (Art/Par) 124,
660, 1360, 1870, 2008, 2091
Circumstances 1919 ( ) 1220
Circumstantial Evidence; or An Innocent
Victim 1908 (V)
Circus Boy, The 1908 (Lubin)
Circus Cyclone, A 1917 (Vogue) 2608
Circus Girl, The see Her Circus
Knight
Circus Imps 1916 (F) 1524
Circus Man, The 1914 (Las) 1201, 2149
Circus Romance, A 1916 (V) 1991
Cissy and Bertie 1914 (V) 908
Cissy's Funnymoon 1914 (V) 908
Cissy's Innocent Wink 1914 (V) 908
City, The 1914 ( ) 2096
City Beautiful, The 1914 ( ) 1028, 2112
City of Beautiful Nonsense, The 1919
(Hep) 812, 2744
City of Comrades 1919 (Go) 950, 1261,
1867, 1998, 2175

City of Darkness 1914 (King-Bee) 473,
1745, 1794, 2096
City of Dim Faces, The 1919 (Par) 1126,
1208, 2018, 2210, 2462
City of Purple Dreams 1918 ( ) 318, 857,
2221
City of Tears 1918 (Un) 95, 1911, 2164
City of Terrible Night 1915 ( ) 108
City of the Dead 1915 (Tri) 1032, 1794
City Slicker, The 1918 (P) 1586
Civilization 1916 (Ince) 315, 334, 473, 906,
960, 1246, 1745, 1793, 1821, 2392,
2488, 2522, 2609
Claim, The 1918 ( ) 2487
Clancarty 1914 (Br) 812
Clarence Crooks and Chivalry 1919 (Br)
1487
Clarence the Cop 1903 (AMB)
Clarence the Cop, on the Feed Store Beat
1904 (AMB)
Clarion Call, The 1916 (Tri) 2547
Classmates 1908 (AMB)
Classmates 1913 (Bio) 141, 1924, 2513,
2680
Classmates' Frolic, The 1913 ( ) 2472
Claw, The 1918 (Select) 1280, 2410, 2811
Claws of the Hun 1918 ( ) 1690, 1948,
2096
Cleaning Time 1915 (Lubin) 1161
Clemenceau Case, The 1915 (F) 116, 1038,
1275, 1524, 1525, 2087, 2381, 2394,
2659
Cleopatra 1912 (V) 985
Cleopatra 1917 (F) 9, 116, 238, 721, 764,
783, 1125, 1534, 1794, 2175
Cleopatra's Lover; or A Night of En-
chantment 1909 (V)
Cleptomaniac, The 1907 (Lubin)
Clever Dummy, A 1917 (Key/Tri) 46,
166, 531, 696, 748, 1153, 2608
Clever Mrs. Carfax, The 1917 (Art/Par)
832
Clever Trick, A 1909 (V)
Climbers, The 1919 (V) 1088, 1748
Clock, The 1917 ( ) 867
Clock Maker's Dream 1904 (Melies)
Clock Struck One, The 1917 (Es) 386, 487
Clodhopper, The 1917 (Tri) 960, 1454,
2090, 2780
Cloister and the Heart, The 1913 (Hep)
2744
Cloister's Touch, The 1910 (Bio) 1363,
1933, 2680
Close Call, A 1912 (Bio)
Close Call, A 1916 (Selig Polyscope) 1849
Close Resemblance 1916 (M) 768, 1707
Close Shave, A 1902 (AMB)
Close to Nature 1919 ( ) 689, 690
Closed Road, The 1916 ( ) 2544
Closed Sunday 1909 (Ed)
Closin' In 1918 ( ) 715
Clothes Make the Man 1915 (Ed) 1161
Clover's Rebellion 1917 (V) 2472
Clown, The 1908 (Lubin)
Clown, The 1916 (Las) 1868, 2686
Clown and the Alchemist, The 1900 (Ed)
Clown Juggler 1906 (Winthrop Press)
Clownland 1912 (Un)
Clown's Adventures, The 1906 (Lubin)

Clown's Christmas Eve, The 1908 (V)
Clown's Love Story, A 1907 (V)
Clown's Triumphs 1912 (Imp)
Clubman and the Tramp, The 1908 (AMB)
Clubs Are Trump 1917 (P) 1586, 2055
Clue, The 1915 ( ) 1208, 2513
Clutch of Circumstances 1918 (V) 1088
Clutching Hand, The--serial 1917 (P)
    1564, 2003
Coax Me 1919 ( ) 835, 1819
Cobbler and the Caliph, The 1909 (V)
Cobweb, The 1917 (Hep) 812, 1289, 2171,
    2531
Cock o' the Walk 1919 (Hep) 1528
Code of Honor, The 1907 (Selig Polyscope)
    258, 1544
Code of Marcia Gray, The 1916 (Morosco)
    518, 2445
Code of the North, The * ( ) 1509
Code of the Yukon 1919 ( ) 1562
Co-ed Professor, The 1911 (Independent
    Moving Picture Co.)
Cohen at Coney Island 1909 (V)
Cohen at Coney Island see At Coney
    Island 1912 (Key)
Cohen Collects a Debt 1912 (Key) 1666,
    1941, 2368, 2465
Cohen Saves the Flag 1913 (Key) 509,
    1941, 2368, 2465
Cohen's Advertising Scheme 1904 (Ed)
Cohen's Fire Sale 1907 (Ed)
Cohen's Outing 1913 (Key) 99, 650, 1613,
    2465
Cold Cash * ( ) 1896
Cold Duck 1917 (Tri) 281, 1188
Coleen Bawn * (Kal) 992
College Chums 1907 (Ed)
College Girl's Affair of Honor, A 1906
    (AMB)
College Orphan 1915 ( ) 689
College Widow, The 1915 (Lubin) 486
Collegian's First Cigar, The 1907 (P)
    1575
Collegian's First Outing, The 1905 (P)
    1575
Colonel of the Red Hussars 1914 ( ) 1656
Colonel's Friend, The 1905 ( )
Colonial Romance, A 1909 (V)
Colored Stenographer, The 1909 (Ed)
Comata, the Sioux 1909 (Bio) 79, 1450,
    1511, 1542
Combat, The 1916 (V) 1632, 2472
Come again Smith 1919 ( ) 1080, 1431
Come Back to Me 1918 ( ) 242
Come on In 1918 (Par) 579, 1774, 2595
Come out of the Kitchen 1919 (Par) 482,
    1105, 1427, 1959
Come Through 1917 (Tri) 1476, 2095,
    2479
Comeback, The 1916 (Mu) 41, 1589,
    2680
Comedy and Tragedy 1909 (Ed)
Comedy of Errors, A 1908 (V)
Comedy of Understanding, A 1911 (Ed)
Comedy Set-To 1898 (Ed)
Comin' thro' the Rye 1916 (Hep) 1233,
    1289, 2171, 2531, 2744
Coming of Angelo, The 1913 (Bio) 1182,
    1714, 1832, 2513

Coming of Columbus, The 1912 (Selig
    Polyscope) 2770
Coming of the Law 1919 (F) 1494, 1849
Commanding Officer, The 1915 (Las) 761,
    1007, 1924
Common Cause, The 1918 (V) 77, 1046,
    2095
Common Cause, The 1919 (Par) 281
Common Clay 1919 (P) 27, 1510, 2683
Common Enemy, A 1908 (Selig Polyscope)
    635
Common Ground 1916 ( ) 756
Common Law, The 1916 (WS) 2535, 2811
Common Level 1919 ( ) 283
Common Property 1919 (Un) 54, 607,
    1535, 1859
Commuter's Wife, The 1912 (Ed)
Compact, The 1912 ( ) 2760
Comrade John 1915 (P) 506, 825, 2169
Comrades 1911 (Bio) 1223, 1224, 2067,
    2368, 2504
Comradeship 1919 (Br) 43, 834, 1931
Concealing a Burglar 1908 (AMB) 1363,
    1511
Condemnation of Faust, The 1904 (Lubin)
Condensed Milk 1903 (AMB)
Coney Island 1917 (FP/Las) 65
Coney Island Princess, A 1916 (FP) 886,
    1550, 1865
Confederate Ironclad 1917 ( ) 554
Confession, The 1919 (F) 406, 2680
Confidence 1909 (AMB) 1336, 1363, 1511
Conflict, The 1916 ( ) 1632, 2478
Conjuror's Outing, The 1909 (Lubin)
Conquered Hearts 1918 ( ) 1753
Conquering Hero, The 1909 (Lubin)
Conqueror, The 1916 ( ) 406, 868,
    1685
Conquest of the Pole 1912 (Melies) 1802
Conscience 1911 (Bio)
Conscience 1918 (F) 295
Conscience of Hassan Bey, The 1913 (Bio)
    1029
Conspiracy, The 1914 (FP) 837, 1589,
    1808, 1844
Conspiracy Against the King, A 1911 (Ed)
Contortionist, A 1894 (Ed) 214
Contrabanders, The 1907 (P)
Contrary Wife, The see His Temporary
    Wife
Contrary Wind 1903 (AMB)
Convenient Burglar, A 1911 (Bio)
Convent Gate, The 1913 (Br) 177
Conversion of Frosty Blake, The /aka/
    Gentleman from Blue Gulch, The
    1915 (Tri) 1032, 1188, 2096
Converts, The 1910 (Bio) 79, 1363, 1542,
    2680
Convict 933 1917 ( ) 435, 1971
Convicted by Hypnotism; or A Double
    Life 1912 (Eclair)
Convict's Bride, The 1906 (AMB)
Convict's Child, The 1911 (V) 2523
Convict's Escape, The 1904 (AMB)
Convict's Parole, The 1912 (Ed) 968,
    1656
Convict's Punishment, A 1903 (AMB)
Convict's Sacrifice, A 1909 (Bio) 79, 816,
    1450, 1593, 1992, 2368, 2680

Cook, The see Dough and Dynamite 1914 (Key)

Cook, The 1918 (FP/Las) 65, 1401, 1476, 2208

Cook in the Parlor, The 1903 (AMB)

Cook in Trouble, The 1904 (Melies)

Cook's Revenge, The 1901 (Lubin)

Cop and the Nurse Girl, The 1898 (Ed)

Cop Fools the Sergeant, The 1904 (Ed)

Cophetua 1912 (Br) 503

Cops and Cussedness 1917 (V) 2367

Cops and Watches see Twenty Minutes of Love

Coquette, The 1910 (Ed)

Corbett-Courtneay Fight /aka/ Corbett and Courtney before the Kinetograph 1894 (Wm. K. L. Dickson) 556, 570

Cord of Life 1909 (AMB) 79, 209, 994, 1336, 1552, 2368

Co-Respondent, The 1918 ( ) 1139

Cork and Vicinity 1912 (V) 332

Cork Leg Legacy 1909 (Lubin)

Corner, The 1915 ( ) 1685

Corner Grocer, The 1918 ( ) 853, 895

Corner in Coleen's Home, A 1916 (Tri) 134, 960, 2096, 2547, 2780

Corner in Cotton, A 1915 (Quality) 105, 106, 353, 496, 612

Corner in Smith's, A 1918 (Go) 630

Corner in the Playroom 1903 (AMB)

Corner in Water, A 1916 (Selig Polyscope) 1849

Corner in Wheat, A 1909 (AMB) 79, 315, 1224, 1363, 1450, 1701, 2062, 2081, 2368, 2513, 2680

Corporal's Daughter, The 1911 (Bio)

Corporation and the Ranch Girl, The 1911 (Es) 50

Corruption see Going Straight 1916 (FA/Tri)

Corsair, The 1914 ( ) 2760

Corset Model, The 1903 (AMB)

Corsican Brothers, The 1912 (Ed)

Corsican Brothers, The 1915 (Un) 108

Corsican Brothers, The 1919 (UP) 866, 1446

Counsel for the Defense 1913 (V) 2523

Count, The 1916 (Mu) 97, 384, 451, 517, 1414, 1840, 2077, 2990, 2219, 2746

Count and the Cowboy, The 1911 (Es) 50

Count 'Em /aka/ The Counts 1915 (V) 2472

Count of Monte Cristo, The 1912 (Selig) 258

Count of Monte Cristo, The 1913 (FP) 218, 1979, 2095, 2221

Count of No Account, The 1908 (Lubin)

Count the Votes 1919 (P) 1586

Count Your Change 1919 (P) 1586

Counted Out see The Knockout

Counterfeit, The 1919 (Art/Par) 888, 1006, 2061

Counterfeit Trial 1917 ( ) 340

Counterfeiters, The 1905 (Lubin)

Countess Betty's Mine, The 1914 ( ) 651, 2112

Countess Charming 1917 (Par) 595, 832, 1756, 2623, 2638, 2648

Country Barber 1913 (V) 2523

Country Boy, The 1915 (Las) 1924

Country Chickens 1914 (Key) 531

Country Cousin 1919 ( ) 1139, 1163, 1673

Country Cupid, A 1911 (Bio) 2513

Country Doctor, The 1909 (Bio) 2047, 2062, 2340

Country Girl, The 1915 (T) 127, 548, 1196, 1468

Country Hero, A 1919 ( ) 1401, 1476

Country Lovers 1911 (Bio) 2513

Country Mouse, The 1914 (Bo) 258, 870

Country That God Forgot, The 1917 (Art/ Par) 457, 875, 1925, 2221

Counts, The see Count 'Em

Count's Wooing, The 1909 (Melies)

County Chairman, The 1914 (FP) 64, 1589

Courage for Two 1919 ( ) 231, 1223

Courage of a Coward, The 1914 (Br) 2138

Courage of Silence, The 1917 ( ) 1388, 1877

Courageous Coward, The 1919 (Par) 60, 1208

Course of True Love, The 1905 (AMB)

Course of True Love, The 1910 (Bio)

Court House Crooks 1915 (Key) 70, 791, 2465

Court Martialled 1915 (Hep) 2171 2531

Courting of Mary, The 1911 (Majestic) 1865, 2047

Cousin Lucy 1914 ( ) 832

Coward, A 1909 (Ed)

Coward, The 1915 (Tri) 473, 509, 960, 1012, 1404, 1564, 2096

Cowardice Court 1919 ( ) 1329

Cowardly Way, The 1915 (FP) 2105

Cowboy and the Lady, The 1903 (AMB)

Cowboy and the Lady, The 1911 ( ) 1117

Cowboy and the Squaw, The 1910 (Es) 50

Cowboy Coward, The 1913 (Es) 50, 487

Cowboy Elopement, A 1908 (AMB)

Cowboy Justice 1904 (AMB)

Cowboy's Mother-in-Law, A 1910 (Es) 50

Cowboy's Romance, A 1909 (Centaur Film Co.)

Cowboy's Stratagem, A 1912 (Ed)

Cowboy's Sweetheart, A 1909 (Centaur Film Co.)

Cowboy's Vindication, A 1910 (Es) 50

Cowpuncher's Glove, The 1910 (Ed)

Cowpuncher's Peril, The 1915 (Selig Polyscope) 1849

Cowpuncher's Ward, The 1910 (Es) 50

Crack up Your Heels 1919 (P) 1586

Cracksman Santa Claus, A 1913 ( ) 651, 2112

Cracksman's Reformation, The 1913 ( ) 651, 2112

Crash, The 1916 ( ) 2480

Craven, The 1915 ( ) 1998, 2112

Crazy by Proxy 1915 (Christie) 525, 1132

Crazy Composer, A 1905 (Melies)

Crazy Quilt, A 1907 (V)

Creaking Stairs 1919 ( ) 1694

Creampuff Romance, A /aka/ His Alibi 1916 (Key/Tri) 65

Creators of Foxy Grandpa 1902 (AMB)

Creatures of Clay 1914 (Br) 2171

Creatures of Habit 1914 (GB) 2604

Cricket on the Hearth, The 1909 (Bio)
79, 209, 1336, 1814, 1865, 2074
Cricket on the Hearth, The 1914 (Las)
1117, 2201
Crime and Punishment 1917 (P) 272, 366,
516, 572, 1002, 1454
Crime's Triangle 1915 ( ) 108
Criminal, The 1915 (V) 297, 715
Criminal Hypnotist, The 1909 (AMB) 1542,
2212
Criminal's Daughter, The 1908 (Lubin)
Crimson Cross, The 1913 (V) 950
Crimson Gardenia, The 1919 (Go) 24, 473,
950, 1756, 1865, 1946, 2468
Crimson Stain Mystery, The--serial 1916
(M) 566, 1058, 1674, 1972, 2492
1. The Brand of Satan
2. In the Demon's Spell
3. The Broken Spell
4. The Mysterious Disappearance
5. The Figure in Black
6. The Phantom Image
7. The Devil's Symphony
8. In the Shadow of Death
9. The Haunting Specter
10. The Infernal Fiend
11. The Tortured Soul
12. The Restless Spirit
13. Despoiling Brutes
14. The Bloodhound
15. The Human Tiger
16. The Unmasking
Crinoline Girl 1914 ( ) 832
Crisis, The 1912 (New York Motion
Picture Co.)
Crisis, The 1916 (Selig) 218, 857, 1924,
2221, 2431
Crissie Sheridan 1897 (Ed)
Critic, The 1906 (AMB)
Crook of Dreams 1919 ( ) 1078, 1309
Crooked Road, The 1911 (Bio) 816, 1223,
1593, 2060
Crooked Romance, A 1917 ( ) 1312
Crooked Straight, The 1919 (Par) 259,
2096, 2780
Crooked to the End 1915 (Key/Tri) 70,
876, 1622, 1666, 2164
Crooked Trails /aka/ Twisted Trails
1916 (Selig Polyscope) 1849
Crooky Scruggs 1915 (V) 636, 1501, 2145
Cross Bearer, The 1918 ( ) 1603
Cross Country Original, The 1910 (P)
Cross Currents 1915 (Bo) 920, 2690
Cross Purposes 1913 ( ) 1711, 2112
Cross Red Nurse, The 1918 (Go) 765
Crossed Currents 1915 ( ) 2068
Crossed Love and Swords 1915 (Key) 210,
878, 2208
Crossing the American Plains in the
Early Fifties 1911 (Bio)
Crossroads of Life 1908 (AMB)
Crow, The 1919 ( ) 1011
Crown Jewels 1918 ( ) 192
Crown Prince's Double, The 1915 (V)
297, 566, 1185, 1837, 2523
Crucial Test, The 1911 (Ed)
Crucible, The 1914 (FP) 482
Cruel, Cruel Love /aka/ Lord Helpus
1914 (Key) 384, 451, 531, 650, 791,
2077

Cruise of the Jolly Roger 1919 ( ) 1518
Crusader, The 1911 (Ed)
Crushed Hat, The 1904 (AMB)
Crushed Tragedian, The 1908 (Lubin)
Cry for Help, A 1912 (Bio) 141, 398,
1028, 1029, 1182, 1665, 1832
Cry from the Wilderness, A 1909 (Ed)
Cry of Justice, The 1919 ( ) 1035
Cry of the Captive, The 1914 (Br) 1289,
2171
Cry of the Weak 1919 ( ) 2683
Crystal Casket, The 1905 (Melies)
Crystal Gazer, The 1917 ( ) 1080, 2683
Cub Reporter, The 1912 (Ed)
Cuore Edarte 1915 ( ) 273
Cup Final Mystery, The 1914 (Br) 834,
1879, 2138
Cup of Chance 1915 ( ) 273
Cup of Fury 1919 (Select) 884
Cup of Life, A 1915 (Tri) 134, 473, 1032,
1745, 2096, 2392
Cup of Tea and She, A 1909 (Ed)
Cupid and Psyche 1897 (Ed)
Cupid and the Motor Boat 1910 (V) 332
Cupid by Proxy 1918 (P) 1988
Cupid Forecloses 1919 (P) 1241, 1519,
1602
Cupid in a Dental Parlor 1913 (Key) 1666
Cupid Incognito 1914 ( ) 2112
Cupid Trims His Lordship 1915 (Christie)
525
Cupid Versus Money 1915 (V) 297, 2523
Cupid's Day Off 1919 (Key/Tri) 2608
Cupid's Hired Man 1913 (V) 332, 901
Cupid's Joke 1911 (Bio)
Cupid's Papa * (Christie) 525
Chpid's Pranks 1908 (Ed)
Cupid's Realm; or A Game of Hearts 1908
(V)
Cupid's Rival 1917 (King-Bee) 1161, 2733
Cupid's Roundup 1918 (F) 1849
Cupid's Target 1915 (Lubin) 1161
Cupid's Uppercut 1915 (Christie) 525
Curate's Love Story, A 1912 (Hep) 2744
Cure, The 1917 (Mu) 97, 204, 384, 451,
517, 1414, 2077, 2090, 2499, 2611
Cure for Bashfulness 1908 (V)
Cure for Crime, A 1911 (Ed)
Cure for Dyspepsia, A 1911 (Ed)
Cure for Pokeritus 1912 (V) 111, 332,
790, 818, 901
Cure That Failed, The 1912 (Un)
Cure That Failed, The 1913 (Key) 1666,
1941, 2465
Cured 1911 (Bio)
Curfew Bell, The 1909 (Ed)
Curfew Must Not Ring Tonight 1912 (Hep)
2531
Curfew Shall Not Ring Tonight, The 1912
( ) 2112
Curing a Jealous Husband 1909 (Lubin)
Curing Cissy 1914 (V) 908
Curing of Myra May, The 1914 (V) 2523
Curing the Office Boy 1912 (Ed)
Curiosity 1911 (Bio)
Curiosity Punished 1908 (Melies)
Curious Dream, A 1919 ( ) 2003
Curious Dream, A 1907 (V)
Curious Mr. Curio 1908 (Ed)

Curse of Eve, The 1917 ( ) 1745
Curse of Gold, The 1909 (Lubin)
Curse of Humanity, The 1914 ( ) 2096
Curse of Iku, The 1918 ( ) 60
Cursed by His Beauty 1914 (Key) 460,
    650, 1906, 2501
Curses! They Remarked 1914 (Key) 531
Curtain Pole, The 1909 (AMB) 79, 2368
Curtain's Secret, The 1915 (Hep) 1289,
    2171, 2744
Cutting California Redwoods 1912 (Es)
    50
Cy Whittaker's Ward 1917 ( ) 1774
Cycle of Fate, The 1916 (Selig Polyscope)
    857, 1364, 1957
Cyclone Higgins, D. F. 1918 (M) 156,
    353
Cyclone Smith Plays Trumpet 1919 (Tri)
    2034, 2056
Cyclone Smith's Comeback 1919 (Tri)
    2034, 2056
Cyclone Smith's Partner 1919 (Tri) 2034,
    2056
Cyclone Smith's Vow 1917 (Tri) 2034,
    2056
Cymbeline 1913 (T) 603, 647, 1468, 2201
Cynthia in the Wilderness 1916 (Br) 1968,
    2179, 2712
Cynthia's Agreement 1912 (Ed)
Czarma Ksiazka /aka/ Zolty Paszport
    1915 ( ) 1922

- D -

Daddy 1917 (Br) 349
Daddy Long Legs 1919 (FN) 138, 528,
    653, 1137, 1523, 1924, 2047
Daddy's Girl 1918 (P) 1988
Dad's a Gentleman Too 1905 ( )
Dad's Knockout 1918 (Go) 2009, 2121
Dad's Out-Laws 1916 (Tri) 1042
Dairy Maid's Revenge, The 1902 (AMB)
Daisy Cowboys, The 1911 (Ed)
Daisy's Doodad's Dial 1914 (GB) 2604
Damaged Goods 1915 ( ) 193
Damages for Breach 1919 (Br) 943
Damnation of Faust, The 1903 (Melies)
Damon and Pythias 1915 (Un) 1580, 1711,
    2095, 2803
Damsel in Distress, A 1919 ( ) 1118
Dan the Dandy 1911 (Bio) 357, 1613,
    2502, 2728
Dance 1894 (Ed) 2207
Dance at Silver Gulch, The 1912 (Es) 50
Dancer and the King, The 1908 (V)
Dancer and the King, The 1914 (W) 2439,
    2509
Dancer's Peril, The 1917 ( ) 1255
Dancing Chinaman, Marionettes 1898 (Ed)
Dancing Darkey Boy 1897 (Ed)
Dancing Darkies 1897 (American Mu-
    toscope)
Dancing Fiend, The 1908 (Lubin)
Dancing Girl, The 1915 (FP) 1984, 2105
Dancing Girl of Butte, The 1910 (Bio)
    122, 1865, 2368
Dandy Donovan 1914 ( ) 1918
Danger Game, The 1918 (Go) 1423
Danger Girl /aka/ Love on Skates 1917

(Key/Tri) 280, 1572, 2510, 2512,
    2564, 2636
Danger-Go-Slow 1918 (Un) 449, 1025,
    1454, 1896, 1907
Danger Mark, The 1918 (Art/Par) 888,
    1049, 1137, 1427
Danger Patrol * ( ) 1509
Danger Signal 1915 (M) 656
Danger Trail, The 1917 (Selig) 358, 1220,
    1273, 2693
Danger Zone, The 1919 ( ) 1266, 2133,
    2581
Dangerous Affair, A 1919 ( ) 2095
Dangerous Game, A 1913 ( ) 2070
Dangerous Hours 1919 ( ) 437, 771, 2128
Dangerous Lesson, A 1912 (Ed)
Dangerous Pair, A 1909 (Ed)
Dangerous Paradise, A 1919 ( ) 2232
Dangerous Play, A 1912 (Ingvald C. Oes)
Dangerous Waters 1919 ( ) 715, 1558
Dangers of a Bride 1917 (Key/Tri) 551,
    796, 1153, 1691, 1835, 2336, 2512,
    2588, 2636
Danger's Peril, The 1917 ( ) 273, 626
Daniel 1916 ( ) 1426
Daniel Boone 1907 (Ed)
Danse du Ventre 1896 (Ed) 872
Danse Vampiresque 1912 (Danish)
Dante's Inferno 1911 (Monopol Film Co.)
Dante's Progress and Experiences
    through Paradise 1912 (National Film
    Distributing Co.)
Dante's Progress and Experiences
    through Purgatory 1912 (National
    Film Distributing Co.)
Daphne and the Pirate 1916 ( ) 724, 1029
Darby and Joan 1919 (Br) 503
Daredevil Dan 1917 ( ) 2486
Daring Hearts 1919 (M) 156, 353
Daring of Diana, The 1917 (V) 1878, 2472
Dark Harum 1915 (FP) 588
Dark Lantern, A 1919 (Relart) 273, 586
Dark Star, The 1919 (Cosmopolitan) 300,
    502, 552, 587, 660, 803, 1076, 1432,
    1473, 1864
Darkening Trail 1915 ( ) 1188, 1332,
    1745
Darkest London 1915 (Br) 503
Darkest Russia 1917 ( ) 265, 273
Darktown Belle, The 1913 (Key) 1666
Darling of Paris, The 1917 (F) 116, 674,
    733, 975, 1244, 1506, 1521, 2745
Darling of the Gallery Gods, The 1905
    (AMB)
Das Leben ein Traum, Die Augen der
    Mumie Ma 1913 ( ) 1349
Das Rasel von Bangalore 1917 (German)
    2632
Das Tagebuch einer Verlorenen 1917
    (German) 2632
Dash of Courage, A 1916 (Key/Tri) 166,
    460, 786, 1086, 1776, 1981, 2512,
    2636, 2799
Dash through the Clouds, A 1912 (Bio)
    83, 315, 1941, 2000, 2045
Dash to Death, A 1909 (Ed)
Daughter Angele 1917 ( ) 1652, 2453
Daughter of Daring, A--serial 1916 ( )
    1011
Daughter of Destiny, A 1917 (FN) 2037

Daughter of Eve, A 1919 (Bw) 414, 522, 941, 1289, 2171, 2515
Daughter of France, A 1918 (F) 2024
Daughter of Israel, A 1914 (V) 297, 2523
Daughter of MacGregor, The 1916 ( ) 1064
Daughter of Maryland, A 1917 (Mu) 401, 1040
Daughter of Mine 1919 (Go) 265, 1423, 1756
Daughter of the City, A 1915 (Es) 377, 487, 638, 1392
Daughter of the Confederacy 1913 (Kal) 992
Daughter of the Dragon 1917 (Las) 1208
Daughter of the Gods, A 1916 (F) 437, 1275, 1411, 1524, 2071
Daughter of the Mines, A 1910 (Ed)
Daughter of the Old South, A 1918 (Par) 957
Daughter of the Poor, A 1917 (Tri) 2479
Daughter of the Sea, A 1915 ( ) 1991
Daughter of the Sun, A 1909 (Ed)
Daughter of the Well Dressed Poor, A 1917 ( ) 2131
Daughter of the West, A 1918 (P) 1988
Daughter of the Wolf 1919 ( ) 1417, 1528
Daughter of Uncle Sam, A--serial 1918 (General Film Corp.) 399, 670, 2432, 2624
Daughters of Destiny 1917 ( ) 1266
Daughter's Strange Inheritance 1915 (V) 297, 2523
Dave's Love Affair 1911 (Bio)
Davey Crockett 1916 ( ) 866, 1446
Davey Jones' Locker 1903 (AMB)
David Copperfield 1913 (Hep) 714
David Garrick 1914 (Hep) 1247, 2744
David Garrick 1916 (Pal) 866, 1446
David Harum 1915 (FP) 1798
Dawn 1919 ( ) 901
Dawn Maker, The 1916 (Tri) 715, 1188, 2742
Dawn of Romance, The 1914 (Un) 1058
Dawn of Freedom, The 1916 ( ) 2068
Dawn of Love 1916 (M) 2520
Dawn of Tomorrow, A 1915 (FP) 365, 579, 2047, 2061, 2155
Dawn of Understanding, The 1919 ( ) 1602
Day After, The 1909 (Bio) 79, 1363, 1542
Day After Day 1909 (Bio) 2513
Day at School, A 1916 (Vim) 1161
Day at the Circus 1901 (Ed)
Day Dreams 1919 (Go) 265, 950, 1423
Day of the Dog, The 1909 (Lubin)
Day She Paid, The 1919 ( ) 1283, 2627
Daybreak 1918 ( ) 1389
Days of Daring * (Selig Polyscope) 1849
Days of '49, The 1917 ( ) 2754
Day's Pleasure, A 1919 (FN) 97, 204, 451, 538, 1529, 2077, 2611, 2782
Dazzling Miss Davison, The 1916 ( ) 2088
Deacon Outwitted, The 1913 (Key) 1941, 2465
Deacon's Love Letter, The 1909 (V)
Deacon's Trouble, The 1912 (Key) 1666, 1941, 2465
Deacon's Waterloo, The 1915 (Christie) 525
Dead Letter, The 1915 (Lubin) 1161

Dead Man's Child, A 1911 (Ingvald C. Oes)
Dead Man's Shoes 1913 ( ) 2112, 2125
Dead Shot Baker 1917 ( ) 785, 1519
Deadwood Sleeper, The 1905 (AMB)
Deaf Burglar, A 1913 (Key) 1666
Dear Little Teacher, The 1912 (Hep) 2531
Dear Old Stars and Stripes, Goodbye 1903 (Lubin)
Dearly Paid for Kiss, A 1908 (V)
Death Dance 1918 ( ) 273, 1137
Death Disc, The 1909 (Bio) 79, 850, 1450, 1701, 1933, 2156
Death Doll, The 1915 ( ) 2002
Death of a Toreador, The 1907 (P) 1575
Death of Nathan Hale, The 1911 (Ed)
Death's Marathon 1913 (Bio) 141, 315, 1182, 1832, 2513, 2680
Debt, The 1917 (Mu) 1208, 2088
Debt of Honor, A 1919 ( ) 831, 1329
Deceived Slumming Party, The 1908 (AMB)
Deceiver, The 1907 (V)
Deception, The 1909 (AMB) 79, 1511, 2729
Deception, The 1918 (Br) 1453
Deciding Kiss, The 1918 (Un) 1080, 2147
Decoyed 1904 (AMB)
Decree of Destiny, A 1911 (Bio) 271, 732, 1074, 2047, 2368, 2502
Deemster, The 1917 ( ) 272
Deep Purple 1915 (W) 2410, 2811
Deep Purple, The 1919 ( ) 1427, 2690
Deep Sea Liar, A /aka/ Landlubber 1916 (Vogue) 2608
Deerslayer, The 1911 (V) 745, 1877, 2111, 2112, 2604
Defeat of the City, The 1917 ( ) 102
Defence of Sevastopol, The 1911 ( ) 1890
Delayed Proposal, The 1911 (Bio)
Delicious Little Devil, The 1919 (Un) 1455, 1907, 2616
Delinquent Bridegroom, The 1916 (Vogue) 2608
Delirium in a Studio 1907 (Melies)
Deliver the Goods 1915 (Br) 150
Deliverance 1919 ( ) 176, 1244, 1409, 1410, 1571, 1573, 1624, 1708, 1766, 1803, 2180, 2335
Delusion, A 1902 (AMB)
Deluxe Annie 1918 (Select) 335, 662, 1319, 1836, 1959, 2449, 2523
Demon, The 1918 ( ) 506, 1717, 2487
Den of Thieves, A 1914 ( ) 2112
Denny from Ireland 1919 ( ) 2549
Dentist, The see Laughing Gas 1914 (Key)
Dentist, The 1917 (M) 768, 1707, 2069
Deputy's Love Affair, The 1910 (Es) 50
Der Abgrund 1910 ( ) 1935
Der Gelbe Schein 1915 ( ) 1922
Der Stier von Oliviera 1918 ( ) 1349
Der Tanz Auf den Vulken 1919 ( ) 1614
Derby Winner, The 1915 (Br) 43
Derelict, The 1915 (Mu) 892, 1080, 1206
Desdemona 1912 (Ingvald C. Oes)
Desert Breed, The 1915 (Rex/Un) 352, 449, 762
Desert Gold 1914 ( ) 1569, 2096
Desert Gold 1919 ( ) 1591, 2780
Desert Hero, A 1919 (FP/Las) 65, 1401, 1719

Desert Law 1919 ( ) 2128
Desert Man, The 1917 (Tri) 1188, 2780
Desert of Egypt, The 1915 ( ) 1684
Desert of Wheat 1919 (Tri) 2341, 2479
Desert Vulture, The 1919 (Reelcraft) 1099
Desert Wooing, A 1918 ( ) 189, 1280
Deserted Hero, A 1919 ( ) 1476, 2208
Deserted Shaft, The 1912 (Imp)
Deserter, The 1912 (New York Motion
    Picture Co.)
Deserter, The 1916 (Tri) 172, 763, 1951,
    2096, 2451, 2606
Desert's Sting, The 1914 ( ) 1613, 1694,
    1809
Desire of the Moth 1917 ( ) 495
Desired Woman, A 1918 ( ) 1877
Despatch Bearer, The 1907 (V) 1511
Desperado, The 1910 (Es) 50
Desperate Crime, A 1906 (Melies)
Desperate Deed, A 1919 ( ) 1273
Desperate Gold 1919 ( ) 2031
Desperate Lover, A 1912 (Key) 1666,
    1941, 2368
Desperate Scoundrel, A see Dirty Work
    in a Laundry
Desperation 1918 ( ) 1570
Destiny 1919 (Un) 1253, 2042, 2700, 2738
Destroyer, The 1916 ( ) 1270, 1632
Destruction 1916 (F) 116, 174, 850, 952,
    970, 1263, 1709, 1887, 1971
Determined Lover, The; or Where There's
    a Will, There's a Way 1908 (V)
Deuce Duncan 1918 (Tri) 715, 1788
Devil, The 1908 (AMB) 994, 1511, 2212
Devil, The 1908 (Ed)
Devil and the Gambler, The 1908 (V)
Devil Between, The 1919 ( ) 2211
Devil Decides, The 1915 ( ) 1685
Devil Dodger, The 1917 (Tri) 186, 1016,
    2479
Devil M' Care 1919 ( ) 2760
Devil Stone, The 1917 (Art/Par) 411, 869,
    1386, 1537, 1721, 1756, 1925, 2112,
    2623, 2648
Devil's Assistant, The 1917 (Mu) 905
Devil's Castle, The see LeManoir du
    Diable
Devil's Darling, The 1918 ( ) 1496
Devil's Daughter, The 1915 (F) 116, 195,
    759, 1213, 1834
Devil's Double, The 1916 (Tri) 1188, 1745
Devil's Needle, The 1916 (FA/Tri) 1753,
    1756, 2523
Devil's Own, The 1916 ( ) 969
Devil's Passkey, The 1919 (Un) 351, 686,
    898, 998
Devil's Pay Day, The 1917 ( ) 2803
Devil's Price, The 1919 ( ) 468
Devil's Riddle, The 1918 ( ) 295
Devil's Slide 1902 (AMB)
Devil's Toy 1916 ( ) 2468
Devil's Trail, The 1919 ( ) 525, 771,
    1494, 1717
Devil's Wheel, The 1918 (F) 295
Dew Drop Inn 1919 (V) 2367
Dewar's Scotch Whiskey 1897 (Inter-
    national Film Co.)
Deyo 1907 (AMB)
Diamond Cut Diamond 1912 (V) 332, 901,
    2112
Diamond from the Sky, The--serial 1915

(AM) 326, 344, 606, 925, 930, 1317,
2032, 2046, 2201, 2538
  1.   The Heritage of Hate
  2.   An Eye for an Eye
  3.   The Silent Witness
  4.   The Prodigal's Progress
  5.   For the Sake of a False
       Friend
  6.   Shadows at Sunrise
  7.   The Fox and the Pig
  8.   A Mind in the Past
  9.   A Runaway Match
 10.   Old Foes with New Faces
 11.   The Web of Destiny or
       Plaything of the Papoose
 12.   To the Highest Bidder
 13.   The Man in the Mask
 14.   For Love and Money
 15.   Desperate Chances
 16.   The Path of Peril
 17.   King of Diamonds and the
       Queen of Hearts
 18.   Charm against Harm
 19.   Fire, Fury and Confusion
 20.   The Soul Stranglers
 21.   The Lion's Bride
 22.   The Rose in the Dust
 23.   The Double Cross
 24.   The Mad Millionaire
 25.   A House of Cards
 26.   The Garden of the Gods
 27.   Mine Own People
 28.   The Falling Aeroplane
 29.   A Deal with Destiny
 30.   The American Earl
Diamond in the Rough, A 1916 ( ) 2002
Diamond Maker, The; or Fortune and
    Misfortune 1909 (V)
Diamond Star, The 1911 (Bio) 122, 1613
Diamonds and Pearls 1918 ( ) 1048
Diana Ardway 1919 (M) 631
Diana of the Green Van 1919 (Tri) 2194
Diana the Huntress 1916 ( ) 275, 2511
Diana's Dress Reform 1914 ( ) 2472
Diane of the Follies 1916 ( ) 686, 1029,
    1490
Dick Carson Wins Through 1917 (Hep)
    812, 2744
Dick Turpin series (4) 1912 (Br) 1873
Dick's Sister 1908 (Lubin)
Dicksville Terrors, The 1916 (F) 1524
Dictator, The 1915 (FP) 140, 2411
Did Mother Get Her Wish? 1912 (Bio)
Did Not Finish the Story 1903 (AMB)
Die Auger der Mumie Ma (Eyes of the
    Mummy, The 1919 ( ) 1922
Die Beastie 1915 ( ) 1922
Die Spinner 1919 (Decla-Bioscop) 624, 719
Die Toten Augen 1918 ( ) 1922
Difficult Way, The 1914 (Br) 43, 349
Dime Novel 1909 (V)
Dime Novel Detective A 1909 (Lubin)
Dimples 1916 ( ) 1841
Dinah's Defeat 1904 (AMB)
Dip into Society, A 1913 ( ) 2748
Diplomacy 1915 (Las) 724, 752, 756
Diplomat of Wolfville 1917 ( ) 1519
Diplomatic Mission, A 1919 (V) 646, 2767
Dirty Work in a Laundry /aka/ A
    Desperate Scoundrel 1915 (Key) 210,
    791, 2208, 2465

Dirty's Daring Dash 1919 (Key) 2143
Disappointed Old Maid, The 1903 (AMB)
Discard, The 1916 (Es) 1142
Disciple, The 1915 (Tri) 627, 1188, 1690
Discord and Harmony 1914 (Gold Seal/Un)
    352, 449, 938, 1705, 1925
Discordant Note, A 1903 (AMB)
Discoverers, The 1908 (V)
Discoveries of Bodies 1903 (AMB)
Dishonored Medal, The 1914 ( ) 2672
Disintegrated Convict 1907 (V)
Disraeli 1916 (Br) 177
Disreputable Mr. Raegen, The 1911 (Ed)
District Attorney, The 1915 ( ) 209
Divident, The 1916 ( ) 2096
Dividing Line, The 1912 (Un)
Divine Sacrifice 1918 ( ) 1048
Diving Displays 1909 (V) 1411
Diving Girl, The 1911 (Bio)
Diving Girl, The 1911 (Key) 1941
Divorce, The 1903 (AMB)
        Detected
        On the Trail
        The Evidence Secured
Divorce Game 1917 ( ) 265, 273
Divorce Trap, The 1919 (F) 295
Divorcee, The 1909 (M) 139
Divorcee, The 1917 (P) 1437
Dixie Madcaps 1916 (F) 1524
Dixie Mother, The 1910 (V) 231, 1426,
    2523, 2604
Dizzy Diver, The * ( ) 750
Dizzy Heights and Daring Hearts 1916
    (Key/Tri) 47, 48, 509, 531, 1776
Do and Dare * (Selig Polyscope) 1849
Do Children Count? 1917 (Es) 1636
Do It Now 1908 (Lubin)
Do-Re-Me-Fa 1915 (Kay) 531
Do You Love Your Wife? 1919 (Rolin/P)
    1502
Doctor, The 1911 (Ed)
Doctor and the Woman, The 1918 ( ) 961,
    1175
Doctor Bridget 1912 (V) 332, 818, 901
Dr. Brompton-Watts' Adjuster 1912 (Ed)
Dr. Bunion and the Mischievous Boys
    1902 (AMB)
Doctor Cupid 1911 (V) 231, 332
Dr. Curem's Patients 1908 (Lubin)
Dr. Dippy's Sanitarium 1906 (AMB)
Dr. Fenton's Ordeal 1914 (Hep) 2744
Dr. Jekyll and Mr. Hyde 1912 (T) 184,
    2430
Dr. Jekyll and Mr. Hyde 1913 (Selig)
    108, 603, 973
Dr. Jekyll and Mr. Hyde 1916 ( ) 1564
Dr. LeFleur's Theory 1907 (Ed) 566
Dr. Phantom, the Scientific Sleuth 1912
    ( )
Doctored Affair, A 1913 (Key) 1941
Doctored Dinner Pail, The 1909 (Ed)
Doctoring a Leak /aka/ Total Loss 1916
    (Vogue) 2608
Doctor's Bride, The 1909 (Lubin)
Doctor's Favorite Patient, The 1903 (AMB)
Doctor's Secret, The 1913 (V) 297, 2523
Dodgin' a Million 1918 (Go) 1941
Dodging His Doom 1917 (Key/Tri) 531,
    966, 2165, 2580, 2799
Dog Catcher's Love, A 1917 (Key/Tri)
    282, 440, 543, 1225, 2023, 2501

Dog Factory, 1904 (Ed)
Dog Gone Shame 1917 ( ) 1872
Dog Lost, Strayed or Stolen, $25.00
    Reward. Apply to Mrs. Brown, 711
    Park Ave., A 1905 (Lubin)
Dog's Life, A 1917 (FN) 97, 204, 451,
    452, 1347, 1380, 1414, 2077, 2116,
    2499, 2611, 2741, 2782
Dog's Love, A 1914 (T) 107
Doing His Best see Making a Living
Doing His Bit 1917 (Br) 2152
Doing Our Bit 1918 (F) 1524
Dolken 1916 ( ) 1155
Doll Shop, The 1917 (Tri) 2479
Doll's House, A 1917 (Bluebird/Un) 449,
    677, 2042, 2490, 2804
Doll's House, A 1918 (Art/Par) 888, 1237,
    2373, 2385
Dollar Did It, A 1913 (Key) 2465
Dollar Mark, The 1914 ( ) 2698
Dollars and Sense /aka/ The Twins 1916
    (Key/Tri) 179, 371, 396, 509, 598,
    2020, 2206
Dollars and the Women 1916 ( ) 1427
Dolly Does Her Bit 1918 (P) 1988
Dolly's Scoop 1916 (Rex/Un) 449, 827,
    990, 1604, 1683
Dolly's Vacation 1919 (P) 1988
Dombey and Son 1918 (Br) 834, 1968,
    2150
Don Caesar de Bazan 1915 (Kal) 1270,
    1826
Don Quichotte--cartoon 1909 (French) 512
Con Quixote 1915 (Tri) 731, 877, 1286,
    2568, 2671
Donkey Party, A 1903 (AMB)
Donkey Party, The 1901 (Ed)
Don't Change Your Husband 1919 (Art/Par)
    83, 506, 606, 724, 877, 1925, 2149,
    2380, 2512
Don't Monkey with a Buzz Saw 1914 (Kal)
    1924
Don't Shoot! 1917 ( ) 2095
Don't Shove! 1919 (P) 1586
Dooley's Scheme 1911 (Bio)
Doomed Ship, The 1911 (Ed)
Door Between, The 1917 ( ) 495
Doorsteps 1916 (GB) 812, 2604
Doorway of Destruction, The 1915 (Un)
    926, 2343
Dora: A Rustic Idyll 1908 (V)
Dora Thorne 1915 ( ) 2430
Dorian's Divorce 1916 ( ) 2614
Dormant Power, The 1917 ( ) 486, 1991
Dorothy Danesbridge--Militant 1915 (V)
    2523
Dorothy Dares 1917 ( ) 2486
Dorothy's Family 1911 (Independent
    Moving Picture Co.)
Double-Barreled Suicide, A 1907 (V)
Double Crossed 1914 (Key) 2465
Double Crossed 1917 (Par) 957
Double Crossed 1919 (Un) 2034
Double Hold Up, The 1919 ( ) 1011
Double Knot, The 1914 ( ) 2672
Double Life, A 1912 (New York Motion
    Picture Co.)
Double Life, A 1917 (M) 768, 1707
Double Life of Mr. Alfred Burton 1919
    (Br) 776, 943
Double Standard 1917 ( ) 1006

Double Trouble 1915 (FA/Tri) 295, 857,
    1083, 1424, 2211, 2573, 2780
Double Trouble 1916 (F) 1524
Double Wedding, A 1913 (Key) 1666, 2465
Dough and Dynamite /aka/ The Doughnut
    Designer; The Cook 1914 (Key) 37,
    73, 451, 460, 531, 815, 1422, 1662,
    1934
Doughnut Designer, The see Dough and
    Dynamite
Dough-Nuts 1917 (King-Bee) 1161, 2733
Dove and the Serpent, The 1912 (Imp)
Down and Out see Laughing Gas
Down by the Sea 1915 (Christie) 525, 1132
Down by the Sounding Sea 1914 (Mu) 1182,
    1751, 2112
Down the Road to Creditville 1914 ( )
    1028, 2112
Down through the Ages * ( ) 992
Down to Earth 1917 (Art/Par) 387, 857,
    1006, 1855, 2031, 2648
Downward Path, The 1902 (AMB)
            The New Soubrette
            The Fresh Book Agent
            The Girl Who Went Astray
            The Suicide
            She Ran Away
Draft 258 1918 ( ) 1832, 2520
Dragnet, The * ( ) 1472
Dragon, The 1916 (Mu) 905
Dragon Painter, The 1919 (Par) 60, 964,
    1208
Dragon's Claw, The 1915 ( ) 1143, 1542
Dragon's Net, The 1919 ( ) 2656
Drake's Love Story 1913 (Hep) 1289, 2744
Drama's Dreadful Deal 1917 (P) 1586
Dramatic Mistake, A 1914 (Sterling) 2465
Dramatist's Dream, The 1909 (V)
Drawing Lesson, The; or The Living
    Statue 1903 (Melies)
Drawing the Color Line 1909 (Ed)
Dream, A see His Prehistoric Past
Dream, The 1911 (Imp) 2047
Dream Girl, The 1916 (Par) 947, 1648,
    1907, 1925, 2149, 2728
Dream Lady, The 1918 ( ) 370
Dream of a Rarebit Fiend, The 1906 (Ed)
    279
Dream of an Opium Fiend, The 1908
    (Melies)
Dream of the Race Track Fiend 1905 (AMB)
Dream of Wealth, A 1908 (V)
Dreamland Frolic, A 1919 (Br) 1487
Dreams 1918 ( ) 1426
Dreams of a Policeman 1908 (V)
Dreamy Knights 1916 (Vim) 1161
Dress Suits in Pawn 1912 (Ed)
Dressmaker's Accident, The 1903 (AMB)
Dreyfus Affair, The 1899 (Melies) 1802
Drifters, The 1919 ( ) 1431
Drink 1918 (Br) 1879
Drink, A 1907 (Melies)
Drink's Lure 1913 (Bio)
Drive for Life, The 1909 (AMB) 1363
Driven 1916 (Br) 1931, 2138
Driven from Home 1909 (Lubin)
Drop of Ink, A 1904 (AMB)
Dropped from the Clouds 1917 ( ) 2354
Droppington's Devlish Dream 1915 (Key)
    531
Droppington's Family Tree 1915 (Key) 531

Drowsy Dick, Officer No. 73 1910 (Ed)
Drummer's Day Off, The 1908 (V)
Drummer's Vacation 1912 (Key) 650, 1666
Drunkard's Child 1090 (Lubin)
Drunkard's Reformation, The 1909 (AMB)
    79, 685, 1363
DuBarry 1917 ( ) 2717
DuBarry 1919 (Decla-Bioscop) 1922
Dub, The 1918 (Par) 1201, 1563, 1970,
    2112
Ducking a Discord 1916 (Vogue) 2608
Ducks out of Water 1917 ( ) 1872
Dude and the Bathing Girls, The 1903
    (AMB)
Dude and the Burglars, The 1903 (AMB)
Duds and Drygoods 1917 (V) 2367
Duel, The 1912 (Key) 1941, 2368
Duel in Mid-Air, A 1909 (Ed)
Duel of Monsieur Myope, The 1907 (P)
    1575
Duel Scene, "By Right of Sword" 1904
    (AMB)
Duel Scene from "Macbeth" 1905 (AMB)
Duet from "Martha" (Flotow) 1909 (Lubin)
Duke's Jester, The or A Fool's Revenge
    1909 (V)
Duke's Plan, The 1910 (Bio) 554, 1060
Dull Care 1919 (V) 2367
Dull Razor, A 1900 (Ed)
Dumb Girl of Portici, The 1916 (Un)
    1007, 1307, 1391, 1397, 2016, 2371,
    2422, 2711, 2779
Dumb Half-Breed's Defense, The 1910
    (Es) 50
Dumb Hero, A 1908 (Ed)
Dumb Messenger, The 1911 (Independent
    Moving Picture Co.)
Dumb Witness, The 1908 (V)
Dumb Wooing, The 1912 (Ed)
Dummy, The 1916 (Br) 1487
Dummy, The 1917 (Art/Par) 1954, 2045
Dunces and Danger 1918 (V) 2367
Dupe, The 1916 ( ) 1800, 2513
Duplicity 1916 (M) 768, 1707
Duplicity of Hargraves, The 1916 ( )
    1426
Durand of the Badlands 1917 (F) 866,
    1523, 1849
During the Roundup 1913 (Bio) 338, 1029,
    2680
Dust 1916 ( ) 1080
Dust of Desire 1918 ( ) 243, 709, 1275
Dust of Egypt 1915 (V) 468, 1876, 2487
Dutch Gold Mine, A 1911 (Bio)
Dutch Gold Mine, The 1912 (Key) 731,
    2368
Dutch Kiddies: Montgomery and Stone
    1907 (Winthrop Moving Picture Co.)
Dutiful Dub, The 1919 (P) 1586
Duty 1911 (Indipendent Moving Picture Co.)
Duty Versus Revenge 1908 (V)
Dynamite Waistcoat, The 1909 (V)
Dynamiter, The see Cannon Ball, The
Dynamiter, The 1908 (W)
Dynamiters, The 1912 ( ) 785
Dynast, The 1917 ( ) 1714

                        - E -

Each Hour a Pearl 1916 ( ) 2683

Each Pearl a Tear 1916 ( ) 28
Each to His Own Kind 1917 (Las) 1208,
    2002, 2613
Eagle, The 1918 ( ) 2211
Eagle's Eye, The--serial 1918 (Wharton/
    Am) 108, 110, 955, 1376, 1737, 2052,
    2400, 2430, 2653
    1. Hidden Death
    2. The Naval Ball Conspiracy
    3. The Plot against the Fleet
    4. Von Rentelen, the Destroyer
    5. The Strike Breeders
    6. The Plot against Organized
        Labor
    7. Brown Portfolio
    8. The Kaiser's Death Messenger
    9. The Munitions Campaign
    10. The Invasion of Canada
    11. The Burning of Hopewell
    12. The Canal Conspirators
    13. The Reign of Terror
    14. The Infantile Paralylis Epi-
        demic
    15. The Campaign against Cotton
    16. The Raid of the U-53
    17. Germany's U-Base in America
    18. The Great Hindu Conspiracy
    19. The Menace of the I. W. W.
    20. The Great Decision
Eagle's Mate, The 1914 (FP) 1450, 2047,
    2701
Eagle's Nest, The 1913 ( ) 579
Eagle's Wings, The 1916 ( ) 2613
Early Bird 1915 ( ) 283
Early Morning Attack, The 1899 (Ed)
Easiest Way, The 1917 (Select) 884, 1437,
    2811
East Is East 1917 (GB) 812, 849, 2604
East Lynne; or Led Astray 1908 (V)
East Lynne 1915 (F) 116, 684, 910, 1260,
    1275, 1962, 2430, 2473, 2477, 2574,
    2738, 2756, 2798
East Lynne with Variations 1919 (Key/Tri)
    2069, 2608
East of Suez 1912 (Martin Johnson Prods.)
    1366
Eastern Flower 1913 (Am) 1431
Easterner, The 1907 (V)
Eastward Ho! 1919 ( ) 1255
Easy Money 1907 (Lubin)
Easy Money 1918 ( ) 486
Easy Street 1917 (Mu) 97, 204, 206, 384,
    451, 517, 1414, 1840, 2077, 2090,
    2499, 2611, 2746
Easy to Make Money 1919 (M) 618, 1631,
    2375
Eating Force 1903 (AMB)
Eavesdropper, The 1909 (AMB) 1542,
    1823, 2212
Eavesdropper, The 1914 (Key) 65
Echo of Youth 1919 ( ) 111, 2129
Eclipse, The 1907 (Melies)
Eddie's Exploit 1912 (Ed)
Eddie's Little Love Affair 1915 ( ) 1630
Eddie's Night Out 1915 (Christie) 525
Edgar Allan Poe 1909 (AMB) 79
Edgar series 1918 ( ) 1379
Edge o' Beyond 1919 (Br) 831, 1918
Edge of Heart's Desire 1919 ( ) 274
Edge of the Abyss 1915 (Tri) 246,
    1690

Edge of the Law, The 1917 ( ) 2486,
    2570, 2753
Edison Bugg's Invention 1916 (Vin) 1161
Edison Kinetoscopic Record of a Sneeze
    1894 (W. K. L. Dickson)
Edna's Imprisonment 1911 (Ed)
Education of Mr. Pipp, The 1914 (Alco)
    173
Effecting a Cure 1910 (Bio)
Efficiency Edgar's Courtship 1917 (Es)
    1276, 1495, 2619
Egg-Crate Wallop, The 1919 (Ince/Par)
    535, 1261, 1588, 1859, 2096
Egyptian Mummy, The 1914 (V) 2081,
    2521
Egyptian Mystery, The 1909 (Ed)
Eighth Grandparent, The 1917 ( ) 2397,
    2754
Eileen of Erin 1913 (King-Bee) 134, 2096,
    2392
Elder Miss Blossom, The 1918 (Br) 831,
    1918
Elder Miss Simpkins Calls, The 1904
    (AMB)
Eldora, the Fruit Girl 1910 (Ed)
Eleanore Cuyler 1912 (Ed)
Elektra 1909 (V) 968
Element of Might, The 1919 ( ) 1186
Elephant on His Hands, An 1913 (Nestor/
    Un) 449
Eleventh Commandment, The 1918 ( )
    1832, 2478
Eleventh Hour, The 1910 (Ed)
Elf King, The 1908 (V)
Elite Ball, The 1913 (Key) 1666, 2368,
    2465
Elmo, the Mighty--serial 1919 (Un) 514,
    578, 610, 1570, 1668, 2454
    1. The Mystery of Mad
        Mountain
    2. Buried Alive
    3. Flames of Hate
    4. A Fiendish Revenge
    5. The Phantom Rescue
    6. The Puma's Paws
    7. The Masked Pursuer
    8. The Flaming Pit
    9. The House of a Thousand
        Tortures
    10. Victims of the Sea
    11. The Burning Den
    12. Lashed to the Rocks
    13. Into the Chasm
    14. The Human Bridge
    15. Craching to Earth
    16. Parachute Perils
    17. The Plunge
    18. Unmasked
Elopement, The 1897 (Ed)
Elopement, The 1907 (AMB)
Elopement at Home, An 1913 (V) 297, 2523
Elopement on Horseback 1898 (Ed)
Elopers Who Didn't Elope, The 1904
    (AMB)
Eloping with Aunty 1909 (Bio) 271, 1511
Elsa's Brother 1915 (V) 297, 2523
Elusive Isabel 1916 ( ) 272
Embarrassed Bridegroom, An 1913 ( )
    785
Embarrassment of Riches 1919 ( ) 731,
    2663

Embezzler, The 1914 (Gold Seal/Un) 352,
   449, 762, 1587, 1705, 2188
Emerald Broach, The 1915 ( ) 2002
Empress, The 1917 ( ) 239
Empty Cab, The 1918 ( ) 2031
Empty Gun, The 1917 (Gold Seal/Un) 449,
   686, 1665
Empty Pockets 1918 (FN) 437, 1631
Empty Sleeve, The; or Memories of
   By-Gone Days 1909 (V)
Enchanted Born, The 1919 ( ) 1602
Enchanted Drawing, The 1900 (Ed)
Enchanted Matress, The 1907 (Lubin)
Enchanted Profile, The 1917 ( ) 102
Enchanted Sedan-Chair, The 1905 (Melies)
Enchanted Well, The 1903 (Melies)
Enchantment, The 1916 (Mu) 2126, 2754
End of Camera Fiend 1904 (Paley &
   Steiner)
End of the Feud, The 1914 (Rex/Un) 352,
   449, 762, 1587, 1705
End of the Game 1917 ( ) 1431, 2754,
   2779
End of the Trail 1916 (F) 856, 868
Enemies of Children 1919 (F) 557
Enemy, The 1916 (V) 223, 1329, 1426,
   1888, 1996
Enemy amongst Us, The 1916 (Br) 150
Enemy to the King, An 1916 (V) 328,
   1731, 2378, 2433, 2487
Engagement Ring, The 1912 (Bio)
Engineer, The 1908 (Lubin)
Engineer's Romance, The 1910 (Ed)
Engineer's Sweetheart, The 1910 (Kal)
   1388
Engelein 1913 ( ) 1935
England's Menace 1914 (Br) 43
Englishman and the Girl, The 1910 (Bio)
   580, 2047
Englishman's Home, An 1914 (Br) 150
Enlighten Thy Daughter 1917 (Go) 709,
   1393, 1402
Enoch Arden, Part I 1911 (Bio) 79, 1060,
   1182, 1224, 1468, 1613, 1701, 1865,
   2000
Enoch Arden, Part II 1911 (Bio) 79, 1060,
   1468, 1613, 1865, 2000
Enoch Arden 1914 (Br) 2712
Enoch Arden 1915 (Mu) 1029, 1175, 1182,
   2112
Entente Cordiale (P) 1575
Entertaining the Boss 1917 ( ) 689
Environment 1917 (Mu) 906, 1841
Equal to the Emergency 1910 (Ed)
Equine Hero, An 1910 (Ed)
Eradicating Aunty 1909 (Bio) 1363, 1593
Erotikon 1919 ( ) 1155
Erstwhile Susan 1919 (Relart) 27, 120,
   226, 2091, 2118
Es Werde Licht 1917 (German) 2340, 2632
Escape, The 1914 (Mu) 595, 1029, 1182,
   1563, 1751, 1865, 2513, 2605
Escape, The 1919 ( ) 2690
Escape from Bondage, The 1912 (Ed)
Escape from Sing Sing 1903 (AMB)
Escape from Sing Sing, The 1905 (V)
Escape from the Flames, An 1904 (AMB)
Escape of Gas, An 1911 (F) 1575
Escape of Jim Dolan 1913 (Selig Poly-
   scope) 1849
Escaped Lunatic, The 1904 (AMB)

Escaped Lunatic, The 1911 (Ed)
Escaped Melody, The 1909 (Lubin)
Eskimo, The 1919 ( ) 539
Esmeralda 1915 (FP) 1282, 1804, 2047,
   2658, 2701
Esther 1916 (Br) 834, 1931, 2138
Eternal City, The 1915 (FP) 957, 1266,
   1600
Eternal Grind, The 1916 (FP) 265, 365,
   2047, 2729
Eternal Magdalene, The 1919 ( ) 823,
   1753
Eternal Mother, The 1912 (Bio) 95, 1941,
   2513
Eternal Mother, The 1917 (M) 139, 2105
Eternal Question, The 1916 (M) 1137,
   1971, 2037
Eternal Sapho 1916 (F) 116, 544, 1574,
   1763, 1971, 2110
Eternal Sin, The 1917 (Select) 143, 2105,
   2381
Eternal Temptress, The 1917 (Par) 438,
   462
Eternal Triangle, The 1917 (Hep) 1289,
   2171, 2744
Ethel's Luncheon 1909 (Ed)
Ethel's Romeos 1915 (Casino) 1161
Etta of the Footlights 1914 (V) 2523
Evangeline 1919 (F) 25, 554, 2175, 2717
Eve in Exile 1919 ( ) 1782, 2405, 2661
Even as You and I 1917 ( ) 998
Even Break, An 1917 (Tri) 2557
Evening at the Cinema, An 1907 (P) 1575
Eventful Elopement, An 1912 (V) 332
Ever Living Isles, The 1915 ( ) 2002
Everlasting Mercy 1912 (Bio) 1665
Every Day Is Sunshine When the Heart
   Beats True 1903 (Lubin)
Every Girl's Dream 1917 (F) 392, 1253
Every Inch a Man 1912 ( ) 2112
Every Mother's Son 1919 ( ) 2661
Every Rose Has It's Stem 1912 (Ed) 1977
Everybody Works but Father 1905 (Ed)
Everybody Works but Father (Black-face)
   1905 (AMB)
Everybody Works but Father (White-face)
   1905 (AMB)
Everybody Works but Mother 1905 (AMB)
Everybody Works but Mother 1906
   (Winthrop Press)
Everybody's Business 1919 (Br) 370, 1488,
   2129
Everybody's Girl 1919 (V) 1388
Everything Comes to Him Who Waits 1912
   (Ed)
Everywoman 1919 (Par) 242, 454, 606,
   635, 1201, 1206, 1220, 1292, 1321,
   1581, 1756, 1925, 2149
Everywoman's Husband 1918 (Tri) 1442,
   1490, 1582, 2022, 2512, 2731
Eve's Daughter 1918 (Art/Par) 333
Evicted 1911 (Hep) 2531
Eviction, The 1904 (AMB)
Evidence, The 1917 (P) 1988, 2392
Evidence Was Against Him, The 1902 (AMB)
Evil Art, The; or Gambling Exposed 1912
   (Eureka Feature Film Co.)
Evil Eye, The 1917 (Art/Par) 454, 935,
   1591, 2513
Evil of the Rich 1919 ( ) 1796
Evil That Men Do, The 1909 (V)

Evolution of Fashion, The 1917 (Nestor/
    Un) 1502
Evolution of Man, The--An Educated
    Chimpanzee 1901 (Lubin)
Evolution of Percival, The 1914 (V) 2081,
    2521
Evolution of the Japanese 1905 (Lubin)
Examination Day at School 1910 (Bio) 315,
    731, 1182, 1426, 1831, 2045, 2047,
    2156, 2368
Excess Baggage 1916 ( ) 690
Ex-Convict, The 1904 (Ed)
        Leaving Home
        The Burglary
        Discharged
        Looking for Employment
        Discouraged
        Desperation
        A Friend at Last
        The Rescue
Execution of Mary Queen of Scots 1893
    (Ed-Kintescope) 2556
Executive Clemency 1911 (Independent
    Moving Picture Co.)
Exile 1917 ( ) 2037
Exit the Vamp 1918 ( ) 269
Exoneration, The 1913 ( ) 2096
Expelled from the Club: The Ladies of
    the Club 1904 (AMB)
Expensive Visit, An 1915 (Lubin) 1161
Experience 1919 ( ) 708
Experimental Marriage 1919 (Select) 454,
    927, 1201, 1248, 2416, 2521
Expiation, The 1909 (Bio) 1363, 1542,
    1865
Exploits of Elaine, The--serial 1915 (P)
    141, 327, 628, 1118, 1564, 1752,
    2095, 2748
        1. The Clutching Hand
        2. The Twilight Sleep
        3. The Vanishing Jewels
        4. The Frozen Safe
        5. The Poisoned Room
        6. The Vampire
        7. The Double Trap
        8. The Hidden Voice
        9. The Death Ray
        10. The Life Current
        11. The Hour of Three
        12. The Blood Crystals
        13. The Devil Worshippers
        14. The Reckoning
Exploits of Tubby series 1917 (Hep) 1289,
    2744
Explorer, The 1915 ( ) 2541
Exquisite Thief, The 1919 (Un) 675
Extension Table, The 1912 (V) 2523
Extra Turn, The 1903 (Ed)
Extraordinary Illusions 1903 (Melies)
Extravagance 1916 (Par) 189, 627, 809
Extremities 1913 (V) 566, 2523
Eye for Eye 1918 (M) 151, 321, 891, 978,
    1919
Eye of Envy, The 1917 (Mu) 2760
Eye of the Night 1916 ( ) 2780
Eyes of Julia Deep, The 1918 ( ) 1841
Eyes of Mystery 1918 ( ) 2487
Eyes of the Mummy, The 1918 ( ) 1349
Eyes of the Soul 1919 (Par) 888, 2444
Eyes of the World 1918 ( ) 595, 1948,
    2026, 2211

Eyes of Youth 1919 (Equity) 569, 1310,
    1563, 1606, 2130, 2369, 2410, 2436,
    2453, 2616, 2811
Eyes That Saw 1915 (Gaumont Co.)
Eyes That See Not 1915 ( ) 2518

                    - F -

Fable of Elvira and Farina and the Meal
    Ticket 1915 (Es) 2512
Face at the Window, The 1908 (Lubin)
Face at the Window, The 1910 (Bio) 477,
    2047, 2680
Face at the Window, The 1919 (Br) 1358
Face in the Dark, The 1918 (Go) 950,
    1751
Face in the Fog 1914 ( ) 141
Face in the Moonlight, The 1915 ( )
Face on the Barroom Floor, The 1908 (Ed)
Face on the Barroom Floor, The /aka/
    The Ham Artist 1914 (Key) 73, 451,
    531, 815, 2336
Face to Face 1916 (Hep) 177, 2171, 2744
Face Value 1918 ( ) 1907, 1957
Faded Lilies, The 1909 (Bio) 2047
Faded Vampire, A see False Beauty
Failure, The 1911 (Bio) 209, 1613
Failure, The 1915 ( ) 2649
Fair and Warmer 1919 (M) 41, 2002
Fair Barrier 1918 ( ) 1764
Fair Dentist, The 1911 (Imp) 2047
Fair Enough 1919 ( ) 720, 930, 1651,
    1753
Fair Exchange, A 1909 (Bio)
Fair Exchange, A see Getting
    Acquainted 1914 (Key)
Fair Exchange Is No Robbery 1899 (Ed)
Fair Pretender, The 1918 (Go) 1423
Fair Rebel, A 1914 (Bio) 79, 1028, 2728
Fairie's Banquet, The 1911 (Ed)
Fairy and the Waif, The 1915 ( ) 1841
Fairyland, The 1903 (Melies)
        The Prince
        The Lords
        The Boudoir of Princess Azurine
        The Armory of the Castle
        The Vision
        The Royal Galley
        The Bottom of the Sea
        The Submarine Cave
        The Entrance of the Cavern
        The Neptune's Empire
        The Devil's Castle
        The Palace of the King
Faith 1919 ( ) 1631, 2468
Faith Endurin' * (Tri) 2479
Faith Healer, The 1912 ( ) 606, 1563
Faithful 1910 (Bio) 122, 1363, 2062, 2368
Faithful Fool, A 1909 (V)
Faithful Husband: A Loving Couple 1904
    (AMB)
Faithful Indian, The 1911 (Es) 50
Faithful Taxicab, The 1913 (Key) 65, 1941,
    2465
Faithful to the Finish 1915 (Komic) 731,
    2568
Faithful Wife, A 1908 (Lubin)
Fake Beggar 1898 (Ed)
Fake Blind Man, The 1905 (Lubin)
Fake Diamond Swindler, A 1908 (Melies)

Fake Windstorm, The 1908 (Lubin)
Faking with Society see Caught in a
  Cabaret
Fall of a Nation, The 1916 ( ) 996, 2398,
  2443
Fall of Babylon, The 1919 (Go) 497, 1756,
  1998, 2408, 2521
Fall of Blackhawk 1912 (Am)
Fall of the Romanoffs, The 1917 (Brenon)
  534, 1245, 1978, 2535, 2596
Fallen Angel 1918 (F) 406
Fallen Idol, The 1909 (Ed)
Fallen Idol, The 1913 (Br) 834
Falling Arrow, The 1909 (Lubin) 2103
Falling Out, The 1911 (Independent
  Moving Picture Co.)
Falls of Minnehaha 1897 (Ed)
False Accusation, A 1909 (V)
False Alarm 1914 (Key) 531
False Alarm in the Dressing Room, A
  1903 (AMB)
False Ambition 1918 (Tri) 2194
Flase Beauty, A /aka/ A Faded Vampire
  1914 (Key) 2368, 2465, 2510
False Colors 1914 (Bo) 920, 2422, 2711
False Evidence 1919 (M) 631, 1976
False Faces, The 1919 (Art/Par) 51, 268,
  449, 814, 2011, 2183, 2680
False Gods 1919 ( ) 643
False Roomers 1919 ( ) 1651
False to Both 1912 (Imp)
Falsely Accused 1908 (Lubin)
Fame and Fortune 1919 (F) 1849
Family Cupboard, The 1915 (W) 239
Family Honor, The 1917 ( ) 1807
Family House see His Trysting Place
Family Mix-up, A 1912 (Key) 1666, 1941,
  2368
Family of Vegetarians, A 1910 (Ed)
Family Outing 1907 (Lubin)
Family Troubles 1903 (AMB)
Family Skeleton 1918 (Par) 281, 1261,
  2096
Family Solicitor, The 1914 (Br) 177
Famous Duel, A 1911 (Ed)
Famous Escape, A 1908 (AMB)
Fan Fan 1919 (F) 557
Fanchon the Cricket 1912 (Un)
Fanchon the Cricket 1915 (Par) 85, 86,
  2045, 2046, 2047, 2442
Fancy Dress 1919 (Br) 776, 1931, 2536
Fanny's Conspiracy 1913 (V) 297, 2523
Fantasmagorie--cartoon 1908 (French)
  512
Fantine; or A Mother's Love 1909 (V)
Fantine 1918 ( ) 1191
Far from the Beaten Track 1912 (Imp)
Far from the Madding Crowd 1909 (Ed)
Far from the Madding Crowd 1916 (GB)
  812, 2604
Farmer and the Bad Boys, The 1901 (Ed)
Farmer Kissing the Lean Girl 1898 (Ed)
Farmer Oatcake Has His Troubles 1902
  (AMB)
Farmer's Daughter, The; or The Wages
  of Sin 1908 (V)
Farmer's Daughter, The 1910 (Ed)
Farmer's Imitation of Ching Ling Foo, A
  1902 (AMB)
Farmer's Troubles 1897 (Ed)
Fascinating Mrs. Frances, The 1909 (AMB)

Fascination of the Fleur de Lis 1915
  (Rex/Un) 449, 1711, 2398, 2781
Fast Company 1918 (Bluebird/Un) 441,
  449, 867, 1091, 1153, 1854
Fat and Fickle 1916 (Vim) 1161, 2070
Fat Girl's Love Affair, The 1905 (AMB)
Fata Morgana 1914 ( ) 1372
Fatal Ball, The 1909 (Melies)
Fatal Card, The 1908 (Lubin)
Fatal Chocolate, The 1912 (Bio)
Fatal Flirt, A 1913 (Key) 65, 2368
Fatal Flirtation, A 1909 (Lubin)
Fatal Flirtation, A 1914 (Key) 1906
Fatal Fortune, The--serial 1919 (SLK
  Serial Corp.) 230, 327, 626, 1273,
  1443, 1555, 1578, 2809
  1. The Trader's Secret
  2. Men of Tigerish Mold
  3. Tortured by Flames
  4. A Climb for Life
  5. The Forced Marriage
  6. Desperate Chances
  7. A Plunge to Death
  8. A Struggle in Midair
  9. The Deadly Peril
  10. Sure Death
  11. A Leap for Life
  12. A Fiendish Plot
  13. Set Adrift
  14. The Hidden Treasure
  15. Unmasked
Fatal Hour, The 1908 (AMB) 994, 1542
Fatal Lie, A 1912 (Ingvald C. Oes)
Fatal Likeness, The 1908 (Lubin)
Fatal Mallet, The /aka/ The Pile Driver
  1914 (Key) 384, 451, 1726, 1941,
  2368, 2510
Fatal Marriage, The 1915 ( )
Fatal Ring, The--serial 1917 (P) 327, 890,
  947, 1068, 1262, 1971, 2363, 2748
  1. The Violet Diamond
  2. The Crushing Wall
  3. Borrowed Identity
  4. The Warning on the Ring
  5. Danger Underground
  6. Rays of Death
  7. The Signal Lantern
  8. The Switch in the Safe
  9. The Dice of Death
  10. The Perilous Plunge
  11. The Short Circuit
  12. A Desperate Chance
  13. A Dash for Arabia
  14. The Painted Safe
  15. The Dagger Duel
  16. The Double Disguise
  17. The Death Weight
  18. The Subterfuge
  19. The Cryptic Maze
  20. The End of the Trail
Fatal Temptation, A 1908 (Lubin)
Fatal Thirty, The--serial 1919 ( ) 2480
Fatal Warning, The--serial 1914 ( ) 2422
Fatality 1912 (Eclair)
Fate 1913 (Bio) 141, 1182
Fate of a Gossip, The 1903 (AMB)
Fate of the Artist's Model, The 1903
  (AMB)
Fates and Flora Fourflush, The (The Ten
  Billion Dollar Vitagraph Mystery
  Serial)--serial 1915 (V) 301, 1634,

2232, 2470, 2811
  1. Treachery in the Clouds
  2. The Temple of Bhosh
  3. A Race for Life
Fate's Boomerang 1916 ( ) 2412
Fate's Chessboard * ( ) 1509
Fate's Funny Frolic 1911 (Es) 353, 2042
Fate's Interception 1912 (Bio) 1182, 1613,
  2047, 2728
Fate's Turning 1911 (Bio) 209, 595, 2728
Father, The 1912 (Ed)
Father and Son 1910 (Br) 177
Father and the Boys 1915 (Broadway/Un)
  173, 449, 459, 461, 583, 652, 1132,
  1484, 1604, 1683
Father Gets in the Game 1908 (AMB)
  1542, 2212, 2368
Fatherhood 1915 (Bo) 258
Father's Bluff 1912 (Ed)
Father's Choice 1913 (Key) 1941, 2465
Father's Dress Suit 1911 (Ed)
Father's Favorite 1912 (Am) 1924
Father's First Half-Holiday 1909 (Ed)
Father's Flirtation 1914 (V) 51, 157, 332,
  901
Father's Glue 1909 (Lubin)
Father's Hatband 1913 (V) 297, 2523
Father's Quiet Sunday 1907 (V)
Father's Time Piece 1914 (V) 2081, 2521
Fatima 1897 (International Film Co.) 872
Fatima at Coney Island 1897 (American
  Mutoscope) 872
Fatty Again /aka/ Fatty the Four Flusher
  1914 (Key) 65
Fatty and Mabel 1915 (Key) 65, 1941
Fatty and Mabel Adrift 1916 (Key/Tri) 65,
  253, 322, 330, 1211, 1941, 2208,
  2580, 2724
Fatty and Mabel at the San Diego Ex-
  position 1915 (Key) 65, 1211, 1941
Fatty and Mabel's Married Life 1915 (Key)
  65, 1941
Fatty and Mabel's Simple Life 1915 (Key)
  65, 1941
Fatty and Minnie-Ha-Haw 1914 (Key) 65,
  791
Fatty and the Broadway Stars 1916 (Key/
  Tri) 65, 211, 519, 600, 895, 1342,
  2208, 2368, 2465, 2710
Fatty and the Heiress 1914 (Key) 65
Fatty at San Diego 1913 (Key) 65
Fatty in Coney Island 1917 (Par) 65, 1401,
  2208
Fatty Joins the Force 1913 (Key) 65, 864
Fatty on the Job 1913 (Key) 65
Fatty's Affair of Honor 1913 (Key) 65
Fatty's Chance Acquaintance 1915 (Key) 65
Fatty's Day Off 1913 (Key) 65
Fatty's Debut /aka/ Fatty Butts In 1914
  (Key) 65
Fatty's Faithful Fido 1915 (Key) 65
Fatty's Fatal Fun 1915 (/Am) 1161
Fatty's Feature Film 1917 (Key) 65
Fatty's Finish 1914 (Key) 65
Fatty's Flirtation 1913 (Key) 65, 1941
Fatty's Gift 1914 (Key) 65
Fatty's Hoo-Doo Day 1914 (Key) 65
Fatty's Jonah Day 1914 (Key) 37, 65, 791,
  1941
Fatty's Magic Pants /aka/ Fatty's Suit-
  less Day 1914 (Key) 65, 2143

Fatty's New Role 1915 (Key) 65
Fatty's Plucky Pup 1915 (Key) 65
Fatty's Reckless Fling 1915 (Key) 65
Fatty's Spooning Day see Mabel, Fatty
  and the Law
Fatty's Sweetheart 1916 (Key) 65
Fatty's Tin Type Tangle 1915 (Key) 65,
  878, 1422
Fatty's Wine Party 1915 (Key) 65, 452,
  1941
Faust 1909 (Ed)
Faust and Marguerite 1900 (Ed)
Faust Aux Enfers 1903 (Melies)
Faust et Marguerite 1904 (Melies)
Favorite Fool, A 1915 (Key/Tri) 70, 351,
  948, 949, 1874
Favorite Son 1913 ( ) 610, 926, 2096
Favourite for the Jamaica Cup, The 1913
  (Br) 1873
Fear Woman, The 1919 (Par) 957, 1248,
  1440, 2410
Feast of Belshazzar, The 1913 ( )
Feast of Life 1916 (WS) 955, 2811
Feathered Nest, The /aka/ Girl Guardian;
  Only a Farmer's Daughter 1916 (Key/
  Tri) 250, 460, 815, 878, 1906, 2336,
  2580
Felix on the Job 1916 (Victor/Un) 449,
  883, 1597, 2570
Fellow Romans 1915 ( ) 1684
Female Cop, The 1914 (Lubin) 1161
Female Crook and Her Easy Victim 1905
  (AMB)
Female Impersonator, The see The
  Masquerader
Female of the Species, The 1912 (Bio)
  209, 1665, 2047
Fencing Master, The 1915 ( ) 1353
Feodora 1918 (Par) 957, 1535
Fettered Woman, The 1918 (V) 1388
Fetters of Fear 1915 (Br) 1329
Feud and the Turkey, The 1908 (AMB)
  731, 994, 1823
Feud Girl, The 1916 ( ) 667
Feud in the Kentucky Hills, A 1915 (Bio)
  315, 1832, 2047, 2680
Feudists, The 1913 (V) 332, 429, 768,
  901
Fibbers, The 1917 (Es) 2619, 2700
Fickle Fatty's Fall 1915 (Key/Tri) 37,
  440, 600, 650, 791, 840, 2208, 2636,
  2799
Fickle Fatty's Romance 1915 (Key/Tri)
  791
Fickle Spaniard, The 1912 (Bio) 2368
Fido's Fate 1916 (Key/Tri) 840, 1211,
  1906, 2336
Fields of Honor 1918 (Go) 1523, 1751,
  1753
Fifth Man, The 1914 (Selig) 857
Fifty-Fifty 1916 (FA/Tri) 446, 1369, 2523
Fight for a Bride, A 1905 (AMB)
Fight for Freedom, The 1906 (AMB)
Fight for Love, A 1919 (Un) 398, 1004,
  1659
Fight for Millions, A--serial 1918 (V)
  785, 1364, 1720, 2163, 2002
  1. The Snare
  2. Flames of Peril
  3. The Secret Stockade
  4. Precipice of Horror

    5. Path of Thrills
    6. Spell of Evil
    7. Gorge of Destruction
    8. In the Clutches
    9. The Estate
   10. The Secret Tunnel
   11. The Noose of Death
   12. The Tide of Disaster
   13. The Engine of Terror
   14. The Decoy
   15. The Sealed Enbelope
Fight for the Right 1913 ( ) 696, 2554
Fight with Fire, A 1911 (Hep) 2531
Fightin' Mad 1917 ( ) 715, 1010
Fighting Back 1917 ( ) 715, 1665
Fighting Blood 1911 (Bio) 141, 315, 357,
    1468, 1751, 1933, 2513
Fighting Brothers 1919 ( ) 1011
Fighting Chance, A 1913 ( ) 2472
Fighting Cigar, The 1909 (Lubin)
Fighting Cressy 1919 ( ) 2412, 2513
Fighting Destiny 1919 ( ) 1877
Fighting Fate--serial 1919 ( ) 1364
Fighting for Gold 1919 (F) 1849, 2216
Fighting Grin, The 1918 ( ) 867
Fighting Hope, The 1918 ( ) 1800
Fighting Odds, The 1917 (Go) 501, 823
Fighting Parson, The 1908 (Lubin)
Fighting Through 1919 ( ) 25, 781, 1569
Fighting Trail, The--serial 1917 (V) 338,
    785, 1271, 1279, 2163, 2202
    1. The Priceless Ingredient
    2. The Story of Ybarra
    3. Will Yaqui Joe Tell?
    4. The Other Half
    5. The Torrent Rush
    6. The Ledge of Despair
    7. The Lion's Prey
    8. Strands of Doom
    9. The Bridge of Death
   10. The Sheriff
   11. Parched Trails
   12. The Desert of Torture
   13. The Water Trap
   14. The Trestle of Horrors
   15. Out of the Flame
Fights of Nations 1907 (AMB)
Figure with Hand on Horse 1889 (Dickson)
    727
Filling His Own Shoes 1917 (Es) 630
Film Favorites 1914 (GB) 2604
Film Johnny, A /aka/ Movie Nut; Million
    Dollar Job 1914 (Key) 65, 451, 791,
    1451
Film Tags series 1919 (Hep) 812, 2531,
    2744
Final Close-Up, The 1919 (Par) 1774
Final Fraud, The 1917 (Es) 2700
Final Judgment, The 1915 (M) 139, 397
Final Settlement, The 1910 (Bio) 1363,
    1450, 1992
Final Verdict, The 1914 ( ) 2672
Find the Woman 1918 (V) 552, 1388
Fine Feathers 1909 (Bio) 209
Fine Feathers 1915 (Br) 834, 943, 2138
Fine Feathers Make Fine Birds 1905 (AMB)
Finger of Destiny 1914 (Br) 2138
Finger of Justice 1919 ( ) 2760
Finish of Bridget McKeen, The 1901 (Ed)
Finish of Futurity 1901 (AMB)
Fire-Bug, The 1905 (AMB)

Fire Chief, The see A Lover's Might
Fire Chief's Daughter, The 1910 (Selig)
    2770
Fire Flingers 1919 (Un) 898, 2133
Fire of Life, The 1912 (Ingvald C. Oes)
Fire the Kaiser 1918 (4th Liberty Loan)
    857
Fireball, The 1904 (Melies)
Firebrand, The 1918 (F) 2024
Firebugs, The 1913 (Key) 1666, 2465
Fired Cook, The 1913 (Kal) 1924
Firefly of France 1918 (Par) 1201, 1580,
    1970, 2112
Firefly of Tough Luck, The 1917 (Tri)
    1101, 2194
Firelight 1913 (Eclair) 1618, 2544
Fireman, The 1916 (Mu) 97, 106, 384,
    451, 517, 1414, 2077, 2090, 2746
Fireman Save My Child! 1918 (P) 1586
Fireman's Daughter, The 1911 (Hep) 2744
Fires of Conscience 1914 ( ) 651, 2112
Fires of Faith, The 1919 (Par) 54, 375,
    709, 1866, 1959
Fires of Fate, The 1913 ( ) 651, 2112
Fires of Rebellion 1917 (Bluebird/Un) 186,
    274, 449, 1493, 1710, 2042
Fireside Brewer 1918 (Key) 878
Fireside Reminiscences 1908 (Ed)
Firing Line, The 1919 ( ) 435, 558,
    1600, 2061, 2459
Firing the Cook 1903 (AMB)
First Baby, The 1904 (AMB)
First Championship Fight Film 1897
    (Veriscope) 912
First Command, The 1916 ( ) 1246
First Heir, The 1914 (Key) 531
First Kiss, The from The Widow Jones
    1886 (Ed) 1339, 2123
First Law, The 1918 (V) 435, 1876, 2430
First Men in the Moon 1919 (GB) 2551
First Misunderstanding, The 1910 ( )
    1865
First Quarrel, The 1907 (Lubin)
First Sleigh-Ride, The 1897 (Ed)
First Violin, The 1912 (V) 231, 332, 565,
    566, 818, 2523
First Woman Jury in America 1912 (V)
    332, 901
Fish Story, A 1907 (V)
Fisher Folks 1911 (Bio) 79, 731, 1613,
    1701, 2573
Fisher Maid, The 1911 (Imp) 2047
Fisherman, The; or Men Must Work and
    Women Must Weep 1909 (V)
Fisherman and His Sweetheart, The 1912
    (Ingvald C. Oes)
Fisherman Kate 1912 ( ) 2070
Fisherman's Luck 1897 (Ed)
Fisherman's Romance, A 1909 (Bison)
    960
Fishy Affair, A 1913 (Key) 2465
Fit to Fight 1918 ( ) 1415
Five Hundred Dollars Reward 1911 (Bio)
Five Hundred or Bust 1918 ( ) 961
Five Little Widows 1919 ( ) 2147
Five Thousand an Hour 1918 (M) 1134,
    2478
$5000 Elopement, A * (Selig Polyscope)
    1849
Flag Lieutenant, The 1919 (Br) 503
Flag of Distress 1912 (Imp)

Flame of the Desert 1919 (Go) 454, 869,
     887, 950, 1165, 2541
Flame of the Yukon, The 1917 (Tri) 627
Flames 1917 (Br) 834
Flames of Chance, The 1918 ( ) 2780
Flames of '49, The 1916 (Tri) 857
Flames of the Flesh 1919 (F) 295, 601,
     680
Flaming Hearts 1913 (V) 332
Flaming Omen, The 1918 ( ) 1519, 2754
Flare-Up Sal 1918 (Tri) 532, 627
Flash in the Dark, A 1914 ( ) 651, 2112
Flash of Fate, The 1918 ( ) 1928, 2728
Flash of Light, A 1910 (Bio) 357, 477,
     1933, 2067, 2728
Flashlight, The 1917 (Bluebird/Un) 341,
     449, 2042, 2490
Flashlight Girl, The 1917 (Un) 34
Flat Dwellers, The 1906 (V)
Flat Dwellers; or The House of Too Much
     Trouble 1907 (V)
Flesh of Fate 1918 ( ) 2095
Flight of Red Wing, The * (101-Bison)
     2103
Flips and Flops 1919 (V) 1161
Flirt, The 1917 (P) 1586, 2055, 2656
Flirtation, A 1902 (AMB)
Flirtation, A: Table D'Hote 1904 (AMB)
Flirting by the Seaside 1906 (Melies)
Flirting Husband, The 1912 (Key) 1941,
     2465
Flirting with Death 1914 (Un) 2095
Flirting with Fate 1916 (FA/Tri) 200, 406,
     857, 993, 1029, 1490, 1514
Flirting with Marriage * ( ) 1767
Flirts, The see Between Showers
Flirt's Mistake, A 1914 (Key) 65
Flivvering 1917 (Par) 1868
Floating Coffin, The 1915 ( ) 2748
Floor Above, The 1914 ( ) 947, 1028,
     1563, 2680
Floor Below, The 1918 (Go) 635, 1780,
     1867, 2055
Floorwalker, The 1916 (Mu) 97, 106, 204,
     384, 451, 517, 1347, 1414, 1840,
     2077, 2219, 2746
Florence Nightingale 1915 (Br) 834, 2138
Flo's Discipline 1911 (V) 1511, 1865
Flossie's New Peach-Basket Hat 1909
     (Lubin)
Flotilla the Flirt 1914 (GB) 2604
Flower Girl, The 1908 (V)
Flower Girl of Paris, The 1908 (V)
Flower of the Dusk 1918 (M) 631
Flower of the Ranch, The 1910 (Es) 50
Fluffy Ruffles 1908 (Lubin)
Fly Cop, The 1917 (King-Bee) 1161
Fly God, The 1918 (Tri) 2479
Flying-A--serial 1916 ( ) 2046
Flying by Hydroplane * (P) 1575
Flying Circus, The 1912 (Nordisk Films
     Co.)
Flying Colors 1917 (Tri) 715, 1710, 2392
Flying Torpedo, The 1916 ( ) 1563, 1602
Flying Train 1903 (AMB)
Flying Wedge, A 1903 (AMB)
Fogg's Millions 1914 (V) 1876, 2523
Foiled by a Girl 1912 (Br) 177
Foiling Fickle Father 1913 (Key) 1941
Follies Girl, The 1918 (Sel) 1092, 1665,
     2557

Follow Me 1918 ( ) 1519
Follow the Crowd 1918 (P) 1586
Follow the Girl 1917 ( ) 2486
Following the Scent 1915 (V) 768
Folly of Anne, The 1914 ( ) 1029
Food Gamblers 1917 ( ) 1613
Fool, The 1913 (Br) 2536
Fool and His Money, A 1908 (Lubin)
Fool and His Money Are Soon Parted, A;
     or The Prodigal Son Up-to-Date
     1908 (V)
Fool Days 1919 ( ) 2208
Fool for Luck, A 1908 (Ed)
Fool There Was, A 1915 (F) 41, 116,
     195, 314, 962, 1259, 1383, 2062
Foolish Virgin, The 1915 ( ) 2811
Fool for Luck 1917 ( ) 1276
Fool's Gold 1919 (V) 286, 1078, 1562,
     2052, 2604
Fools of Fate 1909 (Bio) 1450, 1542, 2062,
     2680
Fool's Revenge, A 1909 (AMB) 122
Fool's Revenge, A 1916 (F) 1971, 2574
Footlight Parade, A 1917 (F) 70
Footlights and Fakers 1917 (V) 92, 2367
Footlights on the Farm, The 1910 (Ed)
For a Baby's Sake 1911 (Hep) 2531
For a Wife's Honor 1908 (AMB) 1336,
     2212
For a Woman's Honor 1919 ( ) 693
For All Eternity 1917 (Br) 1592
For Better--but Worse see That Little
     Band of Gold
For Better, for Worse 1919 (Art/Par) 83,
     724, 935, 1126, 1201, 1206, 1280,
     1321, 1387, 1800, 2149, 2512
For Cash 1915 (Victor/Un) 449, 1431
For France 1917 (V) 804, 1786, 2649
For Freedom 1919 (F) 868, 1532
For Freedom of the East 1918 ( ) 1799
For Freedom of the World 1917 ( ) 437,
     1569
For Her Brother's Sake 1911 (Bio) 2047,
     2096, 2392
For Her Country's Sake 1909 (V)
For Her Father's Sins 1914 (Mu) 2112,
     2513
For Her Mother's Sake 1912 (Br) 177
For Her People 1914 (GB) 2604
For Her Sake; or Two Sailors and a Girl
     1909 (V)
For Her Sister's Sake 1910 (Ed)
For Her Sweetheart's Sake 1909 (V)
For He's a Jolly Good Fellow 1908 (V)
For His Master 1914 ( ) 2672
For His Sister's Sin 1908 (Lubin)
For His Son 1912 (Bio) 2513
For Honor of the Name 1911 ( ) 2748
For Husbands Only 1918 (Jewel/Un) 506,
     1175
For Liberty--serial 1916 (Un) 295, 2056,
     2656
For Love and Gold 1917 ( ) 1364
For Love of Gold 1908 (AMB) 1089, 1336,
     2212
For Massa's Sake 1911 ( ) 2760
For Sale 1918 ( ) 1312
For Sale--a Baby 1909 (Melies)
For Ten Thousand Bucks 1916 (Vogue)
     2608
For the Cause of Suffrage 1909 (Melies)

For the Cause of the South 1912 (Ed)
For the Commonwealth 1912 (Ed)
For the Defense 1916 (FP/Las) 83, 486,
    1065, 2051, 2460, 2683
For the Family Name 1917 ( ) 865
For the Flag 1912 (Am) 1431
For the Love of Mabel 1913 (Key) 65,
    1941, 2368
For the Little Lady's Sake 1908 (Hep) 2744
For the Queen 1911 (Ed)
For the Queen's Honor 1911 (Imp) 2047
For the Wearing of the Green 1914 ( )
    1580, 2096
For Those Unborn 1914 (Mu) 1182, 2513
For Valour 1912 (Ed)
Forbidden City 1918 (Select) 1634, 1800,
    2523
Forbiddin Fruit 1919 ( ) 102
Forbidden Path 1918 (F) 116, 847, 1506,
    1536, 1760, 1775, 2560
Forbidden Paths 1917 (Art/Par) 935, 1208,
    1764
Forbidden Room, The 1914 (101-Bison/Un)
    348, 352, 449, 1705
Forbidden Room, The 1919 (F) 295
Forced Bravery 1913 (Key) 2465
Forcing Dad's Consent 1914 (V) 2081, 2581
Forecastle Tom 1909 (Lubin)
Foreign Spy, A 1913 ( ) 2112, 2125
Foreman of the Bar Z * (Selig Polyscope)
    1849
Foreman of the Jury, The 1913 (Key) 1666,
    1941
Foreman's Treachery, The 1913 (Ed) 1930
Forest on the Hill, The 1919 (Hep) 43,
    2531
Forest Ranger, The 1910 (Es) 50
Forest Rivals 1919 ( ) 656, 1078
Forester Made King, A 1907 (Melies)
Forester's Remedy, The 1908 (Melies)
Forfeit 1919 ( ) 2035
Forged Will, The 1908 (Lubin)
Forgiven; or Father and Son 1909 (V)
Forgiven: A Young Lady 1904 (AMB)
Forgotten 1911 (V) 2523
Forgotten Latchkey, The 1913 ( ) 2472
Forgotten Umbrellas: I Must Hurry to the
    Office 1904 (AMB)
Forgotten Watch, The 1908 (Lubin)
Forked Trails 1914 (Selig Polyscope) 1849
Fortune, The 1913 (V) 332, 901
Fortune at Stake, A 1918 (Br) 43, 1289
Fortune Favors the Brave, The 1909
    (Melies)
Fortune Hunter, The 1914 (Lubin) 277, 288,
    486, 825, 2438
Fortune Hunter, The 1918 (FN) 452
Fortune Teller see Maid Mad
Fortune Teller, The 1909 (Lubin)
Fortune's Child 1919 ( ) 1078, 1547
Fortune's Fool 1910 (Ed)
Fortunes of a Composer 1912 (V) 2523
Fortunes of Fifi 1917 (Par) 482
Fortunes of War, The 1914 (King-Bee)
    1745, 2096
45 Minutes from Broadway 1919 ( ) 720
Forty Winks; or A Strenuous Dream 1907
    (V)
Foster Mother, The 1902 (AMB)
Fougere 1902 (AMB)
Foul Play 1906 (V)

Foul Play 1911 (Ed)
Foundling, The 1907 (Lubin)
Foundling, The 1916 (FP) 1174, 1450,
    1765, 1885, 2047, 2734
Foundling, The--A Dressing Room Waif
    1909 (V)
Fount of Courage 1919 ( ) 274
Fountain of Youth, The 1907 (V)
Four Beautiful Pairs 1904 (AMB)
Four-Flusher, The 1919 (M) 1134, 1717,
    2486
Four from Nowhere 1916 (Un) 926
Fox Hunt, The 1906 (AMB)
Fox Hunt, The 1909 (Ed)
Fox Trot Finese 1915 (V) 768
Fox Woman, The 1915 ( ) 1998
Foxy Grandpa and Polly in a Little
    Hilarity 1902 (AMB)
Foxy Grandpa Shows the Boys a Trick or
    Two with the Tramp 1902 (AMB)
Foxy Grandpa Tells the Boys a Funny
    Story 1902 (AMB)
Foxy Grandpa Thumb Book 1903 (AMB)
Fozzle at a Tea Party, A 1915 (P) 1586
Fra Diavolo 1912 (Solax) 2081
Frailty 1916 (Br) 1879, 1945, 2791
Franc Piece, The 1917 ( ) 1364
Francesca Da Rimini 1912 (V) 671, 2098,
    2604
Francesca Di Rimini; or The Two
    Brothers 1907 (V)
Frankenstein 1910 (Ed) 1970
Frankenstein's Trestle 1902 (AMB)
Frankly Chaste 1917 (Tri) 2557
Franks 1909 (Bio) 2081
Frau Eve; Die Ehe der Luise Rohrbach
    1915 ( ) 1349
Frauds and Frenzies 1918 (V) 1502, 2367
Freckled Fish 1919 (L-Ko) 1161
Freckles 1912 (V) 332, 901
Freckles 1917 (Las) 258, 1309, 1537, 2045
Fred Ott's Sneeze 1893 (Ed) 1994
Freddy Versus Hamlet 1916 (V) 634, 718
Freeze-Out, The * (Un) 398
Freezing Auntie 1912 (Ed)
French Duel, The 1909 (Bio)
French Milliner, The 1916 (Tri) 2568
Frenzied Finance, A 1916 (Vim) 340, 346,
    1156, 2497
Fresh Air Fiend; or How He Was Cured
    1908 (V)
Fresh from the Farm 1915 (P) 1586
Fresh Lover, The 1902 (AMB)
Fricot e le Uova 1914 ( ) 1068
Friday, the 13th; or Just Like the Gaytons
    1911 (Ed)
Friend, The 1914 (King-Bee) 1745, 2096
Friend Husband 1918 (Go) 658, 1423
Friend in Need Is a Friend Indeed, A
    1906 (AMB)
Friend in Need Is a Friend Indeed, A
    1909 (V)
Friend in the Enemy's Camp, A 1909 (V)
Friend of the Family, The 1909 (Bio)
Friend Wilson's Daughter 1915 ( ) 1649
Friendly Call, The 1919 ( ) 1832
Friendly Enemies see Hushing the
    Scandal
Friendly Husband 1918 ( ) 884
Friends 1912 (Bio) 141, 398, 1182, 1714,
    2047, 2680

Frightened Flirts 1917 (Vogue) 2608
Frills 1916 ( ) 2558
Fringe of Society 1917 (P) 2169, 2410
Fringe of War, The 1914 (Br) 43
From Broadway to a Throne 1916 ( ) 689
From Hand to Mouth 1919 (P) 1586
From Headquarters 1915 (V) 2472
From Italy's Shore 1914 (Un) 1586, 1948
From out the Shadows 1908 (AMB) 95,
  2728
From Patches to Plenty 1915 (Key) 815,
  1712, 1906, 2510
From Shopgirl to Duchess 1915 (Br) 834,
  2138
From Show Girl to Burlesque Queen 1903
  (AMB)
From the Bottom of the Sea 1911 (Imp)
  2047
From the Manger to the Cross 1912 (Kal)
  236, 481, 992, 1270, 1672
From the Submerged 1912 ( ) 377, 2486
From Two to Six 1918 ( ) 947
From Tyranny to Liberty 1910 (Ed)
Front for a Hotel 1917 ( ) 2649
Frontier Flirtation, A 1903 (AMB)
Frontier Hero, A 1910 (Ed)
Frontier of the Stars 1919 ( ) 1800
Frou-Frou 1918 (Par) 2094
Fruit of Evil, The 1914 ( ) 651, 2112
Fuel of Life 1917 (Tri) 186, 1099, 2392
Fugitive, The 1910 (Bio) 95, 315, 363,
  400, 567, 651, 731, 2729
Fugitive, The see The Taking of Luke
  McVane 1915 (Ince)
Fugitive Apparitions, The 1904 (Melies)
Full of Pep 1919 (Un) 1134, 1714, 1717,
  2058
Fun in a Bakery Shop 1902 (Ed)
Fun in a Butcher Shop 1901 (Ed)
Fun in a Chinese Laundry 1901 (Lubin)
Fun in a Fotograf Gallery 1907 (V)
Fun in Camp 1899 (Ed)
Fun in a Photograph Gallery 1902 (AMB)
Fun on a Sand Hill 1903 (AMB)
Fun on the Farm 1905 (Lubin)
Fun on the Joy Line 1905 (Lubin)
Fun with the Bridal Party 1908 (Melies)
Funeral That Flashed in the Pan, A 1912
  (Ed)
Furnished Room House, The 1904 (AMB)
Furnished Rooms to Let 1909 (Ed)
Furs, The 1912 (Bio)
Further Adventures of Sherlock Holmes,
  The--series 1915 (Br) 1945
Fuss and Feathers 1909 (Ed)
Fuss and Feathers 1918 ( ) 189, 1697
Future Safeguard 1916 (Br) 150
Futurity 1902 (AMB)

- G -

Gall and Gold 1917 (V) 2367
Gallant Gob, A * ( ) 750
Gallant Knight, A 1908 (Lubin)
Gallegher 1910 (Ed)
Galley Slave, The 1909 (V)
Galley Slave, The 1915 (F) 116, 1226,
  1275, 1449, 1512, 1525, 2756
Gallopin' Through 1919 ( ) 1307
Galloping Romeo 1913 ( ) 785

Gamble, The 1919 ( ) 1877
Gamble for Love, A 1917 (Br) 43, 1289
Gambler, The 1908 (V)
Gambler of the West, A 1910 (Es) 50
Gamblers, The 1919 ( ) 889, 1426
Gamblers All 1919 (Br) 1918
Gambler's Life and End, The 1904 (Lubin)
Gambling in Souls 1919 ( ) 2581
Game of Liberty, The 1916 (Br) 43
Game of Poker, A 1913 (Key) 2465
Game of Pool, A 1913 (Key) 2465
Game Old Knight, A 1915 (Key/Tri) 73,
  250, 878, 1422, 1906, 2501
Game with Fate, A 1918 ( ) 243, 1877
Game's Up, The 1919 ( ) 495
Gangsters, The 1912 (Key) 65, 1666
Gangsters and the Girl, The 1915 ( ) 2096
Gangsters of New York 1913 (Bio) 1563,
  2680
Garage, The 1919 (FP/Las) 65, 1401,
  1476, 1651, 1719, 2208
Garden of Allah, The 1917 (Selig) 1595,
  2221, 2690
Garden of Lies, The 1915 (Las) 576, 2201
Garden of the Resurrection, The 1919 (Br)
  776, 1931
Gardener's Daughter, The 1913 (Br) 177
Gardener's Ladder, The 1911 (Ed)
Garret in Bohemia, A 1915 (Br) 2712
Gas Logic 1918 (M) 768, 1707
Gasoline Engagement, A 1911 (Imp) 2047
Gasoline Wedding, A 1918 (P) 1586, 2055
'Gater and the Pickaninny, The 1903 (AMB)
Gates of Brass 1917 ( ) 1404
Gates of Doom, The--serial 1917 ( )
  1120, 1685
Gates of Duty 1919 (Br) 1453
Gates of Eden, The 1916 (Ed) 804
Gates of Gladness, The 1918 ( ) 853
Gaumont chase comedies 1904 (GB) 1873
Gauntlet of Washington, The 1913 ( )
  1656
Gay Deceiver, A 1915 ( ) 1132
Gay Lord Quex, The 1917 (LFC) 374, 834,
  2712
Gay Lord Quex, The 1919 (Go) 468, 630,
  1283, 1297
Gay Lothario, A see Giddy, Gay and
  Ticklish
Gay Old Boy, A 1903 (AMB)
Gay Old Boy, A 1907 (Lubin)
Gay Shoe Clerk, The 1903 (Ed)
General's Daughter, The 1911 (V) 2523
Genii of Fire, The 1908 (Melies)
Genius, The 1917 (King-Bee) 1161
Genius Pierre, The 1919 ( ) 656
Gentle Ill Wind, A 1917 ( ) 2753
Gentleman Burglar, The 1908 (Ed)
Gentleman from Blue Gulch, The see
  The Conversion of Frosty Blake
Gentleman from Indiana, A 1915 (Las)
  866
Gentleman of Fashion, A 1913 (V) 332,
  901
Gentleman of France, A 1904 (V) 178
Gentleman of Quality, A 1919 (V) 646,
  2767
Gentleman Rider, A 1919 (Br) 1289, 2171
Gentleman's Agreement, A 1918 ( )
  2397, 2754
Gentlemen Highwaymen, The 1905 (AMB)

Gentlemen of Nerve 1914 (Key) 37, 451,
    460, 531, 650, 791, 1941, 2465,
    2501, 2510
Gentlemen's Ball 1915 (Kal) 1136
George Robey Turns Anarchist 1914 (Br)
    2152
George Robey's Day Off 1918 (Br) 2152
Geranium, The /aka/ Mission of a
    Flower 1911 (V) 564, 565
Get Me a Stepladder 1908 (V)
Getting a Start in Life * (Selig Polyscope)
    1849
Getting Acquainted /aka/ A Fair Exchange
    1914 (Key) 37, 73, 451, 1422, 1651,
    1941, 2510
Getting Even 1909 (Bio) 95, 1992, 2047,
    2081, 2368
Getting Evidence 1906 (Ed)
Getting His Goat see The Property Man
Getting Married see Better Late Than
    Never
Getting Mary Married 1919 (Cosmopolitan)
    158, 347, 660, 1057, 1217, 1432,
    1864, 2500
Getting Strong 1904 (AMB)
Getting up in the World 1903 (AMB)
Ghost, The 1911 (Bio)
Ghost Breaker, The 1914 (Las) 2149, 2693
Ghost Flower, The 1918 (Tri) 2194
Ghost House, The 1917 (Art/Par) 1309,
    2002, 2045
Ghost of Canyon Diablo, The 1917 ( )
    1010
Ghost of Rosy Taylor, The 1918 ( ) 1841,
    2032
Ghost of the Rancho 1918 (Par) 2700
Ghost Story, The 1907 (V)
Ghost Train, The 1911 (Ed)
Ghosts 1914 (Br) 503
Ghosts 1915 (Mu) 27, 242, 680, 2649, 2680
Ghosts of Yesterday, The 1917 (Select) 644,
    1236, 1275, 1959, 2523
Ghost's Warning, The 1911 (Ed)
Giant Powder 1917 ( ) 1364
Gibson Goddess, The 1909 (Bio) 850,
    1363, 1450, 1542, 1933, 2047, 2081,
    2368
Giddy Dancing Master, The 1903 (AMB)
Giddy, Gay and Ticklish /aka/ A Gay
    Lothario 1913 (Key/Tri) 37, 452
Gift from Santa Claus, A 1909 (Ed)
Gift o' Gab, The 1917 (Es) 889, 986
Gift of the Desert 1916 ( ) 2736
Gift of Youth, The 1909 (V)
Gilbert Dying to Die 1915 (Br) 834
Gilbert Gets Tiger-itis 1915 (Br) 834,
    2138
Gilded Cage 1916 ( ) 273, 606, 626, 950,
    1603
Gilded Lady, The * ( ) 1907
Gilded Spider, The 1916 (Bluebird/Un)
    170, 449, 827, 1141, 1604, 1683,
    2696
Gilded Youth 1915 ( ) 193
Ginger 1919 ( ) 1105, 1310
Gipsy Man 1911 (Hep) 2744
Girl across the Way, The 1908 (Lubin)
Girl and Her Trust, The 1912 (Bio) 95,
    209, 1182, 1613, 1714, 2000, 2728
Girl and the Cat, The 1904 (AMB)
Girl and the Game, The--serial 1915

(Mu) 1273, 1654, 1672, 1720
    1. Helen's Race with Death
    2. The Winning Jump
    3. A Life in Peril
    4. Helen's Perilous Escape
    5. The Fight at the Signal
        Station
    6. Helen's Wild Ride
    7. Spike's Awakening
    8. A Race for the Right of Way
    9. A Close Call
    10. A Dash through Flames
    11. The Salting of Superstition
        Mine
    12. Buried Alive
    13. A Fight for a Fortune
    14. Helen's Race against Time
    15. Driving the Last Spike
Girl and the Graft, The 1917 ( ) 102
Girl and the Half Back 1911 (Independent
    Moving Picture Co.)
Girl and the Judge, The 1913 ( ) 2540
Girl and the Motor Boat, The 1911 (Ed)
Girl and the Mummy, The 1916 (Tri)
    1286
Girl and the Outlaw, The 1908 (AMB)
    1336, 1511
Girl Angle, The 1918 ( ) 1439
Girl at Bay, A 1919 (V) 296, 1088, 1832
Girl at Home, The 1917 (Las) 1764, 1925,
    2045
Girl at Lancing Mill, The 1913 (Hep) 2531
Girl at the Key, The 1912 (Ed)
Girl at the Lunch Counter, The 1913 (V)
    332, 901
Girl at the Window, The 1903 (AMB)
Girl behind the Counter, The 1911
    (Ingvald C. Oes)
Girl Boy Scout, The 1914 (Br) 149, 150
Girl by the Roadside, The 1917 ( ) 1814
Girl Detective, The--serial 1916 (P) 2169
Girl Dodger, The 1919 ( ) 543, 720,
    1928, 2096
Girl for Sale 1919 ( ) 1907
Girl from Beyond, The 1918 ( ) 2397,
    2754
Girl from Bohemia, The 1917 ( ) 435
Girl from Montana, The 1907 (Selig)
Girl from Nowhere, The 1919 ( ) 1613
Girl from Outside, The 1919 (Go) 24,
    543, 1292, 1483, 2533
Girl from Prosperity, The 1914 ( ) 2472
Girl from the Country, The 1912 (Ed)
Girl from the Sky, The 1914 (Br) 503
Girl Guardian see The Feathered Nest
Girl in Bohemia, A 1919 ( ) 2335, 2405
Girl in His House, The 1918 (V) 646,
    2767
Girl in the Checkered Coat, The 1917
    (Bluebird/Un) 449, 2042, 2490, 2752
Girl in the Dark 1918 (Un) 1911
Girl in the Next Room, The 1912 ( )
    2748
Girl Like That, A 1917 (Art/Par) 1865,
    2557
Girl Next Door, The 1916 ( ) 2619
Girl of Gopher City, The 1917 ( ) 1010
Girl of Hell's Agony, The 1918 (Frohman)
    464, 1099, 2128
Girl of My Dreams 1918 ( ) 1710, 2121
Girl of Mystery, The 1914 ( ) 2343

Girl of the Golden West, The 1915 (Par) 677, 770, 828, 866, 1096, 1168, 1201, 1439, 1500, 1701, 1985, 1986, 2035, 2149, 2623

Girl of the Night, The 1915 (Tex/Un) 352, 449, 2420

Girl of the Rancho 1919 (Reelcraft) 1099

Girl of the Timber Claims 1917 (Select) 2521

Girl of the West, A 1910 (Es) 50

Girl of Today, The 1918 (V) 1088, 1656

Girl of Yesterday, A 1915 (FP) 595, 1743, 1761, 1924, 2045, 2047

Girl on Triple X, The 1910 (Es) 50

Girl Philippa, The 1917 (V) 381, 616, 769, 2472

Girl Problem, The 1919 (V) 1047, 1088, 1360

Girl Reporter, The 1913 ( ) 2748

Girl Spy, The--series * (Kal) 992

Girl Who Came Back, The 1918 (Art/Par) 486, 554, 724, 763, 935, 1166, 1925, 2728

Girl Who Couldn't Grow-Up, The 1918 ( ) 905

Girl Who Joined the Bushrangers 1909 (Hep) 2744

Girl Who Lived in Straight Street, The 1914 (Hep) 2171, 2531, 2744

Girl Who Played the Game, The 1914 (Br) 1289, 2171

Girl Who Stayed at Home, The 1919 (Art) 143, 315, 355, 706, 875, 1182, 1552, 1756, 2107, 2370, 2516

Girl Who Won Out, The 1917 ( ) 1714

Girl Who Wouldn't Quit, The 1918 ( ) 1604

Girl with Champagne Eyes, The 1918 (F) 406

Girl with No Rights, The 1919 ( ) 1329

Girl Woman 1919 (V) 566, 1547

Girls 1919 (Go) 443, 482, 927

Girls and Daddy, The 1909 (AMB) 209, 315, 1182, 1336, 1363, 1511, 1613, 2212, 2368, 2729

Girls and the Burglar, The 1904 (AMB)

Girls behind the Scenes, The 1904 (AMB)

Girl's Folly, A 1917 ( ) 1387, 1429

Girl's Stratagem, A 1913 (Bio)

Girls, the Burglar, and the Rat, The 1905 (AMB)

Giving the Bride Away 1919 (P) 635, 2055

Giving Them Fits 1915 (P) 1586

Gladys' Day Dreams 1917 (Mu) 1586

Glass Coffin; or The Crystal Casket 1912 (Eclair)

Glimpse of Los Angeles, A 1914 (Key) 1941

Gloomy Gus Gets the Best of It 1903 (AMB)

Gloria's Romance--serial 1916 (K) 143, 171, 333, 401, 1184, 1460, 1670, 2061, 2064, 2176, 2706
  1. Lost in the Everglades
  2. Caught by the Seminoles
  3. A Perilous Love
  4. The Social Vortex
  5. The Gathering Storm
  6. Hidden Fires
  7. The Harvest of Sin
  8. The Mesh of Mystery
  9. The Shadow of Scandal
  10. Tangled Threads
  11. The Fugitive Witness
  12. Her Fighting Spirit
  13. The Midnight Riot
  14. The Floating Trap
  15. The Murderer at Bay
  16. A Modern Pirate
  17. The Tell-Tale Envelope
  18. The Bitter Truth
  19. Her Vow Fulfilled
  20. Love's Reward

Glorious Adventure, A 1918 (Go) 950, 1751

Glorious Lady 1919 (Sel) 286, 1046, 1864, 2557

Glory 1917 ( ) 1153, 1459, 1796

Glory of Yolanda, The 1917 (V) 2472

Go and Get It 1919 (Art/Par) 1855

Go Get 'Em Garringer 1919 (Go) 443

Go West Young Man 1919 (Go) 396, 1867

Goat, The 1918 (King-Bee) 1161, 1847, 1949, 2482

Gobs of Love * ( ) 750

God and the Man 1918 (Br) 349

God Bless the Red, White and Blue 1918 (Br) 831, 1918

God of Gold 1912 (Selig) 857, 2095, 2221

God Within, The 1912 (Bio) 141, 1665, 2513, 2680

Goddess, The--serial 1915 (V) 634, 904, 2233, 2472, 2767

Goddess of Lost Lake 1918 ( ) 242, 1032

Goddess of Sagebrush Gulch, The 1912 (Bio) 209, 2000, 2513, 2728

Godmother, The 1912 ( ) 2472

God's Country and the Woman 1916 ( ) 2397

God's Good Man 1919 (Br) 834, 1018

God's Law and Man's 1917 (M) 631, 1128, 2039

God's Man 1917 ( ) 2693

God's Outlaw 1919 ( ) 156

Goebel Tragedy, The 1908 (Lubin)

Going! Going! Going! 1919 (P) 1586

Going Straight 1909 (Bio) 2047

Going Straight /aka/ Corruption 1916 (FA/Tri) 1563, 2002, 2483, 2523, 2573

Going West to Make Good 1915 (Selig Polyscope) 1849

Gold and Glitter 1912 (Bio) 141, 1028

Gold and the Woman 1916 (F) 116, 136, 493, 698, 800, 1138, 1150, 1323, 1709, 1777, 1928a, 2671, 2757

Gold Cure, The 1919 (M) 631

Gold Dust Twins, The 1903 (AMB)

Gold Is Not All 1910 (Bio) 1542, 2156, 2680

Gold Necklace, A 1910 (Bio) 2047

Gold Seekers, The 1910 (Bio) 2680

Gold Ship, The 1915 ( ) 1818

Golden Bird 1915 (FP) 482

Golden Chance, The 1915 (Par) 411, 454, 1201, 1386, 2112, 2132

Golden Chariots, The 1902 (Ed)

Golden Claw, The 1915 ( ) 1188

Golden Fetter, The 1917 (Art/Par) 1581, 1591, 1756, 1975, 2112

Golden Fleece 1918 ( ) 192

Golden Goal, The 1918 ( ) 1877

Golden God, The 1917 ( ) 1326

Golden Idiot, The 1917 (Es) 2619, 2700
Golden Lie, A 1909 (Lubin)
Golden Louis, The 1909 (AMB) 315, 1542, 1613, 1865, 2368
Golden Pavement, The 1915 (Hep) 2171, 2531
Golden Rule Kate 1917 (Tri) 473, 1016, 1032
Golden Shower, The 1919 ( ) 1878
Golden Supper, The 1910 (Bio) 1665, 2728, 2729
Golden Trail, The * (Es) 50
Golden Wall, The 1918 ( ) 231, 853
Golem, The 1914 (Deutsche-Bioscop) 807, 2715
Golf Game and the Bonnet, The 1913 (V) 332, 901
Gondolier's Daughter, The 1908 (Lubin)
Goo Goo Eyes 1903 (Ed)
Good Bad Man, The 1915 (Tri) 200, 686, 857, 1602, 2415
Good Boy, A 1908 (V)
Good Catch, A 1912 (Es) 156, 353
Good-for-Nothing 1910 (Es) 50
Good-for-Nothing, The see His New Profession 1914 (Key)
Good for Nothing 1917 ( ) 987, 1603
Good Glue Sticks 1907 (Melies)
Good Gracious, Annabelle! 1919 (Art/Par) 333, 1427, 1960, 2095
Good Indian, The 1913 ( ) 785
Good Joke, A 1901 (Lubin)
Good Little Devil, A 1908 ( ) 1415
Good Little Devil, A 1914 (FP) 194, 534, 1942, 2047, 2595
Good Luck of a Souse, The 1908 (Melies)
Good Night 1906 (Winthrop Press)
Good Night Nurse! 1918 (Key) 65, 253, 1401, 1476, 2208
Good Night, Paul 1918 ( ) 927, 1432, 2521
Good Sport, The 1918 ( ) 913
Good Turn, A 1911 (Lubin) 1511, 2442
Goodbye 1917 (Br) 834
Goodbye Bill 1918 (Par) 1774, 2595
Goodbye John 1907 (Winthrop Moving Picture Co.)
Goodbye Summer 1914 (V) 297, 1876, 2523
Goodfellow's Christmas Eve, The 1911 (Es)
Goodness Gracious! or Movies as They Shouldn't Be 1914 (V) 768, 904, 1027, 1469, 2070, 2569, 2811
Goody, Goody Two Shoes 1903 (Lubin)
Goose Girl, The 1915 (FP) 482, 2211
Gordon Sisters Boxing 1901 (Ed)
Gosh Darn the Kaiser 1919 (Par) 1774
Gossip, The 1911 (V) 332, 790, 901
Gossipers, The 1906 (AMB)
Got a Match? 1912 (Bio)
Governor's Double, The 1913 ( ) 2003
Governor's Lady, 1915 (Mu) 41, 935
Gown of Destiny 1918 (Tri) 2194
Graduation Celebration, A 1907 (P) 1575
Graft--serial 1915 (Un) 302, 398, 1228, 1290, 1683, 1948, 2195, 2341, 2450, 2723, 2745, 2807
   1. Liquor and the Law
   2. The Tenement House Evil
   3. The Traction Grab
   4. The Power of the People
   5. Grinding Life Down
   6. The Railroad Monopoly
   7. America Saved from War
   8. Old King Coal
   9. The Insurance Swindlers
  10. The Harbor Transportation Trust
  11. The Illegla Bucket Shops
  12. The Milk Battle
  13. Powder Trust and the War
  14. The Iron Ring
  15. The Patent Medicine Danger
  16. The Pirates of Finance
  17. The Queen of the Prophets
  18. The Hidden City of Crime
  19. The Photo Badger Game
  20. The Final Conquest
Grafters, The 1917 ( ) 2356
Grail, The 1915 ( ) 2803
Grain of Dust, The 1918 (Crest) 668, 2663
Grain of Sand, A 1917 (Hep) 2171, 2744
Grand Babylon Hotel 1916 (Hep) 1289, 2171, 2531
Grand Hotel to Big Indian 1906 (AMB)
Grand Passion, The 1918 (Jewel/Un) 34, 62, 449, 1896, 2042, 2361, 2490
Grandfather, The 1912 (Ed)
Grandfather as a Spook 1904 (AMB)
Grandma and the Bad Boys 1900 (Ed)
Grandmother's Lamb 1908 (Ambrosio) 391, 2528
Grandmother's Story, A 1908 (Melies)
Grandpa's Reading Glass 1902 (AMB)
Granny 1914 ( ) 1028
Grasp of Greed 1916 (Bluebird/Un) 449, 1518, 1604
Gratitude 1908 (V)
Gratitude of Wanda 1913 ( ) 2112
Graustark 1915 (Es) 156, 353, 524, 612, 781
Gray Ghost, The--serial 1917 (Un) 88, 420, 540, 582, 597, 675, 677, 945, 1183, 1365, 2056, 2403
   1. The Bank Mystery
   2. The Mysterious Message
   3. The Warning
   4. The Fight
   5. Plunder
   6. The House of Mystery
   7. Caught in the Web
   8. The Double Floor
   9. The Pearl Necklace
  10. Shadows
  11. The Flaming Meteor
  12. The Poisoned Ring
  13. The Tightening Snare
  14. At Bay
  15. The Duel
  16. From out of the Past
Gray Horizon 1919 (Par) 60, 1208, 2031
Gray Towers of Mystery, The 1919 ( ) 1878, 2130
Greased Lightning 1919 (Par) 1206, 1261, 1588, 1690, 1746, 2096, 2794
Greaser, The 1915 ( ) 2672
Greaser and the Weakling, The 1912 (Am) 1924
Greaser's Gauntlet, The 1908 (AMB) 79, 732, 994, 1363
Great Adventure, The 1915 (Br) 22

Great Adventure, The 1918 ( ) 1602
Great Anarchist Mystery 1912 (Br) 1873
Great Chances, The 1918 (M) 2061
Great Coup, A 1919 (Br) 2171
Great Divide, The 1915 (W) 486, 2035
Great Expectations 1916 (FP) 1309, 2045,
    2074
Great Gamble, The--serial 1919 (P) 439,
    541, 1326, 1622, 1871, 1923
    1.   The Great Gamble
    2.   The Clock of Doom
    3.   Into the Chasm
    4.   In the Law's Grip
    5.   Draught of Death
    6.   Out of the Clouds
    7.   The Crawling Menace
    8.   The Ring of Fire
    9.   Through Iron Doors
    10. Written in Blood
    11. The Stolen Identity
    12. The Wolf Pack
    13. Barriers of Flame
    14. Under Arrest
    15. Out of the Shadows
Great Gold Robbery, The 1913 (Br) 834
Great Green Eye 1913 ( ) 141
Great Jewel Mystery, The 1905 (AMB)
Great Jewel Robbery, The 1908 (Lubin)
Great Leap, The 1914 ( ) 2672
Great Leap, The see The Village Vam-
    pire 1916 (Key/Tri)
Great Love, The 1918 (Art) 31, 84, 875,
    1029, 1182, 1283, 1729, 1852, 2356,
    2408, 2448, 2554, 2680
Great Mail Robbery, The 1906 (Lubin)
Great Nickel Robbery, The 1914 (Key) 531
Great Pearl Tangle, The 1916 (Key/Tri)
    14, 211, 791, 1086, 1651
Great Price, The 1916 (M) 2520
Great Radium Mystery, The--serial 1919
    (Un) 274, 1461, 1711, 2109, 2354
    1.   The Mystic Stone
    2.   The Death Trap
    3.   The Fatal Ride
    4.   The Swing for Life
    5.   The Torture Chamber
    6.   The Tunnel of Doom
    7.   A Flash in the Dark
    8.   In the Clutches of the Mad
         Man
    9.   The Roaring Volcano
    10. Creeping Flames
    11. Perils of Doom
    12. Shackled
    13. The Scalding Pit
    14. Hemmed In
    15. The Flaming Arrow
    16. Over the Cataract
    17. The Wheels of Death
    18. Liquid Flames
Great Red War, The 1916 (Br) 150
Great Romance, The 1919 ( ) 709, 1589
Great Secret, The 1910 (Ed)
Great Secret, The--serial 1917 (M) 113,
    156, 234, 313, 353, 357, 534, 781,
    862, 1004, 1209, 1985, 2137, 2449,
    2814
    1.   The Whirlpool of Destiny or
         The Secret Seven
    2.   The Casket of Tainted Trea-
         sure

    3.   The Hidden Hand
    4.   From Sunshine to Shadow
    5.   The Trap
    6.   The Dragon's Den
    7.   The Yellow Claw
    8.   A Clue from the Klondike
    9.   Cupid's Puzzle
    10. The Woman and the Game
    11. A Shot in the Dark
    12. Caught in the Web
    13. The Struggle
    14. The Escape
    15. Test of Death
    16. The Crafty Hand
    17. The Missing Finger
    18. The Great Secret
Great Spy Raid, The 1914 (Br) 1879
Great Train Robbery, The 1903 (Ed) 1,
    50, 125, 1145, 1908
Great Train Robbery, The 1904 (Lubin)
Great Vacuum Robbery, The 1915 (Key/Tri)
    250, 463, 878, 1422, 1906, 2501,
    2580
Great While It Lasted 1916 (P) 1586, 2055
Great White Trail, The 1917 ( ) 1429
Great Wrong Righted, A 1909 (Lubin)
Greater Devotion, The 1914 ( ) 651, 2112
Greater Law, The 1917 ( ) 539, 1518
Greater Love, The 1910 (Ed)
Greater Need, The 1916 (Br) 43, 2179
Greater Than Art 1915 ( ) 1649
Greater Woman, The 1917 (Mu) 2088
Greatest Power, The 1917 (M) 658
Greatest Question, The 1919 (FN) 218,
    601, 875, 1029, 1067, 1182, 1933,
    2480, 2782
Greatest Thing in Life, The 1919 (Art)
    315, 355, 1029, 1182, 1343, 1552,
    1570, 1717, 2026, 2616
Greatest Wish in the World, The 1918
    (Bio)
Green Cat, The 1915 (V) 2081, 2521
Green Cloak, The 1915 (M) 656
Green Eyed Devil, The 1914 ( ) 1029
Green-Eyed Monster, The 1912 (Ed)
Green Eyes 1918 (Tri) 627, 1690
Green God, The 1918 ( ) 243, 1656,
    1877, 2406
Green Goods Man, The 1905 (V)
Green Magic 1917 ( ) 1120, 1518
Green Terror, The 1919 (GB) 2551
Grell Mystery, The 1918 (V) 2767
Gretchen, the Greenhorn 1916 ( ) 315,
    1028, 1563, 2002, 2483
Gretna Green 1915 (FP) 482, 1282, 1623,
    1811
Grey Chiffon Veil, The 1918 (Sel) 927,
    2521
Grey Sentinel, The 1914 ( ) 2096
Griffo-Barnett Fight 1895 (Latham) 128,
    1093
Grim Game, The 1919 (Un) 939, 1295,
    1351, 1756
Grim Justice 1916 (GB) 812, 2604
Grin and Win; or Converted by a Billiken
    1909 (V)
Grind, The 1915 (Rex/Un) 352, 449, 2186,
    2187
Grip 1915 (Br) 2138
Grip Home 1915 (Br) 834
Grip of Ambition, The 1914 (Br) 2171

Grip of Evil, The--serial 1916 (P) 260,
    1652, 2227
    1. Fate
    2. The Underworld
    3. The Upper Ten
    4. The Looters
    5. The Way of a Woman
    6. The Hypocrites
    7. The Butterflies
    8. In Bohemia
    9. The Dollar Kings
    10. Down to the Sea
    11. Mammon and Moloch
    12. Into the Pits
    13. Circumstantial Evidence
    14. Humanity Triumphant
Grip of Jealousy, The 1916 (Bluebird/Un)
    170, 449, 1604, 1683, 1882, 2559
Grit 1915 ( ) 1188
Grit of a Jew, The 1917 (Br) 834
Grocery Clerk's Romance, The 1912 (Key)
    1941, 2465
Grotto of Surprises, The 1904 (Melies)
Grouch, The 1912 (Ed)
Grouch, The 1919 ( ) 1603
Grudge, The 1915 ( ) 1188
Guardian of the Peace, A 1903 (AMB)
Guarding Angel, The 1909 (Lubin)
Guerrilla, The 1908 (AMB) 1912, 2212
Guest of the Evening, The 1914 (Br)
Guff and Gunplay 1917 (V) 2367
Guilt of Silence, The 1918 ( ) 495, 2211
Guilty Cause, A 1919 ( ) 2221
Guilty Conscience, A 1908 (V)
Guilty One, The 1916 (Vim) 1161
Guilty Party, The 1912 (Ed)
Gulf Between, The 1917 ( ) 646, 2719
Gulliver's Travels 1903 (Lubin)
Gun Fighter, The 1917 (Tri) 1188
Gun Fightin' Gentleman, A 1919 (Un) 398,
    2570
Gun Law, The 1919 ( ) 1010, 1011
Gun Packer, The 1919 ( ) 1011
Gun Woman, The 1918 (Tri) 1099, 1658
Guns and Greasers 1918 (V) 2367
Gus and the Anarchists 1915 (Lubin) 1161
Gusher, The 1913 (Key) 1941, 2465
Gussle Rivals Jonah 1915 (Key) 452
Gussle, the Golfer 1914 (Key) 452, 463,
    2510
Gussle Tied to Trouble 1915 (Key) 452
Gussle's Backward Way 1915 (Key) 452
Gussle's Day of Rest 1915 (Key) 73, 452,
    2501
Gussle's Wayward Path 1915 (Key/Tri)
    37, 452
Gutter Magdalene, A 1916 ( ) 1581, 2683
Guy Fawkes and the Gunpowder Plot 1913
    (Br) 150
Gypsy Blood see Carmen 1919
Gypsy Duel, A 1903 (AMB)
Gypsy Flirt, The 1912 ( ) 2748
Gypsy Girl, The 1907 (Bio) 2047
Gypsy Joe 1916 (Key/Tri) 697, 723, 1135,
    1342, 1749, 1889, 2165
Gypsy Queen, The 1913 (Key) 65, 1941
Gypsy Romance, A 1914 ( ) 2112
Gypsy Trail, The 1915 (V) 1876
Gypsy Trail, The 1918 (Par) 1206, 2700
Gypsy's Revenge 1907 (Lubin)
Gypsy's Revenge 1908 (V)

Gypsy's Warning, The 1907 (V)

- H -

Habit of Happiness 1916 (FA/Tri) 857,
    875, 2729
Hair Restorer and the Indians, The 1911
    (Ed)
Hairdresser, The 1903 (AMB)
Half-Breed, The 1916 (FA/Tri) 200, 406,
    686, 857, 2194
Half Million Bride, The 1916 ( ) 2430
Hall Room Boys series 1919 (Cohn, Brandt,
    Cohn/Columbia Pictures Corp.) 813
Halloween 1905 (AMB)
Halloween Night at the Seminary 1904 (Ed)
Ham and the Garbage 1915 (Kal) 1136
Ham and the Villain Factory 1914 (Kal)
    1924
Ham Artist, The see The Face on the
    Barroom Floor
Ham at the Garbage Gentleman's Ball 1915
    (Kal) 2169
Ham, the Piano Mover 1914 (Kal) 1136,
    2169
Hamlet 1903 ( ) 212
Hamlet 1907 (Melies)
Hamlet 1913 (GB) 17, 44, 89, 126, 199,
    263, 542, 822, 923
Hamlet 1914 (V) 1047, 2811
Hamlet 1917 (Rodolfi-Film) 289
Hamlet 1919 ( ) 1614
Hamlet Made Over /aka/ Hamlet
    Up-to-Date 1916 (Lubin) 829
Hand at the Window, The 1918 ( ) 2780
Hand Invisible, The 1919 (W) 1142, 1603,
    1991
Hand of Fate, The 1908 (Lubin)
Hand of Uncle Sam, The 1909 (Es) 1431
Hand That Rocked the Cradle, The 1912
    (Un) 95, 2361
Hands Down 1918 ( ) 2211
Hands Up!--serial 1918 (P) 242, 464,
    1353, 1494, 1603, 1613, 1859, 2169,
    2675
    1. Bride of the Sun
    2. The Missing Price
    3. The Phantom and the Girl
    4. The Phantom Trail
    5. The Runaway Bride
    6. Flames of Vengeance
    7. Tossed into the Torrent
    8. The Fatal Jewels
    9. A Leap through Space
    10. The Sun Message
    11. Stranger from the Sea
    12. The Silver Book
    13. The Last Warning
    14. The Oracle's Decree
    15. The Celestial Messenger
Handsome Chap, The 1917 ( ) 2002
Handy Henry 1917 (M) 768, 1707
Handy Man, The 1918 (King-Bee) 1161
Hanging Judge, The 1918 (Hep) 812, 2744
Hank and Lank 1910 (Es)
Hansel and Gretel 1909 (Ed)
Hansom Driver, The 1913 (Key) 1941,
    2368, 2465
Happiness a la Mode 1919 (Par) 927,
    2335, 2521

Happy Accident, A 1909 (Ed)
Happy Family, No. 99 1897 (AMB)
Happy-Go-Lucky 1912 (V) 2767, 2811
Happy Heels * ( ) 750
Happy Hooligan 1903 (AMB)
Happy Hooligan April-Fooled 1901 (Ed)
Happy Hooligan in a Trap 1903 (AMB)
Happy Hooligan Surprised 1901 (Ed)
Happy Hooligan Turns Burglar 1902 (Ed)
Happy Hooligan's Interrupted Lunch 1903
   (AMB)
Happy Jack, a Hero 1910 (Bio)
Happy though Married 1919 (Art/Par)
   189, 543, 1697, 2570, 2613
Happy Warrior, The 1917 (Br) 1300, 1453
Harbinger of Peace, The 1912 (Ed) 968
Harbor Bar 1919 ( ) 286
Harbor Island 1908 (Selig) 1589, 2770
Hard Boiled 1919 (Par) 473, 627, 1248
Hard Cash 1913 ( ) 1970
Hard Rock Breed, The 1918 ( ) 2780
Hard Times 1915 (Br) 177
Hard to Beat 1909 (Ed)
Hard Wash, A 1896 (AMB)
Hard Wash, A 1903 (AMB)
Harem, The see Poultry a la Mode
   1916 (Vogue)
Harold, the Last of the Saxons 1919 (M)
   768, 1707
Harper Mystery, The 1913 (GB) 2604
Harvest of Flame, The 1913 ( ) 2112
Hash and Havoc 1915 (V) 2367
Hash-House Count, The 1913 (Kal) 1924
Hash House Fraud, A 1915 (Key) 531, 878,
   2336
Hash-House Hero see The Star Boarder
Hash House Mashers 1915 (Key) 460, 465,
   531, 1981, 2336
Hashimura to Go 1917 (Art/Par) 935,
   1208, 1591, 2623
Hat of Fortune, The 1908 (Lubin)
Hate 1917 ( ) 1640
Haunted Bedroom, The 1919 (Par) 189,
   1311
Haunted Castle, The see Le Manoir du
   Diable
Haunted Hat, The 1909 (Lubin)
Haunted Hat, The 1915 (Lubin) 1161
Haunted Hotel, The 1907 (V)
Haunted House, The 1899 (V)
Haunted House, The 1911 (Independent
   Moving Picture Co.)
Haunted Pajamas, The 1916 (FA/Tri)
   612, 1589, 1911
Haunted Queen, The 1914 (Kal) 2169
Haunted Sentinel Tower, The 1911 (Ed)
Haunting of Silas P. Gould 1914 (Br) 503
Have a Light, Sir 1906 (V)
Have You Seen My Wife? 1908 (Lubin)
Having a Good Time see High Spots on
   Broadway
Havoc, The 1916 (Es) 1154, 2485, 2700
Hawk, 1917 ( ) 1053, 1326, 2593
Hawk's Trail, The--serial 1919 ( ) 108,
   1847
Hawlin' Jones 1913 ( ) 785
Hawthorne of the U. S. A. 1919 (Art/Par)
   264, 345, 927, 1528, 1756, 1970,
   1975, 2112, 2149, 2468
Hay Foot, Straw Foot! 1919 (Par) 25,
   532, 1588, 2096

Hayseed, The 1919 (FA/Las) 65, 1401,
   1919
Haystacks and Steeples 1916 (Key/Tri)
   280, 883, 1886, 2073, 2512, 2514,
   2550, 2564, 2636
Hazards and Home Runs 1917 (V) 2367
Hazards of Helen, The--serial 1914 (Kal)
   11, 56, 500, 1010, 1011, 1273, 1307,
   1672, 2027, 2585, 2703, 2765
   1.   Helen's Sacrifice
   2.   The Plot at the R. R. Cut
   3.   The Girl at the Throttle
   4.   The Stolen Engine
   5.   The Flying Freight's Captive
   6.   The Black Diamond Express
   7.   The Escape on the Limited
   8.   The Girl Telegrapher's Peril
   9.   The Leap from the Water
        Tower
   10. The Broken Circuit
   11. The Fast Mail's Danger
   12. The Little Engineer
   13. Escape of the Fast Freight
   14. The Red Signal
   15. The Engineer's Peril
   16. The Open Drawbridge
   17. The Death Train
   18. Night Operator at Buxton
   19. Railroad Raiders of '62
   20. The Girl at Lone Point
   21. A Life in the Balance
   22. The Girl on the Trestle
   23. The Girl Engineer
   24. A Race for a Crossing
   25. The Box Car Trap
   26. The Wild Engine
   27. A Fiend at the Throttle
   28. The Broken Train
   29. A Railroader's Bravery
   30. The Human Chain
   31. The Pay Train
   32. Near Eternity
   33. In Danger's Path
   34. The Midnight Limited
   35. A Wild Ride
   36. A Deed of Daring
   37. The Girl on the Engine
   38. The Fate of #1
   39. The Substitute Fireman
   40. The Limited's Peril
   41. A Perilous Chance
   42. Train Order #45
   43. The Broken Rail
   44. Nerves of Steel
   45. A Girl's Grit
   46. A Matter of Seconds
   47. The Runaway Boxcar
   48. The Water Tank Plot
   49. A Test of Courage (First
        episode with Helen Gibson
        1915)
   50. A Mile a Minute
   51. Rescue of the Brakeman's
        Children
   52. Danger Ahead
   53. The Girl and the Special
   54. The Girl on the Bridge
   55. The Dynamite Train
   56. The Tramp Telegrapher
   57. Crossed Wires
   58. The Wrong Train Order

59.   A Boy at the Throttle
60.   At the Risk of Her Life
61.   When Seconds Count
62.   The Haunted Station
63.   The Open Track
64.   Tapped Wires
65.   The Broken Wire
66.   Peril of the Rails
67.   A Perilous Swing
68.   The Switchman's Story
69.   A Girl Telegrapher's Nerve
70.   A Race for Life
71.   The Girl Who Dared
72.   The Detective's Peril
73.   The Tapping of "Peeler White"
74.   The Record Run
75.   The Race for a Siding
76.   The Governor's Special
77.   The Trail of Danger
78.   The Human Telegram
79.   The Bridge of Danger
80.   One Chance in a Hundred
81.   The Capture of Red Stanley
82.   Spiked Switch
83.   Treasure Train
84.   A Race through the Air
85.   The Mysterious Cypher
86.   The Engineer's Honor
87.   To Save the Road
88.   The Broken Brake
89.   In Death's Pathway
90.   A Plunge from the Sky
91.   A Mystery of the Rails
92.   Hurled through the Drawbridge
93.   With the Aid of the Wrecker
94.   At Danger's Call
95.   Secret of the Box Car
96.   Ablaze on the Rails
97.   The Hoodoo of Division B
98.   Defying Death
99.   The Death Swing
100. The Blocked Track
101. To Save the Special
102. A Daring Chance
103. The Last Messenger
104. The Gate of Death
105. The Lone Point Mystery
106. The Runaway Sleeper
107. The Forgotten Train Order
108. The Trial Run
109. The Lineman's Peril
110. The Midnight Express
111. The Vanishing Box Car
112. A Race with Death
113. The Morgul Mountain Mystery
114. The Fireman's Nemesis
115. The Wrecked Station
116. Railroad Claim Intrigue
117. The Death Siding
118. The Prima Donna's Special
119. The Side Tracked Sleeper

Hazel from Hollywood 1918 ( ) 720
Hazel Kirke 1916 (P) 1198, 1706, 2748
Hazers, The 1908 (V)
He Almost Eloped 1915 (Christie) 525
He Answered the Ad 1913 (V) 332, 901
He Comes up Smiling 1918 (Art/Par)
     387, 664, 857, 1448, 1702, 1855,
     2441
"He Cometh Not, " She Said 1903 (AMB)

He Couldn't Dance, but He Learned 1909
     (V)
He Danced Himself to Death 1914 ( )
     1332
He Did and He Didn't /aka/ Love and
     Lobsters 1916 (Key/Tri) 65, 1354,
     1941, 2208, 2608
He Fell in Love with His Mother-in-Law
     1913 (V) 2523
He Fell on the Beach 1915 ( ) 1132
He Forgot His Umbrella 1902 (AMB)
He Got His Hat 1905 (Paley & Steiner)
He Got into the Wrong House 1905 (AMB)
He Got Soap in His Eyes 1908 (V)
He Leads, Others Follow 1919 (P) 1586
He Looked Crooked see Why Ben Bolted
He Loved Her So see Twenty Minutes of
     Love
He Loves Her Still 1912 ( ) 2733
He Loves Me, He Loves Me Not 1903
     (AMB)
He Never Knew 1914 ( ) 2472
He Never Touched Me 1917 (V) 2367
He Tried on Handcuffs 1909 (V)
He Tries the Fire Escape 1904 (AMB)
He Went to See the Devil Play 1908 (V)
He Who Laughs Last 1910 (V) 332
He Winked and Won 1916 (Vim) 346, 1161
He Would a Hunting Go 1913 (Key) 65
He Wouldn't Go under a Ladder 1909 (Ed)
He Wouldn't Stay Down 1915 (Key) 2465
Headin' South 1918 (Art/Par) 387, 664,
     857, 1661
Headwaiter, The 1919 (V) 2367
Healthy and Happy 1919 (V) 1161
Healthy Neighbor, A 1913 (Key) 2465
Heap Big Chief 1919 (P) 1586, 2055
Hear 'Em Rave 1918 (P) 1586
Heard over the Phone 1908 (Ed)
Heart and Soul 1917 (F) 116, 733, 975,
     1253, 1278, 1475, 1506, 2110, 2745,
     2756
Heart Beat 1918 (Un) 398
Heart Beats of Long Ago 1911 (Bio) 79,
     1613, 1701
Heart o' the Hills 1910 (V) 2523
Heart of a Clown, The 1909 (Ed)
Heart of a Cowboy 1909 (Es) 50
Heart of a Cracksman, The 1913 (Powers)
     1711, 2112
Heart of a Fool, The 1916 ( ) 2784
Heart of a Girl, The 1918 ( ) 437
Heart of a Gypsy, The 1912 (Un)
Heart of a Jewess, The 1917 (Un) 1911
Heart of a Lion, The 1918 ( ) 868
Heart of a Rose 1919 (Br) 2637
Heart of a Savage, The 1911 (Bio)
Heart of a Sheriff, The * (Selig Poly-
     scope) 1849
Heart of an Indian, The 1913 (Ince) 802,
     1580, 2392
Heart of Big Dan, The * ( ) 1509
Heart of Gold 1919 ( ) 1255, 1309
Heart of Humanity, The 1918 (Un) 54,
     1104, 1311, 1728, 2042, 2490, 2649
Heart of Mary Ann, The 1917 ( ) 2486
Heart of Maryland, The 1915 ( ) 421,
     1659, 2381
Heart of Midlothian, The 1914 (Hep) 1289,
     2171, 2531
Heart of Nichette, The 1911 (Ed)

Heart of Nora Flynn, The 1916 (Par) 724, 752, 756, 999, 1344, 1386, 1648, 1793, 2728
Heart of Oyama, The 1908 (AMB) 1511
Heart of Paula, The 1916 (Pal) 659, 2445, 2610
Heart of Rachel 1918 (Un) 28, 134, 1120, 1244, 1283, 1558, 1794
Heart of Romance 1918 (F) 392
Heart of Sister Anne, The 1915 (Br) 1931
Heart of Texas Ryan, The 1916 (Selig Polyscope) 857, 1849
Heart of the Blueridge 1915 (W) 130, 2811
Heart of the Hills 1914 ( ) 2112
Heart of the Hills 1918 (FN) 651, 686, 1016, 1041, 1321, 1665, 1688, 1800, 1864, 2047, 2535
Heart of the Rose, The 1910 (Ed)
Heart of the Sunset 1918 ( ) 1244, 1939
Heart of the Wilds 1918 (Art/Par) 626, 888, 1800, 1864
Heart of Wetona, The 1918 (Select) 1321, 1346, 1800, 2523, 2610
Heart of Youth 1919 (Art/Par) 935, 1454, 1528, 1975, 2401, 2416,
Heart Punch, The 1919 (Un) 2763
Heartbeats of Long Ago see Heart Beats of Long Ago
Heartease 1919 (Go) 24, 342, 443, 950, 1867, 2462, 2554
Hearts Adrift 1914 (FP) 1589, 2047
Hearts and Diamonds 1912 (Ed)
Hearts and Diamonds 1914 (V) 332, 818, 901
Hearts and Flags 1911 (Ed)
Hearts and Flowers 1918 ( ) 2465
Hearts and Horses 1913 ( ) 2112, 2125
Hearts and Planets 1915 (Key) 531, 791, 2368
Hearts and Saddles 1916 (Selig Polyscope) 1849
Hearts and Sparks 1916 (Key) 187, 460, 509, 1424, 1726, 2512, 2636
Hearts Asleep 1919 ( ) 2613
Heart's Desire 1917 ( ) 752, 992
Heart's in Exile 1915 (W) 1637, 2460, 2811
Hearts in Pawn 1919 ( ) 60, 2613
Hearts of Love 1916 (Es) 1346, 1795
Hearts of Men 1919 ( ) 160, 2623
Hearts of the First Empire 1919 ( ) 111
Hearts of the World 1918 (Art) 28, 54, 315, 562, 574, 601, 775, 778, 795, 825, 838, 875, 1028, 1029, 1030, 1178, 1179, 1180, 1181, 1182, 1207, 1265, 1538, 1552, 1609, 1610, 1742, 1859, 1933, 2059, 2142, 2356, 2408, 2504, 2649, 2679
Hearts or Diamonds? 1918 (Mu) 2201
Hearts United 1909 (Bison) 960
Heaven Avenges 1912 (Bio) 209
Heavenly Twins at Lunch, The 1903 (Ed)
Heavenly Twins at Odds 1903 (Ed)
Hebrew Fugitive, The 1908 (Lubin)
Hedda Gabler 1917 (Mu(1978
Heinie and Louis comedies 1915 (Starlight) 92
    Merry Chase, A
    Monkey Shines
Heinze's Resurrection 1913 (Key) 1666, 1941, 2465
Heir Apparent, The 1912 (Ed)

Heir of the Ages, The 1917 ( ) 2002
Heirs of Hate 1917 (Mu) 2760
Heiress for a Day, An 1918 (Tri) 2557
Held by the Enemy 1919 ( ) 1280
Held for Ransom 1908 (Lubin)
Held for Ransom 1913 (Hep) 2744
Helen Grayson's Strategy 1917 ( ) 2405
Helen of the Chorus 1916 (Ed) 602
Helene of the North 1915 (Par) 481, 1600, 2535
Helen's Marriage 1912 (Bio)
Helgon, the Mighty 1919 ( ) 2221
Hell Bent 1918 (Un) 398, 1004
Hell Cat, The 1913 (Selig) 2221
Hell Cat, The 1918 (Go) 869, 1685, 2410
Hell Morgan's Girl 1917 (Bluebird/Un) 34, 449, 1025, 2042, 2490
Hell Roarin' Reform 1919 (F) 1849
Hell-to-Pay Austin 1916 ( ) 27, 1602, 1613, 2002
Hellcat of Alaska, The 1917 ( ) 186
Hello, Judge 1917 ( ) 1872
Hello, Mabel 1914 (Key) 1941
Hello Trouble 1918 ( ) 460
Hello, Who's Your Lady Friend? 1917 (Br) 1487
Hell's End 1918 ( ) 715
Hell's Hinges 1916 (Tri) 334, 1016, 1032, 1188, 1242, 1268, 1461, 1690, 1957, 2172, 2442, 2765
Help! 1916 (M) 768, 1707
Help! Help! 1912 (Bio)
Help! Help! Help! 1916 (V) 2367
Help! Help! Hydrophobia 1913 (Key) 65
Help! Police! 1909 (Lubin)
Help! Help! Police! 1919 ( ) 286, 2671
Help Wanted 1911 (Bio)
Helpful Sisterhood, The 1914 (V) 297, 2523
Helping Hand, The 1908 (AMB) 79, 1182, 1363, 1511, 1823, 2212, 2368
Helping Hand, The 1908 (Melies)
Helping Hand, The 1912 (Imp)
Helping Himself see His New Profession
Helping John 1912 (Ed)
Henpecked Ike 1912 (Imp)
Henry VIII 1910 ( ) 22, 262, 575
Henry VIII 1911 (Barker) 6, 376, 447, 542, 593, 965
Henry VIII 1911 (Br) 1018
Henry, O.--series (25) 1917 ( ) 102
Henry's Ancestors 1917 (M) 768, 1707
Her American Husband 1918 ( ) 2216
Her Anniversaries 1917 (M) 768, 1707
Her Awakening 1911 (Bio) 1328, 1363, 1941, 2112
Her Awakening 1914 (Mu) 1563, 2513
Her Better Self 1917 ( ) 610, 1270
Her Big Story 1913 ( ) 1431
Her Birthday 1911 (Independent Moving Picture Co.)
Her Birthday Present 1913 (Key) 1666
Her Bitter Cup 1916 ( ) 1216
Her Body in Bond 1918 ( ) 1907
Her Bounty 1914 (Rex/Un) 352, 449, 1442, 2620
Her Boy 1918 ( ) 2719
Her Breezy Affair 1918 (Christie) 632, 1767
Her Brother's Crime 1911 ( ) 2774
Her Brother's Photograph 1911 (Ed)
Her Busted Trust 1916 (Key/Tri) 2724

Her Cave Man see The Stone Age
Her Celluloid Hero 1915 (Christie) 525
Her Chance 1915 (Rex/Un) 352, 449, 686
Her Choice 1912 ( ) 2472
Her Choice 1915 (Lubin) 1161
Her Circus Knight /aka/ The Circus Girl
   1917 (Key/Tri) 179, 371, 396, 509,
   598, 2020, 2206
Her City Beau 1919 ( ) 2147
Her Code of Honor 1919 ( ) 606, 715,
   950, 955, 2105
Her Country Calls 1918 ( ) 1841
Her Country First 1918 ( ) 1764
Her Country's Call 1917 ( ) 1841
Her Crooked Career 1915 (Christie) 525
Her Cross 1919 (Br) 503
Her Crowning Glory 1911 (V) 332, 565, 566
Her Crowning Glory 1913 (Hep) 901, 2744
Her Darkest Hour 1911 (Imp) 2047
Her Deceitful Lover see Mabel's Awful
   Mistake
Her Decision 1918 (Tri) 942, 1465, 2392,
   2512
Her Double Life 1916 (F) 116, 1151, 1275,
   1506, 1521, 1524, 1525, 1861
Her Dramatic Debut see Mabel's
   Dramatic Career
Her Economic Independence 1917 (M) 768,
   1707
Her Escape 1917 (Rex/Un) 352, 449, 762,
   2188
Her Excellency, the Governor 1917 ( )
   1288
Her Face 1912 (Ed)
Her Face Was Her Fortune 1909 (Lubin)
Her Fame and Shame 1917 (Key/Tri) 83,
   250, 878, 1422, 1874, 1906, 1981,
   2501
Her Father's Footsteps 1915 (Key/Tri) 460
Her Father's Pride 1910 (Bio) 315, 1831
Her Father's Silent Partner 1914 (Bio) 398,
   1028, 1665
Her Father's Son 1916 (Pal) 1764, 2754
Her Final Reckoning 1918 (Par) 957
Her First Adventure 1908 (AMB)
Her First Appearance 1910 (Ed)
Her First Biscuits 1909 (Bio) 79, 526,
   1336, 1363, 1511, 1824, 1912, 2047,
   2502
Her First Cigarette 1903 (AMB)
Her First Commission 1911 (Ed)
Her First Game 1917 (M) 768, 1707
Her First Mistake 1918 (Key) 878
Her Friend, the Bandit /aka/ Mabel's
   Flirtation 1914 (Key) 384, 451, 1906,
   1941
Her Friend, the Chauffeur 1915 (Christie)
   525
Her Friend, the Doctor 1915 (Christie) 525
Her Game 1919 ( ) 2535
Her Grace, the Vampire 1917 (Art/Par)
   832
Her Grandparents 1915 ( ) 1028
Her Grave Mistake 1914 (Nestor/Un) 449,
   1197, 1705, 2635
Her Great Chance 1918 (Realart) 273
Her Greatest Love 1917 (F) 116, 620, 975,
   1253, 1591, 2226, 2576, 2745
Her Greatest Performance 1916 (Br) 1879
Her Greatest Triumph 1916 ( ) 2430
Her Guardian 1911 (Br) 177

Her Heritage 1919 (Br) 324
Her Hero 1911 (V) 332, 901, 2523
Her Hero 1917 (Strand) 2121
Her Hour 1918 ( ) 1048
Her Indian Hero 1909 ( ) 651
Her Innocent Marriage 1913 ( ) 2112,
   2125
Her Inspiration 1919 (M) 41
Her Kingdom of Dreams 1919 (FN) 25,
   138, 618, 1137, 1690, 1756, 1939,
   2221, 2472
Her Lesson 1917 (M) 768, 1707
Her Life's Story 1914 (Rex/Un) 352, 449,
   977, 1956, 2620, 2670
Her Luck in London 1914 (Br) 834, 2138
Her Man 1918 (Go) 1139, 2091
Her Marble Heart 1916 (Key/Tri) 250,
   878, 1211, 1291, 1906, 2430, 2580
Her Marriage Lines 1917 (Hep) 1289,
   2171, 2744
Her Mistake 1919 ( ) 1929
Her Moment 1918 ( ) 1622
Her Morning Exercise 1902 (AMB)
Her Mother Interferes 1911 (Bio)
Her Mother's Daughter 1915 ( ) 27, 1028
Her Mother's Necklace 1914 ( ) 1028
Her Mother's Oath 1913 (Bio) 731, 1028,
   1182, 1714, 1751
Her Nameless Child 1915 (Br) 834, 2138
Her Nature Dance 1917 (Key/Tri) 1476,
   2069, 2336, 2550
Her New Beau 1913 (Key) 1666, 1941,
   2368
Her New Party Gown 1903 (AMB)
Her New York 1917 ( ) 1312
Her Newsboy Friend 1908 (V)
Her Obsession 1917 (M) 1707
Her Official Fathers 1917 ( ) 686, 1028
Her Old Sweetheart 1912 (V) 332, 901
Her Old Teacher 1914 ( ) 1028
Her One Mistake 1918 (F) 295
Her Only Way 1918 (Select) 1305, 1959,
   2523
Her Own People 1917 ( ) 2610
Her Painted Hero 1915 (Key/Tri) 250,
   396, 1134, 1874, 1906, 2501
Her Pet 1911 (Bio)
Her Picture Idol 1912 ( ) 1476
Her Polished Family 1912 (Ed)
Her Price 1918 (F) 2024
Her Private Husband 1914 (Key) 531
Her Purchase Price 1919 (F) 134, 1460,
   2175
Her Right to Live 1917 (V) 1047, 1876
Her Sacrifice 1911 (Bio) 1224, 1533, 2067,
   2728
Her Screen Idol 1918 (Key) 878, 2465
Her Secret 1917 ( ) 552
Her Sentimental System 1913 (Bio) 1924
Her Silent Sacrifice 1918 ( ) 273
Her Sister 1918 ( ) 2540
Her Sister's Children 1911 (V) 332, 564,
   565, 566, 2523
Her Steady Carfare 1915 (Christie) 525
Her Strange Wedding 1917 (Art/Par) 935,
   2683
Her Terrible Ordeal 1910 (Bio) 122, 1865,
   1933, 1992
Her Torpedoed Love 1917 (Key/Tri) 250,
   460, 878, 1422, 2465, 2580
Her Triumph 1915 (FP) 2050

Her Two Sons 1911 (Lubin) 1363, 1511, 1912
Her Wedding Bell 1914 (Mu) 2513
Her Wedding Ring 1911 (Ed)
Her Western Adventure 1917 ( ) 610
Her Winning Punch 1915 (Key) 2501
Here Come the Girls 1918 (P) 1586
Here Comes the Bride 1918 (Par) 140, 227, 1245, 1600
Here He Is, in Jail 1904 (AMB)
Heredity 1912 (Bio) 398, 1933, 2000, 2045, 2502
Heredity 1918 ( ) 437
Here's to the Prettiest 1906 (Winthrop Press)
Heritage of Hate 1916 (Un) 2056
Hermit Doctor of Garja 1918 ( ) 960
Hero, The 1907 (V)
Hero, The 1914 (V) 2523
Hero, The 1917 (King-bee) 1161
Hero of Liao Yang 1904 (AMB)
Hero of Little Italy, The 1913 (Bio) 357, 398, 1714, 2513, 2573, 2728
Hero of Submarine D-2, The 1916 (V) 1402, 1888, 2091, 2129, 2795
Heroes, The 1916 (Vim) 1161, 2733
Heroes Three 1911 (Ed)
Heroic Harold 1913 ( ) 2748
Heroine of the Forge, The 1908 (V)
He's a Devil 1915 (Christie) 525
Hessian Renegades, The see 1776, or The Hessian Renegades
Hey There! 1918 (P) 1586
Hiawatha 1909 (Imp) 1312
Hickery, Dickery, Dock 1903 (Lubin)
Hickory Hiram 1918 (Nestor/Un) 1502
Hidden Aces 1917 ( ) 1326
Hidden City, The 1915 (Un) 610, 926, 2056
Hidden Fires 1918 (Go) 1495, 1751
Hidden Hand, The--serial 1917 (P) 1137, 1429, 1564, 2068
   1. The Gauntlet of Death
   2. Counterfeit Faces
   3. The Island of Dread
   4. The False Locket
   5. The Air-Lock
   6. The Flower of Death
   7. The Fire Trap
   8. Slide for Life
   9. Jets of Flame
  10. Cogs of Death
  11. Trapped by Treachery
  12. Eyes in the Wall
  13. Jaws of the Tiger
  14. The Unmasking
  15. The Girl of the Prophecy
Hidden Letters, The 1914 (V) 297, 618, 1032, 1876, 2523
Hidden Mine, The 1911 (Es) 50
Hidden Pearls, The 1918 (Art/Par) 1208, 1975
Hidden Pit, The * ( ) 1509
Hidden Scar, The 1916 (WS) 239
Hidden Truth, The 1919 (Select) 426, 2129
Hidden Valley 1916 (P) 2617
Hidden Voice, The 1915 ( ) 2748
Hide and Seek 1913 (Key) 509, 1273, 1941, 2465
Hide and Seek, Detectives 1918 (Key/Tri) 2608

Hieroglyphic, The 1912 ( ) 2112
High and Dry 1917 (Key/Tri) 1651, 1874
High Cost of Living, The 1912 (Ed)
High Cost of Living, The 1917 (M) 768, 1707
High Diver's Last Kiss, The 1917 (Key/Tri) 2501
High Sign, The 1914 (Un) 2095
High Sign, The 1919 ( ) 2208
High Spots on Broadway /aka/ Having a Good Time 1914 (Key) 1830
High Stakes 1918 (Tri) 1907, 2392
High Tide 1918 ( ) 1818
Highbinders, The 1915 ( ) 2002
Highest Trump, The 1919 (V) 646, 2767
Highway of Hope, The 1918 (Par) 2770
Highway Robbery 1905 (Lubin)
Highwayman's Honour, A 1914 (Br) 43
Hilarious Posters, The 1906 (Melies)
Hilda 1918 ( ) 853
Hill Billy, The 1918 (Un) 398, 1719
Hillcrest Mystery, The--serial 1918 (P) 435, 1357, 1407
Hillman, The 1917 (V) 1047
Hills Are Calling, The 1914 (Hep) 2531
Hindle Wakes 1918 (Br) 834
Hindoo Fakir 1902 (Ed)
Hindoos and Hazards 1918 (V) 2367
Hindu Charm, The 1913 ( ) 564
Hindu Dagger, The 1909 (AMB) 1182, 1542
Hindu's Prize, The 1912 (Un)
Hired and Fired /aka/ The Leading Man 1915 (Vim) 1161, 2608
Hired Man, The 1918 ( ) 960, 1791, 2096
Hiring a Girl 1909 (Lubin)
His Auto Ruination 1916 (Key/Tri) 787, 877, 1086, 1651, 2510, 2724
His Baby 1915 (Christie) 525
His Better Half 1919 ( ) 901
His Birthright 1918 (Par) 60, 1208, 1417, 2210
His Bitter Half see Those College Girls
His Bitter Pill /aka/ Big-Hearted Sheriff 1916 (Key/Tri) 1114, 1422, 1788, 2510
His Blowout /aka/ The Plumber 1916 (Vogue) 2608
His Bogus Boast /aka/ A Cheerful Liar 1917 (Bogue) 2608
His Bread and Butter 1916 (Key/Tri) 787, 1726, 2023, 2501
His Bridal Night 1919 (Realart) 273, 804, 2160
His Busted Trust 1916 (Key/Tri) 787, 815, 1135, 2023, 2501
His Busy Day 1918 (Br) 1487
His Chum, the Baron 1913 (Key) 2465
His Conscious Conscience 1916 (V) 2367
His Cooling Courtship 1915 (Br) 1487
His Country's Bidding 1914 (Hep) 2171, 2531
His Crooked Career 1913 (Key) 2368, 2465
His Curiosity 1917 (M) 768, 1707
His Daredevil Queen see Mabel at the Wheel
His Daughter 1911 (Bio) 95, 122
His Daughter 1912 (Ed)
His Daughter's Dilemma 1916 (Br) 2712
His Day of Rest 1908 (AMB)
His Day Out 1918 (King-Bee) 1161

His Deadly Calm 1917 (M) 768, 1707
His Dearest Possession 1919 (Hep) 812, 2744
His Debt 1919 ( ) 1948
His Diving Beauty see The Sea Nymphs
His Divorced Wife 1919 ( ) 977, 2728
His Dress Shirt 1911 (Independent Moving Picture Co.) 2047
His Duty 1909 (Bio) 2062
His Enemy, the Law 1918 ( ) 2128
His Ear for Music 1917 (M) 768, 1707
His Excellency, the Governor 1917 ( ) 1613
His Father's Deputy 1913 ( ) 785
His Father's Footsteps 1915 (Key/Tri) 2465
His Father's House 1914 (V) 1876
His Father's Son 1917 ( ) 141
His Father's Wife 1919 ( ) 835
His Favorite Pastime /aka/ The Bonehead 1914 (Key) 65, 451, 2023
His First False Step 1916 (Kay/Tri) 531, 1884, 2116, 2165, 2564, 2724
His First Girl 1909 (V)
His First Love 1918 (M) 768, 1707
His First Ride 1907 (Selig)
His First Trip 1911 (Ed)
His First Valentine 1910 (Ed)
His Guardian Angel 1916 ( ) 2002
His Halted Career 1914 (Key) 1906
His Heart, His Hand and His Sword-- serial 1914 ( ) 1431
His Hereafter /aka/ Murray's Mixup 1916 (Key/Tri) 250, 878, 1412, 1422, 1572, 1874, 1906, 2580
His Hidden Purpose 1919 (Key) 2069
His Highness, the Beggar 1919 (Par) 1208
His Home, Sweet Home 1919 (V) 2367
His Honor, the Mayor 1913 (V) 332, 818, 901
His Hour of Manhood 1915 ( ) 1188
His House in Order 1919 (FP) 888
His Just Deserts 1910 (Ed)
His Last Burglary 1910 (Bio) 1664, 1933, 2680, 2729
His Last Dollar 1910 (Bio)
His Last Fight 1913 ( ) 2472
His Last Laugh 1916 (Key/Tri) 48, 187, 371, 598, 877, 1650, 1651, 2136, 2564
His Last Pill 1915 (Christie) 525
His Last Scent 1916 (Key/Tri) 73, 650, 1666, 2058, 2336
His Lesson 1912 (Bio) 209
His Little Girl 1909 (Lubin)
His Little Page 1913 (V) 297, 2523
His Lordship's Dilemma 1915 ( ) 896, 2733
His Lost Love 1909 (Bio) 1542, 1865, 2047
His Luckless Love 1915 (Key) 1941
His Lying Heart 1916 (Key/Tri) 815, 1345, 1788, 2116, 2465
His Madonna 1912 (Un)
His Majesty Bunker Bean 1918 (Par) 2045
His Majesty, the American 1919 (UA) 387, 664, 796, 857, 1397, 1490, 2342, 2436
His Masterpiece 1903 (AMB)
His Masterpiece 1909 (Ed)
His Message 1912 (Un)
His Misjudgment 1911 (Ed)

His Mother-in-Law 1912 (V) 332
His Mother's Boy 1918 ( ) 473, 1454, 2096
His Mother's Oath 1913 (Bio) 1526, 2680
His Mother's Scarf 1911 (Bio) 1613, 2728, 2729
His Mother's Son 1913 (Bio) 1182, 1526, 1751, 1831, 1832, 2112
His Mother's Thanksgiving 1910 (Ed)
His Move 1905 (AMB)
His Musical Career /aka/ Musical Tramps; The Piano Movers 1914 (Key) 37, 253, 451, 460, 1304, 2336, 2510
His Name Was Mud 1903 (AMB)
His Naughty Thought 1917 (Kay/Tri) 1461, 1627, 1874, 2165, 2510, 2550
His Neighbor's Wife 1913 (FP) 1491, 1775
His Nemesis 1912 (New York Motion Picture Co.)
His New Family 1910 (Ed)
His New Job 1915 (Es) 102, 384, 451, 517, 1336, 1840, 2077, 2512, 2608, 2746
His New Lid 1910 (Bio)
His New Profession /aka/ Good-for-Nothing; Helping Himself 1914 (Key) 451, 460, 791, 1651
His New Wife 1912 (Independent Moving Picture Co.)
His Obsession 1917 (M) 768
His Official Appointment 1913 (V) 2523
His Official Fianceé 1918 (Art/Par) 1925, 2416, 2445
His Only Father 1919 (P) 2055
His Only Son 1912 ( ) 651, 1011, 2112
His Other Self 1912 (Un)
His Own Fault 1912 (Bio)
His Own Home Town 1918 ( ) 960, 1261, 1661, 2096
His Own People 1918 ( ) 243, 1547, 1877
His Pajama Girl 1918 ( ) 961
His Pal 1915 ( ) 242
His Parisian Wife 1919 (Art/Par) 888, 920, 1600, 2061, 2766
His Partner's Share 1912 (Un)
His Perfect Day 1917 (M) 768, 1707
His Phantom Sweetheart 1915 (V) 2472
His Picture in the Papers 1916 (FA/Tri) 233, 857, 1148, 2649
His Precious Life 1917 (Key/Tri) 878, 1906, 2165, 2501, 2580
His Prehistoric Past /aka/ The Hula Hula Dance; A Dream 1914 (Key) 73, 451, 1750, 2208, 2336, 2510
His Pride and Shame 1916 (Key/Tri) 787, 1153, 2465, 2636, 2799
His Reformation 1909 (Es) 50
His Regeneration 1915 (Key) 451
His Rival 1916 (M) 768, 1707
His Robe of Honor 1918 (Paralta) 457, 1474, 2002, 2680, 2779
His Royal Highness 1911 (Independent Moving Picture Co.)
His Royal Highness 1918 (W) 231
His Royal Slyness 1919 (P) 663, 1586, 1856, 2025
His Salad Days 1918 (Br) 1487
His Second Childhood 1914 (Key) 1906
His Second Wife 1913 ( ) 2472
His Secretary 1912 (Ed)
His Silver Bachelorhood 1913 (V) 297, 2523

His Sister-in-Law 1910 (Bio) 122, 731
His Sister's Kids 1913 (Key) 65
His Son's Wife 1914 (Key) 531
His Taking Ways 1914 (Key) 531
His Talented Wife 1914 (Key) 1906, 2368
His Temporary Wife /aka/ The Contrary
  Wife 1918 ( ) 246
His Tired Uncle 1913 (V) 332, 695, 769
His Trust 1911 (Bio) 1613
His Trust Fulfilled 1911 (Bio) 315, 477,
  1224, 1613, 1665
His Trysting Place /aka/ Family House
  1914 (Key) 37, 451, 791, 1941, 2510
His Uncle Dudley 1917 (Key/Tri) 250, 796,
  1211, 1874, 2428
His Ups and Downs 1913 (Key) 2465
His Ward's Love 1909 (AMB)
His Wedded Wife 1915 ( ) 1132
His Wedding Night 1917 (Par) 65, 1401,
  1476, 1724, 2208
His Week's Wages; or Where's That
  Quarter? 1908 (Lubin)
His Wife's Good Name 1916 ( ) 2478
His Wife's Mistakes 1916 (Key) 65, 791,
  803, 1069, 1354, 2208
His Wife's Mother 1909 (AMB) 526, 1336,
  1511, 1824
His Wife's Sweethearts 1911 (Bio)
His Wife's Visitor 1909 (Bio) 2047, 2062,
  2081
His Wild Oats 1916 (Key/Tri) 815, 1086,
  1114, 1874, 2465, 2510, 2514, 2799
His Young Friends Arrive 1904 (AMB)
Hist at Six o'Clock 1915 (Christie) 525
Hist ... Spies! 1917 (M) 768, 1707
History Repeats Itself
Hit Him Again 1918 (P) 1586
Hit or Miss 1919 ( ) 231, 1640
Hit the Trail Holiday 1918 (Art) 143, 146,
  487, 510
Hitting the High Spots 1919 ( ) 1631
Hoarded Assets 1919 ( ) 1877
Hobbs in a Hurry 1918 (Mu) 2201, 2736
Hobo, The 1917 (King-Bee) 1161
Hobo's Dream 1908 (Lubin)
Hobo's Revenge 1908 (Lubin)
Hoffmeyer's Legacy 1912 (Key) 1666, 2368,
  2465
Hogan out West 1915 (Key) 1906
Hogan, the Partner 1915 (Key) 1906
Hogan's Alley 1912 (Ed)
Hogan's Annual Spree 1914 (Key) 1906
Hogan's Mussy Job 1915 (Key) 1906
Hogan's Romance Upset 1915 (Key) 787,
  1906
Hogan's Wild Oats 1915 (Key) 1906
Hold the Line 1917 (Key/Tri) 2501
Hold-up, Held Up, The 1909 (Ed)
Hold up in a Country Grocery Store 1904
  (Ed)
Hold-up of the Rocky Mountain Express,
  The 1906 (AMB)
Holding the Fort 1912 (Ed)
Hollow of Her Hand, The 1918 ( ) 558,
  2458
Holy City, The 1912 (Un)
Holy Orders 1917 (Br) 2592
Home 1911 (Ed)
Home 1915 (Br) 2138
Home 1916 (Tri) 134, 763, 1032, 1049,
  1175, 1241, 1454, 2096, 2364

Home at Last, A 1909 (V)
Home Breaker, The 1919 (Art/Par) 627,
  1697, 2468, 2616
Home Breakers, The /aka/ Other
  People's Wives 1915 (Key) 460, 531,
  650, 791, 2501, 2510
Home Breaking Hound, A 1915 (Key) 118,
  1111, 2514
Home Cure, The 1915 (V) 768
Home Defense 1917 (Par) 1868
Home Folks 1912 (Bio) 315, 1182, 1613,
  1714, 1751, 2047, 2368, 2513, 2680
Home-Made Turkish Bath, The 1904 (AMB)
Home of the Seal, The 1911 (Ed)
Home Rule 1914 (Key) 531
Home Run Ambrose 1917 (L-KO) 2510
Home, Sweet Home 1914 (Mu) 25, 27,
  200, 338, 554, 595, 601, 731, 920,
  947, 1028, 1029, 1182, 1450, 1563,
  1751, 1865, 2045, 2356, 2513, 2568,
  2680
Home Town Girl, The 1919 (Par) 454,
  1067, 1261, 1764
Home Trail, The 1918 ( ) 2397, 2754
Home Wanted 1919 ( ) 853, 1532
Homeless 1912 (Ingvald C. Oes)
Homer's Odyssey, The; or The Adventures
  of Ulysses 1911 (Monopol Film Co.)
Homespun 1919 ( ) 1841
Homunculus--serial 1917 (Bioscop) 407,
  919
Honest Man, A 1918 (Tri) 715, 951
Honesty Is the Best Policy 1908 (Ed)
Honeymoon, The 1917 (Select) 947, 1049,
  2521
Honeymoon Baby, The 1915 (V) 768
Honeymoon for Three 1915 (Br) 834, 2138
Honeymoon for Three, A 1915 (FP) 482
Honeymooners, The 1914 (V) 332, 457,
  1132
Honor of His Family, The 1910 (Bio)
  1450, 1992, 2680
Honor of His House, The 1918 ( ) 1118,
  1208, 1280, 2638
Honor of the Mounted, The 1914 (Gold
  Seal/Un) 352, 449, 1705, 1925
Honor of the Slums 1909 (V)
Honor of Thieves, The 1909 (AMB) 1865,
  2062
Honor System 1916 ( ) 554, 1411, 2410,
  2671
Honor Thy Father 1912 (Majestic) 2047
Honor Thy Name 1916 (Tri) 473, 1032,
  1241, 1404, 2096
Honorable Algernon, The 1913 (V) 297,
  2523
Honorable Algy 1916 ( ) 2096, 2780
Honorable Cad, An 1916 ( ) 673
Honorable Clergy, The 1916 ( ) 960
Honorable Friend, The 1916 ( ) 1201,
  1208
Honorable William's Jonah 1914 (Br) 503
Honor's Cross 1918 ( ) 1474, 1847
Honour's Altar 1915 ( ) 2485
Hooded Helper, The 1915 ( ) 2748
Hoodlum, The 1919 (FN) 63, 528, 596,
  657, 1166, 1241, 1563, 1816, 2047
Hoodoo Ann 1916 (Tri) 1175, 1751
Hoodooed 1916 ( ) 690
Hooligan as a Safe Robber 1903 (AMB)
Hooligan Assists the Magician 1900 (Ed)

Hooligan in Jail 1903 (AMB)
Hooligan to the Rescue 1903 (AMB)
Hooligan's Christmas Dream 1903 (AMB)
Hooligan's Roller Skates 1903 (AMB)
Hooligan's Thanksgiving Dinner 1903 (AMB)
Hoop and the Lovers, The 1904 (AMB)
Hoop-La of the Circus 1919 ( ) 2121
Hoosier Romance, A 1913 (Selig/Mu) 1211,
   1353, 1651, 1859
Hoot Man 1919 (Rolin/P) 1502
Hop the Bellhop 1919 (L-KO) 1161
Hop, the Devil's Brew 1916 ( ) 2656
Hope Chest, The 1918 (Art) 143, 686, 706,
   875, 1028, 1065, 2573
Hopes of Blind Alley, The 1914 (101-Bison/
   Un) 352, 449
Hopi Legend, A 1913 ( ) 651, 2112
Hopper, The 1918 ( ) 1853
Hornet's Nest, The 1919 ( ) 2613
Horse of Another Color, A 1907 (V)
Horse Thief, The 1905 (AMB)
Horse Thief, The 1913 (Key) 1434
Horse Wranglers, The 1914 ( ) 2002
Horsley's Cub comedies 1915-1917 (Mu)
   1997
Hostage, The 1917 ( ) 165, 1581, 1949,
   2112, 2401
Hot Dogs see Mabel's Busy Day
Hot Head, The 1915 ( ) 1796
Hot Finish see Mabel at the Wheel
Hot Meals at All Hours 1903 (AMB)
Hot Mutton Pies 1902 (AMB)
Hot Stuff 1912 (Bio)
Hot Time at Home 1904 (AMB)
Hotel Mixup see Mabel's Strange
   Predicament
Hour before the Dawn, An 1913 ( ) 2035
House Built upon Sand, The 1917 (Tri)
   1029, 2479
House Cat, The 1917 (Select) 884
House Divided, A 1918 (Par) 281
House of a Thousand Candles, The 1915
   (P) 1818, 1876, 2693
House of a Thousand Relations 1915 ( )
   2554
House of Betty, The 1919 ( ) 2564
House of Bondage 1914 ( ) 1580, 2096
House of Cards, The 1909 (Ed)
House of Darkness, The 1913 (Bio) 141,
   1029, 1665, 1714
House of Discord 1913 (Bio) 141, 1028,
   1450, 1876, 1896, 1924, 2513
House of Distemperly 1914 (Br) 852
House of Fortescue, The 1916 (Br) 1289,
   2171
House of Glass 1918 ( ) 462
House of Gloom 1917 ( ) 1518
House of Granada, The see Rose of
   Granada
House of Hate, The--serial 1918 (P) 327,
   734, 1023, 1876, 2376, 2748
   1.   The Hooded Terror
   2.   The Tiger's Eye
   3.   A Woman's Perfidy
   4.   The Man from Java
   5.   Spies Within
   6.   A Living Target
   7.   Germ Menace
   8.   The Untold Secret
   9.   Poisoned Darts
   10. Double Crossed
   11. Haunts of Evil
   12. Flashes in the Dark
   13. Enemy Aliens
   14. Underworld Allies
   15. The False Signal
   16. The Vial of Death
   17. The Death Switch
   18. At the Pistol's Point
   19. The Hooded Terror Unmasked
   20. Following Old Glory
House of Intrigue, The 1919 ( ) 601
House of Mystery, The 1913 (Br) 177
House of Silence 1918 (Par) 1126, 1580,
   2112
House of Temperley, The 1913 (Br) 1784,
   2712
House of Terror, The 1908 (Lubin)
House of the Seven Gables, The 1910 (Ed)
House on the Bridge, The 1908 (Lubin)
House on the Hill, The 1910 (Ed)
House Opposite, The 1917 (Br) 503, 1289,
   1488
House That Jack Built, The 1909 (Lubin)
House That Jack Built, The 1914 (Bio) 79
House to Let; or The New Tenants 1908 (V)
House with the Closed Shutters, The 1910
   (Bio) 2680, 2729
House with the Golden Windows, The 1916
   ( ) 664, 2132, 2623
House with the Tall Porch, The 1912 (Ed)
House without Children 1919 ( ) 1191,
   2582
Houseboat Mystery, The 1914 (Br) 1873
Household Pest, The 1910 (V) 2523
Housekeeping 1916 ( ) 1912, 2554
How a French Nobleman Got a Wife
   through the New York Herald Personal
   Columns 1904 (Ed)
How a Pretty Girl Sold Her Hair Restorer
   1908 (Lubin)
How Bella Was Won 1911 (Ed)
How Betty Made Good 1913 ( ) 785
How Bobby Joined the Circus 1912 (Ed)
How Bridget Made the Fire 1902 (AMB)
How Bridget's Lover Escaped 1907 (Melies)
How Brown Got Married 1909 (Lubin)
How Bumptious Papered the Parlor 1910
   (Ed)
How Buttons Got Even with the Butler
   1903 (AMB)
How Championships Are Won and Lost
   1910 (V) 2604
How Charlie Lost the Heiress 1903 (AMB)
How Cissy Made Good 1915 (V) 332, 901,
   908
How Could You, Jean? 1917 (Par) 25, 887,
   1602, 2047, 2051, 2441
How Dry I Am 1919 (P) 635, 2055
How Father Accomplished His Work 1912
   (Ed)
How Happy Jack Got a Meal 1908 (Lubin)
How Hazel Got Even 1915 ( ) 1028, 2002
How He Prepared the Room 1912 (V) 332,
   901
How Heroes Are Made 1914 (Key) 531,
   1651, 1941
How Hiram Won Out 1913 (Key) 2465
How Hubby Got a Raise 1910 (Bio)
How Jim Proposed 1911 (Kal) 1924
How Jones Lost His Roll 1905 (Ed)
   Jones Meets Skinflint

Skinflint Treats Jones
Skinflint's Cheap Wine
Invitation to Dinner
Game of Cards
Jones Loses
Jones Goes Home in a Barrel
How Jones Saw the Baseball Game 1907 (Lubin)
How Jones Saw the Carnival 1908 (V)
How Lt. Pimple Captured the Kaiser 1914 (Br) 851, 852
How Little Willie Put a Head on His Pa 1902 (AMB)
How Max Went Around the World 1911 (P) 1575
How Men Love Women 1915 (Br) 1873
How Mr. Bullington Ran the House 1912 (V) 2070, 2604, 2663
How Mr. Butt-in Benefits by Chauncey's Mishaps 1905 (Paley & Steiner)
How Molly Made Good 1915 (Un) 599, 673, 809, 832, 1460, 2160, 2344
How Mrs. Murray Saved the Army 1911 (Ed) 1275, 1970
How Old Is Ann? 1903 (Ed)
How Patrick's Eyes Were Opened 1912 (Ed)
How Rastus Got His Pork Chops 1908 (Lubin)
How She Loves Him 1905 (Paley & Steiner)
How She Married Him 1912 (Imp)
How She Triumphed 1911 (Bio) 1468, 2067, 2513
How Shorty Won Out 1912 (Un)
How Simpkins Discovered the North Pole 1908 (V)
How Sir Andrew Lost His Vote 1911 (Ed)
How Spriggins Took Lodgers 1911 (Ed)
How the Athletic Lover Outwitted the Old Man 1903 (AMB)
How the Boys Fought the Indians 1912 (Ed)
How the Cook Made Her Mark 1904 (AMB)
How the Dutch Beat the Irish 1901 (Ed)
How the Hungry Man Was Fed 1911 (Ed)
How the Kids Got Even 1909 (V)
How the Landlord Collected His Rents 1909 (Ed)
How the Masher Was Punished 1907 (Lubin)
How the Office Boy Saw the Ball Game 1906 (Ed)
How the Squire Was Captured 1910 (Ed)
How the Telephone Came to Town 1911 (Ed)
How the Tramp Got the Lunch 1909 (Ed)
How They Fired the Bum, Nit 1903 (AMB)
How Washington Crossed the Delaware 1912 (Ed)
How Willie Raised Tobacco 1911 (Ed)
How Would You Like a Wife Like This? 1907 (AMB)
How'd You Like to be the Iceman? 1902 (AMB)
Hubby Buys a Baby 1913 (V) 332, 901
Hubby Decides to Go to the Club 1904 (AMB)
Hubby Does the Washing 1912 (Solax) 2081
Hubby's Cure 1914 (Key) 878
Hubby's Job 1913 (Key) 1666, 1941
Hubby's Night Out 1915 (Christie) 525
Hubby's Toothache 1913 (V) 332, 901, 909

Hubby's Vacation 1908 (Lubin)
Huck and Tom 1918 (Par) 1050, 1104, 1292, 2045
Hugo, the Mighty 1918 ( ) 2211
Hula Hula Dance, The see His Pre-historic Past
Hula Hula Land 1917 (Key/Tri) 71, 2456, 2705, 2799
Hulda from Holland 1916 (Las) 146, 265, 579, 1600, 2047
Hulda's Lovers 1908 (AMB)
Human Clay 1918 (P) 1444
Human Driftwood 1916 (WS) 462, 2698
Human Hearts 1912 ( ) 108
Human Hen, The 1896 (AMB)
Human Hounds 1916 (Vim) 1161
Human Hound's Triumph, A 1915 (Key) 1651, 2336, 2510
Humanity through Ages 1908 (Melies)
Humbus and Husbands 1918 (V) 2367
Humdrum Brown 1918 ( ) 457, 2680
Hun Within, The 1919 (Art/Par) 315, 657, 875, 1006, 1028, 1697, 2649
Hunchback, The 1909 (V)
Hunchback, The 1914 ( ) 1029
Hungry Actor, The 1909 (Lubin)
Hungry Heart, A 1918 (Par) 462, 950, 957
Hungry Hearts 1916 (Vim) 273, 1161
Huns and Hyphens 1918 (V) 1502, 2367
Hunt, The 1915 (Key/Tri) 460, 840, 1111, 1874, 1981, 2336, 2465, 2636
Hunted Woman 1916 ( ) 552
Hunting of the Hawk 1917 ( ) 2430
Hunting the Teddy Bear 1908 (Melies)
Husband and Wife 1916 (WS) 239, 486, 853
Husband's Revenge, A; or The Poisoned Pills 1908 (V)
Hushed Hour 1919 (Par) 28, 1283, 1613, 2410, 2444, 2513, 2554
Hushing the Scandal /aka/ Friendly Enemies 1915 (Key) 452, 531
Hustling for Health 1919 (Rolin/P) 1502
Hypnotic Cure, The 1909 (Lubin)
Hypnotic Nell 1912 (Kal) 2169
Hypnotist's Revenge 1907 (AMB)
Hypnotist's Revenge 1909 (Melies)
Hypochondriac, The 1917 (M) 768, 1707
Hypocrisy 1916 (V) 2024, 2444

- I -

I Did It, Mama 1909 (AMB)
I Had to Leave a Happy Home for You! 1903 (AMB)
I Love You 1918 (Tri) 2194
I Want a Baby 1910 (P) 1575
I Want to Forget 1919 ( ) 579, 1929
I Will 1919 (Br) 776, 1931
I Will Repay 1918 (V) 1088
I Wish I Had a Girl 1912 (Imp)
Ice 1916 (P) 1586
Iconoclast, The 1910 (Bio) 732, 1533, 1865, 2045, 2212
Ida's Christmas 1912 (V) 297, 332, 564
Idle Wives 1916 (Un) 998, 1216, 1694
Idol of Paris 1914 (Br) 834, 2138
Idolators, The 1917 (Tri) 1032
Idyll of the Hills, An 1915 (Rex/Un) 352, 449, 2781

If My Country Should Call 1916 (Red Feather/Un) 449, 870, 1518, 1548, 1928, 2042, 2757
If Thou Wert Blind 1917 (Br) 2712
If We Only Knew 1913 (Bio) 2513, 2680
If Wm. Penn Came to Life 1907 (Lubin)
Ike Gets a Goat 1914 ( ) 1032
I'll Get Him Yet 1918 (Par) 143, 875, 1028, 1067, 2026
I'll Just Try the Bed 1904 (AMB)
I'll Only Marry a Sport 1909 (Lubin)
I'll Say 1917 ( ) 1640
I'll Say So 1918 (F) 2671
Illumination, The 1912 ( ) 2112, 2554
Illusions Fantasmagoriques 1903 (Melies)
Illustrious Prince, The 1919 ( ) 114
Im Banne der Leidenschaft 1914 ( ) 1349
I'm on My Way 1919 (P) 1586
Immigrant, The 1915 (Las) 1020, 2503
Immigrant, The 1917 (Mu) 97, 204, 384, 451, 517, 1414, 2077, 2090, 2219, 2611
Immigrant's Violin, 1912 (Imp)
Imp of the Bottle, The 1909 (Ed)
Impalement, The 1910 (Bio) 1593, 2062
Impartial Lover, An 1903 (AMB)
Imperceptible Transmutations, The 1904 (Melies)
Impossible Catharine 1919 ( ) 658
Impossible Susan 1918 ( ) 905, 1311
Impossible Voyage, The 1904 (Melies) 1802
Impossible Woman, The 1919 (Br) 349
Imposter, The 1918 ( ) 1223
Imro Fox Rabbit Trick 1897 (American Mutoscope Co.)
In a Hamper Bag see In a Hempen Bag
In a Hempen Bag 1909 (Bio) 79, 315, 1182, 2369
In a Pinch 1919 ( ) 689, 690
In Again 1912 ( ) 2733
In Again--out Again 1917 (Art/Par) 857, 1651, 1855, 1874, 2004, 2068, 2649
In and Out 1918 ( ) 961
In Bad 1918 (Mu) 2201
In Bondage 1919 (Br) 831
In Bridal Attire 1914 (V) 2081, 2521
In Convict Garb 1913 ( ) 2486
In Defiance of the Law * (Selig Polyscope) 1849
In for Thirty Days 1919 (M) 41
In Her Boudoir 1904 (AMB)
In His Brother's Place 1919 (M) 1134, 1440, 1472, 2430
In His Father's Steps 1912 (Ed)
In Honor's Web 1919 ( ) 2458
In Judgment Of 1918 ( ) 867, 1939
In Life's Cycle 1910 (Bio) 1593, 2680, 2728
In Little Italy 1909 (Bio) 1542, 1933, 2680
In Loving Memory see Ambrose's First Falsehood
In Mizzoura 1919 (Par) 165, 242, 365, 653, 2031, 2058, 2401, 2698
In My Lady's Boudoir 1903 (AMB)
In Neighboring Kingdoms 1911 (V) 2523
In Nutsyville 1914 ( ) 1028
In Old California 1910 (Bio) 1060, 1363, 1542, 1831, 2680, 2728
In Old Kentucky 1909 (Bio) 315, 357, 477, 1865, 2047, 2680

In Old Kentucky 1919 (FN) 1137, 2472
In Old Madrid 1911 (Imp) 2047
In Old Tennessee 1912 (Un)
In Peace and War 1914 (Br) 177
In Prehistoric Days 1913 (Bio) 1182, 1751, 2408
In Pursuit of Polly 1918 (V) 333, 1600, 1800
In Sagebrush Country 1915 ( ) 1188
In Search of a Wife 1915 ( ) 2803
In Search of Arcady 1919 ( ) 2052, 2121
In Slavery Days 1913 (Un) 905
In Swift Waters 1912 (Victor/Un) 1511, 1865
In the Aisles of the Wild 1912 (Bio) 398, 1029, 1665, 2680
In the Arctic Night 1911 (V) 332
In the Baggage Coach Ahead 1911 (Ed)
In the Balance 1917 (V) 1966, 2767
In the Barber Shop 1908 (Melies)
In the Bishop's Carriage 1913 (FP) 1309, 2047
In the Blood 1915 (Br) 177, 2712
In the Bogie Man's Cave 1908 (Melies)
In the Border States 1910 (Bio)
In the Clutches of a Gang 1914 (Key) 65, 1726, 1830, 2208, 2368, 2465
In the Clutches of a Vapor Bath 1911 (V) 332, 950
In the Cow Country 1914 (Kay-Bee) 1745, 2096
In the Days of Chivalry 1911 (Ed)
In the Days of '49 1911 (Bio) 1223, 1665, 1831, 2728
In the Days of the Pilgrims 1908 (V)
In the Days of the Thundering Herd 1914 (Selig Polyscope) 1849, 2103
In the Days of the Trojan 1913 ( ) 1431
In the Days of Witchcraft 1909 (Ed)
In the Dressing Room 1903 (AMB)
In the Hands of Imposters 1911 (Ingvald C. Oes)
In the Form of a Hypnotist * ( ) 992
In the Gloaming 1919 (Br) 1289
In the Grip of the Vampire 1913 ( )
In the Hallow of Her Hand 1918 ( ) 273, 1748
In the Haunts of Rip Van Winkle 1906 (AMB)
In the Kingdom of Fairyland 1903 (Lubin)
In the Land of Upsidedown 1909 (Lubin)
In the Latin Quarter 1914 (V) 1876, 2487, 2521
In the Long Ago 1913 (Selig) 2221
In the Nick of Time 1908 (Lubin)
In the Nick of Time 1910 (Ed)
In the Northern Woods 1912 (Independent Moving Picture Co.)
In the Palace of the King 1915 (Es) 581, 2582
In the Park see Caught in the Rain 1914 (Key)
In the Park 1915 (Es) 106, 451, 1347, 2077, 2746
In the Ranks 1914 (Br) 1329
In the Season of Buds 1910 (Bio) 1182, 2047, 2502
In the Sewing 1912 (Un)
In the Shadow of Big Ben 1914 (Hep) 2531
In the Springtime, Gentle Annie! 1904 (AMB)

In the Stretch 1914 ( ) 1275
In the Sultan's Garden 1911 (Imp) 2047
In the Talons of the Eagle 1917 ( ) 1364
In the Tennessee Hills 1914 (Kay-Bee)
    1745, 2096
In the Tombs 1906 (AMB)
In the Valley of the Esopus 1906 (AMB)
In the Watches of the Night 1909 (Bio)
    816, 1933, 1992, 2047, 2368
In the Window Recess 1909 (Bio)
In Wrong see Between Showers 1914
    (Key)
In Wrong 1919 (FN) 693, 1292, 1454, 2045
Incident from Don Quixote 1908 (Melies)
Incompetent Hero, An 1914 (Key) 65
Incorrigible Dukane 1915 (FP) 140, 2718
Incorruptible Crown, The 1915 (Br) 2171
Independence B'Gosh 1918 ( ) 742, 1306
Indestructible Wife, The 1919 (Reelart)
    273, 558, 1311, 1748
Indian Bitters; or The Patent Medicine
    Man 1908 (V)
Indian Brothers, The 1911 (Bio) 1613
Indian Day School 1898 (Ed)
Indian Friendship, An 1912 (Es) 50
Indian Girl's Love, An 1910 (Es) 50
Indian Love Story, An 1907 (V)
Indian Maiden's Lesson, The 1911 (Es) 50
Indian Massacre, The 1912 (New York
    Motion Picture Co.)
Indian Raiders 1912 ( ) 2112
Indian Romeo and Juliet 1912 (V) 1877,
    2112
Indian Runner's Romance, The 1909 (Bio)
    1363, 1450, 2047
Indian Sorcerer, The 1908 (Melies)
Indian Summer, An 1912 (Bio) 315, 1831,
    2047
Indian Trailer, The 1909 (Es) 50
Indian Uprising at Santa Fe 1912 (Bio)
    231, 1751
Indian Wife's Devotion, An 1910 (Selig
    Polyscope) 1849
Indian's Friendship, The 1907 (Lubin)
Indian's Honor, An 1908 (V)
Indian's Lament, The 1917 ( ) 2656
Indian's Loyalty, An 1913 (Bio) 338, 641,
    731, 1029
Indian's Revenge, The; or Osceola, the
    Last of the Seminoles 1906 (V)
Indianrubber Head, The 1901 (Melies) 1802
Indiscreet Corrine 1918 (Tri) 192, 2557
Infant of Snakeville, The 1911 (Es) 50
Infatuation 1918 (P) 713
Infelice 1915 (Br) 1329
Infernal Caldron, The 1903 (Melies)
Infernal Machine, The 1909 (V)
Infidelity 1916 ( ) 1329
Influence of the Unknown 1913 (Bio) 1182,
    1751, 2680
Influence of Bronco Billy 1913 (Es) 50
Informer, The 1912 (Bio) 141, 315, 398,
    1028, 1182, 1831, 2047, 2680
Ingeborg Holm 1913 (SB) 1097, 1155, 1497,
    1576, 1577, 1619, 2417,
Ingomar 1908 (Ed)
Ingrate, The 1908 (AMB) 1363, 1511
Inheritance, The 1911 (Ed)
Inn of Death, The 1908 (V)
Inn of the Blue Moon, The 1919 ( ) 1429
Inn Where No Man Rests 1903 (Melies)

Inner Circle, The 1912 (Bio) 1552, 2000,
    2047, 2060, 2513, 2680
Inner Shrine, The 1917 ( ) 1330
Innocence of Ruth, The 1916 (Ed) 804
Innocent 1918 ( ) 2683
Innocent Adventuress, An 1919 (Par) 1764
Innocent Bystander, The 1909 (Lubin)
Innocent Conspirator, An 1903 (AMB)
Innocent Life, The 1916 ( ) 1064
Innocent Magdalene, An 1916 ( ) 686,
    1029
Innocent Sinner, The 1917 ( ) 554
Innocent Victim, An 1903 (AMB)
Innocents' Progress 1918 ( ) 2453
Inquisitive Boy, The; or Uncle's Present
    1907 (V)
Inquisitive Girl, An 1907 (Lubin)
Inquisitive Ike 1914 (Br) 834, 2138
Insanity; or The Madman 1912 (Eclair)
Inside the Lines 1918 (W) 487, 2485
Insurgent Senator, The 1912 (Ed)
Insurrection 1915 (Lubin) 1205, 1819
Intelligence 1918 ( ) 763
Intelligent Camera, An 1912 (Ed)
Interference of Bronco Billy 1914 (Es) 50
Interloper, The 1918 (W) 606, 1048
Intermittent Alarm Clock, The 1907 (V)
International Heart-breaker, An 1911 (Ed)
International Marriage, An 1916 (FP) 920,
    1372
International Sneak, An 1918 (Key) 2534
Interrupted Elopement, An 1912 (Bio)
Interrupted Flirtation, An 1904 (Paley &
    Steiner)
Interrupted Game, An 1911 (Bio)
Interrupted Honeymoon, An 1904 (AMB)
Interrupted Joyride, The 1909 (Ed)
Interrupted Kiss, An 1903 (AMB)
Interrupted Outing 1907 (Lubin)
Interrupted Picnic, The 1902 (Ed)
Interscholastic Run 1911 (Independent
    Moving Picture Co.)
Into the Jaws of Death 1910 (Ed)
Into the Light 1916 (Br) 150
Into the Night 1916 ( ) 1216
Into the North 1913 ( ) 377, 2042
Intolerance 1916 (Wark) 25, 27, 190, 242,
    305, 308, 311, 315, 387, 406, 497,
    554, 559, 595, 601, 615, 645, 655,
    657, 680, 686, 706, 731, 784, 830,
    857, 875, 993, 996, 1029, 1083, 1146,
    1175, 1182, 1222, 1223, 1284, 1286,
    1322, 1334, 1391, 1490, 1508, 1514,
    1520, 1563, 1565, 1570, 1602, 1613,
    1644, 1645, 1693, 1751, 1753, 1756,
    1850, 1858, 1859, 1865, 1911, 1964,
    1998, 2000, 2002, 2112, 2194, 2207,
    2346, 2352, 2356, 2408, 2434, 2448,
    2453, 2480, 2521, 2522, 2549, 2584,
    2605, 2626, 2646, 2649, 2671, 2679,
    2736, 2780, 2782, 2814
Intrepid Davy 1911 (V) 332, 901
Intrigue 1916 (V) 533, 866, 1329, 1656,
    2232, 2610, 2639
Introducing Charlie Chaplin 1915 (Es) 451
Intruder, The 1914 ( ) 651, 2112
Intrusion of Isabel, The 1919 ( ) 1841
Invaders, The 1913 ( ) 231
Inventions of an Idiot 1909 (Lubin)
Inventor's Secret, The 1911 (Bio)
Invisible Bond, The 1919 ( ) 435

Invisible Man, The 1912 ( ) 1876
Invisible Ray, The--serial 1914 (T) 272
Invisible Ray, The 1916 (Fromman) 662,
    2391
Iola's Promise 1912 (Bio) 1363, 1714,
    2000, 2047
Ireland, a Nation 1916 ( ) 843, 1958,
    2114
Irene's Infatuation 1912 (V) 332, 901
Iris 1915 (Hep) 22, 2171, 2531
Irish Eyes 1919 ( ) 2453
Irish Hero, An 1909 (V)
Iron Claw, The--serial 1916 (P) 788, 954,
    1118, 1564, 2748
        1. The Vengeance of Legar
        2. The House of Unhappiness
        3. The Cognac Mask
        4. The Name and the Game
        5. The Incorrigible Captive
        6. The Spotted Warning
        7. The Hooded Helper
        8. The Stroke of 12
        9. Arrows of Hate
       10. The Living Dead
       11. The Saving of Dan O'Mara
       12. The Haunted Canvas
       13. The Hidden Face
       14. The Plunge for Life
       15. The Double Resurrection
       16. The Unmasking of Davy
       17. The Vanishing Fakir
       18. The Green-Eyed God
       19. The Dave of Despair
       20. The Triumph of the Laughing
            Mask
Iron Heart, The 1917 ( ) 1445
Iron Justice 1915 (Payne & Morgan) 860
Iron Master, The 1911 (Ed)
Iron Mitt, The 1916 (Vogue) 2008
Iron Strain, The 1915 (Tri) 866, 1032,
    1745
Iron Test, The--serial 1918 (V) 1271,
    1876
        1. Ring of Fire
        2. Van of Disaster
        3. Blade of Hate
        4. The Noose
        5. Tide of Death
        6. Firey Fate
        7. The Whirling Trap
        8. The Man Eater
        9. The Pit of Lost Hope
       10. In the Coils
       11. The Red Mask's Prey
       12. The Span of Terror
       13. Hanging Peril
       14. Desperate Odds
       15. Riding with Death
Iron Woman, The 1916 ( ) 286, 2416
Irresistible Flapper, The 1919 (Br) 43,
    503, 1018, 1289
Is He Eligible? 1912 (Ed)
Is Marriage Sacred?--series 1917 ( ) 377
Island Comedy, An 1911 (Ed)
Island of Desire, The 1916 (F) 2671
Island of Intrigue 1919 ( ) 1894
Island of Regeneration, The 1915 (V) 468,
    1876, 2487
Isle of Conquest 1919 (Select) 1003, 1006,
    1288, 2423, 2444, 2522, 2523, 2756
Isle of Content 1915 ( ) 2002

Isle of Intrigue 1919 (M) 41, 926
Isle of Jewels 1914 ( ) 1275
Isle of Love 1916 ( ) 832, 1411, 2616
It Happened at Midnight 1908 (Lubin)
It Happened in Pikersville 1916 (Vim) 1161
It Is for England 1916 (Br) 1873
It Is Very Pretty 1904 (AMB)
It Might Have Been Worse 1909 (Lubin)
It Pays to Advertise 1910 (Ed)
It Pays to Advertise 1919 (Art/Par) 595,
    618, 1248, 1975, 2700, 2779
It Pays to Exercise 1917 (Key/Tri) 2501
It Served Her Right 1911 (Ed)
It Was Coming to Him 1906 (Winthrop
    Press)
Italian, The 1915 ( ) 160, 189
Italian Barber, The 1911 (Bio) 1074, 2047,
    2728, 2729
Italian Blood 1911 (Bio) 1074, 1539, 1613,
    2067
It'a a Bear 1919 ( ) 1276
It's a Boy 1918 (Key) 878
It's a Hard Way to Die 1919 (P) 2055
It's a Hard Life 1919 (P) 635
It's a Long, Long Way to Tipperary 1914
    (Br) 834, 2138
It's a Shame to Take the Money 1905 (AMB)
It's a Wild Life 1918 (P) 1586
It's Great to Be Crazy 1918 (Nestor/Un)
    502
It's Happiness That Counts 1918 ( ) 2558
It's Never Too Late to Mend 1908 (Lubin)
It's Never Too Late to Mend 1913 ( ) 968
It's No Laughing Matter 1914 ( ) 64, 2458
It's Unlucky to Pass under a Ladder 1902
    (AMB)
Ivan Koschula 1914 ( ) 2340
Ivanhoe 1913 (Imp) 108, 111, 285
Ivory Snuff Box, The 1915 (W) 239
Ivy's Elopement 1914 (Br) 503

                        - J -

Jack and Jill 1903 (Lubin)
Jack and Jill 1905 (Paley & Steiner)
Jack and Jill 1916 (Las) 1309, 2045
Jack and Jim 1903 (Melies)
Jack and the Beanstalk 1902 (Ed)
Jack and the Beanstalk 1903 (Lubin)
Jack and the Beanstalk 1912 (Ed)
Jack and the Beanstalk 1917 (F) 410, 557,
    1477, 1563, 2529
Jack Fat and Jim Slim at Coney Island
    1910 (V) 332, 2070
Jack Jaggs & Dum Dum 1903 (Melies)
Jack London's Adventures in the South
    Seas 1908-12 (Martin Johnson Prods.)
    1366
Jack, Sam and Pete 1919 (Br) 1873
Jack Spurlock--Prodigal 1918 ( ) 2671
Jack the Kisser 1907 (Ed)
Jack the Peeper 1904 (AMB)
Jackanapes 1910 ( ) 258
Jacques et Jim 1903 (Melies)
Jacques of the Silver North 1919 ( ) 318,
    1562
Jaguar's Claw, The 1917 (Las) 318, 664,
    869, 935, 1208, 1867, 2623
Jail Bird and How He Flew, The 1906 (V)
Jailed 1916 (P) 1586

Jam Closet, The 1912 (Ed)

Jane 1915 (Morosco) 687, 1063, 1079, 1246, 2445

Jane and the Stranger 1907 (Imp) 108, 1683

Jane Eyre 1914 (Imp) 606, 1058, 1214

Jane Eyre 1915 (Bio) 1117, 2612

Jane Goes A-Wooing 1919 (Par) 25, 887, 1764, 2719

Janet of the Chorus 1915 (V) 297, 2523

Janitor, The 1914 (Key) 1874

Janitor's Bottle, The 1909 (Ed)

Janitor's Busy Day, The 1915 (Christie) 525

Janitor's Joyful Job, A 1915 (Novelty) 1161

Janitor's Wife's Temptation, The 1915 (Key/Tri) 1036, 1086, 1559, 1666, 1749

Japanese Nightingale, A 1918 ( ) 2683

Japanese Peach Boy, A 1910 (Ed)

Jar of Cranberry Sauce, A 1910 (Ed)

Jarr Family series 1914 ( ) 1415

Jay Bird, The 1919 ( ) 1011

Jazz Band see Ragtime Band, The

Jazz Waiter see Caught in a Cabaret

Jazzed Honeymoon, A 1919 (P) 1586

Jealous Cavalier, The 1910 (Br) 177

Jealous Guy, A 1916 (V) 2367

Jealous Husband, The 1911 (Bio)

Jealous Jolts 1916 (Vogue) 2608

Jealous Monkey, The 1897 (Ed)

Jealous Old Maid, The; or No One to Love Her 1908 (V)

Jealous Waiter, The 1913 (Key) 1666, 2368, 2465

Jealous Wife, The 1907 (V)

Jealousy! 1908 (V)

Jealousy! 1916 (F) 1056, 2503

Jealousy and the Man 1909 (Bio)

Jealousy of Miguel and Isabella 1913 ( ) 785

Jean and the Calico Doll 1910 (V) 1212

Jean Intervenes 1912 (V) 2112

Jeanne Dore 1915 (Un) 212

Jeanne of the Gutter 1919 (M) 631

Jean's Evidence 1913 (GB) 2604

Jed's Trip to the Fair 1915 (Christie) 525

Jeffries-Sharkey Fight 1899 (AMB) 1355, 2377

Jeffs 1715 (Br) 22, 43

Jego Ostatni Czyn 1915 ( ) 1922

Jenny's Pearls 1913 (Key) 1666

Jephthah's Daughter 1909 (V)

Jerry's Uncle's Namesake 1914 (V) 768, 1634

Jessie, the Stolen Child 1908 (V)

Jester, The 1908 (Ed)

Jesus 1911 ( ) 1098

Jesus of Nazareth 1912 (Kal)

Jewel in Pawn 1917 ( ) 1120, 2399

Jewel Thieves Outwitted, The 1913 (Br) 1289

Jeweled Girdle, The see The Naulahka

Jeweled Hand, The--serial 1919 ( ) 296

Jewels, The 1912 (Ed)

Jilt, The 1909 (AMB) 1933, 2368

Jilted in Jail 1919 ( ) 2147

Jilted Jane 1918 ( ) 905

Jilted Janet 1918 ( ) 1710

Jim Bludson 1916 ( ) 2794

Jim Carmon's Wife 1914 ( ) 1188

Jim Greenberg's Boy 1916 ( ) 1745

Jim the Mule Boy 1911 (Ed)

Jim, the Penman 1915 (FP) 146, 1772

Jimmy Aubrey--one reelers 1917 (Starlight) 1161

Jimmy Dale Alias the Grey Seal--serial 1917 (Mu) 1569, 1845, 2003
1. The Grey Seal
2. The Stolen Rubies
3. The Counterfeit Five
4. The Metzer Murder Mystery
5. A Fight for Honor
6. Below the Deadline
7. The Devil's Work
8. The Underdog
9. The Alibi
10. Two Crooks and a Knave
11. A Rogue's Defeat
12. The Man Higher Up
13. Good for Evil
14. A Sheep among Wolves
15. The Tapped Wires
16. The Victory

Jim's Atonement 1912 (Imp)

Jim's Wife 1912 (Ed)

Jinks Joins the Temperance Club 1911 (Bio)

Jinx 1919 ( ) 473, 1483

Jitney Elopement, A 1915 (Es) 106, 451, 1045, 1676, 2077, 2746

Joan of Arc 1915 ( ) 1581

Joan of Plattsburg 1918 (Go) 1918

Joan of the Woods 1918 (WS) 265, 835

Joan, the Woman 1917 (Par) 258, 411, 485, 532, 664, 828, 869, 1073, 1201, 1280, 1307, 1386, 1457, 1537, 1591, 1756, 1925, 1949, 1953, 2038, 2112, 2132, 2149

Johanna Enlists 1917 (Art/Par) 166, 242, 1321, 1365, 1697, 2047, 2337

John Barleycorn 1914 ( ) 258

John Brown's Heir 1911 (Ed)

John Ermine of Yellowstone 1918 ( ) 926

John Halifax--Gentleman 1914 ( ) 1329, 2558

John Linworth's Atonement 1914 (Br) 2171

John Needham's Double 1916 (Selig) 2065, 2656

John Petticoats 1919 (Art) 1186, 1188, 2375, 2736

John Rance--Gentleman 1914 (V) 297, 1876, 2523

John Smith, Barber 1912 (Imp)

John Tobin's Sweetheart 1913 (V) 301, 332, 901

Johnie and the Telephone, The 1903 (AMB)

Johnny and the Indians 1909 (Centaur Film Co.)

Johnny Get Your Gun 1919 ( ) 887, 2482, 2485

Johnny on the Spot 1919 (M) 1134

Johnny's in the Well 1903 (AMB)

John's New Suit 1908 (V)

Joke at the French Ball, A 1904 (AMB)

Joke on Grandma 1901 (Ed)

Joke on the Joker 1912 (Bio)

Joke on Whom?, A 1902 (AMB)

Joke They Played on Bumptious, The 1910 (Ed)

Jolly Lawn Party, A 1904 (Paley & Steiner)

Jolly Monks of Malabar, The 1906 (AMB)
Jolts and Jewelry 1917 (V) 2367
Jones and His New Neighbors 1909 (AMB)
    209, 526, 1511, 1912
Jones and His Pal in Trouble 1899 (Ed)
Jones and the Lady Book Agent 1909 (AMB)
    209, 526, 901, 1182, 1511, 1912,
    2368
Jones at the Ball see Mr. Jones at the
    Ball
Jones Entertains see Mr. Jones Enter-
    tains
Jones Have Amateur Theatricals, The
    1909 (AMB) 526, 1511, 1912
Jones' Interrupted Sleighride 1899 (Ed)
Jones Makes a Discovery 1899 (Ed)
Jones' Return from the Club 1899 (Ed)
Jonsey 1907 (AMB) 209, 2047
Jordan Is a Hard Road 1915 (Tri) 387,
    1028, 1563, 1591, 1865
Joselyn's Wife 1919 ( ) 28, 134, 601
Joseph in the Land of Egypt 1914 (T) 603,
    2430
Josh and Cindy's Wedding Trip 1911 (Ed)
Josh's Suicide 1911 (Bio)
Journey's End 1918 (Par) 486, 2444
Joy and the Dragon 1917 (P) 1441, 1988
Joy of Freedom, The 1917 (M) 768, 1707
Joyous Liar, A 1919 ( ) 763, 2663
Joyriding 1910 (Es) 2058
Jubilo 1918 (Go) 2168, 2355
Judge, The 1916 (Key/Tri) 37, 250, 878,
    1906, 2368, 2580
Judge Not 1915 (Un) 420, 673, 1929
Judge Not That Ye Be Not Judged 1909 (V)
Judgement 1909 (Es) 50
Judge's Whiskers and the Magic Hair
    Restorer 1909 (V)
Judgment 1918 ( ) 1829
Judgment House 1917 ( ) 1220, 1613
Judgment of Solomon, The 1909 (V)
Judgment of the Guilty 1916 ( ) 186
Judgment of the Mighty Deep, The 1910
    (Ed)
Judith 1916 ( ) 2453
Judith of Bethulia 1914 (Bio) 141, 315,
    362, 398, 731, 1028, 1029, 1182,
    1353, 1714, 1751, 1876, 1924, 2156,
    2513, 2680
Judith of the Cumberlands 1916 (FA/Tri)
    2194
Judy Forgot 1915 (Un) 364
Juggernaut, The 1915 (Selig) 2767, 2770
Juggling with Fate 1913 ( ) 785
Jules of the Strong Heart 1918 ( ) 160
Julius Caesar 1908 (Lubin)
Julius Caesar 1908 (V) 1333
Julius Caesar 1911 (Co-operative Cinemat-
    ograph Co.) 196, 197, 417
Julius Caesar 1913 (FP) 874
Julius Caesar 1914 (K) 1950
Jumps and Jealousy 1916 (V) 2367
June Friday 1915 ( ) 1649
June's Birthday Party 1905 (Ed)
Jungle Child, The 1916 (Tri) 627
Jungle Master, The 1914 ( ) 2656
Jungle Trail 1919 (F) 868, 1532, 1622
Jupiter's Thunder-Bolts 1903 (Melies)
Jury of Fate, The 1917 ( ) 2520
Just a Girl 1916 (Br) 1918
Just a Woman 1918 ( ) 2661

Just before the Raid 1904 (AMB)
Just Brown's Luck 1913 (Key) 650, 1666,
    1941, 2465
Just Dropped In 1919 (P) 1586
Just for Her 1911 (Independent Moving
    Picture Co.)
Just for Tonight 1919 (Go)
Just Gold 1913 (Bio) 141, 315, 1028, 1029,
    1714, 2000, 2728
Just Like a Girl 1904 (Paley & Steiner)
Just Like a Woman 1912 (Bio) 1613, 1714,
    2047
Just Married 1907 (Lubin)
Just Neighbors 1919 (P) 635, 1586
Just Nuts 1915 (P) 1586, 1948, 2479
Just Plain Folks 1908 (V)
Just Rambling Along 1918 (Rolin/P) 1502
Just Reward, A 1909 (Lubin)
Just Show People 1913 (V) 2523
Just Sylvia 1919 ( ) 437, 1255
Just the Cheese 1904 (AMB)
Justice 1914 (Hep) 777, 834, 2171, 2531
Justinian's Human Torches 1908 (Melies)
Juvenile Dancer 1916 ( ) 145
Juvenile Stakes 1903 (AMB)

- K -

Kaintuck 1912 ( ) 2112
Kaiser, the Beast of Berlin, The 1918
    (Renown/Un) 135, 449, 495, 680,
    1025, 1264, 1391, 1472, 1518, 1570,
    2084, 2627
Kaiser's Bride, The 1918 ( ) 1495
Kaiser's Finish, The 1918 (FN) 2756
Kaiser's Last Squeal, The 1919 ( ) 2465
Kaiser's Shadow, The 1918 (Tri) 627
Kara-Kiri 1919 ( ) 624
Karina 1902 (AMB)
Karussell des Lebens 1919 ( ) 1922
Katchem Kate 1912 (Bio)
Kathleen Mavourneen 1906 (Ed)
Kathleen Mavourneen 1919 (F) 116, 725,
    1096, 1128, 1174, 1656, 1688, 1961,
    2563
Katie Bauer 1916 ( ) 1028
Katrina's Valentine 1909 (Lubin)
Katzenjammer Kids 1912 (Selig) 1481, 1537
Katzenjammer Kids and School Marm 1903
    (AMB)
Katzenjammer Kids Have a Love Affair,
    The 1903 (AMB)
Keep 'Em Home 1917 ( ) 689
Keep the Home Fires Burning 1916 (Br)
    150
Keeper of the Door 1919 (Br) 834, 1018
Keeper of the Light, The 1909 (Ed)
Keith of the Border 1918 (Tri) 2479
Kenilworth 1909 (V)
Kennedy Square 1916 (V) 1426, 1876, 1991
Keno Bates, Liar /aka/ The Last Card
    1915 (Ince) 1032, 1188, 1794, 1898,
    2561
Kentuckian 1908 (AMB)
Kentucky Cinderella, A 1917 (Un) 495,
    1365, 1391, 1518
Kentucky Feud, A 1905 (AMB)
Kentucky Girl, The 1912 (Bio) 231, 1751,
    2733
Kentucky School Master, The 1917 ( ) 2780

Kentucky Squire, The 1904 (AMB)
Kerry Gow, The 1915 ( ) 1270
Key of Life, The 1910 (Ed)
Key of the World 1918 (GB) 2551
Key to Power 1919 (Select) 12
Key to Yesterday, The 1914 (Kal) 231, 1795
Key under the Mat, The 1908 (Lubin)
Keys of the Right House 1918 ( ) 189
Keys of the Righteous 1918 ( ) 1933, 2164, 2514
Keystone Kids, The 1434
Keystone Kops, The 2817
Keystone Pets, The 1435
Kick In--serial 1917 (P) 270, 1444
Kicked Out 1918 (P) 1586
Kicking the Germ out of Germany! 1918 (P) 1586
Kid, The 1910 (Bio)
Kid and the Sleuth, The 1912 (Imp)
Kid Auto Races at Venice 1914 (Key) 451, 909, 1090, 1344, 1523, 2213
Kid from the Klondike 1911 (Ed)
Kid Is Clever, The 1918 ( ) 2018, 2671
Kid Regan's Hands 1914 (Un) 2095
Kidder & Company 1918 (Par) 2700
Kidnapped 1917 (Ed) 335, 1688
Kidnapped Child, The 1904 (Lubin)
Kidnapper, The 1903 (AMB)
    At Work
    In the Den
    The Rescue
Kids and Kidlets 1917 ( ) 1177
Kids and Skids 1916 (F) 1524
Kildare of the Storm 1918 (Un) 108, 1427
Kilkenny 1916 ( ) 2445
Kill Joy, The 1917 (Es) 1636
Kill or Be Killed 1919 ( ) 2095
Kilmeny 1915 (Morosco) 2610
Kind-Hearted Bootblack; or Generosity Rewarded 1908 (V)
Kindling 1915 (Par) 623, 828, 935, 1201, 1490, 1648, 1800, 2661
King and the Jester, The 1908 (Melies)
King Charles 1913 (Br) 177
King Cotton 1910 (Ed)
King John 1899 (Tree) 378
King Lear 1909 (V) 94
King Lear 1916 (T) 68, 298, 729, 1313, 1754, 2689
King of Detectives, The 1902 (AMB)
King of Diamonds 1919 ( ) 1877
King of Sharpshooters, The 1905 (Melies)
King of the Cannibal Island, The 1908 (AMB)
King of the Detectives 1903 (AMB)
King of the Forest 1912 (Selig) 2221
King Robert of Sicily 1912 (Hep) 2531
King Solomon 1918 (King-Bee) 1161
King, the Detective 1911 (Independent Moving Picture Co.)
Kingdom of Love 1918 (F) 406
Kingdom of the Fairies 1903 (Melies) 1802
Kingdom of Youth, The 1918 (Go) 1423, 1867
King's Daughter, The 1916 (Br) 43, 834
King's Diamond, The 1908 (Lubin)
King's Game, The 1916 ( ) 1564, 2748
King's Messenger, The 1908 (AMB)
King's Minister, The 1914 (Br) 349
King's Outcast, The 1914 (Br) 43

King's Pardon, The 1908 (Ed)
King's Power, The 1911 (Ingvald C. Oes)
Kinsman, The 1919 (Br) 812
Kismet 1919 ( ) 1794, 2418, 2554, 2717
Kiss, The 1900 (Ed)
Kiss, The 1913 ( ) 2112
Kiss and a Tumble, A 1904 (AMB)
Kiss for Susie, A 1918 (Art/Par) 935
Kiss Me 1904 (AMB)
Kiss of Glory, The * (FdA) 1856
Kiss of Hate, 1916 (M) 139
Kiss of the Vampire 1915 ( )
Kiss or Kill 1918 (Un) 675
Kisses Sweet 1906 (Winthrop Press)
Kissing Cup 1913 (Hep) 2744
Kissing Sister 1915 ( ) 1132
Kit Carson 1903 (AMB)
Kitchen Countess, The 1914 (Br) 43
Kitchen Lady, The 1917 (Key/Tri) 878, 2501
Kitchen Maid's Dream, The 1907 (V)
Kitty and the Cowboys 1911 (V) 332, 950
Kitty Kelly, M. D. 1919 ( ) 1280
Kitty McKay 1917 (V) 380, 2663
Kitty's Hold Up 1912 (Ed)
Kleptomania Tablets 1912 (Br) 150
Kleptomaniac, The 1905 (Ed)
    Arriving at Police Station
    Court Room
    Tableau
    Home of Thief
    Stealing Bread
    Leaving Store
    Superintendent's Office
    Interior of Department Store
    Arriving at Store
    Leaving Home
    Arriving at Police Station in Patrol Wagon
Knickerbocker Buckaroo, The 1919 (Art/Par) 387, 454, 664, 857, 1702, 2721
Knife, The 1918 ( ) 273, 558, 1270, 1427, 1878, 2662
Knight for a Night, A 1909 (Ed)
Knight of Black Art 1908 (Melies)
Knight of the Range, A 1915 (Un) 398, 969, 1011
Knight of the Road, A 1911 (Bio) 2062, 2729
Knights of the Square Table 1917 ( ) 1415
Knockout, The /aka/ The Pugilist; Counted Out 1914 (Key) 65, 384, 451, 460, 499, 791, 1304, 1422, 1726, 2208, 2368, 2501, 2510
Knot in the Plot, A 1910 (Bio)
Kohn's Bad Luck 1907 (Lubin)
Komtesse Doddy 1917 ( ) 1922
Kreutzer Sonata 1915 (F) 116, 204, 622, 1049, 1905, 1978, 2381, 2505, 2629
Kreuzigt Sie 1919 ( ) 1922
Küsse die Man Stiehlt in Dunkeln 1919 ( ) 1922
Kuz delem a Letert 1918 ( ) 1614

- L -

L' Aiglon 1913 ( ) 462
L' Apache 1919 (Par) 627, 824
L' Apprentie 1912 ( ) 462

La Belle Russe 1919 (F) 116, 658, 980,
    1403, 2642, 2773
La Boheme 1916 (WS) 130, 273, 389,
    835, 1402, 2489
La Cigale 1913 (Br) 503
La Dame Aux Camelias 1912 (French-
    American Film Co.) 212, 2541
La Du Barry 1914 (Ambrosio) 421
La Faute des Autres 1919 ( ) 710
La Fille du Peuple 1919 ( ) 710
La Folie du Docteur Tube 1916 (FdA) 730
La Mano di Fatima 1915 ( ) 1372
La Masque D'Horreur 1912 ( ) 710
La Fafale 1919 ( ) 2683
La Rubia 1916 ( ) 2811
La Scandle Rouge 1913 ( ) 1881
La Sposa Della Morte 1915 ( ) 438
La Tosca 1908 (AMB)
La Tosca 1911 ( ) 212
La Tosca 1918 (Par) 934, 957, 1600, 2094
Labour Leader, The 1917 (Br) 527, 1918
Lache Bajazzo 1914 ( ) 2340
Lachinvar 1915 (Br) 2536
Lackey and the Lady, The 1919 (Br)
    1300, 1968
Lad and the Lion, The 1917 (Selig Poly-
    scope) 1678
Ladder of Lies 1919 ( ) 606
Laddie 1909 (Ed)
Ladies First 1918 ( ) 1086
Ladies' World 1911 (Es) 353
Lady and Her Maid, The 1913 (V) 2070,
    2523
Lady and the Burglar, The 1910 (Ed)
Lady and the Lake, The 1912 ( ) 1332
Lady and the Mouse, The 1913 (Bio) 141,
    1028, 1029, 1182, 1751, 2573, 2680
Lady Audley's Secret 1912 (Imp) 108
Lady Audley's Secret 1915 (F) 116, 314,
    568, 1198, 2130
Lady Baffles and Detective Duck 1915
    (Un) 81
Lady Barbers 1908 (Lubin)
Lady Bountiful Visits the Murphys on
    Wash Day 1903 (AMB)
Lady Clare, The 1912 ( ) 1656
Lady Clare, The 1919 (Br) 1258, 1358,
    1968
Lady Drummer, The 1916 (Tri) 2568
Lady Frederick 1919 ( ) 139
Lady Godiva 1911 (V) 1047
Lady Helen's Escapade 1909 (AMB) 1511,
    1823
Lady in Black, The 1913 (Bio) 731, 1028
Lady in the Library, A 1916 (M) 768,
    1707
Lady Jane's Flight 1908 (V)
Lady Mary's Love 1911 (Ingvald C. Oes)
Lady of Quality, A 1913 (FP) 1590, 2035
Lady of Red Butte, The 1919 (Par) 627,
    1266, 1756
Lady of Shallot, The 1912 (Br) 503
Lady of Shallot, The 1915 (V) 901, 2521
Lady of the Dugout, The 1918 ( ) 2480
Lady of the Lake, The 1912 (V) 1032,
    1877, 2487, 2767
Lady or the Tiger, The 1909 (Ed)
Lady Raffles Returns 1916 (Un) 610, 926
Lady Sheriff, The 1917 ( ) 1519
Lady Windermere's Fan 1916 (Br) 2179,
    2791

Lady's Name, A 1918 ( ) 927, 1537,
    2521, 2625
Lafayette, We Come 1918 ( ) 434, 1569
Lair of the Wolf, The 1917 ( ) 1714
Lamb, The 1915 (FA/Tri) 857, 1490,
    1998, 2211, 2573
Lamb, The 1918 (P) 1586, 2055
Lamb and the Lion, The 1919 ( ) 998
Lamb, the Woman, the Wolf, The 1914
    (101-Bison/Un) 352, 449, 1705
Lamp Explodes, The 1902 (AMB)
Lancashire Lass, A 1915 (Hep) 2171, 2531
Land of Darkness, The; or The Great
    Mine Disaster 1912 (Eclair)
Land of Promise, The 1912 (Imp)
Land of Promise, The 1917 (Art/Par)
    27, 333, 1800
Land Salesman, The 1913 (Key) 2465
Landlady's Portrait, The 1909 (Ed)
Landloper, The 1918 (M) 1589
Landlord's Trouble, A 1913 (Key) 2465
Landlubber, The see A Deep Sea Liar
Landon's Legacy 1916 (Un) 1431, 2032,
    2416
Lanterne Magique, La 1903 (Melies)
Larks behind the Scene 1899 (Ed)
Lasca 1919 ( ) 2147, 2753
Lash, The 1916 (Las) 724, 752, 756,
    1308
Lash of Power 1918 ( ) 1166
Lass o' the Looms 1919 (Br) 2637
Lass of the Lumberlands--serial 1916
    (Mu) 455, 1041, 1221, 1273, 1325,
    1579, 1720
    1.   The Lumber Pirate
    2.   The Wreck in the Fog
    3.   First Blood
    4.   A Deed of Daring
    5.   The Burned Record
    6.   The Spiked Switch
    7.   The Runaway Car
    8.   The Fight in Camp
    9.   The Double Fight
    10. The Gold Rush
    11. The Ace High Loses
    12. The Main Line Wreck
    13. *
    14. The Indian's Hand
    15. Retribution
Lass unto Herself, A 1918 ( ) 1032
Lassie's Birthday, The 1910 (Ed)
Last Adventure, The 1916 ( ) 377
Last Adventures of Sherlock Holmes,
    The--series 1915 (Br) 1945
Last Card, The see Keno Bates, Liar
Last Card, The 1916 (M) 41, 1188, 2175
Last Cartridge, The 1907 (V)
Last Dance, The 1912 (Selig) 2770
Last Deal, The 1910 (Bio) 122, 1450,
    1865
Last Drop of Water, The 1911 (Bio) 357,
    1074, 1182, 1223, 1701, 1831, 2513,
    2728
Last Egyptian, The 1914 ( ) 1659
Last Lesson, The 1912 (Ambrosio)
Last Man, The 1916 (V) 785, 1088
Last of His People 1919 ( ) 1216, 2514
Last of the Carnabys, The 1917 ( ) 1312
Last of the Dandy, The 1910 (B) 852
Last of the Duanes 1918 ( ) 868, 1604
Last of the Frontignacs, The 1912 (Ambrosio)

Last of the Line, The /aka/ Pride of Race 1914 (Ince) 1208
Last Rebel, The 1918 ( ) 186
Last Resource, The 1912 (New York Motion Picture Co.)
Last Round Ended in a Free Fight, The 1903 (AMB)
Last Roundup, The 1913 (Es) 50, 487
Last Volunteer, The 1914 (P) 606, 2003
Late Lamented, The 1917 (Key/Tri) 46, 228, 1476, 2564
Latent Spark 1911 (V) 332, 473, 2096, 2392
Latin Quarter, The 1914 (V) 1876
Laughing Ben 1902 (AMB)
Laughing Bill Hyde 1918 (Go) 1532, 2168
Laughing Gas 1907 (V)
Laughing Gas 1907 (Ed)
Laughing Gas /aka/ The Dentist; Down and Out; Turning His Ivories 1914 (Key) 451, 531, 1304, 2336, 2501, 2508, 2510, 2514
Laundry Liz 1916 (Tri) 2568
Laura Comstock's Bag-Punching Dog 1901 (Ed)
Laurel of Tears, The 1915 ( ) 2416
Law and the Outlaw 1913 (Selig Polyscope) 785, 1849
Law North of 65, The 1918 ( ) 857
Law of Compensation, The 1917 (Select) 130, 458, 1789, 2523
Law of Men 1919 ( ) 189, 2719
Law of Nature, The 1919 ( ) 1522
Law of the Great Northwest, The 1918 ( ) 2780
Law of the Land, The 1917 ( ) 1690, 2037
Law of the North, The 1918 (Par) 720, 960, 1283, 1690, 2096
Law unto Herself, A 1918 ( ) 763, 2124
Lawless Love 1918 (F) 406
Law's Outlaw, The * (Tri) 2479
Lazy Bill Hudson 1912 (Ed)
Lazy Bones 1919 ( ) 539
Lazy Farmer Brown 1910 (Ed)
Le Enchanteur Alcrofrisbas 1903 (Melies)
Le Manoir du Diable /aka/ The Haunted Castle; The Devil's Castle 1896 (Robert-Houdin Film)
Le Poison de L'Humanitie 1913 ( ) 462
Le Retour d'Ulysse 1908 (FdA) 142
Le Tango Rouge 1908 ( ) 710
Lead Kindly Light 1912 (Ed)
Lead Kindly Light 1918 (Br) 177
Leading Lady, The 1911 (V) 297, 332, 2112
Leading Lizzie Astray 1914 (Key) 65, 791, 2510
Leading Man, The 1912 (Bio)
Leading Man, The see Hired and Fired
Leah Kleschna 1913 (FP) 972, 1938, 2035, 2581
Leah, the Forsaken 1908 (V)
Leander Sisters 1897 (Ed)
Leap for Love, A 1912 (Imp)
Leap to Fame 1918 ( ) 231, 1991
Leap Year Proposals 1912 (V) 332, 901
Leap Year Proposals of an Old Maid 1908 (V)
Leap Year Tangle, A 1915 (Christie) 525

Learnin' of Jim Benson, The 1917 (Tri) 2479
Leather Pushers, The 1919 (Un) 708, 1583
Leather Stocking Tales 1911 ( ) 2112
Leather Stockings 1909 (Bio) 1865, 2680
Leave It to Susan 1919 (Go) 1248, 1268, 1423, 1662
Leaves of a Romance 1911 (Ed)
Led Astray 1909 (V)
Left Handed Man, The 1913 (Bio) 398, 1029, 2728
Left Out 1909 (Ed)
Legal Advice * (Selig Polyscope) 1849
Legal Hold-Up, A 1902 (AMB)
Legend of Polichinelle, The 1907 (P) 1575
Legend of Sterling Keep, The 1909 (Ed)
Legend of the King, The 1912 (Br) 503
Legion of Death, The 1918 ( ) 1717, 2487
Lem's College Career 1915 (Christie) 525
Lena 1914 (Ed) 631
Lena and the Geese 1912 (Bio) 1539, 1665, 1714, 1751, 2047
Lend Me Your Name 1918 (M) 1589
Leopard, A 1917 ( ) 1614
Leopard Queen, The 1909 (Selig Polyscope)
Leopard's Foundling, The 1914 (Selig) 2770
Leo's Air Rifle 1908 (Lubin)
Leprechaun, The 1908 (Ed)
Les Allumettes Animées--cartoon 1909 (French) 512
Les Enfants d'Edouard 1914 (Cosmograph) 32
Les Miserables 1913 (Electric) 1463
Les Miserables 1918 (F) 209, 406, 868, 1191, 1891
Les Pieds Nickeles--cartoon 1918 (French) 512
Les Vampires--serial 1915 (French)
Less Than Kin 1918 (Par) 165, 1580, 1970, 1975, 2112, 2648
Less Than the Dust 1916 (FP) 27, 146, 1068, 1389, 2047, 2061, 2649
Lesser Evil, The 1912 (Bio) 95, 1751, 1865, 2000, 2513, 2728
Lesson, The 1910 [Bio) 477, 1593, 1831
Lesson, The 1918 (Go) 1248, 1867, 2521
Lesson in Mechanics, A 1914 ( ) 1028
Lesson Learned, A 1911 (Ed)
Lessons to Husbands 1911 (Independent Moving Picture Co.)
Lest We Forget 1914 (Br) 834
Lest We Forget 1917 (M) 768, 1372, 1707
Let 'Er Run 1918 ( ) 720
Let Katy Do It 1915 ( ) 1756
Let No Man Put Asunder 1912 (Un)
Let the Gold Dust Twins Do Your Work 1903 (AMB)
Let Uncle Reuben Show You How 1904 (AMB)
Let Willie Do It 1912 (Imp)
Let's Be Fashionable 1919 ( ) 1791
Let's Elope 1919 (Par) 482
Let's Get a Divorce 1918 (Art/Par) 333
Let's Go! 1918 (P) 1586
Letters of Fire 1919 (Reelcraft) 1099
Letty 1919 ( ) 1601
Levitsky's Insurance Policy; or When Thief Meets Thief 1908 (V)
Liar, The 1918 (F) 2024

Liberty, a Daughter of the U. S. A.--
  serial 1916 (Un) 325, 839, 1965,
  1186, 1280, 1952, 2056, 2479, 2656,
  2723
    1. The Fangs of the Wolf
    2. Riding with Death
    3. American Blood
    4. Dead or Alive
    5. Love and War
    6. The Desert of Lost Souls
    7. Liberty's Sacrifice
    8. Clipped Wings
    9. A Daughter of Mars
   10. The Buzzard's Prey
   11. The Devil's Triumph
   12. For the Flag
   13. Strife and Sorrow
   14. A Modern Joan of Arc
   15. Flag of Truce
   16. Court-Martialled
   17. A Trail of Blood
   18. The Wolf's Nemesis
   19. An Avenging Angel
   20. A Daughter of the U. S. A.
Liberty Bells 1914 (Bio) 25, 1028, 1714,
  2045, 2573
Liberty Bond 1918 (   ) 1029
Liberty for an Four; or An Act of Un-
  selfishness 1909 (V)
Liberty Hall 1914 (Br) 349, 2712
Librarian, The 1912 (Ed)
Lie, The 1909 (Ed)
Lie, The 1912 (Imp)
Lie, The 1914 (Gold Seal/Un) 352, 449,
  1587, 1686, 1705, 1925, 2185, 2188
Lie, The 1918 (Art/Par) 888, 1748, 2061
Lt. Daring and the Dancing Girl 1913
  (Br) 1913
Lt. Daring and the Plans of the Minefield
  1912 (Br) 1873
Lt. Daring and the Secret Service Agents
  1911 (Br) 1873
Lt. Pie's Love Story 1913 (Hep) 2744
Lieutenant Pimple on Secret Service 1913
  (Br) 851, 852
Lt. Rose and the Stolen Submarine 1910
  (Br) 177
Lieutenant's Bride, The 1912 (Hep) 2744
Lieutenant's Last Fight, The 1912 (New
  York Motion Picture Co.)
Life against Honor 1917 (   ) 1888
Life Drama of Napoleon Bonaparte and
  Empress Josephine of France, The
  1909 (V)
Life for a Life 1909 (Lubin)
Life in the Balance, A 1913 (Key) 864,
  2465
Life Line, The 1919 (Go) 166, 506, 1280,
  1756, 1998, 2453
Life Mask, The 1918 (Fn) 2037
Life of a Cowboy 1906 (Ed)
Life of an American Fireman 1903 (Ed)
  2631, 2740
Life of an American Policeman 1905 (Ed)
Life of an American Soldier 1904 (Lubin)
Life of an Oyster, The 1907 (Lubin)
Life of Buffalo Bill, The 1909 (Panzer)
  507, 2003
Life of Buffalo Bill, The 1912 (Buffalo
  Bill & Pawnee Bill Film Co.)
Life of Honor 1918 (   ) 111

Life of Villa 1914 (   )
Life of William Shakespeare, The 1914
  (B&C) 154, 918
Life Savers 1916 (Vim) 1161
Life Story of David Lloyd George, The
  1918 (Br) 834
Life without Soul 1915 (Ocean Film Corp.)
  511, 567, 617, 681, 2443
Lifeguardsman, The 1916 (Br) 1231
Life's a Game of Cards 1908 (Ed)
Life's Blind Alley 1916 (   ) 1589
Life's Dark Road 1914 (Br) 1289, 2171
Life's Funny Proposition 1919 (   ) 715
Life's Greatest Problem 1919 (   ) 1562
Life's Pathways 1917 (   ) 1029
Life's Shop Window (F) 1275, 2756
Life's Whirlpool 1918 (   ) 139, 141
Lifted Veil, The 1917 (M) 139, 960, 1446,
  1498
Light, The 1915 (Br) 1879
Light, The 1919 (F) 116, 1760, 1984,
  2118, 2664, 2717
Light at the Window, The 1908 (Lubin)
Light in Darkness 1917 (   ) 1878
Light of the Western Stars, The 1918 (   )
  387, 866, 1446, 2053
Light of Victory 1919 (Christie) 525, 1416
Light That Came, The 1909 (Bio) 315,
  1074, 1363, 1450, 1542, 1865, 2047,
  2368
Light That Didn't Fail, The 1902 (AMB)
Light That Failed, The 1916 (P) 521, 809
Light Within, The 1918 (FN) 2037
Lighthouse by the Sea, The 1911 (Ed)
Lighthouse Keeper, The 1911 (Imp) 2047
Lighthouse Keeper's Daughter, The 1908
  (Lubin)
Lighthouse Keeper's Daughter, The 1912
  (Ed) 2231
Lightning Bolt, The 1913 (   ) 651, 2112
Lightning Bryce--serial 1919 (Arrow) 448,
  490, 555, 1307, 1320, 1325, 1580,
  1612, 2013
    1. The Scarlet Moon
    2. Wolf Nights
    3. Perilous Trails
    4. The Noose
    5. The Dragon's Den
    6. Robes of Destruction
    7. Bared Fangs
    8. The Yawning Abyss
    9. The Voice of Conscience
   10. Poison Waters
   11. Walls of Flame
   12. A Voice from the Dead
   13. Battling Barriers
   14. Smothering Tides
   15. The End of the Trail
Lightning Raider, The--serial 1919 (P)
  1397, 1971, 2363, 2748
    1. The Ebony Block
    2. The Counterplot
    3. Underworld Terrors
    4. Through the Doors of Steel
    5. The Brass Key
    6. The Mystic Box
    7. Meshes of Evil
    8. Cave of Dread
    9. Falsely Accused
   10. The Baited Trap
   11. Bars of Death

12. Hurled into Space
13. The White Roses
14. Cleared of Guilt
15. Wu Fang Atones
Lightning Sketches 1907 (V)
Lights and Shadows 1914 (Rex/Un) 352, 449
Like Wildfire 1917 ( ) 1004
Lil o' London 1914 (Br) 2712
Lilliputian Minuet, The 1905 (Melies)
Lily and the Rose, The 1915 (V) 1029, 1613, 1632
Lily of the Tenements, The 1911 (Bio) 1363, 1933, 2729
Lily's Lovers 1912 (Bio)
Limb of Satan, A 1917 ( ) 2486
Limousine Life 1918 (Tri) 192, 2557
Lincoln Cycle, The 1917 ( ) 450
Lincoln, the Lover 1914 ( ) 2472
Lincoln's Gettysburg Address 1912 ( ) 1332
Lineman, The 1911 (Independent Moving Picture Co.)
Lines of White on a Sullen Sea 1909 (Bio) 79, 1223, 1933, 2728, 2729
Link That Held, The 1911 (Ed)
Linked by Fate 1919 (Br) 831
Lion and the Girl, The 1916 (Key/Tri) 1202, 1342, 1419, 1626, 1889, 2724
Lion and the Lamb, The 1919 ( ) 2121
Lion and the Mouse, The 1919 (V) 486, 1388, 2091, 2232
Lion Hunt 1906 ( )
Lion Man, The--serial 1918 (Un) 88, 135, 476, 1963, 2034, 2392, 2664, 2806
    1. Flames of Hate
    2. Rope of Death
    3. Kidnappers
    4. A Devilish Device
    5. In the Lion's Den
    6. House of Horrors
    7. Doomed
    8. Dungeon of Despair
    9. Sold into Slavery
    10. Perilous Plunge
    11. At the Mercy of Monsters
    12. Jaws of Destruction
    13. When Hell Broke Loose
    14. Desperate Deeds
    15. Furnace of Fury
    16. Relentless Renegades
    17. In Cruel Clutches
    18. In the Nick of Time
Lion, the Lamb, the Man, The 1914 (Rex/Un) 352, 449, 2781
Lion's Claw, The--serial 1918 (Un) 34, 88, 95, 476, 1149, 1186, 1492, 1579, 2645, 2656
    1. A Woman's Honor
    2. Beasts of the Jungle
    3. Net of Terror
    4. A Woman's Scream
    5. The Secret Document
    6. The Dungeon of Terror
    7. Quicksand
    8. Into the Harem
    9. The Human Pendulum
    10. Escape thru the Flames
    11. Caught in the Toils
    12. The Spies' Cave
    13. In Disguise

14. Hell Let Loose
15. Bridge of the Beast
16. The Jungle Pool
17. The Well of Horror or The Danger Pit
18. The Doom of Rej Hari or Triumph
Lion's Den, The 1919 ( ) 1631
Little American, The 1917 (Art/Par) 28, 166, 258, 454, 1201, 1280, 1432, 1537, 1591, 1791, 1859, 1925, 1949, 1975, 2047, 2051, 2793
Little Angel of Cannon Creek 1917 ( ) 2401
Little Angels of Luck 1910 (Bio) 477
Little Artist of the Market 1912 (Ed)
Little Billy's City Cousin 1914 (Key) 1345
Little Billy's Strategy 1914 (Key) 1345
Little Billy's Triumph 1914 (Key) 1345
Little Bit off the Top, A 1904 (AMB)
Little Boss, The 1919 ( ) 1602
Little Boy Scout, The 1917 (Art/Par) 1865, 2028
Little Bread Winners, The 1908 (Lubin)
Little Bride of Heaven 1912 (Ed)
Little Brother 1917 ( ) 206
Little Brother of the Rich, A 1915 ( ) 1796, 2392
Little, but Oh, My! 1919 ( ) 2595
Little Cafe, The /aka/ The Miracle of the Wolves 1919 ( ) 1575
Little Catamount, The 1915 ( ) 1028, 1563
Little Child, A 1911 (Bio) 2680
Little Child Shall Lead Them, A 1914 (Br) 149, 150
Little Child Shall Lead Them, A 1919 ( ) 2558
Little Comrade, The 1919 (Par) 473, 1764, 2462
Little Country Mouse, The 1914 (Mu) 27, 2112, 2513
Little Coward, The 1908 (Lubin)
Little Darling, The 1909 (Bio) 1182, 1363, 2046, 2047, 2081, 2368
Little Delicatessen Store, The 1912 (Ed)
Little Detective, The 1908 (V)
Little Diplomat, The 1919 (P) 525, 1988
Little Dove's Gratitude 1911 (Kal) 642
Little Dutchess, The 1917 (WS) 853
Little Easter Fairy, The 1908 (Lubin)
Little Father, The; or The Dressmaker's Loyal Son 1909 (V)
Little Fiddler, The 1910 (Ed)
Little German Band 1904 (Ed)
Little Girl Next Door, The 1912 (Ed)
Little Girl Who Did Not Believe in Santa Claus, A 1907 (Ed)
Little Gypsy 1909 (Bio) 209
Little Hero, A 1907 (V)
Little Hero, A 1913 (Key) 1941
Little Hour of Peter Wells, The 1919 (Hollandia) 2551
Little Intruder, The 1919 ( ) 1255, 1275, 1309
Little Lady Eileen 1916 (FP) 482, 2395, 2460
Little Lady of the Big House 1917 ( ) 396
Little Leader, The 1911 (Independent Moving Picture Co.)

Little Lord Fauntleroy 1914 ( ) 372, 811,
848, 1990, 2455, 2641, 2722
Little Man, A 1902 (AMB)
Little Marian's Triumph 1919 ( ) 2570
Little Mary Sunshine 1917 (P) 1988
Little Meena's Romance 1916 (FA) 356,
1028, 1753, 1865, 2573
Little Milliner and the Thief, The 1910
(Hep) 2531
Little Minister, The 1912 (V) 2811, 2812
Little Miss Brown 1919 ( ) 2130
Little Miss Deputy 1919 (Tri) 1099
Little Miss Happiness 1916 (F) 392
Little Miss Hoover 1918 (Par) 482, 1959
Little Miss Moffit and Simian Stone 1909
(Ed)
Little Miss Muffet 1903 (Lubin)
Little Miss No Account 1918 ( ) 1547
Little Miss Nobody 1917 ( ) 1814
Little Miss Optimist 1917 (Art/Par) 1006,
1764
Little Miss Rebellion 1912 ( ) 875
Little Missionary, The 1917 (Es) 1636
Little Mix-up in a Mixed Ale Joint, A
1902 (AMB)
Little Organist, The 1912 (Ed)
Little Orphan, The 1909 (V)
Little Orphan, The 1917 ( ) 1120, 1518
Little Orphan Annie 1918 (Selig/Mu) 218,
1859, 2221
Little Pal 1915 (Par) 49, 146, 1924, 2047
Little Partner, The 1916 ( ) 1308
Little Patriot, A 1918 (P) 853, 1988,
2025
Little Peacemaker, The 1908 (Melies)
Little Piece of String, A 1902 (AMB)
Little Princess, A 1917 (Art/Par) 454,
1091, 1432, 1949, 1975, 2047, 2051,
2149, 2337, 2401, 2648
Little Rag Doll, The 1908 (Lubin)
Little Railroad Queen, The 1912 (Ingvald
C. Oes)
Little Ray of Sunshine after the Rain
1902 (AMB)
Little Red Decides 1918 ( ) 619
Little Red Riding Hood 1911 (Es) 2075
Little Red Riding Hood 1911 (Majestic)
2047
Little Reformer, The 1918 ( ) 1602
Little Roman, The * (P) 1575
Little Rowdy 1919 (Go) 630, 1253
Little School Ma'am, The 1916 ( ) 497,
601, 1028, 2483
Little Scrub Lady, The 1918 ( ) 1764
Little Shepherd of Kingdom Come, The
1919 (Art/Par) 1925, 2453
Little Shepherd of Tumbling Run, The
1909 (Ed)
Little Shoes 1917 (Es) 457, 1636
Little Sister 1909 (Ed)
Little Sister of Everybody, The 1918 ( )
1602
Little Snowdrop 1903 (Lubin)
Little Station Agent, The 1910 (Ed)
Little Stocking, The 1911 (Independent
Moving Picture Co.)
Little Straw Wife, The 1916 (Es) 1795, 2700
Little Teacher, The 1909 (Bio) 731, 1363,
2047, 2081
Little Teacher, The /aka/ A Small Town
Bully 1914 (Key) 65, 1865, 1941, 2368

Little Tease, A 1903 (AMB)
Little Tease, The 1913 (Bio) 315, 1182,
1751, 1831, 2680
Little Tom Thumb 1903 (Lubin)
Little Train Robbery, The 1905 (Ed)
Little Waifs, The 1910 (Bio)
Little White Savage, The 1917 (Es) 1636
Little White Savage, The 1919 (Un) 1253,
1911
Little Widow Is a Dangerous Thing, A
1913 (Hep) 2531
Little Woolen Shoe, The 1912 (Ed)
Little Women 1917 (Br) 2179
Little Women 1919 (W) 209, 916, 1124,
1418, 1479, 1550, 1914
Little Yank, The 1917 ( ) 340, 1028,
2356, 2573
Littlest Rebel, The 1914 ( ) 1569, 2815
Live Wire, The 1914 (Br) 1873
Live Wire, The 1919 ( ) 522 (Film
never released)
Lively Pranks with a Fake Python 1908
(Melies)
Living Doll, The 1909 (Melies)
Living Peach, The 1911 (Ed)
Living Pictures 1903 (AMB)
Living Playing Cards 1905 (Melies)
Livingston Case, The 1910 (Ed)
Lizzie and the Iceman 1914 ( ) 2748
Loaded Cigar, The 1904 (AMB)
Loaded Dice 1918 (P) 1404
Loan Shark, The 1912 (Imp)
Loan Shark, The 1914 ( ) 156
Loan Shark King, A 1914 (V) 297, 1876,
2523
Local Color 1916 (Selig Polyscope) 469,
932, 1381, 1849
Lochinvar 1909 (Ed)
Lochinvar 1915 (Br) 1329
Locked House, The 1914 (V) 332
Locked Out 1917 (M) 768, 1707
Locket, The 1911 (V) 111, 332, 818, 901
Locket, The 1915 (Br) 177
Lodging for the Night, A 1912 (Bio) 2047,
2728
Logan's Babies 1911 (Ed)
Lola 1915 (W) 950, 1438, 1863, 2811
Lombardi, Ltd. 1919 (M) 7, 369, 1152,
1153, 1353, 1565, 1710, 1790
Lon of Lone Mountain 1915 (Rex/Un) 341,
449, 1862, 2398
London Nighthawks 1915 (Br) 1873
London's Enemies 1916 (Br) 1873
London's Yellow Peril 1915 (Br) 834,
2138
Lonedale Operator, The 1911 (Bio) 731,
1060, 1074, 1223, 1613, 2513
Lonely Gentleman; or Incompatibility of
Temper 1908 (V)
Lonely Villa 1909 (Bio) 685, 816, 1450,
1542, 1543, 1714, 1865, 2047, 2368
Lonesome Junction 1908 (AMB)
Lonesome Luke, Circus King 1916 (P)
635, 1586
Lonesome Luke from London to Larramie
1917 (P) 635, 1586

Lonesome Luke in Tin Can Alley 1917
(P) 635, 1586, 2055
Lonesome Luke, Lawyer 1917 (P) 1586
Lonesome Luke Loses Patients 1917 (P)
635, 1586
Lonesome Luke, Mechanic 1917 (P) 635,
1586
Lonesome Luke, Messenger 1917 (P)
635, 1586
Lonesome Luke, Plumber 1917 (P) 635,
1586
Lonesome Luke, Social Gangster 1915
(P) 1586, 2055
Lonesome Luke's Double 1915 (P) 635,
1586, 2055
Lonesome Luke's Honeymoon 1917 (P)
635, 1586
Lonesome Luke's Lively Life 1917 (P)
635, 1586, 2055
Lonesome Luke's Lively Rifle 1917 (P)
635, 1586
Lonesome Luke's Wild Women 1917 (P)
635, 1586
Lonesome Miss Wiggs 1912 (Imp)
Long Ago, The 1913 (Selig) 857, 1957
Long Arm of Mannister, The 1919
( ) 2680
Long Chance, The 1919 ( ) 1928
Long Green Trail, The 1918 ( ) 487
Long Flib the King 1916 ( ) 460
Long Lane's Turning, A 1919 ( ) 457,
2680
Long Road, The 1911 (Bio) 1539, 2513,
2573, 2728
Long Trail, The 1910 (Selig/Polyscope)
1849
Long Trail, The 1917 (Art/Par) 272,
968, 2541
Lonely Woman, The 1918 ( ) 186
Lonore (L'Onore) di Morire 1915 ( )
1372
Look out Below 1919 (P) 1586, 2055
Look Pleasant Please 1918 (P) 1586
Look Up 1913 ( ) 315, 731, 1511
Looking for John Smith 1906 (AMB)
Looking for Trouble 1919 (P) 635, 2055
Looking Them Over see A Lover's
Lost Control
Loot 1919 ( ) 396, 1025
Loot and Love 1915 (V) 2367
Lord and Lady Algy 1919 (Go) 114, 342,
468, 950, 1007, 1052, 1535, 1867
Lord and the Peasant, The 1912 (Ed)
Lord Chumley 1914 ( ) 1029
Lord Feathertop 1908 (Ed)
Lord Helpus see Cruel, Cruel Love
Lorelei, Siren of the Sea, The 1917 ( )
2065
Lorraine of the Timberlands 1919 ( )
2221
Losing Weight 1916 (V) 2367
Losing Winner, The 1917 ( ) 689
Loss of the Birkenhead, The 1914 (Br)
834, 2138
Lost--a Cook 1917 (Key/Tri) 1345, 2206,
2510, 2534, 2608
Lost and Regained 1910 (Ed)
Lost and Won 1959 (GB) 812, 2604
Lost Won 1917 ( ) 724, 752
Lost Appetite, The 1919 ( ) 2147

Lost Art of Making up One's Mind, The
1913 (Bio) 1182
Lost Battalion, The 1919 ( ) 626, 2160,
2814
Lost Bridegroom, The 1916 (FP) 140,
1450
Lost Child, The 1904 (AMB)
Lost Child, The 1904 (Lubin)
Lost Collar Button, The; or A Strenuous
Search 1906 (V)
Lost Cord, The 1917 (Br) 177
Lost Dispatch, The 1913 ( ) 2096
Lost Express, The--serial 1917 (Mu) 319,
1216, 1273, 1579, 1692, 1720
    1. The Lost Express
    2. The Destroyed Document
    3. The Wreck at the Crossing
    4. The Oil Well Conspiracy
    5. In Deep Waters
    6. High Voltage
    7. The Race with the Limited
    8. The Mountain King
    9. The Looters
    10. The Secret of the Mine
    11. A Fight for a Million
    12. Law Is Law or Daring Death
    13. Disowned or The Escape
    14. Trapped or Unmasked
    15. The Found Express or Return
        of the Lost Express
Lost Handbag, The 1909 (Ed)
Lost Hat, The: He Got It Alright 1906
(Lubin)
Lost Heir, The 1909 (Lubin)
Lost House, The 1915 ( ) 1029, 2112
Lost in a Folding Bed 1909 (V)
Lost in an Arizona Desert 1907 (V)
Lost in the Alps 1907 (V)
Lost in the Jungle--serial 1913 (Selig)
2770
Lost in Transit 1917 (Art/Par) 160, 595,
1565
Lost Invitation, The 1909 (Ed)
Lost Kitten, The 1912 (Ed)
Lost Lady, The 1917 ( ) 1422
Lost Lord Lowell, The 1915 ( ) 1028
Lost Millionaire, The 1913 ( ) 2472
Lost New Year's Dinner, The 1908 (Ed)
Lost Paradise 1914 ( ) 2693
Lost Sheep, The 1909 (V)
Lost, Strayed or Stolen 1907 (V)
Lost--Three Hours 1912 (Ed)
Lost--24 Hours 1916 (Es) 2582
Lost Years 1915 (M) 353
Lottery Man, The 1919 (FP/Las) 83, 264,
927, 1080, 1206, 1528, 1756, 1821,
1970, 1975, 2092, 2112, 2149, 2468,
Lotus Woman 1915 ( ) 1270
Lousiana 1919 (Par) 33, 165, 926, 935,
1537, 1764
Love 1919 (FP/Las) 65, 2208
Love among the Roses 1910 (Bio) 1542,
1593, 2047
Love and a Savage 1915 (Christie) 525
Love and Bullets /aka/ The Trouble
Mender 1914 (Key) 1906
Love and Courage 1913 (Key) 65, 1941
Love and Duty 1916 (Vim) 1161
Love and Dynamite 1914 (Key) 2465
Love and Friendship 1912 (Ingvald C. Oes)

Love and Gasoline /aka/ The Skidding
   Joy Riders 1917 (Key) 1941
Love and Hate 1916 (F) 1524
Love and Hatred 1911 (Ed)
Love and Honor--serial 1917 ( ) 1364
Love and Jealousy behind the Scenes
   1904 (AMB)
Love and Justice 1917 ( ) 1032
Love and Lobster 1918 (Br) 1487
Love and Lobsters see He Did and
   He Didn't
Love and Locksmiths 1915 (Christie) 525
Love and Lunch see Mabel's Busy Day
Love and Marriage in Posterland 1910
   (Ed)
Love and Molasses 1908 (Melies)
Love and Pain 1913 (Key) 1666, 2465
Love and Passion 1914 ( ) 1922
Love and Rubbish 1913 (Key) 2465
Love and the Law 1910 (Ed)
Love and the Law 1913 ( ) 2112, 2745
Love and the Stock Market 1911 (Ed)
Love and the Woman 1919 ( ) 835
Love and Vaccination 1915 (Christie) 525
Love and War 1899 (James H. White)
Love and War 1909 (Ed)
Love at 55 1903 (AMB)
Love Auction 1919 (P) 2024
Love Brokers, The 1918 (Tri) 1099, 2194
Love Bugs, The 1917 (Vim) 1161
Love Burglar, The 1919 (Par) 166, 337,
   1202, 1939, 2112, 2547
Love by the Light of the Moon 1901 (Ed)
Love Call, The 1919 ( ) 2121, 2753
Love Chase see Too Many Brides
Love Cheat, The 1919 ( ) 1119
Love Chest, The 1919 (Fox) 392
Love Comet 1916 (Key/Tri) 179, 396
Love Defender 1919 ( ) 835, 853
Love Doctor, The 1917 (V) 1088, 2767
Love Drops 1910 (Ed)
Love Egg, The 1914 (Key) 531
Love Finds a Way 1909 (AMB)
Love Finds a Way /aka/ Love Laughs
   at Blacksmiths 1913 ( ) 2473
Love-Friend see Twenty Minutes of
   Love
Love Germs 1908 (Lubin)
Love Heeds Not the Showers 1911
   (Majestic) 2047
Love Hunger, The 1919 ( ) 2405
Love in a Hammock 1901 (Ed)
Love in a Hammock 1903 (AMB)
Love in a Hurry 1919 ( ) 231
Love in a Laundry 1912 (Br) 1289
Love in a Tepee 1911 (Independent
   Moving Picture Co.)
Love in a Wood 1916 (LFC) 43, 613, 834,
   943, 2138
Love in an Apartment Hotel 1913 (Bio)
   141, 398, 731, 732, 1182, 1751,
   1832, 2513, 2573, 2680
Love in Armor 1915 (Key) 65, 460, 657
Love in Quarantine 1910 (Bio)
Love in the Cornfield 1902 (AMB)
Love in the Dark 1903 (AMB)
Love in the Hills 1911 (Bio) 1074, 2513,
   2728
Love in the Suburbs 1903 (AMB)
Love in the Tropics 1912 (Ingvald C.
   Oes)

Love Insurance 1919 (Art/Par) 595, 2700,
   2779
Love Is Best 1911 (Independent Moving
   Picture Co.)
Love Is Blind 1909 (Ed)
Love Is Love 1919 ( ) 856
Love Laughs at Blacksmiths see Love
   Finds a Way 1913
Love Laughs at Locksmiths 1908 (V)
Love Letters 1917 (Tri) 532, 627
Love, Loot and Crash 1915 (Key) 460,
   531, 2165, 2336, 2514
Love, Luck and Gasoline 1914 (V) 332,
   2663
Love Mask, The 1916 (Las 947, 1201,
   2112, 2122
Love Me 1918 (Tri) 627, 1690
Love Me for Myself Alone 1918 ( ) 612
Love Me, Love My Dog 1903 (AMB)
Love Me, Love My Dog 1908 (Lubin)
Love Microbe 1907 (AMB)
Love Nest, The 1919 ( ) 853, 2582
Love of an Actress, The 1914 (Br) 177
Love of Crysanthemus 1910 (V) 2523
Love of Lady Irma, The 1910 (Bio)
Love of Madge O'Mara, The 1917 (Selig)
   857
Love of the Pasha's Son, The 1909 (V)
Love on Skates see Danger Girl
Love on the Luck Ranch 1912 (Es) 50
Love Or Fame 1919 ( ) 1139
Love Riot, A 1916 (Key/Tri) 250, 650,
   878, 1906, 2165, 2580
Love Sickness at Sea 1912 (Key) 1941,
   2368, 2465
Love, Speed and Thrills 1915 (Key) 531,
   791, 2465
Love Sublime, A 1917 ( ) 2794
Love Swindle, The 1918 (Un)
Love Test, The 1911 ( ) 377
Love That Dares, The 1919 ( ) 2581
Love That Lies 1917 (Par) 957
Love Thief, The 1914 (Key) 531
Love Tragedy in Spain, A 1908 (Melies)
Love Vs. Title; or An up-to-Date
   Elopement 1906 (V)
Love Watches 1918 (V) 1047, 1088, 2547
Love Will Conquer 1916 (Key/Tri) 294,
   1086, 1651, 1666, 1874, 2510, 2514
Love Will Find a Way 1908 (Ed)
Love Wins 1909 (Centaur Film Co.)
Lover and the Count, The 1911 (Ed)
Lover, Coal Box, and Fireplace, The
   1901 (Ed)
Lover's Guide, The 1908 (Ed)
Lover's Hazing, A 1908 (Melies)
Lover's Knot, The 1902 (AMB)
Lover's Lost Control, A /aka/ Looking
   Them Over 1915 (Key) 452
Lover's Luck 1914 (Key) 65
Lover's Might, A /aka/ The Fire Chief
   1916 (Key/Tri) 71, 877, 1086, 1666,
   1889
Lover's Post Office 1914 (Key) 65, 1941
Lover's Quarrell, The: Meeting in the
   Park 1904 (AMB)
Lover's Ruse, The 1904 (AMB)
Lover's Ruse, The; or The Miser's
   Daughter 1908 (V)
Lover's Stratagems, A 1908 (V)
Lover's Telegraphic Code, The 1908 (Ed)

Lover's Tryst 1909 (Bio) 2047
Lover's Yarn, A 1902 (AMB)
Love's Conquest 1918 ( ) 438
Love's Crucible 1916 ( ) 1163
Love's Diary 1912 (Un)
Love's False Faces 1919 ( ) 2069
Love's Lariat 1916 (Imp) 398, 969
Loves, Laughs and Lather 1917 (P) 1586,
  2055
Love's Law 1916 (FP) 920
Love's Legacy 1915 (Br) 1258
Love's Old Dream 1914 (V) 332, 901,
  1584
Love's Pay Day 1919 ( ) 2554
Love's Perfidy 1905 (AMB)
Love's Prisoner 1919 (S) 2557
Love's Quarantine 1913 (V) 332, 901
Love's Sacrifice 1909 (Ed)
Love's Sunset 1913 (V) 533, 2811
Love's Sweet Melody 1908 (Lubin)
Love's Way 1915 (V) 157, 1426, 1876,
  2487
Love's Western Flight 1914 ( ) 2112
Love's Young Dream 1902 (AMB)
Lovesick Maidens of Cuddleton, The 1912
  (V) 332, 818, 2523
Loyalty 1918 ( ) 1208
Lubin's Animated Drop-Curtain Announcing
  Slides 1901 (Lubin)
Lucile 1912 (T) 603, 1468, 2201, 2430
Lucille Love Girl of Mystery--serial 1914
  (Un) 245, 610, 926, 2093, 2393
Luck and Pluck 1919 ( ) 931, 2671
Luck in Pawn 1919 (Par) 482, 1807, 2717
Luck of Roaring Camp, The 1910 (Ed)
Luck of the Irish 1919 ( ) 2784
Lucky Card, The 1911 (Es) 50
Lucky Deal, A 1915 (Selig Polyscope)
  1849
Lucky Dog 1912 (Ed)
Lucky Dog, A 1917 (M) 1021, 1161, 1502,
  2146
Lucky Elopement, The 1914 ( ) 2472
Luck Horseshow, A 1908 (Lubin)
Lucky Jim 1907 (Lubin)
Lucky Jim 1909 (AMB) 1224, 2368
Lucky Kitten 1903 (AMB)
Lucky Leap, A 1915 (Key) 509
Lucky Stone, The 1913 (GB) 2604
Lucky Strike, A 1915 (Lubin) 1161
Lucky Toothache, A 1910 (Bio) 79, 2047
Lucky Wishbone, The 1905 (Paley &
  Steiner)
Lucretia Borgia 1916 (P) 2105
Ludwig from Germany 1911 (Ed)
Luke and the Bang-Tails 1916 (P) 635, 1586
Luke and the Bomb Throwers 1916 (P)
  635, 1586
Luke and the Mermaids 1916 (P) 635,
  1586, 2055
Luke and the Rural Roughnecks 1916 (P)
  635, 1586
Luke, Crystal Gazer 1916 (P) 635, 1586,
  2055
Luke Does the Midway 1916 (P) 635, 1586,
  2055
Luke Foils the Villain 1916 (P) 635, 1586,
  2055
Luke, Gladiator 1916 (P) 635, 1586
Luke Joins the Navy 1916 (P) 635, 1586,
  2055

Luke Laughs Last 1916 (P) 635, 1586,
  2055
Luke Leans to the Literary 1916 (P) 635,
  1586, 2055
Luke Locates the Loot 1916 (P) 635, 1586
Luke Lugs Luggage 1916 (P) 635, 1586,
  2055
Luke, Patient Provider 1916 (P) 635,
  1586
Luke Pipes the Pippins 1916 (P) 635,
  1586, 2055
Luke Rides Roughshod 1916 (P) 635, 1586,
  2055
Luke Rolls in Luxury 1916 (P) 635, 1586,
  2055
Luke the Candy Cut-up 1916 (P) 635,
  1586, 2055
Luke the Chauffeur 1916 (P) 635, 1586
Luke Wins Ye Ladye Faire 1917 (P) 635,
  1586
Luke's Busy Days 1917 (P) 635, 1586
Luke's Double see Lonesome Luke's
  Double
Luke's Fatal Flivver 1916 (P) 635, 1586,
  2055
Luke's Fireworks Fizzle 1916 (P) 635,
  1586
Luke's Last Liberty 1917 (P) 635, 1586
Luke's Late Lunches 1916 (P) 635, 1586
Luke's Lost Lamb 1916 (P) 635, 1586,
  2055
Luke's Movie Muddle 1916 (P) 635, 1586
Luke's Newsie Knockout 1916 (P) 635,
  1586
Luke's Preparedness Preparation 1916
  (P) 635
Luke's Shattered Sleep 1916 (P) 635, 1586
Luke's Society Mixup 1916 (P) 635, 1586,
  2055
Luke's Speedy Club Life 1916 (P) 635,
  1586, 2055
Luke's Trolly Trouble 1917 (P) 635, 1586
Luke's Wishful Waiting 1916 (P) 635, 1586
Lumber Yard Gang, The 1916 (Un) 610,
  926
Lunatics in Power 1909 (Ed)
Lunch Time 1908 (Lubin)
Lupin Gal 1917 ( ) 2780
Lure of a Woman, The 1915 (WS) 273,
  835, 2096
Lure of Ambition, The 1919 (F) 116, 658,
  764, 984, 1009, 1769, 2006, 2701,
  2814
Lure of Broadway, The see Bright
  Lights
Lure of Heart's Desire 1916 ( ) 283, 286
Lure of London, The 1914 (Br) 503
Lure of Luxury, The 1918 ( ) 495, 1216
Lure of the Circus--serial 1918 (Un)
  2056, 2354, 2355
  1. The Big Tent
  2. The Giant's Leap
  3. Beaten Back
  4. The Message on the Cuff
  5. The Lip Reader
  6. The Aerial Disaster
  7. The Charge of the Elephant
  8. The Human Ladder
  9. The Flying Loop
  10. A Shot for Life
  11. The Dagger

12. A Strange Escape
13. A Plunge for Life
14. Flames
15. The Stolen Record
16. The Knockout
17. A Race with Time
18. The Last Trick
Lure of the City, The 1911 (Ed)
Lure of the Gown, The 1909 (AMB) 1336,
  1511, 2368
Lure of the Picture, The 1912 (Imp)
Lure of Woman, The 1915 (Broncho) 1032
Lurking Peril, The--serial 1919 (Arrow)
  161, 219, 797, 1494, 1622, 2376
        1. The $25,000 Contract
        2. At the Edge of the Cliff
        3. The Aviator's Victim
        4. A Bolt from Heaven
        5. The Man Trap in the Woods
        6. A Duel of Wits
        7. A Satanic Plot
        8. Helpless in a Madhouse
        9. The Hiding Place in the Slums
       10. The Den in Chinatown
       11. At a Maniac's Mercy
       12. Six Inches of Steel
       13. Trapped by Telegraph
       14. The Dynamite Ship
       15. The Last Plot of Bates
Lurline Baths 1897 (Ed)
Lust of the Ages 1917 (V) 2663
Lydia Gilmore 1916 (FP) 619, 957
Lying Lips 1916 ( ) 1080
Lyons and Moran comedies 1909 ( ) 1872

- M -

Mabel and Fatty's Viewing the World's
  Fair at San Diego 1915 (Key) 65, 1941
Mabel and Fatty's Wash Day 1915 (Key)
  65, 1941
Mabel at the Wheel /aka/ His Daredevil
  Queen; Hot House Fiend 1914 (Key)
  384, 451, 531, 1651, 1941, 2208,
  2357, 2368
Mabel, Fatty and the Law /aka/ Fatty's
  Spooning Day 1915 (Key) 65, 791,
  1086, 1211, 1941
Mabel Lost and Won 1915 (Key) 1865,
  1941, 2510
Mabel's Adventures 1912 (Key) 1666, 1941,
  2510
Mabel's Awful Mistake /aka/ Her De-
  ceitful Lover 1913 (Key) 1941, 2368
Mabel's Bare Escape 1914 (Key) 1941
Mabel's Blunder 1914 (Key) 1941
Mabel's Busy Day /aka/ Charlie and the
  Sausages; Hot Dogs; Love and Lunch
  1914 (Key) 451, 531, 1651, 1662,
  1941, 2501
Mabel's Dramatic Career /aka/ Her
  Dramatic Debut 1913 (Key) 65, 1941,
  2368, 2465
Mabel's Dramatic Moment * (P) 1575
Mabel's Flirtation see Her Friend the
  Bandit
Mabel's Greatest Moment 1915 (Key) 1941
Mabel's Heroes 1913 (Key) 509, 1666,
  1941, 2368

Mabel's Latest Prank /aka/ A Touch of
  Rheumatism 1914 (Key) 1941
Mabel's Lovers 1912 (Key) 650, 1666,
  1941, 2368
Mabel's Married Life /aka/ The Square-
  head; When You're Married 1914
  (Key) 451, 1304, 1651, 1662, 1726,
  1906, 1941, 2510
Mabel's Nerve 1914 (Key) 1941
Mabel's New Hero 1913 (Key) 65, 1941
Mabel's New Job 1914 (Key) 460, 631,
  650, 1941
Mabel's Stormy Love Affair 1914 (Key)
  1941
Mabel's Strange Predicament /aka/ Hotel
  Mix-up 1914 (Key) 451, 531, 650,
  1651, 1726, 1941, 2208
Mabel's Stratagem 1912 (Key) 1666, 1941
Mabel's Wilful Way 1915 (Key) 1941
Macbeth 1908 (V)
Macbeth 1909 (Cines of Rome) 390
Macbeth 1910 (FdA) 702
Macbeth 1911 (Co-operative Cinematograph
  Co.) 196, 197, 417
Macbeth 1913 ( ) 262
Macbeth 1916 (FA/Tri) 25, 27, 28, 354,
  410, 518, 537, 798, 937, 1053, 1613,
  2584, 2649
Macbeth, Shakespeare's Sublime Tragedy
  1908 (V)
Mack at It Again 1914 (Key) 1941, 2368
McTeague 1915 (W) 239, 1741
M'Liss 1918 (Art/Par) 242, 1756, 1800,
  1970, 2047, 2149, 2491
Mad Cap, The 1916 ( ) 690
Mad Dog 1909 (Lubin)
Mad Lover, The 1917 ( ) 1139, 2698
Mad Talon, The 1919 ( ) 1971
Mad Woman, The 1919 (Un) 1066, 1245,
  1978
Madam of the Slums 1915 (W) 239
Madam Spy 1918 ( ) 1896
Madame Bo-Peep 1917 ( ) 1177, 1998
Madame Butterfly 1915 (FP/Las) 401,
  1068, 1171, 1924, 2047, 2732
Madame De Mode 1912 (Ed)
Madame DuBarry 1918 (F) 116, 238, 471,
  485, 764, 1601, 1757, 1794, 2224
Madame DuBarry 1919 (Union/UFA) 207,
  1349
Madame Flirt's Manicure Parlor 1908
  (Lubin)
Madame Jealousy 1918 (Par) 957
Madame La Presidente 1916 (Morosco)
  1219, 2036, 2445
Madame Rex 1911 (Bio) 95, 1593
Madame Sans-Gene 1912 (French-American
  Film Co.) 2117
Madame Sphinx 1917 (Tri) 1331, 1658,
  1662, 2194
Madame Spy 1919 ( ) 2147
Madame Who? 1918 ( ) 2002
Madame X 1916 (P) 265, 747, 957
Madcap Ambrose 1916 (Key/Tri) 840,
  1211, 1422, 1874, 1889, 2510, 2724
Madcap Madge * (Tri) 2557
Made a Coward 1913 ( ) 785
Made in America 1919 ( ) 1445
Madeline's Rebellion 1911 (Ed)
Madge of the Mountains 1911 (V) 332, 695

Madonna and Her Child, The 1913 (Bio) 1029
Mae's Suitors 1911 (Ed)
Maestor Do-Mi-Sol-Do, The 1906 (Melies)
Magda 1917 (Select) 462, 1266, 2811
Magdalene of the Hills, A 1916 (M) 2520
Maggie Pepper 1919 (Art/Par) 486, 724, 1080, 1756
Maggie's First False Step 1913 (Key/Tri) 166, 250, 650, 878, 1906, 2564
Magic Fountain Pen, The 1909 (V)
Magic Lantern, The 1903 (Melies)
Magic of Catchy Songs 1908 (Melies)
Magic Wand, The 1912 (Es) 156, 353, 2010
Magician, The 1900 (Ed)
Magnetic Eye, The 1908 (Lubin)
Magnetic Vapor 1908 (Lubin)
Magnificent Meddler, The 1917 (V) 51, 1876
Maid Mad /aka/ The Fortune Teller 1916 (Key/Tri) 250, 878, 1906, 2580
Maid o' the Storm 1918 ( ) 134, 509, 763, 1558
Maid of the Mist 1915 (Rex/Un) 352, 449, 977
Maid or Man 1911 (Imp) 2047
Maid to Order, A 1916 (Vim) 1161
Maiden of the Piefaced Indians, The 1911 (Ed)
Maiden's Trust, A 1917 (Key/Tri) 650, 876, 1086, 1567, 1572, 2465, 2580
Maid's Stratagem, The 1912 (Imp)
Make-Believe Wife, The 1918 (M) 333, 2061
Make It Snappy 1915 ( ) 1684
Make Yourself at Home 1908 (Lubin)
Making a Living /aka/ A Busted Johnny; Doing His Best; Troubles 1914 (Key) 531, 650, 791, 1451, 1533, 1941
Making an Impression 1903 (AMB)
Making an Impression * (Selig Polyscope) 1849
Making Good 1915 (Selig Polyscope) 1849, 2112
Making Her His Wife 1918 ( ) 1049
Making of a Man, The 1911 (Bio) 1074, 1223, 2513
Making of a Mother, The 1915 (Christie) 525
Making of Madalena, The 1916 ( ) 2445
Making Soap Bubbles 1897 (Ed)
Making U. S. Currency 1912 (Un)
Male and Female 1919 (Art/Par) 138, 337, 345, 365, 550, 635, 637, 677, 877, 1201, 1417, 1528, 1537, 1800, 1975, 2102, 2149, 2351, 2512, 2800
Malestrom 1917 ( ) 2406
Mama's Boys 1916 (Vim) 1161
Mamma's Angel Child 1909 (Lubin)
Man, The 1910 (Bio)
Man above the Law 1917 ( ) 2128
Man Afraid of His Wardrobe, A 1919 (Un) 9
Man and Beast 1917 ( ) 2354
Man and His Money, A 1919 (Go) 24, 679, 1550, 1867, 1998
Man and the Woman, The 1908 (AMB) 79, 994
Man Behind, The 1915 ( ) 242

Man behind the Times, The 1917 (Hep) 2171, 2744
Man Beneath, The 1919 (Par) 1208
Man for All That, A 1911 (Ed)
Man for All of That, A 1915 ( ) 2672
Man from Egypt, The 1916 (V) 2367
Man from Funeral Range, The 1918 (Par) 1580, 1756, 2046, 2112
Man from Home, The 1914 (Par) 411, 623, 914, 1369, 1439, 1493, 1854, 1897, 1925, 2149, 2211, 2623
Man from India, The 1914 (Br) 1289, 2171
Man from Mexico, The 1914 (FP) 140
Man from Montana, The 1918 (Un) 1186
Man from Nowhere, The 1915 ( ) 1188
Man from Painted Post, The 1917 (Art/Par) 242, 387, 857, 2031, 2441
Man from Texas, The * (Selig Polyscope) 1840
Man from the East, The 1914 (Selig Polyscope) 1849
Man from the West, The 1912 (Imp)
Man, Hat and Cocktail 1907 (V)
Man Hater, The 1917 ( ) 610
Man Higher Up, The 1913 (V) 332
Man Hunter, The 1919 (F) 868
Man in Possession, The 1915 (Br) 1487, 1815
Man in the Box 1908 (AMB)
Man in the Making 1912 (Ed)
Man in the Moonlight, The 1919 (Un) 1859, 2211, 2490
Man in the Open 1919 (UP) 771, 866
Man Next Door, The 1913 (Key) 1666, 2465
Man of Bronze, The 1918 (W) 2485
Man of Courage 1919 ( ) 25
Man of Honor 1919 (M) 857, 1589
Man of Might, A--serial 1919 (V) 785, 1364, 2202
   1. The Riven Flag
   2. The Leap through Space
   3. The Creeping Death
   4. The Gripping Hand
   5. The Human Shield
   6. The Height of Torment
   7. Into the Trap
   8. The One Chance
   9. The Crashing Horror
  10. Double Crossed
  11. The Ship of Dread
  12. The Volcano's Prey
  13. The Flood of Despair
  14. The Living Catapult
  15. The Rescue
Man of Sorrow, A 1916 (F) 209, 868
Man of the Hour 1914 ( ) 950, 1255, 2698
Man Overboard 1905 (AMB)
Man She Married, The 1916 (V) 1991
Man the Army Made, A 1917 ( ) 2558
Man Trap, The 1917 ( ) 1928, 2095
Man under the Bed, The 1910 (Ed)
Man Wanted 1905 (V)
Man Who Could Not Lose, The 1914 ( ) 231
Man Who Couldn't Beat God, The 1915 (V) 566
Man Who Disappeared, The--serial 1914 (Ed) 1656, 1930, 1977
   1. The Black Mask
   2. The Hunted Animal

3. The Double Cross
4. The Light on the Wall
5. With His Hands
6. The Gap
7. Face to Face
8. A Matter of Minutes
9. The Living Dead
10. By the Aid of a Film
Man Who Forgot, The 1919 (Br) 1453
Man Who Laughed Last, The 1915 ( ) 1208
Man Who Learned, The 1910 (Ed)
Man Who Made Good, The 1912 (Ed)
Man Who Might Have Been, The 1919 ( ) 1566
Man Who Stayed at Home, The 1915 (Hep) 812, 1289, 2531, 2744
Man Who Stayed at Home, The 1919 ( ) 108, 2756
Man Who Took a Chance, The 1917 ( ) 1308
Man Who Turned White, The 1919 ( ) 402, 437, 2693
Man Who Was Afraid, The 1916 (Es) 2700
Man Who Went Out, The 1913 (Domino) 906, 2561
Man Who Woke Up, The 1918 ( ) 1853, 2453
Man Who Won, The 1919 (Br) 831, 1877, 1918
Man Who Wouldn't Shoot, The 1919 (Un) 398
Man Who Wouldn't Tell, The 1919 (V) 2767
Man with the Ladder and the Hose, The 1906 (V)
Man with the Weak Heart, The 1910 (Ed)
Man with the White Gloves, The 1906 ( ) 1081
Man with Three Wives, A 1909 (Ed) 2513
Man Within, The 1914 ( ) 651, 2112
Man without a Country, The 1909 (Ed)
Man without a Soul, The 1916 (Br) 2179
Mandrin's Gold, The 1919 ( ) 606, 1048, 1971
Manhattan Madness 1916 (FA/Tri) 200, 201, 406, 857, 1432, 2130
Manhattan Nights 1917 (F) 1832
Maniac Barber, The 1902 (AMB)
Maniac Chase 1904 (Ed)
Maniac Cook, The 1908 (AMB) 1542
Manicure Fools the Husband, The 1903 (AMB)
Manicure Lady, The 1911 (Bio)
Manicurist and the Mutt, The 1913 (Kal) 1924
Manja 1919 ( ) 1922
Manly Man, A 1911 (Imp) 2047
Manon Lescaut 1914 (Playgoers) 438, 1901, 2374
Man's Country, A 1919 (Robertson-Cole) 449, 763, 991, 1268, 2175, 2194, 2775
Man's Desire 1919 ( ) 192, 619, 2485
Man's Duty, A 1912 ( ) 2112, 2356
Man's Enemy 1914 (Bio) 1029
Man's Fight, A 1919 ( ) 866, 1241, 2627
Man's Genesis 1912 (Bio) 357, 1182, 1526, 1613, 1714, 1751, 1831, 2000, 2368
Man's Lust for Gold 1912 (Bio) 357, 1182, 2513

Man's Man, A 1917 (Paralta) 1166, 1431, 1558, 2002, 2627, 2779
Man's Perogative 1915 (Las) 809
Man's Way, A 1915 (Mu) 344, 989
Mansard Mystery, The 1917 ( ) 1658
Mansion of Misery, A 1913 (Selig) 1589, 2770
Mantle of Charity, The 1918 ( ) 905, 1894
Manxman, The 1916 (Br) 22, 1931, 2138
Many a Slip 1915 (Christie) 525
Manya 1918 ( ) 2210
Marathon, The 1919 (P) 1586, 2055
Marathon Craze, The 1909 (V)
Marble Heart, The 1913 (Bio) 1832
Marble Heart, The; or The Sculptor's Dream 1909 (V)
Marcellini Millions, The 1917 ( ) 2002
March Hare, The 1919 (Br) 776, 1931, 2536
Maria Marten 1913 (Br) 834, 2138
Maria Rosa 1916 (Par) 411, 683, 869, 1386, 1439, 1925, 2112, 2541
Marian, the Holy Terror 1914 ( ) 785
Marie Ltd. 1919 (Reelart) 273, 1600
Marionettes, The 1917 (Select) 132, 462, 950, 1438, 2811
Marjorie's Diamond Ring 1912 (Ed)
Mark of Cain, The 1917 (Red Feather/Un) 435, 449, 885, 1141, 1518, 1876, 2042, 2209, 2570, 2757
Marked Cards 1918 ( ) 192
Marked Man, A 1916 (Br) 943
Marked Man, A 1918 (Un) 398, 1011, 1719
Marked Men 1919 (Un) 398, 1659, 2736
Marked Time-Table, The 1910 (Bio) 1224
Marked Trail, The 1910 (Es) 50
Market of Souls 1919 (Par) 627
Market of Vain Desire, The 1916 ( ) 2693
Marquise, The 1915 ( ) 333
Marriage 1918 ( ) 375
Marriage a la Carte 1916 (Es) 663, 2700
Marriage Blunder, The 1918 ( ) 2416
Marriage Bubble, 1918 ( ) 715, 1622
Marriage by Telephone * (P) 1575
Marriage Is a Puzzle 1911 (P) 1575
Marriage Lie, The 1917 (Un) 1911
Marriage Market, The 1918 (WS) 231, 835
Marriage of Convenience, A 1909 (V)
Marriage of Convenience, A 1919 ( ) 375
Marriage of Kitty, The 1915 (Las)
Marriage of the Molly O', The 1916 (Tri) 1182, 1751
Marriage of the Underworld 1914 ( ) 1450
Marriage of William Ashe 1916 (Hep) 22, 1289, 2171, 2531
Marriage Price, The 1919 (Par) 91, 888, 2444
Marriage Ring, The 1918 ( ) 189, 998, 1280, 1690
Marriage Virgin, The see All Night
Marriages Are Made 1919 ( ) 1329
Married for Millions 1906 (AMB)
Married in Haste 1919 ( ) 856
Married in Name Only 1917 ( ) 2410
Marrying Gretchen 1914 ( ) 785
Marshall's Capture, The 1913 ( ) 785
Marta of the Lowlands 1914 (FP) 1394, 2052
Martha's Rebellion 1912 (V) 332, 901

Martha's Vindication 1916 (FA/Tri) 1254,
   1530, 1563, 1756, 1998, 2483, 2523
Martin Chuzzlewit 1912 (Ed) 299, 968,
   1117, 1656, 1970, 2379
Martin Johnson's Voyage 1912 (Martin
   Johnson Prods.) 1366
Martyrs of the Alamo, The 1915 (Key/Tri)
   396, 686, 1153
Mary Ann in Society 1917 ( ) 2486
Mary Girl 1917 (Br) 834
Mary Gusta 1917 ( ) 1764
Mary Had a Little Lamb 1903 (Lubin)
Mary Had a Little Lamb 1912 (Ed)
Mary in Stage Land 1912 (Ed)
Mary Jane's Lovers 1909 (Ed)
Mary Jane's Pa 1917 ( ) 1191, 1360
Mary Moreland 1917 (Mu) 336, 824, 2088
Mary Regan 1919 (FN) 1239, 1796, 1827,
   2378, 2472
Mary Stuart 1913 (Ed) 547, 968, 1656
Mary's Little Lobster 1917 (Key/Tri)
   2501
Mary's Masquerade 1911 (Ed)
Ma's Apron Strings 1913 (V) 332
Masher, The 1907 (Selig)
Masher, The 1910 (Bio) 2047
Mashing the Masher 1908 (V)
Mask, The 1918 ( ) 1946
Mask of Love, The 1917 (Laemle Big U/
   Un) 352, 449
Masked Avenger, The 1918 ( ) 612
Masked Mirth 1917 (Vogue) 2608
Masked Raider, The--serial 1919 (Arrow)
   1397, 1912, 2003, 2486
Masked Wrestler, The 1917 (Es) 2700
Masks and Faces 1914 (Bio) 1117
Masks and Faces 1917 (Ideal) 43, 553,
   777, 923, 1488, 2712
Masquerader, The /aka/ The Female
   Impersonator; The Picnic; Putting
   One Over 1914 (Key) 65, 73, 451,
   460, 531, 791, 815, 1651, 1906,
   2336
Masqueraders, The 1906 (AMB)
Masqueraders, The 1908 (Lubin)
Masqueraders, The 1915 (FP) 667, 724,
   1600
Massacre, The 1912 (Bio) 731, 1182,
   1223, 1613, 1665, 1714, 2045, 2513,
   2728
Master and Pupil 1912 (Ed)
Master and the Man 1911 (Imp) 2047
Master Crook Outwitted by a Child, The
   1914 (B) 149, 150
Master Crook Turns Detective, The 1914
   (Br) 150
Master 44 1916 ( ) 612
Master Hand, The 1915 (F) 1043, 1524
Master Key, The--serial 1914 (Un) 420,
   933, 1120, 1199, 1245, 1544
Master Magician Alcrofrisbas, The 1903
   (Melies)
Master Man 1919 ( ) 1404
Master Mind, The 1914 ( ) 283
Master Mystery, The--serial 1919 Octagon
   Films, Inc.) 292, 327, 1054, 1295,
   1753, 2049, 2486
Master of His House 1917 (V) 2081, 2194,
   2521
Master of Men, The 1917 (Br) 177
Master of Men, The 1919 ( ) 1448

Master of the Black Rock, The 1909
   (Lubin)
Master of the Merripit, The 1915 (Br) 177
Master Thief, The 1915 (Es) 353
Matching Billy 1918 (Go) 2009
Matchmakers, The 1917 (M) 768, 1707
Mate of the Sally Ann 1918 ( ) 1841,
   2032
Maternal Spark, The 1917 ( ) 2355
Maternity 1917 (Mu) 265, 273, 853, 2061
Mates and Models 1919 (V) 1161
Matilda's Legacy 1915 (Lubin) 1161
Mating, The 1915 (V) 1547
Mating of Marcella 1918 (Tri) 627, 1153
Matrimaniac, The 1916 (FA/Tri) 406,
   676, 857, 1911, 2521, 2695, 2736
Matrimonial Deluge, A 1913 ( ) 785
Matrimonial Maneuvers 1913 (V) 565
Matrimonial Mixup, A 1916 (P) 1586
Matrimony 1916 (Tri) 673, 1246, 1476,
   2213
Maud 1911 (Br) 177
Maude Miller 1911 (Selig) 2770
Maude's Naughty Little Brother 1900 (Ed)
Max-Aeronaut 1909 (P) 1575
Max and His Mother-in-Law's False
   Teeth 1909 (P) 1575
Max and His Taxi 1917 (Es) 1575
Max and Jane Go to the Theatre * (P)
   1575
Max and Jane Make a Dessert * (P) 1575
Max and Maurice 1912 (Ed)
Max and the Clutching Hand 1915 (P) 1575
Max and the Statue 1912 (P) 1575
Max Attends an Inauguration * (P) 1575
Max between Two Women /aka/ Max
   between Two Fires 1915 (P) 1575
Max Comes Across 1917 (Es) 1575, 1733
Max Creates a Fashion 1912 (P) 1575
Max Does Not Like Cats * (P) 1575
Max Does Not Speak English 1912 (P)
   1575
Max Embarrassed 1911 (P) 1575
Max Gets the Reward 1912 (P) 1575
Max--Heartbreaker 1918 (Es) 1575
Max Hypnotized 1911 (P) 1575
Max in a Dilemma 1910 (P) 1575
Max in a Museum 1909 (P) 1575
Max in a Taxi 1917 (Es) 1575, 1733
Max in the Alps 1911 (P) 1575
Max in the Arms of His Family 1911 (P)
   1575
Max in the Movies 1911 (P) 1575
Max Is Absent-Minded 1910 (P) 1575
Max Is almost Married 1910 (P) 1575
Max Is Decorated * (P) 1575
Max Is Distraught 1911 (P) 1575
Max Is Forced to Work 1911 (P) 1575
Max Is Jealous 1912 (P) 1575
Max Is Stuck Up 1910 (P) 1575
Max, Jockey for Love 1911 (P) 1575
Max--Magician 1912 (P) 1575
Max Makes a Conquest 1912 (P) 1575
Max Makes Music 1912 (P) 1575
Max on Skis 1911 (P) 1575
Max--Pedicurist 1910 (P) 1575
Max--Photographer 1909 (P) 1575
Max Plays Detective 1918 (Es) 1575
Max Plays in Drama * (P) 1575
Max Searches for a Sweetheart 1911 (P)
   1575

Max Takes a Bath 1909 (P) 1575
Max Takes up Boxing 1911 (P) 1575
Max Teaches the Tango /aka/ Too Much
  Mustard 1910 (P) 1575
Max--Toreador 1912 (P) 1575
Max, Victim of Quinquina 1911 (P) 1575
Max--Virtuoso 1912 (P) 1575
Max Wants a Divorce 1917 (Es) 1496,
  1575, 1733
Max Wears Tight Shoes 1910 (P) 1575
Max's Astigmatism 1911 (P) 1575
Max's Double 1912 (P) 1575
Max's Duel 1912 (P) 1575
Max's Hanging 1909 (P) 1575
Max's Hat * (P) 1575
Max's Honeymoon 1912 (P) 1575
Max's Marriage 1912 (P) 1575
Max's Mother-in-Law 1912 (P) 1575
Max's Neighborly Neighbors 1911 (P) 1575
Max's New Landlord 1909 (P) 1575
Max's Vacation 1912 (P) 1575
May and December 1910 (Bio) 2047
May Blossom 1915 (Las) 1924
May to December 1912 (Imp) 2047
Mayblossom 1912 (P) 931, 2748
Mayor of Filbert, The 1919 ( ) 186, 2128,
  2392
Mazeppa 1910 (Selig) 2770
Mazie Puts One Over 1914 ( ) 486
Me and Jack 1902 (AMB)
Me and My Moke 1916 (Br) 43
Measure for Measure 1909 (Lubin)
Measure of a Man, The 1915 (Rex/Un)
  352, 449, 762
Mechanical Statue and the Ingenious
  Servant, The 1907 (V)
Mechanical Toy, The 1904 (AMB)
Meddlers and Moonshine 1918 (V) 2367
Medicine Bend 1916 ( ) 1273
Medicine Bottle, The 1909 (AMB) 685
Medicine Man, The 1917 (Tri) 2479
Meet Me at the Fountain 1904 (Lubin)
Meet Me at the Station 1908 (Lubin)
Meet Me Down at Luna, Lena 1905 (Lubin)
Meg o' the Woods 1918 ( ) 2558
Meg, the Lady 1916 (Br) 834, 2138
Melodrama of Yesterday 1912 (Imp)
Melomaniac, The 1903 (Melies)
Melting Pot, The 1915 (Kal) 1064, 1193,
  2750
Member of the Tattersalls 1919 (Br) 831
Memories in Men's Souls 1914 (V) 297,
  1876, 2523
Memories of a Pioneer 1912 (Un)
Men 1918 ( ) 1532, 2661
Men and Muslin 1913 (Bio) 1029
Men and Woman 1914 (Mu) 141, 1117,
  1665, 1914, 1924, 2513
Men from Bitter Roots, The 1916 (F) 868
Men of the Desert 1917 ( ) 2794
Men, Women and Money 1919 (FP/Las)
  83, 486, 606, 1080, 1417, 1925,
  2051, 2788
Men Women Marry 1919 (Go) 405, 1288
Menace, The 1918 (V) 1088
Menace to Carlotta, The 1914 (Rex/Un)
  348, 352, 449, 762, 1705
Mended Lute, The 1909 (Bio) 1450, 1865,
  2081, 2103
Mender of the Nets, The 1912 (Bio)
  1753, 1941, 2047, 2728

Mennett 1909 (Lubin)
Mental Suicide 1913 ( ) 2112
Mephisto's Affinity 1908 (Lubin)
Merchant of Venice 1908 (V) 1333
Merchant of Venice, The 1911 (FdA) 215
Merchant of Venice, The 1912 (T) 52,
  184, 268, 1468, 2201
Merchant of Venice, The 1914 (Un) 1007,
  1391, 2422, 2711
Merchant of Venice, The 1916 (Bw) 293,
  428, 1488
Mercy Merrick 1913 ( ) 968
Merely a Married Man 1915 (Key) 1651
Merely Mary Ann 1916 (Pal) 272, 887,
  1764
Merely Mrs. Stubbs 1917 (Hep) 812, 2531
Merely Players 1918 ( ) 1048
Mermaid, The 1904 (Melies)
Mermaid, The 1912 (Hep) 2744
Merry Chase, A 1915 (Starlight) 92
Merry Frolics of Satan, The 1906 (Melies)
  The Laboratory of Satan
  The Devilish Kitchen
Merry-Go-Round 1898 (Ed)
Merry Widow Hat, The 1908 (Lubin)
Merry Widow Hat, The 1908 (V)
Merry Widow Waltz Craze, The 1908 (Ed)
Merry Widower, The; or The Rejuvenation
  of a Fossil 1908 (V)
Mesmerist and Country Couple 1899 (Ed)
Message, The 1909 (Bio) 1450, 1182
Message from the Moon, A 1912 (Bio)
Message in the Bottle, The 1911 (Imp)
  2047
Message of the Lillies 1919 ( ) 116
Message of the Mouse, The 1917 (V) 1047,
  2472
Message of the Violin, The 1910 (Bio)
  1593, 2728
Messenger, The 1918 (King-Bee) 1161,
  2733
Messenger Boy and the Ballet Girl, The
  1905 (AMB)
Messenger Boy's Mistake, The 1903 (Ed)
Meteor, The 1902 (AMB)
Metropolitan Handicap 1903 (AMB)
Mexican Bill 1909 (Lubin)
Mexican Love Story, A 1908 (V)
Mexican Sweethearts 1909 (Bio) 2047
Mexican's Gratitude, A 1909 (Es) 50
Mice and Men * (FP) 482, 1924
Michael McShane, Matchmaker 1912 (V)
  332
Michael O'Halloran 1919 ( ) 269, 2124
Michael Strogoff 1910 (Ed)
Michael Strogoff 1914 (Lubin) 18
Mickey 1918 (Go) 506, 1105, 1896, 1933,
  1941, 1957, 2687
Mickey 1918 (Sennett) 791, 1113, 1504,
  1424
Mickey Gets Ready 1919 (Go) 1941
Microbe, The 1919 (M) 631
Microscope Mystery, The 1916 (Tri) 242,
  315, 1613, 2521, 2736
Mid the Cannon's Roar 1910 (Ed)
Middleman, The 1915 (Br) 43
Midget's Revenge, The 1912 (V) 2523
Midnight Adventure, A 1909 (Bio) 315,
  1363, 2047, 2081, 2368
Midnight Cupid, A 1910 (Bio) 1224, 1933,
  2368

Midnight Disturbance 1909 ( ) 2608
Midnight Elopement, A 1912 (Key) 1941, 2465
Midnight Express, The 1908 (Lubin)
Midnight Intruder 1904 (Ed)
Midnight Madness 1918 ( ) 495, 1166
Midnight Man, The--serial 1919 (Un) 556, 939, 1025, 1317, 1367, 1373, 1896, 2057, 2229, 2415, 2797
   1. Cast Adrift
   2. Deadly Enemies
   3. Ten Thousand Dollars Reward
   4. At Bay
   5. Unmasked
   6. Elevator Mystery
   7. The Electric Foe
   8. Shadow of Fear
   9. The Society Hold-up
  10. Blazing Torch
  11. The Death Ride
  12. The Tunnel of Terror
  13. A Fight to the Finish
  14. Jaws of Death
  15. Wheel of Terror
  16. Hurled from the Heights
  17. The Cave of Destruction
  18. A Wild Finish
Midnight Marauder, The 1911 (Bio)
Midnight Phantasy, A 1903 (AMB)
Midnight Ride of Paul Revere 1907 (Ed)
Midnight Romance, A 1919 (FN) 780, 1153, 1280, 2472, 2711
Midnight Sons, The 1909 (Lubin)
Midnight Stage 1919 ( ) 763, 998, 1404
Midnight Supper, A 1909 (Ed)
Midnight Trail, The 1918 (Mu) 2201
Midnight Wedding, The 1914 (Br) 150
Midshipman Easy 1915 (Br) 834, 2138
'Midst Woodland Shadows 1914 ( ) 2472
Midsummer Night's Dream, A 1909 (V) 8, 453, 564, 565, 566
Midsummer Night's Dream, A 1913 (Deutsche Bioscop) 203, 492
Midsummer-Tide 1912 (Ingvald C. Oes)
Midwinter Night's Dream; or Little Joe's Luck 1906 (V)
Mifanwy 1913 (Br) 503
Might and the Man 1917 (FA/Tri) 1911
Mignon 1895 (W) 1820
Mignon 1915 (W) 221, 2035
Mikado, The 1919 (F) 557
Mike and Jake at the Beach 1913 (Joker/Un) 81, 878, 1651, 2636
Mike Got the Soap in His Eyes 1903 (AMB)
Mike the Miser 1911 (Ed)
Mike's Hero 1911 (Ed)
Milady o' the Beanstalk 1919 (P) 1988
Mile-a-Minute Kendall 1918 (Par) 852, 2045, 2046
Mile-a-Minute Mary 1918 ( ) 720
Milestones 1916 (Br) 831, 1918
Militant Schoolman, A * (Selig Polyscope) 1849
Militant Suffragette see A Busy Day
Military Judas, A 1914 ( ) 2096
Milker's Mishap, The 1897 (Ed)
Mill Girl, The 1907 (V)
Mill Girl, The 1909 (Lubin)
Mill Girl, The 1913 (Hep) 2531
Mill of Life, The 1914 (V) 2523
Miller's Daughter, The 1905 (Ed)

Millinery Bomb, A 1913 (V) 332, 901
Million a Minute, A 1916 (M) 656
Million Bid, A 1914 ( ) 1877, 2472
Million Dollar Dollies, The 1918 (M) 743, 744, 1046
Million Dollar Job see A Film Johnny
Million Dollar Mystery, The--serial 1914 (T) 272, 603, 606, 871, 1118, 1468, 1562, 2430
   1. The Airship in the Night
   2. The False Friend
   3. A Leap in the Dark
   4. The Top Floor Flat
   5. At the Bottom of the Sea
   6. The Coaching Party of the Countess
   7. The Doom of the Auto Bandits
   8. The Wiles of a Woman
   9. The Leap from an Ocean Liner
  10. *
  11. In the Path of the Fast Express
  12.-14. *
  15. The Borrowed Hydroplane
  16. Drawn into the Quicksand
  17. A Battle of Wits
  18.-21. *
  22. Million Dollar Mystery
  23. The Mystery Solved
Millionaire, The 1917 (King-Bee) 1161, 2733
Millionaire and the Girl, The 1910 (Es) 50
Millionaire Baby, The 1915 ( ) 2221
Millionaire Cowboy, 1910 (Selig Polyscope) 1849
Millionaire for a Day 1912 (Imp)
Millionaire Paupers, The 1915 (Rex/Un) 449, 1518, 1862, 2398, 2559, 2781
Millionaire Pirate 1919 (Un) 495, 898, 2211
Millionaire Vagrant, The 1917 (Par) 281, 1016, 1241, 2096, 2392
Millionaire's Double, The 1917 ( ) 141, 286
Mills of the Gods, The 1909 (Bio) 79, 1363, 1542
Mind Cure, The 1912 ( ) 2748
Mind-the-Paint Girl, The 1919 (V) 698, 2232, 2472, 2535
Mine at Last 1909 (V)
Mine on the Yukon, The 1912 (Ed)
Miner and Camille, The 1910 (Ed)
Miner's Daughter, The 1908 (Lubin)
Miner's Daughter, The 1908 (V)
Miner's Heart, The 1912 (Eclair)
Miner's Romance, A 1914 (Nestor/Un) 449, 1197, 1705, 2635
Minerva's Mission 1915 ( ) 1028
Mingling Spirits 1915 (Christie) 525
Minister's Daughter, The 1909 (Ed)
Minister's Hat, The 1903 (Bio)
Minister's Wooing, The 1903 (AMB)
Minstrel Mishaps 1908 (Ed)
Mints of Hell 1919 ( ) 715
Miracle Man, The 1919 (Art/Par) 358, 449, 525, 763, 779, 856, 1327, 1523, 1800, 1919, 2605
Miracle of Life, The 1915 (Mu) 905

Miracle of Love 1919 (Par) 567, 804, 2227, 2444
Miraculous Eggs 1907 (Ed)
Miraculous Recovery, A 1911 (Br) 177
Mirandy Smiles 1918 (Par) 164, 958, 1417, 1697, 1764
Mirror, The 1911 (Imp) 2047
Misadventures of a Mighty Monarch, The 1914 (V) 332, 901
Misadventures of a Piece of Veal 1896 (GB) 1102
Misappropriated Turkey, A 1913 (Bio)
Mischances of a Photographer, The 1908 (Melies)
Mischievous Boys 1904 (Paley & Steiner)
Mischievous Sketch, A 1907 (Melies)
Mischievous Willie's Rocking Chair Motor 1902 (AMB)
Miser, The 1908 (Melies)
Miser, The 1915 ( ) 1581
Miser Murphy's Wedding Present 1914 (V) 2523
Miser's Heart, The 1911 (Bio) 731, 1613, 1714
Miser's Hoard, The 1907 (V)
Miser's Reversion, The 1916 ( ) 272
Misguided Love 1911 (Ingvald C. Oes)
Mishaps of Musty Suffer, The 1916 (K) 2702
Misleading Lady, The 1916 (Es) 1795, 2130
Misleading Widow, The 1918 (Art/Par) 333, 586, 1836
Misplaced Foot, A 1914 (Key) 65, 791, 1941
Misplaced Jealousy 1911 (Bio)
Miss Adventure 1919 ( ) 1329
Miss Ambition 1918 (V) 243, 1088, 1673, 2232
Miss Crusoe 1919 ( ) 442, 1142, 2518
Miss Dulcie from Dixie 1919 ( ) 1047, 1426, 1547
Miss Fatty's Seaside Lovers 1914 (Key) 65
Miss George Washington 1916 (FP) 482, 2719
Miss Innocence 1918 (F) 392
Miss Jackie of the Navy 1918 ( ) 905
Miss Jerry 1894 (Black) 155, 571
Miss Nobody 1917 ( ) 1312
Miss Petticoats 1916 ( ) 273, 1255
Miss Robinson Crusoe 1917 (F) 1832
Miss Sherlock Holmes 1908 (Ed)
Miss Sticky Maufit Kiss 1915 (V) 768
Miss U. S. A. 1917 (F) 392
Missing 1918 (Par) 281, 1050, 1800
Missing Bank Notes, The 1915 (V) 2521
Missing Link, The 1917 (Br) 1487
Missing Links, The 1915 (FA/Tri) 497, 1182, 1353, 2521, 2523
Missing the Tide 1918 (Br) 43, 503, 1018, 1289
Mission Bells 1914 (Bio) 79
Mission of a Flower see The Geranium
Missionary and the Maid, The 1909 (Ed)
Mistake, The 1913 (Bio) 2513, 2680
Mistake in Rustlers, A 1916 (Selig Polyscope) 1849
Mistake Slight, A 1911 (V) 871
Mistaken Bandit, The 1910 (Es) 50
Mistaken Identity, A 1908 (Melies)

Mistaken Identity, A 1919 ( ) 1439
Mistaken Masher, The 1913 (Key) 1941, 2368, 2465
Mistakes Will Happen 1911 (Ed)
Mr. Aladdin of Broadway 1917 ( ) 1519
Mr. Barnes of New York 1914 (V) 566, 769, 1119
Mr. Bolter's Infatuation 1912 (V) 332
Mr. Bolter's Niece 1913 (V) 332, 565, 901
Mr. Bolter's Sweetheart 1912 (V) 2523
Mr. Bragg, a Fugitive 1911 (Bio)
Mr. Bullington Ran the House 1912 (V) 901
Mr. Bumptious, Detective 1911 (Ed)
Mr. Bumptious on Birds 1910 (Ed)
Mr. Bunny in Disguise 1914 (V) 157, 332, 901
Mr. Bunnyhug Buys a Hat for His Bride 1914 (V) 332, 901
Mr. Butler Butles 1912 (V) 2523
Mr. Butt-In 1906 (AMB)
Mr. Butt-in-Sky 1906 (Winthrop Press)
Mr. Butterburn 1918 ( ) 1621
Mr. Dauber & the Mystifying Picture 1905 (Melies)
Mr. Easymark 1903 (AMB)
Mr. Fix-It 1912 (Key) 1666, 1941, 2368, 2465
Mr. Fixit 1918 (Art/Par) 387, 664, 857, 1206, 1661
Mr. Gay and Mrs. 1907 (AMB)
Mr. Gilfil's Love Story * (Br) 1968
Mr. Goode, Samaritan 1916 ( ) 1286, 1753
Mr. Haygood Producer 1912 (Selig Polyscope) 1849
Mr. Hurry-up of New York 1907 (AMB)
Mr. Inquisitive 1909 (Lubin)
Mr. Jack Caught in the Dressing Room 1904 (AMB)
Mr. Jack Entertains in His Office 1904 (AMB)
Mr. Jack in the Dressing Room 1904 (AMB)
Mr. Jones at the Ball 1908 (AMB) 209, 526, 994, 1336, 1511, 1701, 2212, 2368
Mr. Jones' Burglar 1909 (Bio) 209, 526, 1151
Mr. Jones Entertains 1908 (AMB) 526, 1511, 1701
Mr. Jones Has a Card Party 1909 (AMB) 526, 2368
Mr. Murray's Wedding Present 1914 (V) 297
Mr. Parker Hero 1917 (M) 768, 1707
Mr. Peck Goes Calling 1911 (Bio)
Mr. Physical Culture's Surprise Party 1909 (V)
Mr. Pickwick's Predicament 1912 (Ed)
Mr. Shoestring in the Hole 1919 ( ) 1987
Mr. Silent Haskins 1914 (Mu) 1188
Mr. Vampire 1916 ( )
Mr. Wee 1919 (Br) 834, 1488
Mrs. and Mr. Duff 1909 (Melies)
Mrs. Black Is Back 1914 (FP) 251, 1339, 1486
Mrs. Carter's Necklace 1912 (V) 2523
Mrs. Dane's Defense 1918 (Par) 957
Mrs. 'Enery 'Awkins 1911 (V) 2523
Mrs. George Washington 1909 (Bio) 2074
Mrs. Jones Entertains 1908 (Bio) 901, 1992

Mrs. Jones' Lover or I Want My Hat 1909 (Bio) 209, 526, 1151
Mrs. Leffingwell's Boots 1918 (Sel) 877, 927, 2521
Mrs. Murphy's Cook * (Selig Polyscope) 1849
Mrs. Nag 1911 (V) 1941
Mrs. Nation & Her Hatchet Brigade 1901 (Lubin)
Mrs. Plumb's Pudding 1915 (Un) 310, 1630, 1700
Mrs. Reynolds 1918 (WS) 231, 835
Mrs. Slacker 1918 ( ) 1312, 1445
Mrs. Smifkins Wants Wood 1904 (AMB)
Mrs. Thompson 1919 (Br) 831
Mrs. Wiggs of the Cabbage Patch 1919 (Par) 296, 415, 482, 1293, 1310, 1640, 1969
Mistress Nell 1915 (FP) 1262, 1282, 1865, 2047
Misunderstanding, A 1907 (Lubin)
Misunderstood 1916 ( ) 2680
Misunderstood Boy, A 1913 (Bio) 141, 1029, 1182, 1714, 2000
Mixed Blood 1917 ( ) 200
Mixed Flats 1915 (Lubin) 1161
Mixed Nuts 1919 (Rolin/P) 1502
Mixup for Mazie, A 1915 (P) 1586
Mix-up in Hearts, A 1917 (King-Bee) 1161
Mix-up in Rain Coats 1911 (Bio)
Mix-up in the Gallery, A 1906 (Melies)
Mixup in the Movies, A * (Selig Polyscope) 1849
Model Wife, A 1915 (V) 157, 1876, 2663
Model Young Man, A 1914 (V) 768
Model's Confession, The 1918 ( ) 1166, 1518, 1696, 2074
Modern Cinderella, A 1911 (Ed)
Modern Cinderella, A 1917 (F) 392, 1878, 2738
Modern Dianas, The 1911 (Ed)
Modern Enoch Arden, A 1916 (Key/Tri) 815, 1342, 1726, 1749, 2165, 2510
Modern Highwayman, The 1912 (Imp)
Modern Husbands 1919 ( ) 771, 2680
Modern Love 1918 ( ) 1907
Modern Musketeer, A 1918 (Art/Par) 387, 664, 857, 1448, 1756, 1984, 2051
Modern Oliver Twist, The; or The Life of a Pickpocket 1906 (V)
Modern Othello, A 1913 (American Beauty) 905
Modern Othello, A 1917 ( ) 2698
Modern Prodigal, The 1910 (Bio) 1218, 1450, 2045
Modern Sappho, A 1905 (AMB)
Modern Snare, A 1913 ( ) 2112, 2125
Modern Taming of the Shrew, A 1916 (Tri) 866, 960
Modern Thelma, A 1916 (Pal) 1764
Modest Hero, A 1913 (Bio) 1029
Modest Young Man, A 1909 (Ed)
Modiste, The 1917 (King-Bee) 1161
Mogg Megone 1909 (V)
Mohawk's Way, A 1910 (Bio) 651, 1665, 2000, 2368
Molly Bawn 1916 (Hep) 1289, 2171, 2531
Molly Entangled 1917 (Art/Par) 927, 1764, 2047
Molly Go Get 'Em 1918 ( ) 905
Molly Make-Believe 1916 (FP) 482

Molly of the Follies 1919 ( ) 905, 1894
Molly Shawn 1917 (Art/Par) 1764
Molly the Drummer Boy 1914 (Ed) 631
Moment Before, The 1916 (FP) 957, 1266
Monday Morning in a Coney Island Police Court 1908 (Bio) 526
Money Corporal, The 1919 ( ) 1126, 1188, 1794, 1948
Money Corral, The see The Money Corporal
Money for Nothing 1916 (Br) 834, 1931
Money Isn't Everything 1918 ( ) 905, 1894
Money Kings 1914 (V) 2527
Money Lender, The 1908 (V)
Money Mad 1908 (AMB) 1336
Money Mad 1918 (Go) 269, 726, 1751
Money Madness 1917 (Tri) 2056
Money Magic 1917 (V) 785, 1876, 2487
Money Master, The 1915 ( ) 2623
Money to Burn 1911 (Ed)
Money to Burn 1916 ( ) 377
Moneyless Honeymoon, The 1916 (Par) 1686
Monkey Business 1905 (AMB)
Monkey Movie Hero 1916 ( ) 676
Monkey Shines 1915 (Starlight) 92
Monkeyland 1908 (V)
Monkey's Feast 1896 (AMB)
Monkey's Feast 1903 (AMB)
Monna Vanna 1915 ( ) 1372
Monroe 1913 ( ) 2002
Monsieur 1911 (Ed)
Monsieur Beaucaire 1905 (V)
Monsieur Stäp--cartoon 1913 (French) 512
Monster, The 1903 (Melies)
Montebank, The 1909 (Lubin)
Moon Riders, The--serial 1919 (Un) 9
Moonlight Serenade, A; or The Miser Punished 1904 (Melies)
Moonshine 1918 (FP/Las) 65, 1401, 1476, 2208
Moonshine Molly 1914 (Mu) 1182, 2112
Moonshine Trail 1913 (V) 297, 1047
Moonshiner, The 1904 (AMB)
Moonshiners, The 1916 (Key/Tri) 253, 1115, 1476, 2208
Moonstone, The 1915 ( ) 1959
Moonstone of Fez, The 1914 (V) 566, 2521
Moral Courage 1917 ( ) 1991
Moral Deadline, The 1919 (WS) 835, 1991
Moral Fabric, The 1916 ( ) 1836
Moral Law, The 1918 ( ) 295
Moral Suicide 1918 ( ) 111, 1117, 1622, 1888
Morals of Marcus 1915 (FP) 752, 756
Morals of Men, The 1917 (Mu) 2760
Morals of Weybury, The 1916 (Br) 43, 2138
More Deadly Than the Male 1919 ( ) 543
More Excellent Way, The 1917 (V) 2129, 2472
More Money Than Manners 1916 (V) 2367
More Precious Than Gold 1912 (Ed)
More Than His Duty 1910 (Ed)
More Trouble 1918 ( ) 763, 1404
More Truth Than Poetry 1917 ( ) 2037
Moriarity 1916 ( ) 1288
Morning Alarm, A 1896 (Ed)
Morning Bath, A 1896 (Ed)

Morphis, the Death Drug 1914 (Hep) 2531
Mortgaged Wife 1917 (Un) 95, 2042
Mortmain 1915 (Las) 809, 1991
Moses Sells a Collar Button 1907 (Lubin)
Moth, The 1917 (Select) 1119, 1806, 1959,
    2523, 2643
Mother 1917 (FN) 2138
Mother and Daughters 1912 (Ed)
Mother and the Law 1919 (Go) 554, 1182,
    1565, 1591, 1751
Mother by Proxy 1910 (V) 2523
Mother Goose 1909 (Ed)
Mother, I Need You 1918 ( ) 1745
Mother-in-Law 1906 (V)
Mother-in-Law and the Artist's Model 1908
    (V)
Mother Instinct, The 1915 (Tri) 1016, 2780
Mother McGuire 1919 ( ) 2221
Mother o'Dreams 1919 ( ) 2221
Mother o'Mine * ( ) 1472
Mother of Dartmour, A 1916 (Br) 2138
Mother of Men, A 1914 ( ) 1064
Mother of the Ranch, The 1912 (Es) 50
Mothering Heart, The 1913 (Bio) 1029,
    1655, 1832, 2023
Motherlove 1916 (Br) 834, 1931, 2138
Mother's Angel Child 1905 (AMB)
Mother's Atonement, A 1915 (Rex/Un)
    449, 1711, 2398, 2781
Mother's Boy 1913 (Key) 65, 509
Mother's Child 1916 (Vim) 1161, 2070
Mother's Crime, A 1908 (V)
Mother's Dream 1907 (Lubin)
Mothers-in-Law 1918 ( ) 495
Mother's Influence, A 1914 ( ) 2112
Mother's Influence, A 1916 (Br) 2138
Mothers of France 1916 (Meres Francoise)
    212, 2409
Mother's Sin, A 1918 (V) 2767
Moths and the Flame, The 1910 (Ed)
Moulding, The 1913 ( ) 2472
Mountain Blizzard, A 1910 (Ed)
Mountain Dew 1917 ( ) 2780
Mountain Girl, The 1915 ( ) 1028, 1563
Mountain Justice 1915 (Rex/Un) 449, 2398,
    2559, 2776
Mountain Maid, A 1910 (Ed)
Mountain Rat, The 1914 ( ) 595, 1028,
    1029, 1450, 2680
Mountaineer, The 1908 (Lubin)
Mountaineer, The 1914 ( ) 2112
Mountaineer's Honor, The 1909 (Bio) 1363,
    2047
Mountaineer's Revenge, The 1908 (Lubin)
Mountaineer's Romance, The 1912 (Br)
    1873
Mourners, The; or The Clever Undertaking
    1908 (V)
Move On 1903 (Ed)
Move On 1917 (P) 2055
Movie Mad 1918 (Christie) 339
Movie Nut see A Film Johnny
Movie Star, A 1916 (Key/Tri) 37, 1084,
    1651, 1788, 2510, 2724
Moving 1917 (Par) 1868
Moving Day; or No Children Allowed 1905
    (V)
Moving Picture Cowboy 1914 (Selig
    Polyscope) 1849
Mud and Sand 1919 (Rolin/P) 1502
Mud Bath, A 1915 (Key) 1941

Muddled in Mud see A Muddy Romance
Muddy Romance, A /aka/ Muddled in
    Mud 1913 (Key) 1830, 1941, 2465,
    2510
Muffled Drums 1919 ( ) 715
Muggsy 1919 ( ) 2227
Muggsy Becomes a Hero 1910 (Bio) 731,
    2047
Muggsy's First Sweetheart 1910 (Bio) 901,
    2047, 2081
Mule Driver and the Garrulous Mate, The
    1910 (Ed)
Mules and Mortgages 1919 (V) 92, 1161
Mulligan's Waterloo 1909 (Ed)
Multiple Applause 1912 (Isidor Kitsee)
Mummer's Daughter, The 1908 (V)
Munition Girl's Romance, A 1917 (Br)
    1289
Murdock Trial, The 1914 (GB) 2604
Murphy's I. O. U. 1913 (Key) 864, 1666,
    2368, 2465
Murphy's Wake 1903 (AMB)
Murray's Mixup see His Hereafter
Music Hall see Tango Tangles
Music Hath Charm 1917 (M) 768, 1707
Music Master, The 1908 (Bio) 1089
Musical Marvels, The 1917 (Vogue) 2608
Musical Ride, The 1901 (Ed)
Musical Tramps see His Musical
    Career
Musketeers of Pig Alley, The 1912 (Bio)
    141, 251, 398, 1028, 1029, 1182,
    1832 1876, 2000, 2045, 2158
Must Be in Bed before Ten 1903 (AMB)
Mustang Pete comedy series 1913 (Es)
    2058
Mutiny on the Black Sea 1905 (AMB)
Mutts and Motors 1918 (V) 2367
My Baby 1912 (Bio) 141, 1029, 2047,
    2680
My Country First 1916 (P) 2546, 2754,
    2801
My Cousin 1918 (Art/Par) 423, 1545,
    2743
My Dog Dick * (P) 1575
My Double and How He Undid Me 1912
    (Ed)
My Dream Lady 1918 (Un) 1911
My Four Years in Germany 1918 (FN)
    633, 1001
My Friend, Mr. Dummy 1909 (Lubin)
My Friend, the Indian 1909 (Lubin)
My Hero 1912 (Bio) 141, 315, 398, 1028,
    1182, 1566, 1714, 2680
My Husband's Other Wife 1919 (Par) 281,
    1050, 1640
My Lady Incog 1916 (FP) 365, 667
My Lady Robin Hood 1919 (Reelcraft) 1099
My Lady's Slipper 1916 (V) 1437, 2472,
    2767
My Little Boy 1918 ( ) 1120
My Little Sister 1919 ( ) 1078, 1929
My Lord in Livery 1909 (Ed)
My Milliner's Bill 1910 (Ed)
My Mother 1918 (Un) 1472
My Official Wife 1914 (V) 1877, 2591,
    2616, 2767, 2811
My Old Dutch 1911 (V) 297, 566
My Old Dutch 1959 (GB) 812, 2604
My Own United States 1918 ( ) 1532
My Partner 1916 ( ) 1679

My Unmarried Wife 1917 (Un) 1911, 2356
My Valet 1915 (Key/Tri) 519, 650, 1257,
    1666, 1865, 1941, 2368
My Wife 1917 ( ) 333, 1223, 1902
Mysteries of Myra, The--serial 1916 (P)
    846, 1904, 2086, 2435, 2737
    1. *
    2. *
    3. The Mystic Mirrors
    4.-8. *
    9. The Invisible Destroyer
    10. Levitation
    11. The Fire-Elemental
    12. The Elixir of Youth
    13. Witchcraft
    14. Suspended Animation
    15. The Thought Monster
Mysteries of the Soul, The 1912 (New
    York Motion Picture Co.)
Mysterious Cafe, The 1901 (Ed)
Mysterious Client, The 1917 ( ) 435,
    1971, 2410
Mysterious Lodger, The 1914 (V) 566, 2521
Mysterious Midgets, The 1904 (AMB)
Mysterious Miss Terry, The 1917 (Art/Par)
    333, 1800
Mysterious Mr. Davey, The 1914 (V) 768
Mysterious Mr. Tiller 1917 ( ) 495
Mysterious Mrs. M., The 1917 ( ) 1677,
    2361
Mysterious Mrs. Musslewhite, The 1916
    (Un) 924, 927, 1694, 2407
Mysterious Phonograph, The 1908 (Lubin)
Mysterious Piano, The 1908 (Ambrosio)
    391, 2528
Mysterious Prince, The 1919 (Par) 1208
Mysterious Princess, The 1919 ( ) 752,
    756
Mysterious Retort, The 1906 (Melies)
Mysterious Rose, The 1914 ( ) 245, 610,
    926, 2343
Mysterious Shot, The 1914 ( ) 595, 1028,
    2045, 2680
Mystery Girl 1919 ( ) 486
Mystery of a Hansom Cab, The 1915 (Br)
    2179
Mystery of the Bridge of Notre Dame
    1912 (Eclair)
Mystery of the Double Cross, The--serial
    1917 (P) 144, 435, 954, 963, 1346,
    1444, 2496
    1. The Lady in Number 7
    2. The Masked Strangers
    3. An Hour to Live
    4. Kidnapped
    5. The Life Current
    6. The Dead Come Back
    7. Into Thin Air
    8. The Stranger Disposes
    9. When Jailbirds Fly
    10. The Hole-in-the-Wall
    11. Love's Sacrifice
    12. The Riddle of the Cross
    13. The Face of the Stranger
    14. The Hidden Brand
    15. The Double Cross
Mystery of the Garrison, The 1908
    (Melies)
Mystery of the Hindu Image 1914 ( ) 2672
Mystery of the Leaping Fish 1916 (Key/
    Tri) 857, 1121, 1602, 2194, 2352, 2467

Mystery of the Sleeping Death 1914 (Kal)
    1128, 1388, 1867
Mystery of the Yellow Aster Mine 1913
    ( ) 2112
Mystery of 13, The--serial 1919 (Burston
    Films) 640, 680, 885, 926, 929,
    1026, 1516, 1785, 1983, 2230, 2554
    1. Bitter Bondage
    2. Lights Out
    3. The Submarine Gardens
    4. The Lone Rider
    5. Blown to Atoms
    6. Single Handed
    7. Fire and Water
    8. Pirate Loot
    9. The Phantom House
    10. The Raid
    11. Bare Handed
    12. The Death Ride
    13. Brother against Brother
    14. The Man Hunt
    15. The 13th Card
Mystery Ship, The--serial 1917 (Un) 181,
    1004, 2774, 2802
    1. The Crescent Scar
    2. The Grip of Hate
    3. Adrift
    4. The Secret of the Tomb
    5. The Fire God
    6. Treachery
    7. One Minute to Live
    8. Hidden Hands
    9. The Black Masks
    10. The Rescue
    11. The Line of Death
    12. The Rain of Fire
    13. The Underground House
    14. The Masked Riders
    15. The House of Trickery
    16. The Forced Marriage
    17. The Deadly Torpedo
    18. The Fight in Mid-Air
Mystic Hour, The 1917 ( ) 1326
Mystic Re-Incarnation, A 1902 (AMB)
Mystic Swing, The 1900 (Ed)
Mystical Flame, The 1903 (Melies)

- N -

Nachenschnur des Tot 1910 ( ) 1614
Naked Fists 1918 (Un) 1186
Naked Yaqui 1912 (P) 1586
Nakhla 1917 (Selig Polyscope) 2106
Nan of Music Mountain 1917 (Art/Par)
    1201, 1307, 1580, 1975, 2112, 2149
Nanette of the Wilds 1916 (FP) 957
Napoleon 1906 (Blackton) 1047, 1318
Napoleon: the Man of Destiny 1909 (V)
Narrow Path, The 1918 ( ) 2683
Narrow Road, The 1912 (Bio) 251, 1328,
    1714, 2047
Narrow Trail, The 1917 (Tri) 281, 1188
Nation's Peril, A 1912 ( ) 2760
Natural Born Gambler, A 1916 (Bio) 2764
Natural Law, The 1918 ( ) 572
Nature Girl, The 1919 ( ) 1814
Nature of the Beast, The 1919 (Hep) 43
    2531
Nature's Gentleman 1918 (BR) 1453
Naughty Little Princess, The 1908 (V)

Naughty! Naughty! 1918 ( ) 189, 1283, 2164
Naulahka, The /aka/ The Jeweled Girdle 1918 (P) 27, 443, 752, 1876, 1971
Neal of the Navy--serial 1915 (P) 274, 532, 569, 1598, 2447
   1. The Survivors
   2. The Yellow Packet
   3. The Failure
   4. The Tattered Parchment
   5. A Message from the Past
   6. The Cavern of Death
   7. The Gun Runners
   8. The Yellow Peril
   9. The Sun Worshipers
  10. The Rolling Terror
  11. The Dreadful Pit
  12. The Worm Turns
  13. White Gods
  14. The Final Goal
Near to Earth 1913 (Bio) 141, 1751, 1832, 1941, 2513
Near-Tragedy, A 1912 (Bio)
Nearer My God to Thee 1917 (Hep) 812, 2531
Nearly a King 1916 (FP) 140
Nearly a Lady 1915 (Bo) 1348, 1865
Nearly a Papa 1915 (Christie) 525
Nearly Married 1917 (Go) 143, 1288, 1423
Nearly Newlyweds 1919 ( ) 1177
Nearsighted Mary 1909 (Lubin)
Nearsighted Professor, The 1908 (Lubin)
Necklace, The 1909 (Bio) 1363, 1511, 1593, 2062, 2047
Necklace, The 1911 ( ) 2748
Necklace of Crushed Rose Leaves, The 1912 (Ed)
Nectorine 1915 ( ) 1563, 1591
Necromancer, The 1903 (AMB)
Need of Gold, The 1907 (V)
Ne'er-Do-Well, The 1916 (Selig) 1595, 1957, 2770
Neglected Wife, The--serial 1917 (P) 260, 1061, 1158, 1652, 2169
   1. The Woman Alone
   2. The Weakening
   3. In the Crucible
   4. Beyond Recall
   5. Under Suspicion
   6. On the Precipice
   7. The Message on the Mirror
   8. A Relentless Fate
   9. Deepening Degradation
  10. A Veiled Intrigue
  11. A Reckless Indiscretion
  12. Embittered Love
  13. Revolting Pride
  14. Desperation
  15. A Sacrifice Supreme
Neighborly Neighbors 1908 (Lubin)
Neighbors 1912 (Bio)
Neighbors 1918 ( ) 853, 1255
Neighbors Who Borrow 1907 (Lubin)
Nell of the Pampas 1912 (Am) 1924
Nellie, the Beautiful Housemaid 1908 (V)
Nellie, the Model 1911 (V) 2523
Nellie, the Pretty Typewriter 1908 (Ed)
Nell's Last Deal 1911 (Ed)
Nelson 1919 (LFC) 374, 834, 1592
Neptune's Daughter 1912 (Es) 353
Neptune's Daughter 1914 (Un) 111, 1411, 2381

Neptune's Daughters 1903 (AMB)
Nero and the Burning of Rome 1908 (Ed)
Nerve and Gasoline 1916 (Vim) 1161
Nerves and the Man 1912 (Ed)
Nervy Jim and the Cop 1907 (Lubin)
Nervy Nat Kisses the Bride 1904 (Ed)
Nevada Girl, A 1909 (Centaur Film Co.)
Never Again 1910 (Bio) 2047
Never Again 1914 (V) 768
Never Again 1916 (Vim) 519, 1161
Never Eat Green Apples 1909 (V)
Never Kiss the Maid 1912 (P) 1575
Never Say Quit 1919 ( ) 2671
Never Too Old 1919 (Key) 1906, 2069
Never Touched Him 1903 (AMB)
Never Touched Me 1919 (P) 1586
New Adam and Eve 1915 ( ) 2614
New Apprentice, The 1907 (Lubin)
New Arrival, The 1907 (Lubin)
New Baby, The 1912 (Bio)
New Black Diamond Express 1900 (Ed)
New Breakfast Food, The 1908 (Lubin)
New Butler, The 1915 (Lubin) 1161, 1294, 2108
New Church Carpet, The 1911 (Ed)
New Conductor, The 1913 (Key) 2465
New Death Penalty, A 1907 (Melies)
New Dress, The 1911 (Bio) 1613, 2573, 2729
New Editor, The 1012 (Ed)
New Exploits of Elaine, The--serial 1915 (P) 67, 628, 1118, 2748
   1. The Serpent Sign
   2. The Cryptic Ring
   3. The Watching Eye
   4. The Vengeance of Wu Fang
   5. The Saving Circles
   6. Spontaneous Combustion
   7. The Ear in the Wall
   8. The Opium Smugglers
   9. The Tell-Tale Heart
  10. Shadows of War
New Governess, The 1909 (Lubin)
New Janitor, The /aka/ The New Porter; The Blundering Boob 1914 (Key) 451, 732, 791, 2208, 2336
New Life, A 1909 (Ed)
New Loves for Old 1918 ( ) 269, 1120
New Magdalene, The 1910 (Powers) 2748
New Maid, The 1903 (AMB)
New Maid, The 1908 (Lubin)
New Mirror, The 1908 (Lubin)
New Moon, The 1919 (Select) 317, 487, 683, 1003, 1006, 1275, 1656, 2523
New Neighbor, The 1912 (Key) 1666, 1941, 2465
New Old Master, A 1909 (Lubin)
New Policeman, The 1909 (Ed)
New Porter, The see The New Janitor
New Secretary, The 1914 (V) 901, 1027, 1684, 2161, 2621, 2663
New Stenographer, The 1904 (AMB)
New Stenographer, The 1908 (Ed)
New Stenographer, The 1911 (V) 332, 566, 901, 2043, 2590, 2604
New Trick, A 1909 (Bio)
New Version of "Personal" 1904 (Lubin)
New Way to Pay Debts, A 1908 (Lubin)
New Year, A 1908 (Lubin)
New Year's Gift, A 1908 (Lubin)
New York 1916 (P) 2105, 2783

New York Girl, A 1914 (Key) 2368
New York Hat, The 1912 (Bio) 141, 1028, 1029, 1182, 1714, 1751, 2045, 2047, 2368
New York Lights 1915 ( ) 2748
New York Luck 1917 (Mu) 2201
New York Peacock, The 1917 ( ) 2756
Newer Woman, The 1914 (Mu) 595, 1028, 1182
Newest Woman, The 1909 (Lubin
Newlyweds, The 1910 (Bio) 1363, 1831, 1992, 2000, 2047, 2368
Newlywed's Mix-up, The 1915 (Christie) 525
Newsboy, The 1905 (V)
Newsboy, The 1908 (Lubin)
Next 1903 (AMB)
Next Aisle Over 1919 (P) 1586
Nicht Lange Tauschte mich des Glück 1917 ( ) 1922
Nichtozhniye (Worthless) 1916 (Russian) 1995
Nick of Time Baby, The 1917 (Key/Tri) 83, 280, 1424, 1627, 2164, 2512, 2537, 2636
Niece and the Chorus Lady, The 1911 (Ed)
Niewolnica Zomyslow 1914 ( ) 1922
Niggard, The 1914 ( ) 2112
Nigger, The 1915 (F) 868, 2756
Nigger in the Woodpile, A 1904 (AMB)
Night and Morning 1915 (Br) 177
Night at the Gayety, A 1907 (Lubin)
Night before Christmas, The 1905 (Ed)
Night before Christmas, The 1912 (V) 565, 566
Night Duty 1904 (AMB)
Night in Dreamland, A 1907 (V)
Night in New York, A 1916 ( ) 2480
Night in the Show, A /aka/ Charlie at the Show 1915 (Es) 451, 1045, 1347, 1414, 1480, 1676, 2077, 2090, 2682, 2746, 2747
Night of Horror, A 1916 (German)
Night of Love 1917 ( ) 1603
Night of Terror, A 1911 (Ed)
Night of the Party, The 1906 (AMB)
Night of Thrills, A 1914 (Rex/Un) 449
Night Off, A 1906 (Lubin)
Night Out, A 1916 (Es) 451, 552, 901, 1045, 1347, 2070, 2077, 2160, 2608, 2746
Night Out, A; or He Couldn't Go Home until Morning 1908 (V)
Night Raider, The 1918 (M) 631, 1099
Night with Masqueraders in Paris, A 1908 (Melies)
Nightbirds of London, The 1915 (Hep) 1289, 2171, 2744
Nightingale, The 1914 (Alco) 139, 644, 2535
Nihilists, The 1905 (AMB)
Nina of the Theatre 1913 (Kal) 1388, 1867
Nina, the Flower Girl 1917 (Tri) 1602, 2000
Nine Lives of a Cat, The 1907 (Ed)
Nine o'Clock Town, A 1918 ( ) 473, 1261, 1948, 2096
Nine-Tenth of the Law 1918 ( ) 1562
Ninety and Nine, The 1916 (V) 1632, 2478
Ninety Nine 1918 ( ) 1614
Niobe 1915 (FP/Las) 2, 667

Nipper and the Curate 1915 (Br) 1487
Nipper's Bank Holiday 1915 (Br) 1487
Nipper's Busy Bee Time 1916 (Br) 1487
Nipper's Busy Holiday 1915 (Br) 1487
No Bill Peddlers Allowed 1905 (Miles Bros.)
No Children Wanted 1908 (Lubin)
No Cooking Allowed 1911 (Ed)
No-Good Guy, The 1916 (Ince) 519
No Liberties, Please 1903 (AMB)
No Man's Land 1918 ( ) 1631, 1939, 2002
No Mother to Guide Him 1919 (Key/Tri) 2608
No One to Guide Him see The Stone Age
No One to Love Her see The Jealous Old Maid
No Parking 1919 ( ) 339
No Place for Father 1913 ( ) 1876
No Place Like Jail 1918 (Rolin/P) 1502
No Salad Dressing Wanted 1902 (AMB)
No Trifling with Love 1908 (Melies)
No Wedding Bells for Him 1906 (AMB)
Noble Crook, A see Two Crooks
Noble Jester, A; or Faint Heart Never Won Fair Lady 1908 (V)
Nobody Home 1916 (M) 388, 467, 497, 768, 1707
Nobody Home 1919 (Art) 875, 1028, 1067
Nobody Works Like Father 1906 (V)
Nobody's Child 1919 (Br) 2536, 2712
Nobody's Wife 1918 ( ) 1604
Noise from the Deep, A 1913 (Key) 65, 1941
Noise of Bombs, The 1914 (Key) 1422, 1906
Noisy Naggers and Nosey Neighbors 1917 (V) 2367
Non-Stop Kid, The 1918 (P) 1586, 2055
Nora's 4th of July 1902 (AMB)
North of '53 1918 (F) 866
Not Guilty 1908 (Melies)
Not Guilty 1919 (Br) 943
Not Like Other Girls 1912 (Un)
Not My Sister 1916 (Tri) 134, 715, 2547
Not of the Flock 1914 (Kay-Bee) 1745, 2096
Not So Bad as It Seemed 1910 (Bio)
Note in the Shoe, The 1909 (AMB) 1511
Nothing but Trouble 1918 (P) 1586, 2055
Nothing Shall be Hidden 1912 (Un)
Nothing to Wear 1917 (M) 768, 1707
Notorious Gallagher 1916 ( ) 2430
Notre Dame de Paris 1911 (Scagl) 32
Novel Way of Catching a Burglar, A 1904 (AMB)
Novice, The 1911 (Selig) 2095
Now I Lay Me Down to Sleep 1897 (Ed)
Nugget Nell 1919 ( ) 355, 356, 388, 467, 865, 914, 1028, 1249, 2223
Number One 1916 (M) 768, 1707
Number 10--Westbound 1917 ( ) 2354
Nun, The 1915 ( ) 1028
Nurse, The 1912 (Ed) 1841
Nurse and the Martyr, The 1915 (Br) 1873
Nursing a Viper 1909 (Bio) 1363, 1542
Nuts in May 1917 (Nestor/Un) 1502
Nymph of the Waves, A 1903 (AMB)
Nymph of the Woods 1919 ( ) 1547

- O -

O. H. M. S., Our Helpless Millions
    Saved 1914 (Br) 1873
Oakdale Affair, The 1918 (W) 708, 1049,
    1075
Oath, The 1919 (FP) 258
Oath and the Man, The 1910 (Bio) 2000
Obdurate Father, The 1909 (V)
Object of Affection * ( ) 46
O'Brien's Busy Day 1912 (Imp)
O'Connor's Mag 1917 ( ) 1658, 2147
Ocean Swells 1917 ( ) 339
Ocean Waif, The 1916 ( ) 1429
Octoroon, The 1913 (Kal) 572
Odalisque, The 1914 (Mu) 554, 1182,
    2112, 2513, 2680
Odd Charges 1916 (Br) 943
Odd Pair of Limbs, An 1908 (V)
Odds against Her 1919 (Br) 2179
Odyssey of the North, An 1915 (Bo) 258
Oeidpus * ( ) 1893
Of Conscience 1913 ( ) 156
Off His Beat 1903 (AMB)
Off the Trolley 1919 (P) 1586
Office Boy's Revenge, The 1903 (Ed)
Office Boy's Revenge, The 1904 (AMB)
Officer John Donovan 1913 (V) 297, 2523
Officer Kate 1912 ( ) 2070
Officer McCue 1909 (Lubin)
Official Chaperone 1916 ( ) 1329
Oh, Boy! 1919 (F) 392, 639, 901, 1118,
    1402
Oh, Daddy 1915 (Mu) 386, 979, 1172,
    1451
Oh, Doctor! 1917 (FP/Las) 65, 1401,
    1476, 2208
Oh, I Don't Know 1904 (AMB)
Oh, Johnny! 1919 * ( ) 847
Oh, Me, Oh My 1907 (Lubin)
Oh, My Feet! 1908 (Lubin)
Oh, Rats! 1909 (Ed)
Oh, That Limburger 1906 (V)
Oh, That Watermelon 1896 (American
    Mutoscope Co.)
Oh, Those Eyes! 1912 (Bio)
Oh, Uncle! 1909 (Bio) 2047, 2081
Oh, What a Night see The Rounders
Oh, You Dirty Boy! 1905 (V)
Oh, You Pearl 1913 ( ) 2748
Oh, You Woman! 1919 ( ) 1309, 2595
O'Hara as Guardian Angel 1913 (V) 2523
O'Hara Helps Cupid 1912 (V) 297, 2070,
    2523
O'Hara, Squatter and Philosopher 1912
    (V) 2523
O'Hara's Godchild 1913 (V) 2523
Oil and Water 1913 (Bio) 141, 1028, 1029,
    1182, 1714, 1832, 2000, 2513, 2680
Oily Scoundrel, An 1916 (Key/Tri) 70,
    876, 966, 1666, 1788, 2164
Ol' Swimmin' Hole, The 1917 ( ) 2069
Olaf--an Atom 1913 (Bio) 398, 1665, 1714
Old Actor, The 1912 (Bio) 96, 315, 1831,
    1981, 2047, 2728
Old Appointment, An 1912 ( ) 1656
Old Army Chest, The 1909 (Lubin)
Old Bachelor, An 1904 (AMB)
Old Bookkeeper, The 1912 (Bio) 1831, 2000
Old Class Reunion, The 1911 (Independent
    Moving Picture Co.)

Old Clerk, The 1913 (Un) 2095
Old Cobbler, The 1914 (101-Bison/Un)
    449, 1705, 2188, 2635
Old Confectioner's Mistake, The 1911
    (Bio) 1613, 1224
Old Curiosity Shop, The 1913 (Hep)
Old Doll, The 1911 (V) 332, 565, 950
Old Dutch 1915 (W) 129, 842, 895, 1195,
    1390, 1764
Old Family Bible, The 1911 (Ed)
Old Fashioned Girl, An 1915 ( ) 1028,
    1998
Old Fashioned Young Man, An 1917
    (FA/Tri) 1175, 1182, 1859, 2194
Old Fire Horse and the New Fire Chief,
    The 1914 (V) 332, 901
Old Flute Player, The 1914 (V) 1426,
    1876, 2487
Old Folks at Home 1916 ( ) 601, 1175
Old Footlight Favorite, The 1908
    (Melies)
Old Gentleman Spinkles 1903 (AMB)
Old Guard, The 1917 ( ) 2068
Old Hall Clock, The 1909 (Lubin)
Old Hartwell's Club 1918 ( ) 715
Old Heidelberg 1915 (Tri) 1028, 1042,
    2112, 2573, 2649, 2725
Old Homestead, The 1915 ( ) 1600
Old Isaac, the Pawnbroker 1908 (AMB)
    1089
Old Loves and the New 1910 (Ed)
Old Maid, The 1914 (Mu) 25, 2513
Old Maid and Fortune Teller 1904 (Ed)
Old Maid and the Burglar, The 1903
    (AMB)
Old Maid Having Her Picture Taken, The
    1901 (Ed)
Old Maid in the Horsecar, The 1901 (Ed)
Old Maid's Baby, The 1914 (V) 332, 901
Old Maid's Baby, The 1919 (P) 771, 1988
Old Maid's Disappointment, The 1902
    (AMB)
Old Maid's Dream, The 1908 (Lubin)
Old Maid's Parrot, The 1908 (Lubin)
Old Maid's Picture, The 1903 (AMB)
Old Maids' Temperance Club 1908 (Ed)
Old Man, The 1914 ( ) 1028, 2680
Old Man's Love Story, An 1913 (V) 2523
Old Man's Pride, An 1909 (Lubin)
Old, Old Song, An 1919 ( ) 2700
Old Mother Hubbard 1903 (Lubin)
Old Organ, The 1909 (V)
Old Peddler, The 1911 (Independent
    Moving Picture Co.)
Old Reliable 1914 (V) 297, 2523
Old San Francisco 1908 ( ) 564
Old Story with a New Ending, An 1910
    (Bio)
Old Sweetheart of Mine, An 1911 (Ed)
Old Sweethearts of Mine 1909 (V)
Old Swimming Hole, The 1908 (AMB)
Old Town Girl, The 1919 ( ) 2738
Old Wives for New 1918 (FP/Las) 83,
    269, 550, 724, 877, 988, 1206, 1377,
    1417, 1537, 1732, 1756, 2149, 2547,
    2638, 2648
Old Woman Who Lived in a Shoe 1903
    (Lubin)
Olden and New Style Conjuring 1906
    (Melies)
Oldest Law, The 1918 (WS) 265, 835

Oliver Twist 1909 (V) 1993
Oliver Twist 1912 (Hep) 1043, 2531
Oliver Twist 1916 (Las) 258, 752, 756,
    1201, 1756, 2776
Omens and Oracles 1912 (V) 2523
On Her Wedding Night 1915 (V) 1426,
    1876, 2487
On His Majesty's Service 1914 (Br) 43
On His Wedding Day 1913 (Key) 2465
On the Banks of Allan Water 1916 (Br)
    1018
On the Border 1914 ( ) 2002
On the Desert's Edge 1910 (Es) 50
On the Eagle's Trail * (Selig Polyscope)
    1849
On the Fire 1919 (P) 1586, 2671
On the Jump 1918 (P) 1586, 2671
On the Lazy Line 1914 (Ed) 2074
On the Level 1917 ( ) 2683, 2803
On the Night Stage /aka/ The Bandit and
    the Preacher 1914 (Mu) 809, 1188,
    1847
On the Quiet 1918 (Par) 140
On the Reef 1910 (Bio) 1542, 2680
On the Road 1903 (AMB)
On the Shore 1912 (Imp)
On-the-Square Girl 1917 (P) 1444
On the Stage; or Melodrama from the
    Bowery 1907 (V)
On the Stroke of Twelve 1908 (Lubin)
On the Stroke of Twelve 1915 ( ) 1649
On the Verge of War 1914 (Un) 2095
On the Western Frontier 1909 (Ed)
On the Window Shades 1904 (AMB)
On Trial 1917 (Es) 437, 957, 1429, 1636
Onawandah; or An Indian's Devotion 1909
    (V)
Once a Man 1919 (M) 768, 1707
Once a Mason 1919 (M) 768, 1707
Once Every Ten Minutes 1915 (P) 1586
Once to Every Woman 1919 ( ) 1728
Once upon a Time 1918 (Br) 1722
Onda of the Orient 1916 ( ) 2656
One A. M. 1916 (Mu) 97, 451
One a Minute 1919 (Un) 2058
One against Many 1919 ( ) 1439
One Busy Hour 1909 (AMB) 731, 1182
One Busy Hour 1912 (Key) 2368
One Dollar Bid 1918 ( ) 1431, 2779
One Every Minute 1919 ( ) 913
One Exciting Night 1913 (P) 1575, 1751
One Flag at Last 1911 (V) 1332
One Good Joke Deserves Another 1913 (V)
    332, 901
One Hour 1917 ( ) 1117, 1402
One Hour of Love 1917 ( ) 1603
One Hundred Dollar Bill, The 1911 (V)
    332
One Hundred Million 1915 (K) 452
100% American 1918 (Propoganda film)
    242, 2047
100% Jealousy 1909 (Ed)
100 to 1 Shot, The; or A Run of Luck
    1906 (V)
One Is Business, the Other Crime 1912
    (Bio) 95, 209, 315, 1751, 2000,
    2513, 2728
One Law for Both 1917 ( ) 111, 1372
One Man Baseball 1907 (V)
$1,000,000 Reward 1919 ( ) 26
One More American 1918 ( ) 160

One Night and Then ... 1910 (Bio) 357
One Night Stand, A 1915 (Key) 351, 531,
    815, 1651
One of Many 1917 ( ) 2719
One of Our Girls 1914 (FP) 667
One of the Discard 1914 ( ) 295, 2096
One of the Family 1917 (M) 768, 1707
One of the Finest 1907 (Selig)
One of the Finest 1919 (Go) 543, 1867,
    1998
One Round Hogan 1915 ( ) 1424
One Round O'Brien 1912 (Bio)
One Shall Be Taken 1914 (Br) 150
One She Loved, The 1912 (Bio) 141, 1029,
    2047, 2680
One Shot Ross 1917 (Tri) 2355, 2479
One Summer's Day 1917 (Br) 527 1918
One Thing after Another 1914 (GB) 2604
One-Thing-at-a-Time o'Day 1919 ( ) 1631
$1,000 1918 ( ) 102, 804
One Thousand Mile Tree 1903 (AMB)
One Thousand Miles through the Rockies
    1912 (Ed)
One Too Many 1916 (Vim) 1161
One Touch of Nature 1908 (AMB) 315, 994,
    1336, 1675
One Touch of Sin 1917 ( ) 295
One Way of Taking a Girl's Picture 1904
    (AMB)
One Week of Life 1919 (Par) 957
One Wonderful Night 1914 (Es) 156, 353,
    767, 2700
Onion Fiend, The 1907 (Selig)
Only a Farmer's Daughter see The
    Feathered Nest
Only a Messenger Boy 1915 (Key) 2465
Only a Nigger 1918 ( ) 1208
Only a Soldier Boy 1903 (Lubin)
Only Kids 1907 (Lubin)
Only Man, The 1915 (Br) 1815
Only Road, The 1918 (M) 242, 631, 887
Only Son, The 1914 (Las) 649, 2184
Only Way, The 1917 (FP) 2149, 2683,
    2813
Onoko's Vow 1910 (Ed)
Onward Christian Soldiers 1918 (Br) 831,
    1918
Open Another Bottle 1915 ( ) 1684
Open Door, The 1913 ( ) 2096
Open Door, The 1919 ( ) 1532, 1832
Open Gate, The 1909 (Bio) 1865, 2156
Open Your Eyes 1919 (WB) 217, 227, 304,
    1031, 1629, 1738
Opportunity 1918 (M) 631
Ora Pro Nobis 1917 (Br) 2637
Oracle of Delphi, The 1903 (Melies)
Oracles and Omens 1913 ( ) 2070
Orchid Lady, The 1916 (M) 2037
Ordeal, The 1909 (Ed)
Ordeal of Rosetta, The 1918 (Un) 273, 337,
    1427
Order in the Court 1919 (P) 635, 2055
Orderly, The 1918 (King-Bee) 1161
Ore the Banster 1905 (AMB)
Oriental Black Art 1908 (Melies)
Oriental Love 1917 (Key/Tri) 45, 179, 371,
    396, 509, 1422, 2020, 2428
Oriental Mystic, The 1909 (V)
Oriental Rugs * ( ) 750
Original Cohens 1909 (Lubin)
Orphan, The; or A Mountain Romance 1908 (V)

Osler-Ising Papa 1905 (AMB)
'Ostler Joe 1908 (AMB) 731, 1089
'Ostler Joe 1912 (Ed)
Othello 1908 (V) 19, 453, 737
Othello 1909 (P) 746
Othello 1918 (Max Mack Film) 728, 861
Othello in Jonesville 1913 (Ed) 3
Other Fellow, The; or A Fight for Love
    1909 (Ed)
Other Girl, The 1917 (Vim) 1161
Other Half, The 1919 ( ) 2051, 2638
Other Man, The 1916 (Key/Tri) 65, 253,
    791, 1115, 1354, 2208, 2372, 2666
Other Man, The 1918 (V) 1877
Other Man's Wife, The 1919 ( ) 286, 433,
    1275, 1361
Other Men's Daughters 1918 ( ) 1329
Other Men's Wives 1919 (Par) 627
Other People's Money 1916 ( ) 1537
Other People's Wives see The Home
    Breakers
Other Side of Eden, The 1918 ( ) 1717
Other Side of the Door 1916 ( ) 2131
Other Side of the Hedge, The 1904 (AMB)
Other Woman, The 1913 (V) 2523
Other Woman, The 1918 ( ) 1329, 2410
Ouda of the Orient 1918 (Un) 2056
Ouija Did It, The 1918 (Christie) 339
Our Baby 1912 (Imp)
Our Better Selves 1919 ( ) 1714, 2683
Our Children (First kiddie comedy) 1913
    (Key) 1434
Our Country in Arms 1909 (Lubin)
Our Dare Devil Chief 1915 (Key) 210, 791,
    2208, 2465, 2510, 2636
Our Deaf Friend, Fogarty 1904 (AMB)
Our Fairy Play 1914 (V) 2521
Our Little Wife 1918 ( ) 658, 1078,
    1423, 2216
Our Mrs. McChesney 1918 (M) 139, 1046,
    1632, 1905, 2478
Our Mutual Girl 1914 (V) 1876
Our Own Little Flat 1908 (Lubin)
Our People 1919 ( ) 2700
Our Teddy 1919 ( ) 2412
Out and In 1913 (Key) 2465
Out for the Coin 1915 (Christie) 525
Out from the Shadow 1911 (Bio) 2000,
    2513
Out of a Clear Sky 1918 (Par) 482, 533,
    1800
Out of Bondage 1915 (Mu) 1028, 1254, 1591
Out of Evil Cometh Good 1914 (Br) 150
Out of Luck 1919 (Art) 875, 1028, 1067,
    2573, 2616
Out of the Air 1914 ( ) 1998
Out of the Ashes 1919 ( ) 2627
Out of the Darkness 1915 (Par) 2661
Out of the Deep 1912 (Ed)
Out of the Drifts 1916 (FP) 482, 536, 569,
    1055, 2411
Out of the Fog 1919 (M) 321, 1169, 1919
Out of the Night 1910 (Ed)
Out of the Night 1918 (Christie) 339, 375,
    2458
Out of the Shadow 1919 (Par) 274, 360,
    957, 2444
Out of the West 1919 (CFC) 1186
Out of the Wreck 1917 (Art/Par) 2770
Out West see The Sheriff
Out Yonder 1919 ( ) 1046

Outcast, The 1912 (New York Motion
    Picture Co.)
Outcast, The 1917 ( ) 1223, 1902
Outcast among Outcasts, An 1912 (Bio)
    2513, 2728
Outcast and the Bride, The 1903 (Lubin)
Outcast Child, The 1912 (Eclair)
Outcast or Heroine? 1909 (V)
Outcasts of Poker Flat, The 1919 (Un)
    398, 1283, 1483, 1659, 1714, 2058
Outer Edge, The 1915 ( ) 377
Outlaw, The 1908 (AMB)
Outlaw and His Wife, The 1918 (SB) 817,
    844, 2417, 2598
Outlaw and the Child, The 1911 (Es) 50
Outlaw Express * (P) 1720
Outlaw's Bride, The * (Selig Polyscope)
    1849
Outlaw's Sacrifice, The 1912 (Es) 50
Outrage, The 1915 (Hep) 22, 1289, 2531
Outside the Gates 1915 (Rex/Un) 352, 449,
    762
Outwitted 1917 (Select) 947
Outwitted by His Wife 1908 (Lubin)
Outwitting Dad 1914 (Lubin) 1161
Over-Anxious Waiter, The 1903 (AMB)
Over Mountain Passes 1910 (Ed)
Over Silent Paths 1910 (Bio) 1542
Over the Fence 1917 (P) 635, 1586, 2055
Over the Garden Wall 1919 ( ) 1519, 1602,
    2625
Over the Hill 1918 ( ) 1312
Over the Hills 1911 (Independent Moving
    Picture Co.)
Over the Hills to the Poor House 1908
    (AMB)
Over the Ledge 1914 ( ) 2112
Over the Rhine 1918 ( ) 832
Over the Top 1918 (V) 243, 841, 1047,
    1888
Over There 1919 ( ) 1939, 2129
Oyster Dredger, The 1915 (Victor/Un)
    449, 1431, 2416,
Oz features 1915 ( ) 1684
Ozark Romance, An 1918 (P) 1586

                        - P -

P. D. Q. 1917 ( ) 1872
Pa Pays 1913 ( ) 731, 1028
Paddy O'Hara 1917 ( ) 2096
Pagan and Christian 1909 (Ed)
Pagan God, The 1919 ( ) 693, 2693
Paid in Advance 1919 (Jewel/Un) 312,
    342, 449, 675, 705, 1025, 2042,
    2492
Paid in Full 1919 (Par) 957, 1600, 1756,
    2444
Paid to Love 1917 ( ) 1353
Painted Lady, The 1912 (Bio) 601, 1028,
    1074, 1714, 2513
Painted Lie, The 1917 (Mu) 2760
Painted Lily, The 1918 (Tri) 2128, 2194
Painted Lips 1918 ( ) 1604
Painted Madonna 1917 ( ) 1191
Painted Soul, The 1915 ( ) 134, 2096
Painted World, The 1914 ( ) 2472
Painter for Love * (P) 1575
Painter's Revenge, The 1908 (Ed)
Painting, The 1908 (V)

Pair of Aces, A 1916 (F) 1524
Pair of Cupids, A 1918 (M) 156, 353
Pair of Gloves, A 1911 (Independent
    Moving Picture Co.)
Pair of Queens, A 1903 (AMB)
Pair of Silk Stockings, A 1918 (Select) 83,
    927, 1050, 1206, 2462, 2521
Pair of Sixes, A 1919 ( ) 339, 1276
Pair of Spectacles, A 1908 (Lubin)
Pair of Spectacles, A 1916 (Br) 1329
Pair of Stockings, A see A Pair of
    Silk Stockings
Pajama Girl, The 1903 (AMB)
Pajama Statue Girls, The 1903 (AMB)
Palace of the Arabian Nights, The 1905
    (Melies)
        Reception Room in the Rajah's
            Palace
        The Temple of Siva
        The Banks of the Sacred River
        The Gondola of the Blue Dwarf
        The Magic Forest
        The Staircase
        The Entrance of the Wonderful
            Caverns
        The Descent in the Crystal Grotto
        The Crystal Grotto
        The Miraculous Caves
        The Palace of the Arabian Nights
        The Palace of the Rajah
Paleface Brave 1914 (Kal) 642
Pallard the Punter 1919 (GB) 2551
Pals; or My Friend, the Dummy 1906 (V)
Pals First 1918 (M) 709, 1589
Pals in Blue * (Selig Polyscope) 1849
Pals of the Range 1910 (Es) 50
Pandora's Box 1912 (V) 332, 901
Panic Is On, The 1916 ( ) 460
Panthea 1917 (Select) 875, 947, 953, 1176,
    1634, 1705, 2188, 2523, 2649
Panther Woman, The 1918 (FN) 2037
Pants 1917 (Es) 1636
Pants and Pansies 1912 (Bio)
Paola and Francesca 1911 (V) 2523
Papa by Proxy 1916 ( ) 2636
Papa's Sweetheart 1911 (Ed)
Papa's Warning: "He Must Go at Eleven"
    1904 (AMB)
Paper Hanger's Helper, The 1915 (Lubin)
    1161
Papered Door, The 1911 (Es) 1976, 2486
Paperhanger, The see Work
Paperhanger in Trouble 1905 (Paley &
    Steiner)
Parade of Buffalo Bill's Wild West Show
    1898 (Ed)
Paradise 1912 (National Film Distributing
    Co.)
Paradise Garden 1917 ( ) 496, 612, 2416
Paradise Green 1918 (M) 1589
Paradise Lost 1911 (Bio)
Parante, The 1912 (Bio) 1751
Parasite, The 1912 ( ) 231, 2733
Pardners 1910 (Ed)
Pardners 1918 ( ) 2661
Parent's Devotion, The 1908 (Lubin)
Paris Hat, The 1913 (FP) 2047
Paris Original, A * (P) 1575
Parisian Romance, A 1915 (V) 1806
Parisian Tigress 1919 (M) 631
Park Honeymooners, The 1915 (V) 1876

Parlez vous Francais? 1908 (V)
Parsifal 1904 (Ed)
Parson of Henry Gulch, The 1907 (Lubin)
Parson of Panamint, The 1916 (Pal) 866,
    1446
Parson Who Fled West, The * (Selig
    Polyscope) 1849
Parson's Umbrella, The 1910 (Ed)
Parted, but United Again 1909 (V)
Parted by the Sword 1915 (Br) 1873
Parted Curtains 1914 ( ) 2680
Parted on Their Honeymoon 1909 (Ed)
Partners 1916 (Hep) 2171, 2744
Partners for Life 1912 (Ed)
Partners Three 1919 ( ) 189, 1720
Pasadena Peach, The 1911 (Kal) 1924
Pasquale 1916 (Morosco) 160, 808, 1928
Pass Key, The 1909 (Lubin)
Passer-By, The 1912 (Ed)
Passing of a Grouch, The 1910 (Bio)
Passing of Izzy, The 1914 (Key) 1906
Passing of J. B. Randell and Company,
    The 1912 (Ed)
Passing of Pete, The 1915 (Selig Poly-
    scope) 1849
Passing of the Beast 1914 ( ) 2112
Passing of the Third Floor Back, The
    1918 (FN) 923
Passing of Two Gun Hicks see Two
    Gun Hicks
Passing the Buck 1919 (V) 2367
Passion Flower, The 1912 (Ed)
Passionels Tagebuch 1915 ( ) 1349
Passions, He Had Three 1913 (Key) 65
Past Redemption * (Ince) 1580
Paste 1916 (Br) 43
Paste and Waste 1916 ( ) 460
Pat Clancy's Adventure 1911 (Ed)
Path of Genius 1914 ( ) 1580, 2096
Pathfinder, The 1911 ( ) 2112
Patience Sparhawk 1917 ( ) 2037
Patient Housekeeper, The 1912 (Ed)
Patria--serial 1917 (P) 327, 435, 1076,
    1713, 1904, 1971, 2410, 2616, 2656
        1. Last of the Fighting Channings
        2. The Treasure
        3. Winged Millions
        4. Double Crossed
        5. The Island God Forgot
        6. Alias Nemesis
        7. Red Dawn
        8. Red Night
        9. Cat's Paw and Scapegoat
        10. War in the Dooryard
        11. Sunset Falls
        12. Peace on the Border or
            Peace Which Passeth All
            Understanding
        13. Wings of Death
        14. Border Peril
        15. For the Flag
Patricia of the Plains 1910 (Es) 50
Patriot, The 1917 (M) 768, 1188, 1707
Patriot, The; or The Horrors of War
    1908 (V)
Patriotism 1918 ( ) 134
Pat's Day Off 1912 (Key) 1666, 2368, 2465
Patsy, The 1916 (F) 1524
Pawn of Fate 1916 (M) 656, 1429
Pawnbroker, The 1908 (Lubin)
Pawnbroker's Heart, The 1917 (Key/Tri)

440, 531, 2023, 2608
Pawnshop, The 1916 (Mu) 97, 384, 451, 517, 1414, 2077, 2090
Paws of the Bear 1917 (Tri) 715, 2765
Pay Me 1917 (Jewel/Un) 449, 496, 771, 2042, 2361, 2490
Pay Your Dues 1919 (P) 1586
Paying His Debt 1918 (Tri) 2479
Paying the Price 1916 (W) 1396
Payment 1916 (Tri) 134
Peace of Roaring River 1919 (Par) 957, 1266, 1449, 2570
Peace, Perfect Peace 1918 (Br) 1968
Peacemaker, The 1914 (V) 297, 1876, 2521, 2523
Peach-Basket Hat, The 1909 (Bio) 79, 1227, 1511, 1824
Peach Brand, The 1914 ( ) 2002
Peaches and Cream 1909 (Lubin)
Peacock Feather Fan, The 1915 (Mu) 905, 2054
Peanuts and Bullets 1915 (Key) 509
Pearl and the Poet 1913 ( ) 2748
Pearl and the Tramp 1913 ( ) 2748
Pearl as a Detective 1913 ( ) 2748
Pearl of Paradise 1916 (Mu) 905
Pearl of the Army--serial 1916 (P) 327, 401, 963, 1407, 2704, 2728
   1.   The Traitor
   2.   Found Guilty
   3.   The Silent Menace
   4.   War Clouds
   5.   Somewhere in Grenada
   6.   Major Brent's Perfidy
   7.   For the Stars and Stripes
   8.   International Diplomacy
   9.   The Monroe Doctrine
  10.   The Silent Army
  11.   A Million Volunteers
  12.   The Foreign Alliance
  13.   Modern Buccaneers
  14.   The Flag Despoiler
  15.   The Colonel's Orderly
Pearl's Hero 1913 ( ) 2748
Pearl's Mistake 1913 ( ) 2748
Peasant Girl's Loyalty, The 1908 (V)
Peck's Bad Girl 1918 ( ) 947
Peculiar Patients' Pranks 1915 (P) 1586, 2055
Peddler, The 1913 (Key) 2465
Peddler, The 1917 ( ) 2625
Pedro's Dilemma 1912 (Key) 932, 1666, 1941, 2368, 2465
Peep behind the Scenes, A 1918 (Br) 43, 503
Peeping Pete 1913 (Key) 509, 2368, 2465
Peeping Tom in the Dressing Room 1905 (AMB)
Peer Gynt 1915 (Morosco) 715, 1784, 2196, 2458
Peg o' My Heart 1919 ( ) 437, 1417, 1919 (never released)
Peg o' the Ring--serial 1916 ( ) 245
Peg of the Pirates 1918 ( ) 1329
Peg Woffington 1910 (Ed)
Peggy 1916 (Tri) 333, 473, 715, 771, 785, 2096, 2562
Peggy Does Her Darndest 1919 (M) 41, 618
Peggy Gets Rid of the Baby 1912 (Br) 150

Peggy Leads the Way 1918 ( ) 1841, 2480, 2520
Peggy Rebels 1918 ( ) 1841
Pelleás and Melésande 1913 (Un) 591, 1783
Penalty, The 1915 ( ) 2002
Penitents, The 1915 ( ) 601, 1998
Pennington's Choice 1915 (Quality) 353
People vs. John Doe, The 1916 ( ) 111, 2361
Pep * ( ) 751
Peppy Polly 1919 (Art) 143, 601, 1028, 2026, 2573
Percy Learns to Dance 1912 (Imp)
Percy, the Masher 1911 (Independent Moving Picture Co.)
Perfect Lady, A 1918 (Go) 1423, 1640, 2077
Perfect Lady, The see A Woman 1915 (Es)
Perfect Lover, The 1919 (Sel) 296, 572, 1332, 1959, 2478
Perfect 36, A 1919 (Go) 1495, 1941
Perfect Villain 1914 (Key) 531
Perfectly Fiendish Flanagan 1918 ( ) 913
Perfidy of Mary, The 1913 (Bio) 141, 1028, 1751, 1832, 2680
Peril, The 1912 (Imp)
Peril of the Plains 1912 ( ) 864
Peril of the Rails 1917 ( ) 1010
Perilous Proceeding, A 1902 (AMB)
Perilous Ride, A 1911 (Ed)
Perils in the Park 1916 (Key/Tri) 650, 1086, 1651, 1723
Perils of Our Girl Reporters--serial 1916 (Mu) 1077, 1402, 1819, 2607
   1.   The Jade Necklace
   2.   The Black Door
   3.   Ace High
   4.   The White Trail
   5.   Many a Slip
   6.   The Long Lane
   7.   Smite of Conscience
   8.   Birds of Prey
   9.   Misjudged
  10.   Taking Chances
  11.   The Meeting
  12.   Outwitted
  13.   The Schemers
  14.   The Counterfeiters
  15.   Kidnapped
Perils of Paris, The--serial 1918 ( ) 2748
Perils of Pork Pie, The 1916 (Br) 1815
Perils of Patrick, The 1918 ( ) 451
Perils of Pauline, The--serial 1914 (P) 206, 314, 404, 1383, 1673, 1689, 2003, 2203, 2478. 2760. 2795
Perils of the Sea 1913 (Kal) 231, 2121
Perils of Thunder Mountain, The--serial 1919 (V) 1271, 1876, 2070, 2674
   1.   Spear of Malice
   2.   The Bridge Trap
   3.   Teeth of Steel
   4.   Cave of Terror
   5.   Cliff of Treachery
   6.   Tree of Torture
   7.   Lightning Lure
   8.   Iron Clutch
   9.   Prisoner of the Deep
  10.   The Flaming Sacrifice

11. In the Ocean's Grip
12. Rushing Horror
13. River of Dread
14. Hut of Disaster
15. Fate's Verdict
Perjury 1908 (Ambrosio) 391, 2528
Perpetual Proposal, The; or An Ardent Wooer 1909 (V)
Persecution of Bob Pretty, The 1916 (Br) 943
Persistency Wins 1908 (Lubin)
Persistent Actor, A 1908 (Lubin)
Persistent Jane 1909 (Lubin)
Persistent Lover, A 1912 (V) 332, 901
Persistent Mr. Prince, The 1914 (V) 1876, 2663
Persistent Suitor, A 1908 (Ed)
Persistent Trombonist, The 1908 (Lubin)
Persnickety Polly Ann 1917 ( ) 1602
Personal 1904 (AMB)
Personal Affair, A 1912 (Ed)
Personal Introductions 1914 (V) 332
Personally Conducted 1912 (Ed)
Persuasive Peggy 1917 (M) 658, 1329
Pest, The 1917 (M) 265, 619, 768, 1161, 1707, 1941, 2733
Pests and Promises 1917 (V) 2367
Petal on the Current, A 1919 (Un) 355, 1694, 2058, 2133
Peter Ibbetson 1917 ( ) 141
Peter's Pledge 1913 (Lubin) 1489
Petticoat Lane on Sunday 1904 (AMB)
Petticoat Pilot 1918 ( ) 1764
Pettigrew's Girl 1919 ( ) 242, 486, 1006
Phantom Buccaneer 1916 (Es) 2582
Phantom Carriage, The 1919 (Swedish) 254
Phantom Happiness, The 1916 ( ) 1819
Phantom Husband, The 1917 ( ) 2486
Phantom of the House 1913 (Bio) 2680
Phantom Riders, The 1918 (Un) 398, 1719
Phantom Ship, The 1918 ( ) 926, 1004
Phantom Violin, The 1914 ( ) 610, 926
Phantom's Secret, The 1917 ( ) 2405
Phil for Short 1919 ( ) 2549
Philadelphia, the Cradle of Liberty 1908 (Lubin)
Phoebe Snow 1905 (Ed)
Phoenix, The 1910 (V) 2112
Phoney Photos 1918 (L-KO) 1502
Photograph Habit, The 1909 (Lubin)
Photographed for the Rogue's Gallery 1909 (Lubin)
Photographer's Mishap 1909 (Ed)
Photographer's Mishap 1901 (Lubin)
Phunphilms 1915 (P) 1586
Piano Movers, The see His Musical Career
Pickaninny and the Pup, The 1910 (Ed)
Picket Guard 1913 ( ) 2112
Pickpocket, The 1903 (AMB)
Pickpocket, The 1913 (V) 332, 818, 801
Pickwick Papers 1913 (V) 332
        Part 1. The Honorable Event
        Part 2. The Adventure of the Westgate Seminary
        Part 3. The Adventure of the Shooting Party
Picnic, The see The Masquerader
Picture of Dorian Gray, The 1913 ( ) 2112, 2422
Picture of Dorian Gray, The 1916 (Br) 2637

Picture Pirates 1915 (Vogue) 2608
Picture the Photographer Took, The 1904 (AMB)
Pidgin Island 1917 (Yorke) 612, 1589
Pie, Tramp and the Bulldog, The 1901 (Ed)
Piece of Ambergris, A 1912 (Imp)
Piece of Lace, A 1910 (Ed)
Pierrot, Murderer 1904 (Gaumont & Co.)
Pierrot's Problem 1902 (AMB)
Pig That Came to Life, The 1904 (AMB)
Pigs Is Pigs 1910 (Ed)
Pigs Is Pigs 1914 (V) 332
Piker's Dream, The 1907 (V)
Pile Driver, The see The Fatal Mallet
Pilgrim's Progress 1912 ( ) 1971
Pillar of Flame 1915 (V) 297
Pillars of Society 1916 (Tri) 200, 601
Pills of Peril 1916 (Key/Tri) 250, 650, 878, 1572, 1906, 2500
Pimple as Hamlet 1916 (Br) 851, 852
Pimple Does the Turkey Trot 1912 (Br) 851, 852
Pimple's Battle of Waterloo 1913 (Br) 851
Pimple's Better 'Ole 1918 (Br) 851, 852
Pimple's Clutching Hand 1916 (Br) 851, 852
Pimple's Ivanhoe 1913 (Br) 851, 852
Pimple's Midsummer Night's Dream 1915 (Br) 851, 852
Pimple's Million Dollar Mystery 1915 (Br) 851, 852
Pimple's Royal Divorce 1915 (Br) 851, 852
Pimple's Three Weeks 1915 (Br) 851, 852
Pinch Hitter, The 1917 ( ) 2096
Pinch Hitter, The 1917 (Par) 281, 763
Pinched 1917 (P) 1586
Pinched in the Finish 1917 (Key/Tri) 1086, 1572, 2166, 2465, 2564
Pine's Revenge, The 1915 (Gold Seal/Un) 449, 1711, 2398, 2781
Pink Lady, The 1916 ( ) 667
Pins Are Lucky 1914 (Lubin) 1161
Pinto Ben * ( ) 1188
Pioneers Crossing the Plains in '49 1908 (Ed)
Pipe Dream, A 1905 (AMB)
Pipe Dreams 1908 (Lubin)
Pipe Dreams 1916 (Vim) 1161
Pipe Story of the Fourth, A 1902 (AMB)
Pipe the Whiskers 1918 (P) 1586
Piper, The 1914 (Key) 531
Piper's Price, The 1917 (Bluebird/Un) 449, 771, 998, 2042, 2490
Pipes of Pan, The 1914 (Rex/Un) 352, 449, 1442, 2041
Pippa Passes 1909 (Bio) 79, 1363, 1450, 1542, 1865, 2047, 2156, 2680
Pirate Gold 1913 (Bio) 2513
Pirates, The 1905 (Lubin)
Pirates, The 1913 (V) 332, 818
Pirate's Gold, The 1908 (AMB) 1992
Pirates of the Sky 1919 ( ) 1206
Pirate's Treasure, The; or A Sailor's Love Story 1907 (V)
Pistols for Breakfast 1919 (P) 1586, 2055
Pit, The 1917 ( ) 2410
Pitfalls of a Big City 1919 (F) 295
Pity the Blind 1904 (AMB)
Place beyond the Winds 1916

(Red Feather/Un) 449, 686, 1896, 2042

Plagues and Puppy Love 1917 (V) 2367

Plain Jane 1916 ( ) 134, 519, 2096

Plain Mame; or All That Glitters Is Not Gold 1909 (V)

Plain Song, A 1910 (Bio) 1831, 2047

Plans and Pajamas 1917 (V) 2367

Planter, The 1917 ( ) 2065

Planter's Wife, The 1908 (AMB) 79, 1363, 1511

Plate of Ice Cream and Two Spoons, A 1903 (AMB)

Play Ball 1917 (Vim) 2497

Playing the Game 1912 (Independent Moving Picture Co.)

Playing the Game 1918 ( ) 960, 1261, 1598, 1690, 1791, 2096

Playing with Fate 1918 ( ) 1877

Playmates 1908 (Ed)

Playmates 1918 (King-Bee) 1161, 2733

Playthings 1918 ( ) 318

Playthings of Passion 1919 ( ) 1048

Please Get Married 1919 (M) 631, 1440, 2399

Please Help Emily 1917 (Mu) 1223, 1663, 1902

Please Help the Blind; or A Game of Graft 1906 (V)

Please Remit 1912 (Ed)

Plot and Counterplot 1913 (V) 2523

Plot and Pash 1912 (Hep) 2744

Plot That Failed, The 1909 (V)

Plow Girl, The 1916 ( ) 1907

Pluck and Plotters 1918 (V) 2367

Plumber, The 1914 (Key) 1906, 2514

Plumber, The see His Blowout

Plump and Runt--Plump series 1916-17 (Vim) 1161

Plunderer, The 1915 (F) 868

Pocahontas 1908 (Ed)

Poet's Revenge, A 1902 (AMB)

Pointing Finger, The 1919 ( ) 1454, 1518, 1694

Poison 1907 (P)

Poison Pen 1919 ( ) 95, 835, 1819

Poisoned Banquet, The 1908 (V)

Poisoned Flume, The 1912 (Am) 1431

Pojkoj Nr 13 /aka/ Tajemnica Hotelu 1915 ( ) 1922

Poker at Dawson City 1899 (Ed)

Poker in the West 1906 (Winthrop Press)

Pokes and Jabs series 1914-15 (Lubin) 1161, 2497

Police 1916 (Es) 71, 451, 517, 1045, 1347, 1414, 2077, 2090, 2197, 2746

Police Raid at a Dog Fight 1906 (AMB)

Policeman for an Hour, A 1908 (Lubin)

Policeman's Pall 1905 (Lubin)

Policemen's Prank on Their Comrades 1903 (Ed)

Polish and Pie 1911 (Ed)

Polished Villain, A see A Rascal of Wolfish Ways

Polishing Up 1914 (V) 332, 901

Politician's Dream, The 1911 (V) 332, 901

Politician's Love Story, The 1908 (Bio) 79, 1363, 2062, 2368

Politics and the Press 1914 (V) 297, 1876, 2523

Polly Ann 1917 ( ) 1308

Polly of the Circus 1917 (Go) 1505, 1751, 2460

Polly Put the Kettle On 1917 ( ) 1782

Polly's Progress 1914 (GB) 2604

Pompey's Honey Girl 1905 (AMB)

Pony Express, The * (Selig Polyscope) 1849

Pony Express, The 1909 (Ed)

Pony Express Rider, The 1910 (Es) 50

Pony Express Rider, The 1912 (Selig Polyscope) 1849

Pool Sharks 1915 (GB) 896

Poor Algy 1905 (Ed)

Poor Gentleman, The 1915 ( ) 1353

Poor Girl, It Was a Hot Night and the Mosquitos Were Thick 1903 (AMB)

Poor Hooligan, So Hungry Too 1903 (AMB)

Poor Jake's Demise 1913 (Imp) 449

Poor John 1907 (Belcher & Waterson)

Poor Little Peppina 1916 (FP) 401, 1068, 1875, 1959, 2045, 2047, 2382

Poor Little Rich Girl, The 1917 (Art/Par) 631, 858, 1174, 1670, 2047, 2074, 2399, 2581, 2720

Poor Musician, The 1909 (V)

Poor Papa 1916 (Tri) 1286

Poor Place for Love Making, A 1905 (AMB)

Poor Relations 1919 (Art/Par) 1398, 1537, 2051, 2638

Poor Rich Man 1918 (M) 156, 353, 1275

Poor Sick Men, The 1911 (Bio)

Poor Snob, The 1918 (Par) 2700

Poppy 1917 (Select) 462, 1705, 1959, 2523

Poppy Girl's Husband, The 1919 ( ) 1153, 1188, 1591

Popsy Wopsy 1913 (Br) 834

Porous Plaster, The 1903 (AMB)

Port of Doom 1913 ( ) 2035

Port of Missing Girls 1919 (Par) 2444

Portugee Joe 1912 (Un)

Possession 1919 (Br) 43, 812

Post No Bills 1906 (V)

Post Telegrapher, The 1912 (New York Motion Picture Co.)

Poster Girls, The 1902 (AMB)

Postman Whitewashed 1904 (AMB)

Pots-and-Pans Peggy 1917 ( ) 1312

Pott Bungles Again 1915 (Christie) 525

Poultry a la Mode /aka/ The Harem 1916 (Vogue) 2608

Powder Flash of Death, The 1913 ( ) 2112

Power, The 1917 ( ) 1714

Power and the Glory, The 1919 ( ) 835, 853

Power of Conscience, The 1912 (Imp)

Power of Destruction, The 1912 (Eclair)

Power of Love, The 1912 (Ingvald C. Oes)

Power of Right, The 1919 (Br) 1453

Power of the Press 1913 ( ) 141

Pranks 1909 (Bio) 1182, 1363, 1542, 2680

Precious Parcel, A 1916 (Vim) 1161

Prehistoric Days /aka/ Wars of the Primal Tribes; Brute Force; In Prehistoric Days 1913 (Bio)

Prehistoric Love, A 1915 (Br) 831, 1247

Prehistoric Love Story, A see A Prehistoric Love

Prejudice of Pierre Marie, The 1911 (V) 2604

Prentis Trio, The 1899 (Ed)

Presidential Possibilities 1912 (Un)
President's Carriage, The 1903 (AMB)
Press Gang, The 1908 (Lubin)
Press Gang, The 1908 (V)
Pressing His Suit 1915 (P) 1586
Pressure of the Poster, The 1915 (Br) 150
Preté pour un Rendu, Un; ou, Une Bonne Farce avec Ma Tete 1904 (Melies)
Pretender, The 1918 ( ) 715
Pretty Mrs. Smith 1915 (Bo) 1865, 2338
Pretty Sister of Jose, The 1915 (FP) 482, 2045
Pretty Smooth 1919 (Un) 675
Price, The 1916 ( ) 2690
Price for Folly, The 1915 (V) 157, 1426, 1876, 1877, 2487
Price Mark, The 1917 (Tri) 532, 627
Price of a Good Time, The 1917 ( ) 1175
Price of a Kiss, The 1902 (AMB)
Price of a Kiss: The Barber 1904 (AMB)
Price of a Man, The 1911 (Ed)
Price of a Soul, The 1909 (Ed)
Price of Folly, The--serial 1918 (P) 2169
Price of Happiness 1916 (Tri) 246
Price of Malice, The 1916 ( ) 2544
Price of Silence, The 1916 (Bluebird/Un) 116, 170, 449, 1329, 1896, 2042, 2361, 2429, 2613, 2757
Price of Victory, The 1911 (Ed)
Price of Virtue, The 1917 (V) 2091
Price She Paid, The 1917 (Select) 1117
Price She Paid, The; or A Fatal Practical Joke 1912 (Powers)
Pride 1919 ( ) 239, 1748, 2232
Pride and the Man 1917 (Mu) 2201, 2399
Pride of Jennico, The 1914 (Las) 1189, 2035
Pride of Lonesome 1913 ( ) 2112
Pride of New York, The 1918 ( ) 2671
Pride of Race see The Last of the Line
Pride of the Clan, The 1917 (Art/Par) 309, 541, 1864, 2047
Prima Donna's Husband, The 1917 ( ) 239
Prima Donna's Understudy, The 1905 (AMB)
Primal Call, The 1911 (Bio) 595, 1060, 1468, 1613, 1665, 2000, 2067, 2513
Primal Lure, The 1916 (Tri) 1188, 1690, 2780
Primeval Test, The 1914 (Un) 905, 1544
Primitive Man 1913 (Bio) 95, 1182, 1613, 1714, 1751, 2000
Primitive Strain, The 1916 (Es) 74, 581, 2560
Primitive Woman, The 1918 ( ) 905, 1894
Primrose Ring, The 1917 ( ) 1126, 1907
Prince and the Pauper, The 1909 (Bio) 2439
Prince and the Pauper, The 1909 (Ed)
Prince and the Pauper, The 1915 (FP) 482
Prince Chap, The 1916 (Selig Polyscope)
Prince Chap, The 1919 (Selig) 457, 857, 875, 1800, 1924
Prince Charming 1912 ( ) 1450
Prince Cosmo 1919 ( ) 1427
Prince for a Day 1917 ( ) 145
Prince in a Pawnshop, A 1916 (V) 208, 533, 1319, 1340

Prince of Darkness, The 1902 (AMB)
Prince of Evil, The 1913 ( ) 2472
Prince of Graustark, The 1916 (Es) 487, 1795, 2700
Prince of Power 1916 (Tri) 242, 1284
Prince Ubaldo 1919 (Art/Par) 423, 1205
Princely Bandit, The 1916 ( ) 610
Princess and the Peasant, The 1910 (Ed)
Princess Clementina 1911 (Br) 1945
Princess from the Poorhouse, The 1916 (Es) 1496
Princess in the Dark 1917 (Tri) 189, 2754
Princess in the Tower, The 1901 (Hep) 714
Princess in the Vase, The 1908 (AMB)
Princess Nicotine; or The Smoke Fairy 1909 (V)
Princess of Bagdad, A 1912 (V) 985
Princess of Happy Chance, The 1916 (Br) 43, 834, 1238
Princess of Park Row, 1917 (V) 296, 2663
Princess of the Dark 1917 (Tri) 1016
Princess Tatters 1917 ( ) 1814
Princess Virtue 1917 ( ) 1907, 2627
Priscilla and the Umbrella 1911 (Bio)
Priscilla's April Fool Joke 1911 (Bio)
Priscilla's Capture 1912 (Bio)
Priscilla's Engagement Kiss 1911 (Bio)
Prison without Walls, The 1916 ( ) 2112, 2458
Prisoner of the Harem, A 1912 (Kal) 992
Prisoner of the Pines 1919 ( ) 1431
Prisoner of War, The 1912 (Ed)
Prisoner of Zenda, The 1913 (FP) 163, 1107, 1117, 2575
Prisoner of Zenda, The 1915 (LFC) 22, 43, 2551
Private Brown 1909 (Cenatur Film Co.)
Private Bunny 1914 (V) 301, 332, 818, 901
Private Preserves * ( ) 751
Private Supper at Hellar's, A 1902 (AMB)
Prize Baby 1915 (Lubin) 1161
Prize Winners 1916 (Vim) 1161
Probation Wife, The 1919 (Select) 224, 950, 1667, 1800, 2500, 2523
Prodigal Liar 1919 (Christie) 525, 715
Prodigal Widow, The 1917 ( ) 1004
Prodigal Wife, The 1918 ( ) 246, 567
Prodigal's Return, The 1897 (American Mutoscope Co.)
Professional Patient, The 1917 (V) 768, 1641, 1707
Professor, The 1903 (AMB)
Professor, The 1911 (Independent Moving Picture Co.)
Professor and the New Hat, The 1911 (Ed)
Professor Bean's Removal 1913 (Key) 1941, 2465
Professor Fix Fixed 1909 (Ed)
Professor of the Drama, The 1903 (AMB)
Professor's Daughter, The 1913 (Key) 1666, 1941, 2465
Professor's Trip to the Country; or A Case of Mistaken Identity 1908 (V)
Profiteers 1919 ( ) 2468, 2683
Profligate, The 1915 (Mu) 258, 1080
Profligate, The 1917 (Br) 177, 349, 1351, 2712
Promise, The 1917 (M) 41, 1589
Promise, The--Henri Promises Never to Gamble Again 1908 (V)
Promised Land, The 1914 (Es) 487, 2700

Property Man, The /aka/ The Roustabout; Getting His Goat 1914 (Key) 37, 451, 1651, 1884, 2336, 2368
Prophetess of Thebes, The 1908 (Melies)
Proposal, The 1910 (Bio)
Prospector, The 1912 (Es) 50
Prospector, The 1917 (King-Bee) 1161
Prospectors, The 1906 (V)
Prostitution 1918 ( ) 2632
Prudence on Broadway 1919 (Sel) 1490, 1658, 2557
Prudence, the Pirate 1916 ( ) 901
Prunella 1919 (Par) 216, 442, 482, 558, 1174
Prussian Cur, The 1918 ( ) 554
Prussian Spy, The 1909 (AMB)
Pseudo Sultan 1912 (V) 332, 901
Public Be Damed, The 1917 ( ) 2129
Public Defender, The 1916 (P) 809
Public Ghost No. 1 1916 ( ) 460
Public Opinion 1916 (Las) 454, 724, 925, 947, 1201, 2513
Puddin' Head Wilson 1916 (Las) 1117, 1800, 2149
Pueblo Legend, A 1912 (Bio) 1182, 1613, 2047 (Biograph's first two reeler)
Pugilist, The see The Knockout
Pull Down the Curtains, Susie 1904 (AMB)
Pull for the Shore, Sailor 1911 (Ed)
Pulling off the Bed Clothes 1903 (AMB)
Pullman Bride, A 1917 (Key/Tri) 531, 1874, 2510, 2512
Pullman Mystery, The 1917 ( ) 1719
Pullman Porter, The 1919 ( ) 2208
Pumpkin Eater 1904 (Paley & Steiner)
Punch the Clock 1919 (P) 2055
Puncher's New Love, The 1911 (Es) 50
Punishment, The 1912 (Bio) 315, 362, 1328, 2513
Puppet Crown, The 1915 (Par) 474, 935
Puppets 1916 (Tri) 1286
Puppy Love 1917 ( ) 601, 1528, 2486
Purgation, The 1910 (Bio) 357, 1074, 1223, 1224, 2156
Purgatory 1912 (National Film Distributing Co.)
Purity 1916 ( ) 1900
Purple Dress, The 1917 ( ) 102
Purple Lily, The 1918 ( ) 1048
Purple Mask, The--serial 1916 (Un) 80, 222, 610, 774, 880, 926, 1000, 1199
   1. The Vanished Jewels
   2. Suspected
   3. The Capture
   4. Facing Death
   5. The Demon of the Sky
   6. The Silent Feud
   7. The Race for Freedom
   8. Secret Adventure
   9. A Strange Discovery
  10. House of Mystery
  11. Garden of Surprise
  12. The Vault of Mystery
  13. The Leap
  14. The Sky Monsters
  15. Floating Signal
  16. A Prisoner of Love
Purple Scar, The 1917 ( ) 2002
Pursuit of a Suit, The 1908 (Lubin)
Puss in Boots 1903 (Lubin)
Pussy's Bath 1897 (American Mutoscope Co.)

Put up Your Hands! 1919 ( ) 905, 2070
Putting It Over 1919 (Art/Par) 2700
Putting It Over on Henry 1917 (M) 768, 1707
Putting One Over see The Masquerader 1914 (Key)
Putting One Over 1919 (F) 2671
Puzzle-Mad 1909 (Lubin)
Puzzle Woman, The 1917 ( ) 610, 926
Pygmalion and Galatea 1912 (Br) 503

- Q -

Quack, The 1914 ( ) 2112
Quakeress, The 1913 ( ) 1032, 2096
Quality of Mercy, The (Hep) 2531
Quality of Mercy, The 1915 (V) 618, 1876, 2487
Quarrel on the Cliff, The 1911 (Ed)
Quarrelsome Washerwoman, The 1904 (AMB)
Quarry Mystery, The 1914 (Br) 1289
Quarter after Two, A 1911 (Independent Moving Picture Co.)
Queen Elizabeth 1912 (FP) 212, 2541
Queen for a Day, A 1911 (V) 332
Queen of Criminals 1912 ( )
Queen of Hearts 1918 (F) 2024
Queen of the Burlesque, A 1910 (Ed)
Queen of the Ranch, The 1909 (Lubin)
Queen of the Sea 1918 (F) 1411, 1591, 2560
Queenie of the Circus 1914 (Br) 1879
Queen's Evidence 1919 (B&C) 2536
Quello Che Videro I Mici Occhi 1917 ( ) 1372
Quest, The 1916 (Mu) 905
Quest of Life, The 1916 (FP) 1553, 2681
Quest of the Big 'Un 1919 ( ) 558
Quest of the Holy Grail 1916 ( ) 1175, 1602, 1751
Quest of Virginia, The 1917 ( ) 2656
Question Mark, The 1911 (Ed)
Question of Clothes, A 1914 (V) 297, 2523
Question of Seconds, A 1912 (Ed)
Quick Recovery, A 1902 (AMB)
Quick Work for the Soubrettes 1904 (AMB)
Quickening Flame, The 1919 ( ) 114, 835, 1603
Quicksands 1919 (Par) 627, 1029, 1186
Quiet Little Wedding, A 1913 (Key) 65
Quiet Supper for Four, A 1915 (Christie) 525
Quinney's 1919 (Br) 22, 831
Quits 1915 (Rex/Un) 449, 2398

- R -

Race, The 1916 (Par) 1868
Race for a Kiss, A 1904 (AMB)
Race for a Wife, A 1906 (V)
Race for Millions, A 1907 (Ed)
Racing Strain, The 1919 (Go) 1751, 2814
Rack, The 1915 (WS) 273, 835, 1429, 2410
Raffles, Amateur Cracksman 1905 (V) 2392
Raffles, Amateur Cracksman 1918 ( ) 140, 1878
Raffles, the Dog 1905 (Ed)
Ragamuffin, The 1916 (Las) 935, 2513

Ragged Earl, The 1918 ( ) 1205
Ragged Messenger, The 1917 (Br) 43, 1289
Ragged Princess, The 1919 (F) 392
Ragged Queen, The 1917 ( ) 1814
Rags 1915 (FP) 1450, 1659, 1730, 2047
Ragtime Band, The /aka/ The Jazz Band 1913 (Key) 1941, 2465
Ragtime Snapshots 1915 (P) 1586
Rah! Rah! Rah! 1916 (V) 2367
Raid on a Cock Fight, A 1908 (AMB)
Raid on a Coiner's Den 1904 (AMB)
Raiders, The 1916 (Selig Polyscope) 1849, 2693
Raiders on the Mexican Border 1912 ( ) 864
Railroad Raiders, The--serial 1917 (Mu) 168, 319, 330, 1221, 1273, 1325, 1579, 1672, 1720, 1762
  1. Circumstantial Evidence
  2. A Double Steal
  3. Inside Treachery
  4. A Race for a Fortune
  5. A Woman's Wit
  6. The Overland Disaster
  7. Mistaken Identity
  8. A Knotted Cord
  9. A Leap for Life
  10. A Watery Grave
  11. A Desperate Deed
  12. A Fight for a Franchise
  13. The Road Wrecker
  14. The Trap
  15. Mystery of the Counterfeit Tickets
Railroaders, The 1919 ( ) 875
Rainbow Island 1917 (P) 1586, 2055
Rainbow Princess, The 1916 (FP) 2028
Rainbow Trail 1918 (F) 868, 1374
Rain-Dear, The 1908 (Lubin)
Rainey's African Hunt 1913 ( ) 2085
Rainmakers 1897 (Ed)
Rajah, The 1911 (Ed)
Rajah, The 1919 (P) 1586, 2055
Rambling Romeo 1919 ( ) 339
Ramon und Mensch 1914 ( ) 2340
Ramona 1910 (Bio) 1059, 1182, 2047, 2680
Ramona 1916 (W. H. Clune) 473, 595, 1033, 2103, 2211
Ranch Girl's Legacy, The 1910 (Es) 50
Ranch Girl's on a Rampage 1912 (Kal) 2169
Ranch Girl's Trail, The 1912 (Es) 50
Ranch Life in the Great Southwest 1910 (Selig Polyscope) 1849
Ranch Romance, A 1914 (Nestor/Un) 449, 1197, 1408, 1705, 2635
Ranchero's Revenge, The 1913 (Bio) 141, 398, 1665
Ranchman's Feud, The 1910 (Es) 50
Ranchman's Rival 1909 (Es) 50
Range Girl and the Cowboy, The 1915 (Selig Polyscope) 1849
Range Law, The 1913 (Selig Polyscope) 785, 1849
Range Rider, The 1910 (Selig Polyscope) 1849
Range Rider series 1912 (P) 617, 1720, 1989, 2749
Ranger of Pike's Peak 1919 ( ) 2133
Ranger's Romance, The 1914 (Selig

Polyscope) 1849
Ransom, The 1916 ( ) 673
Ransom of Red Chief, The 1911 (Ed)
Ranson's Folly 1910 (Ed)
Ranson's Folly 1916 (Ed) 804, 1656, 2597
Rascal of Wolfish Ways, A /aka/ A Polished Villain 1915 (Key) 70, 351, 2336
Rasputin 1918 (WS) 835
Rasputin, the Black Monk 1917 (W) 1603
Rasputin, the Mad Monk 1917 ( ) 534, 606
Rat Trap Pickpocket Detector, The 1905 (AMB)
Rations 1918 (Br) 852
Raven, The 1912 (Eclair) 1975
Raven, The 1915 (Es) 1302, 2680
Razzle, Dazzle 1903 (Ed)
Reaching for the Moon 1917 (Art/Par) 387, 607, 857, 1984, 2031, 2649, 2708
Reading the Death Sentence 1905 (AMB)
Ready in a Minute 1910 (Ed)
Ready Money 1914 (Las) 134, 2149
Real Thing at Last, The 1916 (British Actors Film Co.) 78, 553, 922, 1103, 1231, 1918, 2536
Reapers, The 1916 ( ) 1971
Reaping, The 1915 ( ) 377
Reason Why, The 1918 ( ) 2535, 2811
Rebecca of Sunnybrook Farm 1917 (FP) 138, 601, 664, 808, 1959, 1970, 2047, 2051, 2573
Rebecca's Wedding Day 1914 (Key) 65
Rebellion of Kitty Belle, The 1914 (Mu) 1028, 1029, 1182
Rebellion of Mr. Minor, The 1917 (M) 768, 1707
Rebellious Bride, The 1919 ( ) 1329
Recalling of John Grey, The 1915 (Hep) 1289, 2171, 2744
Reckless Romeo, A /aka/ A Creampuff Romance; His Alibi 1917 (FP/Las) 65, 396, 1401, 1476, 2208
Reckless Wrestlers 1916 (P) 1586
Reckoning, The 1908 (AMB) 731, 2212
Reckoning Day 1919 ( ) 186
Reckoning Roads 1919 ( ) 1440
Reclaimed 1918 ( ) 2719
Reclamation 1916 ( ) 1080
Recording Day 1918 ( ) 2392
Recreation /aka/ Spring Fever 1914 (Key) 451
Recreation of an Heiress, The 1910 (Bio)
Red Ace, The--serial 1917 (Un) 66, 290, 1367, 1682, 1848, 2038, 2384, 2656, 2723
  1. Silent Terror
  2. Lure of the Unattainable
  3. A Leap for Liberty
  4. The Undercurrent
  5. In Mid-Air
  6. Fighting Blood
  7. The Lion's Claws
  8. Lair of the Beast
  9. A Voice from the Dead or Voice from the Past
  10. Hearts of Steel
  11. The Burning Span
  12. Overboard
  13. New Enemies

14. The Fugitives
15. Hell's Riders
16. Virginia's Triumph
Red and White Roses 1913 (V) 1047
Red Blood and Yellow 1919 ( ) 50
Red Circle, The--serial 1915 (P) 1652,
   1796, 2169, 2205
   1. Nevermore
   2. Pitty the Poor
   3. Twenty Years Ago
   4. In Strange Attire
   5. Weapons of War
   6. False Colors
   7. Third Degree or Two Captives
   8. Peace at Any Price
   9. Dodging the Law
   10. Excess Baggage
   11. Seeds of Suspicion
   12. Like a Rat in a Trap
   13. Branded as a Thief
   14. Judgment Day
Red Cross Pluck 1914 (Br) 150
Red Cross Seal, The 1910 (Ed)
Red Girl, The 1908 (AMB) 1336, 1363,
   1992, 2502
Red Glove, The--serial 1919 (Un) 34, 692,
   1579, 1976, 2361, 2625, 2656, 2657
   1. Pool of Lost Souls
   2. Claws of the Vulture
   3. The Vulture's Vengeance
   4. Passing of Gentleman Geoff
   5. At the Mercy of a Monster
   6. Flames of Death
   7. A Desperate Chance
   8. Facing Death
   9. A Leap for Life
   10. Out of Death's Shadow
   11. In the Depths of the Sea
   12. In Death's Grip
   13. Trapped
   14. The Lost Millions
   15. The Mystery Message
   16. The Deadly Peril
   17. The Rope of Death
   18. Run to Earth
Red-Haired Cupid, A 1918 (Tri) 2479
Red Hot Dollars 1919 ( ) 532, 997, 1714,
   2096
Red Hot Romance, A 1913 (Key) 1666,
   1941, 2465
Red Ink Tragedy 1912 (V) 332, 901
Red Lantern 1919 (M) 165, 321, 618, 1126,
   1460, 1919, 2790
Red Lights 1919 ( ) 1476
Red Margaret--Moonshiner 1913 (Gold Seal/
   Un) 352, 449, 1705, 1925
Red Mask, The 1914 ( ) 2-96
Red Pottage 1918 (Br) 43, 2424
Red Prince, The 1917 ( ) 1519
Red, Red Heart, The 1918 ( ) 496, 1518,
   1613, 2211
Red Riding Hood of the Hills 1914 (Es) 50
Red Robe, The--serial 1919 ( ) 2656
Red Stain, The 1916 ( ) 1719
Red Star Inn, The 1909 (Melies)
Red Viper, The 1919 ( ) 1310
Red, White and Blue Blood 1917 (M) 156,
   353, 1297
Red Widow, The 1916 (FP) 140, 2816
Red Wing's Gratitude * (V) 2103
Redeemed from Sin 1908 (Lubin)

Redeeming Love 1917 (Art/Par) 1266,
   2770
Redemption 1909 (Bio) 1511
Redemption 1912 (Eclair)
Redemption 1917 ( ) 1929, 2553
Redemption of Dave Darcey 1916 ( ) 1888
Redemption of His Name, The 1918 (Br)
   1873
Redhead, The 1919 (Reelart) 273, 1914,
   2072
Redman and the Child, The 1908 (AMB)
   1336, 2212, 2526
Redman's View, The 1909 (Bio) 1450, 1831
Reflections from the Firelight 1912 (Imp)
Reform Candidate, The 1911 (Ed)
Reform Candidate, The 1915 ( ) 2445
Reformation of Sierra Smith, The 1912
   (Am) 1924
Reformer, The 1916 (Vim) 1161
Reformers, The; or The Lost Art of
   Minding One's Own Business 1913
   (Bio) 1182, 1714, 1751, 1831, 1909
Reforming a Husband 1909 (Lubin)
Refugee, The 1918 (Hep) 812, 2531, 2744
Regenerates 1917 (Tri) 2194
Regeneration 1914 ( ) 884, 2112
Reggie Mixes In 1916 (FA/Tri) 190, 857,
   1602, 1608, 2194, 2415
Regiment of Two, A 1913 (V) 768, 1332,
   1707, 2472, 2487
Regular Fellow, A 1919 ( ) 1276, 1490,
   1864
Regular Girl, A 1919 ( ) 694, 1348, 1560,
   1633, 1864, 1903, 2814
Rehearsal, The 1903 (AMB)
Reilly's Wash Day 1919 (Key) 1906, 2069
Reincarnation of Karma 1912 (V) 920,
   2554, 2663
Rejected Lover's Luck, The 1913 ( ) 785
Reliable Henry 1917 (M) 768, 1707
Relief of Lucknow, The 1912 (Ed)
Religion and Gun Practice 1913 ( ) 785
Remember Mary Magdalen 1914 (Victor/Un)
   352, 449, 1705
Remodeling Her Husband 1919 ( ) 1029
Renegade, The 1915 (Tri) 1032, 1794, 2096
Reno, All Change 1917 ( ) 1177
Rent Jumpers, The 1915 (Key) 351, 460,
   1981, 2336
Renunciation, The 1908 (V)
Renunciation, The 1909 (Bio) 95, 2047,
   2081, 2212
Repaid 1914 ( ) 2096
Reporter, The 1911 (V) 2112
Reprieve, The 1908 (V)
Reprieve from the Scaffold, A 1905 (AMB)
Reputation 1917 (Mu) 1254
Rescue, The 1917 (Bluebird/Un) 88, 449,
   771, 1518, 1719, 2042, 2490
Rescue of Child from Indians 1903 (AMB)
Rescued by Carlo 1906 (Lubin)
Rescued by Rover 1905 (AMB)
Rescued by Rover 1905 (Hep) 1232, 1233,
   1234
Rescued by Wireless 1912 (Imp)
Rescued from an Eagle's Nest 1908 (Ed)
   1089
Rescuing Angel, The 1919 (Par) 454, 1774,
   1925
Resourceful Lovers 1911 (Bio)
Responsibility 1917 ( ) 1745

Restless Souls 1919 (Tri) 537, 2194
Restoration, The 1909 (Bio) 1450, 1542,
  1865, 2047
Restored by Repentence 1908 (Lubin)
Resurrection 1909 (Bio) 271, 1363, 1511,
  1865
Resurrection 1912 (Masko Film Co.) 824,
  2669
Resurrection 1918 (Par) 957, 1496
Resurrection of John, The 1911 (Ed)
Retribution 1913 ( ) 2112
Retribution; or The Brand of Cain 1907
  (V)
Retrospect /aka/ Sweet Memories 1909
  (Bio) 2047
Return of Draw Egan, The 1916 (Tri) 1032,
  1188, 1690, 2780
Return of Eve 1916 (Es) 1787, 1795, 1959
Return of Mary 1919 (M) 41, 1613
Return of Richard Neal 1915 (Es) 353, 581
Return of the Riddle Rider--serial 1917
  ( ) 610
Return of "Widow" Pogson's Husband
  1911 (V) 332
Reuben in the Subway 1905 (AMB)
Reunited by the Sea 1912 (Un)
Reve d'un Maitre de Ballet, Le 1903
  (Melies)
Reve de l'Horloger, Le 1904 (Melies)
Revelation 1918 (M) 321, 618, 1919
Revelry see The Rounders
Revenant, Le 1903 (Melies)
Revenge 1904 (AMB)
Revenge 1918 ( ) 2487
Revenge Is Sweet 1912 (Ed)
Revenge of Mr. Thomas Atkins 1914 (Br)
  43
Revenue Man and the Girl, The 1911
  (Bio) 2729
Revolt, The 1916 ( ) 2690
Revolution 1915 (Br) 150, 2637
Reward of Bronco Billy 1912 (Es) 50
Reward of Valor, The 1912 (Am) 1924
Rex's Bath 1902 (AMB)
Reynard the Fox 1903 (Lubin)
Rheumatic Joint, A 1915 (P) 1161
Rice and Old Shoes 1917 ( ) 689
Rich Man, Poor Man 1918 (Par) 143, 482
Rich Man's Darling, A 1918 ( ) 1604
Rich Revenge, A 1910 (Bio) 1363, 2047,
  2081
Richard, the Brazen 1917 ( ) 102
Richard III 1908 (V) 94, 1333
Richard III 1911 (Co-operative) 21, 213,
  323, 863
Richard III 1913 (Sterling) 2689
Richelieu 1914 (Un) 352, 449, 454, 762,
  1587, 1705, 1716, 1925, 2188
Riches and Rogues 1913 ( ) 1160
Richest Girl, The 1917 ( ) 1902
Riddle Gawne 1918 (Art/Par) 449, 1188,
  1428, 1518, 1661, 2183, 2401, 2567
Riddle of the Green Umbrella 1914 (Kal)
  1388
Riddle: Woman, The 1919 (Go) 869
Ride for a Rancho, A 1917 (Tri) 2056
Riders of the Dawn 1919 ( ) 763
Riders of the Law 1919 (Un) 398, 1283,
  1307
Riders of the Night 1918 (M) 631
Riders of the Plains 1910 (Ed)

Riders of the Purple Stage 1918 (F) 868,
  1374, 1849
Riders of Vengeance 1919 (Un) 398
Right and Wrong of It, The 1914 ( ) 2472
Right Clue, The 1912 (Imp)
Right Decision, The 1910 (Ed)
Right Girl, The 1915 (V) 2472
Right of the Seigneur, The 1908 (V)
Right of Way, The 1914 (V) 297, 2523
Right to Happiness, The 1919 (Un) 1728,
  2042, 2738
Right to Labor, The 1909 (Lubin)
Rightful Heir, The 1914 ( ) 2096
Rights of Youth, The 1912 (Ingvald C. Oes)
Riley and Schultz 1912 (Key) 1666, 1941,
  2465
Rimrock Jones 1918 (Art/Par) 1580, 1975,
  2112, 2648
Ring, The 1914 ( ) 2748
Ring up the Curtain 1919 (P) 1586
Ringmaster's Wife, The 1907 (Lubin)
Rink, The 1916 (Mu) 97, 106, 204, 384,
  451, 517, 1414, 1840, 2077, 2090
Riot, The 1913 (Key) 65, 1941, 2465
Rip 1905 (Melies)
Rip and the Dwarf 1902 (AMB)
Rip Leaving Sleepy Hollow 1896 (American
  Mutoscope Co.)
Rip Leaving Sleepy Hollow 1902 (AMB)
Rip Meeting the Dwarf 1896 (American
  Mutoscope Co.)
Rip Meeting the Dwarf 1902 (AMB)
Rip Passing Over Hill 1902 (AMB)
Rip Van Winkle 1902 (AMB) 1352
Rip Van Winkle 1903 (Lubin)
Rip Van Winkle 1912 (Eclair)
Rip Van Winkle 1912 (V) 565
Rips and Rushes 1917 (V) 2367
Rip's Toast 1896 (American Mutoscope Co.)
Rip's Toast 1902 (AMB)
Rip's Toast to Hudson and Crew 1897
  (American Mutoscope Co.)
Rip's Toast to Hudson and Crew 1902 (AMB)
Rip's Twenty Years' Sleep 1897 (American
  Mutoscope Co.)
Rip's Twenty Years' Sleep 1902 (AMB)
Rise and Fall of Weary Willie 1911 (Ed)
Rise of Jennie Cushing, The 1917
  (Art/Par) 724, 888
Rise of Susan 1916 ( ) 2811
Risks and Roughnecks 1917 (V) 2367
Risky Road, The 1918 (Un) 2042
Rival Candidates, The 1911 (Ed)
Rival Mashers, The see Those Love
  Pangs
Rival Models, The 1904 (AMB)
Rival Sculptors, The 1911 (Ed)
Rival Stage Lines, The * (Selig Polyscope)
  1849
Rivals, The 1903 (AMB)
Rivals, The 1907 (Ed)
Rivals, The 1912 (Key) 1941, 2368, 2465
Rivals for a Week 1908 (Lubin)
River of Romance 1916 (M) 41, 1589
River Pirates, The 1905 (AMB)
River Pirates, The 1906 (Lubin)
Road Called Straight, The 1919 ( ) 1205
Road of Strife, The--serial 1915 (Lubin)
  277, 288, 457, 1846, 2442, 2760
    1. The House of Secrets
    2. Face of Fear

3. The Silver Cup
4. The Ring of Death
5. No Other Way
6. Strength of Love
7. Into the Night
8. In the Wolf's Den
9. The Iron Hand of Law
10. The Unsparing Sword
11. The Valley of the Shadow
12. The Sacrifice
13. The Man Who Did Not Die
14. A Story of the Past
15. The Coming of the Kingdom
Road Side Inn, A 1906 (Melies)
Road through the Dark 1918 ( ) 2811
Road to France, The 1918 (W) 231, 1075, 1223
Road to Love, A 1909 (Ed)
Road to Love, The 1916 ( ) 2610
Road to the Heart, The 1909 (AMB) 1227, 1450, 1511
Roaring Oaks--serial 1919 ( ) 572, 1971
Roaring Road, The 1919 (Art/Par) 1580, 1975, 2112, 2149
Roasted Chestnuts 1907 (Lubin)
Robbed of Her All 1905 (AMB)
Robber of the Golden Star 1917 ( ) 1010
Robbery of the Citizens' Bank, The 1908 (Lubin)
Robbie's Pet Rat 1908 (Lubin)
Robert Macaire and Bertrand behind the Scene 1907 (Melies)
Robin Hood 1912 (Ed) 950, 955, 1975, 2544
Robin Hood 1912 (Eclair)
Robin Hood 1913 (T) 1272, 2201
Robin Crusoe 1903 (Lubin)
Robin Crusoe 1913 (Rex/Un) 1544
Robinson's Trousseau 1917 ( ) 1872
Robust Romeo, A 1914 (Key) 65
Rock of Ages 1902 (Ed)
Rock of Ages 1903 (AMB)
Rock of Ages 1918 ( ) 2558
Rocks of Valpre, The 1919 (Br) 834, 1018
Rocky Road, The 1910 (Bio) 79, 315, 580, 1450, 1593, 1613, 1831, 1933, 2062, 2513
Rogue, The 1918 (King-Bee) 1161, 2733
Rogue's Romance, A 1919 (V) 998, 2616, 2767
Rogues' Tricks 1907 (Melies)
Roi Du Maquillage, Le 1904 (Melies)
Roller Skate Craze, The 1907 (Selig)
Rolling Stones 1916 ( ) 572
Roman, The 1908 (Selig) 258, 1189
Roman Cowboy, The 1917 (F) 1381, 1849
Romance and Arabella 1918 (M) 242, 473, 927, 1925, 2399, 2521
Romance and Kings 1919 (M) 768, 1707
Romance and Rough House 1916 (V) 2367
Romance of a Dry Town, The 1911 (Kal) 1924
Romance of a Gypsy Camp 1908 (Lubin)
Romance of a Jewess 1908 (AMB) 994, 1336, 1511
Romance of a War Nurse 1908 (Ed)
Romance of an Actor 1914 (Powers) 95, 96, 2387
Romance of an American Duchess, The 1915 (Es) 24, 2345, 2486, 2512, 2582
Romance of an Egg 1908 (AMB)

Romance of an Old Maid 1912 (Imp)
Romance of an Umbrella 1909 (V)
Romance of Bar "O" 1910 (Es) 50
Romance of Elaine, The--serial 1915 (P) 141, 628, 1118, 2748
1. The Lost Torpedo
2. The Gray Friar
3. The Vanishing Man
4. The Submarine Harbor
5. The Conspirators
6. The Wireless Detective
7. The Death Cloud
8. The Searchlight Gun
9. The Life Chain
10. The Flash
11. The Disappearing Helmet
12. The Triumph of Elaine
Romance of Engine 999 1909 (Lubin)
Romance of Happy Valley, A 1919 (Art/Par) 315, 706, 875, 1029, 1065, 1182, 1552, 1933, 2494, 2570
Romance of Hefty Burke, The 1910 (Ed)
Romance of Lady Hamilton, The 1919 (Br) 1592
Romance of Old Bill, The 1918 ( ) 2756
Romance of Old Madrid, A 1909 (Ed)
Romance of Old Mexico, A 1909 (V)
Romance of Rome, A 1917 ( ) 1253
Romance of Tarzan, The 1918 (National Film Corp.) 242, 1353, 1570, 1711, 1745
Romance of the Air, A 1918 ( ) 668
Romance of the Alps, A 1908 (V)
Romance of the Cliff Dwellers, A 1911 (Ed)
Romance of the Forest Reserve 1914 ( ) 785
Romance of the Fur Country, A 1908 (Lubin)
Romance of the Ice Fields 1912 (Ed)
Romance of the Rail, A 1903 (Ed)
Romance of the Rancho 1914 (Par) 677
Romance of the Redwoods 1917 (Art/Par) 724, 1126, 1201, 1591, 1756, 1970, 2047
Romance of the Underworld, A 1918 (Keeney) 375, 1959, 2061
Romance of the Western Hills, A 1910 (Bio) 315, 1363, 2000, 2047, 2513, 2728
Romans and Rascals 1918 (V) 2367
Romantic Peggy 1915 (V) 768
Romantic Redskins 1910 ( ) 864
Romany Lass, The 1918 (Br) 1453
Romany Rye 1919 ( ) 166
Romany Tragedy, A 1911 (Bio) 357, 816, 1074, 1665
Romeo and Juliet 1908 (GB) 59, 109, 2536
Romeo and Juliet 1908 (V) 19, 90, 424, 453, 1151, 2003
Romeo and Juliet 1911 (FdA) 215
Romeo and Juliet 1915 (Cricks and Martin) 484
Romeo and Juliet 1916 (F) 116, 147, 733, 806, 975, 1278, 1506, 1574, 2579, 2745
Romeo and Juliet 1916 (M) 117, 156, 180, 252, 255, 350, 353, 358, 608, 625, 656, 781, 833, 1253
Rommates 1909 (Lubin
Rooms and Rumors 1918 (V) 2367

Rooms for Gentlemen Only 1905 (AMB)
Root of Evil, The 1912 (Bio) 209, 1328
Roped 1918 (Un) 398, 1004, 1659
Ropin' Fool 1919 ( ) 2124
Roping a Sweetheart 1916 (Selig Polyscope)
    1849
Roping Her Romeo 1917 (Key/Tri) 1874,
    2501, 2608
Rosary, The 1911 (Es) 353, 2042
Rose, The 1903 (AMB)
Rose, The 1916 (Par) 1439
Rose Bernd 1918 ( ) 1349
Rose Carnival 1912 (Un)
Rose Marie 1919 ( ) 2753
Rose o' Salem-Town 1910 (Bio) 1363, 2729
Rose of California, The 1912 (Imp)
Rose of Granada /aka/ The House of
    Granada, 1919 (Art/Par) 438, 1901
Rose of Hell 1919 ( ) 192
Rose of Kentucky, The 1911 (Bio) 1613,
    2502
Rose of Old Mexico, A 1913 ( ) 2112
Rose of Paradise 1918 ( ) 134, 1432
Rose of Surrey 1913 (GB) 2604
Rose of the Blood 1917 (F) 116, 238, 485,
    1442, 1794, 1982, 2224, 2603
Rose of the Rancho, The 1914 (Las) 134,
    649, 828, 866, 1369, 1493, 1701,
    1925, 2211
Rose of the River 1919 ( ) 1528
Rose of the South 1916 (V) 1329, 1426,
    1876, 2527
Rose of the Tenderloin, A 1909 (Ed)
Rose of the West 1919 ( ) 1928, 2581
Rose of the World 1918 (Par) 888, 1748,
    2444
Rosemary 1915 (Quality) 105, 353, 496,
    612
Rosemary Climbs the Heights 1918 (Mu)
    938, 1841
Rosen die der Sturm Entblättert 1918
    ( ) 1922
Rose's Story, The 1911 (Imp) 2047
Rosie O'Grady 1917 (M) 631
Roue's Heart, The 1909 (AMB) 685, 1542,
    2212
Rouge and Riches 1919 ( ) 2753
Rough and Ready * ( ) 868
Rough House, The 1917 ( ) 1401, 2208,
Rough House in a New York Honky-Tonk
    1905 (AMB)
Rough Knight, A 1916 (Kay-Bee) 1135,
    1286, 2568
Rough Lover, The 1918 ( ) 1153
Rough Neck, The 1915 ( ) 1188, 1603
Rough Ride with Nitroglycerine, A 1912
    (Selig) 785
Rough Riding Romance 1919 ( ) 1153,
    1928
Rough Toughs and Rooftops 1917 (V) 2367
Round Up, The 1919 ( ) 606
Rounders, The /aka/ Oh, What a Night;
    Revelry; Two of a Kind 1914 (Key)
    37, 65, 451, 460, 791, 1662, 2208,
    2336
Rounding up of the "Yeggmen" 1904 (Ed)
Roustabout, The see The Property Man
Rowdy and His New Pal 1912 (Ed)
Royal Blood 1916 (Vim) 1161
Royal Democrat 1919 ( ) 1753
Royal Power 1917 ( ) 1496

Royal Rogue, A 1917 (Key/Tri) 71, 543,
    1092, 1153, 1225, 2200, 2588
Royal Romance, A 1917 (F) 606, 2024
Royal Wild West, The 1914 (V) 768
Rubbing It In 1917 (M) 768, 1707
Rube and Fender 1903 (Ed)
Rube and Mandy at Coney Island 1903 (Ed)
Rube and the Baron, The 1913 (Key) 1666,
    1941, 2368, 2465
Rube and the Boob, The 1913 (Kal) 2367
Rube Couple at a County Fair, A 1904
    (Ed)
Rube in an Opium Joint 1905 (AMB)
Rube in the Subway, A 1905 (AMB)
Rubes in the Theatre 1901 (Ed)
Rude Awakening, A 1908 (Melies)
Rude Hostess, A 1909 (AMB) 1363, 1542
Rug Maker's Daughter, The 1916 ( ) 2445
Ruggles of Red Gap 1918 (Es) 757, 1276
Ruler of the Road, The 1918 ( ) 1404
Ruling Passion, The 1911 (Bio) 816
Ruling Passions 1916 ( ) 673, 2756
Rummies and Razors 1918 (V) 2367
Runaway, The 1917 (Mu) 1223, 2217, 2587
Runaway Freight 1916 ( ) 2002
Runaway in the Park 1896 (Ed)
Runaway June--serial 1915 (Reliance) 38,
    1369, 1605, 1768
    1. The Runaway Bride
    2. The Man with the Black
        Vandyke
    3. Discharged
    4. The New Governess
    5. Trapped in a Gambling House
        or A Woman in Trouble
    6. The Siege of the House of
        O'Keefe
    7. The Tormentors
    8. Her Enemies
    9. Kidnapped
    10. Trapped on a Liner
    11. In the Clutch of the River
        Thieves
    12. The Spirit of the Marsh
    13. Trapped
    14. In the Grip of Poverty
    15. At Last, My Love
Runaway Match 1903 (AMB)
Runaway Romance 1917 (P) 1346
Runaway Romany 1917 (P) 229, 523, 660,
    683, 1205, 1346, 1437, 1864
Rupert of Hentzau 1915 (Br) 22, 43
Rupert of Hentzau 1918 ( ) 1806
Rural Cinderella, A 1914 (Key) 531
Rural Demon, A 1914 (Key) 65
Rural Elopement, A 1909 (AMB)
Rural Romeos 1914 (Warner) 864
Rural Roughnecks 1916 (P) 2055
Rural Third Degree, The 1913 (Key) 1666,
    1941
Rural Tragedy, A 1909 (Ed)
Ruse, The 1916 (Tri) 1188
Ruses, Rhymes, Roughnecks 1915 (P) 1586
Rush Hour 1919 ( ) 355
Rush Orders 1915 ( ) 1684
Rustic Heroine, A; or In the Days of King
    George 1908 (V)
Rustlers, The 1919 ( ) 1010, 1011
Rustling a Bride 1919 ( ) 242, 1455,
    1528
Ruy Blas 1909 (V)

- S -

Sable Lorcha 1915 ( ) 1353, 1756
Sacred Flame, The 1919 (Par) 957, 1991
Sacred Silence 1919 ( ) 102, 1888
Sacrifice 1917 ( ) 1330
Sacrifice, The 1909 (AMB)
Sacrifice of Kathleen, The 1913 (V) 2523
Sadie Goes to Heaven 1917 (Es) 1636
Sadie Love 1919 (Art/Par) 333
Safe for Democracy 1918 ( ) 30, 709,
     1562
Safe in Jail 1913 (Key) 2465
Safe Investment 1915 (V) 768
Safety Curtain, The 1918 (Select) 1014,
     1124, 1959, 2091, 2457, 2523
Safety First Ambrose /aka/ Sheriff Am-
     brose 1916 (Key/Tri) 280, 1382,
     1461, 2510, 2724
Safety Worst 1915 (Lubin) 1161
Sagebrush Hamlet, A 1919 ( ) 693, 715
Sagebrush Tom * (Selig Polyscope) 1849
Sahara 1919 ( ) 680, 1032, 1864, 1866
Sailors Ashore 1904 (AMB)
Sailor's Heart, A 1912 (Bio) 1613, 2513
Sailor's Love Letter, The 1911 (Ed)
St. Elmo 1910 (V) 1511, 2604
St. George and the Dragon 1910 (Ed)
St. George and the Dragon 1912 (Powers)
Saint's Adventure, The 1917 ( ) 457
Sale of a Heart, The 1913 (V) 566
Saleslady, The 1916 (FP) 606, 667
Saleslady's Matinee Idol, The 1909 (Ed)
Sallie's Sure Shot 1913 ( ) 785
Sally Bishop 1916 ( ) 1329
Sally's Blighted Career 1918 ( ) 961
Salome 1918 (F) 116, 238, 754, 959,
     1065, 1244, 1952, 2175
Salome; or The Dance of the Seven Veils
     1908 (V)
Salome and the Devil to Pay 1908 (Lubin)
Salome vs. Shenandoah 1919 (Key/Tri)
     530, 2069, 2608
Salomy Jane 1914 (Alco) 1379, 1820, 1936,
     2035
Salt Did It, The; or If You Want to Catch
     a Bird, Put Salt on Its Tail 1908 (V)
Salutary Lesson, A 1910 (Bio) 816, 1542,
     2067, 2729
Salvation Army Lass, The 1909 (AMB)
     79, 731, 1511, 1865, 2368
Salvation Joan 1916 (Es) 1360, 1795, 1916
Salvation of Nance O'Shaughnessy 1914
     (Selig) 857, 1957
Sammy in Siberia, A 1919 (P) 1586
Samson 1914 (Un) 1417, 1431, 1586
Sand 1919 ( ) 1186
Sand Baby, The 1903 (AMB)
Sand Fort, The 1903 (AMB)
Sand Witches 1918 (Christie) 339
Sandman, The 1909 (Ed)
Sands of Dee, The 1912 (Bio) 95, 1182,
     1665, 1714, 1751, 1831
Sands of Fate 1914 (Mu) 1028, 1182, 2672
Sands of Sacrifice 1917 (Mu) 2201
Sands, Scamps and Strategy 1916 (V) 2367
Sandwich Man, The 1902 (AMB)
Sandy 1917 (Art/Par) 200, 2045
Sandy Burke of the U-Bar-U 1919 ( ) 847
Sandy McPherson's Quiet Fishing Trip
     1908 (Ed)

Sandy, the Substitute 1910 (Ed)
Sane Fourth of July, A 1911 (Ed)
Santa Claus and the Club-Man 1911
     (Ed)
Santa Fe Mac 1912 (P) 617, 1720, 1989,
     2749
Santa Filling Stockings 1902 (AMB)
Sap, The 1912 ( ) 2733
Sapho 1900 (Lubin)
Sapho 1917 ( ) 462
Satan in Prison 1907 (Melies)
Satan Junior 1919 (M) 631, 1311, 1455
Satanas 1919 ( ) 2632
Satan's Fan 1909 (Lubin)
Saturday's Shopping 1903 (AMB)
Sauce for the Goose 1918 (Sel) 927,
     2521
Saucy Sue 1908 (Lubin)
Saucy Madeline 1918 (Key/Tri) 2608
Saul and David: The Biblical Story of
     the Shepherd Boy Who became King
     of the Israelites 1909 (V)
Sausage Machine, The 1902 (AMB)
Savage, The 1918 (Bluebird/Un) 495,
     1859, 2211
Savage Princess, The 1909 (Bio) 2047
Savage Woman, The 1918 (Select) 2410,
     2811
Save the Pieces 1916 ( ) 2636
Saved! 1904 (AMB)
Saved by a Watch * (Selig Polyscope)
     1849
Saved by Fire 1912 (Br) 177
Saved by Her Horse * (Selig Polyscope)
     1849
Saved by Love 1908 (Ed)
Saved by Wireless 1915 (Key/Tri) 45,
     396, 509, 531, 1452, 1651, 2510
Saved from Himself 1911 (Bio) 1074, 1941
Saved from the Vampire 1914 ( )
Saved from the Vigilantes 1913 ( ) 785
Saving an Audience 1911 (V) 1786, 1888,
     1932, 2066, 2767
Saving Grace 1914 ( ) 1028, 2356
Saving Mabel's Day 1913 (Key) 1666, 1941
Saving the Family Name 1916 (Un) 1694,
     2341
Sawdust and Salome 1914 (V) 297, 2523
Sawdust Doll 1919 (P) 771, 1988
Sawdust Ring, The 1916 (Tri) 1602
Say! Young Fellow 1918 (Art/Par) 387,
     454, 664, 857, 1925, 2149
Scales of Justice 1909 (V)
Scales of Justice 1913 ( ) 1637
Scamps and Scandals 1919 (V) 2367
Scandal 1917 (Select) 1346, 1394, 2521
Scapegoat, The * (Selig Polyscope) 1849
Scar, The 1919 ( ) 1048
Scarecrow Pump 1904 (Ed)
Scarlet Car, The 1917 (Bluebird/Un) 449,
     686, 867, 900, 1364
Scarlet Crystal, The 1917 ( ) 1364
Scarlet Days 1909 (Bio)
Scarlet Days 1919 (Art) 143, 218, 315, 706,
     875, 1067, 1591, 2370, 2504, 2694
Scarlet Drop, The 1918 (Un) 398, 1719, 1782
Scarlet Lady, The 1915 ( ) 2002
Scarlet Letter, The 1913 (Bio) 79, 108
Scarlet Letter, The 1917 (F) 1275, 1763,
     2110
Scarlet Oath, The 1916 ( ) 1117

Scarlet Pimpernel, The 1917 (F) 866, 1446
Scarlet Road, The 1918 ( ) 295, 2405
Scarlet Runner, The--serial 1916 (V) 53,
   223, 940, 1303, 1402, 1426, 1467,
   1673, 1837, 2153, 2487, 2495, 2655,
   2767
   1. The Car and His Majesty
   2. The Nuremberg Watch
   3. The Masked Ball
   4. The Hidden Prince
   5. The Jacoben House
   6. The Red Whiskered Man
   7. The Mysterious Motor Car
   8. The Glove and the Ring
   9. The Gold Cigarette Case
   10. The Lost Girl
   11. The Missing Chapter
   12. The Car and the Girl
Scarlet Shadow, The 1919 ( ) 1782, 1907,
   2068, 2221
Scarlet Sin, A 1915 ( ) 1208
Scarlet Woman, The 1916 ( ) 1959
Scars and Strings 1919 (Rolin/P) 1502
Scheme That Failed, The 1907 (Lubin)
Schemers, The 1913 (V) 332, 901
Schemers, The 1914 (Hep) 1289, 2171,
   2531
Schemers, The 1916 (Vim) 1161
Schemers, The 1919 (Key/Tri) 2510
Scheming Gambler's Paradise, The 1905
   (Melies)
Schneider's Anti-Noise Crusade 1909 (AMB)
Schnitz, the Tailor 1913 (Key) 2465
Scholar, The 1918 (King-Bee) 1161
School for Husbands, The 1917 (Las) 2683
School for Lovemaking, A 1909 (Lubin)
School for Scandal, The 1914 (Kal) 98,
   546, 1388, 2181
School Master's Surprise 1902 (AMB)
School Teacher and the Waif, The 1912
   (Bio) 95, 2047
Science 1911 (Imp) 2047
Scoundrel's Tale, A 1916 (Key/Tri) 966,
   1092, 1422, 2166, 2513
Scourge of the Desert 1914 (Mu) 1188
Scrambling for Eggs 1902 (Ed)
Scrap in Black and White, A 1903 (Ed)
Scrap in the Dressing Room, A 1904 (AMB)
Scrap of Paper, A 1914 (Bio) 1117
Scrapper, The 1912 ( ) 2733
Scrapper, The 1917 (Un) 928
Scrappy Bill 1909 (Centaur Film Co.)
Scraps 1919 (FN) 2047
Screaming Shadow, The--serial 1918 ( )
   2774
Scrooge 1913 (Br) 1247
Scrub Lady, The 1917 (Go) 765
Scrubbing Clothes 1905 (AMB)
Sculptor's Love, The 1909 (V)
Sculptor's Nightmare, The 1908 (AMB)
   2368
Sculptor's Welsh Rabbit Dream, A 1908
   (Ed)
Sea Dogs 1916 (Vim) 1161
Sea Flower, The 1919 ( ) 1153
Sea Food * ( ) 750
Sea Master, The 1917 (Mu) 2201
Sea Nymphs, The /aka/ His Diving
   Beauty 1914 (Key) 65, 1941, 2510
Sea Panther 1918 ( ) 715
Sea Urchin, The 1913 (Powers/Un) 449,

1544, 1701
Sea Waif 1919 ( ) 1309
Sea Wolf, The 1913 (Selig) 258, 2095
Seal of Death, The 1918 ( ) 1794
Seal of Silence, The 1918 (V) 533, 646,
   2767
Sealed Envelope 1919 ( ) 318
Sealed Hearts 1919 ( ) 809, 1445, 1959,
   2478
Sealed Room, The 1909 (Bio) 1363, 1542,
   2047, 2408, 2680
Search for Evidence, A 1903 (AMB)
Seashore Baby, The 1904 (AMB)
Seashore Frolics 1902 (AMB)
Seashore Gymkana, A 1902 (AMB)
Seaside Romeos 1917 (Kal) 782
Second in Command, The 1915 (Quality)
   353, 2430
Second Mrs. Roebuck, The 1914 (Mu) 27,
   2112, 2513
Second of August, The 1914 (P) 1575
Second Sight 1911 (Imp) 2047
Second String, The 1915 (Hep) 1289, 2171,
   2744
Secret, A 1908 (Lubin)
Secret Code, The 1918 (Tri) 1442, 2392,
   2476, 2512, 2665
Secret Game, The 1917 ( ) 1208
Secret Garden, The 1919 ( ) 1528
Secret Kingdom, The--serial (V) 790, 904,
   1413, 1437, 2068, 2129, 2720
   1. Land of the Intrigue
   2. Royalty at Red Wing
   3. Sealed Packet
   4. Honorable Mr. Oxenham
   5. Carriage Call #101
   6. Human Flotsam
   7. Ghost Ship
   8. Rum Cay
   9. Swamp Adder
   10. A Goat without Horns
   11. The White Witch
   12. The Shark's Nest
   13. The Tragic Masque
   14. The Portrait of a King
   15. The Tocsin
Secret Life 1914 (Br) 177
Secret Man, The 1917 (Un) 398
Secret Marriage, The 1919 ( ) 1694
Secret of Black Mountain, The 1917 ( )
   2613
Secret of the Locket, The 1909 (Ed)
Secret of the Lone Star, The 1919 ( )
Secret of the Storm Country, The 1917
   (Select) 952, 2523, 2643, 2719
Secret of the Submarine, The--serial
   (Am) 191, 461, 475, 810, 1153, 1269,
   1371, 2538, 2707
Secret Orchard, The 1915 ( ) 231, 2132,
   2149, 2513
Secret Service; or The Diamond Smug-
   glers 1906 (V)
Secret Service 1919 (Art/Par) 454, 606,
   887, 1022, 1206, 1537, 1975, 2149,
   2698
Secret Service Man, The 1912 ( ) 2112
Secret Sin, The 1915 (Las) 1208, 1800,
   2513
Secret Strings 1919 ( ) 2540
Secret Wire, The 1916 (Mu) 41, 1589
Secret Woman, The 1918 (Br) 2637

Secrets of a Beauty Parlor 1917 (Key/Tri)
    83, 650, 787, 796, 876, 2069, 2164
Section Foreman 1912 (Imp)
See a Pin and Pick It Up, All That Day
    You'll Have Good Luck 1909 (Ed)
See Eva's Hair, Mama 1904 (AMB)
See the Paint 1908 (Lubin)
Seeing Double 1913 (V) 332
Seeing Things 1919 ( ) 2147
Seek and You Shall Find 1907 (Melies)
Seekers, The 1916 ( ) 1216
Seepore Rebellion, The 1912 ( ) 2112
Seeress, The 1904 (AMB)
Selecting His Heiress 1911 (V) 332, 901
Selfish Man, The 1908 (V)
Selfish Woman, The 1916 (Par) 454, 2112,
    2132
Selfish Yates 1918 (Art) 1188, 1948
Self-Made Widow, A 1917 ( ) 265, 273
Selling Old Master 1911 (Ed)
Seminary Girls 1897 (Ed)
Seminary Scandal, A 1916 (Christie) 16,
    131, 1132, 2121
Senator and the Suffragettes, The 1910
    (Ed)
Sennett Bathing Beauties, Mack 2818
Senorita's Repentance, The 1913 ( ) 785
Sentimental Lady 1915 (M) 656
Sentimental Sister, The 1914 (Mu) 2513
Sentinel Asleep, The 1911 (Independent
    Moving Picture Co.) 2047
Sequel to the Diamond from the Sky,
    The--serial 1916 (Am) 344, 1317,
    1847, 2201, 2538
        1.   Fate and Death
        2.   Under Oath
        3.   Sealed Lips
        4.   The Climax
Serenade, The 1916 (Vim) 1161
Serenaders, The 1902 (AMB)
Serious Sixteen 1910 (Bio)
Serpent, The 1916 (F) 116, 422, 580,
    1157, 1200, 1739, 1880, 1921, 1971
Serpents, The 1912 (V) 1332, 2487
Serpent's Tooth, The 1917 (Mu) 1396,
    2754
Servant Girl Problem, The 1905 (V)
Servant Question, The 1919 ( ) 520
Servant Question out West, The 1914
    ( ) 785
Service Star, The 1918 (Go) 1423, 2814
Service Stripes 1912 ( ) 2733
Service Stripes 1919 ( ) 1580
Set Free 1919 ( ) 2147
Setting the Style 1914 (V) 157, 332
Settled at the Seaside 1915 (Key) 351, 460
Seven Ages, The 1905 (Ed)
        Schoolmates
        Lovers
        The Soldier
        The Judge
        What Age?
        Second Childhood
        Infancy
        Playmates
Seven Ages, The 1907 (V) 1333
Seven Ages, The 1913 (FP) 740
Seven Deadly Sins, The 1917 (McClure)
    314, 1531, 1774, 1902, 1978, 2661,
    2693
        Envy

        Greed
        Passion
        Pride
        Sloth
        Wrath
        and--The Seventh
Seven Keys to Baldpate 1917 (Art/Par)
    510, 1288, 1939
Seven Pearls, The--serial 1917 (P)
    144, 327, 789, 1118, 1444, 2363
        1.   The Sultan's Necklace
        2.   The Bowstring
        3.   The Air Peril
        4.   Amid the Clouds
        5.   Between Fire and Water
        6.   The Abandoned Mine
        7.   The False Pearl
        8.   The Man Trap
        9.   The Message on the Wire
             or The Warning on the Wire
        10. The Holdup
        11. Gems of Jeopardy
        12. Buried Alive
        13. Over the Falls
        14. The Tower of Death
        15. The Seventh Pearl
777 [sic] 1918 (V) 1876
Seven Sisters 1915 (FP) 119, 379, 482,
    853, 881, 971, 1628, 1775, 1875,
    2474, 2535
Seven Swans 1917 (Art/Par) 143, 842
Seventeen 1916 (FP) 853, 1248, 1309,
    2045
1776; or The Hessian Renegades 1909
    (Bio) 79, 315, 357, 477, 1450, 1613,
    1865, 1933, 2047, 2062, 2081, 2368,
    2680
Seventh Day, The 1909 (Bio) 1450, 2047,
    2062, 2368
Seventh Person, The 1919 ( ) 2671
Seventh Son, The 1912 (V) 1332, 2112,
    2767
Seventh Word, The 1915 (Br) 177
Severed Hand, The 1916 (Un) 1711, 1853
Sexton of Longwyn, The 1908 (Lubin)
Sexton Pimple 1915 (Br) 851, 852
Seymour Hicks and Ellaline Terriss 1913
    (Br) 1247
Shadow, The 1913 (Kal) 1388
Shadow of Suspicion 1919 ( ) 397
Shadow of the Past 1914 ( ) 1332, 1877,
    2472
Shadow on the Blind, The 1912 (Ed)
Shadowing Henry 1917 (M) 768, 1707
Shadows 1919 (Go) 869, 1685, 2221, 2410
Shadows of a Great City 1913 (Hep) 2744
Shadows of Doubt 1909 (Bio) 1542, 1865,
    2047
Shadows of Suspicion 1919 (M) 468, 998,
    1589
Shakespeare 1907 (Melies)
Shakespeare's Tragedy: King Lear 1909
    (V)
Shall We Forgive Her? 1918 (WS) 835
Shame 1918 ( ) 1402
Shamus O'Brien 1912 (Imp)
Shanghaied 1915 (Es) 71, 267, 451, 1045,
    1347, 1676, 2077, 2090, 2197, 2746
Shanghaied Jonah, A 1917 (Key/Tri) 71,
    2705, 2799
Shappo 1913 ( ) 2148

Shark Malone 1918 ( ) 1661
Shark Monroe 1916 (Tri) 1188
Shark Monroe 1919 (Art/Par)
Sharpshooter 1913 ( ) 2096
Shaughraun, The 1908 (V)
She 1908 (Ed)
She 1911 ( ) 2430
She 1916 (Br) 2637
She Brings It Home 1904 (AMB)
She Calls on the Manager 1904 (AMB)
She Came, She Saw, She Conquered 1916
  (Kal) 1805
She-Devil, The 1919 (F) 116, 249, 295,
  1654, 2175, 2717
She Fell Fainting into His Arms 1903
  (AMB)
She-Going Sailor, A * ( ) 750
She Hired a Husband 1919 (Un) 675
She Kicked on the Cooking 1904 (AMB)
She Loses Me 1919 (P) 1586
She Loved a Sailor 1916 (Key/Tri) 46,
  876, 1135, 1651
She Loved Him Plenty 1918 (Key/Tri)
  2608
She Loves Me Not 1918 (P) 1586, 2055
She Meets with Wife's Approval 1902
  (AMB)
She Needed a Doctor 1917 (Key/Tri) 250,
  303, 748, 1874, 2550, 2580
She Paid the Price 1917 ( ) 2811
She Stoops to Conquer 1914 (Br) 22, 527
She Wanted to be an Actress 1908 (V)
She Wanted to Rise in the World 1904
  (AMB)
She Was Good to Him 1906 (Winthrop
  Press)
She Who Laughs Last 1916 (V) 2367
She Wolf 1918 (Frohman) 464, 1099, 2128
She Won the Prize 1916 (V) 1876
She Would Be an Actress 1909 (Lubin)
Sheath Gown, The 1908 (Lubin)
Sheba 1919 (Hep) 43, 2531
Shell-43 1916 ( ) 1745
Shells and Shivers 1917 (V) 2367
Shepherd Lassie of Argyle, The 1914 (GB)
  2604
Shepherd of Souls, The 1914 (Br) 1289,
  2171
Shepherd of the Hills, The 1919 ( ) 1104,
  1379, 2053
Shepherd's Daughter, The 1909 (V)
Sheridan's Ride 1908 (V)
Sheriff, The 1911 (Ed)
Sheriff, The /aka/ Out West 1918 (FP/
  Las) 65, 525, 791, 1188, 1401, 1476,
  2208
Sheriff Ambrose see Safety First
  Ambrose
Sheriff Nell's Come Back 1915 (Key) 1874
Sheriff Nell's Tussle 1918 (Key/Tri) 2608
Sheriff's Baby, The 1913 (Bio) 141, 315,
  398, 731, 732, 1182, 1655, 2000,
  2680
Sheriff's Blunder, The 1916 (Selig Poly-
  Scope) 1849
Sheriff's Brother, The 1911 (Es) 50
Sheriff's Child, The 1913 (Es) 50
Sheriff's Chum, The 1911 (Es) 50
Sheriff's Daughter, The 1909 (Hep) 2744
Sheriff's Duty, The * (Selig Polyscope)
  1849

Sheriff's Girl, The * (Selig Polyscope)
  1849
Sheriff's Honeymoon, The 1913 (Es) 50
Sheriff's Inheritance, The 1912 (Es) 50
Sheriff's Luck, The 1912 (Es) 50
Sheriff's Prisoner, The 1914 ( ) 2002
Sheriff's Reward, The 1914 (Selig Poly-
  scope) 1849
Sheriff's Sacrifice, The 1910 (Es) 50
Sheriff's Sister, The 1911 ( ) 1431
Sheriff's Son, The 1919 (Par) 960, 1261,
  1523, 1998, 2096
Sheriff's Story, The 1913 (Es) 50
Sheriff's Streak of Yellow, The 1915 ( )
  1188
Sherlock Holmes 1916 (Es) 1022, 1400
Sherlock Holmes Baffled 1903 (AMB)
Shielding Shadow, The--serial 1916 (P)
  144, 646, 1407, 2581
  1. The Treasure Trove
  2. Into the Depths
  3. The Mystic Defender
  4. The Earthquake
  5. Through Bolted Doors
  6. The Disappearing Shadow
  7. The Awakening
  8. The Haunting Hand
  9. The Incorrigible Captive
  10. The Vanishing Mantle
  11. The Great Sacrifice
  12. The Stolen Shadow
  13. The Hidden Menace
  14. Absolute Black
  15. The Final Chapter
Shifting Sands 1918 (Tri) 1442, 1490, 1833,
  2512
Ship Ahoy 1919 ( ) 460
Ship of Doom, The 1917 ( ) 1665
Ship's Husband, The 1910 (Ed)
Shirley Kane 1917 ( ) 2756
Shoal Light, The 1915 ( ) 763, 2096
Shocking Stockings, The 1904 (AMB)
Shoddy the Tailor 1915 (Lubin) 1161
Shoemaker of Coepenick, The 1908 (V)
Shoes 1916 (Un) 145, 1694, 2341
Shoes That Danced, The 1918 ( ) 2453
Shoo Fly 1903 (AMB)
Shootin' Mad 1918 (Golden West Producing
  Co.) 50, 471, 1190, 1561, 2571
Shooting of Sadie Rose, The 1918 ( ) 2554
Shooting up the Movies * (Selig Polyscope)
  1849
Shop Girls 1915 (GB) 2604
Shop Girls 1915 (Mu) 41, 1589
Shorty's Sacrifice 1914 ( ) 2096
Shot, A 1904 (AMB)
Shot in the Excitement 1914 (Key) 37, 460,
  531, 1304
Shot in the Fracas 1916 (Vogue) 2608
Shot That Failed, The 1912 (Un)
Shotgun Ranchman, The 1912 (Es) 50
Shotguns That Kick 1914 (Key) 65
Should a Husband Forgive? 1919 (F) 554
Should a Wife Forgive? 1915 ( ) 1599
Should a Woman Tell? 1919 (Key/Tri) 618,
  1016, 1215, 1454, 1476
Shoulder Arms 1918 (FN) 97, 204, 451,
  452, 1380, 2077, 2611, 2778, 2782
Show Down, The 1917 ( ) 539, 1308
Shrine of Happiness 1916 ( ) 2227
Shuffle the Queens 1918 (Christie) 339

Shulamite, The 1915 (Br) 43
Shut Up! 1902 (AMB)
Shut Up! Getting Ready to Retire 1904
    (AMB)
Shuttle, The 1918 (F) 781, 887, 1379, 2175
Shylock 1913 (Kleine/Eclipse) 152, 248,
    1192, 1385, 2029
Shyness of Shorty, The 1910 (Ed)
Si, Senor 1919 (P) 1586
Sic 'Em Sam 1918 (Art/Par) 857
Sic 'Em Towser! 1918 (P) 1586
Sideshow Wrestlers 1908 (Melies)
Side-Tracked 1916 (Vim) 1161
Siege of Petersburg 1912 ( ) 1939
Sierra Jim's Reformation 1914 ( ) 2112,
    2672
Sight in Darkness 1917 ( ) 1878
Sightseeing 1907 (Melies)
Sign Invisible 1918 (FN) 1562
Sign of the Cross 1904 (Lubin)
Sign of the Cross 1914 (Las) 853, 868,
    1229, 2549
Sign of the Rat 1919 ( ) 1025
Sign of the Three Labels, The 1911 (Ed)
Signet of Sheba 1916 (Mu) 2201
Silence Sellers, The 1917 ( ) 2-37
Silent Avenger, The * (V) 1364
Silent Lady, 1917 ( ) 1518
Silent Lie, The 1917 ( ) 554
Silent Man, The 1917 (Art) 1188, 1690,
    2613
Silent Master, The 1917 (Mu) 1580, 1939,
    2540, 2698
Silent Message, The 1910 (Es) 50
Silent Mystery, The--serial 1918 (Silent
    Mystery Corp.) 926, 990, 2554, 2628
Silent Partner, The 1917 (Las) 935, 1800,
    2513, 2623
Silent Rider, The 1919 (Tri) 2479
Silent Sands 1914 ( ) 1416
Silent Sandy 1914 ( ) 1028, 1029
Silent Strength 1919 ( ) 1877
Silent Terror, The 1917 ( ) 2656
Silent Tongue, The 1911 (Ed)
Silent Voice, The 1915 (M) 105, 353, 2430
Silent Woman, The 1919 ( ) 2487
Silk Lined Burglar 1919 (Un) 675, 686
Silks and Satins 1915 (FP) 482
Silveon and Emerie "On the Web" 1903
    (Lubin)
Silver Cigarette Case, The 1913 (V) 2523
Silver Dollar, The 1909 (Lubin)
Silver Girl, The 1919 ( ) 1404
Silver Greyhound, The 1919 (Br) 1453
Silver Grindstone, The 1913 ( ) 785
Silver King, The 1919 ( ) 437, 874, 980,
    1071, 2507
Silver Lining, The 1919 (Br) 2688
Silver Threads among the Gold 1911 (Ed)
Silver Wedding, The 1906 (AMB)
Simp and the Sophomores, The 1915 (Ed)
    1161
Simple Charity 1910 (Bio) 95, 2047
Simple Home Dinner, A 1909 (Ed)
Simple Life, The 1906 (AMB)
Simple Life, The 1919 (V) 2367
Simple Simon's Surprise Party 1904
    (Melies)
Sin 1915 (F) 116, 1545, 1971, 2101, 2381
Sin of Olga Brandt, The 1915 (Rex/Un)
    352, 449, 762

Sinews of War 1913 ( ) 2096
Single Applause 1912 ( )
Single Code, The 1917 ( ) 2131
Single Shot Parker * (Selig Polyscope)
    1849
Singular Cynic, A 1914 (Un) 1511, 1864
Sinless Summer, A 1919 (Br) 2536
Sins and Sorrows of a Great City 1905
    (Lubin)
Sins of Ambition 1917 (Es) 437, 1613,
    1636, 2581
Sins of Men, The 1916 ( ) 1275
Sins of the Children 1919 ( ) 1275
Sins of the Man 1916 ( ) 209
Sins of the Mothers 1914 ( ) 2472
Sins of the Parents 1916 (F) 295, 2647
Sioux, The 1908 ( ) 1450
Sir Arne's Treasure 1919 (SB) 76, 202,
    1619, 1937, 2190, 2359, 2360, 2481
Sir George and the Heiress 1911 (Ed)
Sir James Mortimer's Wager 1916 (B&C)
    1329, 2536
Siren, The 1914 ( ) 2112
Siren of Corsica 1915 (Lubin) 432, 1106,
    1549
Siren of Impulse, A 1912 (Bio) 209, 2728
Sirene, La 1904 (Melies)
Siren's Necklace, The 1909 (V)
Sirens of the Sea 1918 (Un) 1604, 1896,
    1911
Siren's Song, A 1919 (F) 116, 959, 1146,
    2175, 2405, 2682, 2717
Sis 1919 (Go) 265, 686, 1353, 1941
Sis Hopkins 1919 (Go) 265, 509, 686,
    930, 1353, 1941
Sis's Wonderful Mineral Spring 1914 (Kal)
    1924
Sister of Six, A 1916 (FA/Tri) 1602
Sister to Carmen, A 1913 (V) 985
Sisterly Scheme, A 1919 (V. B. K. Corp.)
    768, 1707
Sisters 1910 (Ed)
Sisters, The 1914 ( ) 497, 1028, 1029
Sister's Burden, A 1915 ( ) 1270, 1939
Sisters in Arms 1918 (Br) 1289
Sister's Love, A 1908 (V)
Sister's Love, A 1912 (Bio) 209, 2512
Six Cylinder Love 1917 (F) 1849
Six Feet Four 1919 (Am) 2201, 2613
Six Shooter Andy 1918 (F) 557, 1849
£66.13.9 3/4 for Every Man Woman and
    Child 1916 (Br) 2152
Skater's Debut, The 1907 (P) 1575
Skating Bug, The 1911 (Independent Moving
    Picture Co.) 2047
Skeleton, The 1914 ( ) 2112
Skeleton Dance, Marionettes 1898 (Ed)
Sketch with the Thumb Print, The 1912
    (Ed)
Skidding Hearts 1917 (Key/Tri) 179, 396
Skidoo Brothers 23 1906 (AMB)
Skids and Scalawags 1918 (V) 2367
Skinner's Baby 1917 (Es) 538, 2700
Skinner's Bubble 1917 (Es) 630, 2700
Skinner's Dress Suit 1917 (Es) 630, 2619,
    2700
Skinny's Finish 1908 (Ed)
Skipper of the Osprey, The 1916 (Br) 943
Skipper's Yarn, The 1910 (Ed)
Skipping Cheese, The 1907 (Melies)
Skirts 1916 (Tri) 2568

Sklaven Fremder Willens 1919 ( ) 1614
Sky Pilot 1911 (V) 2523
Sky Pirate, The 1914 (Key) 65
Skylight Sleep 1915 (P) 1586
Slacker, The 1917 (M) 1832, 2469
Slander 1916 (F) 1394, 1507
Slave, The 1907 (V)
Slave, The 1909 (Bio) 1511, 2047, 2201,
     2212, 2368
Slave, The 1918 (King-Bee) 1161, 2733
Slave Island, The 1916 (FP) 957
Slave Market 1917 (Par) 957
Slavers of the Thames 1915 (Br) 1873
Slave's Devotion, A 1913 ( ) 2090
Sleep, Gentle Sleep 1911 (Ed)
Sleeper, The 1902 (AMB)
Sleeping Beauty 1902 (Lubin)
Sleeping Child 1902 (AMB)
Sleeping Fires 1917 (Par) 957
Sleeping Lion, The 1919 ( ) 2211
Sleepy Cop, The 1907 (Lubin)
Sleepy Soubrette, The 1905 (AMB)
Sleuthing 1913 (V) 2070, 2523
Sleuths 1919 (Key/Tri) 2069, 2608
Sleuths at the Floral Parade, The 1913
     (Key) 1699, 1941, 2368, 2465
Sleuth's Last Stand, The 1913 (Key) 99,
     1666, 1941, 2368
Slight Mistake, A 1911 (V) 332
Slim Higgins 1914 (Selig Polyscope) 1849
Slip Powder 1909 (Lubin)
Slippery 1917 ( ) 686
Slippery Jim's Repentance 1908 (V)
Slippery Slim series 1919 (Un) 2058
Slips and Slackers 1917 (V) 2367
Slocum Disaster, The 1904 (AMB)
Slumberland 1908 (V)
Small Change 1915 (Christie) 525
Small Time Act, A 1913 (Key) 2465
Small Town Bully, A see A Little
     Teacher 1914 (Key)
Small Town Girl, A 1917 (F) 392
Small Town Guy, The 1917 ( ) 1276
Small Town Romance, A 1918 ( ) 552
Smashing Barriers--serial 1919 (V) 515,
     648, 785, 1364, 1643, 2163, 2446
     1. Test of Courage
     2. Plunge of Death
     3. Tree-Hut of Torture
     4. Deed of a Devil
     5. Living Grave
     6. Downward to Doom
     7. The Fatal Flight
     8. The Murder Car
     9. The Dynamite Tree
     10. Overpowered
     11. The Den of Deviltry
     12. Explosive Bullets
     13. Dead Fall
     14. Trapped Like Rats
     15. The Final Barrier
Smashing Through 1918 ( ) 2095, 2364
Smile of a Child, A 1911 (Bio) 2060, 2513
Smile, Smile, Smile 1909 (Lubin)
Smiles 1919 (F) 1524, 2717
Smith 1917 (Br) 834, 1931, 2138
Smoked Husband, A 1908 (AMB) 209, 526,
     1511
Smoker, The 1910 (Bio) 2047
Smoky Stove, The 1903 (AMB)
Smouldering Fires * ( ) 957

Smouldering Flame, The 1917 (Selig) 857
Smuggled into America 1907 (Lubin)
Smugglers, The 1916 (Las) 287, 2539,
     2540, 2652, 2672
Smuggler's Daughter, The 1909 (Lubin)
Smuggler's Daughter, The 1912 (Es) 50
Smuggler's Daughter, The 1914 (Lubin)
     1161
Smuggler's Stepdaughter, The 1911 (Hep)
     2531
Snail, The 1919 ( ) 2549
Snakeville comedy series 1911 (Es) 1384,
     2058, 2571
Snakeville's New Doctor 1914 (Es) 50
Snap Judgment 1917 (Mu) 2201
Snapshot Fiend; or Willie's New Camera
     1906 (V)
Snare, The 1913 (Es) 110, 156, 278
Snare, The 1918 (Br) 1289
Snare for Lovers, A 1904 (AMB)
Snare of Fate, The 1913 ( ) 1468
Sneak, The 1919 (F) 295, 1253
Snobs 1914 (GB) 2604
Snobs 1915 (Las) 1439, 1868
Snookums series--cartoon 1913-15 (French)
     512
Snow Cure, The 1916 (Key/Tri) 650, 748,
     1723, 2336, 2465
Snow in the Desert 1919 (Bw) 522, 1289,
     1778, 2171, 2810
Snow Man, The 1909 (Bio) 94, 731
Snow Men 1897 (American Mutoscope Co.)
Snow Storm 1898 (Ed)
Snow White 1903 (Lubin)
Snow White 1917 (Art/Par) 482
Snowball and His Pal 1912 (New York
     Motion Picture Co.)
Snowbird, The 1908 (Lubin)
Snowbird, The 1916 (M) 397, 2520
So Near, Yet So Far 1912 (Bio) 141, 251,
     1182, 1714, 1832, 1876, 2047
So Runs the Way 1913 ( ) 1029
Soaking the Clothes 1915 (P) 1586
Soap Bubbles 1906 (Melies)
Soap Girl, The 1918 ( ) 1047, 1547
Soapsuds and Sapheads 1919 (V) 2367
Soapsuds and Sirens 1917 (Key) 2143
Social Ambition 1918 ( ) 1246
Social Briars 1918 ( ) 1841
Social Buccaneers 1916 ( ) 272, 1583
Social Club, A 1916 (Key/Tri) 723, 1086,
     1886, 2512, 2514, 2636
Social Gangster 1915 (P) 1586
Social Highwayman, The 1916 ( ) 1603
Social Hypocrites 1918 (M) 41
Social Pirates, The 1916 (Kal) 244, 835,
     1447, 2210
Social Quicksands 1917 (M) 156, 353
Social Secretary, The 1916 (FA/Tri) 857,
     952, 1346, 2204, 2523, 2649, 2714
Society Exile, A 1919 (FP) 401, 403,
     888, 980, 2063
Society for Sale 1918 (Tri) 715, 755, 1490,
     2074, 2512, 2731
Society Palmist, The 1905 (AMB)
Society Raffles, The 1905 (AMB)
Society Sensation, A 1918 (Un) 1911, 2616
Society Sinners 1916 ( ) 1246
Society's Driftwood 1918 ( ) 610
Soft Boiled Yegg 1914 (Key) 531, 676
Soft Money 1919 (P) 1586, 2055

Soft Tenderfoot, A 1917 (F) 1849
Sold 1915 (FP) 957
Sold Again 1908 (V)
Sold for Marriage 1916 ( ) 1029
Soldiers Dream, The 1907 (V)
Soldier's Honor, A 1912 (Un)
Soldiers of Chance 1917 ( ) 1047, 1426
Soldiers of Fortune 1914 (Las) 866
Soldiers of Fortune 1919 (P) 176, 539,
    587, 1432, 1458, 1613, 1652, 1939,
    2453
Soldiers of Misfortune 1914 (Key) 1906
Sole Survivor, The 1917 (Selig) 857
Solitaries 1913 (V) 2523
Solitary Sin, The 1919 ( ) 1896
Some Baby 1915 (P) 1586
Some Boy 1917 ( ) 2018, 2671
Some Bride! 1919 (M) 631
Some Chaperone 1915 (Christie) 525
Some Dudes Can Fight 1903 (AMB)
Some Duel 1915 (Selig Polyscope) 1849
Some Family 1917 ( ) 1872
Some Kid 1915 (Christie) 525
Some Liar 1919 ( ) 2031, 2201
Some Liars 1916 (Vogue) 2608
Some Nerve see Gentlemen of Nerve
Some Nurse 1917 (Mu) 170, 2121
Some Runner 1913 (Nestor) 1630
Some Widow 1914 (V) 1684
Somebody's Baby * (Christie) 525
Someone Must Pay 1919 ( ) 283
Something in Her Eye 1915 (Novelty) 1161
Something on His Mind 1908 (Lubin)
Something to Do 1919 (Art/Par) 1006,
    2700
Somewhere in America 1917 ( ) 1496
Somewhere in Turkey 1918 (P) 1586
Somnambulist, The 1903 (AMB)
Somnambulistic Hero, A 1909 (Ed)
Son of David, A 1919 (Bw) 522
Son of Erin, A 1914 (Las) 866
Son of His Father 1917 ( ) 960, 1690,
    1933, 2096, 2613
Son of the Hills, A 1917 (V) 1876
Son of the Wolf 1914 (Selig) 1957
Song Bird of the North, The 1913 ( )
    2472
Song of Songs, The 1918 (Art/Par) 888,
    915, 1427, 1600
Song of the Ghetto 1914 (V) 1360, 1876
Song of the Hills, A 1917 (V) 1047
Song of the Red Flower 1918 (SB) 42
Song of the Shell, The 1912 ( ) 2472
Song of the Shirt 1908 (AMB) 994, 1363,
    1511, 2212, 2368
Song of the Soul, The 1918 (V) 1388, 1673
Song of the Wage Slave 1915 ( ) 283
Song of the Wildwood Flute, The 1910
    (Bio) 641, 2047
Song That Reached His Heart, The 1910
    (Ed)
Sons of Satan, The 1915 (Br) 43
Son's Return, The 1909 (Bio) 2047, 2081
Sorcellerie Culinaire, La 1904 (Melies)
Sorrowful Example, A 1911 (Bio) 1613,
    1665, 2060
Sorrowful Shore, The 1913 (Bio)
Sorrows of the Unfaithful, The 1910 (Bio)
    731, 1542, 2047, 2680
Sort of a Girl Who Came from Heaven,
    The 1915 (V) 2472

Soubrette and the Simps, The 1914 (Lubin)
    1161
Soubrettes in a Bachelor's Flat 1903
    (AMB)
Soubrette's Slide, The 1904 (AMB)
Soubrette's Troubles on a Fifth Avenue
    Stage 1901 (Ed)
Soul Adrift, A 1919 ( ) 434
Soul for Sale, A 1918 (Un) 2042
Soul Herder, The 1917 (Un) 398, 1011,
    1242, 1719, 2133
Soul in Bondage, A 1913 (V) 297
Soul in Trust, A 1918 (Tri) 186
Soul Market, The 1916 (M) 286, 1432,
    2037
Soul Master, The 1917 ( ) 1047
Soul of a Magdalen, The 1917 ( ) 2037
Soul of a Woman, The 1915 (M) 1531,
    2469
Soul of Broadway, The 1915 (F) 1524
Soul of Buddah, The 1918 (F) 116, 1421,
    1760, 1812, 2134, 2560, 2697
Soul of Honor, The 1914 (Mu) 2513, 2680
Soul of Kura San 1916 ( ) 2458
Soul of the South 1913 ( ) 2096, 2392
Soul of Youth, The 1919 ( ) 2223
Soul without Windows, The 1918 ( ) 486
Souls Adrift 1917 ( ) 2410
Soul's Crucifixion, A 1919 (Br) 1018,
    1289
Souls in Bondage 1913 (Imp) 111, 2767
Souls in Pawn 1917 (Mu) 1697, 2754
Souls Triumphant 1917 ( ) 1029
Souls United 1917 ( ) 1814
Sound Money Parade 1897 (American
    Mutoscope Co.)
Sound of Her Voice, The 1914 (Br) 834,
    2138
Sound Sleeper, A 1909 (AMB) 1182, 1363,
    2081, 2368
Source, The 1918 (Par) 165, 1201, 1580,
    1970, 2112, 2149
Southern Blood 1914 (Br) 177
Southern Justice 1917 ( ) 539
Southern Romance, A 1907 (Selig)
Southern Romance of Slavery Days 1908
    (Lubin)
Sowers, The 1916 (Las) 1201, 1800, 2149,
    2513, 2623
Sowing the Wind 1916 (Hep) 22, 1289,
    2171, 2531, 2744
Spades Are Trumps 1917 (V) 2081, 2521
Spaghetti 1916 (Vim) 1161
Spaghetti a la Mode 1915 (Lubin) 1161,
    2070
Spaghetti and Lottery 1915 (Lubin) 1161
Spanish Cavalier, The 1912 (Ed)
Spanish Dilemma, A 1912 (Bio)
Spanish Girl 1909 (Es) 50
Spanish Gypsy, The 1911 (Bio) 1613, 2000
Spanish Romance, A 1908 (V)
Spark Divine, The 1919 (V) 1388
Spark of Manhood, The 1914 ( ) 2112
Sparks of Fate 1917 (Es) 2700
Sparring Film 1895 (American Mutoscope
    Co.) 431
Speak-Easy, The 1919 ( ) 1906, 2069
Special Today 1918 (M) 768, 1707
Spectacular Start, A 1902 (AMB)
Spectre Bridegroom, The 1913 (V) 950
Speed Demon, The 1912 (Bio) 2045

Speed Maniac, The 1919 (F) 1170, 1374, 1714, 1849, 1947
Speed Queen, The 1913 (Key) 65, 509, 1941, 2465
Spell of the Poppy, The 1915 ( ) 2002
Spell of the Yukon 1916 ( ) 283, 286
Spender, The 1919 ( ) 1631
Sphynx, The 1917 ( ) 1615
Spider, The 1916 (FP) 957, 1600
Spider and Her Web, The 1914 ( ) 2112, 2422
Spider and the Fly, The 1903 (AMB)
Spider and the Fly, The 1916 (F) 1144, 1524, 1734
Spies and Spills 1918 (V) 2367
Spike, the Bag-Punching Dog 1903 (AMB)
Spill, A 1902 (AMB)
Spindle of Life, The 1917 ( ) 1004
Spinner o'Dreams 1918 (Br) 1018, 1968
Spirit Awakened, The 1912 (Bio) 731, 1539, 1751, 2000, 2513
Spirit of Lafayette, The 1917 ( ) 824
Spirit of Merry Christmas 1917 (M) 768, 1707
Spirit of '17, The 1917 (Art/Par) 1309, 2045
Spirit of '76, The 1905 (AMB)
Spirit of the Bell, The 1915 ( ) 1745, 1794, 2096
Spirit of the Flag, The 1913 ( ) 2112
Spirit of the Gorge, The 1911 (Ed)
Spirit of the Lake 1919 ( ) 2221
Spirit of the Red Cross 1918 (Select) 12, 15, 1688
Spirits in the Kitchen 1902 (AMB)
Spiritualist Photographer, A 1903 (Melies)
Spiritualistic Meeting, A 1906 (Melies)
Spit Ball Sadie 1915 (P) 1586
Spite Bride, The 1919 (Sel) 771, 2557
Spite Husband, The 1917 (Mu) 2760
Spitfire, The 1914 (FP) 231
Spitfire of Seville, The 1919 ( ) 1720, 1946, 2356
Splash Me Nicely 1917 (Br) 1487
Splendid Coward, The 1918 (Br) 1453
Splendid Romance, The 1918 (Art/Par) 423, 1205
Splendid Sin, The 1919 ( ) 2581
Splendid Sinner 1918 (Go) 397, 982, 2091
Spoiled Girl, The 1918 ( ) 913
Spoilers, The 1914 (Selig) 480, 857, 868, 1957, 2221, 2770
Spooks and Spasms 1917 (V) 2367
Spooks at School 1903 (AMB)
Sport Girl, The 1918 ( ) 988
Sport of Kings, The 1918 ( ) 1864
Sporting Blood 1909 (Lubin)
Sporting Blood 1916 ( ) 209, 272, 2745
Sporting Chance, A 1919 ( ) 318, 486, 1280, 1441, 2201
Sporting Duchess, The 1915 (Lubin) 277, 1725, 2079, 2438, 2565
Sporting Life 1918 (Art/Par) 226, 227, 345, 580, 818, 1067, 1433, 2130, 2730
Sports and Splashes 1917 (V) 2367
Spotlight Sadie 1919 (Go) 405, 1248, 1662, 1751, 2564
Spotted Lily, The 1917 ( ) 1120, 1714
Spreading Dawn, The 1917 (Go) 367, 576, 1606, 1638, 2463

Spring Fever see Recreation 1914 (Key)
Spring Fever 1919 (P) 1586, 2055
Spurs of Sybill 1918 ( ) 265, 273, 656
Spy, The 1907 (V)
Spy, The 1917 (F) 866
Spy's Defeat, The 1913 (Es) 353, 2486
Squabs and Squabbles 1919 (V) 1161
Square Deal 1917 ( ) 905, 1188, 1991
Square Deal: The End of the Bad Men 1907 (V)
Square Deal Man, The 1917 (Tri) 1188
Square Deal Sanderson 1919 ( ) 1186, 1188, 1580
Square Deceiver, The 1917 (M) 617, 1589
Square Shooter, The 1919 (CFC) 1186
Squared 1919 (M) 768, 1707
Squarehead, The see Mabel's Married Life
Squaw Man, The 1914 (Las) 61, 712, 828, 866, 899, 967, 1446, 1456, 1493, 1500, 1854, 2103, 2211, 2414
Squaw Man, The 1918 (Par) 9, 165, 242, 319, 724, 781, 877, 996, 1125, 1126, 1131, 1238, 1280, 1580, 1661, 1756, 1771, 1866, 1970, 1975, 2149, 2441, 2468
Squaw Man's Son, The 1916 (Par) 651, 1581, 2112, 2623
Squaw's Love, The 1911 (Bio) 641, 1941, 2729
Squeedunk Sherlock Holmes 1909 (Ed)
Squelched: Rest 1904 (AMB)
Staff of Age, The 1912 (Imp)
Stage Coach Driver, The 1914 (Selig Polyscope) 1849
Stage Coach Guard, The 1915 (Selig Polyscope) 1849
Stage Memories of an Old Theatrical Trunk 1908 (Ed)
Stage Romance, A 1911 (Ed)
Stage Rustler, The 1908 (AMB)
Stage Struck 1904 (Lubin)
Stage Struck 1907 (Ed)
Stage Struck 1917 (FA/Tri) 25, 1028, 1911, 2573
Stage Struck Daughter, The 1908 (V)
Stage Struck Lizzie 1911 (Ed)
Stain, The 1914 (P) 116, 2024
Stainless Barrier, The 1917 (Tri) 1099
Stamp in Tramps, A 1914 (V) 2081
Stampede, The 1911 (Imp) 2047
Star Boarder, The /aka/ Hash House Hero 1914 (Key) 451, 650, 1090, 1422
Star Boarder, The 1917 (King-Bee) 1161
Star Boarder, The 1919 (V) 2367
Star Gazer, The 1917 (V) 2663
Star of Bethlehem, The 1909 (Ed)
Star of Bethlehem, The 1912 (T) 1468, 2201
Star of the Sea, The 1915 (Rex/Un) 352, 449, 762, 1956
Star over Night, A 1919 ( ) 169, 1706, 1883, 2120, 2138
Star Spangled Banner, The 1911 (Ed)
Star Spangled Banner, The 1914 ( ) 1415
Star Theatre 1902 (AMB)
Starring of Flora Finchurch, The 1915 (V) 901
Stars and Bars 1917 (Key/Tri) 840, 876, 1086, 2166, 2465
Stars and Stripes, The 1910 (Ed)

Stars of Glory 1918 ( ) 1569
Start Something 1919 (P) 635, 2055
Starting for the Fire 1896 (Ed)
Startled Lover, The 1902 (AMB)
Starving Artist, The; or Realism in Art 1907 (V)
Station Content 1918 (Tri) 1251, 1833, 2112, 2512, 2677
Station Master, The 1917 (King-Bee) 1161
Steady Company 1915 (Rex/Un) 352, 449
Stealing a Dinner 1903 (AMB)
Steel Alarm, The 1918 ( ) 857
Steel King, The 1919 ( ) 835, 1603
Steelheart--serial 1917 ( ) 1364
Stella Maris 1917 (Art/Par) 57, 601, 1732, 2047, 2124, 2535, 2701
Stenographer Troubles 1913 (V) 332, 901
Stenographer Wanted 1912 (V) 111, 332, 818, 901, 1032, 2070, 2663
Stenographer's Friend, The 1910 (Ed)
Step Lively 1917 (P) 635, 1586
Step Lively, Please 1914 (Key) 531
Stepping Out 1919 (Par) 189, 473, 877, 2719
Stepping Stone, The 1916 (Tri) 246, 1404, 1690
Stick Around 1919 ( ) 2595
Stickey Affair, A 1916 (Vim) 1161
Still Alarm 1903 (Ed)
Still Alarm 1918 ( ) 2221
Still Small Voice, The 1919 ( ) 318, 1565
Still Water Runs Deep 1902 (AMB)
Still Waters 1915 (FP) 482
Still Waters Run Deep 1916 (Br) 2179
Sting of Victory, The 1916 (Es) 524, 2660, 2676, 2680
Stingaree 1915 (Kal) 244
Stitch in Time, A 1919 ( ) 1547
Stolen Actress, The 1917 ( ) 2486
Stolen Booking, The 1916 (Vogue) 2608
Stolen Bride, The 1913 (Bio) 2513
Stolen by Gypsies 1905 (Ed)
Stolen Claim, The 1910 (Ed)
Stolen Dog, The 1911 (Ed)
Stolen Father, The 1910 (Ed)
Stolen Flask, The 1908 (Lubin)
Stolen Glory 1912 (Key) 1666, 1941, 2368, 2465
Stolen Goods 1915 (W) 2035, 2132, 2149, 2513
Stolen Honor 1918 (F) 2024
Stolen Hours 1918 ( ) 486
Stolen Jewels, The 1908 (AMB) 816
Stolen Love 1909 (Bio) 1865
Stolen Love 1912 ( ) 2733
Stolen Magic 1915 (Key/Tri) 650, 1211, 1257, 1941, 2368
Stolen Moccasins 1913 ( ) 785
Stolen Nickel, The 1912 (Ed)
Stolen Orders 1918 (WS) 231, 835, 853, 1603
Stolen Paradise, The 1917 ( ) 486
Stolen Pig, The 1907 (V)
Stolen Plans, The; or The Boy Detective 1908 (V)
Stolen Purse, The 1913 (Key) 1666, 2368, 2465
Stolen Sweets 1903 (AMB)
Stolen Treaty, The 1917 (V) 2767
Stolen Wireless, The 1909 (Melies)
Stone Age, The /aka/ Her Cave Man;

No One to Guide Him 1916 (Key/Tri) 37, 452, 472, 2208, 2564, 2580
Stool Pigeon, The 1915 (Victor/Un) 449, 1431, 2032
Stop! Luke! Listen! 1917 (P) 635, 1586
Stop That Alarm 1908 (Lubin)
Stop Thief! 1902 (AMB)
Stop Thief! 1905 (Melies)
Stop Thief! 1919 (Go) 630
Storm, The 1916 ( ) 1800, 2149, 2513
Storm Woman, The 1912 (Bio) 1665
Stormy Petrel, The 1913 (V) 297
Story of a Glove, The 1915 (V) 768, 1707
Story of a Picture, The 1910 (Hep) 2531
Story of a Story, The 1915 ( ) 2002
Story of Eggs, A 1907 (Melies)
Story of Lavinia 1913 (Selig) 857
Story of the Blood Red Rose 1914 (Selig) 1957, 2770
Story of the Indian Ledge, The 1911 (Ed)
Story of the Rose, The 1911 (Independent Moving Picture Co.)
Story of Treasure Island, The 1907 (V)
Story That Boots Told, The 1908 (V)
Stout Heart, but Weak Knees 1914 (Key) 1906
Stowaway, The 1909 (Lubin)
Straight and Narrow, The 1918 (King-Bee) 1161, 2733
Straight Part, The 1918 ( ) 27
Straight Road, The 1914 (Las) 1154, 2201
Straight Shootin' 1917 (Un) 398, 1011, 1719
Stranded 1916 (Vim) 1161, 1602
Stranded in Arcady 1917 ( ) 435
Strange Adventure of New York Drummer 1899 (Ed)
Strange Case of Mary Page, The--serial 1916 (Es) 24, 563, 605, 786, 1795, 2680
    1.   The Tragedy
    2.   The Trial
    3.   The Web
    4.   The Mark
    5.   The Alienist
    6.   The Depths
    7.   A Confession
    8.   The Perjury
    9.   The Accusing Eye
    10. The Clew
    11. The Raid
    12. The Slums
    13. Dawning Hope
    14. Recrimination
    15. The Verdict
Strange Meeting, A 1909 (Bio) 1363, 1593, 1992, 2047
Strange Unknown, The 1915 ( ) 808
Strange Woman, The 1918 ( ) 295
Stranger, The 1917 (King-Bee) 1161, 2733
Stranger and the Taxicab, The 1912 (Ed)
Stranger at Coyote, The 1912 (Am) 1431, 1924
Straphanger, The 1917 ( ) 1872
Strategy of Anne, The 1911 (V) 901
Street Arab, A 1898 (Ed)
Street Beautiful, The 1912 (Ed)
Street Called Straight, A 1919 ( ) 2124, 2410
Street Car Chivalry 1903 (Ed)
Street of Seven Stars, The 1918 ( ) 1429

Street Parade, The 1896 (International
Film Co.)
Street Waif's Christmas, A 1908 (Ed)
Streets of Illusion, The 1917 ( ) 1312
Strength of Love, The <u>see</u> When the
Earth Trembled
Strength of the Weak 1916 ( ) 1360, 2232
Strenuous Life, The 1904 (AMB)
Strenuous Life, The; or Anti-Race Suicide
1904 (Ed)
Stress of Circumstances 1914 (Br) 1289,
2171
Stricken Blind; or To Forgive Is Divine
1908 (V)
Strictly Business 1918 ( ) 1429, 2547
Strictly Confidential 1919 (Go) 247, 265,
930, 1423, 1895, 1940, 2441, 2570
Strike at the Mines, The 1911 (Ed)
Strike One * ( ) 1767
String Beans 1918 (Par) 899, 1261, 1588,
1657, 1948, 2096
String of Pearls, A 1912 (Bio) 1223, 1224,
1328
Stripped for a Million 1919 ( ) 2760
Stripes and Stumbles 1918 (V) 2367
Stroke of Midnight * ( ) 1155
Strolling Players 1909 (Ed)
Strong Man Poses 1896, (Ed) 2218
Strong Man's Love, A 1913 (Br) 177
Strong Revenge, A 1913 (Key) 1941, 2368,
2465
Strong Way, The 1918 (WS) 835
Stronger Love, The 1916 (Pal) 1582, 1764,
2026
Stronger Mind, The 1915 (UP) 352, 449,
1705
Stronger Than Death 1915 (Rex/Un) 449,
1604, 2398, 2781
Stronger Than Death 1919 (M) 321
Stronger Vow, The 1919 (Go) 869, 2221,
2402, 2410
Strongheart 1914 (Mu) 141, 1117, 1876,
2513, 2680
Struggle, The 1912 (Bio) 231, 398, 1182,
1831, 2157
Struggle Everlasting, The 1917 (Par) 1450,
2105, 2410, 2444
Stubb's New Servants 1911 (Bio)
Studenci 1916 ( ) 1922
Student Days 1909 (V)
Student Von Prag 1913 (Deutsche Bioscop)
203, 2715
Student's Prank, The; or A Joke on His
Parents 1908 (Lubin)
Studio Girl, The 1918 ( ) 947, 2521
Studio Stampede, A 1917 (Vogue) 2608
Study in Tramps, A 1915 (V) 2521
Stuff Dreams Are Made Of, The 1914 ( )
1312
Stuff Heroes Are Made Of, The 1911 (Bio)
2502, 2513
Stuff That Americans Are Made Of, The
1911 (Ed)
Stuff That Dreams Are Made Of, The 1911
(Ed)
Subduing of Mrs. Nag, The 1911 (V) 332,
901, 1941
Subject for the Rogue's Gallery, A 1904
(AMB)
Submarine Pirate, A 1915 (Key/Tri) 37,
440, 452, 2197

Subpoena Server 1906 (AMB)
Substitute for Smoking 1906 (Winthrop
Press)
Subub Surprises the Burglar 1903 (Ed)
Suburbanite, The 1904 (AMB)
Suburbanite's Ingenious Alarm, A 1908
(Ed)
Successful Adventure, A 1918 (M) 41, 1253
Such a Cook /aka/ The Bungling Burglars
1914 (Key) 1906
Such a Hunter 1914 (V) 332, 901
Such a Little Pirate 1918 (Par) 927, 1528
Such a Little Princess 1917 ( ) 1432
Such a Little Queen 1914 (FP) 146, 231,
875, 1282, 1589, 2047
Such Is Life 1915 (Rex/Un) 352, 449, 762,
1037
Sudden Gentleman, A 1917 ( ) 715
Sudden Jim 1917 (Par) 281, 763, 1454,
2096
Sudden Riches 1916 (WS) 853
Sue of the South 1919 ( ) 865, 1104, 2147
Suffer Little Children ... for of Such Is
the Kingdom of Labor 1909 (Ed)
Suffragette, The 1913 ( ) 785
Suffragette's Battle, The 1914 ( ) 1028
Suicidal Poet, The 1908 (Lubin)
Suicide Club, The 1909 (AMB)
Suicide Club, The 1914 (Br) 834, 2138
Suing Susan 1912 (V) 332, 901
Suit Case, A 1909 (Lubin)
Suit Case Mystery, The 1910 (Ed)
Suit of Armor, The 1904 (AMB)
Suit of Armor, The 1912 (V) 332, 901
Sultan's Power, The 1909 ( ) 258, 2221
Sultan's Wife, The 1917 (Key/Tri) 371,
1203, 2512, 2537, 2636
Summer Boarders, The 1905 (AMB)
Summer Girl, The 1903 (AMB)
Summer Girl, The 1911 (Ed)
Summer Girl, The 1916 (WS) 82, 1444
Summer Girls, The 1917 (Key) 878
Summer Idyl, A 1908 (V)
Summer Idyl, A 1910 (Bio) 209, 1182,
2046, 2156, 2680
Summer Tragedy, A 1910 (Bio)
Sun Shining Through, The 1918 ( ) 2095
Sunbeam, The 1912 (Bio) 1665
Sunbeam, The 1916 (M) 2520
Sunday 1915 (George W. Lederer Filmotions
Inc.) 661
Sunday Morning in a Coney Island Police
Court 1908 (Bio) 2212
Sundown Trail 1919 ( ) 2211
Sunken Rocks 1919 (Hep) 43, 2531
Sunlight's Last Raid 1918 ( ) 2754
Sunnyside 1918 (FN) 97, 451, 1380, 2077,
2611, 2782
Sunset, A 1917 (Un) 111
Sunset Gun, The 1912 (Ed)
Sunset Princess 1919 ( ) 664
Sunset Trail, The 1918 ( ) 1764, 2683
Sunshine Alley 1917 (Go) 1751
Sunshine and Shadows 1914 (V) 297, 1876,
2523
Sunshine Dad 1916 ( ) 731, 1286, 1287,
1541, 2002, 2564
Sunshine in Poverty Row 1910 ( ) 2003
Sunshine Maid 1917 (F) 392
Sunshine Nan 1917 (Art/Par) 2028
Sunshine Sue 1910 (Bio) 2502, 2728

Sunshine through the Dark 1911 (Bio) 209, 731, 1224
Super Woman 1919 ( ) 139
Supreme 1916 ( ) 145
Supreme Temptation, The 1916 (V) 1426, 1876
Surf Girl, The 1916 (Key/Tri) 65, 440, 600, 877, 966, 1019, 1092, 2336
Surgeon's Temptation, The 1911 (Ed)
Surprise Party, The 1910 (Ed)
Surprises of an Empty Hotel, The 1917 ( ) 2068
Susan Rocks the Boat 1916 ( ) 315, 1028, 1865
Susie Snowflake 1916 (FP) 569, 2028
Susie, the Sleuth 1916 (V) 1876, 2487, 2527
Susie's New Shoes 1916 (Mu) 905, 2054
Suspect, The 1916 (V) 296, 552, 1878, 2472
Suspense 1919 (P) 1444
Suspended Ordeal, A 1914 (Key) 65
Suspended Sentence 1915 (Christie) 525
Suspicious Henry 1913 (V) 332, 901
Sverchok Na Pechi (The Cricket on the Hearth) 1915 (Russian) 1995
Swan Girl, The 1913 ( ) 2472
Swat the Crook 1919 (P) 1586
Swat the Spy 1919 (F) 1524
Sweater, The 1915 (Hep) 2171, 2744
Sweedie comedies 1914-16 (Es) 166
Sweedie Goes to College 1916 (Es) 166, 2512
Sweeney series 1913 (Selig) 1481, 1537
Sweet and Twenty 1909 (Bio) 2047, 2081
Sweet and Twenty 1919 (Br) 349
Sweet Kiss, A 1905 (Lubin)
Sweet Kitty Bellairs 1916 (Las) 186, 935, 1907
Sweet Lady Peggy 1916 (Selig) 2770
Sweet Lavender 1915 (Hep) 22, 2171, 2531, 2744
Sweet Little Home in the Country, A 1902 (AMB)
Sweet Memories see Retrospect
Sweet Revenge 1909 (Bio) 1182
Sweetheart of the Doomed, The 1917 ( ) 1032
Sweethearts 1902 (AMB)
Sweethearts 1912 ( ) 2733
Sweets for the Sweet 1903 (AMB)
Swindler, The 1919 (Br) 834
Swing Your Partner 1918 (P) 1586
Swiss Family Robinson 1903 (Lubin)
Swiss Guide, The 1910 (Ed)
Switches and Sweeties 1919 (V) 1161
Switchman's Tower, The 1911 (Ed)
Sword and the King, The 1909 (V)
Swords and Hearts 1911 (Bio) 1060, 1613, 1665, 1831, 2729
Sylvia of the Secret Service 1918 (P) 435, 724, 2649
Symphony in "A-Flat" 1903 (AMB)

- T -

Tables Turned 1912 (Imp)
Tables Turned, The 1913 (V) 2523
Tacky Sue's Romance 1917 ( ) 2486
Take a Chance 1918 (P) 1586

Take Me out to the Ball Game 1910 (Es) 50
Taking a Chance 1915 (Selig Polyscope) 1849
Taking a Rest 1916 (M) 768, 1707
Taking His Medicine 1906 (Winthrop Press)
Taking His Medicine 1911 (Bio)
Taking His Photograph 1909 (Ed)
Taking of Luke McVane, The /aka/ The Fugitive 1915 (Ince) 1188, 1745, 2425, 2479
Taking the Count 1919 ( ) 520
Tale of a Black Eye, The 1913 (Key) 1666
Tale of a Pig, The 1908 (Lubin)
Tale of a Shirt, The 1908 (V)
Tale of a Shirt, The 1916 (Br) 1815
Tale of the Crusades, A 1908 (V)
Tale of the Harem, A 1908 (V)
Tale of the Sea, A 1907 (V)
Tale of the West, A 1909 (Es) 50
Tale of the Wilderness, A 1912 (Bio) 95, 209, 1714, 2728
Tale of Two Cities, A 1911 (V) 566, 1888, 2523, 2604, 2663
Tale of Two Cities, A 1917 (F) 95, 406, 868, 1563, 2514, 2638
Tale of Two Coats, A 1910 (Ed)
Tale of Two Nations, A 1917 (Independent all color feature) 95, 544, 1210
Tale of Two Worlds 1918 ( ) 2124
Tale the Autumn Leaves Told 1908 (Ed)
Tale the Ticker Told, The 1908 (Ed)
Tales the Searchlight Told 1908 (Ed)
Talk of the Town, The 1918 (Bluebird/Un) 449, 875, 1432, 1563, 1714, 2042, 2364, 2490
Talked to Death 1909 (Lubin)
Tally Ho--Arrival 1896 (Ed)
Tally Ho--Departure 1896 (Ed)
Tambourine Dance 1897 (American Mutoscope Co.) 2751
Taming a Husband 1910 (Bio) 1363
Taming a Tenderfoot 1913 ( ) 785
Taming of Grouchy Bill 1916 (Selig Polyscope) 1849
Taming of Texas Pete, The 1913 ( ) 785
Taming of the Shrew 1908 (AMB) 1363, 1511, 2212
Taming of the Shrew 1911 (Co-operative Cinematograph Co.) 417
Taming of the Shrew 1915 (B&C) 103, 104
Taming of the Whirlwind 1917 (Tri) 627
Taming Target Center 1917 (Key/Tri) 2608
Tangled Affair, A 1913 (Key) 1941
Tangled Fates 1916 ( ) 273
Tangled Hearts 1916 (Bluebird/Un) 170, 449, 827, 1604, 1683, 2635
Tangled Lives 1918 ( ) 243, 1360, 1877
Tangled Tangoists 1914 (V) 51, 157, 332, 901
Tangled Threads 1919 ( ) 28, 134, 1266
Tango Tales 1914 (Key) 65
Tango Tangles /aka/ Charlie's Recreation; Music Hall 1914 (Key) 451, 531, 2465
Tankville Constable 1912 (Imp)
Tapped Wires 1912 ( ) 377
Tar Heel Warrior, The 1918 ( ) 939
Tarantula, The 1916 (V) 1360, 1426, 2487
Tares 1918 (Hep) 812, 2531
Tarzan of the Apes 1918 (National Film

Corp.) 244, 961, 1090, 1353, 1448, 1570, 1745, 2002
Taste of Life, A 1919 ( ) 2147
Tattered Arm, The 1913 ( ) 2002, 2112, 2125
Tattered Duke, The 1914 (Kal) 1924
Tattooed Will, The 1914 (Br) 150
Tavaszi Vihar 1917 ( ) 1614
Tavern Keeper's Daughter, The 1908 (AMB) 994, 995, 2502
Tavern of Tragedy, The 1914 ( ) 595, 1028
Tax on Bachelors, A 1909 (V)
Taxi 1919 ( ) 1276
Taxidermist's Dream, The 1909 (Lubin)
Teaching Dad to Like Her 1911 (Bio) 1223, 2067
Tear That Burned, The 1914 (Mu) 1029, 2513
Tears and Smiles 1918 (P) 1988
Teasing 1905 (AMB)
Teasing the Sail 1916 ( ) 690
Teddy at the Throttle 1916 (Key/Tri) 166, 840, 2040, 2512, 2537, 2636
Teddy Bears, The 1907 (Ed)
Teddy in Jungleland 1909 (V)
Teddy Telzlaff and Earl Cooper, Speed Kings 1913 (Key) 65, 549, 1345, 1941, 2465, 2542
Teeth of the Tiger 1919 ( ) 572, 1006, 2061, 2232, 2458
Telepathic Warning, A 1908 (V)
Telephone, The 1898 (Ed)
Telephone Girl, The 1912 (V) 2112, 2487
Telephone Girl and the Lady, The 1912 (Bio) 1665, 1751
Tell it to the Marines 1919 (F) 1524
Tell Tale Heart, The 1914 ( ) 2356
Tell-Tale Step, The 1917 ( ) 1774
Tell That to the Marines 1918 ( ) 913
Telltale Kiss: The Boarder 1904 (AMB)
Telltale Light, The 1913 (Key) 65, 99, 650, 1941
Tempered Steel 1918 (FN) 2037
Temperamental Husband, A 1912 (Key) 1666, 1941, 2465
Temperamental Wife, A 1919 (FN) 1226, 1360, 1395, 2444, 2521, 2522
Tempest, The 1904 (Beerbohm) 542
Tempest Cody's Manhunt 1919 ( ) 2656
Temple of Dusk, The 1918 (Par) 1208, 1948
Temple of Terror 1916 ( ) 471, 2354
Temporary Truce, A 1912 (Bio) 1182, 1665, 1714, 1751, 2000, 2513, 2728
Temporary Wife 1919 ( ) 283
Temptation 1909 (Ed)
Temptation 1916 (Par) 683, 869, 1201, 1205, 1208, 2149, 2776
Temptation and the Man 1916 ( ) 272
Temptation of John Gray 1909 (Centaur Film Co.)
Temptation of St. Anthony 1902 (AMB)
Temptations of a Large City 1911 (Ingvald C. Oes)
Tempted but True 1912 (Imp)
Temptress, The 1919 ( ) 438
10 Femmes Dans un Parapluie (10 Ladies in an Umbrella) 1903 (Melies)
Ten Minutes with Shakespeare 1908 (Lubin)

Ten Nights in a Bar-Room 1903 (AMB)
    Murder of Willie
    The Fatal Blow
    Death of Little May
    Death of Slade
Ten Nights in a Barroom 1903 (Lubin)
Ten Nights in a Bar-Room 1911 (Selig) 2770
Ten Nights without a Barroom 1917 (Key/Tri) 2501
Ten of Diamonds 1918 (Tri) 627
Ten Pickaninnies 1908 (Ed)
Ten Seconds 1917 ( ) 1872
Tenacious Solicitor, A 1912 (Ed)
Tender Hearted Boy, The 1913 (Bio) 315, 731, 1182, 1751
Tender Hearts 1909 (Bio)
Tenderfoot, The 1917 ( ) 785, 1271
Tenderfoot Messenger, The 1910 (Es) 50
Tenderfoot's Triumph, The 1910 (Bio)
Tenderhearted, The 1909 (Bio) 141
Tenderloin at Night 1899 (Ed)
Tenderloin Tragedy 1907 (AMB)
Tennessee's Pardner 1916 (Las) 672, 2683
Tenth Case, The 1918 (WS) 835
Terje Vigen 1916 ( ) 2417
Terrible Bourreau Turc, Le 1904 (Melies)
Terrible Discovery, A 1911 (Bio) 1613, 1714, 2000
Terrible Kids, The 1906 (Ed)
Terrible Night, A 1908 (AMB)
Terrible Tec, The 1916 (Br) 1815
Terrible Teddy, the Grizzly King 1901 (Ed)
Terrible Tragedy, A 1916 (Vim) 1161
Terrible Turkish Executioner, The 1904 (Melies)
Terribly Stuck Up 1915 (P) 1586
Terrier vs. Wild Cat 1906 (AMB)
Terror, The 1917 ( ) 192
Terror of the Air, The 1914 (Br) 1289, 2171
Terror of the Range, The--serial 1919 (P) 396, 411, 525, 1494, 1717
    1. Prowlers of the Night
    2. The Hidden Chart
    3. The Chasm of Fear
    4. The Midnight Raid
    5. A Threat from the Past
    6. Tangled Tales
    7. Run to Earth
Tess of the D'Ubervilles 1913 (FP) 331, 907, 2575
Tess of the Storm Country 1914 (FP) 969, 1037, 1190, 1589, 2047
Test, The 1909 (Bio) 1029, 2047
Test, The 1914 (Nestor) 1585, 2112, 2221
Test of a Code, The 1919 ( ) 2130
Test of Friendship 1908 (AMB) 79, 1182, 1363, 1511, 1542, 1814, 1823, 2212, 2368
Test of Friendship, The 1911 (Ed)
Test of Honor 1919 (Par) 139, 140, 226, 1732, 2334
Test of Love, The 1911 (Ed)
Testing of Mildred Vane 1918 (M) 41
Texas Star, A 1915 (Selig) 2065
Thais 1917 (Go) 982, 1427, 2120, 2592
That Chink at Golden Gulch 1910 (Bio) 1223
That Colby Girl 1916 ( ) 1028

That Daredevil 1911 (Bio)
That Devil Bateese 1918 (Bluebird/Un) 449, 1033, 1371, 2159 2211
That Gal of Burke's 1916 (Mu) 256, 1580
That Girl of Dixon's 1910 (Ed)
That Girl Philippa 1918 ( ) 1878
That Hero Stuff 1918 ( ) 960
That Little Band of Gold /aka/ For Better --but Worse 1915 (Key) 65, 878, 1651, 1712, 1941, 2465, 2510
That Minstrel Man 1914 (Key) 65, 2465
That Other Girl 1913 ( ) 2748
That Poor Insurance Man 1904 (Paley & Steiner)
That Springtime Feeling 1915 (Key) 452
That Winsome Winnie Smile 1911 (Ed)
That's a Bad Girl 1918 ( ) 1859
That's Good 1919 (M) 1134, 1499
That's Him! 1918 (P) 1586
That's Me 1916 ( ) 689, 690
Thaw-White Tragedy 1906 (AMB)
Theatre Hat 1903 (AMB)
Theatre Hats Off 1903 (AMB)
Their Compact 1918 (M) 156, 353
Their Fates Sealed 1911 (Bio)
Their First 1916 (M) 768, 1707
Their First Acquaintance 1914 (Mu) 554, 1028, 1182
Their First Divorce Case 1911 (Bio) 2368
Their First Execution 1913 (Key) 2368
Their First Kidnapping Case 1912 (Bio)
Their First Misunderstanding 1911 (Imp) 2047
Their Hero 1912 (Ed)
Their Honeymoon 1916 (Vim) 1161
Their Quiet Honeymoon 1915 (Christie) 525
Their Seaside Tangle * (Christie) 525
Their Social Education 1909 (Ed)
Their Social Splash 1915 (Key) 1874, 1906, 1941, 2501
Their Ups and Downs 1914 (Key) 65
Their Vacation 1916 (Vim) 1161
Thelma 1909 (T) 847, 2174
Thelma 1918 (Br) 1592
Them Was the Happy Days 1916 (P) 1586
Then and Now 1909 (Ed)
Then I'll Come Back to You 1916 ( ) 273
Then You'll Remember Me 1911 (Ed)
There and Back 1916 (V) 2367
There He Is 1904 (AMB)
There Never Was a Girl Like You 1909 (Lubin)
There's Good in Everyone 1915 (Br) 834, 2138
There's Good in the Worst of Us 1913 (Br) 150
There's Music in the Hair 1913 (V) 111, 332, 901
They Found the Leak 1902 (AMB)
They Meet on the Mat 1906 (AMB)
They Would Elope 1909 (Bio) 2047, 2081
Thief and the Girl, The 1911 (Bio) 1468, 1613, 2060
Thief and the Pie Woman, The 1903 (AMB)
Thieves' Gold 1918 (Un) 398, 1719, 1782
Thieving Hand, The 1908 (V)
Thin Ice 1919 (V) 1088, 1832, 2547
Thing, The 1917 (Art/Par) 1865
Thing We Love, The 1918 (Par) 1756, 1970, 2112, 2541, 2770
Third Degree, The 1919 (V) 1288, 1388, 2690

Third Judgement, The 1917 (V) 100, 1034, 1731
Third Kiss, The 1919 (Par) 927, 1448, 1764
Thirst 1917 (Key/Tri) 266, 840, 1345, 1627, 2510, 2534, 2550
Thirst for Gold, The 1912 (Imp)
Thirteen Club, The 1905 (AMB)
Thirteenth at the Table, The 1909 (Lubin)
Thirteenth Chair, The 1919 ( ) 370, 1118, 1656, 2404
Thirteenth Girl, The 1917 ( ) 2068
Thirteenth Hour, The--serial 1918 (Un) 2056
Thirty a Week 1918 (Go) 115, 1867
Thirty Days 1916 (Vim) 1161
Thirty Days at Hard Labor 1912 (Ed)
This Hero Stuff 1919 ( ) 2671
This Is Hard Work 1904 (AMB)
This Is the Life 1918 ( ) 2671
This Way Out 1916 (Vim) 340, 1156, 1161, 2497
Thomas Graal's First Child 1918 (SB) 1851, 1937, 2417, 2598, 2785
Thompson's Night Out 1908 (AMB)
Thor, Lord of the Jungle 1913 (Selig) 2221
Thoroughbred, A 1911 (Ed)
Thoroughbred, The 1916 ( ) 1404
Those Awful Hats 1909 (AMB)
Those Bitter Sweets 1915 (Key) 1651, 2501
Those Boys 1909 (AMB)
Those Children 1915 (Br) 149, 150
Those College Girls /aka/ His Bitter Half 1915 (Key) 1874, 1906, 2501
Those Country Kids 1914 (Key) 65, 1941
Those Dangerous Eyes 1914 (Key) 531
Those Good Old Days 1913 (Key) 1941
Those Happy Days 1914 (Key) 65
Those Hicksville Boys 1912 (Bio) 731, 1182, 1223, 1714, 2368
Those Little Flowers 1913 (Bio) 1028, 2573
Those Love Pangs /aka/ Busted Hearts; The Rival Mashers 1914 (Key) 73, 451, 531, 815, 1422, 1651, 1934
Those Troublesome Tresses 1913 (V) 332, 901
Those Wedding Bells 1915 (Christie) 525
Those Wedding Bells Shall Not Ring Out 1902 (AMB)
Those Who Pay 1918 ( ) 134
Those without Sin 1917 (Las) 200, 935, 1970, 2513
Thou Art the Man 1915 (V) 1437
Thou Shalt Not 1910 (Bio) 1593, 2680
Thou Shalt Not 1919 (F) 1427, 1445, 1929, 2024, 2756
Thou Shalt Not Covet 1912 (V) 332, 901
Thou Shalt Not Steal 1914 (Br) 2171
Thousand Dollar Husband, The 1915 (Par) 935, 2513
Thread of Destiny 1914 (Lubin) 1929, 2552
Threads of Fate, The 1915 (Rex/Un) 352, 449, 762
Three Acrobats 1899 (Ed)
Three Bad Men and a Girl 1915 (Un) 610, 926
Three Bears, The 1903 (Lubin)
Three Black Bags, The 1913 (V) 332, 901
Three Black Eyes 1919 ( ) 1276, 1987
Three Brothers, The 1915 ( ) 601, 2112

Three Cavaliers of the Road 1905 (AMB)
Three Friends 1913 (Bio) 141, 2047, 2513, 2680
Three Gamblers, The 1913 (Es) 50
Three Girls in a Hammock 1904 (AMB)
Three Green Eyes 1919 ( ) 231, 835, 1255, 1603
Three Jolly Dutchmen 1905 (Paley & Steiner)
Three King Fishers, The 1910 (Bio)
Three Kisses 1909 (Ed)
Three Little Maids 1904 (AMB)
Three Little Orphans 1914 (Br) 149, 150
Three Little Pigs 1903 (Lubin)
Three Men and a Girl 1919 (FP/Las) 143, 482, 626, 1748, 2012
Three Mounted Men 1918 (Un) 398, 1004, 1120
Three Musketeers, The 1911 (Ed) 133, 161, 444, 700, 968, 1521, 1656, 1930, 2379
Three of a Kind 1906 (Winthrop Press)
Three of a Kind 1911 (Ed)
Three of Us, The 1915 ( ) 1118, 2520
Three Rings and a Goat 1915 (P) 1161
Three Sisters 1911 (Bio) 271, 1182, 2047, 2067, 2368, 2502
Three Slims, The 1916 (Key/Tri) 2058, 2206, 2501
Three Thanksgivings 1909 (Ed)
Three Weeks 1914 (Reliable) 2048, 2581
Three Wise Men 1913 (Selig) 857, 1957, 2221
Three X Gordon 1919 ( ) 1431
Thrilling Detective Story, A 1906 (Lubin)
Through Darkened Vales 1911 (Bio) 1074, 2513, 2728
Through His Wife's Picture 1911 (Bio)
Through Jealousy 1909 (Lubin)
Through Shadow to Sunshine 1909 (Lubin)
Through the Air 1911 (Independent Moving Picture Co.)
Through the Breakers 1909 (Bio) 685, 1450, 1542
Through the Clouds 1910 (Ed)
Through the Dells of Wisconsin 1911 (Independent Moving Picture Co.)
Through the Flames 1912 (Br) 150
Through the Flames 1912 (Imp)
Through the Key-Hole in the Door 1903 (AMB)
Through the Matrimonial Agency 1905 (Lubin)
Through the Toils 1919 ( ) 656, 1603
Through the Valley of Shadows 1914 (GB) 2604
Through the Wall 1916 ( ) 2397
Through the Wrong Door 1919 (Go) 265, 1423, 2335, 2441
Through Trials to Victory 1912 (Ingvald C. Oes)
Through Turbulent Waters 1915 ( ) 1649
Throw of the Dice, A 1913 (Br) 2171
Thumb Print, The 1911 (V) 2523
Thunderbolt 1919 ( ) 25, 2445
Thunderbolt Jack 1918 ( ) 926, 2210
Thunderbolts of Fate 1919 ( ) 1532, 2035
Thwarted Vengeance, A 1911 (Es) 50
Ticklish Man, The 1908 (Lubin)
Tidebrook 1918 ( ) 763
Tides of Barnegat, The 1917 (Las) 724,

927, 935, 2513
Tides of Retribution 1915 ( ) 1659, 1896
Tides That Meet 1919 ( ) 2700
Tied to Her Apron Strings 1904 (AMB)
Tiger, The 1913 ( ) 2472
Tiger Lady, The 1913 (V) 1047, 2767
Tiger Lily 1919 ( ) 905, 2032
Tiger Man, The 1918 (Mu) 960, 1188, 1948
Tiger of the Sea 1919 (V) 2397
Tiger Woman, The 1917 (F) 116, 237, 483, 674, 716, 733, 1244, 1277, 1760, 1763, 2110, 2177, 2745
Tiger's Trail, The--serial 1919 (P) 892, 1458, 1494, 1857, 2169, 2493, 2675
    1. The Tiger Worshipers
    2. Glowing Eyes
    3. The Human Chain
    4. Danger Signals
    5. The Tiger Trap
    6. The Secret Assassin
    7. Flaming Waters
    8. Danger Ahead
    9. Raging Torrent
    10. Bringing in the Law
    11. In the Breakers
    12. The Two Amazons
    13. The False Idol
    14. The Mountain Hermit
    15. The Tiger Face
Tigress, The 1914 ( ) 2037
Till I Come Back to You 1918 (Par) 242, 359, 502, 877, 996, 1024, 1126, 1338, 1537, 2119, 2483, 2638, 2700
Till Our Ship Comes In series 1919 (Br) 943
Tillie Wakes Up 1917 (Go) 765, 1255
Tillie's Punctured Romance 1914 (Key) 37, 187, 188, 206, 253, 451, 460, 531, 650, 765, 791, 1090, 1304, 1422, 1567, 1651, 1662, 1726, 1906, 1941, 2208, 2501, 2506, 2510
Tillie's Tomatoe Surprise 1915 (Lubin) 765
Tilly the Tomboy Goes Boating 1910 (Hep) 2531, 2744
Time, the Great Healer 1914 (Hep) 1289, 2171, 2531 2744
Timely Interception, A 1913 (Bio) 141, 357, 1029, 1182, 1655, 1831, 2000
Timely Repentance 1912 (Imp)
Timothy Dobbs 1916 ( ) 689, 690
Tin Pan Alley 1919 ( ) 2070
Tinker, Tailor, Soldier, Sailor 1918 (Br) 831, 1918
Tinkering with Trouble 1915 (P) 1586
Tinsel 1918 ( ) 1048, 1067, 1991
Tip, The 1917 (P) 1586, 2055
Tired, Absent-Minded Man, The 1911 (V) 332, 901
Tired Tailor's Dream, The 1907 (AMB)
'Tis an Ill Wind That Blows No Good 1909 (AMB) 1363, 1992, 2074
'Tis Now the Very Witching Time of Night 1909 (Ed)
Tit for Tat; or A Good Joke with My Head 1904 (Melies)
Tit for Tat; or Outwitted by Wit 1908 (V)
To Have and to Hold 1916 (Las) 1631, 1907, 2112

To Hell with the Kaiser! 1918 (M) 618,
633, 1062, 1640, 2540
To Him That Hath 1919 ( ) 1603
To Save Her Brother 1912 (Ed)
To Save Her Soul 1909 (Bio) 1363, 2047
To the Highest Bidder 1918 (V) 1388
Tobacco Mania 1909 (Ed)
Toby's Bow 1919 (Go) 509, 1297, 1425,
1466, 1472, 1867, 2018, 2039, 2341
Today 1917 (P) 2105
Todd of the Times 1919 ( ) 1404, 2124
Together 1918 ( ) 1814
Toilers, The 1919 (Diamond) 121, 722,
1235
Toilers, The 1919 (Super) 522, 2555
Toilette, The 1904 (AMB)
Told in the Hills 1919 (Art/Par) 242, 935,
1580, 1596, 1970, 1975, 2698
Toll Gate, The 1916 (Tri) 1188, 2780
Tom and Jerry Mix 1917 (F) 1849
Tom Brown of Harvard _see_ Brown of
Harvard 1918 (Go)
Tom Brown's Schooldays 1916 (Br) 1258
Tom Butler's Mysterious Adventures 1912
(Eclair)
Tom Cringle in Jamaica 1913 (Br) 1873
Tom Jones 1917 (Br) 349
Tom Sawyer 1917 (Art/Par(1050, 1104,
1292, 1309, 2045, 2399
Tom Tight Et Dum-Dum 1903 (Melies)
Tom, Tom, the Piper's Son 1903 (Lubin)
Tom, Tom, the Piper's Son 1905 (AMB)
Tomboy Bessie 1912 (Bio)
Tomboy on Bar Z, The 1912 (Es) 50
Tommy Atkins, Bobby and Cook 1899 (Ed)
Tommy's Geography Lesson 1912 (Ed)
Tom's Sacrifice 1916 (Selig Polyscope)
1849
Tom's Strategy 1916 (Selig Polyscope)
1849
Tong Man, The 1919 (Par) 1208
Tong War 1918 ( ) 2638
Tongues of Flame, The--serial 1919 ( )
2656, 2754
Tonnerre de Jupiter, Le 1903 (Melies)
Tony America 1919 ( ) 1656
Tony and the Stork 1911 (Independent
Moving Picture Co.)
Tony's Oath of Vengeance 1912 (Ed)
Too Ardent Lover, A 1903 (AMB)
Too Fat to Fight 1918 ( ) 1630
Too Good to Be True 1919 ( ) 2595
Too Many Brides /aka/ The Love Chase
1914 (Key) 2465
Too Many Burglars 1911 (Bio)
Too Many Crooks 1919 ( ) 1046, 1547,
Too Many Husbands 1914 (V) 768, 1684,
1876
Too Many Millions 1918 (Par) 396, 1756,
1970, 2112
Too Much Champagne 1908 (V)
Too Much Henry 1917 (M) 768, 1707
Too Much Johnson 1903 (AMB)
Too Much Mother-in-Law 1907 (Lubin)
Too Much Mustard _see_ Max Teaches
the Tango
Too Much of a Good Thing 1903 (AMB)
Too Much Woman 1914 ( ) 2554
Too Scrambled 1918 (P) 1586
Toodles and Her Strawberry Tart 1903
(AMB)

Toodles Recites a Recitation 1903 (AMB)
Toodles' Tea Party 1903 (AMB)
Tools of Providence 1915 ( ) 1188
Tootsie 1917 (M) 768, 1707
Tootsies and Tamales 1919 (V) 1161
Top Dog 1918 (Br) 943, 1968
Toplitsky and Company 1913 (Key) 1666,
2465
Toreador, The 1919 ( ) 539, 1422
Torero Song "Carmen" 1909 (Lubin)
Tornado, The 1917 ( ) 928
Tortured Heart, The 1916 (V) 2024
Tosca 1908 (FdA) 212
Toss of a Coin, The 1911 (Independent
Moving Picture Co.)
Tossing Eggs 1902 (Ed)
Total Accident, A 1903 (AMB)
Total Loss, A _see_ Doctoring a Leak
T' Other Dear Charmer 1919 ( ) 1309
Toto 1919 (Sel) 2557
Toton, the Apache 1917 (Tri) 2034
Touch Down, The 1917 ( ) 1872
Touch of a Child, The 1918 (Hep) 812,
2171, 2531
Touch of Rheumatism, A _see_ Mabel's
Last Prank
Tough Dance, A 1902 (AMB)
Tough Kid's Waterloo 1902 (AMB)
Tough Luck 1919 (P) 635, 2055
Tough Luck and Tin Lizzies 1917 (V)
2367
Tourists, The 1912 (Bio)
Tout's Remembrance, The 1910 (Es) 50
Towards the Light 1918 (Hep) 812, 2744
Tower of Ivory 1918 ( ) 437, 2364
Tower of London, The 1905 (Melies)
Toymaker, The 1911 (V) 565
Toymaker, the Doll and the Devil, The
1910 (Ed)
Toys of Fate 1918 (M) 321, 534, 618,
1919 Tracked by a Woman 1908 (Lubin)
Trading His Mother 1911 (Ed)
Trading Stamp Craze, The 1906 (Lubin)
Traffic in Soles 1914 (Un) 81
Traffic in Souls 1913 (Imp) 439, 582,
1058, 1864
Tragedy of a Dress Suit, The 1912 (Bio)
Tragedy of Basil Grieve 1914 (Br) 1289,
2171
Tragedy of Japan, A 1908 (V)
Tragedy of the Desert * ( ) 992
Tragedy of Whispering Creek, The 1914
(101-Bison/Un) 348, 352, 449, 552,
583, 762, 1587, 2195
Tragic Love 1909 (AMB) 79, 1363, 1823
Trail of Books, The 1911 (Bio) 685
Trail of the Holdup 1919 ( ) 1011
Trail of the Lonesome Pine, The 1916
(Par) 306, 947, 1188, 1800, 2149,
2461, 2661
Trail of the Octopus--serial 1919 (Hall
Mark Pictures Corp.) 418, 582,
799, 1004, 2015, 2774
    1.   The Devil's Trade-Mark
    2.   Purple Dagger
    3.   Face to Face
    4.   The Hand of Wang
    5.   The Eye of Satan
    6.   Behind the Mask
    7.   The Dance of Death
    8.   Satan's Soulmate

9. The Chained Soul
10. The Ape Man
11. The Red Death
12. The Poisoned Talon
13. The Phantom Mandarin
14. The House of Shadows
15. The Yellow Octopus
Trail of the Rails 1917 ( ) 1010
Trail of the Serpent 1915 ( ) 2416
Trail to Yesterday 1918 (M) 397, 1631,
    1939
Trailed by the West 1910 (Es) 50
Trailing the Counterfeiter 1911 (Bio)
Train of Incidents, A 1914 (V) 51, 332,
    901
Trainer's Daughter, The; or A Race for
    Love 1907 (Ed)
Traitor, The 1918 (Go) 153
Traitor's Fate, A 1912 (Un)
Tramp, The 1915 (Es) 71, 106, 451, 1045,
    1347, 1676, 2077, 2746
Tramp and the Dump Cart 1905 (Paley &
    Steiner)
Tramp and the Bathers, The 1903 (AMB)
Tramp and the Matress Maker, The 1906
    (Melies)
Tramp and the Muscular Cook, The 1902
    (AMB)
Tramp and the Nursing Bottle, The 1901
    (Ed)
Tramp in the Kitchen, The 1898 (Ed)
Tramp on a Farm 1904 (Paley & Steiner)
Tramp on the Roof, A 1904 (AMB)
Tramp, Tramp, Tramp 1913 ( ) 1132
Tramps, The 1915 (Lubin) 1161
Tramp's Dream, The 1901 (Ed)
Tramp's Miraculous Escape, The 1901
    (Ed)
Tramp's Nap Interrupted 1901 (Lubin)
Tramp's Revenge 1905 (Lubin)
Tramp's Strategy That Failed 1901 (Ed)
Tramp's Unexpected Skate, The 1901 (Ed)
Transformation of Mike, The 1912 (Bio)
    1613, 2513
Transgressor, The 1913 ( ) 1032, 2096
Transients in Arcadia 1918 ( ) 804
Trap, The 1913 (Powers/Un) 449, 1711
Trap, The 1918 (Un) 273, 1052, 1117,
    1427, 1796, 2124, 2540
Trap for Santa Claus, A 1909 (Bio) 816,
    1542
Trapped in a Forest Fire 1913 (Am) 101,
    344
Trapped Wires 1917 ( ) 1010
Trapper's Five Dollar Bill, The 1911 (Ed)
Traps and Tangles 1919 (V) 2367
Traveling Salesman, The 1917 (Par) 1429,
    1680
Travels of a Lost Trunk 1905 (Paley &
    Steiner)
Treachery of Bronco Billy's Pal 1914 (Es)
    50
Treason 1917 ( ) 1216, 1275
Treasure, The; or The House Next Door
    1909 (V)
Treasure Island 1912 (Ed)
Treasure Island 1918 (F) 557, 1570
Treasure Island 1919 (Art/Par) 1855
Treasure of Desert Island, The 1913 ( )
    2472
Treasure of Heaven, The 1916 (Br) 177, 349

Treasure of the Sea 1918 (F) 506, 2487
Treasure Trove 1911 (V) 332
Treat 'Em Rough 1918 (F) 1849
Treatin' 'Em Rough 1918 (Key) 878
Trelawney of the Wells 1916 (Hep) 1289,
    2171, 2531, 2744
Trembling Hour, The 1919 ( ) 2356,
    2480
Trey o' Hearts, The--serial 1914 (Un)
    1149, 1494, 1711, 2018, 2419, 2673
    1. Flower o' Flame
    2. White Water
    3. The Sea Venture
    4. Dead Reckoning
    5. The Sunset Bride
    6. The Crack o' Doom
    7. Stalemate
    8. The Mock Rose
    9. As the Crow Flies
    10. Steel Ribbons
    11. The Painted Hills
    12. The Mirage
    13. Jaws of Death
    14. The First Law
    15. The Last Trump
Trial Marriages 1907 (AMB)
Trial of Captain Dreyfuss at Rennes,
    France 1899 (Lubin)
Triangle, The 1912 (Ed)
Tribal Law, The 1912 ( ) 2112
Tribe's Penalty, The 1911 (Es) 50
Tribulations of a Photographer 1908
    (Lubin)
Trick Bears 1899 (Ed)
Trick Elephants 1897 (Ed)
Trick of Fate, A 1919 ( ) 134, 2514,
    2754
Trick on the Cop, A 1904 (AMB)
Trick That Failed, The 1909 (Bio) 1363,
    2047, 2368
Tricky Painter's Fate, A 1908 (Melies)
Tried for His Own Murder 1915 (V) 111,
    566
Tried in the Fire 1913 (Hep) 2531
Trilby 1915 (Equitable/W) 130, 1470, 2811
Trilby and Little Billee 1896 (American
    Mutoscope Co.)
Trinity, The 1912 (Independent Moving
    Picture Co.)
Trip to Mars, A 1903 (Lubin)
Trip to Mars, A 1910 (Ed)
Trip to the Moon 1899 (Lubin)
Trip to the Moon, A 1902 (Melies) 10, 55
Triple Trouble 1918 (Es) 71, 97, 451,
    1347, 1414, 2077, 2197, 2746
Trips and Tribunals 1918 (Br) 1487
Triumph 1917 (Bluebird/Un) 449, 771,
    799, 1388, 2042, 2490
Trixie from Broadway 1919 ( ) 905
Trop Crédule 1908 ( ) 466
Trouble Buster, The 1917 (Art/Par) 935,
    1764, 2772
Trouble Enough 1916 (P) 1586
Trouble for Nothing 1916 (Br) 834, 1931
Trouble in Hogan's Alley 1903 (AMB)
Trouble Mender, The see Love and
    Bullets
Troublemakers 1918 (F) 1524
Troubles see Making a Living
Troubles of a Butler, The 1911 (Ed)
Troubles of a Flirt 1908 (V)

Troubles of a Manager of a Burlesque
Show 1904 (AMB)
Troubles of a Stranded Actor 1908 (Lubin)
Troubles of an Amateur Detective, The
1909 (V)
Troubles of a Too Ardent Admirer 1908
(Lubin)
Troublesome Baby, The 1910 (Bio)
Troublesome Fly, The 1902 (AMB)
Troublesome Satchel, A 1909 (AMB)
Troublesome Stepdaughters, The 1912 (V)
332, 1032, 1129, 1413, 1941, 2487,
2523, 2663
Trovatore, II 1909 (Lubin)
Truant, The; or How Willie Fixed His
Dad 1909 (V)
Truant Soul, The 1917 ( ) 457
Truants, The 1907 (AMB)
True Blue 1918 (F) 853, 868, 1374
True Heart Susie 1919 (Art) 315, 388,
706, 875, 1029, 1182, 1249, 1964,
2370
True Hearts Are More Than Coronets
1908 (V)
True Indian's Heart, A 1909 (Bison) 960
True Love Never Runs Smoothly 1909 (Ed)
True Patriot, A 1909 (Lubin)
True Till Death 1912 (Melies)
True Till Death 1912 (V) 2487
Truer Love, The 1909 (V)
Trumpet of the Weak, The 1918 ( ) 1673
Trust, The 1915 (Victor/Un) 449, 2080
Truth Game, The 1915 ( ) 333
Truth in the Wilderness 1913 (Am) 1431
Truthful Tolliver 1917 (Tri) 1188, 2194
Try and Get It 1919 ( ) 2700
Try Out, The 1911 (Ed)
Try-Out, The 1916 (Vim) 340, 1156, 1161,
2497
Trying It on the Dog 1906 (Winthrop Press)
Trying to Fool Uncle 1912 (Bio)
Trying to Get Along 1919 ( ) 1906, 2465
Trying to Get Arrested 1909 (AMB)
Tsveti Zapozdaliye (Belated Flowers) /aka/
Doktor Toporkov 1917 (Russian) 1995
Tubby Turns the Tables 1916 (V) 2367
Tugboat Romeo, A 1916 (Key/Tri) 531,
1723, 2588, 2799
Tumultuous Elopement, A 1909 (Melies)
Turf Conspiracy, A 1918 (Br) 43, 1289
Turmoil, The 1916 (M) 1445, 2618
Turn in the Road, The 1919 ( ) 28, 617,
808, 1126, 1311, 1710, 1933, 2638
Turn of a Card, A 1918 ( ) 1431, 2002,
2779
Turn of the Wheel 1919 (Go) 869, 1220,
1748, 2095, 2402
Turned to the Wall 1911 (Ed)
Turning His Ivories see Laughing Gas
Turning over a New Leaf 1908 (Ed)
Turning Point, The 1919 ( ) 1166, 1248,
1853
Turning the Tables 1903 (Ed)
Turning the Tables 1910 (Bio)
Turning the Tables 1911 (Ed)
Turning the Tables 1919 (Art) 218, 875,
1028, 2573
Turning the Tables; or Waiting on the
Waiter 1908 (V)
Turtle Doves 1914 (Br) 349
'Tween Two Loves 1911 (Independent

Moving Picture Co.) 2047
Twelfth Night 1910 (V) 1047, 1426, 2210
Twelve Good Hens and True 1917 (M) 768,
1707
Twelve in a Barrel 1901 (Lubin)
Twelve: Ten 1919 (Br) 2712
Twelve: Ten 1919 (Select) 395, 752, 756,
2215
Twentieth Century Tramp, The; or Happy
Hooligan and His Airship 1902 (Ed)
Twenty Dollars a Week 118 ( ) 1276
Twenty Minutes of Love /aka/ Cops and
Watches; He Loved Her So; Love-
Friend 1914 (Key) 451, 531, 791,
1090, 1442, 2514
Twenty One 1918 (Par) 2700
Twenty Thousand Leagues under the Sea
1907 (Melies) 1802
Twenty Thousand Leagues under the Sea
1916 (Un) 973, 1025, 1281, 1864
23 1/2 Hours Leave 1919 (Par) 259,
1100, 1261, 1697, 1791, 1928, 2448
Twenty Years in Sing-Sing 1911
(America's Feature Film Co.)
Twilight 1919 ( ) 1429
Twilight Baby 1913 ( ) 1651
Twin Brothers 1909 (AMB)
Twin Flats 1916 (Vim) 1161
Twin Husbands 1917 ( ) 689
Twin Pawns 1919 ( ) 1907, 1971
Twin Sisters 1915 (Lubin) 1161
Twin Towers, The 1911 (Ed)
Twins, The see Dollars and Sense
Twisted Trail, The 1910 (Bio) 2047
Twisted Trails 1917 (Selig) 857
Twixt Cup and Lip 1915 (Br) 1329
Twixt Love and Duty 1908 (V)
Two Affinities; or a Domestic Reunion
1908 (V)
Two-Bit Seats 1917 ( ) 1276
Two Bottle Babies 1904 (AMB)
Two Brides 1919 ( ) 438, 920, 2485
Two Broken Hearts 1908 (V)
Two Brothers, The 1910 (Bio) 315, 1542,
2047, 2081
Two Chappies in a Box 1903 (Ed)
Two Cinders 1912 (V) 332
Two Convicts, The 1912 (Ingvald C. Oes)
Two Cousins 1909 (Lubin)
Two Crazy Bugs 1908 (Melies)
Two Crooks /aka/ A Noble Crook 1917
(Key/Tri) 1086, 2069
Two Cylinder Courtship, A 1917 (Strand)
2121
Two Daughters of Eve, The 1912 (Bio)
251, 1029, 1430, 1665, 1832, 1876,
1933, 2680
Two Father Christmases 1913 (Br) 150
Two Flats, The 1912 (Ed)
Two Gun Betty 1918 ( ) 134
Two Gun-Gussie 1918 (P) 1586
Two Gun Hicks /aka/ Passing of Two
Gun Hicks 1914 (Bio) 1188
Two Heroes, The 1911 (Ed)
Two Hours after Chickens Leave the
Shells 1902 (AMB)
Two Is Company, Three a Crowd 1904
(Paley & Steiner)
Two Knights in a Barroom 1912 (Ed)
Two Little Dogs 1908 (Lubin)
Two Little Dromios 1914 (T) 52

Two Little Imps 1916 (F) 1524
Two Little Shoes 1908 (Lubin)
Two Little Waifs 1910 (Bio)
Two Memories 1909 (Bio) 1182, 1363,
   1542, 1865, 2046, 2047, 2368
Two Men of the Desert 1913 (Bio) 1832,
   1924, 2513, 2680
Two o'Clock Train, The 1916 (Tri) 2568
Two of a Kind see The Rounders
Two of a Kind 1909 (Ed)
Two Officers 1911 (Ed)
Two Old Cronies 1903 (AMB)
Two Orphans, The 1911 (Selig) 1018, 1537,
   1960, 2452, 2770
Two Orphans, The 1915 (F) 116, 205, 240,
   285, 291, 1038, 1905, 2381, 2435,
   2436
Two Overcoats 1911 (V) 332, 901
Two Paths, The 1911 (Bio) 122, 595,
   1542, 1552, 2728
Two Rebels 1916 ( ) 2341
Two Reformations 1910 (Es) 50
Two Roads 1915 (Br) 2712
Two Rubes at the Theatre 1901 (Lubin)
Two Seedy Rubes: They Have a Hot
   Time in the Old Town 1916 (Lubin)
Two Sides, The 1911 (Bio) 357
Two Sides of the Wall 1908 (Lubin)
Two Sons, The 1908 (V)
Two Souled Woman 1918 (Un) 675, 1025
Two Strenuous Rubes 1905 (Paley &
   Steiner)
Two Talented Vagabonds 1908 (Melies)
Two Thousand Miles without a Dollar
   1907 (V)
Two Tough Tenderfeet 1918 (Key/Tri)
   2608
Two Traveling Boys, The; or The Adven-
   tures of Percy White and Pauline
   Wells 1908 (V)
Two Valentines 1911 (Ed)
Two White Roses 1911 (Ed)
Two Widows, The 1913 (Key) 2465
Two Women 1915 (V) 1047, 2472, 2767
Two Women and a Man 1909 (Bio) 1593,
   2062
Two's Company 1902 (AMB)
Two's Company, Three's a Crowd 1908
   (V)
Two's Company, Three's a Crowd 1913
   ( ) 2472
Typhoon, The 1914 (Kal) 60, 1208
Tyrant Fear 1918 (Tri) 627, 1125
Tyrant Is Dead, The 1910 (V) 566

                    - U -

Ugly Tempered Tramp, The 1903 (AMB)
Ulysses and Giant Polyphemus 1905
   (Melies)
Umbrellas to Mend; or Mr. Niceman's
   Umbrella 1912 (V) 332, 901
Umbrella They Could Not Lose, The 1912
   (Br) 1289
Unafraid, The 1915 (Par) 664, 828, 981,
   1201, 1372, 1406, 2035, 2036, 2038,
   2149
Unappreciated Genius 1909 (Ed)
Unbeliever, The 1918 (Ed) 572, 1482,
   1550, 1688, 2173, 2466, 2649, 2709

(This was Edison's last film)
Unchanging Sea, The 1910 (Bio) 79, 1363,
   2047
Unchastened Woman 1917 ( ) 2614
Unclaimed Goods 1918 ( ) 927, 1764
Uncle Bill 1914 (V) 1047, 2091, 2472,
   2521
Uncle Hiram's List 1911 (Ed)
Uncle Josh at the Moving Picture Show
   1902 (Ed)
Uncle Josh in a Spooky Hotel 1900 (Ed)
Uncle Josh's Nightmare 1900 (Ed)
Uncle Pete's Ruse 1911 (Independent
   Moving Picture Co.)
Uncle Rueben at the Waldorf 1903 (AMB)
Uncle Rueben's Courtship 1909 (Lubin)
Uncle Tom 1910 ( ) 2149
Uncle Tom Wins 1909 (Ed)
Uncle Tom without the Cabin 1919 (Key/
   Tri) 2608
Uncle Tom's Cabin 1903 (Ed)
Uncle Tom's Cabin 1903 (Lubin)
Uncle Tom's Cabin 1909 (V) 231, 1426
Uncle Tom's Cabin 1913 (Un) 29, 606,
   905, 2054, 2388, 2401
Uncle Tom's Cabin 1914 (Peerless) 819,
   1611
Uncle Tom's Cabin 1918 (Par) 482, 1600
Uncle Tom's Cabin (Burlesque) 1919 (Key)
   531, 2069
Uncle's Birthday Gift 1911 (Ed)
Uncle's Visit 1911 (Independent Moving
   Picture Co.)
Unconquered 1917 ( ) 1756, 2623
Under a Flag of Truce 1912 ( ) 1939
Under a Shadow 1915 (Rex/Un) 449, 1518,
   2398, 2781
Under Burning Skies 1912 (Bio) 362, 1613,
   2513
Under Cover 1917 (Art/Par) 667, 1865
Under False Colors 1907 (V)
Under False Colors 1914 (V) 297, 1876,
   2523
Under False Colors 1917 (P) 801, 2689
Under Handicap 1917 ( ) 612
Under Northern Skies 1909 (Ed)
Under Royal Patronage 1914 (Es) 156,
   353, 612, 2700
Under Sheriff, The 1914 (Key) 65
Under Suspicion 1918 (M) 156, 353, 396,
   2445
Under the Bamboo Tree 1905 (AMB)
Under the Crescent--serial 1915 (Un) 762,
   1316, 1770, 2041, 2419, 2804
   1.   The Purple Iris
   2.   The Cage of the Golden Bars
   3.   In the Shadow of the Pyramids
   4.   For the Honor of a Woman
   5.   In the Name of the King
   6.   The Crown of Death
Under the Daisies 1913 (V) 297, 2523
Under the German Yoke 1915 (Br) 177
Under the Greenwood Tree 1918 (Par)
   462, 888, 1959, 2061
Under the Handicap 1918 (M) 1589
Under the Mistletoe 1903 (Ed)
Under the Old Apple Tree 1907 (AMB)
Under the Seas 1907 (Melies)
Under the Steam Hammer 1909 (Lubin)
Under the Top 1919 (Art/Par) 595, 1120,
   1975, 2482

Under the Tree 1904 (AMB)
Under the Tropical Sun 1911 (Ed)
Under the Yoke 1918 (F) 116, 1952, 2175, 2567, 2682
Under Two Flags 1916 (F) 116, 580, 592, 1244, 2738, 2756
Under Western Skies 1910 (Es) 50
Undercurrent 1919 ( ) 243, 1216
Undersea Loot 1919 ( ) 2002
Undine 1912 (T) 1468, 2201, 2430
Undying Flame, The 1917 ( ) 2037
Une Partie de Cartes 1896 (Melies) 1802
Uneasy Money 1918 ( ) 1276, 2619
Uneven Road, The 1917 (Es) 1636
Unexpected Fireworks 1905 (Melies)
Unexpected Guest, An 1909 (Lubin)
Unexpected Help 1910 (Bio) 816, 1363
Unexpected Knockout, An 1902 (AMB)
Unexpected Meeting, An 1907 (P) 1575
Unexpected Places 1918 ( ) 1631, 1847, 2554
Unexpected Review, An 1911 (V) 332
Unexpected Reward, The 1910 (Ed)
Unexpected Santa Claus, An 1908 (Ed)
Unexpected Treasure 1918 (Br) 1487
Unfaithful 1918 (Tri) 627
Unfaithful Odalisque, The 1903 (AMB)
Unfaithful Wife, The 1903 (AMB)
    The Lover
    The Fight
    Murder and Suicide
Unfinished Letter, The 1911 (Ed)
Unfit 1914 (Br) 1289, 2171
Unforseen, The 1918 (M) 980, 2061, 2540
Unfortunate Sex, The 1919 ( ) 1494
Unfriendly Fruit 1916 (P) 1586
Unknown 274, 1917 (F) 392
Unknown, The 1915 ( ) 2541
Unknown Claim, The 1910 (Es) 50
Unknown Language, An 1911 (Ed)
Unknown Love 1919 ( ) 434, 824
Unknown Quantity, The 1919 (V) 1046, 1088
Unknown Violinist, The 1912 (V) 332, 695
Unlawful Trade, The 1914 (Rex/Un) 352, 449, 552, 762, 1587, 1705
Unlucky at Cards; Lucky at Love 1905 (AMB)
Unlucky Horseshoe, The 1908 (Lubin)
Unlucky Jim 1917 (Mu) 2760
Unlucky Lover, An 1903 (AMB)
Unmarried Look, The 1917 (M) 768, 1707
Unmasked 1917 ( ) 610, 926
Unpainted Woman, The 1919 ( ) 355, 1125, 1694
Unpardonable Sin, The 1919 (Garson-Neilan-Equity) 27, 138, 166, 239, 533, 1855, 1864, 2468, 2513
Unprotected, The 1916 (Par) 935, 1591, 2149, 2513
Unprotected Female, An 1903 (AMB)
Unseen Enemy, An 1912 (Bio) 251, 398, 1028, 1029, 1182, 1224, 2663
Unseen Terror, An 1914 (Kal) 1388, 1867
Unselfish Love, An 1910 (Ed)
Unspoken Goodbye, The 1909 (V)
Unsuccessful Substitution, An 1909 (Ed)
Untamable Whiskers, The 1904 (Melies)
Untamed, The 1918 (Tri) 2453, 2479
Until They Get Me 1917 ( ) 619, 2453
Unto the End 1919 ( ) 2760

Unusual Sacrifice, An 1912 (Ed)
Unveiling, The 1911 (Bio) 357, 1182, 1224, 1941
Unveiling Hand, The 1919 ( ) 606, 1048
Unwelcome Guest, The 1912 (Bio) 251, 398, 1029, 1665, 1714, 1831, 2045, 2047
Unwelcome Guest, The 1919 ( ) 901
Unwelcome Mother, The 1916 ( ) 1506
Unwelcome Mrs. Hatch, The 1914 (FP) 590, 599, 1313, 1589, 1940
Unwelcome Visitor, An 1898 (Ed)
Unwritten Code, The 1919 (Par) 1774
Unwritten Law, The 1907 (Lubin)
Up a Tree 1910 (Bio)
Up against It 1912 (Imp)
Up in Alf's Place 1919 ( ) 1906
Up or Down? 1917 ( ) 539, 2133
Up Romance Road 1918 (Mu) 2201
Up San Juan Hill 1910 (Selig Polyscope) 1849
Up the Ladder with Tom Bowline 1909 (Ed)
Up the Road 1918 ( ) 2026
Up the Road with Sally 1918 (Sel) 1432, 2521
Up-to-Date Clothes Cleaning 1908 (Melies)
Upholding the Law 1916 ( ) 1188, 2780
Uplifters, The 1919 (M) 41
Uplifting of Mr. Barker, The 1909 (Ed)
Upper and Lower 1917 ( ) 1872
Ups and Downs 1911 (V) 332
Ups and Downs 1915 (Vim) 340, 1156, 1611, 2497
Upside Down 1919 ( ) 1276, 1532
Upstairs 1919 (Go) 543, 1483, 1941, 2468
Upstairs and Down 1919 (Sel) 355, 457, 826, 1448, 2159, 2554, 2557
Usurer, The 1910 (Bio) 122, 315, 357, 1224, 1363, 1933, 2680
Usurer's Grip, The 1912 (Ed)
Usurper, The 1919 (V) 857, 1490, 2767

- V -

V. C. 1914 (Hep) 2712, 2744
Vad Izalmabogy 1914 ( ) 1614
Vagabond, The 1916 (Mu) 97, 106, 384, 451, 517, 1414, 1840, 2077, 2090, 2746
Vagabond Luck 1919 ( ) 856
Vagabond Prince, The 1916 (Tri) 627, 2693
Valentine and Orson 1903 (Lubin)
Valentine Girl, The 1917 (Art/Par) 482, 1600, 1806
Valet's Vindication, The 1910 (Ed)
Valet's Wife, The 1908 (AMB) 1182, 1363, 1511, 1865
Valley of the Giants 1919 (Art/Par) 165, 646, 1307, 1563, 1970, 1975, 2112, 2547
Valley of the Moon 1913 ( ) 537, 2458
Vamp, The 1918 ( ) 189, 1690
Vampe di Gelosia (The Vamp's Jealousy) 1912 (Italian)
Vampire, The 1912 (Messter)
Vampire, The 1913 (Kal) 572, 1270
Vampire, The 1914 (Lubin) 2037
Vampire Ambrose 1916 (Key/Tri) 840,

1874, 2510
Vampire Dance, The 1912 (Ingvald C. Oes)
Vampire of the Coast 1909 ( )
Vampire out of Work, A 1916 (V)
Vampires, The 1915 (GB) 1554, 1556,
    1779, 1910
Vampire's Clutch, The 1915 (Knight)
Vampires of the Night 1914 (Feature Photo
    Plays)
Vampires of Warsaw 1914 ( )
Vampire's Tower, The 1914 (Ambrosia)
Vampire's Trail 1910 ( )
Vampire's Trail, The 1914 (Kal) 1270,
    1388, 1867
Vampryn 1912 (Swedish)
Van Bibber's Experiment 1911 (Ed)
Vanishing Lady 1898 (Ed)
Vanishing Lady, The 1904 (Melies)
Vanishing Vault, The 1917 (V) 2081, 2521
Vanity Fair 1911 (V) 332, 695, 790, 950,
    985, 1368, 2070, 2527
Vanity Fair 1915 (Ed) 907, 1774, 2601
Vanity Pool 1918 ( ) 1266, 1694, 2210
Vaquero's Vow, The 1908 (AMB) 850,
    1363, 1511, 1701, 2212
Varmint, The 1918 (Art/Par) 1050, 1309,
    2045
Vases of Hymen, The 1914 (V) 332, 901
Vavasour Ball, The 1914 (V) 2523
Vavawert Ball, The 1913 (V) 297
Veiled Adventure, The 1919 (Par) 927,
    2416, 2506, 2521, 2738
Veiled Beauty, The 1907 (V)
Veiled Mystery, The 1918 ( ) 552
Velvet Hand, The 1918 ( ) 318
Vendetta 1916 ( ) 1349
Venetian Looking-Glass, The 1905 (Melies)
Vengeance 1912 (Ingvald C. Oes)
Vengeance 1918 ( ) 437, 1603
Vengeance and the Woman--serial 1917
    (V) 39, 338, 785, 1271, 1279, 1301,
    1359, 2163
    1.   The Oath
    2.   Loaded Dice
    3.   The Unscaled Peak
    4.   The Signalling Cipher
    5.   The Plunge of Destruction
    6.   Lure of Hate
    7.   Wolf Trap
    8.   Mountain of Devastation
    9.   Buried Alive
    10. The Leap for Life
    11. The Cavern of Terror
    12. The Desperate Chance
    13. Sands of Doom
    14. The Hand of Fate
    15. The Reckoning
Vengeance Is Mine 1918 ( ) 435
Vengeance of Allah, The 1915 ( ) 2558
Vengeance of Durand 1919 ( ) 1748
Vengeance of Galora, The 1913 (Bio) 141,
    1028, 2513, 2680
Vengeance of the West 1917 (Bluebird/Un)
    449
Venom of the Poppy, The 1911 (Ed)
Ventriloquist's Trunk, The 1911 (V) 332,
    818, 901
Ventures of Marguerite, The--serial
    1915 (Kal) 572, 2076, 2177, 2390
    1.   When Appearances Deceive
    2.   The Rogue Syndicate

    3.   The Kidnapped Heiress
    4.   The Veiled Priestess
    5.   A Society Schemer
    6.   The Key to a Fortune
    7.   The Ancient Coin
    8.   The Secret Message
    9.   The Oriental's Plot
    10. The Spy's Ruse
    11. The Crossed Clues
    12. The Tricksters
    13. The Sealskin Coat
    14. The Lurking Peril
    15. The Fate of America
    16. The Trail's End
Venus in the East 1918 (Par) 2700
Venus Model, The 1918 (Go) 950, 1423,
    1495, 1941
Verdict, The 1916 (Un) 2056
Versatile Villain, A 1915 (Key) 460, 878
Very Good Young Man, A 1919 (Art/Par)
    595, 2700
Very Much Engaged 1912 (Ed)
Veteran's Pension, The 1911 (Hep) 2531
Via Cabaret 1913 ( ) 2112
Via Wireless 1915 ( ) 1324, 1637
Vicar of Wakefield, The 1913 (Hep) 1289,
    2744
Vicar of Wakefield, The 1916 (Br) 2712
Vicar of Wakefield, The 1917 ( ) 1547
Vice Versa 1916 (Br) 834, 1931
Victim, The 1917 ( ) 1116, 2002, 2756
Victim of Bridge, A 1910 (Ed)
Victim of Circumstances, A 1911 (Bio)
Victim of Circumstantial Evidence, A
    1903 (AMB)
Victim of Jealousy, A 1910 (Bio) 1074,
    1450, 2047
Victim of the Mormons, A 1911 (Ingvald
    C. Oes)
Victim Snared, The 1904 (AMB)
Victor of the Plot, The 1918 ( ) 857
Victoria Cross, The /aka/ Charge of the
    Light Brigade 1912 (V) 1047, 2112,
    2487, 2527
Victoria Cross, The 1916 (Las) 2623
Victorine 1915 ( ) 1028
Victory 1919 (Art/Par) 166, 449, 684,
    1280, 1855, 1933, 1998, 2787
Victory and Peace 1918 (Br) 1488
Victory Cross, The 1916 (Las) 2541
Victory Leaders, The 1919 (Br) 834
Victory of Conscience, The 1916 ( )
    2541
Viking's Daughter, The 1908 (V)
Villa of the Movies 1917 (Key/Tri) 787,
    2023, 2501
Village Blacksmith, The 1916 (Key/Tri)
    440, 815, 983, 1424, 1726, 1874
Village Chestnut, The 1918 (Key) 878
Village Cut-Up, The 1906 (AMB)
Village Hero, The 1911 (Bio)
Village Scandal, A 1915 (Key/Tri) 65,
    1257, 1422, 1651, 2208, 2816
Village Smithy, The 1918 (Key) 878
Village Vampire, The /aka/ The Great
    Leap 1916 (Key/Tri) 294, 657, 966,
    1622, 1666, 2164, 2514
Villain, The 1917 (King-Bee) 1161
Villain Foiled, The 1911 (Bio)
Villainous Villain, A 1916 (V) 2367
Violin Maker, The 1915 (Victor/Un)

449, 1518
Violin Maker of Cremona, The 1909 (Bio)
1822, 1823, 1865, 2047
Violin of Monsieur, The 1912 (V) 1027,
2386, 2811, 2812
Violin Player (Dickson Experimental Sound
Film) 1895 (Ed) 727
Virginian, The 1914 (Par) 411, 677, 770,
828, 866, 1096, 1369, 1439, 1448,
1493, 1646, 2211, 2461
Virginius 1909 (V)
Virtue Its Own Reward 1914 (Rex/Un)
276, 352, 449, 935
Virtue of Rags, The 1912 (Es) 353
Virtuous Men 1919 ( ) 643, 1332, 1569
Virtuous Sinners 1919 (Par) 1206, 1432,
2535, 2616
Virtuous Thief, The 1919 (Par) 532, 1311,
2719
Virtuous Vamp, A 1919 (FN) 115, 1070,
2437, 2521, 2535
Virtuous Vampire, A 1919 ( ) 856
Virtuous Wives 1919 (FN) 1288, 2472,
2513, 2535
Vision of Mary 1903 (AMB)
Visit to Baby Roger 1902 (AMB)
Vital Question, The 1915 (V) 2024
Vive La France! 1918 (Tri) 189, 627,
1523, 1606
Vivette 1918 ( ) 1764, 2002
Vixen, The 1916 (F) 116, 483, 1002, 1244,
1763, 1967, 2622
Voice from the Dead, A 1908 (Ed)
Voice from the Deep, 1912 (Bio)
Voice from the Fireplace, A 1910 (Es)
1431
Voice in the Fog, The 1915 (Las) 287, 1033
Voice of Conscience 1912 (Es) 353, 2700
Voice of Destiny 1918 (P) 1988
Voice of the Child, The 1911 (Bio) 701,
1074, 2513
Voice of the Million 1912 ( ) 1876
Voice of Viola, The 1914 ( ) 2112
Voice on the Wire, The--serial 1917 (Un)
582, 1004, 1011, 1025, 1658, 2393,
2572, 2774
    1. The Oriental Death Punch
    2. The Mysterious Man in Black
    3. The Spider's Web
    4. The Next Victim
    5. The Spectral Hand
    6. The Death Warrant
    7. The Marked Room
    8. High Finance
    9. A Stern Case
    10. The Guarded Heart
    11. The Thought Machine
    12. The Sign of the Thumb or
       The Fifth Victim
    13. 'Twixt Death and Dawn
    14. The Light of Death
Volcano, The 1919 ( ) 111
Volunteer, The 1917 (WS) 853, 1314
Von Webber's Last Waltz 1912 (Ed)
Voyage to the Moon 1902 (Melies) 1802
Vultures of Society 1916 ( ) 377

- W -

Wager, The 1910 ( ) 2554, 2767

Wages No Object 1917 (M) 768, 1707
Wages of Sin, The 1903 (AMB)
Wages of Sin, The 1908 (V)
Wages of Sin, The 1918 (Br) 943, 1968
Waggin' Tale, The 1917 ( ) 689
Wagon Tracks 1919 ( ) 1188, 1948
Wagon Trail, The * (Selig Polyscope)
1849
Waif, The 1904 (AMB)
Waif, The 1911 (Independent Moving
Picture Co.)
Waifs 1916 (Tri) 785, 1082
Waifs 1918 ( ) 1312
Waiter, The see Caught in a Cabaret
Waiter No. 5 1910 (Bio) 2047
Waiter's Ball, The 1916 (Key/Tri) 65,
253, 1476, 2005, 2070, 2208
Waiter's Picnic, The 1913 (Key) 65, 1941,
2465
Waiting at the Church 1906 (Ed)
Waiting at the Church 1907 ( )
Waiting at the Church 1911 (Independent
Moving Picture Co.)
Waiting for Bill 1903 (AMB)
Waiting for Santa Claus 1902 (AMB)
Wake in Hell's Kitchen, A 1903 (AMB)
Wall Between, The 1916 (M) 656
Wall Invisible, The 1919 (Par) 1774
Wall of Money, The 1913 ( ) 2112
Wallace Jewels, The 1909 (Ed)
Walls of Jericho 1914 ( ) 283, 1379
Wand Dance, Pueblo Indians 1898 (Ed)
Wanderer, The 1913 (Bio) 141, 398, 731,
1665, 1714, 1751, 1832, 1924, 2680
Wandering Jew, The 1904 (Melies)
Wanted: a Bad Man 1917 (Vim) 1161
Wanted, a Child 1909 (Bio)
Wanted: a Dog 1905 (AMB)
Wanted, a Home 1916 ( ) 2480
Wanted--a Husband 1907 (Lubin)
Wanted: a Husband 1915 (Christie) 525,
1486
Wanted: a Leading Lady 1915 (Christie)
525, 1630
Wanted--a Military Man 1908 (Lubin)
Wanted: a Mother 1918 ( ) 853
Wanted--a Nurse 1906 (AMB)
Wanted: a Nurse 1915 (V) 768
Wanted--a Strong Hand 1913 (V) 297,
2523
Wanted: a Widow 1916 (Br) 1231
Wanted, a Wife 1905 ( ) 2527
Wanted--$5,000 1919 (P) 1586
Wanted for Murder 1918 ( ) 1139
War 1913 (V) 2767
War and the Woman 1917 (FP) 1468
War Bridegrooms 1917 (Nestor) 1630,
1872, 2147, 2554
War Brides 1916 (WS) 143, 205, 321,
437, 901, 1635, 1919, 2692, 2759
War Is Hell 1915 (Br) 150
War o' Dreams 1915 (Selig) 2668
War of the Primal Tribes 1913 ( ) 2356
War on the Mosquito, The 1912 (Ed)
War on the Plains 1912 (New York Motion
Picture Co.)
War Relief 1917 (Propaganda Film) 832,
857, 1188, 2047, 2149
Ware Case, The 1917 (Br) 1289, 1488
Warfare of the Flesh 1917 ( ) 1564
Warm Occasion, A 1904 (AMB)

Warm Reception, A 1916 (Vim) 1161
Warning, The 1914 ( ) 1028
Warrens of Virginia, The 1915 (Par) 664,
    1175, 1296, 1357, 1493, 1648, 1925,
    2035, 2036, 2513, 2623
Warrior, The 1917 (FN) 1681, 1999
Warrior Bold, A 1910 (Ed)
War's Women 1916 ( ) 1745
Was He a Coward? 1911 (Bio) 1613, 2513
Was Justice Served? 1909 (Bio) 477, 1450,
    2062, 2212
Was She a Vampire? 1915 (Un)
Washerwoman's Revenge, The 1908 (Lubin)
Washington under the American Flag 1909
    (V)
Washington under the British Flag 1909
    (V)
Washwoman's Daughter, The 1902 (AMB)
Washwoman's Troubles 1897 (Ed)
Wasp, The 1918 ( ) 1048
Watch Out, William 1916 ( ) 2736
Watch Your Neighbor 1918 (Key/Tri)
    1906, 2564
Water Cure, The 1916 (Vim) 1161
Water Dog, The 1914 (Key) 65
Water Duel 1903 (AMB)
Water Nymph, The 1912 (Key) 1666, 1941,
    2368, 2465
Water Nymphs 1902 (AMB)
Water, Water Everywhere 1919 (Go) 2168
Wawona, Big Tree 1903 (AMB)
Way of a Man, The 1909 (Bio) 1363, 1511,
    2047
Way of a Man with a Maid, The 1919
    (Art/Par) 857, 1206, 2700
Way of a Woman, The 1914 ( ) 2112
Way of a Woman, The 1919 (Select) 651,
    1275, 1305, 1531, 1640, 2402, 2523,
    2535
Way of an Eagle, The 1918 (Br) 831, 1968
Way of the Cross, The 1909 (V)
Way of the Redman, The 1913 (Selig
    Polyscope) 1849
Way of the Strong, The 1919 ( ) 1939,
    2644
Way of the World, The 1910 (Bio) 1831
Way Out, The 1918 (WS) 231, 835
Way They Fooled Dad, The 1908 (Lubin)
Ways of Fate, The 1913 ( ) 2112, 2125
Wayward Daughter, A 1914 (V) 2523
We Are French 1917 ( ) 1120
We Can't Have Everything 1918 (FP/Las)
    83, 281, 724, 828, 1125, 1201, 1206,
    1386, 1756, 1925, 1970, 2149, 2770
We Never Sleep 1917 (P) 635, 1586, 2055
We Should Worry 1918 (F) 1524
Weaker Sex, The 1916 (Tri) 627, 960,
    1032, 1690, 2096, 2392
Weaker Vessels 1919 ( ) 1125, 1694
Weakness of Man, The 1916 (WS) 239,
    1150, 2795
Weakness of Strength 1916 ( ) 283
Weary Goes Wooing * (Selig Polyscope)
    1849
Weary Hunters and the Magician, The
    1902 (Ed)
Weary Willie and the Gardener 1901 (Ed)
Weary Willie Kidnaps a Child 1904 (Ed)
Weary Willie's Revenge 1908 (Lubin)
Wearybones Seeks Rest and Gets It 1909
    (V)

Weary's Christmas Dinner 1908 (V)
Weaver of Dreams 1919 (P) 631, 663
Weavers of Life, The 1917 ( ) 1212
Web, The 1913 ( ) 2472, 2554
Web of Desire 1917 (WS) 853, 884
Web of Fate, The 1909 (Ed)
Webb Singing Pictures 1917 ( ) 382, 423,
    529, 2191, 2771
Wedded, but No Wife 1907 (Bio) 2047
Wedding, The 1905 (AMB)
Wedding Bell, The 1911 (Ed)
Wedding Bells out of Tune 1918 (Key) 878
Wedding Blues 1918 (Christie) 339
Wedding by Correspondence, A 1904
    (Melies)
Wedding Gown, The 1914 (Bio) 1924
Wedlock 1918 ( ) 1032
Wee Lady Betty 1917 ( ) 1602
Week End Shopping 1916 ( ) 2070
Weighing the Baby 1903 (AMB)
Welcome Burglar, A 1909 (AMB) 731,
    1542, 2212
Welcome Intruder, A 1913 (Bio) 1665, 1714,
    2728
Well, I'll Be ... 1919 (V) 2367
Wells of Paradise 1915 ( ) 473, 2096
Welsh Rabbit, A 1903 (AMB)
Welsh Singer, A 1915 (GB) 812, 849,
    2604
Wen Vier Dassebbe Tun 1917 ( ) 1349
Wenn das Herz in Hass Erglüht 1918
    ( ) 1922
Werther 1909 (FdA) 316
Western Blood 1918 (F) 1374, 1849
Western Chivalry 1910 (Es) 50
Western Courtship 1908 (V)
Western Girls 1912 (Es) 50
Western Justice 1907 (Selig Polyscope)
Western Maid, A 1909 (Es) 50
Western Masquerade, A 1916 (Selig
    Polyscope) 1849
Western Night, A 1911 (Ed)
Western Prince Charming, A 1912 (Ed)
Western Romance, A 1910 (Ed)
Western Romance in the Days of '49
    1908 (Lubin)
Western Stage Coach Hold Up 1904 (Ed)
Westerners, The 1919 (Tri) 1523, 1613,
    1690, 1731, 2479
Westerner's Way, A 1910 (Es) 50
Wharf Rat, The 1916 (FA) 25, 1182,
    1751, 2453
What a Cinch! 1915 (Lubin) 1161
What a Woman Will Do 1912 (Un)
What Am I Bid? 1919 ( ) 1907
What Are the Wild Waves Saying Sister?
    1903 (AMB)
What Boys Will Do 1903 (AMB)
What Burglar Bill Found in the Safe 1904
    (AMB)
What Could a Gentleman Do? 1918 ( )
    2558
What Could Be Sweeter? 1916 ( ) 690
What Could She Do? 1915 ( ) 1649
What Demoralized the Barber Shop 1901
    (Ed)
What Drink Did 1909 (Bio) 685, 1902,
    2047, 2212
What Every Woman Learns 1919 ( ) 189,
    606, 1454, 2410
What Every Woman Wants 1919 ( ) 646, 771

What Happened in the Tunnel? 1903 (Ed)
What Happened to Jones? 1903 (AMB)
What Happened to Mary?--serial 1912 (Ed)
   968, 1656, 1970, 1977, 2654, 2774
     1. The Escape from Bondage
     2. Alone in New York
     3. Mary in Stageland
     4. The Affair at Raynor's
     5. A Letter to the Princess
     6. A Clue to Her Parentage
     7. False to Their Trust
     8. A Will and a Way
     9. A Way to the Underworld
    10. The High Tide of Misfortune
    11. A Race to New York
    12. Fortune Smiles
What He Forgot 1915 (Lubin) 1161
What Love Forgives 1919 ( ) 437, 1991
What Might Have Been 1918 (Select) 1305
What Money Can't Buy 1917 ( ) 1309,
   2045, 2541
What One Small Boy Can Do 1908 (V)
What Shall We Do with Our Old? 1911
   (Bio) 1552, 1831, 1933, 2728
What the Cards Foretold 1909 (Ed)
What the Daisy Said 1910 (Bio) 2047, 2156
What the Doctor Ordered 1912 (Bio)
Whatever the Cost 1919 ( ) 1439
What's His Name? 1914 (Par) 412, 677,
   704, 897, 1500, 1854, 2149, 2151
What's Sauce for the Goose 1916 (Vim)
   1161
What's the Use of Grumbling 1918 (Br)
   1018
What's Your Hurry? 1909 (Bio) 2047
What's Your Husband Doing? 1919 ( )
   1791
Wheel of Life, The 1914 ( ) 651, 1051,
   2112
When a Girl Loves 1919 ( ) 1175
When a Man Loves 1911 (Bio) 1223, 2047
When a Man Rides Alone 1919 ( ) 2201
When a Man Sees Red 1917 (F) 868
When a Woman Sins 1918 (F) 116, 238,
   959, 2170, 2175, 2514
When a Woman Strikes 1919 ( ) 2554
When a Woman Wars 1912 ( ) 111
When Ambrose Dared Walrus 1915 (Key)
   531, 815, 2510
When Baby Forgot 1917 (P) 1988
When Bearcat Went Dry 1919 (Photo-
   plays/W) 274, 449, 792, 1126, 2615,
   2755, 2781
When Big Dan Rides * ( ) 1509
When Broadway Was a Trail 1915 (W)
   1618, 2544
When Casey Joined the Lodge 1908 (V)
When Do We Eat? 1919 ( ) 189
When Doctors Disagree 1919 (Go) 1248,
   1919, 1933
When Dreams Come True 1913 (Key) 2465
When East Meets West 1915 (Br) 177
When False Tongues Speak 1918 (F) 2024,
   2756
When Fate Decides 1919 ( ) 771, 2581
When Fate Frowned 1915 ( ) 554
When Jim Returned 1913 ( ) 2002, 2112,
   2125
When Johnny Comes Marching Home 1918
   ( ) 1583, 1697
When Kings Were the Law 1912 (Bio)

1613, 2000
When Knighthood Was in Flower * ( ) 750
When Knights Were Bold 1908 (AMB) 79,
   1089, 2212
When Knights Were Bold 1916 (Br) 43,
   834
When Knights Were Cold 1919 (Rolin/P)
   1502
When Lips Are Sealed 1908 (Lubin)
When Lizzie Disappeared 1915 (Christie)
   525
When London Sleeps 1914 (Br) 150
When Love and Honor Called 1913 (Es)
   50, 487
When Love Is Blind 1919 (Key/Tri) 2069,
   2608
When Love Is Mocked 1915 ( ) 2002
When Love Took Wings 1915 (Key) 65
When Luck Changes 1913 ( ) 2112, 2125
When Ma Goes Shopping 1908 (Lubin)
When Men Are Tempted 1918 ( ) 2754
When Men Betray 1918 (Select) 115, 1275
When Men Desire 1919 (F) 116, 820,
   1252, 1760, 1952, 2684
When My Lady Smiles 1915 ( ) 2518
When Our Ship Comes In 1908 (Lubin)
When Papa Died 1916 (Vogue) 2608
When Passion Blinds Honesty 1912
   (Ingvald C. Oes)
When Reuben Comes to Town 1908 (Ed)
When Seconds Count 1917 ( ) 1010
When She Was about Sixteen 1912 (Ed)
When Souls Meet 1912 (Es) 353, 434
When the Cartridges Failed 1914 ( ) 2774
When the Cat's Away 1911 (Imp) 2047
When the Clouds Roll By 1919 (UA) 387,
   494, 857, 1094, 1563, 1855, 2154
When the Cook Fell In 1914 (Selig
   Polyscope) 1849, 1957
When the Desert Smiled 1919 (Arrow) 1186
When the Earth Trembled /aka/ The
   Strength of Love 1913 ( ) 2554
When the Fire-Bells Rang 1912 (Bio)
When the Flag Falls 1909 (Lubin)
When the Germans Entered Loos 1916
   (Br) 150
When the Gods Played a Badger Game
   1915 (Rex/Un) 352, 449
When the Losers Win 1915 (Christie) 525
When the Mummy Cried for Help 1915
   ( ) 1630
When the Press Speaks 1913 (V) 332, 818,
   901
When Two Hearts Won 1911 (Kal) 768
When We Were in Our Teens 1910 (Bio)
   2047
When We Were Twenty-One 1902 (AMB)
When Wifey Holds the Purse Strings 1911
   (Bio)
When Women Are Police 1913 (Kal) 1924
When Women Vote 1907 (Lubin)
When You're Married see Mabel's
   Married Life
Where Are My Children? 1916 (Selig)
   232, 2065, 2122, 2167
Where Bonds Are Loosed 1919 ( ) 1522
Where Breakers Roar 1908 (AMB) 1336,
   1511
Where Charity Begins 1913 ( ) 2748
Where Hazel Met the Villain 1914 (Key)
   65

Where Is My Mother? 1917 (Es) 1636
Where Is My Wandering Boy Tonight? 1909 (Ed)
Where Love Leads 1916 ( ) 1205
Where Paths Meet 1912 (Imp)
Where Peril Lurkes * ( ) 1509
Where the Devil Drives 1916 ( ) 2068
Where the Forest Ends 1915 (Rex/Un) 352, 449, 686, 762
Where the Heather Blooms 1915 (Christie) 525
Where the Trail Divides 1914 (Las) 809, 1369, 1446, 2149
Where the West Begins 1919 ( ) 1483, 2031, 2201
Where There's a Will, There's a Way 1909 (V)
Which Was the Happiest Time in Your Life? 1908 (Lubin)
Which Way Did He Go? 1913 (V) 332, 901
Which Woman? 1918 ( ) 1120
While Father Telephoned 1913 (Kal) 1494, 2169
Whim, The 1917 ( ) 1166
Whim of an Apache, The 1907 (P)
Whims of Society 1918 ( ) 486
Whipping Bear 1906 ( )
Whirl of Life, The 1915 ( ) 435, 436
Whirlpool 1918 ( ) 273, 1117, 1237
Whirr of the Spinning Wheel, The 1914 (Hep) 2171, 2531
Whispering Chorus, The 1918 (Art/Par) 165, 307, 454, 550, 724, 877, 1201, 1377, 1625, 1756, 1925, 1975, 2648, 2770
Whispering Smith 1916 ( ) 1273
Whistles and Widows 1918 (V) 2367
White Boys, The 1916 (Hep) 1289, 2171, 2744
White Chief, The 1908 (Lubin)
White Feather, The 1914 (Br) 834
White Heather, The 1919 ( ) 25, 28, 114, 1016, 1053, 1067, 1237,
White Hope, The 1915 (Br) 1289, 2171
White Lie 1919 ( ) 134, 1426
White Man's Chance, The 1919 (Hodkinson) 1431, 2663
White Man's First Smoke, The; or Puritan Days in America 1907 (V)
White Man's Law 1918 (Par) 1208, 2638, 2728
White Messenger 1916 (Un) 2056
White Pearl, The 1915 (FP) 752, 756, 1266
White Raven, The 1917 (M) 139, 658
White Rose of the Wilds, The 1911 (Bio) 1182, 1613, 2513
White Roses 1910 (Bio) 95, 2045, 2047
White Savior, The 1912 (Un)
White Scar 1915 ( ) 1216
White Sister, The 1915 (Es) 24, 524, 638, 2582
White Squaw, The * (Kal) 2103
White Winged Monkey 1916 ( ) 676
White Wings on Review 1903 (Ed)
Whitewashed Walls 1918 ( ) 318, 715
Whither Thou Goest 1917 ( ) 1558

Whitler's Witless Wanderings 1909 (Ed)
Who Cares? 1919 (Par) 25, 927, 2521
Who Gets the Order? 1911 (Ed)
Who Goes There? 1918 (V) 1088, 1877
Who Got Stung? see Caught in the Rain
Who Got the Reward? 1912 (Bio)
Who Is Number One?--serial 1917 (Par) 494, 1483
    1. The Flaming Cross
    2. The Flying Fortress
    3. The Sea Crawler
    4. A Marine Miracle
    5. Halls of Hazard
    6. The Flight of the Fury
    7. Hearts in Torment
    8. Walls of Gas
    9. Struck Down
    10. Wires of Wrath
    11. The Rail Raiders
    12. The Show Down
    13. Cornered
    14. No Surrender
    15. The Round-Up
Who Killed Max? 1912 (P) 1575
Who Killed Cock Robin? 1903 (Lubin)
Who Killed Walton? 1918 ( ) 2392
Who Looks, Pays 1906 (Melies)
Who Needed the Dough? 1908 (V)
Who Pays?--serial 1915 (P) 274, 1017, 1441, 1647, 2169
Who Pays for the Drinks? 1903 (AMB)
Who Said Chicken? 1901 (Lubin)
Who Said Chicken? 1903 (AMB)
Who Shall Take My Life? 1918 ( ) 318, 857, 2221
Who Stole Bunny's Umbrella? 1912 (V) 332
Who Stole Jones' Wood? 1908 (Lubin)
Who Stole the Dogies? 1915 (Lubin) 1161
Who Was the Other Man? 1918 ( ) 926
Who Wears Them? 1912 (Imp)
Who Will Marry Mary?--serial 1913 (Ed) 968, 2774
    1. A Proposal from the Duke
    2. A Proposal from the Spanish Don
    3. A Proposal from the Sculptor
    4. A Proposal from Nobody
    5. A Proposal Deferred
    6. A Proposal from Mary
Who Will Marry Me? 1919 ( ) 1911
Who Wins?--serial 1916 (P) 2169
Who Wins? /aka/ The Price of Folly 1918 ( ) 1796
Whole Dam Family and the Dam Dog, The 1905 (Ed)
Whole World Kin, The 1909 (Ed)
Whom the Gods Destroy 1919 (FN) 1426, 1755, 1896, 2453
Who's Boss of the House? 1907 (Lubin)
Who's Got the Red Ear? 1903 (AMB)
Who's Guilty?--serial 1916 (P) 846, 1867, 1939, 2716
Who's to Win? 1912 (V) 332, 818
Who's Who? 1909 (Ed)
Who's Your Brother? 1919 ( ) 296, 1346
Who's Your Neighbor? 1918 (V) 286, 1878, 2091
Whose Baby? 1917 (Key/Tri) 796, 1153, 1835, 2336, 2512, 2588, 2636
Whose Little Wife Are You? 1919 (Key/Tri) 2608

Whose Wife? * (Christie) 525
Whose Wife Is Kate? 1917 ( ) 1872
Whose Zoo? 1918 (L-KO) 1502
Whoso Diggeth a Pit 1914 (Nestor) 2112
Whoso Diggeth a Pit 1915 (Br) 43
Whoso Is without Sin 1916 (Br) 2179
Whosoever Shall Offend 1917 (Es) 1636
Whosoever Shall Offend 1919 (Br) 943,
   1968
Why Am I Here? 1913 ( ) 2472
Why Ben Bolted /aka/ He Looked Crooked
   1917 (Vogue) 2608
Why Bronco Billy Left Bear Country 1913
   (Es) 50
Why Curfew Did Not Ring 1903 (AMB)
Why Divorce? 1919 ( ) 689, 690
Why Foxy Grandpa Escaped a Ducking
   1903 (AMB)
Why Germany Must Pay 1919 ( ) 1118
Why Girls Leave Home 1909 (Ed)
Why He Gave Up 1911 (Bio)
Why He Signed the Pledge 1908 (Lubin)
Why Henry Left Home 1918 (M) 768, 1707
Why I Would Not Marry 1918 ( ) 658
Why Jones Discharged His Clerks 1900
   (Ed)
Why Krausmyer Can't Sleep 1899 (Lubin)
Why Marry? 1912 ( ) 2733
Why Mr. Nation Wants a Divorce 1901 (Ed)
Why Mrs. Jones Got a Divorce 1900 (Ed)
Why Papa Cannot Sleep 1897 (American
   Mutoscope Co.)
Why Pick on Me? 1918 (P) 1586
Why Smith Left Home 1919 (Art/Par) 595,
   1126, 1248, 1417, 1596, 2682, 2700,
   2779
Why That Actor Was Late 1908 (Melies)
Why the Check Was Good 1911 (Independent
   Moving Picture Co.)
Why the Cook Was Not Fired 1905 (Lubin)
Why the Mail Was Late 1909 (Lubin)
Why the Sheriff Is a Bachelor 1913 (Selig
   Polyscope) 1849
Wicked City, The 1916 (Vogue) 2608
Wicked Darling, The 1919 (Un) 25, 88,
   449, 675, 2052
Widow and the Only Man, The 1904 (AMB)
Widow by Proxy 1919 (Par) 132, 473, 482,
   899, 1015, 1940
Widow Visits Sprigtown 1911 (V)
Widow's Claim, The 1912 (Un)
Widow's Kids, The 1913 (Bio) 1028
Widow's Might, The 1918 ( ) 2638
Wife, The 1914 (Bio) 79, 1028, 1029
Wife and Auto Trouble 1916 (Key/Tri)
   179, 351, 519, 650, 2020
Wife by Proxy, A 1917 ( ) 2520
Wife He Brought Back, The 1918 (Un) 1911
Wife in a Hurry, A 1916 (Br) 1487
Wife on a Wager, A 1914 ( ) 2112
Wife or Country 1918 (Tri) 1518, 1818,
   2128, 2512, 2728
Wife Wanted 1914 (Key/Tri) 864, 2472,
   2733
Wife's Awakening, A 1911 (Independent
   Moving Picture Co.)
Wife's Devotion, A 1908 (V)
Wife's Ordeal, A 1909 (Ed)
Wife's Sacrifice, A 1916 (F) 1144, 1734
Wifey Away, Hubby at Play 1909 (Lubin)
Wifey's Mistake 1904 (Ed)

Wifey's Strategy 1908 (Ed)
Wild and Woolly 1917 (Art) 242, 361,
   419, 686, 857, 1378, 2031, 2350,
   2415, 2467, 2782
Wild Ass' Skin, The * ( ) 1917
Wild Cat, The 1911 (V) 2523
Wild Cat, The 1917 ( ) 1613, 1814
Wild Girl, The 1917 ( ) 1275
Wild Girl of the Sierra 1916 (Tri) 1613,
   1751, 1182
Wild Goose Chase, The 1915 (Par) 474,
   935, 1201, 1386, 1581, 1747, 2149,
   2427
Wild Honey 1919 ( ) 1429
Wild Life 1918 ( ) 715, 2355
Wild Primrose 1918 (Go) 1360, 1423,
   1547
Wild Ride, A 1913 (Selig) 857, 2221
Wild Strain, The 1917 ( ) 2397, 2754
Wild Sumac 1917 ( ) 2780
Wild West Love 1914 (Key) 531
Wild Winship's Widow 1917 (Tri) 627
Wild Women 1918 (Un) 398, 1719, 1782
Wild Youth 1918 ( ) 1309, 1896, 2149
Wildcat of Paris 1918 (Un) 675, 1498
Wilderness Mail, The 1914 (Selig
   Polyscope) 1849
Wilderness Trail, The 1919 (F) 821,
   1849, 1859, 1928
Wildfire 1915 (W) 2198
Wildflower 1914 (FP) 482, 1589, 2045
Wilful Ambrose 1915 (Key) 878, 2510
Wilful Peggy 1910 (Bio) 315, 1182, 1665,
   2047, 2680
Will He Marry the Girl? 1902 (AMB)
Will of Her Own, A 1915 (Br) 834, 2138
Will of the People, The 1917 (Br) 1592
Willful Murder 1904 (AMB)
Willie Becomes an Artist 1912 (Bio)
Willie Westinghouse and the Doctor's
   Battery 1903 (AMB)
Willie Wise and His Motor Boat 1911 (Ed)
Willie Work comedies 1914 (P) 1586
Willie's Camera 1903 (AMB)
Willie's Fall from Grace 1908 (V)
Willie's First Smoke 1899 (Ed)
Willie's Hat 1902 (AMB)
Willie's Party 1908 (Lubin)
Willie's Vacation 1904 (Paley & Steiner)
Willie's Water Sprinkler 1909 (Lubin)
Willy Boy Loses the Heiress 1904 (AMB)
Wilson or the Kaiser 1918 ( ) 1118
Winchester Woman, The 1919 (V) 1388,
   1748
Winding Trail, The 1918 (M) 631
Window Opposite, The 1919 ( ) 111
Winds of Fate, The 1911 (Ed)
Wine Girl, The 1918 (Un) 1166, 1911
Wine, Women and Song 1906 (AMB)
Winged Idol, The 1915 (W) 2035
Winged Mystery, The 1917 ( ) 2554
Wings and Wheels 1916 (Key/Tri) 179, 396
Wings of the Morning 1919 ( ) 1604, 1794
Winifred, the Shop Girl 1916 (V) 2487
Wink, The 1914 (V) 1684
Win(k)some Widow, The /aka/ The
   Winsome Widow 1914 (V) 908, 1634,
   1684, 2621
Winner Takes All 1918 ( ) 1928, 2211
Winnie's Dance 1912 (Ed)
Winning a Widow 1912 (Kal) 992

Winning Back His Love 1910 (Bio) 95,
    1450, 1593, 1613, 1701, 2067
Winning Coat, The 1909 (AMB) 1511,
    1865, 2212
Winning Girl, The 1919 (Par) 454, 1774
Winning Grandma 1918 (P) 1988
Winning Miss, The 1912 (Independent
    Moving Picture Co.)
Winning of a Bride 1919 ( ) 2133
Winning of Beatrice 1918 (M) 41, 1134
Winning of Miss Langdon 1910 (Ed)
Winning of Sally Temple, The 1917 ( )
    2002, 2683
Winning Punch, The 1916 (Key/Tri) 787,
    902, 2023, 2501
Winning Stroke, The 1919 (F) 1639, 2671
Winsome Widow, The see Win(k)some
    Widow, The
Winsor McCay's Drawings 1911 (V) 332
Winter's Tale, A 1909 (Ed)
Winter's Tale, A 1910 (T) 123, 584, 873,
    2174
Wireless Romance, A 1910 (Ed)
Wise Old Elephant 1913 (Selig) 258, 2770
Wishbone, The 1906 (Lubin)
Wishbone, The 1908 (V)
Wished on Mabel 1915 (Key) 1941
Wishful Girl, The 1918 ( ) 115
Wishing Hour, The 1914 (W) 1764
Wishing Ring, The 1910 ( ) 108
Wishing Ring Man 1919 ( ) 771, 2625
Wishing Seat, The 1913 (Am) 1431
Wisp in the Woods, A 1917 ( ) 1839
Witch, The 1906 (Melies)
Witch, The 1908 (V)
Witch, The 1916 ( ) 1978
Witch of Salem, The 1913 ( ) 2096
Witch Woman 1918 (Un) 486, 675
Witchcraft 1917 ( ) 1537
Witching Hour, The 1916 (WS) 75, 688,
    2391, 2404, 2424
Witch's Revenge, The 1903 (Melies)
With a Kodak 1912 (Bio)
With All Her Heart * (Br) 1968
With Bridges Burned 1910 (Ed)
With Eyes of the Blind 1913 ( ) 968
With Her Card 1909 (Bio) 1542, 2062
With Hoops of Steel 1918 ( ) 457, 1474,
    2680
With Interest to Date 1911 (Ed)
With Neatness and Dispatch 1918 (M) 156,
    353
With the Enemy's Help 1912 (Bio) 2045,
    2047, 2513
With the Eyes of the Blind 1913 ( ) 1656
Within the Cup 1918 ( ) 134, 1241, 1583
Within the Law 1917 (V) 749, 1388, 1673,
    1877, 2091
Without Honor 1917 ( ) 2780
Without Limit 1916 ( ) 955
Witness for the Defense 1919 (Par) 888,
    1971, 2444, 2460
Wives and Other Wives 1919 ( ) 1841
Wives of Men 1918 ( ) 1557, 1836, 2105
Wizard of Oz, The 1910 (Selig)
Wizard of Oz, The 1914 ( ) 1175
Woes of a Wealthy Widow, The 1911 (V)
    332, 901
Woes of Roller Skaters, The 1908 (Melies)
Wolf, The 1919 (V) 2767
Wolf and His Mate, The 1918 ( ) 1604

Wolf-Face Man, The--serial 1918 ( )
    1717
Wolf Hunt, The 1908 (Oklahoma Natural
    Mutoscene Co.)
Wolf Lowry 1917 (Tri) 1188, 2780
Wolf Woman, The 1916 (Tri) 473, 1032,
    2096, 2444
Wolfville 1917 (V) 785
Wolfville Tales 1919 (V) 1356
Wolverine, The 1919 ( ) 1720
Wolves of Kultur--serial 1918 (P) 111,
    116, 295, 1326, 1564
    1. The Torture Trap
    2. The Iron Chair
    3. Trapping the Traitor
    4. The Ride to Death
    5. Through the Flames
    6. Trails of Treachery
    7. The Leap of Despair
    8. In the Hands of the Hun
    9. Precipice of Death
    10. When Woman Wars
    11. Betwixt Heaven and Earth
    12. Towers of Tears
    13. The Huns' Hell Trap
    14. Code of Hate
    15. Reward of Patriotism
Wolves of the Border 1918 (Tri) 2355,
    2479
Wolves of the Night 1919 (F) 868, 1604,
    2124
Wolves of the North, The * (V) 1364
Wolves of the Trail 1918 (Art) 1188, 2613
Woman, A /aka/ Charlie and the Perfect
    Lady; The Perfect Lady 1915 (Es) 71,
    451, 531, 1036, 1336, 2077, 2113,
    2746
Woman, The 1918 ( ) 227, 491, 1471,
    2130
Woman Alone 1916 ( ) 273
Woman and the Law 1918 ( ) 554
Woman and Wife 1918 (Select 273, 724,
    853
Woman Beneath, A 1918 ( ) 486
Woman between Friends, A 1918 (V) 1388
Woman from Mellon's, The 1910 (Bio)
    1933, 2047, 2081
Woman God Forgot, The 1917 (Par) 258,
    869, 877, 1083, 1201, 1462, 1591,
    2112
Woman Hater, The 1909 (Lubin)
Woman Hater, The 1916 (Es) 1795
Woman Haters, The 1913 (Key) 65
Woman He Feared, The 1916 ( ) 2613
Woman in Chains 1919 ( ) 2089
Woman in 47, The 1916 ( ) 273
Woman in Gray, The--serial 1916 ( )
    2068
Woman in the Case, The 1916 (FP) 957,
    1117
Woman in the Suitcase, The 1919 ( )
    997
Woman in the Web, A--serial 1918 (V)
    1034, 1519, 1946
    1. Caught in the Web
    2. The Open Switch
    3. The Speeding Doom
    4. The Clutch of Terror
    5. The Hand of Mystery
    6. Full Speed Ahead
    7. The Crater of Death

8. The Plunge of Horror
9. The Fire Trap
10. Out of the Dungeon
11. In the Desert's Grip
12. Hurled to Destruction
13. The Hidden Menace
14. The Crash of Fate
15. Out of the Web
Woman in Ultimate, A 1913 (Bio) 1029
Woman Michael Married, The 1919 ( )
    134
Woman Next Door, The 1919 ( ) 165, 486,
    1365, 2788
Woman of Impulse, A 1918 ( ) 438
Woman of Lies 1919 ( ) 835, 1819
Woman of Pleasure, A 1919 (Par) 25, 138,
    1613, 2513, 2514
Woman of Redemption 1918 (WS) 835
Woman of 1776, The 1908 (Lubin)
Woman on the Index, The 1919 (Par) 957,
    2814
Woman Pays, The 1915 (Br) 150
Woman Scorned, A 1911 (Bio) 850, 1552,
    1613, 1665, 1714, 2067, 1513
Woman That God Sent, The 1919 ( ) 1402
Woman the Germans Shot, The 1918 (V)
    77, 1118, 2574
Woman There Was, A 1919 (F) 116, 658,
    824, 2021
Woman Thou Gavest Me, The 1919 (Art/
    Par) 1280, 1661, 2149, 2410
Woman under Cover 1919 ( ) 318, 1498,
    2536
Woman under Oath 1919 ( ) 1310, 1445,
    1566, 1640, 2061, 2105
Woman Who Dared, The 1916 ( ) 1523
Woman Who Did, The 1915 (Br) 1879
Woman Who Gave, The 1919 ( ) 606,
    1929
Woman Who Was Nothing, The 1917 (Br)
    834
Woman Wins, The 1918 (Br) 1289
Woman with a Record, A 1904 (AMB)
Woman, Woman 1919 ( ) 442, 1622, 1929
Womanhood 1917 (V) 1388, 1673, 1888
Woman's Experience, A 1918 ( ) 246,
    1162
Woman's Eyes, A 1916 ( ) 969
Woman's Fool, A 1918 (Un) 398, 1719
Woman's Law, The 1916 (P) 2105
Woman's Power, A 1916 (W) 1444
Woman's Strategy, A 1910 (Ed)
Woman's Way, A 1908 (AMB) 1511
Woman's Way, A 1909 (V)
Woman's Way, A 1916 (WS) 231, 486,
    1603
Woman's Weapons, A 1918 ( ) 486
Women and Roses 1914 ( ) 2112
Women Go on the Warpath 1913 (V) 901,
    2811
Won by a Fish 1912 (Bio) 2047
Won by Losing 1916 ( ) 2558
Won in a Cabaret 1915 (Christie) 525
Won in a Closet 1914 (Key) 1941
Won in the Clouds 1918 ( ) 2095
Won through a Medium 1911 (Bio)
Wonder, Ching Ling Foo, The 1899 (Lubin)
Wonderful Charm, The 1908 (Melies)
Wonderful Eye, The 1911 (Bio)
Wonderful Rose Tree, The 1904 (Melies)
Wonderful Statue, The 1913 (V) 332,

901, 920
Wood Nymph, The 1916 (Tri) 752, 756,
    1613
Wood Violet, The 1913 (V) 2472
Woodchopper's Child, The 1909 (Ed)
Wooden Indian, The 1909 (V)
Wooden Indian, The 1912 (Ed)
Wooden Leg, The 1909 (AMB)
Wooden Shoes 1917 (Tri) 134, 1582
Wooing of Aunt Jamima, The 1915
    (Christie) 525
Wooing of Princess Pat, The 1918 (V)
    1034, 1547
Word of His People, The 1914 ( ) 2096,
    2392
Words and Music By ... 1919 ( ) 856,
    2002
Work /aka/ The Paperhanger 1915 (Es)
    71, 451, 1036, 1336, 1676, 2077,
    2746
Work Made Easy 1907 (V)
Working for Hubby 1912 (V) 111, 332
Workingman's Dream, A 1908 (V)
Workman's Lesson, The 1912 (Ed)
World and the Woman, The 1916 (P) 801
World and Its Woman, The 1919 (Go)
    394, 738, 869, 950, 2541, 2570
World Aflame 1919 ( ) 771, 1404
World Apart 1917 (Par) 2002, 2112, 2458
World to Live In, A 1919 (Reelart) 273,
    558, 1142, 1819
World's Desire, The 1915 (Br) 1879
World's Great Snare, The 1916 (FP) 957
Worm Will Turn, The 1909 (Ed)
Worries and Wobbles 1917 (V) 2367
Worst of Friends, The 1916 (Key/Tri)
    351, 650, 895, 1086, 2710
Worth of a Man 1912 (Imp)
Would-Be Shriner, The 1912 (Bio) 83,
    315, 731, 2045, 2728
Wrath of a Jealous Wife, The 1903 (AMB)
Wrath of the Gods, The 1914 (Ince) 189,
    1208
Wreath in Time, A 1909 (AMB) 1542,
    2368
Wreath of Orange Blossoms, A 1911 (Bio)
    122
Wreck, The 1913 ( ) 1877, 2472
Wreck and Ruin 1914 (Br) 177
Wreckers of the Limited Express 1906
    (Lubin)
(W)ringing Good Joke 1903 (AMB)
Wringing a Good Joke 1899 (Ed)
Writing on the Blotter, The 1911 (Ed)
Writing on the Wall, The 1916 ( ) 1437
Wrong Burglar, The 1908 (Lubin)
Wrong Flat, The 1907 (V)
Wrong Grip, The 1908 (Lubin)
Wrong Overcoat, The 1908 (Lubin)
Wrong Patient, The 1911 (V) 332
Wrong Room, The 1904 (AMB)
Wrong Weight, The 1912 (Un)

- Y -

Yank from the West, A 1918 ( ) 601
Yankee Doodle in Berlin 1919 (Key/Tri)
    1589, 2069, 2143, 2608
Yankee from the West, A 1915 ( ) 1998,
    2112, 2356

Yankee Girl, The 1915 (Bo) 2135, 2445
Yankee Prince, The 1908 (Bio) 595
Yankee Princess, A 1919 ( ) 1241, 1602,
   2570
Yankee Way, The 1917 ( ) 1745, 2671
Yaps and Yokels 1919 (V) 1161
Yaqui Cur, The 1913 (Bio) 141, 315, 1182,
   1751, 1832
Yard of Frankfurters, A 1903 (AMB)
Yard of Puppies, A 1903 (AMB)
Yarn of the Nancy Bell, The 1912 (Ed)
Ye Olden Grafter 1915 (Key) 1086, 2510
Ye Wooing of Peggy 1917 ( ) 2558
Year of the Locust, The 1916 (Las) 1591,
   2683
Yellow Dog, The 1918 ( ) 2399
Yellow Dove, The 1918 ( ) 468
Yellow Girl, The 1916 ( ) 2638
Yellow Menace, The--serial 1916 (Serial
   Film Co.) 561, 976, 1087, 1122,
   1471, 1718, 2468, 2583
      1. Hidden Power
      2. The Mutilated Hand
      3. The Poisonous Tarantula
      4. Plot of a Demon
      5. The Haunted House
      6. The Torture Chamber
      7. Drops of Blood
      8. The Time-Clock Bomb
      9. The Crystal Globe
     10. A Message from the Sky
     11. The Half-Breed's Hatred
     12. Aeroplane Accident
     13. The Spy and the Submarine
     14. Interrupted Nuptials
     15. The Pay of Death
     16. The Final Strand
Yellow Passport 1916 (WS) 95, 2811
Yellow Pawn, The 1916 (Las) 935, 2112,
   2132
Yellow Peril, The 1908 (AMB)
Yellow Streak, The 1914 (Un) 141, 2056
Yellow Sunbonnet, The 1915 ( ) 1270
Yellow Ticket, The 1918 ( ) 296, 1532,
   1769, 1971, 2410, 2683
Yens Yensen, the Swedish Butcher Boy;
   or Mistaken for a Burglar 1908 (V)
Yiddisher Boy, The 1908 (Lubin)
Yorkshire School, A 1910 (Ed)
You 1916 (Br) 43
You Can't Believe Everything 1918 (Tri)
   942, 1665, 2026, 2128, 2512
You Can't Win--serial 1917 (F) 1832
You Never Know Your Luck 1919 ( ) 2035
You Never Saw Such a Girl 1919 (Par) 1764
You Will Send Me to Bed, Eh? 1903 (AMB)
You Won't Cut Any Ice with Me 1906
   (Winthrop Press)
Young America 1903 (AMB)
Young Man Who Figered, The 1915 (V)
   2081, 2521
Young Mr. Jazz 1919 (P) 1586
Young Mother Hubbard 1917 (Es) 1636
Young Patriot, A 1912 (Bio) 1714
Young Romance 1915 (Par) 935
Younger Brother, The 1911 (Ed)
Your Girl and Mine 1914 ( ) 2693
You're Fired! 1919 (Par) 1201, 1206, 2112,
   2149
Youth 1915 (V) 1370, 1876
Youth and Jealousy 1913 ( ) 2112, 2125

Youth of Fortune 1916 ( ) 690
Youthful Affair, A 1919 (M) 533, 768,
   1707
You've Got to Love Me a Lot 1909 (Lubin)
Yvonne from Paris 1919 ( ) 1841

                    - Z -

Zavani 1915 ( ) 1372
Zaza 1915 (FP) 853, 957
Zazhivo Pogrebenni (Buried Alive) 1919
   (Russian) 1996
Zeppelin's Last Raid, The 1918 ( ) 1745
Zero Hour 1919 (WS) 835
Zigomar 1911 (Eclair)
Zigomar vs. Le Rouguin 1912 (Eclair)
Zip, the Dodger 1914 (Key) 65
Zollenstein 1918 ( ) 2211
Zona 1916 ( ) 1922
Zongar 1918 (MacFadden) 1494
Zudora (The Twenty Million Dollar
   Mystery)--serial 1914 (T) 184, 272,
   603, 871, 921, 2430
      1. The Mystic Message of the
          Spotted Collar
      2. The Mystery of the Sleeping
          House
      3. The Mystery of the Dutch
          Cheese Maker
      4. The Mystery of the Frozen
          Laugh
      5. The Secret of the Haunted
          Hills
      6. The Mystery of the Perpetual
          Glare
      7. The Mystery of the Lost
          Ships
      8. The Foiled Elopement
      9. Kidnapped or The Mystery of
          the Missing Heiress
     10. Zudora in the $20,000,000
          Mystery or The Gentleman
          Crooks and the Lady
     11. A Message from the Heart
     12. A Bag of Diamonds
     13. The Raid on the Madhouse or
          The Secret of Dr. Munns'
          Sanitarium
     14. The Missing Million
     15. The Ruby Coronet
     16. The Battle on the Bridge
     17. The Island of Mystery
     18. The Cipher Code
     19. The Prisoner in the Pilot
          House
     20. The Richest Woman in the
          World
Zulu's Heart, The 1908 (AMB) 1511
Zuzu, the Band Leader 1914 (Key) 1112,
   1941, 2465